IS THERE AN AFTERLIFE?

David Fontana

BOOKS

*In memory of three of my dearest friends who
have made the transition we call death.*

*Ralph Noyes
Arthur Ellison
Montague Keen*

*Distinguished researchers into life's mysteries
and noblest of spirits.*

....

Copyright © 2005 O Books
Reprinted 2006
Deershot Lodge, Park Lane, Ropley, Hants, SO24 OBE, UK.
Tel: +44 (0) 1962 773768 Fax: +44 (0) 1962 773769
E-mail: office@johnhunt-publishing.com
www.0-books.net

U.S.A. and Canada
Books available from:
NBN,
15200 NBN Way
Blue Ridge Summit, PA 17214, U.S.A.
Email: custserv@nbnbooks.com
Tel: 1 800 462 6420
Fax: 1 800 338 4550

Text: © 2004 David Fontana

Text set in Weiss by Andrew Milne Design, UK
Cover design: Krave Ltd, London

ISBN 1 903816 90 4

A CIP catalogue record for this book is available from the British Library.

Printed by Maple-Vail Ltd, USA

CONTENTS

FOREWORD

It is now more than a century since serious research into ostensible paranormal phenomena began. Psychical research has been conducted in many countries throughout the world attracting the attention of some of the most famous scientists, renowned for their important work in disciplines such as psychology, physics, astronomy, biology, to name only a few.
It has also engaged the efforts and allegiance of respected physicians, philosophers and statesmen. Many have been members of the Society for Psychical search or the American Society for Psychical Research. It is a remarkable fact, for example, that in the first century of the S.P.R.'s existence, among the fifty-one Presidents of the Society there were nineteen Professors, ten Fellows of the Royal Society, five Fellows of the British Academy, four holders of the Order of Merit, and one Nobel prize-winner.

In their studies of the field, often conducted for decades of years, most of them accepted that a wealth of evidence has been collected leading them to the conclusion that a wide variety of different kinds of paranormal phenomena occur. Many concluded that unless one accepts an explanation involving super-telepathy, clairvoyance and precognition (the so called super-ESP theory, never ever demonstrated in a Para psychological laboratory), the possibility that some human beings survive death, retaining their essential personalities, memories, characteristics, skills and concern for those they have left behind, has to be taken very seriously indeed.

And yet more than a century of such evidence is still ignored by the majority of scientists and of course the materialist reductionist. With respect to scientists it might be thought that they have carefully examined the evidence and considered it to be inadequate or faulty. But that is not so. The simple answer is that they have no track record in psychical research, never having studied the evidence or experimented in the subject. At best they may have seen some newspaper or magazine article or some slanted TV programme. With respect to the materialist sceptic who maintains vociferously that no paranormal phenomenon has ever been proven to occur, he or she is equally ignorant of the evidence or so Flat Earth minded that no amount of hard evidence would ever change his or her mind.

For these reasons and more, Professor David Fonanta's new book is of great importance. In it he displays an almost encyclopaedic knowledge of the vast field of psychical research and gives a careful and balanced account not only of past investigations, but also of modern significant studies being carried out. The bibliography itself if of great value. His own significant contributions to that subject in the study of mediumship, both mental and physical, poltergeists and the Electronic Voice Phenomenon are also described.

I have not doubt that Professor Fontana's book will become a modern classic, allowing anyone coming fresh to the subject and of open mind to realise why psychical research is of such importance, providing perhaps the best road to our understanding of what a human being is. It gives hope of extending our knowledge of human personality and it shows why many psychical researchers over the past century have taken very seriously indeed the possibility that survival of that inescapable appointment we call death takes place.

Archie E. Roy

Professor Emeritus of Astronomy in Glasgow University,
Former President of the Society for Psychical Research.

INTRODUCTION

The Sure Facts of Life

It is rightly said that birth and death are the two sure facts of life. We know a great deal about birth, the prelude to independent existence, but death remains shrouded in mystery. Is death the end of this existence, as many people believe and as many scientists assume is demonstrated by the facts? Or is death the transition to another phase of life, with all the challenges and promises that such a transition may present?

The purpose of this book is to survey the evidence that may help us answer these questions. Some critics may claim that all such evidence can be dismissed as fraud, delusion, or wishful thinking. Others may be surprised that a psychologist should even consider a book on survival, as psychologists are known to be the most skeptical of all scientists on matters relating to any aspect of the so-called paranormal. My reply to these critics is that one should not pronounce on the quality of evidence in any field until one has studied it, and that far from avoiding the subject psychologists should regard it with particular interest as psychology is about people, and people want answers to fundamental questions such as whether or not there is life after death.

Many scientists consider that such questions can never be answered, as they cannot be subjected to proper scientific test. Others insist that even without proper test, science has demonstrated that the chances we live after death are vanishingly small. Science has never found anything resembling a soul or a spirit in the body, and when the body dies that must therefore be the end of it. Even those relatively few scientists (known as parapsychologists) who do take a professional interest in the paranormal prefer for the most part to ignore the issue of survival, preferring to focus instead on paranormal abilities in the living, such as telepathy, clairvoyance, and precognition. We will explore the reasons for this at appropriate points in the book, but among them is the fear that the question of survival is so closely associated with fraudulent mediumship, spiritualism, religion, ghost stories, and other doubtful areas that any active interest in the subject is likely to give parapsychology a bad name (see e.g. Alvarado 2003). Despite the fact that parapsychologists (by which I mean those based in university and other research laboratories, not those who simply decide to call themselves by that name), using methods as rigorous as those in the other sciences, have established the existence of paranormal abilities beyond reasonable doubt, parapsychology still struggles to obtain acceptance by orthodox science. Thus it prefers to ignore anything, such as survival research, which may make that struggle even more difficult.

This generally dismissive attitude towards survival research is not only unfair to a vitally important subject and to the large number of people who seek explanations for personal experiences that suggest deceased loved ones still survive – for example some 50 per cent of those who have lost a spouse report receiving evidence that suggests they have survived (Gallup and Proctor 1984) – it ignores the fact that research into survival does not necessitate the abandonment of scientifically respectable methods, as we shall see in due course. However, as in very many other areas of psychological research, it does mean that at times we have to place some reliance upon human testimony, and take into account the fact that some of this testimony may be influenced by exaggeration and faulty memory. With this proviso in mind, it is fair also to recognize that some people are accurate witnesses. Were this not the case, no court of law and very few social institutions could function. As in all areas of human psychology, the first prerequisite is to pay attention to what people say before dismissing it, and to accept that they may just know what they have experienced, particularly if they do not change their story from one telling to the next. Many of the people I have interviewed, in 30 years and more of active involvement in researching the evidence for survival, have had nothing to gain by pretending to experiences that they have not had. In fact many of them have been fearful of ridicule, and only spoken of these experiences when they are convinced they will not be treated as foolish or as mentally unbalanced. They have answered questions put to them readily and directly, and if they have no answers they say so. Far from wishing to impose their own interpretations upon their experiences, they are often deeply puzzled by them, and anxious for explanations. Not infrequently their experiences have been life changing for them, and not infrequently the details are recalled with great clarity from many years ago. Having listened to many of these experiences I have also been impressed by the degree of consistency demonstrated by them. They conform for the most part to an identifiable pattern, even if the individuals who recount them have read nothing on the subject and have never previously discussed their experiences with others. In addition, far from exaggerating them, the tendency has been to understate them, and to talk of them almost apologetically, as if in this scientific age no rational person should have such experiences.

I am sometimes asked what prompted my interest in survival and in psychical research. My answer is that I cannot remember a time in my life when I was not interested in these things, or a time when I wasn't surprised that not everyone shared this interest. For me, the study of the mind naturally raises the question whether or not the latter survives death, and whether or not it has the paranormal abilities that from time immemorial have been claimed for it. It was my concern to study the mind that brought me into psychology, and it has made sense to research these questions alongside my mainstream work as a scientific psychologist. As will become clear during the book, this research has not been confined to studying the discoveries made by others. I have sought to investigate paranormal phenomena at first hand, and have been fortunate to experience sufficient of these phenomena to leave me in no doubt of their reality. I will refer to some of this experience as we go along.

Problems of Selection When Writing About Survival

The field of psychical research (my preferred term for research into the paranormal) is so vast, and the areas of it that relate to survival so extensive, that it is impossible to cover more than a small part of it in any one book, no matter how long. Any writer on the subject is therefore faced with the dilemma of what to select and what to leave out. In tackling this dilemma one of my regrets is that I have had to confine myself primarily to phenomena reported in the English-speaking world. Much careful and highly successful work has been carried out over the years in countries such as Italy, France, Germany, Russia and Brazil, but problems of language and the absence of available translations mean that a great deal of the literature describing this work is inaccessible to readers of this book. There is little point in referencing numerous original sources in foreign languages knowing that readers cannot go to them in order to take their studies further, and I have therefore kept such references to a minimum. But no reader should be left with the impression that the English-speaking world has a monopoly of good psychical research. In some areas, such as reports of apparent spirit communications through electronic media (discussed in Chapter 14), the English-speaking world in fact lags significantly behind a number of other European countries.

Another aspect of the dilemma as to what to select is whether to refer to older cases, or whether to keep exclusively to those of recent date. Many of the older cases have already been dealt with at some length in the literature, and it would be superfluous to devote too much space to them. On the other hand, some of the older cases have stood the test of time, having been subjected to every form of criticism without being found wanting. If the picture I hope to present is to be anywhere near complete, they cannot therefore be ignored. In looking at these older cases it is also important not to be beguiled by the myth of eternal progress – the myth that we always do things better nowadays than our parents and forebears. Many of the older cases were meticulously researched, and there is no reason to suppose we could do things very much better. In addition, there is no area of study that ignores seminal findings in its own field simply on the basis of age. Each area of study advances by accumulating findings over the years, and this is particularly true of areas that rely upon observation rather than only upon experimentation. Furthermore, survival research depends upon the availability of data, and availability has fluctuated markedly over the years. For example, although it is untrue to say that there are no good ("good" in the sense of providing material worthy of investigation) mediums working today, mediumship, like so many human abilities, appears to be more of an art than a science. And in all areas, great artists are few and far between. Two of the most thorough and objective earlier attempts to survey the evidence on survival, with critical appraisals at each point of the various arguments for and against the strength of this evidence (Hart 1959 and Jacobson 1973), deal both with earlier cases and with those contemporary at the time of writing, and I have no doubt that this approach produces the most illuminating results.

The Dangers of Theory-Building

The final part of the dilemma is whether or not to spend time trying to build elaborate theories or hypotheses about survival. There is a tendency these days for writers in any field of science – perhaps particularly in psychical research where it is said we have no theory to explain data seemingly at odds with other scientific facts – to feel they must build theories if they are to be taken seriously. No matter how unlikely the theory, it seems it is better than nothing. But there are areas where theories can actively be a hindrance to further thought and research (note that theories are not the same as conclusions; we can arrive at the latter without necessary recourse to the former). Survival is one of these areas. As I shall point out at more length later in the book, some scientists and philosophers reject the possibility of survival (or find great difficulty with it) because they argue that there is no acceptable theory as to what might survive the death of the body and the brain. Others reject it because they have no theory as to where an afterlife might take place, or no theory as to what it might be like, or no theory as to how existence could be possible outside space and time. Yet others hinder things by putting forward theories designed to wean people away from the possibility of survival by stressing that if paranormal phenomena of any kind should prove to occur the whole edifice of science would collapse. We shall meet some of these theories in due course. However, in an area such as survival research, observation and description should precede theory. The need is to observe and describe, accurately and objectively, the evidence before us, even in the absence of any plausible theory to explain it. As Sir William Crookes said of the physical phenomena he witnessed when investigating the medium Daniel Dunglas Home (Chapter 12), "I do not say it is possible. I say that it happened." I can think of no better advice.

CHAPTER 1
SURVIVAL OF DEATH:
QUESTIONS AND BELIEFS

Unanswered Questions

Imagine we are looking at a photograph of a busy street scene, taken some one hundred years ago. In the absence of traffic some people are casually crossing the road, and all are frozen in time with their period clothes and their serious expressions. Some of the women are pushing perambulators, and here and there errand boys ride ancient bicycles. The photograph is taken from an upstairs window, giving us a bird's-eye view of the street. There are shops on either side, and conscious of the novelty of being photographed many of the shopkeepers and their assistants are standing at the shop doors, the men in their aprons and carefully rolled shirt sleeves, and the women in their long skirts and mob caps. Although we cannot know the details, we are conscious that each person has his or her own life history, and that as the shutter clicked each person was busy with his or her own thoughts.

Now imagine that time is being slowly wound forward as we continue to watch the picture. As the days and months and years pass, one by one the individuals in the street disappear from the scene, claimed by death. After ten years the ranks have visibly thinned, after 30 more than half the people have disappeared, and after 50 there are very few left. In the end, the street stands empty and lifeless. Where have all these people gone? Their bodies, of course, went to the grave, but what has become of the richness of their lives, their experiences, their hopes and dreams, their laughter and their wisdom, their gifts and their achievements, their decency and their shortcomings? And what has become of the countless millions who have also departed this life down the centuries, leaving behind the places and the people they loved, the things they possessed and cared for? Death is an unavoidable part of life, but how much do we know of what happens afterwards? We may believe that life goes on, but is there any evidence that it does? Has research thrown any light on the matter? *Can* research throw any light on the matter?

The United States Government devotes some $350 billion dollars to its military budget dedicated to the technology of death. How much does it, or any other Western government, spend on research into the possibility of survival of death? The answer, of course, is nothing. Governments are effective at finding new ways of killing our fellow men and women, but have no interest in what happens to their own taxpayers when death takes them off the electoral role. It is almost as difficult to attract private funding for research into survival. People who have drawn their last breath are no longer of interest to the multinationals that fund research into so many other areas of science. Dead people are no longer consumers, with money to spend. Once gone, they are of interest only to their grieving relatives and friends. Death remains in many ways the most neglected of topics. We most of us live our lives as if it will never happen to us or to those we love, and the reality of it only strikes home when we are bereaved or if our own lives are threatened in some way. We rarely even wonder what has become of the great men and women of the past, the towering geniuses, the brilliant scientists and scholars, the explorers, the saints, the founders of the world's great religions. What has become of Mozart, Bach, Beethoven, Dante, Goethe, Shakespeare, Einstein, Galileo, Leonardo da Vinci, Michaelangelo, Copernicus, St. Francis, St. Theresa of Avila, Mother Julian of Norwich, Newton, Walt Whitman, and the many other luminaries who have graced this life and beautified our culture? Does all their hard work, their creativity, their suffering, their learning, their compassion live on only in the things they have left behind, and in the minds of those who value their achievements?

Questions on what if anything happens after death relate to animals as well as humans. No one who has lived close to dogs or cats doubts their extraordinary intelligence, the warmth of their affection, their loyalty, their concern for their owners and for their own offspring, their distinctive personalities, and the many other qualities that enrich the lives of their owners. It is a sign of our arrogance as a species that we assume animals have no self-consciousness, no awareness of their own mortality, and no profound emotions and feelings comparable to our own. All too often this arrogance leads us all to suppose that if survival is a fact, it applies exclusively to humans.

Later in the book we will look in detail at what aspects of the individual may survive physical death, and what the nature of that survival may be like. For the moment it is enough to say that if survival is to be meaningful – that is if the individual is to feel that the state after death is in some major way connected with the state before – we have to suppose that it involves a continuation of earthly thoughts, ideas, concerns, feelings, and memories. Moreover, we must suppose that individuals still have their senses, and can see and hear and feel things much as before death. In other words, that there is an important sense in which the person still recognizes him as himself, much as we recognize that the person we are on waking in the morning is the same person who went to sleep the night before. This may seem a tall order. After all, we are talking of a disembodied state. In this world, much of our experience is registered through the body and its organs. Without them, many people confess they cannot even conceptualize a life after death, and this inability is one of the reasons why physical science ignores or firmly rejects any discussion of survival, and makes no effort to mount research into the subject.

However, the absence of extensive formal research into what happens to life when it leaves the physical body does not mean that no evidence exists on the matter. In fact, evidence of various kinds has existed since the dawn of history, and has accumulated copiously down the centuries. The purpose of this book is to detail this evidence, and to draw conclusions as to what it tells us. It is particularly important to bring the story up to date, and in order to do so the book will also summarize a selection of the most important modern developments, and include some of my own experiences as a scientific investigator into what is surely the most fascinating and challenging question addressed by the human mind.

Evidence from Shamanism and Early Spiritual Traditions

All the major religious and spiritual traditions from both the Western and Eastern worlds teach survival after death. Some of their followers may not subscribe to this belief, but it remains a central feature of religious and spiritual doctrine. Humans, we are told, possess some quality – referred to as a soul in the Western traditions – which is non-physical, and which lives on when the physical body reaches the end of the road. Discussion of what is meant by this quality can be left to Part III, but it is generally taken to be a non-physical element that animates the physical body, and although influenced by the experiences of this body is in no sense dependent upon it. When the body dies, this element leaves the physical world and exists in a subtler dimension, though perhaps destined one day to take on another physical body and to return to this or some other material existence.

A belief that at death something leaves the body and continues its existence elsewhere appears to have existed since the earliest times. Archaeology reveals that some 50,000 years ago the dead were carefully buried with food and weapons. More than 10,000 years earlier, Neanderthal man buried the dead with flowers, and conducted rituals over their bodies, perhaps indicative of a belief in an afterlife. Wherever we look, we find similar historical evidence for this belief. Even in the present day, among misleadingly so-called less "developed" cultures such as those in Africa, parts of South America and Asia, this belief remains widespread. The Western mind, reared currently on a diet of scientific materialism, is quick to dismiss such a belief as primitive superstition. Yet, without prematurely entering the debate (to be returned to at several points in the book) on the status of science in relation to issues such as life after death it is at least of value to hold back on charges of superstition until we have asked what evidence, if any, did and do these various cultures have for their widespread belief.

The rapid technological developments that have been fuelled by the advances in the physical sciences over the last three hundred years have progressively alienated Western man from his biological and spiritual roots. Living much closer to nature and to three of the areas that link humankind to nature – birth, procreation, and death – than the modern Westerner, people in less "developed" cultures grow up with an enhanced sensitivity to their environment. Sensitivity of this kind, like the potential for many abilities and skills, depends greatly upon early experience. Without such experience, the potential may be irretrievably lost (much as people born blind who later acquire sight are unable to perceive the world as we do). Normally we think of this sensitivity in terms of a heightened physical awareness, but the cultures concerned speak of a non-physical awareness, one that renders them receptive to realities beyond normal ways of seeing and hearing. It is thought that this awareness allows contact with the spirits of the dead, either through apparitions or dreams. Particularly gifted individuals are claimed to be able to make these contacts at will, even traveling in some cases to the dimensions where these spirits are said to continue their existence. In Africa, remote areas of Siberia, and in the Native American cultures of both North and South America, such gifted men and women are known as shamans.

There is ample evidence that many respected anthropologists have taken this claim seriously. Joan Halifax, a medical anthropologist and author of scholarly research into the subject (including the classic *Shamanic Voices*, first published in 1979) gives a number of accounts drawn from the literature and her own fieldwork, of the shaman's reported contacts with the spirit world. After undergoing a lengthy period of training and many initiations, the shaman's gifts develop to the point where he or she is said to visit the spirit world at will, sometimes to bring back news of departed relatives, and at others to receive guidance on how to heal members of the community. The shaman is also instructed during these other-world journeys on how to deal with cases of spirit possession in which the newly dead, reluctant to accept the fact of their death, overshadow and control living individuals in order to continue to enjoy the sensations of the material life.

In shamanic and other cultures living close to nature, the awareness of the spiritual world, and of the souls of the departed, seems so real and intense that the dead are thought to remain, as it were, members of the community, sometimes acting as a source of wisdom and guidance or, occasionally, of fear. Thus in these cultures belief in a life after death appears to rest less upon mere superstition than upon what is claimed to be direct experience. As we shall see later in the book, the very acceptance that men and animals survive death may facilitate this direct experience, although critics may argue that this acceptance leads individuals to misinterpret normal experience in paranormal terms, and this is another matter that will be looked at later.

Earlier cultures were so conscious of the ever-present reality of death and of the supposed afterlife, that they prepared extensive manuals to be studied by the living and read to the dying that gave precise instructions on how to meet death and what comes next. The state of mind in which one dies, not just the way one has lived life, was said to determine the nature of the afterlife experience. The *Tibetan Book of the Dead* (Tibetan *Bardo Thodol*) is one such manual, still very much used and revered by the *Nyingma*, the oldest Tibetan Buddhist sect. The Western medieval world had the *Ars Moriendi* (the *Art of Dying*), while the Egyptians had a number of texts that have since been collected under the title *The Egyptian Book of the Dead*. The writings of the Mayan Indians of South America have also been collected as *The Maya Book of the Dead* (see Grof and Grof 1980 for further details).

If these various texts were based only on folklore and religious speculations, they would be of interest only to anthropologists and would merely throw light on the patterns of belief of long-vanished cultures. But the claim is that they arose from the direct experience of exceptional men and women who had penetrated the veil between the worlds and visited the realms concerned. Critics contend that the marked differences between these various manuals in their descriptions of the afterlife demonstrate that they are cultural rather than spiritual products; for example, whereas the Christian *Ars Moriendi* speaks of a single soul, the Egyptian texts talk of the *ka*, the vital force that leaves the body at death, the *ab*, the conscience or heart, the *akh*, the transfigured spirit, and the *ba*, the vital force that animates the individual after death. However, the more one studies these texts, the more it becomes clear that these various differences are more apparent than real. Although the distinction has been rather lost over the years, early Christians also spoke of a soul and a spirit, the former the changing individual nature, and the latter the divine animating principle. The Western mystery traditions, influenced both by the pre-Christian cults that flourished around the Mediterranean basin and by Christian and Jewish mysticism, speak in addition of what is best called a vehicle of vitality that animates the physical body and that usually disintegrates over the three days or so following death, while the soul and the spirit go on to higher things. These various non-physical bodies are discussed more fully in Chapter 18. Also discussed in Chapter 18 is the fact that cultural differences in accounts of the afterlife are partly explained by the claim that experiences in the next world are greatly influenced by the power of thought. Thus the preconceptions we have of it at death help determine the nature of what awaits us. The idea is not so unlikely when we remember that thought also influences the way we experience this world. Modern physics tells us that the world "out there" is very different from the way we perceive it. From the moving flux of sub-atomic particles that make up physical reality – including our own bodies – we somehow mentally "'create" the solid, stable world of experience.

Evidence From Mysticism

We could describe shamans as mystics in that they are said to have access to realms of consciousness beyond those of their fellows, but the latter term is usually applied to men and women from within the three theistic religions of the West: Judaism, Christianity, and Islam. Mystical experiences, in which the individual is reported either as experiencing direct contact with an absolute reality outside him- or herself (transcendent mysticism), or as feeling the boundaries of the separate self dissolve into this reality (imminent mysticism), have been consistently reported by saints and visionaries down the centuries, typically imbuing them with the abiding conviction that there is no death, and that love is the abiding divine principle. These mystical experiences are taken by the spiritual traditions as providing additional first-hand support for the idea that death is not the end of us, and that the afterlife, for some people at least, is more glorious and all-embracing than our sojourn on earth.

Both transcendent and imminent mysticism offer equal reassurance that life is not restricted to – or created by – the physical body. In some cases mystical experience also provides reassurance that meetings with loved ones take place in the afterlife. For example, Saint Teresa of Avila, the sixteenth-century Spanish mystic and one of the first women to be given the title of Doctor of the Church, speaks of being taken up to Heaven during one of her experiences, where she met her deceased parents. The meeting took from her all fear of death, of which previously she confesses herself to have been "much afraid" (Saint Teresa of Avila 1974). Experiences of meeting deceased loved ones are not of course restricted to the saints, and we shall look at many examples in the chapters that follow. Sir Alister Hardy, the founder of the Religious Experience Research Unit at Manchester College, Oxford (now renamed the Alister Hardy Religious Experience Research Unit and based at the University of Wales, Lampeter), in a wide survey of religious experiences, found that 8 per cent involved encounters with the dead (Hardy 1979).

In recent years, the attempt by some Western theologians to "demythologize" religion has contributed to the relative neglect currently extended by much of the Christian church to survival. This is unfortunate. Without the concept of life after death, religion becomes little more than a set of moral codes for social living, and ends up even denying the reality of the mystical experiences upon which it is based. This neglect also risks harming interest in survival in general since it appears to acknowledge that scientific materialism rather than religion has the last word on such matters.

CHAPTER 2
EVIDENCE FROM MODERN PARAPSYCHOLOGY

The Development of Parapsychology

Reference has already been made to the fact that many parapsychologists fear that an interest in survival is likely to disqualify parapsychology from being taken seriously by scientists. Nevertheless, the discoveries of parapsychologists over the last half-century and more have indirectly done much to support the possibility that we have a dimension within us that lives on after death. Dating from the foundation of the first parapsychology laboratory at Duke University North Carolina by J. B. and Louisa Rhine in 1927, parapsychology quickly broke away from the methodology used by the British Society for Psychical Research (founded in 1882 as the first scientific society set up to research into the paranormal), which focused upon spontaneous cases such as apparitions, and upon mediumship and other survival-related experiences. In their experiments, the Rhines deliberately set out to avoid areas such as these, where scientific proof of the paranormal is difficult if not impossible to obtain (Fontana 1998). Instead they employed the more mundane method of investigating whether or not an individual (referred to as the "receiver") can guess, more often than would be expected by chance alone, the identity of cards at which another person (referred to as the "sender") is looking. In spite of its unspectacular nature, the virtue of such a method is that it can be used under carefully controlled scientific conditions. Either people can succeed in guessing cards correctly under conditions that rule out cheating, or they cannot. If they can, then there is a strong possibility that telepathy, direct mind-to-mind contact between sender and receiver, is involved (Rhine, J. B. 1937, 1948, 1954).

Using the so-called Zener cards, which consist of five sets (stars, circles, squares, crosses, and wavy lines) with five cards in each set, receiver and sender were hidden from each other while the sender concentrated on each card in turn and the receiver attempted to guess what it might be. By chance alone, the receiver would be expected to average five correct guesses each time the sender went through the 25 cards. But if the receiver consistently scored more than five, then the odds against chance being the explanation increased. If odds of 20 to one or more against chance were obtained, the experimenters could feel justified in supposing that telepathy (now more usually called *anomalous cognition*) was responsible. Over a period of time, even though the receivers were simply volunteers and made no claim to paranormal abilities, the results obtained in these experiments at Duke

University were so successful that the odds against chance mounted up impressively, and the success rate of some receivers was found not to diminish even if the distance between receiver and sender was increased, sometimes to many miles, which suggests that telepathy is unaffected by space.

As a variant of this experiment, the Rhines worked without a sender. The cards were mechanically shuffled, and the receiver was asked to guess their order even though no other human mind was now involved. Again successful results were obtained with sufficient consistency for chance to be ruled out. As telepathy could not now be involved, it was proposed that these results were due to clairvoyance (the ability, now often called *remote viewing*, to gain information paranormally directly from the environment). As with telepathy, clairvoyance appeared unaffected by distance. A further variant in the experiments was to ask the receiver to guess what the order of the cards would be after shuffling *before* they were put into the mechanical shuffler. Once more the results were positive, leading to the suggestion that precognition, the ability to obtain paranormal knowledge of the future, was responsible.

Thus the Rhines' results appeared to demonstrate the existence of no fewer than three paranormal abilities: telepathy, clairvoyance, and precognition. But there was more to come. In addition to the work with the Zener cards, the Rhines constructed experiments to see if individuals can influence the fall of an unbiased dice (one equally weighted on all six sides), thrown mechanically so that no sleight of hand could be involved. Results proved sufficiently successful to suggest the existence of a fourth ability, psychokinesis, the direct action of mind upon matter (Rhine, L. E. 1977).

I remember how impressed I was when, as a postgraduate at Cambridge, I came across two of J. B. Rhine's books, *New Frontiers of the Mind* and *The Reach of the Mind*, in one of the postgraduate libraries. My interest in psychical research goes back to boyhood, but Rhine's books were the first indication, together with Donald West's *Psychical Research Today* (1954) and Robert Thouless' *Experimental Psychical Research* (1963) (which I came across by chance at around the same time; both West and Thouless were distinguished Cambridge University academics) that psychic abilities had apparently been successfully demonstrated under strict scientific conditions. To my surprise, neither of Rhine's books had been taken out by a previous user of the library. Was there so little interest, even in Cambridge – the home of some of the world's most exciting scientific discoveries, and the *alma mater* of the founders of the Society for Psychical Research – in findings as momentous as those of the Rhines? I discussed the matter with my tutor and with fellow students, but to little effect. Then as now, the great majority of my academic colleagues showed at best only polite interest in psychical research, and showed a puzzling tendency to change the subject at the first convenient moment.

Then as now, they were neither gripped by psychical research, nor prepared to recognize its relevance for our understanding of the human mind.

However, from further reading I found that hardened critics of this research had not been slow to react to the Rhines' results, horrified by the fact that they seemingly contradicted the scientific laws that tell us minds cannot interact directly with each other or with the environment, cannot gain knowledge of the future, and cannot directly influence the behavior of material objects. The Rhines' results were variously dismissed as due to faulty techniques, to mistakes in statistical analysis, and to outright fraud by members of the research team. Nevertheless, since the time of the Rhines, and inspired initially by their work, an impressive amount of parapsychological research has been carried out in universities and other research centers in the USA and Europe. More details of this work will be given at appropriate points later in the book, but for present purposes it is sufficient to refer to only a small part of it, and to make clear that despite the best efforts of critics, published results since the time of the Rhines' pioneering experiments have provided strong support for their general findings. Some of the best of these results have come while using the *ganzfeld* (German for "whole field") technique, developed independently during the 1970s and 1980s by the late Charles Honorton at the Maimonedes Medical Center in New York, Professor William Braud then at the University of Houston in the USA, and Dr. Adrian Parker then at the University of Edinburgh in Britain (see Radin 1997 for an excellent survey). In the *ganzfeld* experiments the sender looks at a picture instead of at the Zener cards, while the receiver is situated in a separate room and in a condition of partial sensory deprivation (i.e. wearing headphones playing white noise into both ears while relaxing on a recliner with eyes shielded from a dim red light by special goggles or half ping-pong balls), describing into an audio tape whatever thoughts and images come to mind. At the end of the session, the receiver is asked to select from a set of four pictures (the genuine target picture plus three others) the one that approximates most closely to these thoughts and images. As a variant, the sender is sometimes dispensed with, and the target images are selected randomly by computer, and seen by no one until the experiment is over, thus converting it from a test of telepathy to one of clairvoyance. A panel of judges, ignorant of the identity of the target picture, is also asked to listen to the thoughts and images recorded by the receiver and decide to which of the pictures they most closely approximate.

The state of partial sensory deprivation experienced by the receiver in the *ganzfeld* appears to help quieten the mental chatter that usually dominates the mind, thus increasing the likelihood of the faint paranormal perceptions received through telepathy or clairvoyance emerging into consciousness. The odds of selecting the right picture in these *ganzfeld* experiments by chance alone are of course one in four. But in spite of attempts by critics to discredit the results, repeated experiments over many years have produced findings well above chance, even though receivers have generally been members of the normal population rather than those professing to possess paranormal abilities.

Further evidence for the reality of the paranormal abilities measured in the *ganzfeld* and in other parapsychological experiments comes from the finding, first reported by James Spottiswoode in 1997 and further developed in the same year by Spottiswoode and Edwin May, both of the Cognitive Sciences Laboratory in California, that these laboratory-based experiments are significantly more successful if they take place between 11.9 hours and 13.9 hours Local Sidereal Time (LST), with a peak in the success rate at 12.9 hours. Sidereal Time is measured not by the period of a complete rotation of the earth's axis in relation to the sun (i.e. Solar Time, our normal way of measuring the 24 hour day), but by its complete rotation in relation to the fixed stars. The complete rotation of the earth against the fixed stars takes 23 hours and 55.91 minutes, i.e. 4.09 minutes less than the complete rotation of the earth against the sun. Thus Sidereal Time and Solar Time are out of phase with each other (e.g. at one point in the calendar year noon in LST time will fall at midnight Solar Time). Parapsychology laboratories, like other scientific laboratories, usually keep a careful record of the Local Solar Time at which their experiments take place, and from these records it is possible to calculate the equivalent Local Sidereal Time. Surveying nearly 3,000 parapsychology experiments, Spottiswoode and May found no correlation between successful results and Local Solar Time (i.e. there is apparently no time during the Solar Day when parapsychology experiments have a better chance of success than at any other), but a highly significant correlation between successful results and Local Sidereal Time. At the peak LST of 12.9 hours, this correlation in fact reaches odds against chance of 10,000 to one (Spottiswoode 1997).

This strong correlation between LST and successful parapsychological experiments would not, of course, appear if successful parapsychological experiments did not exist. Furthermore, if the results of successful parapsychological experiments were due not to the existence of paranormal abilities but to faulty experimental methods, then we would expect these successful experiments to be randomly distributed across the working day rather than to cluster around 12.9 hours LST. Together with the various other findings summarized above and the many others for which I have no space, a very strong case emerges for the existence of telepathy, clairvoyance, psychokinesis, and precognition. Readers wishing to know more are strongly advised to study Radin (1997 referenced above), formerly of the University of Nevada and now of the Institute of Noetic Science in California, or Broughton (1992), Director of Research at the Institute for Parapsychology.

The Relevance of Parapsychological Research to Survival –
Outside Space and Time

However, since, as we have said, the attempt by parapsychologists to put the study of the paranormal upon a firm scientific footing has distracted attention away from the more challenging subject of survival of death, the reader may be wondering why we have just spent so much time describing this attempt. The reason becomes clear if we consider what is meant by death. Death means coming to an end in what relativity theory terms *the space-time continuum*. In other words, death means that we cease to exist in space and within time, the dimensions that compose the material world. And this is where the findings of parapsychology summarized above are highly relevant to the question of survival, for they demonstrate not only that telepathy and clairvoyance are realities, but that they appear to operate outside space (telepathy and clairvoyance are unaffected by distance) and outside time (precognition allows knowledge of future events). From this it follows that although death means coming to an end in the space-time continuum, there is an element of mind that appears able to operate during one's lifetime *outside* space and time. If this is the case, it further follows that the element of mind concerned is unaffected by death.

It might be objected that if the only part of the mind to persist after physical death is that represented by fleeting, fragmentary paranormal abilities such as telepathy, clairvoyance, and precognition, then this can hardly be said to represent anything worth having, or indeed anything that we can usefully classify as survival. But this is to confuse the way in which the mind *uses* its abilities with these abilities themselves. Living as we do in material bodies in a space-time world, it is hardly surprising that the mind's abilities to acquire information and to process and express this information and to conceptualize itself normally function only within the sensory and other constraints imposed by this world (although as suggested earlier, this may be less true of cultures living more naturally and instinctively than of cultures dominated by materialism). Once these constraints are removed by physical death, then it is possible that these abilities may attune fully to an existence outside space-time. Rupert Sheldrake's theory of the *extended mind* (e.g. Sheldrake 2003), which suggests that even in the present world minds are not limited by the physical body and extend beyond it into fields that link organisms to their environment and to each other, is also relevant to this possibility, and the theory will be returned to at greater length in Chapter 18.

Research into the efficacy of distant prayer lends weight to the suggestion that the mind can operate outside space. In 1988 physician Randolph Byrd published the results of an experiment at San Francisco General Hospital involving 393 patients in coronary care. The experiment was designed to determine whether those who were prayed for regularly by a prayer group showed better clinical progress than those who were not. The patients were divided into two groups matched on variables such as severity of disease, age, etc., and the members of the prayer group did not see or know the patients for whom they were to pray, being given only their first names and brief medical details. The 393 patients were not told whether they were assigned to the group receiving prayer (the experimental group) or to the group who were not (the control group). At the end of a 10-month period, a panel of physicians, who also did not know to which group the patients belonged, assessed their medical progress. Findings showed that patients in the experimental group had needed significantly less antibiotics and mechanical ventilation. They also had a lower incidence of fluid in the lungs and of pneumonia and cardiopulmonary arrest, needed fewer diuretics, and had fewer deaths. None of these differences were very large, but they were sufficient to have been hailed by the medical profession as an important breakthrough had conventional drugs rather than prayer been involved (Dossey 2002).

Distant spiritual healing, in which the healer claims to be channeling healing energy from outside him or herself, also appears to have some effect. Dr. Elizabeth Targ and Frederick Sicher of the Sausalito Consciousness Research Laboratory in California carried out a similar study to that of Byrd, the difference being that the patients were suffering from AIDs rather than cardiac disease, and the healers directed at them healing rather than prayers for healing. Writing in 1998 in one of America's most prestigious medical journals, Sicher reports that the 20 AIDs patients receiving distant healing showed significantly fewer severe illnesses and fewer AIDs-related illnesses, and they required fewer medical visits, fewer hospitalizations, and fewer overnight stays during each hospitalization, than a matched group of 20 controls. In an earlier study at Kaplan Hospital in Israel with hernia patients, Zvi Bentwich and Shulamith found that those receiving distant healing did significantly better than controls on four medically assessed post-operative variables – scar healing, elevated body temperature, intensity of pain, and patient attitude. Healers were informed only of the time of operation of subjects in the experimental group.

It is possible of course that distant prayer and distant healing act directly on the body of the receiver without going through any part of the receiver's mind. Controlled laboratory experiments by William Braud, now of the Institute of Transpersonal Psychology, showed in 1990 that even senders unpracticed in distant healing may, through visualization and directed attention, reduce the rate of destruction in blood cells placed in a saline solution. Braud's experiments produced results with odds against chance of 5,000 to one, and since no receiver was involved direct action upon the blood vessels must be supposed. However, in all the other experiments summarized above, a receiver is involved, and the idea that the mind of the sender can paranormally influence the body of the receiver at a distance and without interacting with him or her through physical energy systems seems both intriguing and well-supported.

The implications of the finding that the mind may be capable of operating outside space-time may take some while to impinge upon the way in which we think about ourselves – either as purely biological beings living in a world without meaning or purpose, or as minds that can reach out beyond our physical boundaries – yet the way in which we think about ourselves can profoundly influence virtually all areas of our lives. It may also help to determine whether or not we experience paranormal events. If we think these events are possible, then they may be more likely to happen to us. Parapsychological research has consistently reported what has come to be known as the sheep-goats effect. Subjects in parapsychological experiments who believe in the paranormal (the sheep) typically obtain more successful results than those who do not (the goats). It is also frequently stated by those who claim psychic abilities that the presence of hardened skeptics who steadfastly refuse to accept the reality of the paranormal even when the evidence for it is good may inhibit the operation of these abilities, possibly through some unconscious telepathic process between the mind of the skeptic and that of the psychic.

Role of the Unconscious

Evidence that the mind's parapsychological abilities may indeed operate at unconscious levels, and may be influencing our thoughts and actions in subtle and usually unrecognized ways, is evident from another important development in parapsychological research known as DMILS (Direct Mental Interaction between Living Systems). In DMILS research, measurements are typically taken of the receiver's electrodermal reactions while he or she is subjected to a series of both arousing and calming thoughts by a sender. Electrodermal activity refers to the fluctuations in the skin's resistance to a very mild electrical current; when aroused by an emotion the skin dampens slightly and the resistance drops, when relaxed it increases. In a DMILS experiment, the sender may visualize the receiver in a very exciting or fearful situation, then switch to visualizing him or her relaxing on a sunlit beach. The receiver and sender are in separate locations, thus ensuring that no signals of any kind pass between them, and the receiver has no idea whether the sender is imagining arousing or relaxing situations in any sending period (typically the whole experiment lasts some 20 minutes divided into 40 sending periods of 30 seconds each, with the sender instructed by a randomizing computer program whether each period should be arousing or relaxing).

In numerous DMILS experiments carried out to date in reputable parapsychology laboratories and each involving many sessions, relatively consistent although small positive results have been obtained (Delanoy 2001,

Schmidt and colleagues 2002). Even on occasions when the receiver is unable to report correctly whether the sender is visualizing arousing or relaxing situations, electrodermal reaction nevertheless turns out to be significantly more activated during the arousing than during the calming sessions. Electrodermal reaction is in most cases beyond the individual's conscious control, and the instruments that are used to measure it are so sensitive that they register an effect even when the reaction is so slight that it fails to impinge on the receiver's conscious mind. Thus the experiments show that even when receivers have no conscious idea of whether they are the recipients of arousing or calming thoughts, their unconscious mind seems to be receiving the information and registering it in physiological reactions. Successful DMILS experiments have also been carried out that support the popular conviction that our unconscious mind tells us when someone is staring at us. The sender, who sees the receiver through a one-way mirror or on a video screen, is instructed for various periods during the session either to stare or not to stare at the receiver. The receiver is told when each of these periods commences, but is not told whether it involves staring or not. He or she is instructed to press buttons to indicate whether or not they intuitively feel that staring is taking place during these periods, and electrodermal measurements of their reactions are also taken (Sheldrake 2003).

The success of these experiments indicates that, more often than might be expected by guessing alone, our unconscious mind does register whether we are being stared at or not. It might be suggested that the unconscious mind has nothing to do with it, and that the act of being stared at has a direct influence upon our bodies as measured by our electrodermal responses. This suggestion is unlikely to be true. In the course of their experiments into the staring effect, Professor William Braud of the Institute of Transpersonal Psychology and Dr. Marilyn Schlitz of the Institute of Noetic Science found that shy and introverted individuals show higher levels of unconscious electrodermal activity when being stared at than do outgoing and extraverted people (Schlitz and Braud 1997). Shyness and introversion are primarily psychological rather than physiological characteristics, so this finding points to the fact that the act of being stared at is registered first by the unconscious mind, which then triggers the body's reaction.

If the vast reservoir of mental life below the surface of awareness that we call the unconscious is indeed responsive to subtle paranormal influences that sometimes fail to register upon consciousness this implies that it may be the frequent recipient of a steady stream of information through paranormal channels from other living systems. Except perhaps for those with highly developed parapsychological abilities, much of this information may emerge only rarely into consciousness, but the unconscious may nevertheless allow it to influence the body. The involvement of the unconscious in this way further emphasizes the point that the mind's parapsychological abilities – and the aspects of the mind that could survive death – may be far more extensive than would appear on the basis of the occasional snippets of telepathic and clairvoyant information that emerge into consciousness. More will be said about this when we look at the evidence for survival arising from research into mediumship, but enough details have been given to suggest that the findings of parapsychology strongly support the view that some part at least of the mind is independent of the constraints of time and space (and the known laws of science), and may therefore survive the death of the body.

In conclusion, it can be said that although laboratory-based work in parapsychology has not focused directly on the question whether or not we survive physical death, it has yielded findings that support the argument that we do. The evidence for survival surveyed in the rest of this book should be read against a background of these findings, which together with much of this evidence render it increasingly difficult for critics to protest that there is no laboratory-based scientific evidence that supports, even if indirectly, the notion of survival.

CHAPTER 3

EVIDENCE FROM APPARITIONS

We can commence the process of exploring more direct evidence for survival by looking at what we can discover from reports of apparitions, not because apparitions provide us with the best kind of evidence but because in the popular mind they provide the most dramatic. From childhood onwards, few things excite and/or scare us more than good ghost stories, and it is a constant surprise to me that these tales of the paranormal do not prompt more people to pursue the question of whether or not they represent any truth about the existence of an afterlife.

Apparitions, Visions, Materializations, and Ghosts

An apparition is something that registers upon the senses of an observer or observers, gives the impression of objective reality, yet isn't physically there. The term comes from the Latin *apparitio*, the root of which also gives us "appear" and "appearance." Apparitions are therefore thought by the observer both at the time and subsequently to be situated in the *external* world, unlike hallucinations (such as dreams and the images sometimes seen in certain forms of mental delusion), which are recognized either later or at the time as occurring in the inner world of the imagination. We tend to think of apparitions as another name for ghosts, the manifestation of someone no longer in the physical world, but we can experience apparitions of a person who is known to be alive at the time (I've seen an apparition of this kind myself, as I explain in Chapter 16). And we can see apparitions of objects or of landscapes or of apparently advanced spiritual beings, although we usually refer to these as "visions." There is also some confusion between the terms "apparitions" and "materializations." The former applies to a figure that appears complete from the outset, while the latter applies to figures that seem to build up in front of the observer, as sometimes happens in the séance room (Chapter 12).

From the standpoint of survival, the most relevant apparitions are those of people who have physically died. Who or what are these apparitions and what are they said to tell us about survival? Sometimes they are associated with hauntings, those curious happenings in which sightings of the same or similar apparition are reported over a number of years and which are dealt with in the next chapter, but often more interesting from the point of view of survival evidence are those apparitions seen only once or only over a short period of time. Unlike hauntings, which often seem purposeless and repetitive, the majority of these cases involve people whose deaths are recent, and frequently they seem to occur as a way of demonstrating the continuing existence of the person concerned.

Both the popular literature and the serious research literature published by the Society for Psychical Research (SPR) in Britain and by comparable scientific societies in Europe and the USA are full of reports of sightings of apparitions defined in this way. Copies of the *SPR Proceedings*, first published in 1882 and available on line from the SPR, are in fact an excellent place to start for anyone who wishes to gain some idea of the vast literature available. However, I intend to begin with examples from some of the cases reported personally to me. The narrator of the first case is a young woman, who had no previous experiences of this kind and knew little about psychic matters.

We live in one of a pair of small cottages. Next door to us there was an old lady with whom we became quite friendly. Eventually she fell ill and was under medical care. One day I was at our kitchen window at the front of the house, and I saw her pass by the window on her way to our front door, as she often did. I was pleased to see that she was better and up and about again. I went to the front door to greet her, but there was no one there. Later that day, I learnt that she had died at about the time I saw her pass by the window. The old lady looked exactly as she did in life – ordinary clothes, no semi-transparency, nothing strange or unusual about her at all.

The narrator was a serious and level-headed woman, who was convinced of what she had seen, and who badly wanted an explanation for the experience. Here is another example, from an account given to me by a sensible and articulate woman known to me for some years. She reports having had many psychic experiences throughout her life; this one took place while she was still a teenager.

One of my friends, a young girl, was diagnosed with cancer. She was operated upon and lost one of her arms, but sadly the operation did not stop the spread of the disease, and she died shortly afterwards. In life, she had been particularly close to my brother, and one day when I entered his room after her death I saw her sitting there in the chair she always occupied when she came to see him. She and I talked about ordinary things, very matter-of-fact.

In this instance the observer accepted the incident without surprise, and remains convinced that the apparition was indeed that of her friend, as fully alive as she ever was when in her physical body. It was this total lack of surprise that explains why they spoke only about "ordinary ... matter of fact" things, as if the visitor wished simply to demonstrate her continuing existence and assure herself that all was well with her earthly friends. We may feel frustrated that she was not asked about the process of dying, the nature of the next world, and her experiences in the afterlife. Instead, the whole incident sounds very much like two old friends meeting up for a brief chat.

But I have found that this is not untypical of people who have been psychic throughout life. For the most part they are well aware of the voluminous information already available purporting to give details on the afterlife (which we look at in Chapter 18), and taking these details for granted they seem to behave as naturally as they would with a living visitor. As with communications through mediums, visitors from the next world seem more intent upon insisting that they are well and happy, and on sending their love to those they have left behind, than on more lofty matters.

In both the above examples the apparitions were as solid and apparently objective as in life, and not the wraith-like ghosts of popular tradition, although we have no way of knowing whether the respective observers saw them clairvoyantly or whether, had anyone else been present, they would have seen them too. Both examples are also unlike popular tradition in that although the apparitions are seen in places familiar to them in life, neither is associated in any way with places said to be haunted. And neither prompted any of the responses said to be typical in those encountering apparitions, such as fear or sensations of sudden cold. Indeed, in the first example the observer took the apparition for a living person.

Here is another example of an apparition who was not associated in any way with a traditional haunting, although he did not appear quite as solid as in the two previous examples. The observer in this case is a highly intelligent professional woman, well known to me, who reports having had only one other psychic experience – many years earlier – in her life.

I was on a residential yoga retreat with a group of other members of our yoga group, and one day when we were taking a walk in single file and in silence through the woods, Brian, one of the founder members of our group who had recently died, was suddenly walking next to me. He was as tall as in life, a big smile on his face, but not quite solid. I would describe him as semi-transparent. He placed his left hand on my shoulder and we walked together through the woods. I was struck by the fact that he still had the two deformed fingers on his hand that were a birth defect, and I said to him "Oh, Brian, I thought we were mended when we get to heaven." We walked together for about a minute and then he disappeared just before I left the wood. Later I realized that he showed me the two deformed fingers as clear proof of his identity.

Again, there is no fear or surprise on the part of the observer, and although the figure of Brian is semi-transparent, it is yet solid enough for her to be aware of his hand on her shoulder, and for her to see the two deformed fingers that he had in life. The wood through which they were walking consisted mainly of small trees, and the light was good. Assuming the truthfulness of the three witnesses (and I have no reason to doubt it, though the point is touched on again in the next section), might there be normal explanations for their experiences? The apparitions were seen by them in daylight and close to, which rules out the possibility of tricks of the light.

This leaves only the possibility that they were either mistaken in what they thought they saw, or each was the victim of a cruel hoax of some kind, with persons unknown impersonating the apparitions. The fallibility of human testimony is discussed in the next section, but what of the possibility that the witnesses were hoaxed? For various reasons, this seems unlikely. In the third of the cases, the apparition is described as semi-transparent and with a deformed hand. In the second of them the apparition was in view of the witness for some little while, and words were exchanged. In the first of them the hypothetical hoaxer not only resembled the old lady closely enough to be mistaken for her, but appeared at or around the time of her death. To dismiss all sightings as explicable by natural means therefore seems likely to stretch credulity a little too far for comfort.

I have chosen these three examples from the many I could quote not only because they appear to be good cases, but because together they illustrate some of the important features of apparitions. These can be summarized as follows:

1. The apparitions were seen whether or not the observer knew that the person concerned was dead.
2. They were seen whether or not the observer had any professed psychic abilities.
3. They were not seen in places thought to be haunted.
4. They aroused no fear or unusual sensations in the observers.
5. They were entirely recognizable, and in the first example the observer mistook the apparition for a living person.
6. They behaved as normal human beings, and were seen walking, smiling and sitting down.
7. They remained in sight for an appreciable time.
8. In two examples they were solid and in one semi-transparent.
9. In two examples words were addressed to them, and in one of these examples a conversation was held.
10. In one example the apparition had a physical defect present during physical life, contrary to the presuppositions of the observer.
11. All three sightings took place in daylight, two of them outdoors.
12. In no instance did the observer report having just woken from sleep before the sighting, or being under the influence of drugs or prone to hallucinations.

Many of the above features are also present in other reports of apparitions I have collected over the years. Contrary to popular conceptions of ghosts, apparitions solid enough to be taken for living people are by no means uncommon; neither is seeing apparitions in places not said to be haunted, or seeing them in broad daylight. Reports of conversations with apparitions are relatively rare, however, although I have another example in my files very similar to the second of those just quoted. A doctoral student in psychology at Cardiff University who had had many psychic experiences confided to me (in private and only when he knew of my interest in the subject – reports of psychic experiences are not greatly appreciated in most university psychology departments) that after the death of his sister she appeared to him in his bedroom, sat beside him on the bed, and as in the second example above exchanged a few words designed simply to reassure him that she lived on.

In each of these cases the apparitions seemed aware they were visitors from the next world, but this is not always the case. The next example comes from one of the security guards at Canterbury Cathedral, primary cathedral of the Anglican community. Churches, cathedrals, castles, and ancient monuments in general have their fair share of reported sightings, but very few of these can be taken seriously. The eeriness of such places at night sets the scene, and the imagination of the observers usually does the rest. But there are exceptions. The security guard at Canterbury Cathedral, Harry Wales, who impressed me as a careful and accurate witness, reported to me that one evening in March 2001 at approximately 11 p.m. he was doing his rounds outside the main building, in a part of the cathedral complex that leads down to the cloisters. The whole area, including the cloisters, is illuminated by powerful electric lights throughout the night. Outside the gate leading into the cloisters he saw the figure of a monk, in his habit and with his hood pulled over his head. Men in ecclesiastical dress are part and parcel of the life of a cathedral, and Harry Wales assumed the man was a guest staying in one of the cathedral precincts taking an evening stroll. He thought no more of it, but when passing the night security post a few minutes later he mentioned the experience to colleagues. They expressed surprise. Harry was new to the job at the time and unfamiliar with the comings and goings of cathedral personnel, but his more experienced colleagues assured him that there were no monks currently in residence, and the figure therefore was suspicious.

Harry quickly returned to where he had seen the monk, only to find that the figure was now the other side of the gate and inside the cloisters. The gate is constructed of heavy iron bars which allow a clear view into the cloisters, but which are too close together to allow access even to domestic animals. As part of his duties Harry had locked the gate earlier in the evening, and he found it was now still locked. There was only one key, and that was on Harry's key ring. His immediate response was to call out through the gate to challenge the monk and demand to know where he was going. The answer was "the scriptorium." The figure then abruptly disappeared, and it was at this point that Harry realized he had seen an apparition. Harry's colleagues back at the security post were puzzled not only by the experience but by the reference to "the scriptorium" (where the monks used to copy the scriptures) which no longer existed, and the following day one of them took Harry to the Cathedral archives, where their research revealed that there were no references to its existence after the twelfth century.

As with the cases already mentioned, can we offer normal explanations for Harry's experience? Could Harry's colleagues have obtained the master key to the cloisters, and disguised one of their number as a monk in order to play a trick on him? Possibly, but tricks only work if the person tricked is subsequently told he has been tricked, and there is general merriment at his expense. Nothing of the kind happened. Harry's colleagues remained as mystified as he, and it seems they had little difficulty in accepting his experiences. Most of them confess to having seen or heard inexplicable things for themselves during their nightly rounds, and it is recognized that the Cathedral and its precincts are haunted. I spoke to one of Harry's colleagues who confirmed that Harry's experience was well known among the security staff, and accepted at face value. Nevertheless, could it simply be a tall story told to impress a gullible tourist? Hardly. Tourists are locked out of the Cathedral grounds at night, and I was there as a guest not as a sightseer. After Harry told me the story I went back over it, questioning him closely on each of the details. He never wavered or tried to change any of them, and seemed fully convinced, two years after the event, that he had seen an apparition.

Could an interloper have gained access to the cloisters? Doubtful. There are no unlocked points of access to the cloisters at night. Could someone have hidden there during the day and avoided Harry when he made his rounds of the cloisters at night before locking up? In which case, could an accomplice dressed as a monk have shown himself to Harry outside the gate, while the first miscreant emerged from his hiding place on Harry's return and carried out his spot of play-acting from behind the bars of the gate? Could the accomplice have then returned to his hiding place, and slipped out unnoticed when the gate was opened in the morning? Could this have been a student prank perhaps? If so it was a prank that had little purpose, as no one tried to make capital out of it afterwards. More importantly, however, I have explored the cloisters in detail and there are no hiding places likely to escape the attention of security staff on their rounds. Even the Dean's Steps that lead from the cloisters up to the Cathedral are a dead-end at night, with the door into the Cathedral securely locked.

The monk has not been seen again, either by Harry or by his colleagues. In answer to my question Harry informed me that he has had a few previous psychic experiences in his life, particularly in the family home in Yorkshire, where he and other family members have seen a child in an apparently oversized coat walking up the stairs. Possibly his psychic abilities played some part in his sighting of the monk, and it is interesting that the apparition, if that is what it was, both heard him enquire where it was heading and gave an audible reply.

If apparition it was, the ability to hear and reply to a witness contradicts the theory that apparitions of this kind are images from the past, impressed upon and retained by the surrounding fabric, and re-played for some unknown reason at various times. As such, it is argued, they resemble little more than old photographs, and have nothing to do with surviving personalities.

Harry's apparition does not fall into this category. But if it was an apparition of a twelfth-century monk does it suggest he has been lingering in the cloisters for eight centuries, forever finding his way to a phantom scriptorium? Perhaps. Communicators have frequently insisted through mediums that time means nothing on the other side, and that so-called earthbound spirits may remain in material surroundings for any number of our years. Another possibility is that the apparition returned to the earthly dimension for some purpose to do with his memories of the scriptorium, and once his mission was accomplished, left the scene for good. The latter certainly seems a more comforting explanation, but a discussion of earthbound spirits must be left to Chapter 18.

Whatever the explanation, the apparition seemed aware of Harry's presence, and responded to his question. However, sometimes words are spoken by apparitions that have no relevance for anyone else present, as is the case in the next example, where the apparition seems to be in a dimension of his own, caught perhaps in a time warp from the past. As such, the case resembles in some ways a traditional haunting. The observer was George Jonas, caretaker of the Yorkshire Museum in York, UK, and the case occurred in 1953. Jonas reports that after locking up the museum and retiring to the basement kitchen, he and his wife both heard footsteps overhead. On going up to investigate he saw an elderly gentleman leaving the museum director's office. Mr. Jonas supposed he must be an eccentric professor, and anxious to help he asked him if he was looking for the director.

He did not answer but just shuffled past me and began to go down the stairs towards the library. Being only a few feet from him, I saw his face clearly ... He looked agitated, had a frown on his face, and kept muttering, "I must find it; I must find it." ... He looked just as real as you or me.

Anxious to finish his duties for the day and go home, but not wishing to leave the elderly and possibly confused gentleman in the building overnight, Mr. Jonas followed him into the darkened library and switched on the lights.

He was standing between two tall book racks ... He seemed anxious to find something ... thinking he was deaf, I stretched out my right hand to touch him on the shoulder. But as my hand drew near his coat he vanished.

The case is cited by Eric Dingwall (at one time research officer of the SPR) and Trevor Hall in *Four Modern Ghosts*, and was also reported by Brian Lumley in the respected regional newspaper, the *Yorkshire Evening Post* (October 10, 1953). Mr. Jonas appeared very sure of his facts, and furnished a detailed description of the apparition, which could have been of someone from the late nineteenth century. He was said to be odd looking, old fashioned, with fluffy side whiskers and very little hair, wearing a frock coat with big black buttons on the back, drainpipe trousers, and elastic sided boots. Mr. Jonas reported seeing the apparition again a month later, this time descending the stairs and passing through a closed door.

It seems that the old gentleman was not subsequently identified with any known person, which is not surprising given the numerous visitors to the museum and the changes of staff over the years. If he was indeed from another dimension, let us hope he found the object of his search, whatever that might have been. If we can rely on Mr. Jonas' account, the gentleman may have been a frequent visitor to the museum library in life. If this was the case, and if he had been hunting down the years for his lost object, it is interesting that there appear to be no previous accounts of his appearance. Or, so life-like was he, that perhaps others before Mr. Jonas indeed saw him on his solitary wanderings, only to pass him by with hardly a glance. Eccentrics are by no means an uncommon sight in museums (there are a fair number of them in universities too, for that matter).

Are Apparitions Good Evidence for Survival?

At face value, apparitions would appear to be genuine sightings of people who have survived death, and who are able, by means unknown to science, to re-appear in their physical forms. The problem is that the only evidence we have for their appearance is the word of witnesses, usually of only one person in each case. There are several possibilities. Witnesses, such as those in the above examples, who report seeing apparitions may simply be untruthful, possibly in order to seek attention, or to lend themselves an aura of mystery. Their memories may be playing tricks. They may be mistaken in what they think they have seen. They may be exaggerating trivial incidents that have a perfectly rational explanation. They may, although not admitting it, have been under the influence of drugs at the time. They may simply have over-active powers of imagination, perhaps fuelled by the fact that they *expect* to see apparitions. They may have had brief psychotic episodes in which they experienced hallucinations, which they projected outwards into apparently objective realities. Dr. Louisa Rhine (1956, 1961 and 1967) proposed that the observer's unconscious mind may generate the experience as an hallucinatory response to an emotional need. Dr. Gardner Murphy, a leading American psychologist who took a keen interest in psychical research, put forward a similar view (Murphy 1945).

Alternatively, witnesses who see apparitions may be having genuinely paranormal experiences, but these experiences may have nothing to do with survival. Edmund Gurney, one of the senior authors of one of the largest collections of cases of apparitions ever published (Sidgwick et al 1886), considered that all of them could be explained as telepathic impressions sent by the person appearing as the apparition (termed the "agent") just before he or she died. In his view, the fact that the apparition is sometimes not 'seen' at the moment it is sent by the agent but some time later is because the telepathic impression may only emerge slowly into the witnesses' consciousness. Gurney explained reported instances of more than one person seeing an apparition simultaneously as telepathy from the principal witness to the minds of his or her companions. H. F. Saltmarsh, another prominent figure in the history of the SPR, took a similar view, insisting that telepathic images received by the agent while the latter was still alive "may [remain] latent in the subconsciousness until a favorable opportunity for emergence" occurs (Saltmarsh 1932). Thus both Gurney and Saltmarsh considered that the apparition could simply be a memory, albeit of a paranormal experience, projected outwards by some means. This is an example of the so-called Super-ESP (or Super-PSI) hypothesis, which we look at in detail in Chapter 5, and which suggests that all supposed contact with the deceased is explicable in terms of telepathy or clairvoyance by or from living people.

Either of the above possibilities – simple hallucinations induced by emotional needs, or projected memories of earlier telepathic impressions conveyed while the agent was still alive – could be true. If they are, then apparitions, although possibly paranormal, have nothing to do with survival. Skeptics will certainly prefer these possibilities to the survivalist explanation. On the other hand, the witnesses themselves (to judge by those I have mentioned and the many others I have interviewed) vehemently reject these possibilities when they are suggested to them. They claim not to be subject to hallucinations, frequently deny that they had any "emotional need" to see the apparition at the time, and regard the idea that they were projecting outwards memories received telepathically from him or her while they were alive as impossibly far-fetched (it is noticeable that those who advance theories to explain away apparitions do not appear to ask witnesses what they think of these theories). However, in the examples I have given so far, none of the apparitions, with the possible exception of the old lady in the first of them, gave information unknown to the witness, such as the fact of their death. The great majority of cases are of this kind; the witness already knows that the apparition is of someone who has died. Can these cases therefore be explained as pure imagination, fuelled by expectation, on the part of the witness? If we believe in psychic phenomena and expect we may see an apparition of someone close to us who has died, this may render us more likely to imagine that we do.

The witnesses in at least three of the cases quoted earlier were certainly believers in psychic phenomena, but this is by no means true of all witnesses. The witness in the next case was certainly not a believer, and had no expectation of any kind of paranormal experience. The sighting was of the late Professor Arthur Ellison, twice President of the Society for Psychical Research, and a man with half a century of involvement in psychical research. If knowledge of this research, together with much first-hand experience of paranormal phenomena, is of any help in achieving a post-mortem appearance, then Professor Ellison was better qualified than most. However, the witness, a young woman related to Arthur by marriage, had no interest in psychical research, had had no previous paranormal experiences, and is described by Arthur's wife Marian as the most firmly skeptical member of his extended family. Consequently she had no expectations of any post-mortem contact with Arthur.

The sighting took place in Arthur's home, in daylight, on the evening of his death in September 2000. Daphne (pseudonym) was alone in the house at the time with Marian, Arthur's wife. Although naturally upset, she was not in tears, and nothing was impeding her vision. However, while in the hall she clearly saw, through the lightly frosted glass door of the lounge, Arthur walk across the room. She reports him as appearing as solid and objective as in real life, and she was able to describe the clothes he was wearing. The only part of her description that did not fit Arthur was that he was no longer limping, and appeared free of the hip problem that had affected him towards the end of his life. In traversing the line of sight afforded by the glass door the apparition was visible for some 12 feet. Marian, to whom Daphne described the experience immediately afterwards, described her to me as "white and shaking." There was no television switched on in the lounge at the time, no pets in the Ellison household, and no object in the line of sight that could conceivably have been mistaken for a human being. Marian detailed Daphne's experience to me the following day, and shortly afterwards I and Montague Keen, Secretary of the SPR Survival Research Committee of which I am chair, interviewed Daphne. Her account agreed in every particular with the details given to me by Marian. She informed us during the interview that for two days after the experience she felt stunned by it, but then was forced to accept it for what it was, namely a clear sighting of Arthur after his physical death. The fact that Arthur's apparition was moving and that she saw it clearly enough to notice the clothes he was wearing and the fact that he was no longer limping (the loss of this disability compares interestingly with the deformed fingers in one of the examples given earlier), further militates against the notion that she may have been mistaken in what she saw. I wrote down the account of her experiences as given to us, and she subsequently confirmed this as a correct record of what had happened (a fuller description of this incident is given in Fontana 2003).

As Daphne does not appear to have mistaken any person or object for Arthur, how might we explain her experience? Her memory was hardly likely to be playing tricks on her, as she described the experience to Marian immediately after it happened, and gave the same account to Montague Keen and myself a few days later. Exaggeration also seems unlikely. Marian describes her as white and shaken immediately after the event. She has no history of psychotic episodes, and she is not a drug-taker. The suggestion by Saltmarsh that people seeing apparitions may be experiencing a latent telepathic image received during the sender's lifetime hardly seems appropriate. Daphne had had no previous experience of receiving telepathic images of any kind and had apparently no ability in that direction. And if it was a latent telepathic image, what had become of Arthur's (very pronounced) limp? Louisa Rhine's proposal that the observer's unconscious mind generates the experience as an hallucinatory response to emotional need is possible – assuming one finds such a proposal credible – but appears unlikely. Although fond of Arthur (as was everyone who knew him), Daphne was not a blood relation and gives no indication of having an "emotional need" to see Arthur or to become converted to a belief in survival.

What other explanations might there be? Daphne is an intelligent, articulate and practical young woman, and suffers from no defects in vision. Marian Ellison, who is a long-serving and highly respected member of the SPR, confirms that the young woman is not of a nervous disposition and is not given to fantasy or deceit. She had no obvious reason for fabricating an experience that undermined the skeptical position she had consistently maintained against Arthur Ellison during his lifetime. She impressed Montague Keen and me during our interview with her as a highly credible witness, and Marian Ellison is in no doubt of the reliability of her account. Unless one rejects the notion of survival out of hand, the one obvious remaining possibility is that Arthur, with his consuming interest in psychical research and his very evident love for his family, was attempting to make known his continuing existence. It is useless to speculate as to whether or not anyone else would have seen him had they been standing beside Daphne. We do not know. Similarly we do not know why the apparition should have appeared while Daphne was the observer rather than Marian, but it is possible that Arthur, if it were he, had no choice in the matter. Alternatively, he may have considered it better evidence if he appeared to Daphne, a known skeptic, than to Marian, a known believer. Equally we do not know why an apparition of Arthur should be seen behind the glass door of the lounge instead of in the hallway. If the deceased has to visualize a location very clearly if they are to appear there, as seems to be the case with apparitions of the living (Chapter 16), then it may be that it was easier for him to picture and focus upon the lounge than upon other downstairs locations. The whole incident certainly provides us with rich material for speculation.

Collective Sightings

Reported sightings of apparitions that do not provide us with any additional evidence that they live on after death are never likely to convince those who have no wish to be convinced. However, what if the apparition is seen simultaneously by more than one person? The testimony of one person may be unreliable, but an account given by two or more people of the same experience is likely to be less so. In addition, although it is conceivable that one person may have picked up a telepathic impression from a deceased person while they were alive and projected it outwards after their death, the chances of two people having picked up the same impression and then projecting it outwards simultaneously seems less credible.

Cases in which two people claim to see the same apparition simultaneously are not uncommon. I have examples in my own files, one of the most interesting of them involving a respectable middle-aged husband and wife who both saw the same woman in their garden disappearing behind an outhouse into a small area of the garden with no hiding place and from which there was positively no other exit. On following her they found the area to be empty. But again, human testimony, even when two or more people are involved, may be unreliable. One person may believe they see something, and the very suggestion may convince the other that they see it as well. Even when both people, at separate interviews, give similar accounts this cannot be taken as final evidence unless – as never seems to happen – they have had no opportunity to discuss the experience with each other beforehand.

G. N. M. Tyrell, author of a classic work on apparitions in 1953, reports identifying 130 cases in the literature in which apparitions were reported as perceived by two or more people, and a collection of such cases was made by Professor Hornell Hart, who took a particular interest in survival. Professor Hart published one of the best of these cases in 1933 and again in 1959, while another full account is given by Sir Ernest Bennet in 1939, and it remains one of the most intriguing accounts that we have of collective sightings. The fact that it occurred many years ago does not lessen its value. It is a great mistake, in psychical research as in other areas of inquiry, to assume that anything more than ten years old can be discounted. More important than the age of a case is the standing of the investigators and the steps they took to be sure of the facts they were reporting.

The case took place in 1932 in a cottage in Oxford Street, Ramsbury, Wiltshire, UK, and concerned the apparition of a chimney sweep, Samuel Bull, who, before his death on June 21, 1931 after four years of suffering from sooty cancer, had lived there with his elderly invalid wife and his grandson, James Bull, aged 21. The local vicar, the Reverend G. H. Hackett, responsible for discovering the case and for the early interviews with the family, described Samuel Bull as a man "of very pleasant and high character," who it seems had had no interest in spiritualism during his lifetime and who had had only one psychic experience, a precognitive conviction of the death of his son, captured by the Germans after the Battle of Mons early in the First World War.

After Samuel Bull's death, a married daughter, Mrs. Edwards, gave up her own home and came with her husband and five children to join Mrs. Bull and James Bull in the cottage (a wretched dwelling by all accounts, with several rooms too unsafe to be used) for the purpose of looking after her mother. In February 1932 Mrs. Edwards and her eldest child, a daughter Mary aged 13, saw the apparition of Samuel Bull ascend the stairs and pass through a closed door into the room in which he had died, and which had been occupied by Mrs. Bull, who had nursed him faithfully during the years of his last illness, before it became unfit for habitation. Shortly afterwards, Mrs. Edwards and James Bull saw the apparition together. Hearing of the sightings, Mrs. Bull confirmed that she had previously also seen it. Subsequently all the members of the family saw the apparition together on several occasions, all those present seeing it every time it appeared. Even the youngest child, a girl of about 5 years old, recognized it as her grandfather.

Until April 9 the apparition appeared frequently, looking solid and lifelike, walking rather than gliding, and manifesting both in daylight and in artificial light. The features were clearly recognizable, and the clothes were those usually worn by Samuel Bull after work, including his muffler. Mrs. Edwards particularly commented on the appearance of his "poor hands," with the knuckles seeming to protrude through the skin. Twice the apparition laid a hand, which felt cold, on Mrs. Bull's forehead, and once she heard him address her by her name, Jane. Mrs. Edwards insisted that the whole family always felt a sense of "presence" for about half an hour before he appeared. On no occasions were the appearances fleeting, and in one instance Samuel Bull was said to be visible intermittently over a period of several hours (sadly we are given no details of the intriguing discussions that must have taken place among the family during these hours, or told whether or not he was invited to participate in them). Except for the last two appearances, by which time there were good prospects that the family was soon to be re-housed, the apparition was reported as appearing saddened, and it was felt by the family that this was due to his concern at their forlorn living conditions. After initial fear, the family became accustomed to the apparition, although they reported the appearances "took a great deal out of them."

It is unfortunate that no one outside the Bull family is reported as witnessing the apparition. We must assume that even the tolerance of the Bull family for overcrowding did not stretch to sharing their humble cottage with a team of investigators for an extended period, but the "sense of presence" felt by the family before a sighting took place should have enabled them to alert in good time neighbors or others interested in the case. However, in addition to the Reverend Hackett, careful interviews were conducted with Mrs. Edwards and with Mrs. Bull by Admiral Hyde Parker, who lived locally and who through Lord Selborne drew the attention of the SPR to the case, and by a formidable duo from the SPR, Lord Arthur James Balfour the former British Prime Minister and a past President of the Society, and Mr. J. G. Piddington, another past President and a meticulous investigator. The witnesses appeared perfectly consistent in their replies to the various questions put to them by these eminent gentlemen. Later Mr. and Mrs. Edwards both signed a statement corroborating the recorded facts. Unfortunately, Mrs. Bull was bedridden and near to her end by April 14, 1932 when Balfour and Piddington, in company with Admiral Hyde Parker and the Reverend Hackett, visited the cottage - although she managed to answer their questions during a 40 minute interview – and the family was in the process of vacating the cottage for their new accommodation. Samuel Bull's last reported appearance was on the 9th April, so regrettably no opportunity for a sighting arose during their visit.

We would certainly like to know more about this case, and about the impressionability of the Bull and the Edwards families. But where several people are involved and remain consistent in their stories, lying becomes less likely as an explanation, as do the possibilities that memory is playing tricks or mistakes in observation may have been made. We are told that Samuel Bull's apparition was as solid as if he were alive, and that it was seen not only simultaneously by all family members present, but on one occasion remained intermittently visible for several hours. This is hardly the kind of occurrence that four adults and five children are all likely to mistake. It is also unlikely that both the Bulls and the Edwards, children included, were suffering psychotic episodes all at the same time. Drugs also seem unlikely. And Saltmarsh's suggested possibility that impressions received by others while the deceased person is alive may later be projected outwards from memory by them hardly stands up if indeed all those present simultaneously obtained the same view of Samuel Bull and of his actions. We can hardly suppose that all of them, including a five-year-old child, were projecting outwards exactly the same impressions of the dead man, and at exactly the same time. Gurney's theory that one of the witnesses may have communicated his or her telepathic memory-image to everyone else also seems unlikely. I know of no results of group telepathy experiments that suggest successful recipients all see images that differ little from each other. Louisa Rhine's suggestion that the observer's unconscious mind generates the experience as an hallucination in response to the observer's emotional needs stands up no better. We can hardly suppose that the four adults and the five children all had the same emotional need in relation to the dead man, and all hallucinated his appearance simultaneously and in correct perspective (the ability of individual observers in collective sightings each to see the apparition correctly from their different positions, just as they would if it were material, is commented upon both by Tyrrell and by Hornell Hart).

On the face of it, this case would therefore seem to be a strong argument for survival. The investigators discussed the possibility that the family may have invented the haunting in order to press their case with the local authorities for re-housing, but both the Reverend Hackett and Admiral Hyde Parker appeared convinced of the good faith of the family, and the Reverend Hackett even considered that any plot to deceive those responsible for re-housing them might well have had the opposite effect from that intended. Lord Balfour and Mr. Piddington also testified to the fact that Mrs. Edwards was a good witness. But even if we discount the possibility of deliberate deception and accept that the accounts of Samuel Bull's post-mortem appearances are correct, they do not necessarily demonstrate his survival. The appearances could have been of some sort of animated thought-form, created consciously or unconsciously by Samuel Bull during his lifetime, which lingered for a while after his death, even showing up in correct perspective to all those present. Such an idea may not be quite as preposterous as it sounds. Most of us carry in our minds a reasonably accurate picture of how we look, and it might be argued that in certain instances this may impress itself upon the environment. If, as is apparent from the research reviewed in the last chapter, the mind can operate outside time and space and transmit thoughts and images from one mind to another, thoughts would seem to be powerful things, and it would be unrealistic to suppose we understand all aspects of their power. In the Tibetan Buddhist tradition, there is a belief that through very intensive meditational practices the mind can indeed create thought-forms – *tulpas* – that under certain circumstances appear to witnesses to have objective reality. Alexandra David-Neel, the French philosopher and linguist who spent many years in Tibet and herself became an initiated Tibetan Buddhist Lama, gives an account in *Magic and Mystery in Tibet* of her own experience of a *tulpa*, and insists that such thought forms can become visible to others, and can be taken for living beings. However, even if such seemingly preposterous accounts of thought-forms can be taken at face value, it seems that their creation is only possible by highly trained meditators who spend several months in solitary confinement for the specific purpose.

We have no evidence that Samuel Bull, whatever his skills as a chimney sweep, was involved in any intensive practices of this kind during his lifetime. His family even testified that was not interested in spiritualism, and had given no indication during his lifetime that he intended to appear to them in any way and by any means after his death. We can probably therefore dismiss thought-forms as offering a feasible explanation for his apparition. Another possibility is that his apparition represented what Crookall, whose work on out-of-body and near-death experiences will be referred to later in the book, and other writers refer to as an "astral shell." We shall say more about such matters when we discuss the nature of survival in Chapter 18, but the idea, which dates back to the ancient Egyptian model of the *ka*, the *ab*, the *akh*, and the *ba* mentioned in the last chapter, is that we possess various different kinds of bodies of progressive levels of subtlety. The physical body is the most solid, then comes the so-called energy body (analogous to the Egyptian *ka*), which permeates and sustains the physical body and acts as a link between it and the soul body and the various other higher-level bodies. At death, the energy body and all higher bodies leave the physical body, but the energy body is itself discarded some three days later. However, instead of disintegrating, in some cases the energy body persists for an indeterminate time, occasionally even for years and centuries. Under certain circumstances it can still be seen by those on earth, usually repeating mechanically (since it lacks consciousness) some of the habitual actions of the deceased physical body. Referred to as an astral shell, this energy body is used by some to explain many apparent hauntings, where the ghosts concerned exhibit this mindless, repetitive behavior (the Egyptians believed that the energy body in fact remained close to the dead body, ready to re-animate it if need be – hence the practice of preserving the body by mummification).

It may be wrong to dismiss the idea of an energy body out of hand. However, if such a body is responsible for at least some apparitions, it is difficult to explain why it is seen in the clothes worn by the deceased. We are told in the spiritualist literature that in the afterlife the soul body clothes itself by thought. Perhaps. But as the energy body has no consciousness, and therefore no capacity for thought, it is difficult to understand how it also can clothe itself in a careful copy of the clothes worn in life. Similarly it is difficult to understand how it can take apparently intelligent action. We are told that Samuel Bull placed his hand on his wife's forehead and spoke her name, and in two of the examples given earlier we are told that the apparitions actually held conversations with the living. There are also examples of apparitions who convey accurate information, and examples of these will be given shortly. On balance, astral shells would seem to be an inadequate explanation for at least many reported apparitions, including that of Samuel Bull.

The theory sometimes put forward that apparitions are images that have been "photographed" in some way by the fabric of a building and that are then replayed from time to time like an old film, also seems an unlikely explanation for the examples at which we have been looking. The theory suffers from the weakness that in many instances – as in the third of the examples given earlier – the apparition may appear in surroundings which he or she did not visit during life. Another weakness is that if it is correct, then why are some incidents (out of the countless millions that take place every day) photographed by the environment, and then replayed after the deaths of those involved and not others? The answer usually given is that some highly emotional incident, such as a violent crime, is responsible, but in none of the examples so far given was any such incident involved.

Recently, another theory that relates apparitions to the environment has been advanced by Tandy (2000), namely that infrasound – sound with a frequency below that of 20 Hertz and undetectable by normal hearing – may give some individuals the sense that there is a "presence" in the room. It is known that exposure to infrasound affects some people in strange ways (e.g. inducing feelings of dizziness or nausea or disorientation). Attempts to develop weapons emitting infrasound have shown that the effect upon people is not apparent if the sound is only airborne, which suggests that it may work inside buildings by setting up resonances in their structure. Readings taken by Tandy in a fourteenth-century cellar, once part of a Benedictine Priory where presences have been reported, revealed that a continuous sound frequency of around 19 Hz exists, which he considers supports the idea that this frequency may be the cause of the reported feelings of presence.

However, these feelings of presence are usually only feelings, and visual sightings seem rarely to be involved. At most, the infrasound theory would therefore seem relevant only to a small number of apparitions. In addition, it fails to account for two of the examples given earlier in which the apparition was experienced in the open, where any infrasound possibly present would have been airborne and thus ineffective. And although no measurements for infrasound were taken at the time Daphne reported seeing Arthur Ellison's apparition walk across the lounge, neither occupants nor visitors have ever reported any sense of "presence" in the Ellison's house before Arthur's death, which seems to rule out infrasound as a likely explanation. Furthermore, even if infrasound is consistently identified when apparitions are reported inside buildings, this does not demonstrate that they are in any sense "caused" by the action of the sound upon the brain. It may simply be that infrasound inhibits the mechanisms in the brain that usually prevent such experiences from emerging into consciousness. Other environmental factors may have a similar inhibitory effect. Certain atmospheric conditions (such as low air pressure) and certain geophysical structures (such as granite rocks and so-called ley lines) are also reported as facilitating genuine psychic experiences. And as we saw from the work of Spottiswoode and May reported in the last chapter, Local Sidereal Time may also, for reasons unknown, have this effect.

Another example of an apparition seen by more than one person is given by Sir Ernest Bennett (1939). In it the narrator, Vivienne Lee, then a 26 year-old woman, recalls an incident that occurred when she was nine years old concerning a favorite uncle who had died a year previously. While kneeling on the kitchen floor playing with her dolls around 11 a.m. she looks up to see her uncle standing outside the window:

... he looked happy – he held out his arms to me, and smiled – telling me not to worry any more ... He did not speak as we speak – my mind seemed to be in contact with his mind – his lips did not move ... I remember perfectly every detail, much more clearly than I remember physical events of a later date. I could clearly see through his body – the features were the same as before – the outline the same ... I rushed to the door in my efforts to get outside and touch him, but he slowly vanished ... From that day I was satisfied ... I know beyond any doubt, I saw my uncle. I was certainly not thinking of him at the time, being far too much engrossed with my dolls. The clearness of this event has never left me.

On sighting her uncle she called out to tell the housemaid who was in the adjoining pantry. The latter confirmed in writing to Sir Ernest that she looked out the pantry window in response to the child's cry and also saw the figure. From her different perspective she could not see the man's face, but recognized the figure as that of the uncle. She immediately joined the child and together they ran out of the back door only to see the apparition, in Miss Lee's words, "slowly vanishing" into thin air.

An interesting feature of this case is that although the uncle tells the child not to worry, his lips do not move and the communication seems to be mind to mind. The fact that the housemaid saw him too – and was prepared to testify to the fact even many years after the event – seems to rule out the possibility that the incident was due to the childish imagination of a nine-year old girl. As in the Bull case, both witnesses saw the apparition from different angles, and both saw it vanishing as they ran out of the back door. Miss Lee describes the figure as translucent rather than solid, but unmistakably that of her uncle.

One of what seems to be the best authenticated examples of collective sightings was reported to William Stead (Stead 1891), an experienced investigator of the paranormal and the crusading founder and editor of the London-based *Review of Reviews*. (Stead once spent two months in prison after showing how easy it was to "buy" a child prostitute and take her out of the country, but his actions led to an outlawing of the practice, which was his intention.) The case involved officers of the British cavalry regiment the 5th Lancers, who were stationed in the cavalry barracks at Aldershot at the time. In the summer of 1880 at around seven in the evening the officers were taking dinner together in the mess when a woman dressed in a white silk evening gown and a long bridal veil entered the room, moved rapidly to the foot of the table, where she paused momentarily before making her way to the door leading into the kitchen, which she passed through. The five officers seated at the top of the table saw her clearly. Women were only allowed in the officers' mess on special occasions, and the officers assumed she had come into the mess by some mistake. Captain Norton, the adjutant of the regiment who was one of the officers at the top of the table, quickly left his place and ran across the room and into the kitchen and demanded of the mess sergeant where the woman had gone. The sergeant replied that no one had entered the kitchen; this was confirmed by the mess cooks, who were also present.

Captain Norton returned to the table with this news, and an animated discussion began among the officers. The woman had looked solid as flesh and blood, but the officers concluded that the only possible explanation was that she was an apparition. There was agreement among those who saw her that she was beautiful, dark-haired, and that her expression was of great sadness. On hearing the description, the commanding officer, Colonel Vaudeleur, who had not been able to see her from his own position at the table, exclaimed that it was the wife of the regiment's veterinary officer, a lady who had died in India during the regiment's tour of duty there.

At the time of the sighting, the veterinary officer was thought to be away from the regiment on sick leave, but later that evening the officers learned from one of the mess servants, whom he had summoned to bring him a brandy and soda, that he had returned prematurely that very afternoon and, still feeling unwell, had gone straight to his room, which was above the kitchen. At eight o'clock the following morning one of the mess servants went to call the veterinary officer, and found him dead in his bed. Captain Norton, who as adjutant had the sad task of making an inventory of the dead officer's possessions, found among them a photograph of the woman he had seen the previous night in the mess, wearing the self-same clothes. Stead's published report of the incident gives the identities not only of Captain Norton and Colonel Vaudeleur, but of the four officers sitting with Norton at the top of the table: Captain Aubry Fife, Captain Benion, Lieutenant Jack Russel, and the Regimental Medical Officer.

The case is difficult to explain by normal means. Army officers, particularly of a cavalry regiment, would hardly have hatched a cruel hoax between them by pretending to see a non-existent collective apparition of the dead wife of one of their senior brother officers (a veterinary officer is an important figure in a cavalry regiment) thought to be at home sick at the time – a hoax moreover designed also to deceive their commanding officer. Even if such a thing were considered possible, the presence of the adjutant, Captain Norton, as one of the five officers who reported seeing the apparition, rules it out. The adjutant of a regiment serves as the Commanding Officer's personal assistant, and carries particular responsibility for regimental discipline and for ensuring appropriate conduct among the regimental officers. My own experiences as an army officer in my National Service years allow me to say categorically that no adjutant would be a party to deceit of this kind, or countenance it in his brother officers. Was it possible therefore that the apparition was in fact an innocent stranger intent upon visiting one of the soldiers, who blundered into the officers' mess by mistake? This is unlikely for a number of reasons. Firstly her behavior –

walking up to the table and standing there for a moment – was not that of a soldier's sweetheart who had inadvertently invaded the hallowed precincts of the officers' mess. Such a woman would have peeped into the room, recognized her mistake, and made herself very scarce. Secondly, her clothes were not those of a soldier's sweetheart. Not only was she wearing white silk, her bridal veil suggests this was her wedding dress. Thirdly, Colonel Vaudeleur recognized her as the wife of the veterinary officer from the descriptions given of her, and Captain Norton recognized her the following day from the photograph among the dead officer's effects in which she was wearing these very same clothes. Fourthly, the woman was not in the kitchen when Norton hurriedly followed her. The mess sergeant and the mess cooks claimed not to have seen her, and the possibility that they would have hidden her or hurried her out of the kitchen by another door and lied to the adjutant as to her presence is unlikely. The penalties for misleading the adjutant (and thus the Commanding Officer) in this way would have led to far worse punishment for the mess sergeant and the mess cooks than admitting to the presence of the woman, a presence moreover for which her own mistake and not that of any of the mess staff would have been to blame. Furthermore, no adjutant would have reported to his Commanding Officer that the woman had inexplicably disappeared without making doubly sure that there was no normal explanation for her disappearance. Finally, we have the sad coincidence between her appearance and the death of the veterinary officer.

Could the apparition be satisfactorily explained by some form of telepathy, as argued by the Super-ESP hypothesis? This is unlikely. It was reported as seen simultaneously by five officers, none of whom seems to have known the dead woman or to have been with the regiment in India when she died. Could she have been a telepathic projection from the mind of the veterinary officer, lying sick in his room above the kitchen? There is no laboratory evidence that such telepathic projections can be seen simultaneously by five other reliable witnesses. It must also be remembered that the officers did not know the woman, did not know that their brother officer was back in the mess, did not know that he was so seriously ill, and had no expectations that an apparition of his wife would appear. On balance, it is difficult to argue against the possibility that the apparition was in fact the dead wife of the veterinary officer, and that her appearance was connected in some way with his impending death.

Apparitions That Give Verifiable Information

It could be argued that the very presence of an apparition is an attempt to convey information, presumably survival of physical death. Where the observer is unaware that death has taken place, as was the case with the young lady who saw the apparition of her elderly neighbor in the first of the examples I gave earlier, it might additionally be argued that the information conveyed also includes notification of the actual fact of the agent's decease. But are there examples of apparitions who actually give verbal information, particularly verbal information that turns out to be correct, relating to the circumstances of this death? Without doubt the credibility of apparitions as evidence for survival is greatly increased if there are. It is possible of course that if apparitions are from an afterlife they may usually find it very difficult to impinge upon more than one of the sensory modalities of the observer. This possibility is lent some credibility by the fact that the apparition often seems to place some kind of embargo upon being touched. Nevertheless, examples of apparitions who also convey hitherto unknown facts relating to their deaths do exist in the literature, as the following example shows.

The case appears in Volume V of the *Proceedings* of the SPR (Guerney and Myers 1889), and is worth dealing with at some length, both because the evidence it presents is particularly good and because it provides us with an opportunity to show how an approximate assessment can be made of the odds against the details supposedly given by the apparition being put together by the witness solely from his own imagination. The case also carries weight by virtue of the fact that the apparition was reported by someone well known to Frederick Myers and Edmund Gurney, two of the founders of the SPR and two of the most illustrious figures in its history, who were also responsible for publishing it. The observer's name is given only as Colonel _____ (regrettably professional people were as coy about being associated with the paranormal then as they are now). The story concerns the Colonel's brother officer, a friend of more than 20 years standing, J. P. (Major Poole) of the Royal Artillery, who was involved at the time (1881) in the First South African War between the British and the Dutch (Boer) settlers in the Transvaal.

The Colonel reports that, after reading late in the library of his London Club, he had gone to bed at nearly one o'clock and had slept "perhaps several hours" when he "awoke with a start."

The grey dawn was stealing in through the windows, and the light fell sharply and distinctly on the military chest of drawers ... at the further end of the room. Standing by my bed, between me and the chest of drawers, I saw a figure, which I at once recognised as that of my old brother officer.

Major Poole was dressed in khaki uniform and wearing a white sun helmet. Across his shoulder was a leather strap, and a belt of the same material around his waist carried his sword and revolver. His face was pale, "but his bright black eyes shone as keenly" as when the Colonel had last seen him, a year and a half ago. Later in his account, the Colonel also mentions that J. P. wore a beard, "which I myself had never seen him wear." So realistic was the experience that the Colonel supposed himself to be back in barracks, and anxiously asked J. P. if he was late for parade.

P. looked at me steadily and replied: "I'm shot."
"Shot" I exclaimed, "Good God, how and where?"
"Through the lungs!" replied P., and as he spoke his right hand moved slowly up the breast,
until the fingers rested over the right lung.
"What were you doing?" I asked
"The General sent me forward," he answered ... at the same moment the figure melted away. I
rubbed my eyes to make sure I was not dreaming, and sprang out of bed ... I felt sure that my
old friend was no more ... That I had seen a spirit and that I had conversed with it were alike
indisputable facts ... The thought disquieted me, and I longed for the hour when the Club
would open and I could get a chance of learning from the papers any news from the seat of
war ... The hours passed feverishly ... I snatched greedily at the first paper. No news of the
war whatever. I passed the day in a more or less unquiet mood ...

The Colonel confided his experience to a brother officer with the same rank as himself at his London Club, "who was as fully impressed as I was with the story ... " The next day he was the first to arrive at the Club and

... seized with avidity the first paper that came to hand. This time my anxiety was painfully
set at rest, for my eye fell at once on the brief lines that told of the battle of Laing's Neck, and
foremost among the list of the dead was poor J. P. I noted the time the battle was fought,
calculated it with the hour at which I had seen the figure, and found that it almost coincided
... the figure had appeared to me in London almost at the very moment that the fatal bullet had
done its work in the Transvaal.

It is unlikely in fact that the Colonel could be very precise as to the moment the bullet struck, since the exact time that Major Poole met his death during the battle is not known. However, the news of his death first appeared in *The Observer* for Sunday January 30, 1881, and there was thus no way in which the Colonel could have known of the death on January 29, the day on which he saw the apparition. Enquiries subsequently made of survivors of the battle confirmed both the details of J. P.'s uniform and equipment and the fact that he was bearded. The khaki uniform and the leather belt with a leather strap over the shoulder (subsequently named the "Sam Browne" after the officer who first improvised this method of carrying his weapons), was a form of dress hurriedly adopted by the British Army in the Transvaal to replace the traditional but highly conspicuous red tunic and white equipment straps, and one with which the retired Colonel probably was not familiar. In fact he mentions in his account of the incident that the first item of proof he sought after learning of J. P.'s death was whether or not he was wearing "that particular uniform at the time of his death." Enquiries of a brother officer present at the battle of Laing's Neck and an old friend of J. P. also confirmed the very spot through the right lung where he had received the fatal bullet. Confirmation of the fact that J. P. was killed "going forward" comes from the subsequent report of the battle in the *London Gazette* that tells us it began (according to General Colley's official dispatch from the front) at 9.30 a.m. local time on January 28, 1881, with the artillery under Major Poole's command bombarding the heights, and that toward the end of the action Poole took part in the attempt at storming these heights. Under the deadly fire of the Boers the British were repulsed, the dead lying in swathes, their white helmets having enabled the hidden enemy to mark them down with deadly precision. Major Poole was found lying dead, well ahead of the bodies of the men he was leading. Even at this distance in time we can feel a special sadness for Major Poole and his men, dying far from home in a conflict not of their own making, and fought primarily to gain control of the gold and diamond reserves in the Transvaal to which in truth neither side had any right.

The Colonel recalled that the last time he saw J. P. they had breakfasted at the Club on the morning of the latter's departure for South Africa. The two men shook hands when they finally parted at the Club door, and the Colonel writes:

"Good bye, old fellow," he said, "we shall meet again I hope. Yes ... we shall meet again."
I can see him now, as he stood, smart and erect, with his bright black eyes looking intently into mine. A wave of the hand ... and he was gone.

This sounds rather like a compact to meet after death, and possibly this was the reason why J. P. appeared to his old friend. Compacts to return to a loved one or a friend to demonstrate survival are not uncommon, and it could be that such a compact creates some form of bond which the deceased person fulfils wherever possible. The Colonel insists he was no believer in ghosts or spirit manifestations at the time, and that although he had slept many times in supposedly haunted houses he had failed to obtain any paranormal experiences. Major Poole's apparition was however

... so remarkable in its phenomena ... so realistic in its nature, so supported by actual facts, that I am constrained, at the request of my friends, to put my experience into writing.

It seems reasonable to suppose that the friends concerned were Myers and Gurney, and that they were impressed both by the story and by the Colonel's veracity. However, even having accepted the truth of the Colonel's account, it is possible to argue that his mind, preoccupied with the dangers facing his old friend, dreamt the whole thing. The obvious objection to this is that unless we decide in advance that the notion of survival and of paranormal phenomena in general are to be dismissed, and that in this case dreaming is the only possible explanation, we have no evidence that suggests a dream.

The Colonel writes that he "woke with a start," hardly the way in which dreams usually commence. He also saw "sharply and distinctly" the details of the furniture on the far side of the room (dreams often confuse such details). After seeing the apparition he rubbed his eyes to make sure he was not dreaming and then "sprang out of bed" (would that we were all so energetic in the mornings).

The skeptic may then suggest the whole thing was a form of waking hallucination. The objection to this (which applies equally to the suggestion of dreaming if the skeptic wishes to continue with that argument) is the accuracy of the details surrounding the experience. The Colonel learnt from this experience that Major Poole had been shot, as opposed to being the victim of artillery fire, knife wounds (as likely a cause of death as gunshot in the bloody hand-to-hand fighting in which attacks often culminated in nineteenth-century warfare), or fever (a hazard as fatal at that time to British troops abroad as battle itself). The actual position of the wound was indicated correctly. The fact that Major Poole was "sent forward" (unusually for an artillery officer with the rank of major, who would normally stay with his gun battery rather than take part in an infantry attack). The unfamiliar khaki uniform and the other details of dress and equipment were correct, as was the fact that he wore a beard. And the date of death, given that Major Poole was killed "towards the end of the action," was correct at least to a few hours.

It is impossible accurately to assess the odds against the Colonel having gained each of these items of information by guesswork alone, but we can make a useful estimate, erring on the side of under- rather than over-calculating them.

1. *He was killed by a bullet.* If we discount artillery fire on the grounds that the Boers had little in the way of ordinance at the time, the odds of his dying of bullet rather than knife wounds or fever is 3:1.

2. *He was shot in the right lung.* Assuming there are only four places where a gunshot wound would prove quickly fatal without immediate medical help (the head/throat, and vital areas of the right torso, the left torso and the abdomen), this gives odds of 4:1 against chance.

3. *The General had sent him forward* – unusually for an artillery officer of his rank who would not normally take part in an infantry attack, but let us be highly conservative and merely say he might either have been killed at his customary post on the gun lines or with the attacking infantry (yielding odds against chance of 2:1).

4. *He was wearing khaki uniform, with a Sam Browne belt.* Again let us be conservative and say that from the Colonel's perspective he could either have been in a scarlet tunic, the standard dress at that time or khaki (odds of 2:1), and that he could have been wearing white equipment or a leather Sam Browne belt and shoulder strap (odds

again of 2:1).

5. *He was bearded*. The fact that he wore a beard even though in the 23 years of their friendship the Colonel had never seen him with a beard, we will again rate conservatively and once more give odds against chance of only 2:1.

This leaves us to calculate one more set of odds, those against the Colonel getting the date of Major Poole's death right by guesswork. It might be reasoned that he had previously learned from the newspapers that a battle was imminent, and that if he had this would lower the odds against chance. But the term "battle" is somewhat misleading. The battles in the First South African War consisted mostly of skirmishes between the British army and Boer irregulars (the war ended in defeat for the British largely because the British commanders could not adapt to the Boers' guerrilla tactics and their deadly marksmanship). In any case, war news in the late nineteenth century took time to travel to Britain. There was no blanket coverage by war reporters, and people at home learnt of events only after they had taken place. Thus the Colonel was highly unlikely to have had prior knowledge of what was to happen at Laing's Neck, or that Major Poole would be involved.

The First South African War began on the 16th December, 1880 with the declaration of independence from Britain by the Transvaal, and as Major Poole had been posted to South Africa a year and a half previously, he was involved in the war from the start. There were thus some 40 days (we can discount the first few days after December 16 as news took time to reach the London newspapers) during which the Colonel could have imagined J. P.'s death before it actually happened, which would give us odds of 40:1. However, although the *Gazette* tells us that the battle commenced at 9.30 a.m. on January 28 and that Major Poole was killed "towards the end of the action," it does not tell us exactly when he died. Battles in the First South African War, particularly those that involved an uphill attack by infantry in conspicuous white sun helmets, were bloody and usually quickly concluded. The fact that the General sent a senior artillery officer forward, presumably accompanied by the gunners under his command, suggests that this was something of a last gasp attempt to storm the heights (it is difficult to think of any other reason why a commander would have ordered his artillerymen to leave their guns and take part in an infantry attack). The newspaper reports also convey the impression that the action was concluded during daylight, as they emphasize that the white sun helmets of the attackers made them easy targets. Thus all the indications are that the battle started and finished on January 28.

Therefore it seems likely that Major Poole was actually killed during the day of January 28 rather than the early morning of January 29. The Colonel is certain that when he saw the apparition on January 29 his friend was already dead, but he only *calculated* subsequently that the fatal bullet struck him "almost at the moment" of the sighting. So we must take both these dates into account when assessing the accuracy with which the Colonel received the actual date of death. This halves the odds against chance, leaving us with 20:1 rather than 40:1. A cumulative calculation of all the above odds gives us a total of 3,840:1 against the Colonel correctly guessing all his items of information. In reality, due to our conservative methods of calculation, the actual odds are probably very much higher than this. Nevertheless, the skeptic will probably object that before arriving at them we should take into account the number of times the Colonel had had hallucinatory experiences of the deaths of people known to him that turned out to be pure fantasy. The reply to this is that we have his word that he had no previous belief in spirits and no previous paranormal experiences. To this we can add that for him the sighting was "so remarkable in its phenomena" and "so realistic in its nature" that it convinced him, many hours before the news arrived, that his old friend had been killed and that he had seen his apparition. It was this conviction that led him to seize the paper "greedily" later that morning and "avidly" the next day. And it was this conviction that led him to detail his experience to another senior officer, and to spend the day of January 29 in a disturbed state. Had he had many similar experiences that turned out to be false alarms, it is unlikely that he would have taken this one so seriously.

The skeptic may then say that in calculating the odds against chance we should look beyond the Colonel and take into account the number of people in the population at large who had similarly vivid, detailed and compelling waking visual and verbal hallucinations on that same day, but which in the event proved inaccurate. This is a spurious argument. We have no idea how many people of sound mind and free from the influence of drugs had such experiences that day. Nor do we in any case know how common such postulated vivid but inaccurate experiences happen to be on any one day, and it remains for the skeptic, if he or she wishes to use this argument against the present case, to supply us with some credible figures.

A different kind of skeptic, while accepting that the Colonel's experience provides a strong case for paranormality, might protest that it nevertheless does not amount to evidence for survival. Major Poole may not have died immediately from his wound, in which case the apparition could have been the result of telepathy from his mind before death. Another possibility is that the Colonel's experience could have been precognitive, involving information about the death before the bullet actually struck. However, the Colonel insists he felt sure that the apparition convinced him that "his old friend was no more." If we are prepared to accept the possibility of a veridical apparition, then it is not unreasonable that we should also be prepared to accept the accuracy of the impression it gives to the observer. The Colonel was not left wondering whether his friend was wounded or dead, or whether he was about to be shot. He was certain Major Poole was already "no more." The impression seems to have been conveyed without the need for further words from the apparition.

Another argument against precognition is that, although the Colonel does not mention the exact time at which he awoke and saw the apparition, he speaks of a gray dawn stealing in through the windows that gave him enough light to see furniture across the room and Major Poole's pale face and dark eyes. On a late January morning in Britain this would place his experience somewhere between 7 and 8 a.m. (5 a.m. and 6 a.m. Transvaal time) on January 29. As we have already said, it is likely that Major Poole died in daylight on January 28, rather than in the early hours of January 29. Added to the Colonel's certainty that Major Poole was already no more when he saw this apparition, there thus seems little support for the argument that he saw the apparition before the fatality actually took place.

There is also little support for the arguments of Louisa Rhine and Gardner Murphy, mentioned earlier, that the apparition was the result of an emotional need on the Colonel's part. It is hard to believe that he had an emotional need to see an hallucination of his old friend shot through the lung, and that he had an emotional need for the distress that the experience caused him. Certainly we do not know for sure the emotional needs of anyone else (or even sometimes of ourselves), but the onus is upon the skeptic to provide a reasoned argument that there is evidence emotional need was at work in this instance. Saltmarsh's theory that the apparition might have been the result of telepathy from Major Poole while he lived, and that the telepathic impression remained latent in the Colonel's unconscious until a favorable opportunity for its emergence occurred, demands more serious consideration. But we do not know if Major Poole lived long enough after being hit to send telepathic impressions, consciously or unconsciously, to anyone, the Colonel included. What happens when a man, at the head of his troops, is fatally wounded through the right lung? Are his thoughts for his men, for the objective he is vainly trying to achieve, for his swiftly ebbing life, or for an old friend back in Britain? We simply do not know. But we can safely surmise that the physical and emotional impact of being shot, if conveyed telepathically to a friend, would be more likely to register immediately upon the latter than wait "until a favorable opportunity for its emergence occurred." And what constitutes a "favorable opportunity"? We do not know. Unless, once again, we have decided in advance that survival must always remain the least likely of the many explanations advanced for paranormal experiences, it would seem to take precedence over a speculative theory of delayed telepathy.

Any attempt to dismiss the J. P. case, as so many are dismissed, on the grounds of its age is unacceptable. The case was not old when it was published in the *SPR Proceedings*, and to suggest that it was fabricated by the

Colonel not only casts unwarranted doubt on his integrity, but calls into question the judgment and competence of Myers and Gurney (who, incidentally, from the title of the paper in which they published the case – *On apparitions occurring soon after death* – appear to have been satisfied that the apparition was seen post-mortem).

There are other examples of apparitions who supply accurate information unknown to witnesses. The best known of these is the so-called Chaffin Will case. It has been written about so frequently (e.g. Berger 1988) that only a brief summary is needed here. James L. Chaffin was a farmer in North Carolina who made a will in 1905 leaving all his possessions to his third son, Marshall, and making no provision for his wife or for this three other sons, John, James P., and Abner. In 1919, prompted by his reading of the twenty-seventh chapter of Genesis, which details how Isaac was deceived by Jacob into giving him the birthright intended for Esau, the first-born, James Chaffin made a second will, dividing the property equally between the four boys and charging them to take care of their mother. The will was not witnessed, but nevertheless was legal under North Carolina law. For some reason he told no one of this second will, and instead secreted it in Genesis 27, folding the page over to make a pocket to hold it. As the same time he wrote a note which said "Read the twenty-seventh chapter of Genesis in my daddy's old Bible," and placed it in the inside pocket of his overcoat, stitching the pocket shut.

We can speculate as to the reasons for this secretive behavior. Perhaps Chaffin was uncertain whether to make the second will or not, and hedged his bets by hiding it away. Perhaps he thought that the ability of his family to find it would be a test of their religious faith, or of the regularity with which they read the Bible. Perhaps he was becoming paranoid and distrusted his sons if they knew they would profit from his death. In any event, in 1921 he died from a fall, and since no one knew of his second will, the first will was probated, and Marshall inherited. The will was not contested by the rest of the family. However, four years later James P. Chaffin had two sightings of his father at his bedside. On neither occasion was he sure whether he was awake or dozing at the time. On the first occasion his father said nothing, but on the second, in June 1925, he appeared wearing his overcoat, which he pulled back to show the inside, and instructed James that "You will find my will in my overcoat pocket." Convinced by the apparition, James went the next day to his mother's home, where he learnt that the coat had been given to his brother John. On July 6 he visited John, and found the inside pocket of the coat to be sewn up, with his father's note inside.

With admirable foresight James obtained a neighbor, Thomas Blackwelder, and his daughter as witnesses, and together with his own daughter they visited his mother to inspect the family Bible. The second will was found in the folded page of Genesis 27 and taken to the court and offered for probate. Marshall was dead by this time, and the case was brought to trial in December 1925. Marshall's wife and son contested the new will, but withdrew their opposition when ten witnesses testified that the handwriting was indeed that of James L. Chaffin. The court annulled the old will, and the new one was accepted and probated.

There are various possible normal explanations for this case. James P. Chaffin may have forged the will. He may have been told of it during his father's lifetime, and only remembered it when he dreamt of his father. He may have received the information telepathically from his father while the latter was alive, and the telepathic memory may have surfaced only when he had the dream. The first of these possibilities is rendered unlikely by the fact that ten people were prepared to testify to James L. Chaffin's handwriting, that Marshall's wife and son accepted it as genuine, and that the court was also satisfied as to its authenticity. In addition, if the young James had forged the will, he had no reason to wait four years before producing it, concocting at the same time the elaborate story of the apparitions. The second possibility also seems unlikely, as a Carolina attorney who was interested in the case interviewed James, his wife, daughter, and mother, and was satisfied by their honesty and sincerity that they had no prior knowledge of the will. The third possibility, the Super-ESP explanation once again, could theoretically be correct, but as made clear earlier, we have no evidence that telepathy does in fact work in this way. This leaves a fourth possibility, that James L. Chaffin did make a second will, did hide it without telling anyone, and did re-appear after death to give this information to his son. This possibility is strengthened by the fact that when appearing to his son, James L. Chaffin made the mistake of saying the *will* was in his coat pocket, whereas in fact it was the note relating to the will that he had hidden there. About a week before the trial James P. Chaffin reported a third apparition of his father, this time in an agitated state asking "Where is my old will?" This suggests his memory of things may have been hazy, and that he could not recall either the position of the will or the content of the note he had left in his coat pocket. We can hardly suppose that this was another example of a delayed telepathic memory. It sounds rather more as if James L. Chaffin had survived death, and was still concerned with the affairs of his family.

Conclusion

Examples of three different categories of reported apparitions have been summarized in this chapter – apparitions that appear to individuals but without conveying information unknown to him or her at the time, apparitions that appear simultaneously to more than one person, and apparitions that convey correct information unknown to witnesses. Professor Ian Stevenson, one of the world's leading authorities on psychical research, considers that parapsychology should only concern itself with the last of these categories, since only these can be checked against known facts (Stevenson 1982). I disagree. The great majority of sightings fall into the first category, and many of them provide convincing evidence of survival for the witnesses concerned. We should not ignore this vast data bank of important human experience.

The examples presented in this chapter help illustrate the fact that apparitions are a genuine part of human experience. We have no reliable current figures as to what percentage of the population claim to have had this experience, but when in 1889 the SPR carried out its massive survey to identify people who had had "hallucinations" (the SPR's preferred word at the time for apparitions), they received 1,684 positive replies from the 17,000 people canvassed (Sidgwick 1889, 1890), a figure of 9.9 per cent. Some of the cases were too fleeting to count as evidence, but on the other hand some people who had had more convincing experiences may have failed to respond to the census. Thus the results suggest that anything up to 10 per cent of people at the time may have seen apparitions. If this figure still holds good (and the climate of opinion at the end of the nineteenth century appears by all accounts to have been as skeptical of the paranormal as it is today), this suggests that the sightings of apparitions is a relatively common experience.

We looked in this chapter at the various explanations for apparitions, and at the difficulties in deciding the strength of their support for survival. One thing emerges relatively clearly from the evidence, namely that apparitions cannot in at least some cases be dismissed as figments of the human imagination, as symptoms of mental illness, or as evidence of human dishonesty. If they are paranormal, we are left then with only two possible explanations, firstly that they are indeed evidence that those who have died can come back and communicate, or secondly that they are examples of telepathy and clairvoyance from the living, i.e. of Super-ESP.

We shall meet these alternative explanations when we discuss other forms of evidence of survival throughout the book, and the various arguments in favor of each of them. For the present, it is fair to say that unless, as an act of faith, we choose to reject the possibility of survival (as many do), then apparitions provide us with an impressive body of evidence that cannot be discounted as providing support for this possibility. For some this may sound an annoyingly over-cautious conclusion, but apparitions provide only one aspect of the case for survival. They cannot be seen in and of themselves as settling the matter.

CHAPTER 4
HAUNTINGS

The Meaning of Hauntings

As mentioned in the previous chapter, the term "haunting" usually applies to those cases where apparitions are reported as being seen, usually by more than one person, over a period of time. Typically, they appear to be associated with a particular location, either indoors or outdoors. In addition to apparitions, hauntings sometimes include mysterious sounds, smells, cold breezes, a sense of presence, or movement of objects. Hauntings are very much the stuff of legend and of fireside stories, and the people (or sometimes animals) believed responsible for the hauntings are popularly referred to as ghosts or specters. For the most part, ghosts are reported as carrying out repetitive actions (for example, appearing at the same spot, disappearing through closed doorways, walking along the same corridors or up the same staircases), and often, though by no means always (as we shall see when we discuss poltergeist hauntings), they are reported as unaware of the presence of human witnesses. Sometimes they seem to conform to the domestic geography of bygone times, passing through recently constructed walls or walking above the level of a floor that has been lowered in modern times. Those that are visible are sometimes described as semi-transparent, unlike all but one of the apparitions dealt with in the previous chapter, and sometimes are said to glide rather than walk. Rarely are they both seen and heard. The reason for dealing with hauntings separately from apparitions is that, as we shall see, they offer rather different challenges to normal explanations, and to the Super-ESP hypothesis.

On occasions ghosts are described as appearing physically incomplete, lacking faces or lower extremities, and in folklore at least are reported sometimes as carrying visible signs of the violent means by which they may have met their deaths. Typically they are said to haunt the place where they either met this violent death or caused it in someone else. The former type of haunting seems rather hard on the victims concerned. Having met a violent death, they now seem doomed to spend the afterlife reliving the tragedy. However, one theory has it that these unhappy shades are simply thought-forms projected by the perpetrators of the crime, who in the afterlife are destined to experience the terror and suffering of their victims over and over again until their evil deeds are expiated in some way. Another theory, which we touched on in the last chapter only to reject it, is that the settings in which hauntings take place retain an impression of the original violent event, perhaps because of the powerful emotions released at the time, and that this impression, like an old film, is projected outwards and for some reason replayed over and over again.

In hauntings where there is no evidence of violent death, one explanation favored by mediums and psychics is that the ghost is that of an earthbound spirit, someone who has died and either does not realize the fact, or who is emotionally so strongly attached to the material world that they are unable to move on. Thus the ghost remains in his or her old haunts, and is often said to be resentful that others now occupy what used to be their home. Poltergeist cases, to which we turn in due course below, are sometimes said to come in this earthbound category. Some Christian denominations take the view that these troublesome ghosts are up to no good, and authorize selected priests and ministers to carry out services of exorcism designed to banish them to the inferior place where it is thought they belong. Spiritualists adopt a much more lenient approach, and use mediums to contact them and gently persuade them to accept the fact of their death and to leave the scene and go "toward the light," that is, to find their way to one or other of the various spiritual realms said to await the souls of the departed. Sometimes mediums claim they can call upon their spirit guides to come and help them in this work. So-called "rescue circles" even hold regular séances at which they attempt to contact these earthbound spirits and assist them to move on, and various collections of the case studies arising from efforts of this kind (of which Wickland 1978 and Dowding 1945 are two of the best-known examples) have been published over the years. We return to the subject of earthbound spirits in Chapter 18.

A feature of hauntings is that, unlike the apparitions discussed in the last chapter, the ghostly visitor is typically not known personally by any of the observers. In this sense, the apparition reported by George Jonas at the Yorkshire Museum and described in Chapter 3 could be considered a haunting, in that the figure seen twice by Mr. Jonas was unknown to him, and exhibited something of the behavior of a so-called earthbound spirit. Accounts of hauntings not dissimilar from that reported by Mr. Jonas abound, and the published literature is vast. There are books on hauntings at stately homes, books covering local hauntings for practically every region of any size in the UK, the USA, and elsewhere. There are books on hauntings at sea, books on phantom armies and battles, books on haunted churches, and books on haunted theatres, and haunted prisons and castles (a good recent collection is by Evans 2002). To bring things up to date, there are now even collections of cases involving supposedly haunted stretches of roadway complete with phantom pedestrians who step into the path of oncoming cars and then mysteriously vanish after being knocked down, and even ghostly hitch-hikers who silently accept lifts from unsuspecting motorists, only apparently to disappear (somewhat ungratefully) without trace from the moving car somewhere on the journey. One moment the motorist is conscious of the silent hitch-hiker on the seat beside him, or visible in the rear-view mirror, apparently as real and solid as life, the next moment, after turning his attention away briefly, he finds they have vanished.

Roadside Hauntings

Michael Goss, a serious student of reported paranormal experiences, has published an interesting collection of these roadside cases from Britain, the USA, and elsewhere. Frequently the cases seem linked to road accidents known to have happened where the phantom pedestrian appears to be knocked down or where he or she vanishes after hitching a lift, and certainly many a distraught motorist has hurried into the nearest police station to blurt out his (the motorist concerned is nearly always male, whereas a vanishing hitch-hiker is more often female) story. The majority of the cases are initially reported in local newspapers, and unfortunately there is little to support them beyond the word of the motorist involved. Many of them sound suspiciously like urban myths, those modern accounts of seemingly gruesome or sensational happenings that spread rapidly from mouth to mouth, but on enquiry are found to have no real substance.

However, if we are prepared to accept the possibility that ghosts haunt the surroundings where they met violent ends, it seems not unreasonable to accept that victims of sudden death on the roads may sometimes haunt the place where they met their end, perhaps because for a time they continue to relive the incident in imagination from the afterlife. In the case of phantom hitch-hikers we might stretch a point and even surmise that, not realizing they are dead and anxious to continue their interrupted journey, they thumb a lift from a passing car only to disappear when they are a certain distance away from the scene of the accident and presumably no longer able to remain visible. In favor of these far-fetched possibilities is the fact that in some cases the police confirm that the motorist reporting the incident appeared neither drunk nor obviously deranged. They also sometimes confirm visiting the stretch of road where the hitch-hiker is said to have disappeared from the fast-moving car or the pedestrian said to have been knocked down, only to find no sign of the mangled bodies that would be present if the incident had a normal explanation. In addition, although we must always be cautious when attempting to assess the motives of those reporting ostensibly paranormal events, it is difficult to know why anyone would want to tell the police invented stories of phantom hitch-hikers and risk not only ridicule but a possible prosecution for wasting police time. However, the motorist may have been genuinely deluded in some way. Most of the cases are reported as happening at night, when shadows can play strange tricks. Another possibility is that the journalist publishing the case may have misreported the facts, or omitted to mention the motorist's uncertainties over what actually happened. Any of these explanations could be the right one. But nevertheless, a small number of cases remain puzzling.

A good example is the account given by Dawie van Jaarsveld, a corporal at that time (1978) in the South African Army. On a long motorcycle ride to visit his girlfriend in Louterwater, Cape Province, van Jaarsveld stopped at night to offer a lift to a young girl standing at the roadside. Keeping the engine of his powerful motorcycle running in case she might be a decoy for a criminal gang preying upon motorists, and with his hearing further affected by the music from a transistor radio playing through the earplug in one ear, he failed to hear her reply or the details of her intended destination, but saw her nod in response to his offer. After donning his spare crash helmet and accepting the spare earplug to the radio, the girl mounted the pillion and they rode off. A few miles down the road van Jaarsveld felt the motorcycle encounter an odd bump and slither slightly. Looking back he saw the pillion was empty.

Fearing the girl had fallen off, van Jaarsveld retraced his journey as far as the spot where she had mounted the pillion, only to find no sign of her. Equally puzzling, he saw now that the spare crash helmet he had given her to wear was clipped loosely to the luggage rack, and that the spare earpiece to his radio was now in his other ear. Deeply disturbed, van Jaarsveld rode on and called at the Petros Cafe, where the proprietress later confirmed his agitation and expressed her belief that he had encountered the apparition of a phantom hitch-hiker, a 22 year-old woman called Maria Charlotte Roux known to have been killed at the spot and thought by locals to haunt the road. When van Jaarsveld arrived at the home of his girlfriend, her family confirmed that he still appeared agitated, and that he told them of the incident the following morning. Subsequently, from a photograph provided by the fiancé of the dead woman, Lieutenant Giel Pretorius of the South African Air Force, he confirmed that his passenger was indeed Maria Charlotte Roux. While traveling in her fiancé's car Maria had been killed at the spot during Easter 1968, and was said to appear each year around the same date.

Van Jaarsveld's story appeared in *Fate* magazine in July 1979 and in May 1980 in *The Trentonian* of New Jersey and the *Middlesex News* of Framlingham, Mass., and subsequently in various other journals and books. It transpired that three other sightings of the apparition had been published previously, although we do not know if van Jaarsveld had heard of them at the time of his experience. Two of these sightings are vague and do not involve clear views of the young woman. But the third concerns a motorist, Anton Le Grange, who reported that he stopped and gave a lift to a young woman in May 1976. Once the car was in motion she gave her destination as De Lange, 2 Porter Street, but when Le Grange recollected there was no such street in the town for which he was heading and turned to ask her for more details, the young woman had vanished. Dismayed, Le Grange reported the incident to the Uniondale Police, a fact confirmed by Constable Potgieter the duty officer, who then followed Le Grange in police transport to the spot where she had first appeared. Both men testify that on the way and while both vehicles were traveling at speed, the right rear door of Le Grange's Mercedes car swung gently open as if controlled by someone in the act of alighting, and Le Grange claims to have heard a woman's scream at that moment. Le Grange also claimed that the woman closely resembled the photograph of Maria Roux although he could not be certain, and Potgieter was sufficiently impressed by the whole incident to report subsequently that in his view something paranormal had indeed occurred.

Cynthia Hind, who investigated the case for *Fate* magazine, interviewed the various interested parties, unfortunately with the exception of Lieutenant Pretorius and Maria Roux's mother, who had left the area. Assuming the truthfulness of those concerned, we thus have some evidence the events concerned were correctly reported. In both incidents the young woman was described as wearing the same clothes, and the police confirmed the descriptions fitted what Maria Roux was known to have been wearing when she met her death. In both incidents, the young woman was not trying to hitch a lift, but was offered one because she was seen standing at the roadside and it was dark and wet at the time. In both incidents she is described as dark-haired, pale-faced and expressionless. Inquiries by Cynthia Hind revealed that Le Grange was correct in believing that there was no number 2 Porter Street in the town to which he had been heading, and the only house answering to that address turned out to be elsewhere in the Province and in use as a hostel for a boys' school. It has no known connection with "De Lange," whatever or whoever "De Lange" might be, and these words may conceivably have been an attempt by the young woman to address Le Grange by name.

We are unlikely ever to discover whether Maria Roux or any other phantom hitch-hiker is fact or fiction, but the case is well reported and at face value appears convincing. Neither van Jaarsveld nor Le Grange had any obvious reason for fabricating events, and neither seems to have been under the influence of drugs at the time. It is unlikely that the woman could have been a living person, as she left both vehicles while they were traveling at speed, and no sign was found of her body, and it seems unlikely that she could be explained as delayed telepathic memories, since when alive Maria Roux had never been on the pillion of the motor cycle or in the back seat of the car. The careful research carried out by Cynthia Hind would seem to rule out the possibility that the stories were based on flimsy details that had become embellished into urban myths. On balance, we are left with a number of suppositions and unanswered questions.

We would much prefer that this case could be dismissed out of hand as an urban myth. We might just be prepared to entertain the idea of ghosts winding their lonely way through cathedrals and dusty libraries, but the idea they should climb onto motorcycle pillions and into the back of cars, only to disappear when it suits their purposes, stretches our credulity to insupportable limits. Yet if apparitions can, as the examples in the last chapter suggests, sit in chairs and on beds, walk up and down stairs, place their hands on the shoulders of the living, pass through locked gates, hold conversations with the living, disappear on passing from one room to another, and walk large as life past kitchen windows, then in theory there is no reason why they should not accept lifts on the back of motorcycles and the back seats of cars. Supporters of the Super-ESP hypothesis would have us believe that as we do not know the limits of telepathy and clairvoyance from the living these abilities may account for all sightings of apparitions; we can equally well argue that as we do not know the limits of an apparition's capabilities it could well take rides on pillions and in the cars of hospitable drivers. This is not to argue that an apparition *can do* these things. It is simply to suggest that in the light of other evidence we should not immediately conclude that it cannot. The reason we conclude in this way is that we have come to associate ghostly sightings primarily with long corridors and dark stairways in ancient buildings bequeathed to us by long-dead generations. But if ghosts there be, they are as likely to be associated with the present as with the past. What matters is not our preconceptions, but the strength of the evidence.

If Maria Roux *was* a ghost, we can only suppose that she was unaware of her own death, and in her confusion believed she should find her way back home – to an address that she could not remember. The reason she appeared only around the time she died may have been because the date of her death still carried the strongest connection with the physical world for her. Possibly she maintained her lonely wait for a lift from passing motorists each day, but with insufficient energy (whatever that word means in this context) to become visible except around the date she died. Possibly, although still earthbound, she was only drawn to the site at that date. One speculation is as good – or as bad – as another.

Other Hauntings

Uncertainties face us in all supposed hauntings. However, if there are frequent reports of a particular sighting the value of the case increases, particularly if the reports are in substantial agreement on points of detail, and if one or more observers report a sighting without having prior knowledge that others have seen the same thing. A good example of such a case is among those collected by Sir Ernest Bennett (1939). It concerns a certain Miss Y. of Shefford, Bedfordshire, UK, and its unsensational nature lends it a degree of conviction. Living with her two sisters in a "quite new" house, Miss Y. describes how all three women on a number of occasions distinctly saw "a middle-aged man wearing a stone-colored golf cap and a dark jacket, walking by the window at the side of the house as if in deep thought." Hastening to the back door, they found no one. Usually the haunting, if such it was, took place between 2 p.m. and 4 p.m., in broad daylight. Miss Y. insists that she and her sisters "are not suffering from delusions, trickery, or bad observations," and both her sisters signed statements corroborating her narrative for Bennett.

The case gains further interest from the evidence of a family friend, Miss Edwards, who while visiting the sisters twice saw the figure herself, again in daylight, without having been told of his previous appearances. Her account of the first sighting describes how, sitting facing the window during tea, she saw "plainly ... the figure of a man of medium height, wearing a darkish cap, and passing with ordinary steps by the window." Thinking it was someone going to the back door she alerted Miss Y., who on opening the door found no one there. On her return " ... all three sisters looked at each other and smiled. I wondered at the time what it meant, but took no further notice." On the second occasion, which took place on a subsequent visit to the sisters, Miss Edwards, again while seated facing the window, once more saw the same man, and this time followed Miss Y. to the back door only to find the area deserted. She reports remarking to the sisters "he has vanished into space; where on earth could he have gone to?", whereupon the sisters replied "We're glad you have seen him too."

Miss Edwards further describes the man as each time "having his head down ... He looked like a man between twenty-six and thirty by his steady firm walk, but as the path was soft earth, we should not in any case have heard footsteps." Bennett comments that as the man was seen by four witnesses and, on several occasions, by three of them simultaneously, and always in the same place, in his view it is difficult to believe that the sighting was that of a living man. Presumably the four witnesses were satisfied that no living man could have made his escape between the sighting and the opening of the back door, but it is unfortunate that Bennett does not include a sketch map to make matters clear. However, assuming that the sighting was a ghost, why should the unknown gentleman haunt a pathway at the side of a relatively new house? In lifetime, had the unfortunate stranger suffered a fatal heart attack or other cause of sudden death when walking up to the back door in the days before the sisters occupied the house? Or was he a former deceased owner retracing the familiar steps of his homecoming? It is unfortunate that the sisters did not speak of the strange visitors to their neighbors as they did "not like publicity" – which also explains why Bennett protected their anonymity. We would like to know if neighbors recognized him from his description.

It might even have been found that the description fitted that of a living man who was known to be elsewhere at the time. If so, it is just possible that this haunting was not a haunting at all, but an example of bilocation, the supposed ability of certain individuals to appear in two places at once. There are various seemingly well-attested accounts of this ability in the case of Christian saints such as St. Anthony of Padua (who in 1226 spontaneously appeared in a chapel at Limoges in order to read the office before disappearing, while at the same time preaching in the Church of St Pierre at the other end of town), St. Alphonsus Maria de'Ligouri (who was seen at the deathbed of Pope Clement XIV in 1774 when in fact he was confined to his monastery cell at Arezzo, four days' journey away from Rome) and in our own time by Padre Pio of Italy, a man described as possessing many divinely inspired paranormal gifts.

These saintly individuals are said by believers to bilocate consciously, but in the case of lesser mortals the individual may be unaware of the existence of his double (or *doppelganger*), which is said by witnesses to act in a mechanical and self-absorbed way. One of the best-known cases is that of the 32-year-old French schoolmistress Emilee Sagée, who in 1845 at the exclusive Pensionat von Neuwelcke in Livonai (modern Latvia) was seen on occasions by all 42 pupils in the school to be in two places at once, sometimes with her double standing beside or behind her physical self, but once sitting in the schoolroom while she herself was plainly visible picking flowers in the garden. Her unconscious ability to project her double allegedly led to the poor woman losing 18 teaching posts over a space of 16 years, including that at the Pensionat von Neuwelcke, and may have been the reason for her later disappearance and presumed suicide. The case is not as good as it sounds, however, because although carefully investigated by Robert Dale Owen and by leading astronomer and psychical researcher Camille Flammarion (Owen 1860), much of the testimony depends upon one witness who was a 13-year-old pupil at the Pensionat von Neuwelcke at the time, Julie von Guldenstubbe, second daughter of Baron von Guldenstubbe (who nevertheless was able to supply the names of the other girls who saw the doppelganger and the relevant dates).

Rather more reliable is the account given by the famous Irish poet and mystic W. B. Yeats, who describes in his *Essays and Introductions* (Yeats 1961), how years previously his double appeared to one of his student friends several hundred miles away when he was thinking intently about him, and that of the great American writer Theodore Dreiser who describes how Welsh novelist John Cowper Powys, another writer with a mystical bent, once appeared to him while he was reading quietly at home, having told him two hours previously "I'll appear to you later this evening."

It may be that phantom appearances of *doppelgangers* are really instances of so-called out-of-body experiences (OBEs), which will be discussed in Chapter 16. But whatever the explanations, hauntings of the kind we have described so far do not provide us with the clear, objective evidence likely to convince skeptics that something paranormal is taking place. Sightings are quirky and unpredictable, with an annoying habit of failing to appear when teams of investigators, complete with cameras, tape recorders, image intensifiers, and the other paraphernalia beloved of ghost hunters, are present. Ghosts refuse to appear to order, refuse to be photographed (the few pictures we have of their shadowy or wispy forms can all be dismissed as possible fakes), and may in any case only be visible to those with so-called clairvoyant abilities. Ghostly footsteps and other sounds can all too easily be dismissed as due to natural causes. Witnesses can be too easily ridiculed by the determined critic, who has made up his or her mind in advance that ghosts do not exist and that those who report them must therefore be psychotic, under the influence of drugs, fraudsters with some dark motives involving personal gain, or credulous simpletons. The fear of attracting odium or ridicule of this kind is often sufficient to deter people – particularly those with professional or social standing to protect – from admitting publicly to possible paranormal experiences.

Poltergeists

Does this mean that hauntings are doomed to remain forever no more than curiosities on the edge of folklore, of no real support to the possibility of survival? Not at all. In addition to the sightings and sounds to which we've referred, there is another class of hauntings, usually termed *poltergeists*, a German word meaning "noisy spirit." Poltergeist hauntings differ from other categories in that they involve the apparently paranormal movement – often the violent movement – of physical objects. Thus investigators are potentially more likely to witness objective phenomena, some at least of which takes place in broad daylight, whose cause they can then seek to determine. Poltergeists also differ from many other hauntings in that they have been particularly well documented down the centuries, and in some cases attested to by seemingly reliable witnesses, including the police. The Roman Catholic Church in particular has long recognized their reality – perhaps because they have a particular habit of plaguing priests and ministers of religion such as the saintly Curé of Ars near Lyon in France, whose simple dwelling was so severely vandalized on occasions by what seems to have been poltergeist activity that the locals attributed the disturbances to the actions of the devil, outraged by his excessive sanctity.

Attempts to equate poltergeist hauntings with demonic activity were in fact not uncommon among churchmen. The scholarly sixteenth-century Jesuit writer Father Martin Del Rio, in Book II of his *Disquisitionum Magicarum*, lists them among his 18 categories of demons, describing them as:

... those specters which in certain times and places are wont to occasion various commotions

and annoyances ... Sometimes they are content just to annoy and disturb, doing no bodily harm, like that throwing spirit of which William of Paris writes, which disturbed his slumbers with clattering of pots and hurling of stones, and, having pulled away his mattress, turned him out of bed.

Others, Father Del Rio indicates, are more malicious, throwing stones at people though without causing much injury. In other accounts we are told of poltergeists that pull people's hair, cause objects to disappear before returning them in the most unlikely places, start small fires, throw water about, upset furniture, scribble on walls, break objects, and generally enjoy discomforting the hapless owners of the property they choose to haunt. Reading the accounts, one is at times reminded of the so-called little people of Celtic folklore, who were said to cause all kinds of mischief unless treated with respect and placated in various ways, at which times they would attempt to be helpful, even carrying out domestic tasks while the family were asleep.

The Cardiff Poltergeist Case

Mischief, whether seemingly malicious or not, seems in fact to be a consistent feature of poltergeist hauntings, so much so that their antics are often blamed upon any children or adolescents who happen to be in the house at the time. Human agency of one sort or another may of course be responsible for many cases, but this is by no means always so. In what has come to be called the Cardiff Poltergeist Case, which I investigated over a period of a little over two years from June 1989 to early 1992, there were no young people involved, and no obvious adult mischief-makers. The case was brought to the attention of the SPR by the proprietor, John Matthews, of the lawnmower repair workshop and adjoining garden-accessories shop where the inexplicable disturbances were taking place, and who was genuinely concerned not only that these disturbances, which principally involved stone throwing and the inexplicable movement of objects, could frighten away potential customers, but that a member of the public might one day be injured while on his premises. With no previous experience or knowledge of psychic phenomena he had discussed the disturbances, which had been going on for nearly two years, with a local minister of religion, and it was the latter who had informed him that a poltergeist might be responsible. Wishing to know more, he contacted the SPR, and the Society asked me to visit the workshop and make a report. This I did, and the case is worth describing in some detail, not only because of its quality but because I was fortunate enough to witness many of the phenomena myself (fuller accounts appear in Fontana 1991 and 1992).

On receiving the request from the SPR in June 1989 I contacted John Matthews by telephone, and found him more than ready to welcome me at his workshop during working hours whenever I was free to call. I was told I could enter via the retail garden-accessories shop, which was directly in front of the workshop with two connecting doors between the two rooms, or go round the building to the workshop door that opened onto the yard at the back. I agreed to pay a visit on an afternoon when the retail shop would be closed and no customers present, but gave no indication of the exact time I would be there. On arrival I walked round the side of the premises (a small end of terrace building dating from the last years of the nineteenth century) to the workshop, my approach remaining unseen as there were no windows between me and the door of the workshop. John Matthews and a visiting salesman, seated opposite each other on low boxes, were the only occupants of the workshop, and as I entered a missile (which I later found was a small stone) hit the piece of machinery on the floor near their feet with a highly audible "ping" – a sound with which I was to become very familiar in the months that followed. Both men, whose hands were clearly visible on their knees, smiled up at me, and John remarked with no hint of surprise "There you are, he's welcoming you." I joined the two men, and the salesman informed me that, after initial skepticism, he had seen enough in the workshop to convince him the case was genuine. There really was some force or other, inexplicable by normal means, responsible.

It turned out that this force, which John had called "he" on my arrival, was nicknamed – with some affection – by John and those who worked with him "Pete" (for convenience I shall use this term myself), and I was told that some months previously he had first made his presence felt by throwing large stones onto the roof of a shed at the back in which John and one of his workmen were watching a televised rugby match on a quiet Saturday afternoon. So persistent had the stone throwing in the yard subsequently become that the police had been called with a view to catching the suspected young culprits, but at no time had they found anyone who might be responsible. Shortly afterwards, the phenomena began to occur inside the workshop, and in the following 18 months they included: the throwing of coins, bolts, and small stones the size of granite chippings (many of which were also found to litter the floor when John opened the workshop in the morning, John at that time being the only one with the key), against the walls of the workshop; the mysterious arrival of objects (termed "apports") of unknown origin such as a pen and keys, old pennies all dating from 1912 which either appeared to fall from the ceiling or which were found on the work surfaces; tools on racks set swinging with no apparent cause; blue flames emerging from a brass shell case which was kept as an ornament in the workshop and which was also sometimes thrown violently around the room; planks of wood apparently too heavy to be thrown by hand hurled from the yard through the open door of the workshop; stones thrown at Pat, John's wife, while she was in the toilet at the back of the workshop with the door locked; dust thrown down John's collar and that of a business associate who worked with him; and loud knocks on the windows of the shop when no one was visible outside. Particularly frequent was the movement of the small floats used in the carburetors of the lawnmowers under repair, of which there was a large stock in the workshop. (These objects consist of plastic flotation chambers supporting the sharp steel needles that control the flow of petrol into the carburetor.)

Sometimes these various events took place when John was alone in the workshop, at other times they happened when he and others were present, or when others were there and he was absent. Rarely were objects actually seen in flight. Normally they became apparent only when they hit the wall or landed on the floor. At times "Pete" apparently attempted to be helpful. For example, on unlocking the premises and entering the small kitchen that led off the workshop, John and Pat would sometimes find there had been rudimentary attempts to lay out cutlery on the table, as if for breakfast. Inexplicable events, usually involving the mysterious appearance of the ubiquitous carburetor floats, had also begun to occur in the homes both of John and Pat and of two other people closely involved in the case, Paul and Yvonne (pseudonyms), who are referred to more fully in the next paragraph.

Over the following days I interviewed not only John but the four other people most closely involved in the case: Pat (his wife), Paul (Pat's brother), Yvonne (pseudonym for Paul's wife), and Michael (pseudonym for the business associate who worked with John in the workshop). Paul, who had recently taken early retirement from his plumbing business, and Yvonne frequently helped out in the workshop and the retail shop. All five of those just named were respectable middle-aged people, practical and unpretentious, and all five had witnessed many of the events described by John. Their accounts of these events tallied in every important respect, and I gained a favorable impression of their honesty. With the exception of Paul, who had had one inexplicable encounter in an apparently haunted house in which he was working during his days as a plumber, none had had any previous psychic experiences. All were mystified by the things they had seen on the premises, and the four family members in particular were eager for explanations. I also interviewed John's daughter, a psychiatric nurse, who had witnessed some of the events and who, after initial skepticism, was now fully convinced of their genuineness.

One of the most persistent occurrences reported to me by these witnesses concerned the small carburetor floats already mentioned. Measuring some two centimeters long by two centimeters across and with a sharp needle end, these floats were often found out of position when John unlocked the workshop in the mornings. In addition, he informed me that on one occasion he had left a float on top of the unlit gas heater before locking up one evening, and "challenged" it to be moved. On the way home, accompanied by Pat, Paul, and Yvonne, he had stopped the car to enable Paul to buy some cigarettes. When given his change, Paul had felt something prick his palm, and on opening his hand discovered the culprit to be the needle end of a carburetor float that had appeared among the coins. Though there was no way of proving the point, he was adamant to me that he did not have a carburetor float in his pocket which he had unwittingly taken out along with the money for cigarettes, and in fact insisted he had never carried one in his pockets (not surprisingly in view of the sharp needle end) nor had any reason for so doing.

When Paul, apparently white-faced and shaken, returned to the car with his cigarettes, his change and the carburetor float, John turned the car around and they made their way back to the workshop to ascertain if there was still a float on top of the gas heater. There was not. John was emphatic when the event was reported to me that on the evening concerned he had been last out of the workshop before locking up, and that no one could have gained access during his absence. The other three family members involved in this strange incident corroborated John's story in every detail. We can regret the fact that the float left on top of the gas heater had not been marked by John. Was the float in Paul's change the same one? The family assumed that it was. If trickery was involved, we would have to suppose that John had secretly picked up the float before leaving the workshop, and had slipped it unseen into Paul's pocket as they sat together in the car. Taken in isolation we would assume that this is what happened. Taken together with all the other strange events surrounding the case and with John's apparently transparent honesty, we can be less sure.

During my initial interview with John, he told me that after a day particularly disrupted by apparent stone-throwing and other mischief from "Pete," he had lost patience and suspecting, in spite of their denials, that Michael and an employee who worked with them at the time were responsible, he determined to put this to the test by insisting the two men join him in the retail shop after closing time, and sit with their hands flat on the counter to check whether the sounds of stone throwing from the now empty workshop would continue. The sounds did so, and the employee (who had left the business before my investigation began and who does not figure in the rest of the story) suggested they ask whoever or whatever was responsible for the disturbances to "bring" named tools from the workshop into the retail shop. In John's words, each time they requested a tool it arrived, seemingly falling from the ceiling and "materializing" on the way down. So swiftly were the tools produced in this way that John was adamant he could not himself have found them in the workshop in such a short space of time. It was this experience that finally convinced him of the genuineness of the phenomena.

I was to witness some of these happenings for myself in the months that followed, but let me digress for a moment. There is a tendency among many psychical researchers, even those who have obtained positive results in the laboratory experiments detailed in Chapter 2, to turn skeptical when told of psychic happenings in the outside world – or at least to turn skeptical when such happenings are claimed to occur in modern times. They may be prepared to believe the accounts of cases described by the illustrious founders and early investigators of the SPR, but they draw the line at anything more contemporary. There is an unspoken assumption that although we can accept the theory that such things may have happened in the past, we cannot accept them as happening in this day and age. We can suspend disbelief about the past, but not about the present. It is difficult to account for this. Perhaps there is a fear that if one is seen to accept contemporary paranormal events not obtained under controlled laboratory conditions as genuine, and these events are then found to be susceptible to normal explanations, credibility will be lost. However, when it comes to psychical research, there is no substitute for direct experience of paranormal events as they happen, spontaneously and unpredictably, in the real world. The laboratory, for all its major contribution to psychical research, is an artificial, controlled environment, and effects that can only be observed there are of limited value. Thus experiences such as those I had while investigating the Cardiff case are indispensable for anyone who wishes to know – and be convinced by – the major effects that paranormal energies, whatever they be, can sometimes produce in daily life.

In investigations outside the laboratory a range of precautions can be taken against fraud, poor observation, mistaken inference or other normal explanations. Thus, far from being slipshod anecdotal affairs, the investigator can usually ensure that the genuine can be distinguished from the spurious. Investigations outside the laboratory (i.e. fieldwork) can rarely be as tightly controlled as those inside the laboratory, but they can be made as thorough and as rigorous as good observation will allow – and good observation is readily accepted as part of the methodology in other areas of science (e.g. astronomy, engineering, psychology, sociology, anthropology). There is no reason why it should not be equally acceptable in psychical research.

If I may continue this digression just a little longer, it is worth mentioning another danger, one that has been referred to by other investigators in the past. During the Cardiff investigation I would spend the day in John's workshop, observe a range of phenomena (of which more in a moment) that could not be accounted for by normal means, and leave for home convinced that what I had seen was genuine. Yet on the journey home doubts would already begin to arise. My rational mind would start to argue that such things can't *really* happen. A natural explanation must be there somewhere, if I could only find it. No matter how unlikely this natural explanation might appear, surely it would be less unlikely than that objects should be seen to move by themselves. Over the following days the doubts would multiply. Even if I failed to spot the natural explanation myself, surely others would do so, to the detriment of any standing I might have as a serious scientist. It is all too easy for hardened critics to make even the best fieldwork sound ridiculous, and hardened critics have brought this form of ridicule to a fine art, prizing it above any real attempt to get at the truth of things. As a result of it, some of the finest scientists Britain has produced – for example Sir William Crookes, Sir Oliver Lodge, and Russell Wallace – have on the strength of their interest in psychical research been dismissed as well-intentioned bunglers.

However, investigators must guard against this "morning-after skepticism," as we can term it. Morning-after skepticism is one of the reasons why many published accounts of fieldwork are so hedged around with ifs and buts that the reader is left wondering if anything of value has been witnessed after all. And morning-after skepticism is one of the reasons why scientists engaged in psychical research are so frequently accused by laypeople of sitting on the fence instead of having the courage to come down unequivocally on one side or the other. The investigator must be cautious before reaching conclusions and must make any reservations clear, but at the same time must be bold enough – as were Crookes, Lodge, and Wallace – to state what he or she has experienced, and leave others to make of it what they will. Thus, over the months of the Cardiff investigation, I gradually learnt, in the light of the range of phenomena that I witnessed together with the conditions under which they were witnessed, to lay my morning-after skepticism to rest. I saw many of the strange happenings that John and the other family members had described to me, together with some even more startling. One of the latter deserves special mention, not only because it is of interest in itself, but because it throws particular light on the question of survival.

The first one commenced when one day, irritated by "Pete's" stone-throwing, John picked up a small stone and threw it, from some 20 feet away, into the far corner of the workshop from where many of the phenomena appeared to originate. The next moment the stone, apparently returned from the same corner, struck the wall near John. John repeated his action several times with the same result, as subsequently did Pat. Informed of this on my next visit, a day or two later, I tried my own hand at stone-throwing, again from 20 feet away and aiming into the same corner of the workshop, and to my surprise a stone was returned, hitting the wall behind me. I tried again, with the same result. Over the following days and weeks John, Pat, and I spent (I was about to say idled away, but this would give the wrong impression) much time in the stone-throwing game. Sometimes we got results; sometimes our stones were ignored. Nothing happened if we threw stones elsewhere in the workshop. Only the one corner, which we named the active corner, prompted a response. Besides the inherent oddity of this responsive stone-throwing game with an unseen partner, we established a number of facts. Firstly, we never saw the stone that was thrown back to us while it was in flight. We would hear it strike the wall or one of the metal storage shelves that lined the wall with a characteristic "ping," and clatter to the floor. The invisibility of objects in flight has been frequently reported in other poltergeist cases, and it applied to all the many objects that either appeared or were thrown around the room while I was present.

The other witnesses who I interviewed during the course of the investigations (salesmen, and acquaintances of John and Pat's family) with one exception all attested to the fact that the objects they had seen fall to the floor were never apparent in flight. For example, one witness, the retired director of playing fields for that part of Wales, informed me that on one occasion, while in the retail shop on his own, he had watched no fewer than 12 large engineering bolts fall from the ceiling, each one "appearing to materialize" just before hitting the floor. The one exception, a salesman, reported having seen coins apparently traveling through the air before falling to the floor or into a basket hanging just under the ceiling. Instead of appearing as if normally thrown, the coins had moved more slowly and followed a flat trajectory (a phenomenon sometimes reported in other poltergeist hauntings).

The reason that the responsive stone-throwing appears to throw light on survival is that it suggests there was a definite intelligence involved. I shall discuss who or what "Pete" might have been later, but it seems clear that he was aware of our stone-throwing, and was prepared to join in the game. Pat also discovered that expressions of anger towards "Pete" (in exasperation she sometimes berated him for being such a nuisance in the workshop) led to a much more active response during the stone-throwing experiment. It was as if he became angry in return.

For the most part the stones returned by "Pete" during the stone-throwing game did not appear to be the ones we had just thrown, which lessens the possibility that our own stones were bouncing back at us. This possibility was further discredited when I experimented, on days when there was no activity from the poltergeist, to ascertain whether or not we could get stones to bounce back the 20 feet or so between where we habitually stood during the stone-throwing game and the active corner, and found that we could not. The few that did bounce back traveled no more than an erratic three feet or so. None of them hit any of the walls, let alone the one behind where we were standing.

Although attempts to initiate the stone-throwing game by throwing stones into the other corners of the workshop produced no results, John and I found we were able to evoke responses when we experimented by throwing stones into the corner of the retail corner adjacent to the active corner in the workshop. The wall dividing the retail shop from the workshop and forming the adjacent corner in each room did not appear to lessen the activity associated with that particular area of the building. During these various stone-throwing experiments I watched the hands of both John and Pat, and on no occasion saw any indication that they were faking matters. For the most part, no one else was present other than the two or three of us at the time. But final confirmation that trickery could be ruled out came when John and Pat, together with Paul and Yvonne, were absent on holiday in Norfolk, some 300 miles away from Cardiff. During their absence I called unannounced at the workshop and spoke to Michael, who was on his own in the workshop. Michael informed me that there had been no poltergeist activity from the day they had left for their holiday, and observed that in his opinion it required the energies of two people to enable anything paranormal to take place. I tested this by throwing stones into the active corner, and immediately stones came back. This seemed to confirm Michael's theory, and he then withdrew into the yard behind the building so that we could ascertain whether or not activity continued while I was alone in the workshop. It did. Each time I threw a stone there came the familiar clatter of a returned stone hitting the wall and falling to the floor. My disappointment at disproving Michael's interesting theory was more than tempered by the fact that faking on the part of anyone associated with the workshop seemed to be finally ruled out.

The second of the particularly startling events witnessed by me personally, and to which I referred earlier, also concerned the stone-throwing. Having established, it seemed, some contact with the poltergeist by throwing stones into the active corner, we attempted to expand this contact in other ways. The most successful of our attempts concerned the brass 25-pounder shell case from the Second World War mentioned earlier and kept in the workshop as a souvenir. The experiment started by chance. In a short break from work one day, John placed the shell case at the far end of the workshop and attempted to hit it with the many small stones often found littering the floor (apparently from overnight poltergeist activity) when he opened the premises in the morning. After several unsuccessful attempts he became exasperated, and on impulse called out "All right Pete, you hit it." At once a stone ricocheted off the surface of the shell with a loud "ping." I was told about this on my next visit, and tried the experiment for myself, with the same results. Standing on the far side of the workshop, with John next to me, I made several unavailing attempts to hit the shell case before calling out to "Pete" to hit it. Immediately, we heard a stone ricochet off the case and fall to the floor. Never once did either John or I, on that or subsequent days, succeed in hitting the shell case from a distance of 20 feet, yet "Pete" appeared able to do so at will.

In spite of the range of objects thrown by "Pete" in both the workshop and the retail shop during my investigation, no one was hurt. I was myself hit on more than one occasion, yet with extreme, almost exaggerated gentleness. This concern for our safety was particularly apparent one Sunday afternoon, when the premises were closed to the public and when only John and I, together with Pat, Paul, and Yvonne were present, and when the activity continued virtually non-stop for four hours. While in the retail shop a large stone narrowly missed Pat, while a little later a stone fell onto Paul's head, but so lightly that, in his own words, it was as if it was placed rather than dropped there. On the same occasion a steel cylinder weighing five ounces (which may not sound very much until one imagines it coming into violent contact with one's head) fell just behind me while I was alone in the retail shop, hitting the shop counter with some force but missing me by several inches. On another occasion, as Pat was coming through the connecting door into the workshop from the retail shop and was in the act of closing the door behind her, a large object (which on inspection turned out to be a heavy steel strimming wheel) thrown from inside the retail shop hit the door on the side of the retail shop with stunning force, much to her alarm. Had the missile arrived a split second earlier, or had she left the door open behind her as she passed through it would have struck her on the back of the head, causing serious injury. The retail shop, as I ascertained to my satisfaction, was empty at the time. So dangerous was the missile, and with such force did it arrive, that only a seriously deranged individual would have thrown it at the back of someone's head. And only someone with a seemingly superhuman sense of timing would have thrown it so that it hit the door behind Pat while she was in the act of closing it, rather than Pat herself.

In spite of my attempts, we never succeeded in making contact with "Pete" by the time-honored method of asking questions and inviting one rap for a "yes" and two raps for a "no." In fact the raps and bangings frequently reported in poltergeist cases were never a part of the experience. However, a further indication that contact had been made in other ways came from our experience with money. Apparently John and the other members of the family had once playfully asked "Pete" if he could bring them money. The result had been three old pennies, all dated 1912 (which I now have in my possession). With admirable persistence, John then asked for something with a little more purchasing power. Obligingly, over the next weeks, crumpled £5 notes were found both in the workshop and the retail shop when John opened up in the morning. Either on the floor or pinned to the ceiling with the sharp needle of a carburetor float, by my reckoning no less than £70 in all arrived in this way (the family assured me the final figure came to over £100). We never ascertained where this money came from. Certainly none of it was taken from cash held in the shop.

John, except for the period of his absence on holiday in Norfolk, was always present in the workshop during my investigation. Pat was very frequently there, and Paul and Yvonne were intermittently in attendance. Michael was sometimes there, and another man who helped in the shop was occasionally there. Thus there were effectively only four people who could have engaged in faking, if faking was the explanation for the phenomena: John, Pat, Paul, and Yvonne. In the light of the wide range of effects attributed to "Pete," I was able to conclude that all four, with the possible exception of Yvonne who was present less often than the others, would have had to be actively engaged in the conspiracy at various times. An unknown accomplice would have also been needed to account for the stone-throwing that took place when the family were away on holiday and I was in the workshop on my own. At no time did any one of the four, in spite of my continuing close observation of their positions in the rooms and of their movements when phenomena were taking place, give me the slightest reason to suspect their honesty. Extensive searches of the workshop and the retail premises assured me that there were no mechanical devices that could have been responsible for the stone throwing, even if such devices could explain the responsive activity in the active corner or the stones hitting the shell case on demand. I also satisfied myself that low-tech. procedures, such as sticking stones to the ceiling so that they could fall as the glue dried, were not apparent.

In addition, there were no places either in the workshop or in the retail shop where an accomplice could hide. The floors were of narrow, tight-fitting tongue and groove boards, and there was no evidence that any of them were disturbed in any way. The ceilings were of the suspended variety, and consisted of large polystyrene tiles resting upon thin metal struts too fragile to bear any weight. The workshop measured 30 feet by 15 feet as did the retail shop, and my investigations satisfied me that neither of them concealed a secret cupboard. The only rooms opening from the retail shop or the workshop were a small office, an equally small kitchen, and a toilet. The office had been formed by partitioning one corner of the retail shop, and doors from it led respectively into the shop and into the workshop. Both these doors were invariably left open, allowing a full view of the inside of the office, in which there were no hiding places. The kitchen door was also invariably left open. Except when occupied, the toilet door was usually also left open.

What of a motive for faking? None was apparent. On the contrary, all four family members seemed concerned that the poltergeist activity would adversely affect the business, and the indications were that it did frighten some customers away (including one man who fled without picking up his change from the counter when a stone clattered to the floor in the retail shop). On occasions I took two of my research students in psychology with me on my visits to help me in observing paranormal activity. Nothing occurred while one of them was present, but the other saw stone-throwing events that she was confident could not be explained by trickery of any kind.

Could the whole thing have been an elaborate joke? Michael was the only one of the personnel who seemed something of a practical joker, yet he was not present when many of the phenomena witnessed by me took place. Even when present he was often far from the activity and only mildly interested in it, and he took no part in the stone-throwing experiments in which I participated, either in the workshop or the retail shop. In sum, I am in no doubt that it would be very difficult for even the most determined critic to fall back on the argument of fraud at any point during the period of my investigation. I was extremely fortunate in witnessing so many phenomena myself and in the company of individuals of whose integrity I had plenty of time and opportunity to satisfy myself.

We are left therefore with what can only be described as an intriguing example of a poltergeist haunting. This being the case, what light does it throw upon the question of survival? In order to reply, we must first try to decide between three possible alternative explanations for what took place. Firstly, did "Pete" appear to be in any sense a separate personality? Secondly, was he in some way a projection from the minds of one or more of the people involved? Thirdly, were all the phenomena simply a consequence of some environmental factors causing local physical disturbances, such as passing traffic or geophysical or electromagnetic activity? If we decide in favor of the first possibility, the case supports the survival of at least some part of the personality of "Pete." If we decide on the second (the Super-ESP hypothesis yet again), the case would support the existence of paranormal abilities on the part of the living, but tell us nothing directly about survival. If we decide on the third, the case has a normal explanation and we can dismiss it as of any relevance either to survival or to paranormality.

Let us take the third of these possibilities first. As the premises fronted onto a relatively busy street, vibrations from passing traffic might seem a possible candidate for at least some of the phenomena, such as the tools set swinging in the tool rack or the displacement of small objects such as the carburetor floats. However, although I carried out careful observations in the retail shop when large trucks passed by outside, neither the walls nor the floor showed any sign of vibration, and no objects either trembled or were displaced. As the workshop was at the back of the premises, it was even less likely to feel the effects of passing traffic than the retail shop. Furthermore, the workshop backed onto the yard mentioned earlier, and beyond that there was a wall and the gardens of houses in the next street. Thus traffic vibration does not appear, therefore, to be a credible explanation.

Geophysical effects can I think be dismissed almost as readily. Only two such effects are advanced with any conviction in the literature as explanations of poltergeist happenings, namely seismic activity and ground water. There were no records of any appreciable seismic disturbances in Cardiff during the period of the haunting (such disturbances are in any case rare in this part of the world). And even if, as Dingwall and Hall suggested in 1958 (Gould and Cornell 1979), localized disturbances too minor to register upon instruments may yet be of sufficient magnitude to unsettle buildings and cause the displacement of objects, this fails to explain the great majority of the events witnessed by myself and by others in the present case. These were not random events such as objects falling from shelves, but seemingly purposeful happenings. Of equal relevance, they frequently involved the movement of single items, sometimes light (as with stones and the carburetor floats), sometimes heavy (as with the shell case and the planks thrown into the workshop from the yard), while all other objects in the immediate vicinity remaining undisturbed. Hardly the kind of indiscriminate manifestations one would expect from seismic disturbance.

The action of groundwater seems equally unlikely. The relevant area of Cardiff is not subject to flooding, and situated as it is to the north of the city is not proximate to the sea and affected by the tides, even though those along the Cardiff coast are particularly high. The ground water theory, advocated particularly by Lambert in the *Journal of the SPR* in the 1950s and 1960s and answered by Gauld and Cornell in the same journal (see Gould and Cornell 1979 for a summary), has it that underground water channels, even the water in underground sewers, may from time to time produce a head of water that produces a heave in properties up above, causing objects to be displaced and creaks and raps to occur in walls and furniture. After the heaving, the property then subsides, producing further disturbances. It is difficult to see what this theory has to commend it in the great majority of reported poltergeist cases, even if we assume those occupying the properties concerned would be unaware of successive heaves and subsidences violent enough to move the objects around them. Certainly it fails to address the seemingly purposeful activity we witnessed in the Cardiff case.

This brings me to the second possibility, namely paranormal action – probably unconscious – by living minds. Such action is seriously advanced by a number of authorities. One argument has it that poltergeist activity is the exteriorized emotional energy – particularly rage and frustration – of some living person, particularly someone going through some kind of emotional crisis at the time. Their desire to hit out at those around them, to express their anger by breaking things and causing general mayhem, is repressed to such an extent that it eventually finds expression through a form of unconscious psychokinesis. Unable to act out their wishes physically, they do so paranormally. Disturbed adolescents, going through the emotional upheaval of puberty, are frequently said to be those responsible. How likely is it that this was the explanation for Pete? Firstly, there were no adolescents, disturbed or not, involved in the case. John, Pat, Paul, Yvonne, and Michael were all in respectable middle age. Secondly, there was no evidence of any particular rage or emotional frustration in any of them and indeed, if such emotions were the cause of the phenomena, they must have lingered on in – or been paranormally transmitted to – the premises in some way even during the absence of whoever among the five was responsible, since I obtained results when in the workshop on my own. In addition, to my knowledge there is no published laboratory evidence that suggests macro psychokinetic effects such as stone-throwing can be accomplished by persons physically absent at the time. Nor is there evidence that whatever energy lies behind the small psychokinetic effects apparent in the laboratory is sufficient to cause the large scale disturbances witnessed by me in Cardiff. On balance, therefore, it seems we can dismiss the idea that Pete was no more than a living person unconsciously venting his or her inner turmoil paranormally on the premises and on those working there.

A more closely argued theory linking poltergeist activity to living beings has been advanced over a number of years by William Roll, one of the leading doyens of psychical research. Roll suggests that under certain circumstances the sudden bursts of electromagnetic energy in the brain to which some people are subject could interact with electromagnetic energy in the environment and give rise to an energy leading to recurrent spontaneous psychokinesis, which is then interpreted by witnesses as poltergeist activity (e.g. Duncan and Roll 1995). One cannot do justice to Roll's ingenious and complex theory in the space available here, but although it may explain some poltergeist hauntings, we have no laboratory evidence for the existence of the interaction between brain and environment that he proposes. Also, Roll's theory does not explain how sudden bursts of electromagnetic energy in the brain, whether allied or not to electromagnetic energy in the environment, could produce the apparently responsive activity seen at Cardiff and in some other reported cases. Valuable as Roll's theory certainly is, and helpful as it is in alerting us to the fact that different poltergeist cases may have different causes, it would seem inappropriate when applied to the happenings at Cardiff.

What of the third possibility, namely that Pete was a surviving personality? Gould and Cornell, in their scholarly and wide-ranging explorations of poltergeist phenomena (1979), set down a number of suggested criteria that should be satisfied if we are to attribute a particular case to a surviving personality rather than to paranormal effects from a living mind. These criteria provide very useful guidelines, although they assume, possibly incorrectly, that even if the poltergeist is a surviving personality there must nevertheless be a living "agent" who in some way provides the energy upon which the poltergeist seems to draw. Rearranged a little and in summary their criteria are:

1. The phenomena should not be strictly tied to the comings and goings of any particular person – for instance they should linger on

after his or her departure, as if the energy drawn from him or her by the poltergeist can be stored in some, or be "transferred" from living person to person.

2. There should be evidence of intelligent behavior, such as the arrangement of objects into patterns in empty rooms.

3. The behavior exhibited by the poltergeist should be alien to the known aims and purposes of the agent (although it is difficult to establish accurately what these might be).

4. On more than one occasion several witnesses should simultaneously see the same phantasmal figure or figures.

5. Paranormal phenomena should take place which so far as is known are beyond the capacities of living agents.

To what extent do the Cardiff phenomena appear to meet these criteria? They satisfy the first of them in that they occurred in the respective absence of each of the five people associated with the case (they were also reported as happening in the homes of John and Pat and (particularly) of Paul and Yvonne, when only the two partners were present in each case). They satisfy the second in that intelligent behavior appeared to take place while the premises were locked and unoccupied overnight – e.g. the attempt to lay out cutlery in the kitchen, and the arrival of the £5 notes. They satisfy the third in that they appeared contrary to the wishes of the five people involved, who feared they might have an adverse effect upon business. And they satisfy the fifth to the extent that, as already indicated, we have no evidence that living agents are able to produce the kind of psychokinetic effects witnessed at Cardiff.

The only criterion they do not satisfy is the fourth, a criterion that can in any case be challenged, as apparitions are not a particularly common feature of poltergeist hauntings. Nevertheless, on three occasions toward the end of the case Paul reported seeing the apparition of a young boy, of which more in a moment. Thus overall the phenomena seem to stand up well to the Gould and Cornell test criteria. To this we can add that Pete showed a number of the qualities normally associated with a separate personality. He made apparent attempts to be helpful, as in the reported table-laying and the money episodes. He responded playfully to our stone-throwing experiments. He appeared to respond in kind when Pat spoke angrily to him. He surprised us with many of his actions, for example hitting the shell case with stones. He showed some intelligence, for example in finding tools at John's request and presumably in obtaining the £5 notes and the other objects he brought to the premises (even the old pennies he initially brought were in response to playful challenges to bring money; and once when playfully asked by John to bring a car he produced a set of car keys). He showed evident kindness in refraining from hurting anyone with his stone throwing. And finally, a less objective but nonetheless significant point, he impressed the four members of the family (John and Pat, Paul and Yvonne) with his apparent distinct existence. In spite of the annoyance he caused on many occasions, they grew fond of him, rejecting any suggestion that he should be banished through exorcism or persuaded to leave through mediumship. The last word on the matter rests with Paul, who told me at the end of the case that his overriding feelings at being involved in it were of privilege.

In terms of the above reasoning, the explanation that "Pete" was indeed a separate personality who had survived death and was able to make his presence felt, appears the most likely of those on offer. Opponents of this explanation might invoke the so-called Occam's Razor defense, much known and quoted within science. This has it that we should not multiply instances unnecessarily. In other words, we should not invoke unknown factors in the explanation of a phenomenon when there are known factors capable of doing so. In the case of poltergeist hauntings, we should not therefore invoke the idea of a surviving personality when living beings can be used to explain the observed events. Thus however unlikely it may at first sight appear, the idea that "Pete" was a consequence of living minds, whether consciously or unconsciously, paranormally or normally, is preferable to any suggestion that he was someone from beyond the grave. But these grounds for rejecting the possibility that "Pete" was a surviving entity also fall foul of Occam's Razor, because to argue that "Pete" was the result of living minds one would have to credit living minds with psychokinetic abilities far beyond those discovered in laboratory research, abilities capable of operating purposively but unconsciously, of moving objects the size of a shell case and wooden planks, of responding immediately to requests, of helpful actions, of finding objects such as £5 notes from elsewhere and bringing them to the shop, of playing mischievous tricks, and of exercising care in avoiding injury to others. It will be objected that we do not yet know the extent of the psychic abilities of living minds, but there is little to be gained by the argument that although we have no evidence for something at present, we may do so one day. We can as easily say that although we do not yet have the evidence for survival likely to convince the most hardened skeptic, we will do so one day.

Having experienced the events in Cardiff, it is difficult to escape the possibility that "Pete" does indeed provide us with evidence for survival. But if he was a surviving personality, who was he? Much of his behavior suggested a young boy, anxious to draw attention to himself, rather than a mature adult. This possibility is lent some support by the fact that a large rubber ball and a teddy bear, left over from gift items sold in the retail shop the previous Christmas, disappeared from the workshop, and were reported as found by John and Paul hidden above the suspended ceiling, their attention having been drawn to the hiding place by a sound described by both men as that of a ball bouncing in the roof space. The possible connection of the haunting with a young child was further suggested when Paul reported seeing the apparition of just such a boy in the workshop on three occasions. These occurred towards the end of the haunting, when he had assumed responsibility on some days for opening the premises in the morning and locking up at night. On the first occasion, on entering through the outer door to the workshop, he reported seeing the boy sitting on the top shelf in the active corner. He described him as around 12 years old, solid and detailed except for the face, which was seen simply as an oval shape, and the hands. The boy was sitting upright, although strangely a living boy of that age sitting in that position would have to crouch as there would have been insufficient headroom, In Paul's description, it was as if the ceiling immediately above the boy's head had "dematerialized." Paul felt no fear, and called out a greeting with a question "What are you doing here?", whereupon a carburetor float was thrown towards him from the active corner and the apparition disappeared. At the time the room was illuminated only by daylight coming through the open workshop door, but this allowed reasonable visibility.

On the second occasion, Paul and John were on their hands and knees, working in good electric light on a petrol engine on the floor between them. Paul looked up, saw the apparition behind John, and called out to him to look up, whereupon the apparition vanished and simultaneously a large stone hit the petrol engine with great force, shaking both men. John confirmed the incident of the stone, but did not catch sight of the apparition. The two men were alone in the workshop at the time. On the third occasion, Paul was leaving the workshop on his own prior to locking up. The light was already extinguished in the workshop, and on his way across the room he saw the apparition silhouetted against the light from the kitchen, which was still on. The figure appeared to be waving, as if in farewell. This time, although unperturbed by the first two sightings, Paul was deeply disturbed, and for some days afterwards found it difficult to discuss the apparition or any other aspects of the haunting with myself or anyone else.

As mentioned earlier, Paul had had one previous apparently paranormal experience in a house in which he was working during his years as a plumber. At the time he was fitting central heating in the house, which was unoccupied, and while kneeling to adjust a radiator valve he felt a hand grip him strongly on the right shoulder. Much alarmed he quickly left the house, and on arriving home it was found that he had under his shirt the clear imprint of fingers where the hand had gripped his shoulder. This event, together with the reported sightings of the young boy in the workshop, suggests that Paul may have certain psychic gifts, and indeed after the conclusion of the Cardiff case he and Yvonne reported to me two strange occurrences in their own home. In one, two photographs were swapped over in their frames, and in the other £1 coins were sometimes discovered in inexplicable or inaccessible places – for example on a wooden ledge high above the stairwell that could be reached only by means of a ladder. The house is occupied only by the couple themselves, and there appears to be no normal explanation for these experiences.

If "Pete" was indeed a manifestation of a young boy, have we any clues to his identity? In the course of the investigation I was told by John that local rumor had it that a small boy had been killed in a traffic accident immediately nearby some years previously, and towards the end of the case, when to the alarm of the family and of myself, it achieved publicity in a national newspaper, I was approached by the young boy's elder brother, now an adult, who confirmed the death and wondered whether there might be a connection with the haunting. We had no concrete information that would have helped us to identify whether or not such a connection might be justified, but the possibility remains.

Although the case persisted for the two years of my investigation – which is longer than most poltergeist hauntings – it came to an end shortly after the third sighting of the apparition by Paul, at a time when a major reorganization and re-decoration of the premises was taking place. Shortly afterwards John and Pat expanded the business and successfully moved to a much larger workshop, where no further disturbances took place. Their old workshop and retail shop have passed into other hands and been converted to a restaurant, and no details of further hauntings have been forthcoming. If "Pete" was the young boy killed on the road just outside the premises, we might suppose that he was attracted by John, Pat, and the family, people noted for their kindness and compassion. Perhaps Paul's possible psychic abilities may have also played some part. Probably we will never know. Yet the impression made upon all of us involved in this case remains a strong one. For John and Pat in particular, it seems as if for a short period the veil between the worlds was lifted.

Other Poltergeist Cases

I have spent some time describing this case firstly because I had extensive first-hand experience of the phenomena, and secondly because it contained a number of features unusual in poltergeist hauntings. Among these were the facts that there were no adolescent children involved, no obvious emotional problems among those involved, and no apparent motives for deception; that "Pete's" behavior, particularly in the stone throwing experiments, was reciprocal; that a significant sum of money was brought in response to requests; that attempts were made to be helpful as in the cutlery incidents in the kitchen; that the incidents did not seem particularly associated with any one person as "agent"; and that a clear impression of a distinct personality was given. Restrictions on space prevent me from dealing with any other cases in the same detail, but there are many that include an extensive range of phenomena, and these are well summarized by the authors already mentioned and others (Roll 1974, Gauld and Cornell 1979, Goss 1979, Wilson 1981, Price, H. H. 1994, and with an incomparable elegance of style Sacheverell Sitwell 1988). No one who has made a study of these and other serious works on the subject is left in much doubt that in a significant number of cases genuine phenomena, inexplicable by normal means, are being described.

There are a number of other cases in my own files based upon evidence gained and which again I do not have space to describe in detail. However, lest it be thought that all poltergeist energies are as benevolent as those associated with "Pete," three of these cases suggest otherwise. The first involved two young women, close friends of each other, living together in a small modern detached house. The many frightening and inexplicable experiences they reported to me, several of which took place while the house was empty during the day, included a fire in the bathroom intense enough to melt the plastic bath and require the attention of the fire brigade, an expensive mattress slashed to ribbons, graffiti written on the door of the fridge in felt pen, and items moved from the dining room and found later in the attic. One of the most frightening experiences was a housecoat hanging on the wall in full view of both women seen suddenly to smolder and burst into flames before they hurriedly extinguished it. Among their other experiences was a loud crash from the living room during the night which woke both of them, and which sounded as if the heavy bookcase in the lounge had been overturned. When they investigated they found nothing had been disturbed, yet two mornings later, when no sounds had been heard during the night, the bookcase was found to be face down on the floor. On another occasion a visiting friend was hit painfully on the head by a set of car keys that had unaccountably gone missing, apparently thrown down at her from the top of the stairs. Fearing that intruders might be involved, the women had changed the locks on both front and back doors on a number of occasions, and the police had been called five times, yet no explanation for the frightening disturbances was ever found. No connection appeared to exist between these events and previous owners of the house, and in the view of both women it seemed that some malevolent energy objected to their relationship.

In the second of the cases, a young Moslem housewife, her husband, and their four young children reported a long history of disturbances in their Victorian terraced house, some of them so worrying that they had decided to put the house on the market in spite of having spent sizeable sums of money restoring it. The woman seemed to be the main focus of these disturbances. For example, she reported discovering her clothes had disappeared from inside the locked bathroom while she was in the bath, eventually to be discovered hidden behind her bed. On another occasion she reported that after drawing a hot bath she found it stone cold when she entered it immediately afterwards, although she had not left the room in the meanwhile. In the presence of a friend, a teacup was seen to move off the coffee table for no apparent reason and fall on the floor. On a number of occasions credit cards bearing the names of other people living in the street – which she hurriedly returned with tales of having found them in the road – would appear on the same table. Anxious not to pass their troubles on to someone else if and when the house was sold, they requested I invite a medium to identify the source of the problem and if possible put things to rights. I obliged, and the medium reported making contact with the spirit of a small girl who had lived in the house many years ago, and whose ill-treatment included being forced into cold baths. The girl, it seems, admitted responsibility for the disturbances, which appeared to be primarily attention-seeking behavior, and addressed with great kindness by the medium, agreed to leave with her. Afterwards, the disturbances apparently ceased and the house was sold.

The third case, which I was invited to investigate in the company of Patricia Robinson, a leading member of the Scottish Society for Psychical Research, and Professor Archie Roy's colleague in the important research into mediumship reported later in Chapter 10, involved two young adult sisters living together, and the disturbances, which included such things as having the blankets forcibly pulled off their beds by unseen hands during the night, were confined largely to their bedrooms. So alarmed had they become by these disturbances that that they had been forced to sleep downstairs. The house was modern, and rather than being connected with a previous occupant the sisters, both of whom seemed intelligent and level-headed, were convinced that the culprit was a deceased uncle of theirs who had been particularly fond of them in life, and who they were sure was still attracted to them after death. Attempts to contact whoever was responsible by mediumship were unsuccessful, and the events finally appear to have subsided of their own accord.

If we accept the statements of the witnesses in these cases at face value, it is nevertheless conceivable that normal explanations might be advanced to account for them. In the first of them it is possible that jealousy or hostility in one of the young women led her to attempt to frighten or harm the other by inventing a spurious haunting. In the second we might suggest that the mother at the center of the case secretly wished to move out of the house and likewise resorted to subterfuge to frighten her family. In the third case, one of the sisters may have been playing elaborate practical jokes on the other. Alternatively, if the events were genuinely paranormal, the energies concerned could have been externalized from one of the participants, as suggested by the Super-ESP hypothesis.

Human agency certainly cannot be ruled out, though in the first case we would have to suppose almost criminal tendencies in one of the women, while in the second we would have to imagine subterfuge (and the ability to steal credit cards) of a high and seemingly unnecessary order, as the husband appeared more than ready to leave decisions on whether or not to sell the house to his wife. If the events were paranormal, we would again have to stretch the Super-ESP theory to breaking point to explain them. We would have to suppose it could start dangerous fires, overturn heavy bookcases, slash a mattress to pieces, move objects from downstairs to the attic, selectively steal credit cards, transport clothes from locked rooms, turn hot water cold in a matter of seconds, wrench bedclothes from beds and frighten two sisters to such an extent that they abandoned the upper story of their house. Doubtless not impossible in the eyes of those who support the hypothesis, but highly speculative nevertheless. These three cases are not untypical of poltergeist disturbances. Assuming genuineness, the second and third of them in particular could be taken to support the argument for survival.

The Enfield Case

There is space to touch on only one other poltergeist case, the so-called Enfield case, and this is chosen as it is one of the best-known cases to have occurred in the last half century. The case is reported by Guy Playfair, well-known author and psychical researcher, in his book *This House is Haunted* (1980). Together with Maurice Gross, subsequently a Council Member of the SPR and Chair of the Society's Spontaneous Cases Sub Committee, who led the investigation, Guy Playfair researched the case intensively for more than a year in spite of some controversial criticisms of the methodology used (criticisms firmly rejected by the investigators). During the course of it, a range of incidents were witnessed by more than 30 people, and in the view of the investigators these cannot be accounted for by fraud or any other normal explanation.

The family in the Enfield case consisted of a mother and two daughters (Rose aged 13 and her younger sister Janet) and a young son with a speech impediment who featured only marginally in the inexplicable events, at least 26 of which the investigators considered could not be accounted for by fraud. These included movement of small and large objects, interference with bedclothes, pools of water on the floor, apparitions, physical assaults, graffiti, equipment malfunction and failure, spontaneous combustion, disappearance and reappearance of objects, and apparent levitations. Particularly remarkable were the gruff male voices that came through Janet when she was apparently taken over (*possessed*) by the entity thought to be responsible for the disturbances. Such voices would be very difficult for a young girl to produce by normal means, and even more difficult for her to sustain for more than a minute or two due to the strain upon the vocal folds, yet the entity spoke through her for up to three hours on occasions, during which time her mouth barely appeared to move. Professor Hasted, then of Birkbeck College in the University of London, who investigated this particular phenomenon, established that the voices came from what are known as the false vocal folds, which normally become inflamed very quickly if used in this way, rather than from her vocal cords. Certainly, if one hears the tapes of these voices without first knowing all the details, it is difficult to suppose that they came from a young girl rather than from an elderly, gruff-voiced man. The voices also gave certain details of the entity to whom they claimed to belong, information that applied correctly to a neighbor who had died some while previously (although the details given may have been previously known to Janet and her family).

The argument for paranormality in this case is difficult to contest if one studies the published records in detail, listens to the recorded voices, and discusses the details with the investigators, Maurice Gross and Guy Playfair. There is also an interesting follow-up to the case that occurred 16 years after the haunting came to an end. Both Maurice Grosse and I were invited speakers at a conference held by a section of the Mensa Society (the UK Society for those with an IQ of 140 plus) on aspects of the paranormal. Maurice's talk focused on the Enfield poltergeist case and, using a reel-to-reel machine he played a tape of one of the gruff voices that had come through Janet. While the voice was speaking, the tape recorder suddenly jammed. I was sitting in the audience at the time and went onto the platform to see if I could help Maurice rectify matters. But on examining the machine we found to our surprise that the tape had become jammed by winding itself *backwards* (i.e. in the opposite direction of travel between the two reels) around the stanchion above the tape head. Such a thing, as we ascertained, is mechanically impossible by normal means unless one stops the machine, unwinds the tape completely from one of the reels and then winds it manually around the stanchion, in the opposite direction to the travel, before reconnecting it to the reel. Such a maneuver takes several minutes of concentrated effort to accomplish, and would have been impossible under the circumstances in which it happened during Maurice's talk. We ascertained, together with an independent witness from the audience, that both ends of the tape had remained firmly wound around both reels during and after the jamming took place, which had happened almost instantaneously. In addition, both Maurice and the machine were in full view of the audience throughout, and when we disconnected the tape and laboriously unwound it from the stanchion we counted more than 40 windings, a number that emphasized even further the length of time it would have taken to produce this puzzling effect by hand. I published a full report of this incident in one of the SPR's publications (Fontana 2001), and invited anyone who could do so to duplicate the phenomenon by sleight of hand. There have never been any takers.

Does the Enfield case throw light on the survival question? Eminent neuropsychiatrist Dr. Peter Fenwick and colleagues at London's prestigious Maudsley Hospital confirmed after a range of tests that Janet was not suffering from any form of brain defect. Guy Playfair reports that at various times during the case he had the impression that he and Maurice Grosse were dealing "with fragments of confused minds" (more voices than one came through Janet during the investigation) "that once belonged to ordinary men and women who just don't understand their present condition." He also quoted Alan Kardec to the effect that such surviving spirits are sometimes used by other spirits "to play fun and games for their amusement."

If Guy Playfair and Maurice Grosse were wrong and discarnate minds were not responsible for the phenomena, a large number of which were considered by the investigators and many other witnesses as inexplicable by normal means, then who or what was? Energy exteriorized unconsciously by Janet and by other family members (some things happened while Janet was not present)? This might account for some of the disturbances but not for others, many of which were witnessed by Maurice Gross during the many hours that he spent observing the family. In particular, can it explain the voices that came from Janet, and which appear to have been beyond her ability to produce by normal methods of vocalization? Could her unaided energies, even if operating paranormally, have been responsible? It seems unlikely, and even if they were, why should her supposedly paranormal energies, instead of being exteriorized into the environment in the form of psychokinetic activity, be diverted into producing spurious voices? And what of the incident of Maurice Grosse's tape recorder at the Mensa conference? No normal explanation has been forthcoming for what seems a physical impossibility. Assuming paranormality, from where did the energy come that produced the malfunction of the tape recorder? Janet and other members of her family were not present at the Mensa conference, and the event was long after the Enfield case had come to an end. Was one spirit, whose gruff voice was recorded on the tape, attracted (and enraged) by Maurice's attempt to play it to the conference?

Unless we decide in advance that survival is an impossibility, it does appear to be one of the plausible explanations for the events at Enfield and at the Mensa conference, just as it does for the other poltergeist cases detailed in this chapter. The other possible explanation is that of Super-ESP, the exteriorization of paranormal energies from the living. The competing claims of these two explanations will be looked at in detail in Chapter 5.

Other Possible Post-Mortem Communications Involving the Movement of Objects

It is relevant to mention two more of my experiences, which, although they were not associated with poltergeist activity or supposed earthbound spirits, did involve the movement of objects (Fontana 2000). They both concerned the late Ralph Noyes, who appeared to want to provide evidence of his survival by this method. Ralph served as Honorary Secretary of the SPR during my years as President, and was a particularly close friend. Shortly after his death I handed Ingrid Slack, a psychologist from the Open University who was also a close friend of Ralph and with whom I was staying at the time, the copy of a magazine that contained an obituary devoted to him. Prior to reading it, Ingrid prepared a cocktail for us both in the kitchen. Having mixed it, she removed the top of the cocktail shaker, placed it on the counter top well away from the edge, and poured out a drink for each of us. We took our drinks into the lounge, where she read the obituary, remarking with great feeling when she came to the end that it was yet more evidence of Ralph's popularity. "Yes," I answered, "he was very much loved." Precisely at that moment, we heard a loud noise from elsewhere downstairs, as of one metallic object forcibly hitting another. Startled, we went to investigate, and found in the kitchen that the top of the cocktail shaker had left the counter top and hit the door of the fridge on the other side of the room.

We carried out experiments in an attempt to establish how this could have happened. However, even when we placed the top of the shaker on the very edge of the counter top and banged hard on the countertop we could not displace it. Jumping up and down on the (solid) kitchen floor was equally unsuccessful. The counter top had no appreciable slope on it, and it was not wet or greasy. There were no windows open in the kitchen, and no animals in the house. As a detached residence, there were no neighbors who could have caused vibration of any kind. There was no building work taking place nearby. No traffic could have shaken the house. The kitchen was at the back of the house and opened onto a private garden some 60 feet long. The front of the house faced a private paved cul-de-sac. There were no washing machines, dryers, or dishwashers operating in the kitchen at the time, and no electrical appliances in use on the counter top. The house is not subject to any disturbance from underground water or from any other environmental factor that might have caused the incident. Nothing else in the kitchen or elsewhere in the house had been disturbed, and such a thing had never happened before.

The second experience apparently connected with Ralph took place the following week. I was working in my own study, compiling a paper for which I needed a quotation from William James. I picked up my copy of *William James on Psychical Research* (Murphy and Ballou 1960), which was on my desk, my thoughts turning at the time to Ralph who much admired James, and who was working on a book about him when he died. I opened *William James on Psychical Research* at random, and the first words that met my eyes were "physical phenomena." At precisely that moment, a pile of psychology journals on the top shelf behind me fell to the floor. My study is not particularly tidy, and I do not stack journals particularly neatly, but in the 20 years I have used that study nothing else of this kind has ever taken place. The back of my chair was two feet away from the shelves, which are securely attached to the wall. There is no sag in the top shelf, which is supported in the middle as well as at both ends, and there is nothing in the study that can cause shelves to vibrate. The study is far enough from the road to be unaffected by passing traffic (and the road is exceptionally quiet), the house is detached and there are no animals or near neighbors to cause disturbance, and there was no window open at the time.

These two events still defy natural explanation, and the fact that they coincided precisely not only with thoughts of Ralph but respectively and exactly to a reference to the love his friends had for him, and to my catching sight of William James' reference to "physical phenomena," something in which Ralph and I shared a lively interest (we had both been involved in the Scole investigation into physical phenomena described in Chapter 13) seem to point strongly to his wish to communicate his continuing existence. There are many instances in the literature of what are taken to be attempts by the deceased to demonstrate their survival to family and friends by means of physical phenomena such as the movement of objects, and where such phenomena defy normal explanation it seems difficult to attribute them to unconscious psychokinesis from the living. One could perhaps accept that violent emotions such as repressed anger or hostility may in certain circumstances lead to direct effects upon the physical environment, but it is more difficult to suppose that a quiet and unrepressed sadness over the death of a friend could have the same effect. Certainly I have come across no argument to suggest that it can, and I would be interested to listen to one if it is put forward.

Incidents such as the two that seem associated with Ralph lend some support to the argument that surviving personalities may be responsible for at least some of the physical phenomena witnessed in poltergeist cases. However, there is one further possibility associated with poltergeists that warrants a mention. Something has already been made of the fact that one explanation for poltergeists is that repressed energies in living people, directed paranormally outwards at the environment by some unknown process, may be responsible. If this is indeed the correct explanation in some cases, it is possible that this process is connected in some way with what is known as *possession*. Belief in possession was once widespread in Western cultures, and is based upon the assumption that earthbound spirits can take over the minds of the living and speak or act through them in some way.

Various mediums claim that possession is in fact a form of uncontrolled mediumship, in that spirits take over the minds (either conscious or unconscious) of living beings, and may in fact even be responsible for some cases of apparent mental illness. Susy Smith, a prolific writer on psychical research and with mediumistic gifts of her own, took this view, and describes in *The Afterlife Codes* (2000) how she herself suffered in this way from spirits who not only invaded her thoughts with their own messages against her will, but sometimes pulled her hands away from the typewriter which she was using and held them away with "a force I could not fathom." She rejects the idea that these episodes were psychotic, insisting that although they were "irritating and tiring ... even frightening ... the thinking part of me was existing aside from these activities, observing what was going on at all times." Equally convinced of the link between possession and some so-called psychotic states was Professor James Hyslop, Professor of Logics and Ethics at Columbia University, one of the leading American supporters of his day for the reality of survival, successful reorganizer of the almost moribund American SPR, and author of a number of influential works on survival of death including *Science and a Future Life* (1905) and *Life After Death* (1918). Hyslop in fact left money in his will to found an Institute for the treatment by mediums of those suffering from obsessional neurosis.

Can Hauntings Be Caught on Camera?

Various attempts have been made by researchers to establish whether or not the energies involved in hauntings, including poltergeist cases, can be registered by electronic devices. Cameras and video cameras have been set up in the hope of capturing ghostly images – or even the movement of objects displaced by poltergeists while in mid-air. Audio tapes have been set up in the hope of capturing paranormal sounds, and thermometers set up to register inexplicable changes in room temperature. On the whole, results have been very disappointing. One or two fleeting images may have been registered on film or video, a few raps and bangs have been caught on audio tape, and strange drops in temperature have been registered (spirits are said to take energy from the environment in order to manifest), but like the old trick of stretching cotton across doorways to see if they are broken by mysterious presences, nothing particularly convincing has been forthcoming. Even if it were we would be reminded that such evidence is all too easily faked.

Whether this failure to capture hauntings on camera or by other electronic means is due to the fact that spirits and modern electronic equipment don't mix or to the fact that spirits are camera shy is unclear. The first possibility would seem to be ruled out by the evidence currently being obtained in ITC experiments and discussed later (Chapter 14). The second is more likely. At poltergeist hauntings, as I know from experience, many of the phenomena happen just out of one's lines of sight (for example behind one's back), even though the instant one turns one's head it is clear that there is no one physically there. Is it possible that typically the phenomena cannot take place under the direct gaze of observers, or under the lens of the camera? If so, why should this be? The only answer one can give is that, as spontaneous paranormal events take place so infrequently, there may be a wide range of physical factors that inhibit their occurrence. This seems particularly true of events that take place in bright light. Light is itself an energy, and may conflict in some way with the "energy" of paranormal events. Thus even the act of observing, which involves using the energy of light, may be a factor here. This is pure speculation, but in the absence of evidence it may represent our best guess.

The Implications for Science

An issue that will arise from time to time throughout the book is what implications do these and other paranormal happenings have for our existing scientific paradigms? Certainly they cannot be accommodated within these paradigms, but the readiness to change paradigms if the evidence warrants it is in fact essential to scientific progress. Without such a readiness, science would indeed still be in the Dark Ages. Thus a certain cautious openness to new discoveries, however strange they may at first sight appear, is essential in the scientist, together with a recognition that the world is indeed a mysterious place and that it is arrogant to suppose that we have uncovered even a small part of that mystery. Such cautious openness leads us to accept that the laws of science are not laws at all, but informed conclusions reached on the basis of certain areas of exploration. Each law has what we might call a limited and not an absolute range of convenience. That is, within certain areas of being it serves us very well, allowing us to manipulate and control the material environment contained by it. However, once we move outside these areas, the law may no longer apply. Thus when we explore the sub-atomic so-called quantum world, the laws of physics that apply to the observable common-sense world cease to be valid. Sub-atomic particles appear able to move from one place to another without any lapse of time, to be in two places at once, even to be in some form of communication with each other by no known means when separated by what is to them vast distances of space. In fact, in the sub-atomic world, terms such as time and place, as we understand them, can no longer be said to apply. We use these terms only because we have no other language – except that of mathematics so advanced as to be beyond the comprehension of the layperson – with which to discuss them.

Similarly, when we move into the remote macro world of outer space, the laws of physics that explain our observable, common-sense world again no longer apply. For example so-called "black holes" in space (stars that have collapsed inwards upon themselves) have a gravity so powerful that nothing, not even time, can escape from their surface. Thus if it were possible (it is not; nothing could survive the intense pull of that gravity) to exist on the surface of a black hole, we would experience time standing still. Even space travel does strange things to time as we understand it. The occupants of a space ship traveling near the speed of light would age less than the rest of us, as such travel would for them slow down time as we know it. Thus if long space journeys become a possibility a spaceman or woman would return after many years away to find their twin brothers and sisters now much older than themselves. The stuff of science fiction perhaps, but the possibility illustrates that even the passage of time, which was once thought of as an invariable constant, does not occur at a uniform rate. If even our concept of time has to change, then it seems we can be sure of very little.

Many scientists, who may be sufficiently open in other areas of their thinking, draw the line at the existence of paranormal phenomena, in the mistaken belief that if a single psychic event is demonstrated to be true, the whole of the scientific edifice, carefully constructed over the years on the foundation of rigorous experimentation and meticulous observation, would come crashing about our ears. The existence of psychic phenomena in no way threatens the edifice. It simply, as with quantum physics and astrophysics, establishes its own range of convenience, a range within which it has its own laws and outside which other scientific laws, for all their value within their own range, no longer apply.

CHAPTER 5.
MEDIUMSHIP: HISTORY AND BACKGROUND

The Nature of Mediumship

Mediumship has been defined in a number of different ways, but basically it is the alleged ability to receive communications from people who have died. There is an important distinction between mediums and psychics not always appreciated by those writing about the subject. While mediums claim to be in touch with the spirit world, psychics are confined to information from this world, which they claim to gather telepathically, clairvoyantly, or precognitively. Many mediums take the view that all those with mediumistic gifts are also psychic, but insist it is possible to have psychic gifts without being mediumistic. This is probably true. Old style fortune-tellers now refer to themselves as psychics, and many of them use a wide range of paraphernalia to help them in their work, including Tarot Cards, Rune Stones, Crystal Balls and the I Ching. By contrast, mediums rarely use physical aids of this kind, relying instead on what the spirits tell them, either directly or through a so-called spirit guide, who is usually someone who claims to have lived once on earth, but not always. Frequently these guides are described as Native Americans or as ancient Chinese sages, and the explanation given for this is that both these cultural groups followed paths (Shamanism and Taoism respectively) that connected not only to the spirit world but to the sacredness of the natural world. The resulting deep-seated spiritual harmony which they enjoyed between heaven and earth gives them a special facility to work with mediums, a facility not shared by other advanced spirits, who, it is said, find it difficult to lower their vibrations sufficiently to penetrate the dense matter of which the physical planes are composed.

The mediumistic gift expresses itself in a number of different ways, from purely mental mediumship at one end of the scale, with the medium consciously relaying messages supposedly from the deceased, to physical mediumship at the other, in which the medium, usually in deep trance, is said to supply a form of subtle energy that is used by the spirits to produce psychokinetic effects. It is often said that all mediumistic gifts first manifest themselves in early childhood, though they may lay dormant in the face of parental disapproval and emerge again later in life, typically as a consequence of working with a development circle run by an experienced medium who helps students (often through meditation and visualization practices) to lower the boundaries between the conscious and the unconscious mind, thus allowing the elusive whispers from the spirit world received at the level of the latter to emerge into consciousness. Importantly, the development circle also tries to help the budding medium to know how to raise these barriers when needed, so that he or she is not 'invaded' by unwanted and possibly ill-intentioned spirits.

Mediumship appears to be at least as old as recorded history, and in early times was often thought to be an indication of contact with the gods. Space does not allow a survey of this historical background (which is very well covered by Lorimer 1984), so let us take just one example, drawing it from the cradle of Western civilization and from one of the wisest men of his time, namely Socrates (469-399 bc). Plato gives us a good description of Socrates' relationship with his daemon (from the Greek *daimm*, a word meaning god or indwelling spirit, and not to be confused with 'demon,' a medieval corruption of the true meaning of the term prompted by the belief that anything not sanctioned by the church was evil). We are told that Socrates would go into a spontaneous trance and remain in rapt contemplation, sometimes for hours and once for a whole day and night, during which he would consult this guiding spirit. On occasions it would break into his thoughts and even his conversation, and as he said himself it would oppose him even about trifles if he was about to make a mistake of some kind, often stopping him in the middle of a speech. Its silence when he was leaving his house to attend the court that sentenced him to death and while he was addressing the judges led him to announce that 'what has happened to me is a good (and not a mistake), and those of us who think that death is an evil are in error.' Spurning the opportunity to escape the death penalty passed on him for allegedly not worshipping the State gods and for corrupting the young with his new religious ideas, Socrates calmly drank the fatal dose of hemlock, and without regrets left the physical world.

During his lifetime Socrates made the first known attempt to explain the phenomenon of mediumship, for such his own experiences seem to have been. For example, although he recognized that similar experiences had been reported over the centuries they were rare in people of his own acknowledged high intellect, and he speculated as to why this might be. His conclusion (which has a very modern sound to it) was that the intellect seems able to inhibit or interfere with spiritual communications, which in his view normally come only in sleep or when the mind is deranged in some way (as in the ecstasies of the prophetess at the shrine of Apollo at Delphi and of the priestesses at Dodona). During this deranged – or altered – mental state, the intellect does not attempt to interfere with or interpret these communications. They are simply given expression. In some ways Socrates saw this process as similar to the creative flights of the poet, who 'does not attain to excellence through the rules of any art,' but gives voice to 'beautiful verses in a state of inspiration' (the term 'inspiration' meaning at that time the act of taking into oneself the divine spirit of life).

For Socrates, individuals who experienced these altered states were used as instruments by the gods, who might also use certain disembodied spirits as their messengers. At the same time, other disembodied spirits, held back by the influence of the material world that they had left behind, haunted monuments and tombs (in modern times such spirits are usually referred to as earthbound). The problem, as Socrates saw it, was to identify how people of intellect could set aside the interference of the conscious mind and achieve these altered states, thus opening themselves to divine guidance. He acknowledged that there were some who, unlike himself, were able to do so at will, and these he placed even above men and women distinguished in the arts and the handicrafts (Lorimer 1984).

How interesting that nearly two and a half thousand years ago, Socrates was giving very much the same explanation of mediumistic gifts and their inhibition by the conscious mind that we might give today. This brings home to us an essential but often forgotten truth, namely that the knowledge of the spiritual dimension possessed by the ancients has hardly been bettered. The myth of eternal progress in human understanding, which lies behind so much of our delusory intellectual arrogance in modern times, can clearly be seen at least in spiritual matters for what it is, a myth. Those who like to draw their metaphors from the Bible might illustrate this by likening modern man to Esau, who is said in his hunger to have sold his birthright for a mess of potage. The desire for yet more knowledge, for yet more control over nature and the natural world, has led us to sell the birthright of our innate spiritual wisdom for the mess of potage of material progress, a mess in every sense of the word and one which is likely to choke us all if we don't curb our greed for it.

What would modern medicine make of Socrates' experiences if he was on earth today? In all probability they would be diagnosed as psychotic, and Socrates would be labeled a borderline schizophrenic, subject to an hallucinatory inner voice that he mistakenly credited with independent existence and that interfered with his ability to live a normal life (thus although Socrates saw the intellect as interfering with his inner voice, modern medicine would see it as the other way round). Socrates would be prescribed drug therapy to put matters right, and materialistic brain scientists would subject him to brain scans to identify which areas of his brain were active when he heard his voice, and subsequently insist that everything was due to cerebral malfunction. This dogmatic approach to inner experience can be highly misleading because it represents a form of circular reasoning. The materialist psychiatrist decides to label mediumistic voices such as those of Socrates as mental illness, and then proceeds to explain them away as mental illness. The materialist brain scientist decides to label them as brain malfunction and then proceeds to explain them away as brain malfunction. The impression of scientific infallibility given by materialistic psychiatrists and brain scientists often serves to lend their pronouncements the aura of holy writ, seemingly disqualifying the layperson from having anything worth saying on the nature of his or her own mental life. Just as once the multitudes were persuaded by the priesthood they had no right to approach the divine except through the intermediation of the church, so the multitudes are now persuaded by the materialistic creed of our times that they have no right to approach mental life except through the intermediation of those who put their faith in prescription drugs and brain scans.

We can go further and say that not only is the dogmatic approach by materialistic science to the mysteries of the human mind misleading, it reveals a disturbing ignorance. Ignorance is not so much the act of not knowing something, it is the act of not knowing something but claiming to know. The materialistic scientist would have us believe that he 'knows' that any claimed inner spiritual experience has nothing to do with spirituality – since he has already decided that spirituality, along with psychic abilities, does not exist – and has everything to do with mental illness and the human powers of self-delusion. Lacking any personal acquaintance with inner spiritual or psychic experiences, the materialistic scientist 'knows' that those who have such experiences are wrong in their interpretation of them, while he or she is of course right. And not only is this a form of ignorance, it is dangerous ignorance. Dangerous in the sense not only that it may lead to misdiagnosis and mistreatment of people who have experiences akin to those of Socrates and need help in understanding and coming to terms with them, but that it builds up a cultural climate of skepticism in which people are taught to become deaf to much of their own inner experience. In most areas of psychological life, if others convince us that some ability is beyond us, then it tends to become so. If we tell ourselves often enough that we cannot do something, then usually we cannot do it. Our prophecy of our own failure becomes self-fulfilling. At a much deeper level, if we tell ourselves that there is no spiritual dimension to existence, there is no intuitive wisdom that can tell us more about ourselves than can our textbooks, there are no psychic abilities in ourselves or in others and no possibility of contact with the deceased, then all these negatives become part of our thinking, and cause us to shut out the possibility of experiencing any or all of these things.

The Fox Sisters and the Rise of Modern Mediumship

It may seem strange to refer to something that happened well over a century and a half ago as modern, yet there is certainly a thread of continuity between the movement initiated by the events that took place in the Fox household in Hydesville, USA in 1848 and mediumship today. These events are credited with inaugurating the modern wave of interest in mediumship and psychical research, and a knowledge of them is essential if we wish to reach some understanding of mediumship. All too often they have been misrepresented in the past by skeptics and believers alike, ridiculed by the former and accepted uncritically by the latter.

The events centered around two of the Fox sisters, Kate aged 12 and Margaret aged 15, to be joined subsequently by their older sister Leah, 19 years senior to Margaret, when her marriage broke up (these ages are those recorded by those investigating the case, but Mrs. Fox later insisted that Kate was only seven and Margaret 10 at the time, ages that if true must make the girls' reported experiences potentially even more remarkable). The house in Hydesville into which the Foxes – a family of practicing Methodists – had moved the previous year had a reputation for mysterious noises. These had apparently driven out the previous tenant, a Michael Weakman, but at first the Fox family experienced nothing unusual. However, in March 1848 strange raps, thumps, and footsteps were heard at night, and on the evening of March 31 Kate and Margaret discovered that if they clapped their hands the raps appeared to answer back. In the presence of eight neighbors, all of them named in Mrs. Fox's signed report submitted four days later to a committee of neighbors and published in the committee's report the following month (*A Report of the Mysterious Noises in the House of Mr. John D. Fox*), the raps were then found to respond with one rap for 'yes' and two raps for 'no' to the letters of the alphabet (see e.g. Dale Owen 1860, Brown 1970, Jackson 1972, Douglas 1976, Moore 1977, Brandon 1983, Owen 1989, Conan Doyle 1989).

By means of these responses the communicator claimed to be Charles Rosa, a 31-year-old peddler, who further claimed he had had his throat cut five years previously for the sake of the 500 dollars in his possession by John Bell, a previous occupant of the house, who had then buried him 10 feet under the cellar floorboards. The night after these revelations, Mrs. Fox reported that some 300 townspeople crowded into the house, and that all heard the rappings. The next day digging commenced in the cellar in an attempt to find human remains, but this was discontinued when water was reached. Mrs. Fox concluded her written report with the words 'I am very sorry there has been so much excitement ... It has been a great deal of trouble to us. It was our misfortune to live here at the time; but I am willing and anxious that the truth should be known and that a true statement should be made ... I certify that the foregoing statement has been read to me and that the same is true; and that I should be willing to take my oath that it is so if necessary.' Her husband signed a corroborative statement.

Digging recommenced in the cellar in the dry weather that summer, and at five feet hair and bones were discovered which medical opinion pronounced human. However, the mysterious peddler was himself never traced, which seems strange in the light of his claim to have had a family and children who surely must have been aware of his disappearance, and who one would suppose would have come forward once the story was generally known – which it soon was, thanks to its sensationalization in the press. Perhaps prompted by a desire to support her family in the midst of the confusion, and freed by the break-up of her marriage, Leah Fox soon joined the household and took over the management of her two sisters, who later found that the rappings followed them to other houses and even to a public hall where they gave a demonstration. Although some newspapers early branded the sisters as frauds, people soon began to pay money to attend their sèances and demonstrations. Rappings were quickly supplemented by the movement of objects and the levitation of tables, and it was claimed that the spirit of Benjamin Franklin, the American scientist famous for the discovery that lightning is caused by electricity and who died in 1790, joined a growing list of communicators. No trickery on the part of the sisters was found at the time, though many theories were advanced to account for the phenomena. In due course, the sisters were even taken up by P. T. Barnum, the well-known impresario and popularizer of the weird and wonderful, who brought them to New York.

Various attempts were then made to discredit the Fox sisters, perhaps as much from a belief that contact with spirits was evil as from a belief that it was contrary to scientific understanding. As early as 1851 a relative, Mrs. Normal Culver, published a supposed confession by Margaret Fox, together with the account of an investigation held in the Fox household at which a servant girl was said to have been caught rapping under the cellar floor each time the sisters called upon the spirits. Yet subsequently it was confirmed that the Fox family had no servant, that Kate was not present during this supposed investigation, and that it did not even take place in the Fox household. Missing from these attempts to discredit the sisters was any credible explanation of the intelligences that ostensibly answered the questions put to them by investigators through the sisters, and when Kate and Leah Fox appeared before a committee of Harvard professors in 1857 in tests organized by the *Boston Courier*, no report of fraud was forthcoming, although the committee stopped short of proclaiming the phenomena genuine.

The three sisters continued to prosper over the following years, but fame and notoriety began to take its toll on Kate and Margaret, and by 1855 they were both said to be drinking heavily (the date, only seven years after the first appearance of the phenomena, suggests the investigating committee rather than Mrs. Fox were correct about the girls' ages in 1848; it seems unlikely that Kate and Margaret would be verging on alcoholism aged 14 and 17 respectively). Margaret even grew disenchanted with spiritualism for a time, seemingly as a consequence of the family pressures that led her to postpone her marriage to Elisha Kane, a naval surgeon and noted Arctic explorer who was an ardent opponent on religious grounds of contact with spirits. In spite of these pressures, Margaret did finally marry Kane (doubts have been expressed over the legality of the ceremony, although in the rather uncertain legal conditions of the time it was probably genuine), and it seems highly likely that during the years of their relationship she was much influenced by his argument (the gist of which is apparent from his published correspondence with her) that what she was doing was sinful. It may have been this fear of sin that led her to convert to Roman Catholicism, and that perhaps contributed to the deep depression that afflicted her on his untimely death in 1857.

However, in spite of these setbacks, Margaret continued working as a medium, as did Kate. The latter even proved able to do automatic mirror writing (writing comprehensible only when reflected in a mirror), and even produced apparent materializations. From 1861 to 1866 she worked exclusively for Charles Livermore, a rich New York banker who had lost his wife Estelle in 1860, and detailed records were kept of the nearly 400 séances she held for him. During these, although the doors and windows of the house were locked, Estelle nevertheless seems to have materialized, remaining silent but writing in handwriting recognizable as her own on cards supplied by Livermore and while Kate's hands were held. It was Livermore who in gratitude for her work financed her trip to England in 1871, where she held joint sittings with mediums D. D. Home and Mrs. Guppy, then both at the height of their fame, and impressed Sir William Crookes who declared her talents unparalleled. During her time in England she met and married an English barrister, Henry Jencken, with whom she had two sons. Ferdinand, the elder, was hailed as a medium from age three, supposedly manifesting unearthly light from his eyes and penning automatic writing by age five. On the death of her husband in 1885, Kate returned to New York, where she was briefly arrested – she believed this was at her sister Leah's instigation – for alleged cruelty to her children, and for a time went in danger of losing their custody.

Meanwhile Margaret had still been earning a modest living as a medium. In 1884 – and ill at the time – she was called before the Seybert Commission in Philadelphia, where she failed to their satisfaction to produce raps while standing upon glass tumblers, though otherwise she seems to have acquitted herself quite well. But things came to a crisis on May 27, 1888 when Margaret published a letter in the *New York Herald* denouncing spiritualism and promising a complete exposure. In August of the same year she kept her promise at a public lecture in the New York Academy of Music, during which she produced raps on the stage by normal means, explained how the rest of the effects had been faked, and pronounced that spiritualism was a complete fraud. Kate gave a similar confession in New York on October 10. Even the early rappings at Hydesville were claimed by the sisters to have been accomplished by nothing more than toe-cracking, and to have been designed as a trick on their mother, who believed the previous disturbances in the house were caused by a ghost (if trick it was it certainly succeeded beyond expectations – Mrs. Fox's hair is said to have turned white due to the stress caused by the disturbances). The two sisters then embarked on a series of meetings designed to continue the exposure (details of which were seized upon by Reuben Davenport in his book *The Death Blow to Spiritualism*). However, this was not in fact the end of the matter. Kate withdrew her confession a few weeks later, and Margaret did so in 1889.

Both the sisters continued to practice mediumship after this debacle, but their health deteriorated further, due not least to their heavy drinking. Kate died from alcoholism on July 2, 1892, and Margaret died destitute on March 8, 1893. Strangely, this meant that the three sisters died on three consecutive years, as Leah had preceded them on November 1, 1891. What conclusions can we reach about the Fox sisters? Still hailed by spiritualists as remarkable pioneers, and vilified by skeptics as frauds, the sisters remain something of an enigma. Psychic abilities were said to be in their family. The girls' grandmother apparently had the habit of dreaming of the funerals of people still living, the details of which turned out afterwards to be correct (one hopes the sad news of their imminent demise was kept from the people concerned). The girls' aunt, Elizabeth Higgins, was said to have dreamt of her own tombstone and to have died on the date she saw inscribed upon it. The Fox sisters may thus have inherited these gifts, together with the belief in the paranormal that helped their expression. The confessions Margaret and Kate both made in 1888 have been supposedly explained by the fact that Margaret, who was in poverty at the time, was offered sums of money (which in the event were not forthcoming) for discrediting spiritualism. The withdrawal of her confession was published in the New York press in November 1889, and in the course of it she insisted that the confession had been made while she was under 'the strong psychological influence of people inimical to Spiritualism,' and that in making it she 'had given expression to utterances that had no foundation in fact.' She further stated that in withdrawing her confession she was responding to 'the silent impulse of the spirits using my organism at the expense of the hostility of the treacherous horde who held out promises of wealth and happiness in return for an attack on Spiritualism, and whose hopeful assurances were so deceitful ... '

The pressures to which Margaret refers seem therefore to have been both psychological and financial, and they may also have included attempts to play upon her earlier concerns that spiritualism was sinful, particularly as 'spiritualism' had now become 'Spiritualism' with a capital 'S,' a growing religion that was roundly condemned by many churchmen. Both she and Kate also nursed hostility towards Leah, who seems to have deserted them in 1857 for marriage to a wealthy businessman, and who they may have felt had exploited them during the years she managed their demonstrations. In spite of her independent means, Leah also seems not to have helped the sisters financially, perhaps because of exasperation at their excessive drinking. Kate, we are given to understand, felt added bitterness towards Leah for the painful events surrounding her arrest on grounds of alleged child cruelty after her return to the USA in 1885 and for the threat to deprive her of her children. Thus the confessions may also have been an attempt by both sisters to discredit Leah, whom Margaret even accused of giving Kate and herself cues on when to produce fraudulent phenomena during their demonstrations.

Leah is something of a shadowy figure compared to Kate and Margaret. In poverty after the desertion of her husband around the time of the first phenomena at Hydesville, she may indeed have seen commercial opportunities in the abilities of her young sisters, and exploited them to the full. She certainly seems to have had little professional contact with Kate and Margaret after marrying into money and becoming Mrs. Underwood. But it is difficult to know what exactly happened. Leah herself is said to have developed psychic powers, and it may be that she was aware of these before the events at Hydesville, which predisposed her to believe in her young sisters' abilities and to determine to assist and protect them. Emma Hardinge Britten, the founder of what later became the British Spiritualists' National Union and who met and stayed with Leah in New York soon after Leah became Mrs. Underwood, described her in her autobiography (1996) as one of the best and most noble-hearted women she had ever known, and as the best 'test, rapping and physical medium I have ever met.' Together with Robert Dale Owen, son of the celebrated British industrialist and philanthropist Robert Owen, and variously during his career a US Congressman and leading US diplomat, she attended sèances at which Leah produced rappings and direct voice (or independent voice – a phenomenon in which spirits are claimed to speak in their own voices, either directly or through a trumpet, from locations in the room remote from the medium). In Dale Owen's account, 'every object in the room was in motion' and 'it seemed as if the very carpet would be torn up, it shook so, and bulged up as if moved by a strong wind' – events which, if accurately reported, would be difficult to fake.

Whatever the truth of the matter, the confessions by Margaret and Kate had little effect upon the fascination with mediumship inspired by the sisters. The example they gave prompted a wave of interest throughout much of the Western world. Many people claimed to discover that they too had mediumistic powers (whether genuine or fraudulent), and sèances became a regular evening entertainment for even the most respectable families in the USA and Britain. It may be that by apparently demonstrating that mediumship is genuine, the sisters removed the inhibitions that prevented people from releasing their own psychic abilities. Or it may be that others saw a chance of making money, just as the sisters at least for a time were able to do.

The sisters were tested quite carefully by the standards of the time in the years following Hydesville without being reliably discredited, but the pity is that the controls against deception that we would now adopt in cases of this kind were not available right at the beginning of their mediumship. If the events at Hydesville happened today, researchers would descend upon the humble family homestead with all the paraphernalia that can be mustered. Hardened skeptics would come, some of them less interested in establishing the truth of the matter than in finding tiny loopholes that would allow them to cry fraud; the credulous would come hoping for miracles, and those with more open minds would come intent upon finding out what was really happening. The Fox sisters would have been discredited if they were found to be fraudulent, and skeptics would have been silenced – at least temporarily – if no fraud was discovered. However, as it stands, there are so many contradictions in this case that it remains an enigma. When Margaret made her confession in 1888 it was said by Dr. Isaac Funk, psychical researcher and director of the publishing house of Funk and Wagnalls in New York, that for five dollars 'she would have denied her mother, and would have sworn to anything,' so money may indeed have been a factor in her behavior. And, confession or no confession, Margaret does not seem to have lost her powers. In 1905 Dr. Mellen, the woman physician who had attended her on her deathbed 12 years previously, testified before the Medico-Legal Society of New York that she had heard raps on the walls, ceilings, and floor in answer to questions put by Margaret to her guide when the dying Margaret was unable through weakness to move hand or foot and was as 'incapable of cracking her toe-joints at this time as I was.' We do not know, however, whether Dr. Mellen was an independent witness or whether she had a prior sympathy towards spiritualism

On balance, and in the context of so much that has happened since the days of the Fox sisters, it would be difficult to justify accusations against them of consistent deception over nearly 50 years of demonstrations and sèances. The evidence of the last century and a half suggests that much mediumship is genuinely paranormal, and if so, the Fox sisters deserve the benefit of the doubt, or at least of suspended judgment. Professor Richet, one of the doyens of psychical research, concluded that we can hardly suppose that two young girls were able to organize a fraud that lasted over so many years and that was tested thousands of times. Robert Dale Owen, mentioned earlier, who studied the Fox sisters at first hand, was convinced they were genuine and wrote of them extensively in his *Footfalls on the Boundary of Another World*. Sir William Crookes, also mentioned earlier, was equally convinced by them. So were a range of other luminaries in both the USA and Britain, including – although he may be dismissed by some as anything but an objective commentator – Sir Arthur Conan Doyle, who devoted two chapters of his *The History of Spiritualism* to an examination of their case. In spite of many attempts and many suspicions, no one unequivocally caught them cheating. They were working at a time when fierce opposition from fundamentalist churchmen and church communities was at its height, and when materialistic scientists were likely to be equally hostile, yet they continued to produce apparent phenomena. If nothing else, they helped to set in train an interest in mediumship which indirectly led not only to the development of a new religion, but to the attention of the scholars and scientists who in 1882 founded the Society for Psychical Research in London, two events that in their different ways served powerfully to stimulate the development of modern psychical research.

But if the Fox sisters were genuine, what light does their work throw upon survival? They could have been psychics rather than mediums, producing their effects by psychokinetic interaction with the physical environment rather than by communicating with the deceased. As already made clear, the mysterious peddler was never tracked down (it is possible that his name and his personal details, communicated only by means of raps, may have been given incorrectly) although a maid, Lucretia Pulver, who had worked for the Bells, testified that a peddler had indeed stayed one night in the Bell household, and that the Bells had packed her off to her parents that same night; when she returned three days later she was told he had left. In addition to the remains in the cellar, a human skeleton was discovered between the earth and the crumbling cellar walls of the Fox household 56 years later, prompting the non-spiritualist *Boston Journal* of November 22, 1904 to comment that the find cleared the Fox sisters 'from the only shadow of doubt held concerning their sincerity in the discovery of spirit communications' (claims have been made that the bones may have been planted, but this statement by the *Journal* seems to confirm that the Fox sisters were not reliably detected in fraud during their lifetimes). A peddler's tin box was also found near the bones. However, John Bell always protested his innocence of any crime, producing 44 character witnesses in his support, and no charges were ever brought against him.

Whatever we choose to think of the peddler and the alleged crime, all three Fox sisters convinced many careful investigators over almost half a century that they were indeed in touch with the spirits of the deceased, and it was the consequent belief that genuine spirit contact could be made that prompted large numbers of other people to try mediumship for themselves. Many practicing mediums and their supporters still consider that the events at Hydesville were intended by spirits to usher in a new era in contact between the worlds, and that the Fox sisters were the instruments chosen to bring this about. Certainly the sisters seemed able to provide answers to questions put to them by investigators that they were unlikely to have known by normal means. If the supporters of the Fox sisters are right, we must suppose that from the first the disturbances at Hydesville were only possible because of the sisters' mediumistic abilities. Many houses may possibly have old ghosts, whether connected to supposed violent events in the past or not, and the great majority of these restless spirits may never have an opportunity to manifest. It could be that only when mediums of the claimed caliber of the Fox sisters are present that the spirits can gather whatever energies they need in order to interact with the physical environment.

Mediumship as Evidence for Survival

For many years after the events at Hydesville, research into survival focused upon mediumship. In theory, the communications received through mediums should be capable of putting the issue of whether or not survival is a reality beyond doubt. For example, let us suppose that during a sitting with a medium she receives communications from an elderly deceased relative of mine that include his name and address and accurate details about his life and death, and that inform me that at the back of a drawer in his desk I will find the picture of a long-dead childhood sweetheart that he kept secret even from his family. Let us further suppose that prior to the sitting the medium knew nothing about my relative or me, and that I booked the sitting under an assumed name that disguised my identity. Finally, let us suppose that after the sitting I obtain permission from the family of my relative to look in his desk, and that I find there the picture hidden at the back of the drawer just as the medium told me.

Surely a case like this would be enough to demonstrate survival to everybody's satisfaction? Unfortunately not. An alternative explanation to survival is that in spite of my precautions, the medium may after all have learned of my identity before the sitting, perhaps because she had been recommended to me by someone who then told her I was going to consult her. Through the extensive information-gathering network with which skeptics credit mediums, she may then have obtained details of one of my deceased relatives, and fed each of these back to me as if they were coming from the beyond. As for the picture in the desk drawer, this may have been just a lucky guess. Any old photograph of an unknown young lady found in his possession could be interpreted as a sweetheart from long ago once the medium has put the idea in my head. And if an old photograph is not found, I am likely to dismiss this as unimportant in the light of all the other correct details the medium has given me.

Although this scenario is an unlikely one, it is nevertheless a possible one, and that is sufficient for the critic to dismiss the case. Suppose, however, that in addition to the other details, the deceased relative reminds me during the sitting that he took me for a walk when I was a small boy, and that we found a valuable penknife with some initials carved on the handle. Suppose I recall the incident, which has not crossed my mind for many years and about which, sworn to secrecy at the time by my relative who wished to keep the knife, I told nobody. Suppose he further tells me that the penknife is now in the possession of another relative, and suppose that after the sitting I find this to be true. Suppose moreover that this second relative assures me he was never told how the penknife was obtained. I may now feel confident that the medium could not have come by this obscure piece of information by normal means. Ah yes, she could have, say the skeptics. How do we know my deceased relative told no one about the discovery of the knife during his lifetime? How do we know the second relative is telling the truth when he assures me he knows nothing of its origins? How do we know he may not have talked about it to someone? And how can we be sure that if the medium obtained all the other details of my deceased relative by normal means she did not also hear about the knife?

Even if my deceased relative, in an attempt to prove survival, has left a written encoded message, to which he hopes to be able to communicate the key after death, and suppose the key is given to me through a medium, the skeptic will insist he may after all have confided it to someone during his lifetime, and that the medium (again through the extensive information-gathering network with which he credits her) learnt of it. We only have my relative's word to me during his lifetime that the code was known only to him, and the critic often has a marked objection to believing that anyone interested in proving survival is capable of telling the truth. Thus no matter how we proliferate examples of what looks like watertight evidence for survival, the skeptical critic can always find some loophole. Strangely, although the critic may in the rest of his scientific work be ready to accept data as significant when the odds in its favor reach a certain level (usually 20:1), he rarely applies the same criteria when it comes to assessing the odds against a medium obtaining her information by non-paranormal means.

Super-ESP

In effect, the skeptic is therefore always able to claim that what is called sensory leakage from the physical world (word of mouth, written records, etc.) rather than communications from the deceased can explain the information obtained through the medium. In the context of survival, sensory leakage implies that there must be some channel, no matter how seemingly incredible, which allows information to reach the medium through her normal senses, thus obviating the need to propose the existence of communications from the dead. But suppose that communications through a medium produce information that is so unlikely to be due to sensory leakage that no unbiased observer would accept it as an explanation, and suppose that the medium obtains such communications consistently and over many sittings with many different people, will this put the issue beyond doubt?

Once more, unfortunately not, for at this point the Super-ESP argument is likely to be introduced. Reference has been made to this argument several times already, and we have reached the point where it now needs to be looked at in some detail. In truth no book that seeks to carry out a comprehensive survey of the evidence for survival can choose to ignore it, since in the view of many it poses the most serious challenge to the survivalist explanation for any information seemingly obtained from the next world.

To recap briefly, the Super-ESP (or Super-PSI) argument has it that all the information obtained through mediums could come not from the deceased but from sources on earth. They may receive it telepathically from the mind of the sitter (even though the latter may not be consciously thinking about the information at the time), telepathically from the minds of people elsewhere, clairvoyantly from the environment, or even precognitively from the future moment when the sitter checks on the facts given in the communications and finds them to be correct. The term Super-ESP was coined by Hornell Hart in 1959, but the concept had already been developed by Podmore in a number of his writings, and it was spelled out later in more detail by Charles Richet (e.g. Richet 1923). The theory has proved attractive not only to Richet but to many others. For example, Rhine considered that there is nothing on record from mediums 'that cannot be explained by the sort of omnibus hypothesis' [i.e. Super-ESP] into which we have expanded the old counter-hypothesis of telepathy' (Rhine 1949), while Professor E. R. Dodds argued that Super-ESP accounts for the limited degree of relevance and continuity in most trance communications (Dodds 1934). In other words, the medium is picking up a range of information by Super-ESP and gives it all to the sitter, not knowing what is relevant to him or her and what is not. In further support of Super-ESP, Professor Gardner Murphy put it that we have direct evidence for the ability of good psychics to 'filch' evidence from the minds of living people (Murphy 1945).

As mentioned on previous occasions, a stumbling block for the Super-ESP theory is that we have no laboratory evidence that telepathy, clairvoyance, and precognition can produce the amount and quality of information sometimes yielded through mediums. Put another way, we have no laboratory evidence that unaided living minds have sufficient paranormal abilities for these abilities to serve as a viable alternative to the survival explanation. Spirits, disembodied individuals, whichever term one chooses to use, appear to be capable of psychic feats beyond those demonstrable by living beings. We can be asked how we know that spirits enjoy this advantage over humans. The answer is by comparing the quality of the paranormal data that comes through mediums with that produced by living subjects. Direct comparisons are not possible because we can stipulate the target information in the laboratory and work out the odds against successful results being produced by chance, whereas we cannot do so in the work with mediums.

However, although it is not possible to make direct comparisons between the quality of the information that comes through mediums and that yielded by laboratory work we can test to see whether or not laboratory subjects can obtain similar information through telepathy, clairvoyance, or precognition and, as we have already seen, there is no evidence that they can. This is even more marked when it comes to the production of paranormal physical phenomena discussed in future chapters. Much of these physical phenomena have indeed never been duplicated even to a very minor degree in the laboratory. Conversely, there is little evidence that, restricting themselves to using only psychic abilities, mediums can get particularly impressive laboratory results. In fact I know of no leading mediums, with the possible exception of Eileen Garrett, who worked for some time with Rhine and his team at Duke University (Garrett 1968), who have shown any interest or enthusiasm in this kind of purely psychic work.

Recently, however, the argument has been put forward that in addition to laboratory evidence for human ESP abilities we should also take into account the 'decent evidence for psychic functioning ... outside the laboratory,' and two examples are put forward of the evidence thought appropriate, namely physical mediumship and the ESP reported in some spontaneous cases (Braude 2003). Thus the inference is that both these examples are evidence of Super-ESP in the living. Such an inference is unwarranted. In the great majority of cases of physical mediumship (and in all cases involving direct voice phenomena and materializations), the medium and sitters claim that the phenomena are due not to themselves but to spirit activity. Even Stella C., probably the least 'spiritual' of successful physical mediums, spoke of her 'spirit guides' (Chapter 12). As such, physical mediumship represents some of the very survival evidence claimed to be under threat from the Super-ESP explanation. To attempt to use it as evidence of ESP from the living is therefore tantamount to using the same evidence both as prosecutor (on behalf of Super-ESP) and as accused (on behalf of survival). We can say the same for many spontaneous cases (e.g. apparitions and hauntings, disembodied voices, paranormal scents, an overwhelming sense of presence), all of which are usually taken by those who experience them to be evidence for survival rather than for ESP from the living.

It is true that we do have apparent evidence for spontaneous telepathy and clairvoyance among the living, but there are few examples that yield the kind of detailed evidence sometimes acquired through mediumship. It is also true that some commentators consider poltergeist phenomena to be associated exclusively with the living, but it is by no means certain that they are correct in this. Most cases – as with the Cardiff case and the others examples discussed in Chapter 4 – can equally well be argued by supporters of survival to be due to earthbound spirits. What other spontaneous cases might we take into account as unequivocal evidence of ESP from the living? Death-bed visions? Hardly. The majority of these visions, seen by the dying and sometimes by those at the bedside, are recognized by the dying as deceased relatives and friends who, it is said, have come to help their transition to the next world (Barrett 1988, Morse and Perry 1994, Bozzano 1998). Furthermore, in many cases the appearance of these visions is greeted with surprise by both the dying and the bystanders, suggesting that their own ESP abilities do not appear to be involved.

Another argument favored by some supporters of Super-ESP is that we have no warrant to suppose that if one paranormal performance is difficult for a living mind, the many performances required by that mind if it is to obtain the detailed information given by mediums must be out of the question. Braude in particular considers 'It may be enough [for a living mind] merely to wish for something to happen, and then it does.' It may simply be sufficient to have a need or make a wish under efficacious circumstances, and 'virtually anything at all can happen ... *Task complexity may simply not be an issue'*. He uses the term 'magic wand' to describe this supposed ability – one simply expresses a wish under the right circumstances, and all ESP abilities operate together to bring it to fruition. This is an interesting idea. Paranormal abilities in the living may indeed all derive from a common source, ensuring that all can be used in conjunction with each other as well as individually. But are we seriously to suppose that if mediums have this ability they would be unable to use it to recognize that their information is coming from the living rather than from the dead? If it may be 'enough merely to wish for something to happen, and then it does' as Braude suggests, surely mediums have only to wish to know the source of their evidence in order to know it – or are we supposed to believe that they do in fact know it and have all been deliberately misleading us over a century or more with their talk of spirits?

Furthermore, what evidence is there that living beings with ESP abilities, even if used in concert, can in fact achieve paranormal effects or obtain paranormal knowledge comparable in quality and extent to that associated with mediumship? For example, as we shall see in Chapter 10, experiments by Roy and Robertson (2001), Robertson and Roy (2001) and by Schwartz and his various colleagues (2001, 2001, 2002) yield evidence that gifted mediums are able to obtain accurate information, ostensibly from the deceased, for sitters who are concealed from them by screens and of whose identity they have no idea. Have we evidence, under similarly controlled conditions, that ESP by the living can produce comparable results? It is for supporters of the 'magic wand' theory to prove that they can by setting up similar experiments using those who claim only psychic abilities rather than mediumship. It should not be difficult to do this. However, there is no evidence as yet that they have made the attempt.

The possible existence of Super-ESP cannot be refuted, and in theory it remains conceivable that any evidence for survival could be explained away as originating in the psychic abilities of the living. However, my experience of mediumship began over 35 years ago, and during these years I have sat with and interviewed any number of mediums and sitters and those reporting spontaneous cases. To date, I have not met anyone (including myself) who has thought it appropriate to attribute highly significant veridical information received through mediums to Super-ESP rather than to survival. As a psychologist, I am deeply concerned that in all areas of research involving people we should listen to their own interpretations of their experiences, as these interpretations often further our understanding of how and why they think, feel, and behave as they do. There are of course many reasons why people may mislead themselves, and why they may prefer survival as an explanation to Super-ESP for their experiences, but the scientists who debate the issues involved may also have personal preferences that affect their thinking. In addition, when discussing their experiences, mediums – who are the ones with first-hand knowledge of the subject – draw the clear distinction mentioned earlier between mediumship abilities (which depend upon apparent spirit help) and psychic abilities (which rely on the individual's own telepathic and clairvoyant abilities). The sample of over 50 mediums surveyed by Montague Keen, Professor Archie Roy, and myself for an unpublished study for the Prism ('Psychical Research Involving Selected Mediums') Research Group, were emphatic that this distinction should be recognized. In their view most mediums can identify the difference between mediumistic and psychic abilities in their own work. We need to know far more about the claimed differences between the two sets of abilities, but it is relevant to give mediums some credit for knowing when they are using mediumship and when they are using telepathy and clairvoyance. One of the most important lessons one can learn as a psychologist is that there are potential dangers in telling people that the abilities or experiences they have are not what they themselves think them to be. Without similar experiences ourselves, there are obvious limits to the extent to which we can know what takes place in the inner lives of others. Thus if we wish to know about these lives, whether we like it or not, we have to pay attention to what the people concerned tell us about them.

Another argument against the Super-ESP explanation is that sometimes the information given by the medium has not been in the sitter's conscious mind for many years, and no feasible explanation has yet been offered as to how the medium can unconsciously rummage through obscure areas of a recipient's unconscious in order to come upon it, or on what basis and by what method she can then select it as relevant from the mass of competing information held in the unconscious. Dodds' (1934) suggestions that rummaging is unnecessary because the emotional charge that the material holds for the sitter may render it particularly accessible to the medium seems to me unconvincing in that many of the facts that come through mediums, although accurate, carry little emotional charge for the sitter at the time. They may be small, relatively inconsequential things, and their significance as indicative of survival may not be apparent to the sitter until they have been confirmed at some later date. Many sitters have told me that they had in their conscious minds many far more relevant and emotionally charged facts that they hoped might come through the medium than those that actually did, and were surprised that the former were neglected in favor of the latter. Another argument against Dodds' suggestion is that although some of the details that come through a medium may have little or no emotional appeal at the time for the sitter, they may have strong emotional appeal for the communicator, and it may be this that determines why they come through. It is unlikely, for example, that anyone would wish to argue that the material communicated during the 30 years and more of the cross-correspondences, discussed in due course below, had more emotional charge for the automatists who received it than for the communicators, or even that it carried any significance for the former at the time it was received. Indeed, with a few exceptions such as the Palm Sunday Case which we will be looking at in some detail (Balfour 1960), the communications were not intended for individual sitters, and their meaning was only teased out over a period of time by scholarly investigators such as Piddington, Lodge, Mrs. Sidgwick, and Gerald Balfour.

Braude (2003) puts forward a different argument to suggest that the medium may not have to rummage through obscure areas of the sitter's mind in order to get her information, namely that we have 'no warrant for imposing any limits on the scope and functioning of paranormal abilities.' Thus although the information produced by mediums may appear so obscure that it stretches credibility to suppose it could be the result of Super-ESP, our conception of what is and what is not obscure applies only 'to normal methods of acquiring information ... we're in no position to insist that normally obscure information is also psychically obscure.' The answer to this is that there is no unequivocal evidence that our conception of what is obscure does not apply. For example, even in the remote viewing experiments carried out in the 'Stargate' program mentioned below, the details given by remote viewers of the target site, although significant, generally fell short of those that could be given by a flesh and blood observer. The psychic abilities of the remote viewers were thus less successful at identifying obscure details than the normal senses of people actually present at the target site.

If we turn now to those instances where, according to the Super-ESP argument, the medium is able to obtain information clairvoyantly from the environment relevant to the sitter but unknown to him or any other living mind at the time, we find no feasible explanation has been offered as to how this can be done in the absence of any link between medium and information.

Even in what are probably the most convincing and well-controlled experiments in clairvoyance yet attempted – the remote viewing 'Stargate' program funded by American military and civil intelligence bodies and in which subjects were asked clairvoyantly to 'view' a distant target location – some link such as a map reference was given to the remote viewers in order to guide their clairvoyant abilities to the target (see e.g. McMoneagle 1997 and 2002, and Graff 1998). Without a link being provided between mind and environment, it seems doubtful that clairvoyant abilities can operate. Supporters of the survival theory claim that in the case of mediumship, both clairvoyance and a link are unnecessary as the information is provided directly by the deceased.

Supporters of Super-ESP have also provided no feasible explanation of how the medium, if she gains her information by precognizing the future moment when the sitter checks up and finds the information to be correct, can select the relevant future events from the countless others competing for the attention of her supposed precognitive abilities. Furthermore, supporters of Super-ESP have not explained why, if precognition is the explanation, the information the medium gives to sitters frequently bears little resemblance to the actual future events surrounding its confirmation. A good example of this is contained in what I have called the Dallas Case (Fontana 1999). In this case the medium was Otto von Bourg and the sitter Helen Dallas, an Honorary Associate of the SPR and a respected investigator and friend of Sir Oliver Lodge. During the sitting Dallas received through the medium a communication ostensibly from a deceased uncle, in the course of which von Bourg informed her he was getting from the uncle the word incorrect very strongly, and that this applied to some papers the latter had helped arrange for her before he died. Helen Dallas recognized that this had to do with the will he had helped draw up for her, and she asked von Bourg if this meant she should alter her will. 'No,' the medium was informed by the communicator, 'the basis is all right, but there is something incorrect, and I think that if you see it he will impress you as to what it is.'

Dallas immediately obtained the will from her solicitor, who had not found it to be in error in any way, and sent it to a retired judge for his comments. The judge wrote in reply that 'The will appears to me to contain a bad blunder which would defeat your intentions to some extent,' and goes on to comment that he had found 'similar blunders ... made by other solicitors.' The reader will see from all this that at the sitting the medium conveys information only of a current event, namely the mistake in the will. His only reference to the future – the fact that if Dallas looks at the will he thinks her uncle will 'impress' her as to the nature of the mistake – turns out to be wrong. It is not her deceased uncle who does the impressing but the judge to whom she sends the will. Further, the medium says he 'gets the word incorrect very strongly,' yet in fact the term is not used by the judge, who speaks instead of 'a bad blunder.'

I am laboring the possibility of precognition because in the Dallas Case it would seem to be the only explanation upon which the supporter of Super-ESP can rely. We can rule out telepathy, as the medium could not have received news telepathically of the blunder from Dallas, from the solicitor or from the judge, none of whom knew about it at the time of the sitting. And we can rule out clairvoyance, as he could not have gained it clairvoyantly from the will itself – unless we wish to make the absurd proposal that the will knew of its own error, or that the medium unconsciously read the will clairvoyantly and, blessed with more legal knowledge than the uncle or the solicitor, unconsciously identified the blunder for himself, unconsciously identified the uncle as the person responsible for it, and then dramatized a communication from him in which the blunder is revealed.

Cases such as this present a significant challenge to the Super-ESP hypothesis and help us to agree with Gauld (1982), who in his excellent review of the hypothesis and of objections to it concludes that it does not suffice to 'explain the quantity of correct and appropriate information [relating to survival] sometimes furnished.' Sir Cyril Burtt, whose eminence as a thinker is undimmed by the alleged errors found after his death in his treatment of data on the inheritability of intelligence, took a similar view, concluding in his analysis of the relationship between psychology and parapsychology that 'a moment's reflection is sufficient to show that any such omnibus theory [as Super-ESP] involves assumptions which strain credulity to the very limit; it is one of those ingenious skeleton-keys that open every lock, and consequently provides a genuine fit to none' (Burtt 1967). The Super-ESP hypothesis also fails to address the question of how mediums obtain the link that allows them to glean information clairvoyantly from the environment.

The final reason why Super-ESP fails to qualify as an adequate alternative to survival is that it is an hypothesis that cannot be falsified. That is, there is no set of circumstances in which we can effectively test whether it is false or not (as Karl Popper made clear, such circumstances are an imperative before a theory can be regarded as scientific). In effect, the supporters of Super-ESP are claiming that, as we do not know the extent of what can be achieved by psychic abilities, it is theoretically possible that clairvoyance, precognition, and telepathy from the living can therefore explain all communications from supposed discarnates. But how can we test this claim in the absence of measures capable of establishing the extent of psychic abilities? No such measures exist. The Super-ESP hypothesis depends upon what 'may be the right explanation if only it were possible to know enough to prove it.' Such a form of reasoning would be summarily rejected if it was advanced in any other context. One cannot construct an hypothesis or even a sound argument on such a basis. I am aware of the argument that survival is itself an hypothesis that cannot be falsified since we cannot prove that survival does not exist. But proving that something does not exist is not what is meant by falsifying an hypothesis. We cannot prove that anything, even a unicorn, does not exist. An hypothesis is therefore falsified either by showing that it does not effectively fit the known facts, or that there are other theories that fit them much better. Unless we reject the concept of survival on principle, it can be argued that it fits the known facts of many of the cases in the literature better than does the Super-ESP theory, since the latter relies upon the extra assumption that ESP may be very much more powerful than has so far been demonstrated in the laboratory, whereas survival depends upon the evidence actually given as part of the information that comes through mediums. Why should much of this information prove to be correct, whereas the repeated assurance that it comes from the deceased, which forms such an integral part of it, always be incorrect? And if incorrect, why should mediums always be deceived into believing it?

Finally, even if the Super-ESP explanation could be shown to be true, it would by no means destroy the case for survival. In fact it could be argued that it would support it in that it would reveal that the mind has a quite extraordinary ability to operate outside time and space (which as we said in Chapter 1 appears in itself to strengthen the evidence for survival, since death simply means coming to an end within the time-space continuum). For example, supporters of Super-ESP tell us that in proxy sittings, when the sitter does not have in mind the information the medium is communicating and this information cannot therefore be taken telepathically from his or her mind, the medium can acquire it telepathically from the mind of somebody elsewhere in the world who has it. The person may be nearby or thousands of miles away. Space it seems is no problem for the medium's hypothetical Super-ESP ability. Where no one living has the information, the Super-ESP theory has it that the medium gleans it clairvoyantly from wherever it happens physically to exist. This of course may again be many hundreds or thousands of miles away. Once more, space seems to be no problem. It might be countered that the medium's mind does not need to travel clairvoyantly to wherever this evidence exists, and that he or she accesses it from some paranormal data bank (akin to the so-called Akashic Records spoken of in Eastern traditions and referred to again in the next section). However, since there is not a scrap of evidence that this supposed data bank exists in physical space, in order to access it the medium's mind would again have to operate outside space-time.

As already discussed, the Super-ESP hypothesis has now been expanded to suggest that instead of obtaining evidence from the mind of the deceased, the medium can precognitively access the moment in time when the sitter acknowledges the evidence as correct, or the evidence is discovered somewhere in the physical world. If this were true, it implies the medium has extraordinary Super-ESP abilities that operate outside time. Which brings us back once more to the point that if some part of the mind can operate intelligently outside time and space, we have a strong case for arguing that part of the mind at least survives the death of the physical body.

Philip the Imaginary Ghost

The case of Philip is sometimes used by supporters of Super-ESP as an instance of the power of a group of sitters to produce strong telepathic and psychokinetic results. Briefly, a group of eight members of the Toronto Society for Psychical Research decided in 1972 to invent an imaginary ghost in order to see whether or not 'he' would then communicate (Mishlove 1975, Owen and Sparrow 1976). They gave him the name 'Philip,' and invented his life history in some detail. For a year they attempted to get 'him' to communicate by meditating upon him, but when this failed they sat around a table in full light, in a mood of jollity, and when the table began one evening to vibrate they asked if this was the work of 'Philip.' A single rap sounded on the table top, signifying assent, and from then on, using one rap for yes and two raps for no, 'Philip' began to respond to their questions, even affirming some of the details they had invented about his 'life.' At one point the table began to take on a life of its own (as for example in the sèances with Stella C. – see Chapter 12), levitating when no one was touching it, and apparently chasing one of the sitters across the room. The table kept time when the sitters sang a song, and 'Philip' produced colored lights on request. The performance was even filmed live in 1974 by Toronto City Television. A minimum of four sitters out of the group of eight seemed necessary in order to produce phenomena.

It seems then that 'Philip' was simply created telepathically and psychokinetically by the group, which would support the Super-ESP hypothesis. However, an alternative explanation is that an earthbound spirit (a spirit referred to several times in this book who is supposedly a deceased person that remains close to the earth plane and produces poltergeist phenomena and other disturbing phenomena) was involved. Attracted by the efforts of the group, an earthbound spirit may have played along with the group's own attempts at deception, and taken on the role of 'Philip.' We need more evidence of the kind produced by the Toronto group before we can decide between these two alternatives. Certainly we have no other evidence that a group, unaided by unseen helpers, can produce phenomena of the kind reported in Toronto. If it is possible to do so, why the need to invent a 'ghost' and pretend that spirits were involved? Inventing a ghost may have helped the group to convince themselves that paranormal phenomena could take place, but it may also have served to attract earthbound spirits. If human paranormal abilities are capable of producing phenomena on the scale witnessed in Toronto, there should be no need to go to the lengths of inventing 'Philip.'

The Toronto group went about their task very much as would any group attempting to contact spirits for physical phenomena. It is said by those particularly experienced in this kind of phenomenon that if a dedicated group sits together regularly for a year or two in this way they will eventually be contacted by spirits. So the Toronto group was going through the motions of a group of this kind, and phenomena occurred as a result. If the results were entirely due to their own efforts, then there should be no need to invent an imaginary ghost. Those who consider that all the phenomena experienced by the Toronto group were as a consequence of the group's own efforts can readily put the matter to the test by replicating the group's activity but without the addition of an imaginary ghost. If sitting regularly around the table produces phenomena in a group of skeptics this would give us an opportunity to ascertain whether such a phenomenon seems related only to the group or whether it introduces elements – for example veridical information unknown at the time to group members and likely to stretch the Super-ESP hypothesis beyond credible limits – that suggest the methodology might attract entities outside themselves. As it stands, the 'Philip' experiment raises more questions than it answers.

The Cosmic Psychic Reservoir Hypothesis

In addition to Super-ESP, another alternative to survival as an explanation for the evidence obtained through mediumship is sometimes advanced, the so-called psychic reservoir hypothesis. First proposed by Professor William James, this has it that a record of every happening since the dawn of time is stored somewhere and somehow in the cosmos, and the medium is someone who is able to draw upon this store. Thus what appear to be communications from the deceased are nothing more than fragments of this cosmic memory. It is difficult to see what such an hypothesis has to commend it. It appears in fact to be weaker than the Super-ESP argument in that, although the latter can point to the proven existence of telepathy between the living and of clairvoyance and precognition, we have no evidence at all that there is such a thing as a cosmic memory. Certainly some Eastern traditions speak of the so-called 'Akashic Records,' which are said to contain this memory, but this is hardly enough to satisfy science. There are also many practical objections to the hypothesis. What is the organizing principle or intelligence behind the cosmic psychic reservoir? If it exists, and if it, rather than survival, is the reason for mediumistic communications, what is its purpose? Why should it function simply to deceive us into a mistaken belief in survival? Why should the material from it be dramatized by the medium as if it really comes from deceased communicators? Why are mediums themselves universally duped into believing they are in touch with spirits of the dead when they are only contacting a cosmic reservoir?

In addition, as with the Super-ESP hypothesis, the notion of a cosmic psychic reservoir cannot be falsified. There is no way in which it can be put to the test. I can only suppose that James, who is unquestionably one of the finest minds ever to be drawn to psychical research, put it forward in order to meet the philosophical difficulties he had with the idea of survival without a physical body (the nature of these difficulties are discussed in due course in Chapter 18).

CHAPTER 6
MENTAL MEDIUMSHIP

Unlike physical mediumship, which we look at in the next chapter, mental mediumship uses only the mind of the medium as a channel, and normally takes place in good light. In the course of it the medium may go into a trance-like state, in which to all intents and purposes consciousness is lost and the spirit communicators speak through her, or she may remain conscious and simply relay messages as she receives them. Sometimes she may, either in trance or consciousness, use automatic writing, i.e. allowing communicators to control her hand and write their messages. Some mediums report that when in trance they black out completely, as in a dreamless sleep, while the spirits take over their bodies (often the voices that speak through them also make use of their hands to gesture, or make other movements characteristic in life of whoever is supposedly speaking through them). Others speak of being taken out of their bodies, usually to paradise-like surroundings where they are able to rest in great peace. Trance mediums usually have no subsequent recollection of what was said through them during the trance, while those who do not work in trance are normally well aware of the messages they give. The term 'clairaudient' is sometimes used for the latter form of mental mediumship, indicating that the medium can hear things the rest of us cannot hear (though some claim to receive impressions or symbolic pictures rather than actual words), and on occasions the medium may claim also to be able clairvoyantly actually to 'see' the communicators.

The communications given through mental mediums tend to take four different (though not mutually exclusive) forms. Firstly, communicators may attempt to prove their identity by referring to events in their life histories. Secondly, they may describe the sitter's own recent experiences, as if they are able to view what takes place on earth. Thirdly, they may offer advice as to the sitter's future course or courses of action. And fourthly, they may comment upon their present condition, usually simply reassuring the sitter that they are well and happy, or offering pious words about spiritual realities. In the context of survival, information that falls into the first of these categories is obviously of most value, and I always advise sitters to request names, or to ask communicators if they can recall and give details of places or things or events well-known to them in their earth lives. If 'Granddad' communicates after death for example, and tells the sitter that when he was alive he accidentally dropped a broken pocket watch behind the chest of drawers and always meant to retrieve it but never did, and the sitter subsequently finds the watch exactly where Granddad said it was, this seemingly humble piece of information is worth more as evidence of

Granddad's continuing existence than many a pious sermon on the supposed wonders of the next world.

Sittings with mental mediums can be a frustrating experience. One may receive nothing of evidential value at all, or even be given information that is palpably incorrect. The best of mediums vary from day to day in the quality of their work, and even from sitter to sitter, and it is not easy to assess why this should be. Erroneous information could simply be the product of the medium's own unconscious, or a confused jumble of genuine facts picked up either from communicators (possibly including some unknown to the sitter who simply wish to make contact) or even from the minds of living people. Furthermore, one assumes that the availability of suitable communicators may also play a part. It would be naive to suppose that everyone who consults a medium has an army of would-be communicators on the other side all clamoring to come through. The sitter him- or herself also appears to influence proceedings. For example, it is often said that hardened skeptics have a strongly inhibiting effect upon the medium's performance. This is not so strange as it may appear. If thoughts really can be transmitted directly from mind to mind during sittings, it is conceivable that the fog of doubt and mistrust emanating from the skeptic may interfere with the medium's ability to receive impressions from the communicators (Dr. Eric Dingwall, when research officer for the SPR, outlined helpful guidance in 1927 for those sitting with mental and with physical mediums, and his advice still remains sound).

Be this as it may, it seems that mental mediumship involves emptying the conscious mind of competing thoughts, and tuning in to the subtle whispers of the unconscious. I have frequently asked mediums how they can distinguish between those whispers that come from their own unconscious and those that originate from elsewhere, and am invariably told that they simply 'know' the difference. I don't doubt they are sincere in what they say, and equally have no doubt that it must be difficult to put this 'knowing' into words. But until we understand rather more about it we cannot advance our knowledge of how mediumship works, or help in devising suitable programs of training for aspirants to the profession. Nevertheless, those who persevere in attending sittings with mediums are likely sooner or later to receive information that appears highly evidential. Typically such information may concern small domestic details. For example, sitting with the medium Doris Smith soon after the death of my mother, I was first given a description of a woman that I recognized related to her followed by facts about her behavior during the last weeks of her life, all of which were correct, if too general to provide much in the way of firm evidence. I was then given three details that were highly specific. These were that Doris was being shown a bag with some embroidery on the front, a green book ('like a diary but not a diary'), and a cigarette case. I recognized the first of these objects as an embroidered bag my mother had been given in the last months of her life by her sister which fastened to the front of her walking frame and in which she kept her letters and everything else that, in her sadly reduced life, seemed important to her. The second I recognized as the green book ('like a diary but not a diary') in which she kept the telephone numbers of her family and friends and that helped her maintain a lifeline to the world outside her residential home. These objects, the embroidered bag and the green telephone book, were the two things that my mother kept always with her during her last months, and that meant much to her. As such, they indeed represented the kind of details that would still have been in her mind soon after her death.

The third object shown to Doris was if anything even more interesting. Doris described the cigarette case as having initials engraved on the outside, then after a pause, as if she was looking closely at what she was being shown, said these were either initials or flowers, she wasn't sure which. I remembered the cigarette case, a family heirloom that my mother passed on to me during her last years, but the reference to initials and flowers meant nothing to me. However, on returning home I checked up and found that there were initials on the front decorated with entwined leaves resembling the petals of flowers. Doris knew I was a non-smoker, and thus would have been highly unlikely to associate me with a cigarette case, let alone one that she described so accurately, and one which I had never mentioned to her or to anyone outside my own immediate family, none of whom had ever had any contact with Doris or even knew of her existence. The cigarette case was given to me by my mother because she recalled that when I was a boy I once joked that it was almost worth being a smoker to own something so attractive (a remark I had completely forgotten until she mentioned it to me). As an adult, and as a lifelong non-smoker as was my mother, I had attached no importance to the cigarette case, and had even forgotten that it was now in my possession. But during her life my mother's memory was especially good (particularly for anything she gave me!), and from time to time she would enquire on the whereabouts of her gifts to me or their usefulness, and thus it was entirely typical of her that she should refer to the case if she was trying to convince me of her survival.

Communications such as this can be very convincing for those who receive them, but just how good are they as evidence for survival? Doris knew my mother had died, but had never met her or spoken to her, was based hundreds of miles from her, and had no idea where she lived. Doris could not have known of the existence of the three objects to which she referred, or the importance that my mother attached to them. And she could not have met anyone who knew of them. But did Doris mention during the sitting a range of things in connection with my mother that were incorrect, thus reducing the evidentiality of three correct items? No she did not. She spoke only of these three items. Did she do any fishing – i.e. asking me questions the answers to which may have inadvertently given her clues? No she did not, and if she had done so I would have spotted it at once. Did I leave anything in my coat pockets outside the room that may have given away details of my mother? No, I did not. Did my body language give anything away about my mother? No it did not, and it is difficult to see how body language could give away information about an embroidered bag, a green book like a diary but not a diary, and a decorated cigarette case.

Finally, if the information given to me by Doris was paranormally acquired, could it have come telepathically from me (the Super-ESP hypothesis yet again)? As it was only a few weeks after my mother died I was not expecting any communication from her – in fact I had other people very much in mind to whom I was sending silent requests to come through. I had no thoughts of the embroidered bag, the green book, or the cigarette case. I had no conscious recollection of the decoration on the cigarette case, which I had not looked at closely since I was a boy. The idea that Doris trawled through my unconscious in order to pick out these details – or that she picked up the idea of the cigarette case from my unconscious and then clairvoyantly 'saw' the details of the decoration for herself – could hardly be taken seriously by anyone other than those unhappy with the very idea of survival. And if Doris had access to my unconscious she would have found far more vivid and far more emotionally charged memories of my mother than obscure details to do with a forgotten cigarette case. At face value, sittings such as this that involve trivial details which may not mean much to the sitter but which were important to the communicator when alive provide important support for the survival hypothesis.

I have said that it is important always to ask the medium if he or she can obtain the name of the communicator. Inability to do so does not discount the evidence – I have had good sittings in which no names were forthcoming – but names add strongly to the value of this evidence. However, names do not always come in the way we expect. For example, during a sitting with medium Leonard Young, I was given details that suggested strongly that an aunt of mine, who had recently died, was trying to communicate (this followed accurate facts about my days years ago as an undergraduate student that Leonard could not have known by normal means). I asked for a name, and Leonard was silent for some moments before saying apologetically that he was simply being given the names 'Mary' and 'David.' My aunt was not called Mary, and her surname had no connection with David. So one might think the quest for a name was a failure. Far from it. Mary was my aunt's daughter, and David her son-in-law. For some years leading up to her death she had lived happily with Mary and David, helping to care for their children while they continued their professional lives as head-teachers. My aunt was one of the kindest and most generous of women, and it is perfectly in character that the names 'Mary and David' would be in her mind at the time, rather than her own name.

On another occasion, medium Mallory Sendall gave me details from the platform (the only time in fact I have ever received a communication from the platform – I get the feeling that mediums who know me rather avoid me during public presentations) that related strongly to a deceased cousin of mine and that even included the fact he had died by his own hand. I acknowledged the contact, and asked if she could get me his name. Mallory was unable to oblige. However, the following day, when I was talking to her about quite other matters, she abruptly announced she was being given the name 'Alan,' with the attendant impression that it was spelt 'Alun.' Alan was indeed my cousin's name, and although to the best of my knowledge he spelt it with an 'a' rather than a 'u,' 'Alun' is in fact the Welsh spelling, and my cousin was Welsh. There is no credible way in which Mallory would have known of his existence, and needless to say I had never mentioned his name or any of his personal details to her or to anyone with whom she might – even with the wildest flight of surmise – have come into contact.

Sometimes names may appear to be given symbolically or in the form of pictures, carrying conviction for the recipient perhaps but providing no hard objective evidence likely to convince others. Here is an example. A young medium, with whom I was not having a sitting at the time, suddenly blurted out to me for no apparent reason that he was being 'taken' first to Devon, and then to France, 'down near the south.' At face value these details might have meant little, but my oldest and best friend Malcolm, had recently tragically died. At the time the medium gave me these words a certain Devon Malcolm was the main strike bowler for the England cricket team, and my friend Malcolm had been passionately fond of cricket. Had there been a fast bowler with this surname in the England cricket team when he and I were boys together, he would have promptly abandoned his usual leg-spin bowling and charged with exaggerated fury up to the wicket in imitation of his England namesake (I shudder to think of the consequent risk to life and limb of opposing batsmen). From the time that Devon Malcolm first appeared in the England cricket team, his name had invariably brought thoughts of my friend to mind. The reference to France also had immediate associations with my friend, who loved France and spent every summer there. His favorite area was the Dordogne, which is indeed 'down near the south.'

Thus both of the two (and only) key words given to me by the medium were particularly applicable to my friend. Cricket and France were two of his main enthusiasms. I shared these enthusiasms with him, and throughout a friendship that went back to our very first day as eleven-year-olds at grammar school, they had been favorite topics of conversation between us. However, if this was indeed a communication from Malcolm, why did he simply not give his own name? Why give the medium what appeared to be mental pictures of Devon and of France? Mediums do in fact often say of the communicator that 'he or she (the communicator) is showing me a picture of ... ' or is 'taking me to... ,' by which they mean that pictures flash on their inner eye. Communicators have explained this by insisting that it is easier for them to get pictures through to the medium than words, perhaps because the former represent an older and more universal language than the latter.

If the above experience was paranormal, what of the chances it was due to Super-ESP, in this case simple telepathy, as I was certainly thinking of Malcolm at the time, and still feeling his loss? Telepathy is doubtless a possibility, but if it was involved, why should the medium have referred to Devon and to France, neither of which was in my conscious mind at the time, rather than simply giving me the name Malcolm, which was? And if he had received the name Malcolm from me, why in any case should he have linked it to Devon (he informed me afterwards that, as a Scotsman, he had no interest in cricket and had never heard of Devon Malcolm)? And why follow a train of associations from my conscious to my unconscious mind in order to do so, and also to pick out the word France? Are we to assume that, like communicators, I was responsible for sending these pictures, that my unconscious 'decided' to use them rather than words, transmitting them to the medium yet not at that point even to my own conscious mind? Experiences such as this, which happen frequently when working with mediums, raise far more questions than they answer. But unless we ask the questions, we stand no chance of finding the answers.

CHAPTER 7
THREE OUTSTANDING MENTAL MEDIUMS

The Mediumship of Mrs. Leonora Piper

Let us turn now to some of the best evidence for survival that has come through mental mediumship, focusing particularly on the American medium Mrs. Leonora Piper (1859-1950), one of the best ever (it is intriguing to speculate on how many comparable mediums may never have come to the attention of researchers). So much has been written about her that only a general summary of her work is needed here.

One of the most frequently quoted comments about Leonora Piper is that made by the philosopher/psychologist Professor William James (1842-1910), already mentioned as one of the finest minds ever to be attracted to psychical research. Referring in a lecture given in 1890 to the fact that one should not judge mediums by those who fail to produce satisfactory results, James declared: 'To upset the conclusion that all crows are black, there is no need to seek demonstration that no crows are black; it is sufficient to produce one white crow; a single one is sufficient.' For William James that one white crow was Mrs. Piper, though one should not make the mistake of assuming this to mean that she was the only person with psychic powers who impressed him. For example, in 1907 he described the well-witnessed and documented case of the location of the drowned body of Bertha Huse by Mrs. Titus of Lebanon, New Hampshire, working in spontaneous trance. Previous attempts by a professional diver to find the body had failed, and when told of the place indicated by Mrs. Titus during her trance he protested that he had already searched there but to no avail. However Mrs. Titus insisted, telling him that the body was head downwards in a hole in the riverbed at the spot, with only one rubber shoe visible.

The diver followed her instructions and found Bertha Huse exactly where and how Mrs. Titus described, in water where the visibility was so bad he found the body only by feel. At the inquest he commented during cross-examination that the body was 'to the inch' where Mrs. Titus had indicated, and that if it wasn't for her 'the body would not have been found." After discussing and dismissing all the possible normal explanations, James concluded that the case was 'a decidedly solid document in favor of the admission of a supernormal faculty of seership.' This does not mean that he accepted it as necessarily demonstrating survival, for James remained to the end of his life undecided on survival, regarding clairvoyance and telepathy or his Cosmic Reservoir as viable alternative explanations for the undoubtedly paranormal effects he investigated. However, his enthusiasm for Leonora Piper's abilities was never in doubt.

It is difficult not to share this enthusiasm. Mrs. Piper (1859-1950) produced results indicative of paranormal abilities over a long career in which she was investigated by researchers who went to extraordinary lengths to eliminate any realistic possibility of her obtaining her information by normal means. When she came to Britain in 1889 (the first of three visits, in all of which she produced successful results) to be tested by the SPR she stayed in turn as a house guest with two of the principal SPR researchers, initially with Frederick Myers (1843-1901) in Cambridge, and subsequently with Sir Oliver Lodge (1851-1940) in Liverpool. Both men had her carefully watched throughout her time with them, and Lodge even engaged a new domestic staff for the duration of her visit to avoid the risk of her obtaining relevant information about the family from his servants. Whenever she left the house she was accompanied by an SPR member, and Lodge even obtained her permission to open and check all her mail before she saw it to ensure that she was not receiving clandestine information about possible sitters. In the course of her stay she gave 88 trance sittings for the investigators and for anonymous sitters, and at the very first sitting with Lodge she gave descriptions of his father, of an uncle called William, and an aunt called Ann, and of one of his children who had died very young. Certain inaccuracies in these descriptions were all corrected at later sittings, and names were given in full, together with many details of the history of the whole family. So impressed was Lodge with the extraordinary familiarity that Mrs. Piper's spirit guide, who claimed to be a deceased French doctor called Phinuit (pronounced 'Phinwee'), showed of the boyhood of two of his uncles that he sent a private detective to Barking where the men had lived when boys to see if he could uncover by normal means any of the facts she had given. At the end of the investigation the detective confessed that 'Mrs. Piper has certainly beat me. My inquiries ... yield less information than she gave ... the most skilful agent could have done no more than secure the assistance of the local record keepers and the oldest inhabitants living'.

Lodge was convinced that in the sèances organized by him, either with himself or individuals unknown to Mrs. Piper, telepathy from the sitters could be ruled out. In no fewer than 38 of these sittings the entranced Mrs. Piper gave correct information not within the conscious knowledge of any of those present, and sometimes allegedly never known to them. At the end of her visit in 1889, Myers and Lodge published a report of these sittings (Myers, Lodge, Leaf, and James 1890) in which Lodge insisted that:

... I have satisfied myself that much of the information [Mrs. Piper] possesses in the trance state is not acquired by ordinary common-place methods, but that she has some unusual means of acquiring information .. she is also in the trance state able to diagnose diseases and

to specify the owners or late owners of portable property, under circumstances which preclude the application of ordinary methods ... That here is more than can be explained by any amount of either conscious or unconscious fraud – that the phenomenon is a genuine one, however it is to be explained – I now regard as absolutely certain; and I make the following two statements with the utmost confidence:

1. That Mrs. Piper's attitude is not one of deception.
2. No conceivable deception on the part of Mrs. Piper can explain the facts.

In his Introduction to the report Myers voiced similar conclusions, namely that:

1. Many of the facts given [by Mrs. Piper} could not have been learnt even by a skilled detective.
2. Others of them, although they might have been learnt, would have required an expenditure of money as well as of time, which it seemed impossible to suppose that Mrs. Piper could have met.
3. [Mrs. Piper's] conduct has never given any ground whatsoever for supposing her capable of fraud or trickery. Few persons have been so long and so carefully observed, and she has left on all observers the impression of thorough uprightness, candor, and honesty.

Mrs. Piper's first recorded mediumistic experience happened at age eight, when while playing in the garden she suddenly felt a sharp blow on her right ear and heard a prolonged sibilant sound that eventually resolved itself into the letter 'S' followed by the words 'Aunt Sara not dead but with you still.' Terrified, she told her mother, who made a note of the exact time. A few days later the family heard that Aunt Sara had indeed died at that time and on that day. Subsequently the young Leonora was sometimes awakened by bright lights in the bedroom that resolved themselves into spaces, but her mediumship proper only began at age 22 when she fell into a short trance while consulting Dr. J. R. Cocke, a blind clairvoyant noted for his medical diagnoses and cures. Prompted by this experience she joined Dr. Cocke's development circle, and on her second visit again went into trance, walked across the room, picked up a pencil, and wrote a message for a member of the circle from his dead son. The member happened to be a well-known judge, Judge Frost, who considered the message the most remarkable he had ever received.

News of this success soon spread, and Mrs. Piper was inundated by requests for sittings. Displeased by this sudden attention, she refused them. However, for some unknown reason she made an exception for a Mrs. Gibbins, who turned out to be the mother-in-law of Professor William James.

So impressed were Mrs. Gibbins and her daughter, Mrs. William James, by the evidence received that they persuaded the initially skeptical Professor James to request a sitting. As a consequence of what he heard then and subsequently, James became so convinced that the results were indicative of paranormality that for the next 18 months he virtually took control of Mrs. Piper's mediumship, writing in the SPR report already mentioned (Myers, Lodge, Leaf, and James 1890) that they left him 'as absolutely certain as I am of any personal fact in the world that she knows things in her trances which she cannot possibly have heard in her waking state,' adding later that ' ... I should be willing now to stake as much money on Mrs. Piper's honesty as on that of anyone I know, and I am quite satisfied to leave my reputation for wisdom or folly, so far as human nature is concerned, to stand or fall by this declaration.'

During her trances, Leonora Piper was frequently taken over by her guides, who then spoke through her. At other times she produced automatic writing while in trance, and on occasions she displayed both the voices of her guides and automatic writing at the same time. When producing automatic writing in trance she typically did so with her eyes closed and her head resting on the table in front of her while her hand busily scribbled away on sheets of paper placed there by an assistant. Early in her career she also produced physical phenomena but was dissuaded from continuing to do so – and encouraged to concentrate on mental mediumship – by Frederick Myers during her first visit to Britain, although she apparently remained able to withdraw the scent from flowers and make them wither in a few minutes, as if she had some control over their life force. She was also remarkably successful at psychometry, the ability to deduce details paranormally about people, both deceased and living, simply by holding objects that had belonged to them.

Apart from the visits to Britain, Mrs. Piper's mediumship was based in the USA, where Dr. Richard Hodgson (1855-1905), sent to the USA by the SPR specifically to investigate her work, took over from Professor William James when pressure of other work led to the latter becoming less actively involved. Initially highly skeptical, Dr. Hodgson came to share the conviction of his colleagues that Mrs. Piper produced genuine phenomena. During many years of intensive investigation of her nothing was discovered to shake this conviction. William James was to write that:

Dr. Hodgson considers that the hypothesis of fraud cannot be seriously maintained. I agree with him absolutely. The medium has been under observation, much of the time under close observation, as to most of the conditions of her life, by a large number of persons ... for (nearly) 15 years. During that time not only has there not been one single suspicious circumstance remarked, but not one suggestion has ever been made from any quarter which might tend positively to explain how the medium ... could possibly obtain information about so many sitters by natural means.

One of the most remarkable features of Mrs. Piper's mediumship during this time was the five-year period when she was controlled by George Pelham (a pseudonym for George Pellew), a friend of Dr. Hodgson who had died aged only 32 in an accidental fall. In life Pelham had been skeptical of survival (and had assured Hodgson that if he died first and should find himself still living he would 'make things lively' in an attempt to prove his continuing existence), but five weeks after his untimely death he began to communicate, firstly through Mrs. Piper's automatic writing, and subsequently through her entranced voice. During the five years concerned he recognized at least 30 of Mrs. Piper's sitters who were known to him in life, never once claimed erroneously to know any of the 120 or so sitters with whom he had been unacquainted, and referred correctly to many other people who were not present but who had been familiar to him. Furthermore, he displayed all the keenness, perspicacity, intelligence, and other characteristics possessed by George Pelham in life, and convinced a large number of Mrs. Piper's sitters that it really was he.

As to survival itself, Dr. Hodgson made clear in his second report to the SPR in 1898 that 'I cannot profess to have any doubt but that the chief communicators' [through Mrs. Piper] ... are veritably the personalities that they claim to be; that they have survived the change we call death, and that they have directly communicated with us ... ' On the question of whether or not telepathy from the living could account for the phenomena Dr. Hodgson was equally categorical – 'I have no hesitation in affirming with the most absolute assurance that the spirit' hypothesis is justified by its fruits, and the other hypothesis [i.e. that of telepathy from the living] is not.'

Mrs. Piper herself does not appear always to have been quite so sure about the spirit hypothesis. On October 20, 1901 the New York Herald published a statement by her – which they described as a 'confession' – to the effect that 'The theory of telepathy strongly appeals to me as the most plausible and genuinely scientific solution of the problem [of the communications] ... I do not believe that spirits of the dead have spoken through me when I have been in the trance state ... It may be that they have, but I do not affirm it.' Mrs. Piper immediately objected to the use of the term 'confession' by the Herald and to the wording of the statement, insisting in The Boston Advertiser for October 25, 1901 that 'I did not make any such statement as that published in the New York Herald to the effect that spirits of the departed do not control me ... Spirits of the departed may have controlled me and they may not. I confess that I do not know.' In fairness to the New York Herald it must be made clear the newspaper also proclaimed

... since little value would be attached to her opinion in favor of the spiritistic hypothesis, it cannot fairly be urged that her opinion on the other side could weigh with us ... [she is] even in a less favorable position for forming an opinion that those who sit with her, since she does

not afterwards remember what passes while she is in trance.

This is of course undoubtedly true. Note also that the *New York Herald* made no charge of fraud against Mrs. Piper. In fact they always referred to her in the most laudatory of terms.

When Dr. Hodgson died suddenly from heart failure at the early age of 50 in 1905, Professor James Hyslop (1854-1920), previously professor of logic and ethics at Columbia University, took over as chief investigator. Initially as skeptical as Hodgson had been in his early days, Hyslop became as convinced as Hodgson of the genuine nature of Mrs. Piper's mediumship, and of the assurance it gave of survival of death. In one of his major works on survival (Hyslop 1918) he wrote forcefully that:

I regard the existence of discarnate spirits as scientifically proved and I no longer refer to the sceptic as having any right to speak on the subject. Any man who does not accept the existence of discarnate spirits and the proof of it is either ignorant or a moral coward. I give him short shrift, and do not propose any longer to argue with him on the supposition that he knows anything about the subject.

Thus, among many others, two of the leading thinkers and psychical researchers in Britain, Sir Oliver Lodge and Frederick Myers, and three of the leading researchers in the USA, Professors William James and James Hyslop and Dr. Richard Hodgson, all came, on the basis of direct experience, not only to accept but to vigorously support the genuineness of Mrs. Piper's mediumship. Of these five, Lodge, Myers, Hodgson, and Hyslop accepted equally readily that her work demonstrated the reality of survival beyond any doubt (Hodgson is even reported as saying enthusiastically 'I can't wait to die!'), and although James remained more ambivalent on this issue his ambivalence, as mentioned when discussing his Cosmic Reservoir hypothesis, appears to have been due more to philosophical reasons – the difficulty of conceptualizing how disembodied minds could survive and what that survival might be like – than from any reservations over Mrs. Piper or the information that came through her. For example, in his 1909 report on the communications that came ostensibly from Hodgson after his death through Mrs. Piper, James wrote that 'if ever our growing familiarity with these [mediumistic] phenomena should tend more and more to corroborate the hypothesis that 'spirits' play some part in their production, I shall be quite ready to undeafen my ears.' As for the deceased Hodgson, his own passionate intensity to demonstrate the truth of survival from beyond the grave is seemingly well illustrated by his emphatic (even exasperated) post-mortem message through Mrs. Piper to William James, when the latter was being at his most cautious ' ... if I am not Hodgson, he never lived!'

Thus Mrs. Piper's mediumship was confirmed by five men who would be outstanding scholars and investigators in any age. Skeptics sometimes quibble that intellectuals and scientists are not the best people to investigate mediumship, and that conjurors would do a much better job. Like most generalizations there are many exceptions to this. Mental mediumship such as that manifested by Mrs Piper involves none of the physical effects – discussed in due course in connection with physical phenomena – that conjurors claim they can readily duplicate by normal means. And one has only to read the lengths to which the investigators went to ensure that Mrs. Piper did not gain her information by normal means to recognize the caution and good sense of the investigators. In addition to the precautions adopted by Lodge and Myers during her time in Britain, Richard Hodgson even had her shadowed in the USA by a private detective, arranged sittings without disclosing the names of the sitters, and forbade her to read newspapers on the days on which sittings were held. No conjuror could have done more, or I suspect as much.

Over the years various attempts have been made, based primarily upon the contention that Mrs. Piper had some knowledge of George Pelham and his circle during his lifetime, and that this may explain Pelham's apparent success as a communicator. James Munves (1997) in particular advances this contention, but his arguments should be read in conjunction with the 297 closely printed pages of Hodgson's 1898 report on Mrs. Piper (mentioned earlier) before one can assess their strength. My view is that Mrs. Piper may have had a few limited opportunities to know something of Pelham before he died, but even so we would have to accuse her – an accusation never leveled at her by any of those who knew her – of consciously tricking both Hodgson and the sitters. Munves tries to avoid this accusation by placing emphasis upon the unconscious, pointing out that Hodgson and his fellow-investigators were writing before Freud's pioneering theories on the importance of unconscious memories were widely known, and therefore may not have realized the existence of unconscious memories. In his view Mrs. Piper may have consciously forgotten having heard of Pelham, but her unconscious may have retained the memories concerned, and it was these that emerged while she was in trance.

Few psychologists would now accept many of Freud's ideas on the workings of the unconscious, and fewer still would accept that the extensive volume of correct information that came through her ostensibly from Pelham could be explained as unconscious memories. It is true that under hypnosis many forgotten memories can sometimes be recalled, but we have little evidence that the hypnotic trance and the mediumistic trance have much in common. A few individuals have appeared to become mediumistic while experiencing the hypnotic trance – for example Aviva Neumann, the medium we mention later in connection with Fisher's writings on so-called earthbound spirits (Fisher 1990), and the young girl known as Reine C. with whom Cornillier worked (Cornillier 1921) – but the great majority who have undergone hypnosis have not. When Eileen Garrett, who is discussed in due course below, had a number of hypnotic sessions with psychiatrist Dr. William Brown, he failed to reach her controls. However, when she voluntarily went into a mediumistic trance, he informed her afterwards that he had indeed been conversing with her main control, Uvani. It thus seems unlikely in the extreme that Mrs. Piper's unconscious memories would have allowed her to refer in trance to intimate facts and events associated with 30 individuals known to Pelham, most of whom she certainly had not met, and then have dramatized these unconscious memories into a fictional Pelham personality impressive enough to convince the individuals concerned that she was really in contact with him.

After five years the Pelham control appears to have taken a back seat in Mrs. Piper's mediumship, and to have been replaced by the so-called Imperator Group, an assembly of supposedly advanced souls whose main spokesperson went under the name of 'Rector' and who communicated through her a range of lofty – yet wise and compassionate – spirit teachings. Anyone reading these teachings cannot fail to be struck by the contrast between them and the much more practical and mundane content of the Pelham communications. If this was Mrs. Piper's unconscious at work again, then it seems to be an entirely different unconscious from that displayed during the Pelham years – so much so in fact that under the influence of the Imperator Group Mrs. Piper became a much revered spiritual counselor even in her waking state. Her daughter, Alta Piper, noted in 1929 that 'the good she has been able to do [in this role] is almost unbelievable.' William James also noted this remarkable change in her, and the fact that the members of the Imperator Group appeared not only to exhibit individual and consistent personalities, but to be able to divine the secret thoughts of Mrs. Piper's sitters.

The Imperator Group claimed to be identical with the group of the same name who had controlled the Reverend Stainton Moses (author of the highly regarded *Spirit Teachings* and *More Spirit Teachings*), and whose professed mission was to uplift the human race (sadly there is little evidence that their efforts have met with much success). Without questioning the moral quality of either sets of teachings, some doubts have, however, been expressed as to whether the two Imperator Groups were in fact one and the same (Mrs. Piper's Group sometimes showed surprising ignorance of important details of Stainton Moses' mediumship). It probably doesn't greatly matter whether they were or not. The important thing is that the Imperator Group who communicated through Mrs. Piper inspired deep reverence in all those present during the receipt of communications. Even reading them at this distance, I find them moving and impressive. Hodgson was apparently even granted some direct communications from this Group when he was alone in his own room, and subsequently they also spoke through Mrs. Minnie Soule, another highly respected Boston medium.

Lest this talk of the quality of Mrs. Piper's work makes her sound too much of a paragon, it is important to stress that, like all mediums, she was very far from infallible. Some sitters claimed to receive unimpressive evidence. She was vague on dates. She was better on the Christian names of communicators than on their surnames, and prior to the arrival of the Imperator Group her communications were mostly about fairly mundane things such as the personal idiosyncrasies, illnesses, and character traits of her sitters. She often failed on test questions. When the deceased Stainton Moses ostensibly communicated through her the names he gave of his spirit guides were incorrect; and when one of her deceased friends, Hannah Wild, communicated through her she failed to give the contents of the sealed letter that she had written while alive to serve as a post-mortem test. Many of the prophecies given by communicators through Mrs. Piper proved to be incorrect. For example, Hodgson was told by the 'Rector' control that Mrs. Piper would die before him (she outlived him ·by 45 years); another communicator (said to be the English novelist George Eliot) predicted that Hodgson would be in charge of Mrs. Piper's mediumship 'to the end' (this could possibly be construed as true in that Hodgson became one of her controls after his death); and Hodgson was told he would marry and have two children (he died a bachelor and, as far as is known, childless).

Various intensive studies were made of the nature of Mrs. Piper's trance states – all of which were published by the SPR – most notably by Professor William Newbold and by Frank Podmore in 1891 (both in *SPR Proceedings* Vol. XIV, Part XXXIV), by Mrs. Sidgwick and by Andrew Lang in 1900 (both in *SPR Proceedings* Volume XV, Part XXXVI), by Professor James Hyslop in 1901 (*SPR Proceedings* Volume XVI, whole issue), by Hereward Carrington in 1901-03 (*SPR Proceedings* Vol XVII, Part XLV), and by Mrs. Eleanor Sidgwick, widow of Professor Henry Sidgwick and herself one of the Society's most brilliant thinkers in a mammoth 652 page contribution (*SPR Proceedings* Vol. XXVIII, Part LXXI). One of the most intriguing suggestions to arise from these various studies comes from Mrs. Sidgwick, who when discussing the reasons why some sitters received excellent communications through Mrs. Piper while others did not, hypothesized that the good sitter is in fact a successful telepathic channel him- or herself. Not only does this mean, in her view, that material is transferred from the mind of the sitter to that of the medium, but that the spirits themselves may be in telepathic communication with the sitter rather than with the medium, and that it is the content of this communication that Mrs. Piper picks up – again telepathically – from him or her. Thus the sitter, albeit unconsciously, acts as it were as the receiving station from the spirit world, and Mrs. Piper acts, again as it were, as the amplifier and loudspeaker.

It is surprising that this hypothesis has not received more attention, not least because it neatly explains why some people make good sitters while others do not, and also explains how contact can be made with people relevant to the sitter but unknown to the medium from the countless millions supposedly in the next world. Unconscious telepathy between deceased minds and living minds may in fact be taking place in this way for much of the time, yet go unrecognized unless a medium is present to receive it from the mind of the sitter. However, Mrs. Sidgwick's hypothesis is less successful in explaining the good results sometimes obtained at proxy sittings – those sittings in which the sitter is representing a third party rather than him- or herself – where neither sitter nor medium has any personal link with the communicators. It also seems strange that, if Mrs. Sidgwick is correct, mediums themselves should remain so unaware that their communications are not coming direct from the deceased but via the mind of the sitter, and that the matter was never referred to by Mrs. Piper's communicators themselves. In fact Phinuit, Mrs. Piper's original control who was with her for many years, when pressed for details on how communications took place insisted he 'entered' and used her body during the trance while she herself vacated it and took his place in the spirit world. When Hodgson repeatedly pressed him as to why, in this case, Mrs. Piper had no recollection of her spirit adventures when she emerged from her trance, he replied that this was because she had no access to her own brain while out of her body, and therefore she could not store memories within it. If correct, this suggests that although the spirit body is able to store memories in its own memory banks (if this were not the case it would be impossible to explain how spirits can recall earthly memories when they are deceased), it needs also to store them in the physical brain if they are to be accessible to it while it is in the body.

The abiding impressions left by the Piper mediumship are two in number. Firstly, the extraordinary quality of many of the communications received by her and the strong support these communications give to the theory of survival. And secondly, the quality and integrity of the investigators and commentators who researched and analyzed these communications, in particular James, Myers, Lodge, Hodgson, and Hyslop. These distinguished individuals had a depth of involvement with their work and brought to it a keenness of intellect rarely seen in psychical research these days. No one who has studied the voluminous material they published in the *SPR Proceedings* can reasonably challenge these two impressions.

The Mediumship of Mrs. Gladys Leonard

A whole book – indeed very many whole books – could be written about the outstanding mediums of the past, but space only allows me to deal in any detail with three of them. Mrs. Leonora Piper of course, Mrs. Gladys Leonard (often referred to as Mrs. Osborne Leonard, Osborne being her maiden name and Leonard her married name), and Eileen Garrett. I am often asked why there are no modern mediums to compare with these three ladies and their contemporaries. The answer is that probably there are, but the sad fact is that we do not have researchers with the time and commitment to investigate them as happened in the past. However, it is certainly true that few people with mediumistic abilities devote themselves to the development of these abilities as they once did. We live in a frantic, frenetic age, full of the lure of superficial entertainment and other equally meaningless distractions. Before the advent of radio, television, videos, computers, and the welter of time-thieves with which we are surrounded, much of middle-class life was spent in the leisurely quiet of fireside evenings, with entertainments that were homemade. This allowed more space for the sort of activities involved in the development of psychic abilities. For example, a favorite occupation for some Victorian families was table turning (or tapping), a pastime in which a circle sat around a small table with their hands on the surface and asked questions of the spirits, who supposedly gave answers by tipping up one side of the table and tapping the legs against the floor to signify assent each time the sitters, who then recited the alphabet, came to appropriate letters. In addition, more time was spent in the quiet silence of home, and in the absence of bright artificial lighting more hours were spent in darkness or near-darkness (an experience that in itself makes the presence of a spirit world, whether real or imagined, more credible). Mediumship has much less chance of flourishing in our modern world, and in an atmosphere of scientific materialism that pours scorn on the very idea that we are anything more than biological machines.

There is also a suggestion that the artificial electro-magnetic soup in which we are immersed from the cradle to the grave (the radio waves scribbled across the world from television and radio broadcasts, from telephones and mobile phones, from power cables, and even from the electrical appliances and circuits in our homes) inhibits mediumship. Perhaps. It is also said that things are made worse by the universal use of the man-made AC current instead of the naturally occurring DC current. Maybe. We cannot know for sure, but it is a hard fact that never before in history have humans been subjected to so much manufactured radiation. We do not know the damage this radiation may be doing to our physical bodies, far less the effect it may have upon the much more subtle mental and spiritual processes upon which psychic abilities and mediumship would seem to depend.

Gladys Leonard (1882-1968) grew up at a time when there were few of these modern hazards to mediumship. In some ways an even more accomplished medium than Leonora Piper, Gladys Leonard was psychic from childhood. In her autobiography *My Life in Two Worlds*, published in 1931, she reports having frequent visions of what she called her 'Happy Valleys,' a beautiful land consisting of gentle slopes, peaceful valleys, lovely trees, and banks covered with flowers, inhabited by radiantly happy people walking in couples or in groups and dressed in graceful, flowing draperies, whose every gesture and every movement spoke of a state of quiet ecstasy. These visions unfolded on the walls around her, as if they were objectively real rather than subjective imaginings, and she says of them that they 'seemed to extend for many miles, and I was conscious that I could see much farther than was possible with the ordinary physical scenery around me.' Unfortunately, one day she made the mistake of telling her father of these visions, presumably in the supposition that he could see them as well. General family consternation followed, especially as the descriptions she gave of her Happy Valleys were so minute that it was clear to others that she was not simply making them up. Sternly she was forbidden to look at such things again, and obediently and with a great effort she managed to suppress them.

One explanation for these visions is that they were a form of eidetic imagery, sometimes called photographic memory, an ability more common in pre-adolescent children than in later life, that enables the individual to recall previous visual experiences with the detailed clarity associated with looking at a photograph. Those with this ability sometimes speak of it as if they see the recalled image objectively in the outer world. However, Gladys Leonard does not mention having previously seen images similar to her Happy Valleys in picture books or elsewhere. Moreover, her visions were more like watching moving pictures than observing static illustrations. Those who study descriptions of the afterlife received through mediums (see Chapter 18) will notice the similarity between Gladys Leonard's Happy Valleys and the so-called Upper Astral World, a level of development said to be reached by the more spiritually advanced souls.

Be this as it may, the tragedy is that her family equated these visions with mental illness and forced her to suppress them, as appears to happen with many children who have early psychic experiences. Madame d'Esperance, a medium well known in her own day, gives a particularly chilling example in her autobiography. She tells how a doctor called in by her mother to comment on the childhood visions to which she had unwisely confessed listened politely to her account of them, reassured her comfortingly that he had heard many people speak of such things, then followed up with the brutal blow: 'and all of them were mad.' As a consequence, much of her early life was spent in the fear of insanity (d'Esperance 1898).

In her teens Gladys Leonard trained as an opera singer but contracted diphtheria, a disease of the throat then often fatal. Fortunately she survived, but her voice was damaged, and she was forced to abandon opera in favor of acting. At the age of 18 she attended a Spiritualist Church and was told by the medium that 'your guides are preparing you for an important spiritual work.' Shortly afterwards, while touring with a theatre company, she awoke at 2 a.m. to see in front of her a circular patch of light about four feet in diameter that illuminated a vision of her mother, looking young and healthy and seeming to convey an intense feeling of relief and well-being. The next morning she learned that her mother – who had been unwell but not it was thought seriously ill – had died in the night at that hour. Her interest in such things now aroused, Gladys Leonard began to sit for table tapping with two of her friends in her dressing room at the theatre, and after 26 futile sessions the table began to respond, tapping out messages from acquaintances and from Gladys' mother, then giving a long name which they could not pronounce but which they shortened to 'Feda.' Feda tapped out that she was to be Gladys' spirit control, and claimed to be her great-great-grandmother who had married an Englishman, William Hamilton, and died at age 14 in childbirth (Gladys recalled that when alive her mother had told her of this long-dead ancestor, but she had taken little notice of the details at the time).

Gladys Leonard was resistant to the idea of going into trance while Feda spoke through her, but during a sitting some months later in the dressing room at the London Palladium she drifted into sleep, and when she awoke her friends told her that Feda had spoken through her. Thus began Gladys' career as a trance medium and her long association with Feda. Who was Feda? The question can be asked in connection with all the spirit controls said to work through mediums. Was Feda who she said she was, or was she the medium's own secondary personality? 'Secondary personality' is a term used by psychologists and psychiatrists to designate an aspect of the self that has been repressed and that in rare cases sporadically takes over from the primary personality. At such times the primary personality appears to be entirely displaced by the secondary personality, which may be very different from the primary personality in every way (e.g. sometimes behaving recklessly and destructively, while the primary personality may be very prim and proper). When the primary personality reasserts itself, it may claim to be unaware of the existence of the secondary personality, and be deeply distressed to hear of her or his behavior. The secondary personality is thought by some psychologists to represent psychological material so repressed in childhood – in response, for example, to extreme parental disapproval of the behavior associated with it – that it literally 'splits off' from the primary personality and forms a separate, hidden identity. Usually it remains in the unconscious, but in certain circumstances – for example, severe stress – it may emerge and temporarily become dominant over the primary personality.

In Gladys' case, a secondary personality could possibly have been created as a result of stern parental disapproval of her Happy Valleys visions, and then emerged during trance, when the primary personality is in a state of quiescence. The theory that spirit controls are manifestations of the medium's secondary personality has been favored by a number of researchers, and Eileen Garrett (another leading medium who we discuss in due course) confessed herself never sure whether her controls were real spirits or her own secondary personalities. However, a weakness of the secondary personality theory within the context of mediumship is that it does not explain the clearly paranormal knowledge that this secondary personality, as distinct from the primary personality, appears to possess. It may be that if all psychic impressions and spirit communications are received initially in the unconscious the secondary personality has readier access to this information than does the primary personality, but this is speculation. Another objection to the theory is that some authors claim that secondary personalities may not be aspects of the individuals concerned but examples of possession. by so-called earthbound spirits. Adam Crabtree, a psychotherapist with considerable expertise in working with individuals apparently troubled by inner states that seem alien to their normal selves and an expert on the condition, assures us that we just do not know whether such states are evidence of fragmented aspects of the self, are a sign of possession by spirits, or are a combination of the two (Crabtree 1985). Crabtree's book is in fact one of the most comprehensive and readable accounts of so-called multiple personality available to us, and is highly recommended for all those interested in the area.

One of my own experiences, some four years ago, gave me further reason to doubt whether controls can be written off as secondary personalities. I was with a small group studying aspects of mediumship who were witnessing an example of trance in the medium Dorothy. Dorothy was sitting a few feet in front of me, facing me, and as she was not in very good health at the time she had two people sitting in support, one on either side of her, Vi Kipling a highly-respected medium and teacher of mediumship on one side, and her own partner on the other. In the course of a few minutes Dorothy went into trance. Her breathing deepened, her eyes closed, and to all intents and purposes she became unconscious (I have been present when Dorothy's physiological state has been technically tested while in trance, and can confirm that her vital signs drop to an alarmingly low level). After a time her control (whose claimed identity was unknown to me) began to speak through her. Her voice deepened somewhat, but otherwise remained unchanged. There was no accent and no attempt at the bizarre use of language that occurs all too often in trance. I watched Dorothy closely and to my complete surprise became aware of another face building up just beside her own. The build up began to her left, and then strengthened and moved until it almost – but not quite – coincided with her own features. Yet it remained transparent, so that simultaneously I could see Dorothy's face, looking as normal, and the new face partially superimposed over it. Due to this transparent quality and the fact that the two faces never fully coincided, both were visible at the same time. The new face was male, and unmistakably Chinese and sage-like in appearance.

The whole thing took place in normal electric light, and I was able to check the faces of the two supporters on either side of Dorothy to ascertain they remained unchanged, and that it was no trick of the light. Fraud – which would have had to involve the projection of a face onto Dorothy's – was out of the question. The room was one with which I was very familiar, and the equipment necessary to create an illusion of this kind was certainly not present. I have good eyesight, and can forestall criticism by confirming that I was not on drugs, am not in the habit of hallucinating, and was not suffering from any illness. The superimposition of a spirit face over that of the medium – a process known as transfiguration – has frequently been reported in the literature, and I have seen several mediums who claim to be able to produce the phenomenon. Not one of them has impressed me in the least. Usually a soft red light is set up to illuminate their faces, and the rest of the room is in darkness. Under such conditions the contours of the face are shown up in relief, and changes in expression can be interpreted by the unwary as transfiguration. The results in my experience range from laughable to pathetic. The phenomenon witnessed with Dorothy was quite different. Moreover, there was no mention of transfiguration before she went into trance, and therefore no risk that the whole thing was an illusion due to the power of suggestion. I had never heard her spoken of as a transfiguration medium, and it was clear from my subsequent enquires that neither Vi Kipling, who arranged the session, nor Dorothy herself, had transfiguration in mind.

The image superimposed on Dorothy's face gradually faded, and she slowly came out of trance. A discussion of trance followed in which I said nothing. Shortly afterwards, one of the sitters (a young man new to mediumship) remarked in a puzzled voice that he had seen the face of a Chinese gentleman superimposed on the face of the medium, and went on to give a description that agreed almost word for word with my own experience. Afterwards I asked Mallory Sendall, a very experienced medium to whom I referred in another context earlier in the chapter, and who was sitting with the group at the time, about the transfiguration. She assured me she had seen it too, and expressed no surprise, informing me simply that Dorothy's control was in fact a Chinese sage, and that this was the face that had appeared. At the time the six other group members said nothing, and the matter was quickly dropped.

I could find no normal explanation for this strange experience. Dorothy seemed only politely interested when I subsequently tried to discuss it with her. Could it have been a manifestation of a secondary personality? I know of no case in the literature where secondary personalities are said to be in the habit of manifesting visually (secondary personalities should not be confused in this instance with so-called doppelgangers, discussed in the last chapter; there is no case in the literature known to me where individuals diagnosed as periodically dominated by a secondary personality have also been associated with doppelgangers). It might be argued that the Chinese face was a thought form projected in some way by Dorothy or by one of the sitters. This is possible, but simply replaces one mystery with another. What evidence is there that we can materialize thought forms and project them onto our faces or those of others? The group present on this occasion were not members of Dorothy's home circle, and therefore not in any special rapport with her. They were simply there to watch a demonstration of trance. Apart from the two mediums present and her own partner she was not well known to any of them. I myself have seen Dorothy on several occasions both before and since, and have had long conversations with her, but transfiguration has never been a subject for discussion. She impresses me as an intelligent, serious, and principled lady of great integrity, whose life is devoted – at considerable personal sacrifice – to spiritual work. Did I indeed see her control, clearly and unexpectedly, on that occasion, a control distinct from her and with the ability to manifest in physical form? One cannot be sure, although there was no doubt of the sighting itself.

Whatever the truth of the matter, Gladys Leonard herself was in no doubt that Feda was exactly who she said she was, namely her Hindu ancestor, and this even though she and Feda never communicated directly with each other during her trances. Gladys had to rely upon what sitters told her of what had been said once the trance was over, although she reported that she did hear Feda's voice when sitting with the direct voice medium Dennis Bradley. One thing is clear: Gladys Leonard and Feda were very different from each other in almost every way. In her biography of Leonard, Susy Smith (1964) described her towards the end of her life as 'quiet and tranquil, forthright simple and direct. She is gracious, with a native dignity and kindliness ... still a vital and interesting person, poised, wise, and serene, she is truly a great lady.' By contrast, Feda was childish and impulsive, struggling frequently with quite simple words and concepts, and sounding very much like a barely literate young Indian girl. Her role was usually restricted to relaying messages from other spirits much wiser than herself, many of whom she seemed only partially to understand. Once again it seems that unless we prefer to reject in advance all arguments in favor of survival, the possibility remains that Feda and the spirit controls of other mediums may have been who they said they were.

A number of attempts were made, particularly by Whately Carington, to test Feda's independent existence by using word association tests – tests devised by Carl Jung in which the subject is given a list of words verbally, and asked to give a spontaneous, one-word response to each of them. The nature of the response, and the reaction time before it is given, are claimed to vary significantly from person to person. Thus if Feda's responses and reaction times differed significantly from those of Gladys Leonard, a good case could be made out for her independent existence. In the event, results over a number of experiments proved inconclusive. Initially Whately Carington felt convinced that Feda (though probably not two of Gladys Leonard's other communicators, 'John' and 'Essa') was only a secondary personality, but later became less sure (Carington, W. 1945). The debate in the *Proceedings* and in the *Journal* of the SPR went on for some time, but no firm conclusion was reached. This is not surprising. The word association test is viewed with suspicion by many psychologists, simply because we do not know enough about the way in which different people, at different times and under different conditions, give their responses. There is also some doubt about the theoretical arguments that underpin the test. Jung considered that results show the unconscious predispositions of the individual concerned, but as there is no obvious way in which this theory can be put to the test – we have no firm measurements of the unconscious against which test results can be assessed – this remains open to debate. In addition, the conclusions reached by Carington on the strength of his results are open to challenge. These results showed that Feda's reaction times to the stimulus words tended to be the opposite of Glady's reaction times. Thus when Feda showed a short reaction time between the stimulus word and her response to it, Gladys tended to show a long one and vice versa. There seems little warrant in assuming this indicated Feda was a 'repressed' aspect of Gladys' own personality.

In any event, one thing is clear, namely that like Mrs. Piper's controls she had access to information inexplicable by normal means. In March 1914 Feda gave instructions that Gladys must start working as a professional medium as 'Something big and terrible is going to happen to the world, Feda must help many people through you.' Gladys obeyed, and four months later the First World War broke out. Her work in channeling communications from some of those slaughtered in this dreadful conflagration helped to bring her to public attention, and the most high profile of these communications led to the publication of a classic work of psychical research, Sir Oliver Lodge's *Raymond* (first published 1916, with a second book in 1922). Lodge, who has already been mentioned in connection with his work with Mrs. Piper, was by this time not only Principal (from 1900) of the newly-established institution that subsequently became Birmingham University, he had been Chairman of the British Association for the Advancement of Science (1913), and President of the SPR (1901–1903). With his pioneering work in the development of radio, his place in the pantheon of scientific greats was assured. After initial skepticism, his interest in psychical research began in 1883 when he took part in successful thought transference experiments with Malcolm Guthrie, and when one of his sons, Raymond, was killed in France on September 17, 1915 while serving with the Second Battalion of the South Lancashire

Regiment, Lodge became deeply concerned as to whether or not contact could be made with the next world. His wife had already had a sitting with Gladys Leonard on September 25 of that year at which Raymond communicated with the message 'Tell Father I have met some friends of his,' mentioning Myers among them. Two days later Alfred Vout Peters, another prominent medium of the time, mentioned during a sitting with Mrs. Lodge that Raymond was speaking of a photograph taken of him while at the front ('he is particular that I should tell you of this'). On November 29 Lodge received a letter from a Mrs. Cheves, a complete stranger whose son was Medical Officer to the Second Battalion of the South Lancashire Regiment (and who had earlier reported to Lodge the nature of Raymond's fatal wound), in which she said she had six copies of a photograph of a group of officers. Her letter did not actually mention that Raymond was one of them or that the officers were from the South Lancashire Regiment, but she offered to send Lodge a copy.

On December 3 Lodge himself had a sitting with Gladys Leonard, in the course of which Raymond gave a full description of the photograph, including the facts that he was seated while others were 'raised up' (standing?) at the back of him, that someone 'wanted to lean on him' (although he was unsure whether or not the photograph was actually taken while the man was doing so), that the officers were 'a mixed lot' some of whom he did not know well, and that the photograph was taken outdoors against a black background 'with lines going down.' The photograph duly arrived at the Lodges' home on December 7, and was found to correspond to the given details, even to the 'lines going down,' which are in fact the very prominent six wooden retaining struts on the sloping roof of the building that forms the background, and the fact that the officers (21 in number) would probably have come from more than one battalion of the Regiment – for example Raymond himself was in fact commissioned into the Third Battalion and was only attached to the Second Battalion at the time – and therefore were a 'mixed' group, with the result that some of them would probably not have been well known to him. Most importantly of all, Raymond is seated on the ground and the officer sitting on the bench behind him has his forearm leaning on Raymond's shoulder (the only example of one officer leaning on another in the photograph).

Later enquiries from the Quartermaster of the Second Battalion, Captain Boast, who had been responsible for arranging to have the photograph taken and developed, elicited the fact that the negative was not sent to Britain for development until October 15, 18 days after Raymond had communicated its existence to Vout Peters. Raymond had not mentioned the photograph in any of his letters home, and he had had no home leave between the taking of the photograph and his death 21 days later. Thus it seemed clear that Vout Peters could have had no normal knowledge of the photograph when he mentioned it to Mrs. Lodge at her sitting with him on September 27. The photograph did not arrive with the Lodge family until December 7, so it seems equally clear that Mrs. Leonard could have had no knowledge when she gave all the above details of it to Lodge at his sitting with her on December 3.

Lodge subsequently obtained, from the photographers who had developed the negative (the highly respected Aldershot firm of Gale and Polden, who specialized in work with the military), prints of two other photographs that had been taken of the group of officers at the same time. In neither of them is the forearm of the officer behind Raymond on his shoulder, which appears to bear out Raymond's statement that he 'did not know' whether or not the photograph had actually been taken with the man leaning on him. Taking all these details into account, Lodge concluded that the incident of the photograph was 'rather exceptionally good as a piece of evidence' for survival. He also ruled out the possibility of telepathy from the living because the whole of the information from the mediums was given before any of the Lodge family saw the photograph. Thus only what he called the 'far-fetched hypothesis of unconscious telepathy from complete strangers' (the Super-ESP hypothesis yet again) could be advanced as an alternative explanation to survival. This seems fair comment. Gladys Leonard might have received unconscious telepathic impressions from Mrs. Cheves, from the staff at Gale and Polden who did the developing, or from Captain Boast or other officers of the South Lancashire Regiment. Alternatively, she might have picked up precognitive knowledge of the moment the Lodge family saw the photograph (or of the moment when she saw it herself, if she ever did so). I can only repeat what I said when discussing the Super-ESP hypothesis, namely that we have no evidence that psychic abilities work in this way

Raymond contains many other examples of communications that bear the stamp of the young man himself, and when the book was published it created a sensation, not least because of Sir Oliver Lodge's standing as an eminent scientist. It also brought fame to Mrs. Leonard. Unfortunately the book was also the subject of some ridicule because in his communications Raymond mentions that those killed with him who requested cigars or glasses of whisky in the spirit world were given them. However, those who exercised merriment at Lodge's expense ignored the fact that Raymond also makes it clear in his communications that these comforts were facsimiles, prepared by mature spirits for the dead soldiers until the latter realize that they no longer have any need for such things (we return to the issue of such facsimiles in Chapter 18).

Another of the many examples that can be given of the extraordinary mediumship of Gladys Leonard is the newspaper tests undertaken in her work with the Reverend Drayton Thomas, a Council member of the SPR

(Drayton Thomas 1922). These followed a series of successful book tests in which the communicator, allegedly Thomas' father, informed him through Gladys Leonard of a relevant text that he would find on a designated page of a certain book whose position on Thomas' bookshelves (or on those of acquaintances) was also indicated. Of 156 book tests given at the instigation of the communicator, Thomas rated 121 as producing 'good' results, 19 as indefinite, and only 16 as failures. In all cases Thomas himself had no prior knowledge of the position of the book concerned or of the information it contained on the designated page. In an example of a good result – from a test using a book located on the shelves in a friend's study that Thomas had never entered – Thomas was told 'In the second book from the right, and on page 2, is a reference to sea or ocean' – the reference turned out to be 'a first-rate seaman, grown old between sky and ocean.' In another example he was told that lower down page 9 of the third book from the right was a reference to changing color – the reference was found to be '... the sky suddenly changes from light blue to a dark lead colour.' (For the skeptic who thinks such close matches could be found by chance alone I can only say try it out with a friend and note your results.)

After the success of these tests, Feda then suggested (in 1919) a new protocol, designed to connect the communicator's memories or present knowledge with items that had not even at that point been made public. This, it was thought, rendered telepathy from the living even less likely than in the book tests. Accordingly, Feda, speaking for Thomas' father, proceeded over a number of trials to give references to items that would appear in designated positions the following day on the front page of *The Times* newspaper, a page which at that time contained only a number of long, closely printed columns giving notices of births, marriages, deaths, memorials, and other personal details. In each case, Thomas posted these references to the offices of the SPR in the afternoon, immediately after the conclusion of the sittings, and many hours before the publication of the issue of the newspaper to which they referred   Again, results proved strongly positive. For example, Thomas was told through Gladys Leonard that on the following day he would find his own name to the 'left of column three, rather more than one-third down'; that a little above his name would be the name of his wife; that his wife's age would appear within an inch of these names, and that two of his father's names would be half-way down column one. Sure enough, Drayton Thomas' own first name, 'Charles' appeared just over half-way down to the left of column three (i.e. in column two), his wife's name 'Clare' appeared a fraction higher. Just over an inch above these names the number '51' appeared (Clare's age prior to her birthday two weeks previously), and three inches below the middle of column one, two of his father's names, 'Thomas' and 'John,' appeared independently of each other.

Sometimes information completely unknown to Thomas and relating to his friends rather than to himself was given. For example, he was told that the name of Dr. Dyson's deceased brother (who was the ostensible communicator at the time) would appear half-way down the first column in The Times of the following day; that close by would be Dr. Dyson's own name 'or one almost similar' to it; that a little below would be the name of a place that the Dyson brothers had visited and enjoyed; that a little above this would be the name of a mutual friend of theirs, and that near the top of column one would be the name of a great friend of Dr. Dyson who has passed on and who was with his deceased brother. In the event, the name 'Dyson' appeared exactly half-way down the first column in *The Times* of the following day, and Dr. Dyson's second name, 'Andrews,' appeared two and a half inches below it. The name 'Filey,' a town where the Dyson brothers had frequently spent holidays together, was given in the designated position, and the names of two of the mutual friends of the Dysons, 'Jones' and 'Davies,' occurred just above it. At the top of column one the name 'Jack' appeared, the name of the only close friend of Dr. Dyson who had passed over at that time. With the exception of the name 'Dyson' and the first name of the deceased friend, none of the facts concerned were previously known to Drayton Thomas. Dr. Dyson had himself had a successful sitting with Mrs. Leonard at some time before the test, but there is no suggestion that he gave her any of this information in the course of it.

Of the 25 newspaper tests that took place in the first phase of this work, 18 produced good results, three were inconclusive, and four were failures. This ratio remained constant for all the subsequent tests. As with the book tests, the odds against these results occurring by chance are so large that chance can be effectively ruled out as an explanation. However, was there a possibility that Mrs. Leonard obtained information of the front page of *The Times* of the following day by normal means? To check this possibility, Drayton Thomas visited the offices of the newspaper and discovered that the contents of the Birth, Marriages, Deaths, and personal columns were not put in their final positions in the print trays until the evening prior to publication, some time after the sittings with Mrs. Leonard had ended and after Thomas had posted off the record of the sittings to the SPR. From his observations while visiting *The Times*, Thomas insists that '... it seems clear that even unimpeded access to the [*Times*] works at 5 p.m. [and thus after the conclusion of the sittings] would not enable an inquirer to learn the ultimate position of any one name, nor even the contents of the majority of the [entries].'

One may wonder why Feda typically restricted herself to giving the position of information in the columns of *The Times* rather than giving the actual names concerned. Drayton Thomas explains this by pointing out the hesitation and bewilderment that Feda often had with names. By focusing only upon the position of the names and their relevance to the sitter, Feda was able to communicate a large amount of verifiable data at each sitting. Drayton Thomas also addressed the question of why he was so convinced that the information usually came, via Feda, from his father rather than from any other spiritual source. Not only had the communicator 'abundantly proved to me that I was really in communication with my father' during the two and a half years he had sat with Gladys Leonard prior to the newspaper tests, but his father further demonstrated it during the tests concerned by communicating messages involving intimate knowledge of family names and events, present and past. In his view it was not the case that a number of positions of names and events were referred to 'on the chance that some of them may be appropriate; there is no fishing for names, no vague suggestions as might be applicable to any sitter ... the impression made upon me has been cumulative and logically compelling.'

Drayton Thomas gives many examples to illustrate his father's intimate knowledge of family names and events. I have chosen the following not because it is the best, but because what seemed initially to be a failure turned out to be a success, thus lessening the possibility that the information came telepathically from the mind of the sitter. During the sitting Feda, speaking for Drayton Thomas' father, said 'He has the idea that soap is mentioned at the top of the page.' However, the word 'soap' did not appear at the top of the page in *The Times* of the following day, with the result that the test was regarded as a failure. Drayton Thomas mentioned this failure to Feda at the next sitting, to which she replied 'He says it was the name of a famous soap maker; he sensed it, so did not know whether soap was mentioned or some name suggesting soap; he was just reminded of it.' Returning to the newspaper, Drayton Thomas found, prominently at the top of the first column, the name of a family known to his own family 20 years previously and engaged in the manufacture of soap. He comments that 'We had been interested in hearing details of the process [they used], and in after years any reference to that well-known firm brought to mind our associations with this family.'

The example is also interesting in that it reveals something of the difficulties communicators may have when attempting to gain information of earthly conditions. We are told that Mr. Thomas senior 'sensed' the name of a famous soap-maker, but did not know how this name was reflected in the newspaper entry. Was it by the word 'soap' or by some name suggesting soap? Note also that in the initial reference to this entry Feda simply said 'He has the idea that soap is mentioned ... ' There is a lack of precision, just as there is in so many mediumistic communications. It is indeed as if something is 'sensed' by the communicator rather than directly observed, and this is in line with the information given through many mediums. Some communicators describe themselves as having to 'lower their vibrations' to try and bring themselves into tune with earthly conditions, while others talk of entering a heavy, foggy atmosphere where powers of thought and memory become dulled and sluggish. F. W. Myers, communicating through medium Geraldine Cummins, famously spoke of the difficulties of making contact with the medium as rather like attempting to dictate through a frosted glass window to a rather obtuse secretary (Cummins 1933). Critics may say all this is very convenient in that it excuses the mistakes and the vagaries so apparent in many communications, but it does not need much stretch of the imagination to recognize that if intercourse is to take place between the dead and the living it is hardly likely to do so with the facility we enjoy when talking to a friend on the telephone.

In spite of the difficulties under which Mr. Thomas senior may have been laboring, these newspaper tests are among the best pieces of carefully controlled mediumistic evidence for survival. Given that the pages concerned had not yet been set up, the position in the columns of *The Times* of the information concerned could not have been known to the sitter, to the medium, or to any other living person at the time of the sitting. Nor, again given the fact that the page had not been set up, could it have been sensed clairvoyantly by the medium. This leaves only precognition as an alternative explanation to survival. Gladys Leonard might have been able precognitively to pick up the moment when Drayton Thomas saw the actual entry in *The Times* of the following day, or the moment when the relevant type was set up in the *Times* offices. However, in this case she would have picked up Drayton Thomas's experiences on seeing the entries the following day, not the obscure clues given by the Reverend Thomas senior. And if her precognition worked by picking up the position of the type as it was set up for the following day, she would have had no way of knowing which entries had significance for Drayton Thomas. Looked at it in whichever way we choose, the evidence points most strongly to the information coming from a surviving Rev. Thomas senior, whose relevant earth memories were intact and who had the precognitive ability to foresee which items in the next issue of *The Times* could be related to them.

The work of Drayton Thomas, Sir Oliver Lodge, and others is sometimes dismissed by critics on the grounds that they were 'convinced spiritualists.' This is a curious argument. The term 'spiritualist' (as opposed to Spiritualism, which is now a recognized religion) has no particular meaning. And the fact that one is 'convinced' by a body of knowledge and personal experience of the truth of something does not mean that one automatically ceases to discriminate between what is good evidence and what is not. We are all convinced that food is good for us, but that does not stop us from recognizing what is edible and what is not. We may be convinced of the rightness of a particular political party, but that does not blind us to faults in its policies. We may be convinced of our abilities as a scientist, but that does not prevent us from recognizing our mistakes. Drayton Thomas, Sir Oliver Lodge, and the other authorities mentioned in this chapter were highly experienced and careful investigators. The fact that they were or may have been 'spiritualists' does not alter this fact.

The Mediumship of Eileen Garrett

The third of the three outstanding mental mediums for whom I have space, Eileen Garrett, differed from Leonora Piper and Gladys Leonard in that she wrote extensively about her own gifts (e.g. Garrett 1939, 1949, 1968). She was also the only one to be tested under carefully controlled laboratory conditions by Dr. J. B. Rhine, head of the parapsychology unit at Duke University, although Rhine was interested only in her psychic abilities – as tested by scores for telepathy and clairvoyance using the card-guessing experiments with Zener cards – and cared little for her mediumistic abilities and her concern with survival.

Like both Leonora Piper and Gladys Leonard, Eileen Garrett (1893-1970) was aware of her gifts as a child. From the age of four until she was 13, she was visited every day by 'The Children,' two girls (one a little older than herself) and a boy. She saw them first 'framed in the doorway; they were strange to me, as were all children.' She looked at them intently and longed to play with them but knew that her aunt, with whom she lived, did not allow her to mix with other children. Next day, out in the garden, she saw them again, and from then onwards they came regularly. 'Sometimes they stayed all day, sometimes but a little while, but no day passed of which they were not a part.' From that first meeting onwards, 'toys lost their meaning ... Other people came and went ... they interested me for a moment, and when they left I was glad; not so with The Children'; anything that interrupted my life with them made me restless.' She never doubted their reality, or 'the fact that we spoke in ways that no grown-up understood.' When she touched them she found they were as soft and warm as herself – 'There was only one way in which they differed from other people. I saw the form of ordinary humans surrounded by a nimbus of light, but the form of The Children' consisted entirely of this light.' She tried to tell her aunt about 'The Children,' and begged her to come and see them, but predictably she was told it was all her imagination, and that God would 'punish her for telling such lies.' Her uncle, whom she adored, was more understanding. She continued to tell him about them, and he would smile and say 'Maybe so.'

'The Children' shared her love of nature, and taught her many things, including the fact that no grown-up 'ever quite spoke the truth.' Often they would come for her at night, and she would leave her bed and join them in the garden, in spite of the punishment this earned from her aunt. She never saw 'The Children' approach, and never saw them go away. They appeared and disappeared spontaneously. At first, she wanted to follow them when they went, but they refused to allow it. They also refused to climb trees with her or paddle in the brook, and disapproved of her tree-climbing, insisting that the trees were meant to be left intact. In every way they seemed like flesh and blood companions. Whey they first appeared she had never heard about fairies, so was unlikely to imagine them, and they did not resemble any of the village children. Certainly it could be argued that they were a form of imaginary compensation for her lonely and unhappy childhood, but this doesn't quite ring true. Throughout her life she remained convinced of their reality, and it was not until many years later that she 'found out that what went on around me became visible to me by a type of sensing that people then termed supernatural but which even today is regarded as supernormal.'

Reading her account of 'The Children' it is difficult to dismiss it as fantasy. As a psychologist who for many years has worked extensively with child psychology, I have never come across a child who gave such a graphic account of imaginary childhood friends, and never met an adult who still considers – as did Eileen Garrett – that these playmates from long ago were anything other than make-believe. But if 'The Children' were not make-believe, who or what were they? Were they the spirits of departed children, or of departed adults who chose to appear as children in order to comfort a lonely sad child? Or were they perhaps some other form of spirit energy that became personalized into the form of young children? I regret never having had the chance to discuss with Eileen Garrett her own adult conclusions on the matter.

'The Children' were not the only early sign of Eileen Garrett's mediumship. One day, while sitting on the porch working at her schoolbooks, she looked up and saw an aunt, Aunt Leon, who lived some 20 miles away, approaching with a small baby in her arms. Greeting her, she noticed how tired Aunt Leon looked, and heard her say clearly and unmistakably 'I must go away now and take baby with me.' Eileen Garrett ran into the house to call the aunt with whom she lived (it is a sign of their strained relationship that she does not name her), but when they got outside Aunt Leon had disappeared. In spite of her minute description of Aunt Leon's clothes and appearance, Eileen was disbelieved and whipped as usual and falsely accused of having learned of Aunt Leon's baby by having 'eavesdropped' on adult conversation. The following day, however, news arrived of the death of Aunt Leon while giving birth to her baby, who had also died, and now Eileen is told by her aunt not to 'speak again of the things that you see for they might come true.'

Between the vision of Aunt Leon and news of her death, Eileen had further unexpected evidence of survival. In order to take revenge on her aunt for the whipping and the false accusation she drowns her aunt's baby ducks and is astonished to see, issuing from each lifeless body, 'a gray smoke-like substance, rising in spiral form. ... [that] ... began to move and curl as it rose and gradually ... [took] on a new shape as it moved away from these little dead ducks ... I knew in that moment that the ducks were coming alive' again.' Subsequently she witnesses the same phenomenon at the death of other small creatures, and witnessed it again some years later when her cousin dies ('I was most interested to discover that this process of separation took, with the human body, hours longer than ... [with] ... the little ducks').

More evidence of survival came when her beloved uncle died (probably from tuberculosis, which ran in the family and from which she herself was also found to be suffering shortly afterwards). A few weeks after his death she was sitting, now aged 13, in her room in the twilight when 'the door opened quietly. There in the lamp light of the hallway I saw my dear uncle, standing clearly before me ... in the weeks before his death he had seemed feeble and worn. Now he appeared as before, erect and strong.' Her uncle speaks to her, asking her to obey her aunt and sympathizing with her for the difficulties she experiences in the relationship. Then he tells her that in two years time she will be free to leave home, and go to London (a precognition that proves correct when two years later she is sent to school in London in the hope that a drier climate will avoid a recurrence of her tuberculosis). Before she has time to question him the door closes and he is gone. She wants to follow him, but finds herself rooted to the spot. At first she feels exhilarated by his visit, but later 'came a sense of terrible emptiness at his going.' However, although she never sees him again, she feels he remains close to her, and ready to hear her whenever she speaks to him.

What she calls the 'rhythmic transformation' that she observed with the dead ducks and then with other living beings at the moment of physical death convinced her of 'the truly simple changes which occurred to all creatures' when dying. Such experiences 'gave me no sense of finality, but rather of a continuous and rhythmic movement toward fresh adventure ... I had come to understand that there seemed little difference between birth and death, to any living creatures excepting humans.' To her, 'both these processes of change . [are] ... joyful and equally creative. Why, since the balance of the whole universe is kept so perfectly by Infinite Direction, must man alone, of all living creatures ... be so lost and frightened in facing what he calls death?'

I have summarized some of the major events in Eileen Garrett's childhood (described in most detail in Garrett 1939) at length, because they illustrate clearly the sensitivity of the born medium. The spirits of 'The Children,' of Aunt Leon, of the dead baby and of her uncle were as real to her as the beings who inhabited the physical world. The ability to see another dimension of reality in this way, an ability that included seeing auras, witnessing the life force leaving the dead ducks and re-forming into recognizable shapes, and feeling a special kinship with nature – survived even the harsh disbelief of her aunt and much other unhappiness. Of all those with mediumistic gifts, Eileen Garrett wrote with the most self-insight. Her gift touched her so deeply, permeating all aspects of her life, that reading her books is like a series of initiations, as if one enters into her vision and recognizes its reality through direct experience. Of all mediums, she also was the one most concerned to penetrate the real meaning of her abilities, and in particular to establish the objective reality or otherwise of the so-called spirit controls that later came into her life.

The first of these controls manifested when, after work as an adult with a development circle in London, she followed advice and consulted a Mr. Huhnli, a man with considerable knowledge of mediumship (Garrett 1949). During the consultation she lapsed into trance, and on emerging was told that a control who gave the name Uvani has spoken through her. From the first she seems to have doubted his independent existence, and argued that since she had the power to avoid the trance state in her mediumship she had no need of controls. However, she was persuaded by Mr. Huhnli that dispensing with trance might lead to 'further mental confusion.' Subsequently she is introduced to Hewat McKenzie, who with his wife was responsible for the College of Psychic Science (now the College of Psychic Studies). Hewat McKenzie appears to have recognized her extraordinary gifts, and after warning her not to become involved in the physical phenomena that were beginning to manifest around her, he focuses upon helping her develop her mental mediumship. Subsequently another control, Abdul Latif, an alleged twelfth-century Persian astronomer and physician from the court of Saladin, manifested in trance and took responsibility for her work on healing.

Interestingly, Eileen Garrett notes that evidence for survival was the only thing that interested McKenzie and the other spiritualists with whom he worked. This is revealing. It implies that Garrett herself was so sure of survival early in her mediumship that her interest focused more upon what happens during mediumship, in particular are the medium's controls separate beings, or aspects of her own unconscious? Certainly she was in no doubt that they operated at a level at which genuine paranormal information could be accessed, but whose mind was it that did the accessing – that of another being who then took over her consciousness while she was in trance, or her own?

I have the impression, for example from her reluctance right from the start to accept Uvani at face value, that she rather disliked the idea of being taken over by another mind during trance. A fiercely independent and self-reliant woman, I am inclined to believe that she preferred to think that her mediumship originated solely in the deeper levels of her own consciousness. Be this as it may, it is clear that after spending a major part of her adult life in seeking to answer this question, Garrett came to the conclusion (Garrett 1968) that 'I prefer to think of the controls as principals of the subconscious. I had, unconsciously, adopted them by name during the years of early training. I respect them, but cannot explain them.' She also seems to have become somewhat ambivalent, not about her own conviction of survival, but about the value of personal conviction without scientific proof. For example she assures us that 'For myself, I do not need to look in terms of survival after death. I feel myself to be part of the known properties of the earth's family, and that is enough,' but then goes on to say 'If I had reached conviction on the basis of my own acceptance of survival after death, I could have been unfaithful to my own driving need to find answers in science. There alone can speculations and results be tested or verified. For me the answer is not yet, nor do I seek it for myself; but there is a large field of unexplored mental phenomena to be tackled by science.'

This is somewhat at odds with her earlier statements about survival. For example, in 1949 she wrote 'It would appear, then, that death is but an exchange of one experience for another, for during all human history there has been a belief ... that through perceptions beyond the five senses men have been able to get in touch with phases of existence unfamiliar to everyday experience.' My impression is that during the course of her mediumship Eileen Garrett became too optimistic about the power of experimental science – the form of science to which she was introduced by Rhine and the other scientists with whom she worked such as Professors McDougall, Grey Walter, and Ira Progoff – both to uncover the mysteries of mediumship and to establish the scientific basis for survival. Such scientists, in spite in some cases of their sympathetic attitude toward the possibility of survival and their courage in involving themselves in the scientifically unfashionable field of psychical research, were naturally cautious in their conclusions on the nature of mediumship, and reluctant to build the notion of a spiritual dimension and an afterlife into their public thinking.

The methodology of experimental science has developed in the context of the physical world, and its remarkable success in unraveling many of the mysteries of this world should not blind us to the limitations of its methodology when it attempts to explore non-physical dimensions of reality. I have many times noticed a tendency among people such as Eileen Garrett, who have had no formal scientific training, to develop over-optimistic ideas as to the power of this methodology. In doing so they neglect the fact that careful observation of what is already there, and not just its manipulation for experimental purposes, can also be regarded as scientific (as is the case in some areas of astronomy, of archaeology, of medicine, and of the social sciences, where experimentation is not always feasible). In fact science had its birth, long before the development of the experimental method, in observation and in deductions based upon this observation – observation not only of the outer world through the five senses, but observation of the workings of the inner world of consciousness, dreams, feelings, and emotions. Even though supplemented by technical aids, the experimental method relies exclusively upon the five physical senses, and is therefore less appropriate for exploring this inner world, which includes the processes of mediumship and of the possible survival of consciousness after death. Eileen Garrett was thus correct in her statement quoted a little earlier, that it is 'through perceptions beyond the five senses [that] men have been able to get in touch with phases of existence unfamiliar to everyday experience.' 'Perception beyond the senses' must, by definition, depend upon observation by those capable of this perception, and upon the recording and verification of the information yielded through this observation by those acting as investigators.

Not surprisingly, Eileen Garrett may have been deeply influenced by the caution of the scientists with whom she worked, and perhaps diffident in recognizing that her knowledge of mediumship and of survival – based as it was upon direct personal experience denied to them – was necessarily greater than their own. Even for a woman as independent as Eileen Garrett, the scientist can take on an image as the white-coated professional, towering above his or her fellows in wisdom and initiated into an arcane understanding of the human mind denied to those outside the charmed inner circle of the illuminati. I cannot protest too often that a true understanding of science (particularly the science of the mind and of consciousness) can only be based upon a knowledge of its limitations. This is not to denigrate experimental science, whose achievements (for good and ill) are beyond doubt. Rather it is to give voice to the humility that it is important for scientists to develop as they come to know more and more about their subject, and to recognize how small is this knowledge when compared with what is not known – and in many cases what can perhaps never be known through the experimental methods of the physical sciences. This does not mean that survival research cannot be scientific. It means that, like other scientific undertakings in which experimentation is not feasible, it should concentrate upon the logical inferences that arise from careful and repeated observations. Thus the careful and repeated observations by those investigating the evidence for survival may lead us to the logical inference that survival is either the most comprehensive and satisfactory explanation of the evidence or it is not.

As mentioned earlier in connection with Mrs. Piper's controls and those of Gladys Leonard, we simply do not know enough about the workings of the unconscious to argue that it can dramatize material received paranormally into enduring and consistent sub-personalities. It is unclear in any case why the unconscious should do such a thing in order to deceive the conscious mind. The trance state has certain affinities with sleep and dreaming. Both sleep and trance appear to involve the closing down of the conscious mind. However, when we wake from sleep we are not deceived into believing that the characters who featured in our dreams are real people, so why should mediums be so easily deceived by what happens in trance. In addition, even those mental mediums who do not use trance still claim to have controls or guides. Once again, it is difficult to see why their unconscious minds should so consistently play tricks upon their consciousness. If the unconscious receives information paranormally, then why not simply give this information in the form in which it is received?

William James' suggested that the answer might be that all consciousness tends to express itself in personalized form. This may suggest that a universal consciousness of some kind exists and expresses itself as the control, and becomes personalized in the process, but this kind of reasoning is always in danger of being circular – i.e. the explanation for controls lies in the tendency of universal consciousness to personalize itself, and it is the very existence of controls that proves universal consciousness personalizes itself. The great William James would not have been guilty of this circularity, but nevertheless it can be implied by his theory. We do not know whether universal consciousness, assuming it exists, has a tendency to personalize itself, and we have no way that I can see of finding out. This does not mean that we should necessarily take controls at face value. Phinuit, Mrs. Piper's control, although allegedly a French physician, proved a failure when invited by investigators to talk in French. This may be because Mrs. Piper did not speak French, and he could not therefore find French words in her entranced mind. It is said that communicators can only utilize the thoughts and concepts and language possessed by the medium when they try to communicate with mortals. Yet it is reported that during Etta Wriedt's séances (her mediumship is discussed in Chapter 11 in connection with the independent voice phenomenon) spirits spoke convincingly in a number of languages understood by sitters from overseas but unknown to Etta Wriedt herself. If this is so, and communicators can indeed use languages unknown to the medium but known by sitters, it is unclear what prevents controls from typically communicating in the foreign languages they knew during their lifetimes if spoken by sitters.

The practical solution to the puzzle is to concentrate not upon the identity of controls but upon the information that they seem instrumental in bringing through from communicators. If this information includes details about the communicator that establishes his or her identity beyond reasonable doubt, then this, rather than the identity of controls, is the best support for the reality of survival. But if in spite of everything, we wish to speculate on the true nature of controls (we humans are much given to speculation) I would suggest that controls may well be distinct from the medium, but often not who they claim to be. Why they should wish to hide their identity I do not know. Possibly they are composite entities, with more than one consciousness involved (perhaps in some cases they represent the 'group soul' discussed in due course in Chapter 18). If they are in fact deceased individuals, their memories of earth life may have faded to the point of forgetfulness, and consequently they simply invent a persona to satisfy (or reassure) the medium and the investigators. Perhaps, though this is more speculative, they are forms of consciousness that have not experienced a life on earth, as some controls have claimed. Or perhaps in some cases at least – for example Gladys Leonard's Feda – they are who they say they are. One guess is perhaps as good as another.

Eileen Garrett's interest in research led her, while living and working in America, to found the Parapsychology Foundation, funding it through royalties from her books and from donations, and this has since become one of the major international bodies for the dissemination of laboratory-based work in the subject. However, it is unfortunate that this concern for research – in particular research aimed at understanding the mental processes of her mediumship and doomed largely to failure, deflected her from more projects designed to yield direct evidence of survival. Thus we do not have the wealth of case material, obtained under carefully controlled conditions, from Eileen Garrett that we have from Leonora Piper and Gladys Leonard. Probably her best-known case, in Britain at least, concerns the crash of the R101, a giant airship built by the British Air Ministry in 1930 at a time when it was thought that airships rather than airplanes might be the best way of reaching the far-flung corners of the Empire (see e.g. Fuller 1979). Dogged with design and construction problems from the start, the R101 crashed near Beauvais in France on her maiden voyage to India, killing all but six of the 54 passengers and crew on board.

It seems clear that an attempt by the Air Ministry team to compete with the private company commissioned by the government to build her sister-ship, the R100 (which was completed successfully and which had already made a triumphant maiden flight to Montreal in Canada while the R101 was still under construction) led to the disaster. The R101 was badly designed, over-weighted with diesel rather than petrol engines, and manifestly a disaster waiting to happen. The attempt to give it extra lift by literally sawing it in half and adding a new mid section with an extra gas bag was clearly ill-conceived. Yet Lord Thompson, then Air Minister and with ambitions to be the next Viceroy of India, insisted that her maiden voyage commenced on October 4, 1930 in order to fly him to India and bring him back in time to attend the Imperial Conference of Dominion Prime Ministers due to be held in London at the end of the month. His impatience seems to have cost him his life and the lives of nearly all his fellow travelers, including that of the pilot, Flight Lieutenant H. Carmichael Irwin.

Two days after the disaster, Eileen Garrett was holding a sitting in West London at the National Laboratory of Psychical Research founded by Harry Price. The object of the sitting was to try and contact the spirit of Sir Arthur Conan Doyle, who had died a few months previously. However, instead of hearing from Sir Arthur, the voice of Eileen Garrett's control Uvani took on a desperate broken urgency as it announced the name 'Irving' or 'Irwin.' Another voice then took over, and in a number of staccato sentences (all taken down by the expert shorthand writer present) gave several pieces of information that in essence amounted to:

The bulk of the airship was too heavy for her engines. The engines themselves were too heavy. The useful lift of the airship was too small. The gross lift was badly computed. The idea of fitting new elevators was totally mad. The elevator had jammed. The oil pipe was plugged. The mixture of carbon and hydrogen as fuel was absolutely wrong. The airship never reached its cruising altitude. The same thing had happened in the trials. The trials themselves were too short. The crew did not know the ship properly. The airscrews were too small. The fuel injection system was bad. The air pump had failed. The cooling system was bad. The bore capacity was bad. The fuel feed was unsatisfactory. The fabric was water-logged. The ship's nose was down and refused to rise. The craft could not be trimmed, and nearly scraped the roofs at Achy. The weather was too bad for a long flight. The added middle section was too heavy for the engines. The superstructure of the craft was not resilient.

Three weeks later, Major Oliver Villers, Senior Assistant Intelligence Officer on the R101 project, after receiving an impression that Irwin wished to talk with him, had a sitting for the purpose with Eileen Garrett. There was no shorthand writer present, but Viller's notes record that, in answer to his questions, Irwin informed him through Garrett that:

The airship was too heavy by several tons; the construction was amateurish and the envelope was too porous, and the movement of the airbags caused internal pressure that led to the leakage; the girders were of unsound material; the gas indicator was going up and down before the flight, which also suggested a leakage; the weather forecast was bad, and he and the other officers knew the flight was doomed and just hoped to get as far as Le Bourget and tie up there.

Villiers had six further sittings with Garrett at which the other officers of the R101 who had died in the crash apparently communicated, as did Sir Sefton Brancker, the Minister of Civil Aviation (who also died in the crash). The details they gave agreed with those of Irwin, and they provided a few additional items of technical information. Furthermore two of these officers, Wing Commander Colmore who had been in overall command of the R101 project, and First Officer Atherston, both spoke of private diaries in which they had expressed their doubts about the safety of the craft.

Harry Price, who continued to take a special interest in the case, and Villiers (who did not know each other previously) decided that the information received during the two sittings should be forwarded to the Court of Inquiry investigating the tragedy, but neither the Court nor the Air Ministry was prepared to consider it, in spite of the fact that there was no question of fraud on the part of Price or Villiers or Garrett herself. None of them knew about the technical details of airship construction to which Irwin had referred, and one of these details, the hydrogen-carbon mix of fuel, was still in the process of development and had not been used in the flight. None of them had access to details of all the faults apparent in the R101 before take-off (Lord Thompson had in fact described the craft as 'safe as houses except for the millionth chance'). The Air Ministry had clamped down on all details surrounding the crash, and the six survivors, none of whom had been stationed in the control car of the R101, could throw no particular light on events. Price also sent a transcript of the first sitting – at which he had been present – to Will Charlton, Chief Supply and Stores Officer to the project, who studied it together with other technical personnel involved in the building of the R101. All apparently confirmed that only Irwin could have known many of the technical points to which he had referred. Charlton in fact listed 53 of these points that were deemed to be correct.

Subsequently Air Vice Marshall Dowding (later Air Chief Marshall Lord Dowding – discussed in more details later in connection with so-called earthbound spirits), who immediately prior to the tragedy had been appointed to the Air Council, the body responsible for granting the R101 its temporary Certificate of Airworthiness, studied these technical points and agreed with all but eight of them. Air Marshall Victor Goddard, himself a former airship commander, was also impressed by them and considered that, despite several technical errors, Irwin's communications had the ring of truth about them.

However, there have been some experts who have proved less enthusiastic. Interviewed in the early 1960s by Archie Jarman, who compiled a carefully researched report on the R101 tragedy, Wing Commander Booth (captain of the R100, the sister ship of the R101, on its successful flight to Montreal) considered that the details given by Irwin in the Price sitting did not assist in determining the reasons for the crash, while those given in the Villiers sittings were also of little value. For example he denied that gas indicators' were fitted to the R101, or that facilities existed at Le Bourget that would have enabled a craft of the size of the R101 to tie up' there, or that Irwin and his crew would have continued with the flight knowing they were doomed. In his view they would have turned around and, with the wind behind them, made it back to their base at Cardington. It even seemed doubtful that the airship had in fact passed over Achy. And far from the details of its construction and its problems being a well-kept secret, he considered that many of them had become public knowledge before the fatal crash. Wing Commander Cave-Brown-Cave who had been involved in the construction of the R101 was also interviewed by Jarman, and gave his opinion that Will Charlton's observations on the technical details were inaccurate and should be disregarded. Doubt was even expressed as to how much technical knowledge Will Charlton, as Supply and Stores Officer for the R101, actually possessed.

But the story does not end there. Both Colimore and Atherston had insisted through Eileen Garrett that they kept private diaries in which faults in the construction of the R101 had been recorded. When interviewed by L. F. C. Darby, the Assessor and Registrar of the Court of Enquiry into the R101 disaster, Mrs. Colimore confirmed the existence of her husband's diaries, and insisted they were kept in his office in the very place Colimore had indicated through Eileen Garrett. Subsequent failure to find the diaries and the denial by officials of their existence thus looked suspiciously, to those who supported the Garrett sittings, like part of a cover-up by the Air Ministry to protect the reputation of Lord Thompson and to hide the constructional errors that led to the failure of the R101. (The findings of the Court of Inquiry, which decided that the cause of the crash could not be determined, did indeed prove to be a whitewash.) Atherston's diary proved easier to find. His wife had refused to confirm or deny its existence at the time of the Court of Enquiry, but 37 years later, when interviewed by Michael Cox for the BBC documentary on the R101, she finally agreed to produce it. Among the entries made by Atherston 12 months before the tragedy, when the pressures to get the R101 completed in time for Lord Thompson's coveted trip to India were intense, appeared the words 'There is a mad rush and panic to complete the ship ... It is grossly unfair to expect the officers to take out a novel ship of this size ... The airship has no lift worth talking about, and it is obviously tail heavy.'

Taken together, the details of this complex case are intriguing. In some ways it appears to be one of the best cases for survival ever reported. Villiers, Dowding, Goddard, Charlton, and many others acquainted with the details of the R101 were convinced by it. Charlton, it seems, even became a spiritualist on the strength of it, and devoted many years to studying the case. Dowding and Goddard, as a consequence of this and other experiences, also became convinced of survival, as did Villiers. And reading through the transcripts and notes of the sittings Garrett gave to Price and to Villiers, it seems inconceivable that she could have mastered from press reports all the technical details that she uttered in such a torrent – especially at the Price sitting where these details were produced so rapidly that the shorthand writer could barely keep up with them (sadly tape recorders were not available at the time). The only normal explanation for her grasp of them is that Garrett had studied the R101 project intensively herself over very many months prior to the tragedy, obtaining much of her information from people actively engaged in it, memorized all these details and then kept her knowledge a secret in the hope that one day it could be used as a fraudulent way of gaining publicity for her mediumship. This seems highly unlikely. No hint of fraud was ever attached to Eileen Garrett throughout her life, and none of the many eminent scientists who worked with her on research into the processes of mediumship ever expressed any doubt as to her integrity. In addition, although at this distance we cannot be certain as to what was in the public domain at the time of the crash and what was not, it certainly appears that at least some of the faults with the craft detailed by Irwin were confidential to the Air Ministry.

A further argument against Garrett using the R101 disaster as a fraudulent way of gaining publicity for her mediumship is that she herself said little about the case, beyond the fact that even before the tragedy she was having visions of an airship in flames (Garrett 1968). She personally told Sir Sefton Brancker of her visions before the flight, and urged that it should be called off. It seems he was impressed by her warnings, which added to his own doubts as to the safety of the craft. Villiers, who had been close to Brancker, when interviewed by Fuller confirmed these facts, and added that Brancker did in fact go on to warn Thompson that the flight should be postponed, only to be told angrily that if he was afraid he could withdraw from it – there were plenty of others only too eager to take his place. Accused of cowardice in this way, Brancker reluctantly allowed his name to remain on the passenger list.

As with so many complex cases in the field of the paranormal and elsewhere, one can use the evidence to slant things whichever way one chooses. Prior convictions are often the determining factor in deciding how to treat the evidence. But I do not consider that anyone who comes to the strange and tragic story of the R101 with as much objectivity as we humans can muster (which admittedly may not be that much) can reach any conclusion other than that a great deal of the information given by Eileen Garrett was paranormally acquired, and that the survival of Irwin and the other unhappy officers is, on balance, the most likely explanation as to its source. Will Charlton may not have been the best person to pronounce on the technical details given by Irwin and his colleagues, but as Chief Supply and Stores Officer for the project it is hardly conceivable that he would not have come to know – indeed have needed to know – a great deal about the construction of the R101, even though as Jarman reveals in his report he may not have been knowledgeable about the past history of airship development. In addition, Charlton discussed the details of Irwin's communications with members of the R101 technical staff, and his list of the 53 correct technical details given by Irwin was then assessed by both Dowding and Goddard, perhaps two of the finest minds to hold high office in the Royal Air Force at that time.

This still leaves the problems of the technical errors in the communication, of which the talk of the 'gas indicators' and of 'tying up' at Le Bourget are perhaps the most obvious. Attempts to account for these cannot be other than speculative. Villiers may have made a mistake in his note-taking, or may not have heard correctly. Irwin may have been confused (possibly understandably after what he had been through). By gas indicators going up and down' he may have been referring to the behavior of the gas envelopes inside the outer structure of the craft. These were known to move around' (their chafing against the metal framework of the craft was one of the hazards that the construction team had been trying to overcome), and this would presumably have been evident even before take-off if gas was escaping. Possibly it was hoped that with the loss of the gas and the consequent lack of buoyancy the R101 would be able to use even the limited facilities for tying up that existed at Le Bourget. Who knows? But however we explain them, it seems that these technical errors are not sufficient to lead us to discount the very many facts that were correct.

Villiers drove Sir Sefton Brancker to the airport at Cardington for the ill-fated flight, and noted his continuing unease about the mission. But by then it was too late. With the inevitability of Greek tragedy, and driven in no small measure by the hubris of Lord Thompson, the doomed craft lurched from its moorings and set out for its rendezvous with a hillside near Beauvais in northern France only a few short miles away.

Let us leave the last word on her mediumship and on our survival to Eileen Garratt herself. Interviewed shortly before her death she confirmed that "it would be impossible to doubt the continuity of consciousness and the survival of the human entity after death" (Psychic Magazine 1973).

CHAPTER 8
DROP IN COMMUNICATORS AND THE CROSS-CORRESPONDENCES

Drop-in Communicators

So-called *Drop-in Communicators* are those entities who make contact during a sitting yet are unknown to anyone present. If such communicators give evidence of identity that subsequently proves to be correct, they provide strong support for the survival hypothesis. Since they are unknown to the medium or to sitters there is no chance that this evidence can be derived telepathically from any of them, and it is unlikely that the medium would have obtained it clairvoyantly if she has no link with the person concerned and therefore no impetus to seek these details or clues as to where they might be found. To this we can add that the personal details given by drop-in communicators would, if obtained clairvoyantly or telepathically from sources outside the sitting, have had in some cases to be pieced together from a number of separate fragments of information obtained from quite different sources. What would have prompted the medium's unconscious mind to identify each of these sources, and how would that same unconscious mind know how to assemble the fragments concerned into a coherent, persuasive whole? The suggestion that these fragments might already be assembled in some vast cosmic memory bank (such as the so-called Akashic Records already mentioned) upon which the medium can draw has little evidence to support it. As already objected, who or what is responsible for organizing the billions of pieces of experience generated daily by the population of the world into a cohesive whole, and if such an organizing principle exists is it likely that it would allow mediums access to its memory store in order consciously or unconsciously to mislead people into a belief that a surviving individual is communicating? It makes more sense to suppose that the agency responsible for organizing the information given by drop-in communicators is the single, surviving mind of the drop-in communicator him or herself.

A carefully researched collection of drop-in cases was published by Dr. Alan Gauld, a Past President of the SPR and one of the most highly respected investigators of the paranormal (Gauld 1971). The group receiving the communications, which did not include a professional medium and which obtained communications through a ouija (a term taken from the French and German words for "yes" and pronounced we-ya) board, was based in Cambridge and was hosted by an SPR member whose identity Dr. Gauld protects with the initials LG. Dr. Gauld reports that of the 240 communicators recorded by the group over a period of 470 sittings, some 37 were drop-ins. A number of these gave information that could not be verified, but in other cases it was possible, after considerable detective work, to check on the facts that were given. Perhaps the most interesting of the cases reported in detail by Dr. Gauld is that of Harry Stockbridge (not his real name). At the time only LG and his wife WG were in physical contact with the board. Two other group members were observing. The most relevant extracts from Stockbridge's communications, interspersed with questions asked by LG, were as follows (these communications were received over several sittings, as shown). The name 'Stockbridge' was given through the ouija board, but before it appeared WG had a vivid mental impression of a pair of stocks, followed by an impression of a bridge, which together gave her his name. Stockbridge made contact through the ouija board intermittently over several sittings, and the communication between him and LG was as follows:

First Communication, July 3, 1950
    Stockbridge: *Stockbridge. Harry.*
    LG: *Did I know you?*
    Stockbridge: *No. You did not know me. I wish to work with you.*
    LG: *Do you know Kenneth?* (One of the guides of the group.)
    Stockbridge: *No. Me. Tyneside Scottish. Tall, dark, thin. Special, features large brown eyes. Second Loot* (slang for 'lieutenant'). *Attached Northumberland Fusiliers. Died fourteen July sixteen.*

Second Communication, July 10, 1950.
    Stockbridge: *Here we are. Harry ... I hung out in Leicester. Do not attempt to find my family.*

Third Communication, December 11, 1950
    Stockbridge: *Harry Stockbridge here.*
    LG. *How's your Mum? Is she with you?*
    Stockbridge: *Yes. All my love. H Stock. Look me up. Leicester holds a record. I would laugh if doubted when you confirm my existence.*

Fourth Communication, January 28, 1952
    Stockbridge: *I am anxious to grow in this work. My last effort was almost in vain. Brick walls in the male.*
    LG: *What are your likes and dislikes?*
    Stockbridge: *Now yes. Problems any. Pepys reading, water coloring. Let's NRHE a story. Off.*

One morning LG awoke with the conviction that he knew the name of the street in which Stockbridge was born. Without giving the name he mentioned this conviction to WG, who responded with the word 'Powis', which was in fact the very name that had come to LG. At the next sitting at which Stockbridge communicated, LG asked him about Powis Street.

Fifth Communication, July 14, 1952
    Stockbridge: *I knew it well. My association took my memory there.*

Dr. Gauld followed up the various details given during these sittings in an attempt to discover whether Harry Stockbridge had actually existed. The War Office official list of officer fatalities, *Officers Died in the Great War of 1914–1919*, contained the name of a 2nd Lieutenant H. Stockbridge of the Northumberland Fusiliers, but it gave the date of death as July 19 and not July 14. However, Stockbridge's death certificate, which was then obtained, gave the date communicated by Stockbridge, namely July 14. Dr. Gauld then wrote to the Army Records Centre to confirm the date of death, and received the reply that "2nd Lieutenant Stockbridge was killed in action on 14th July 1916." Unfortunately, Dr. Gauld was unable to trace a regimental history of the Northumberland Fusiliers that contained any reference to Stockbridge.

A copy of Stockbridge's birth certificate was obtained next, and it was found that he was born in Leicester, a fact also reported in a book by Joseph Keating, *Tyneside Irish Brigade*, which further lists Stockbridge as belonging to one of the Tyneside Irish Battalions of the Northumberland Fusiliers. Records in the War Office consulted by Gauld revealed, however, that at the time of his death Stockbridge was attached to (i.e. was temporarily serving with) one of the Tyneside *Scottish* Battalions of the Fusiliers (Stockbridge himself names his battalion as the "Scottish Battalion," and mentions that he was "attached," although he refers to attachment to his regiment rather than to his battalion). Two of Stockbridge's brothers were then traced but neither appeared to have known him well (he seems to have been isolated from his family, hence perhaps his comment "Do not attempt to find my family"), although a more distant relative was able to confirm his description of himself as tall and with large dark eyes. It was also confirmed that Stockbridge's mother was indeed dead in 1950, as Stockbridge had implied in answer to LG's questions "How's your Mum? Is she with you?" His brothers were unable to comment on his description of his likes and dislikes, though his reference to an apparent liking for "problems any" may have been borne out by the fact that he had won a prize for mathematics and physics while at school, and had commenced a science course at university before interrupting it to join the army.

Further research by Dr. Gauld revealed that two local Leicester newspapers for July 19, 1916 contained notices of Stockbridge's death, giving his age and details of his old school and his Regiment, but mistakenly giving his rank as Lieutenant instead of Second Lieutenant. His death was also listed in the July 26 issues of the *Daily Telegraph*, the *Manchester Guardian* and the *Morning Post*, but in each case the only details given were his name, rank, and regiment. None of these newspapers printed a photograph of him or gave any description of his appearance. Dr. Gauld was unable to find "In Memorium" notices for Stockbridge in any of the Leicester newspapers in the years after his death or in any of the national newspapers consulted. His name and correct date of death do appear on the Roll of Honor at his old school in Leicester, which may explain his reference to "Leicester holds a record," but no copy of a school magazine from the period concerned (which might have given some of his other details) was found to be in existence either at the school or in the local library. The death notices in the local Leicester newspapers gave Stockbridge's home address as Gordon Road Leicester and not Powis Street, but there is in fact a Powis Street (a somewhat unusual street name to appear in an English city) a few hundred yards away from Gordon Road, and in his communications with the group Stockbridge only claimed he *knew* Powis Street well, not that he was born there or lived there, and it seems from his reply that it held a special association for him of some kind.

The obscurity of the various sources in which Stockbridge's details appeared renders it highly unlikely that LG or WG would have come across them by chance. Neither LG nor WG had ever been to Leicester or had had contacts there. They thus could not have seen the Roll of Honor at Stockbridge's old school, or browsed through elderly copies of local newspapers in the Leicester public library – and had they done so they would in fact have been misinformed as to Stockbridge's rank. If they had come across the War Office publication *Officers Died in the Great War 1914–1919* they would have been misinformed as to the date of his death. And if they had happened upon Keating's obscure *Tyneside Irish Brigade* (Gauld tells us there were no copies of it in the Cambridge City Library or in the Cambridgeshire County Library, and that the sitters did not have access to the Cambridge University Library) they would have been misled as to the battalion in which Stockbridge was serving when he died. The Army Records Office gave only his rank and date of death. On balance, it is clear that unless they had gone through the very careful research undertaken by Dr. Gauld, LG and WG would have been unable to assemble all the correct details given by Stockbridge. And had they done this research, they would perforce have had to do so deliberately and methodically. They could not have picked up the information unconsciously in passing. And if they had acted deliberately and methodically, then they would stand accused of blatant fraud – not at all the picture of them to emerge from Gauld's report of the case.

If we wish to argue that the picture of Harry Stockbridge to emerge at the sitting was the result of unconscious telepathy/clairvoyance by LG or WG from persons and published details unknown to them at the time, was there a single source from which this information could have come? Clearly not. The local and national newspapers gave no details of his appearance, did not mention he was attached to the Tyneside Scottish, and gave his rank incorrectly. The only source to confirm that he was attached to the Tyneside Scottish at the time of his death was a record in the War Office Library. Keating's book does not mention the date of death or make reference to the Tyneside Scottish. The Roll of Honor at the school also does not mention the Tyneside Scottish, and of course gives no details of Stockbridge's appearance or the fact that his mother had died prior to the date of his first communication with the sitters. The details of his appearance and the confirmation of her death came from a distant relative. Thus if unconscious telepathy/clairvoyance was involved, the necessary fragments of information would have had to be drawn from a number of disparate sources. Not impossible, the supporters of the Super-ESP theory will say, but they will be bound to concede yet again that there is no evidence that, particularly without an emotional link and without any motivation in that particular direction, such extensive powers of unconscious telepathy and clairvoyance exist.

The Case of Patience Worth

One of the most remarkable of all drop-in communicators, who, as in the Stockbridge case, first made contact through a ouija board (but later by direct dictation), gave her name as Patience Worth and claimed to have been born in 1649 in Dorsetshire, England, to a poor family, and to have emigrated to America, where she was killed by Indians (Prince 1927, Litvag 1972, Roy 1996). Patience Worth announced her presence on July 8, 1913 with the words "Many moons ago I lived. Again I come. Patience Worth my name." For the next nine years Patience Worth dictated through the recipient, Pearl Curran a St. Louis housewife and non-professional medium, a number of extraordinary books. In the first five years alone these totaled over four million words in 29 volumes that consisted of six full-length historical novels, 2,500 poems usually on devotional themes and always full of love and compassion, and a number of short stories and plays. The most notable novel, *The Sorry Tale*, was an epic about the life of Christ that ran to 300,000 words and took two years to dictate. Also popular with the reading public were *Hope Trueblood* and *Telka*, set in Victorian and medieval England respectively, some of the latter in poetic form. The other novels, *The Merry Tale*, *The Pot Upon the Wheel*, and *Samuel Wheatton* were also well received. The books showed considerable literary merit, and some of the poems were equally striking. A few lines from one of them, entitled *The Inheritance of Ages* are all I have space for:

Strange, is it not, beloved, that even as I lay my cheek to thine,
Even as my eyes behold thine, even as we together,lip to lip,
     declare through our silence adoration;
Strange, is it not, that these atoms which are thee and me
Have held this wine since first they sifted through the ether from the great God's
     fingertips?
My lips, beloved, have kissed a thousand kisses,
My arms, beloved, have embraced a thousand thousand loves.
Mine eyes, beloved, have beheld seven thousand thousand thousand beauteous things.
Yea, even as I embrace thee,
I am encircled with that understanding
Which is born within me through the common usage of my clay.

This amazing output has been scrutinized carefully by a number of scholars, and the historical details found to be correct. The literary style, the creation of plot and of characters have also been highly praised, and it has been suggested by experts that *The Sorry Tale* is one of the finest accounts of the life and times of Christ penned since the Gospels themselves. Pearl Curran had herself left school at age 14, and it seems unlikely that she would have had such a detailed grasp of historical facts – or the opportunity to carry out the extensive and detailed research that would have been necessary in order to acquire them – and such a high level of literary skill. Sometimes she would produce 5,000 words and more in an evening, and at other times without pausing would produce passages of different works interleaved with each other. The form of English used in her writings was never later than the seventeenth century, and some of it from even earlier.

Who was Patience Worth? Was she a fictional character created by Pearl Curran? Was she the creation of Pearl Curran's unconscious? Was she a living individual who transmitted the material telepathically to Pearl Curran (as the Super-ESP hypothesis would suggest)? Was she a past incarnation or incarnations of Pearl Curran, or someone who once lived on earth and who wished to fulfill a role as a creative writer? In view of Pearl Curran's lack of education the possibility that she was a fictional character created by Peal or that everything came from her own unconscious can be effectively ruled out. It is equally difficult to argue that she was a living individual working telepathically through Pearl Curran. Not only do we have no evidence that telepathy can work in this intensive and extended way, we have no possible motive to explain why anyone with the creative gift manifested by Patience Worth would wish to channel it through someone else instead of owning it for him- or herself. If a fear of publicity was the problem, a pseudonym would surely have served far better than the doubtful process of telepathy. Pearl Curran's own previous incarnations are a possibility in view of the novels written by Joan Grant (Chapter 17) that supposedly were a result of her "far memory" of previous lives, but Joan Grant recognized her personal link with these novels while Pearl Curran regarded herself simply as the mouthpiece of an energy that seemed beyond herself.

The final possibility is that Patience Worth was who she said she was, a deceased individual who used Pearl Curran as her medium. It has been suggested that the fact she used some words in her script that pre-dated the seventeenth century and an archaic English dialect not recognized by scholars makes this seem unlikely, but I do not regard this as a problem. We have little idea of what might or might not be learned or forgotten in the afterlife, and if Patience Worth was a spirit she had had 300 years of our time for her command of the English language to improve. It is unfortunate that no accurate records exist of individuals killed by American Indians defending their homeland in the seventeenth century, and it has not been possible to ascertain whether or not an historical figure called Patience Worth – even if that was her name when on earth – existed at that time. Records from seventeenth-century England are also not complete enough to provide any clues. But Walter Franklin Prince, a cautious and careful investigator, concludes his book on Patience Worth with the words that either we must radically alter our notion of the unconscious "to include potencies of which we hitherto have had no knowledge, or else some cause operating through, but not originating in, the subconscious of Mrs. Curran must be recognized" (Prince 1927). It is difficult to disagree with this conclusion.

If Patience Worth was an historical figure, we are still left with the question why she should have wished to communicate so much literary material 300 years after her death. However, communicators tell us that creativity plays a major role in the development of spirits in the afterlife as we shall see in Chapter 18, and there have been many other claimed instances of writers, musicians, and painters channeling new works through mediums on earth. One of the best-known examples is Rosemary Brown (1984), who with only moderate knowledge of music has supposedly channeled new compositions from Liszt, Chopin, Schubert, Beethoven, Debussy, Brahms, Berlioz, and Rachmaninov. Experts are divided as to whether or not the compositions are up to the standard of the composers concerned, but some of them are sufficiently impressive to have been recorded and to have featured on television programs. Renowned conductors such as Leonard Bernstein and Colin Davis have shown serious interest in her work, and John Lill, regarded by many as Britain's finest pianist, has expressed himself as satisfied that the compositions bear the stamp of the original composers. Another example is Frederick Lewis Thompson who without warning or previous artistic inclinations found himself channeling the landscape artist Robert Swain Gifford (Hyslop 1909). In addition to artists, medical doctors have also frequently been claimed by spiritual healers such as Stephen Turoff to be working through them while in trance, often with impressive results (e.g. Solomon 1997).

Creativity is a strange gift. Where do creative ideas come from? Frequently they rise unbidden, as if from outside ourselves. Mozart is reported as saying he often "heard" his music and simply had to write it down. Bach thought he was divinely inspired. The ancient Greeks considered that all creative gifts came from the Muses, the goddesses of inspiration. We psychologists suggest that creative insights come from the unconscious, which works below the threshold of awareness endlessly permeating ideas and memories until it recognizes something of possible value, which it then pushes up into the conscious mind. But this is only a theory. We have no idea whether it is true or not and if true how it really works. Even the thoughts that are continually popping into the mind are a mystery. Where do they come from? The answer is we do not know. If mediums are correct in assuming that the information they give during sittings comes from deceased individuals, it is not unreasonable to suppose that creative ideas could sometimes come from the same source. If so, Patience Worth could indeed have been who she said she was.

The Case of Runolfur Runolfsson

One of the strangest drop-in communicators was Runolfur Runolfsson, who announced his presence through Hafsteinn Bjornsson, a highly regarded Icelandic trance medium, in 1937. The case was extensively investigated by Elinborg Larusdottir, who interviewed the five sitters at Bjornsson's circle and obtained signed affidavits from them that her report of the case, first published in 1946, was correct. Subsequently another investigation, with additional enquiries, was carried out by Professors Haraldsson and Stevenson (Haraldsson and Stevenson 1975).

Runolfsson made his abrupt and uninvited appearance at a Bjornsson sitting with his regular circle, and surprised those present by his rudeness and his rough and uncouth demands. Initially he refused to give his name ("Call me anything you like ... What the hell does it matter to you what my name is?"), and demanded snuff and coffee and became angry when refused rum (presumably he derived or hoped to derive vicarious pleasure from these if taken by the medium). When asked what he wanted, he gave the surprising reply that he was "looking for his leg," which he claimed was "in the sea." At this point he still refused to give his name, but when Ludvik Gudmundsson a fish merchant, joined the circle of sitters Runolfsson greeted him as if he knew him, insisting that his leg was in his house at Sandgerdi. Gudmundsson, who could not place him and had no idea what he meant by his references to a leg, declined to help him unless he revealed his identity. Runolfsson refused to do so, and left in an apparent huff, only to return some months later in a rather more co-operative mood, although his abrupt reappearance gave sitters the impression that he took over the medium by shouldering other would-be communicators aside.

This time he gave his name and told a strange story. Returning drunk to his home near Sandgerdi one evening in October 1879 he had paused to rest on the beach, and consumed more of the alcohol he was carrying with him with the result that he had fallen asleep and been washed out to sea by the storm that was raging that night. His body had not been recovered until January of the next year, by which time "dogs and ravens" had torn it to pieces. The remains, less a missing thighbone, were buried at Utskalar Churchyard, four miles from Sandgerdi. The thigh-bone had been carried out to sea, and when subsequently washed up again "it was passed around and now it is in Ludvik [Gudmundsson's] house." When asked where proof could be found of this Runolfsson replied in the "church book of Utskalar Church." He also gave the information that he had been 52 when he died, and that he was a very tall man. In response to the story Ludvik Gudmundsson, who had found the skulls of two fishermen in the house he had purchased in Sandgerdi along with his fish processing factory but no other bones, questioned some of the oldest men in Sandgerdi in order to discover whether or not anything had been heard of a missing thighbone. One of the men recalled that the carpenter who had built the inner walls of what was now Gudmundsson's house had spoken of putting a bone between the outer and inner walls as it "would not be in the way there" (it seems it could not be buried in consecrated ground as the identity of the owner was not known).

A fruitless search was made in Gudmundsson's house, which was large and had undergone a number of alterations, until (as established by Professor Haraldsson during his enquiries) the carpenter, Asbjorn Palsson, joined the search and proved able to identify the correct spot. The wall was opened and an unusually long thighbone was found. Gudmundsson had a casket made for it, and it was duly buried in a religious ceremony at Utskalar Church. Runolfsson communicated to express his thanks, and over the years became the medium's chief control, reformed in character and now anxious to help other communicators. As evidence for survival this is potentially a strong case. It was exhaustively researched by Larusdottir and by Professors Haraldsson and Stevenson, who interviewed more than 20 people connected with the case, including the medium and the sitters, and who examined published records to establish whether or not the medium could have come by his information by normal means. As claimed by Runolfsson, the Utskalar Church records did mention the date of his death and his age at death, but reported only that he was believed to have been carried out to sea in the storm, and that his bones were found dismembered much later. A book by the Rev. Sigurdur Sivertsen (*Annals of Sudurnes*), the Minister at Utskalar Church at the time of Runolfsson's death, gave similar details, but was not published until 1953. Neither the church records nor the book made any mention that any of the bones were missing. The two biweekly Icelandic newspapers published at the time of the death made no mention of Runolfsson.

It thus seems highly unlikely that the medium or the sitters could have known of the thighbone, let alone where it was hidden, by normal means. The only possible source of telepathy would seem to have been the carpenter, Asbjorn Palsson. However Palsson would not have known to whom the bone belonged when he found it, as there was no mention of its having been lost. Had he known the identity, he would in any case have simply handed it over for Christian burial (it is assumed he put it in the wall space as it would have been considered disrespectful in Iceland simply to throw away a human bone). Clairvoyance is a possibility, but highly unlikely. Even had the bone been identified clairvoyantly, this would not have told the medium to whom it belonged or led him to the church records to ascertain the details of death. In addition clairvoyance would not explain the continuing presence of Runolfsson after the bone was discovered and buried, and the fact that his personality appeared consistent with what was known of him in life. It is also interesting that Runolfsson initially refused to give his name and incorrectly informed the circle that his bone was "in the sea." It was only when Gudmundsson joined the group that Runolfsson seemed to remember, or to realize for the first time, that the bone was on land and somewhere in Gudmundsson's house. It is also possible that he did not give his name because he did not remember his name, and his absence for some months from the group may have been in order to recall it from some source.

Professors Haraldsson and Stevenson, two of the most perceptive and meticulous investigators of the paranormal and whose names occur at a number of points in this book, go through all the various alternative possibilities to survival and find none of them convincing. They leave the reader to make up his or her own mind, but in my view few who study the evidence with sufficient care can readily dismiss survival as a strong possibility. There are many other cases in the literature of deceased people who have supposedly retained concern for the fate of their mortal remains, and who have not it seems rested easily until these were granted an appropriate burial.

Misleading Drop-in Communicators

Another collection of cases of drop-in communicators is *Hungry Ghosts* by Joe Fisher (1990). I include mention of the book because unless the author was misled throughout by trickery, which seems unlikely for reasons that will become apparent as we progress, it throws important light upon the dangers of taking drop-in communicators – and perhaps some established communicators – at face value. Fisher's experiences took place in Canada, with Australian-born medium Aviva Neumann, who worked primarily in an hypnotic trance established initially in an attempt to help her recover from a life-threatening illness, but which subsequently uncovered her unsuspected mediumistic powers. In the course of many sittings with Avival Neumann at a home circle composed of the hypnotist Roger Belancourt and a small group of friends, a number of drop-in communicators made their presence known. The majority of them claimed to be the spirit guides of those present, and in many cases gave details of their earth lives that contained information that seemed convincing and capable of verification. One of the best examples was "Earnest" (his preferred name, not his real name, which was given later) who over a number of sessions provided a wealth of such details. These, in sum, were as follows:

Real name: *Flying Officer William Alfred Scott of 99 Squadron, Group Three, Bomber Command.*

Description: *Five foot eleven inches tall, dark hair and eyes, weight 11 stone (154 pounds).*

Life history prior to RAF: *Born in Brighton, lived at Hill Road in Bristol, educated at Princess Victoria School and Bristol University, where he read mathematics and engineering and claimed one of his professors was Jonathan Langley.*

RAF career: *Joined up in 1937 aged 20. Stationed at Mildenhall in Suffolk in 1939, then at Newmarket Heath and finally Waterbeach (an air base "cut into the Fens in Cambs." (Cambridgeshire). Flew the "Wimpey," the Vickers Wellington Bomber (which was fully described, down to its 1,000 horsepower Pegasus engines). Participated in anti-shipping strikes including that on the German battleship "Tirpitz" and in leaflet dropping and bombing missions over Norway and Germany (specifically Cologne and the Ruhr).*

"Earnest" gave a quite remarkable series of descriptions of his wartime experiences, including the Latin motto for his squadron, the squadron badge (a leaping puma), the squadron nickname (*The Madras Presidency Squadron*), the name of his commanding officer (Wing Commander Linnell), and the names of senior officers successively in charge of Group Three (Air Vice Marshalls Cochrane and Harrison), the bombing by a German Dornier DO 17 of the White Hart Hotel and the post office in Norwich Road, Newmarket, the fact that he and his colleagues had to sleep in the grandstands at Rowley Mile Racecourse when they first moved to Newmarket, that two Wellingtons had crashed on take-off at Waterbeach (one of them piloted by Harry Sergeant), that the Wellingtons carried 4,000 pound bombs and that some of them were equipped with 48-foot hoops under the wings to counter Nazi "tactical weapons," and that his squadron moved to Ambala in India in 1942 although he did not accompany them as he was transferred to 147 squadron. He also gave the names of his nephew (William Scott of Bristol), his uncle (Wilfred

Scott of Lyme Regis) and his aunt (Lilly Williams of Brighton), and the names of two friends, Flying Officer Willie Douglas (later killed) and Flight Lieutenant Derek Watford. His own death occurred not while on active service but in a bombing raid on Coventry, which he was visiting at the time. He gave the exact location of his death as Sandrich Street, north-east of the cathedral.

So spontaneous and confident was Earnest's delivery through the entranced medium that Fisher set out enthusiastically to seek verification. Research in Toronto libraries confirmed that RAF bases had indeed existed at Mildenhall, at Newmarket Heath, and at Waterbeach. 99 Squadron was also found to exist, and its badge and nickname were confirmed, as was the nickname, Wimpey, of the Wellington bomber. As an Australian living in Canada, born after the war and with no expressed interest in RAF Bomber Command, the medium appeared unlikely to have known these details, although she had been in England for four months in 1967, without apparently visiting any of the places mentioned in Earnest's account.

It was clear that research into the other details given by Earnest could only be satisfactorily undertaken in England, to which Fisher traveled in 1987, leaving behind a deposition of the transcribed Earnest material with a Toronto lawyer as proof that it had all been obtained before the trip. Once in England, Fisher visited the Public Records Office at Kew, and looked up details of 99 Squadron's war record. He soon confirmed the existence of Wing Commander Linnell, from a signature at the bottom of a document, and also found details of the bombing and leaflet-dropping raids over Germany and Norway, and of the attacks on shipping. The Squadron's moves from Mildenhall to Newmarket Heath to Waterbeach were also confirmed, together with the fact that sleeping accommodation in Newmarket was provided at the Rowley Mile grandstands. The German bombing raid on Newmarket High Street, which demolished the post office and damaged the White Hart while the squadron was stationed there, was also confirmed. Even the type of German bomber that carried out the raid, the Dornier Do 17, was correct.

Everything seemed to fit, and there was a further breakthrough in that the name of the British pilot whose plane shot down the Dornier (one of the few instances in the whole war of one bomber shooting down another) was given in the records, J. R. Goodman (later Group Captain Goodman). Fisher was then able to track Goodman down to Frogmore in Devon, and to speak to him by telephone. This resulted in the first set-back, as Goodman had no recollection of a Flying Officer Scott in 99 Squadron – he recalled only a pilot, 'a fat sergeant', called Malcolm Scott. Fisher returned to the Public Record Office and looked through all the 99 Squadron Log Books, but found no mention of a Flying Officer William Alfred Scott (although Sergeant Malcolm Scott was there), and no mention of Harry Sergeant who was said by "Earnest" to be the pilot of one of the two Wellingtons that crashed at Waterbeach. Worse was to follow. It transpired that Wing Commander Linnell had in fact left the squadron in 1936, a year before "Earnest" said he himself joined the RAF. Neither of Earnest's two claimed friends, Willie Douglas and Derek Watford, appeared in the RAF List of all personnel, and – by now perhaps predictably – there was no mention of Flying Officer William Scott.

Even worse was to come. At St. Catherine's House in London, which then kept the record of all births, marriages, and deaths from 1837 onwards, no William Alfred Scott who had been born in Brighton in 1917 or who had died in Coventry in 1944 was listed. Further enquiries revealed that there was no Hill Road or Princess Victoria School in Bristol, that no William Alfred Scott had entered Bristol University in the years 1935–37, and that no Professor Jonathan Langley had been on the academic staff. Other enquiries revealed there was no Sandrich Street in Coventry, where "Earnest" said he had been killed. However, Fisher then visited Norman Didwell, who had served with 99 Squadron in 1939–41 and who had formed the Squadron Association in 1976, and played him all the tapes on which "Earnest" had communicated. Didwell's response to them was encouraging. "He was there. He must have been there. It's very convincing. Who would have known about us sleeping in the grandstands? You'd only know that – and several other things mentioned there – if you'd been in the squadron." Didwell also confirmed the crashes at Waterbeach, the 4,000 pound bombs (99 Squadron was one of the first to be equipped with them), the Squadron's move to Ambala, India, the chasing of the battleship *Tirpitz*, the names of Air Vice Marshalls Cochrane and Harrison who successively commanded Group 3 between 1942 and 1945, and the 48-foot hoops under the wings to detonate mines. He knew of no Flying Officer Scott, but found the rather pompous English accent which had come from Earnest as he communicated through the entranced Avuva Neumann was "very, very familiar," and reminiscent of none other than Sergeant Malcolm Scott. Subsequently Jim Ware, a rear-gunner who had flown with Scott and whom Fisher also consulted, agreed. "That's right, that's right. There's a lot there that's strikingly true and it sounds quite like Scotty. He spoke quick like that ... He was a wealthy bloke ... I think his only worry was that he wasn't commissioned." Scott had joined the Squadron after the outbreak of war, and Jim Ware believed he had been killed while serving with an Operational Training Unit.

Fisher later learned that "Earnest," communicating through the medium, had become very evasive and defensive once Fisher had left for England, and on Fisher's return he parried all the angry questions put to him by Fisher with the excuse that he had "covered his tracks" as he did not wish Fisher to identify him. He was, he claimed, involved in trying to work off a karmic debt, and knowledge of his identity would have impeded his progress. "Scott" was his real name, but he had given false Christian names, "I gave you all the information you needed. You could have tracked me down but I'm rather glad that you did not because I did not want to imperil my charge [i.e. the individual in the group for whom he claimed to be the guide] in any way whatsoever." This sorry attempt to excuse himself hardly improved matters, and Fisher discovered that other communicators whose details he tried to investigate – in Engand again and also in Greece – had given the same mish-mash of accurate general facts but misleading personal details. Even his own self-styled "guide," a Greek girl "Filipa" who had communicated with him through the medium and of whom he had become inordinately fond – she even began to contact him directly, presumably through his own incipient mediumship – was found to be as guilty of this dissembling as the others.

Fisher's conclusions at the end of his investigation were that much of the information received through the medium was paranormal in origin. So many obscure details were correct that on the balance of probabilities it seemed unlikely in the extreme that they could have come from the medium's own mind. He was also greatly impressed with the extraordinary insight "Filipa" seemed to have into his own inner being. "Even in duplicity, she knew and understood me more precisely than anyone." However, rather than propose unconscious telepathy/clairvoyance and dramatization by the medium's sub-personalities, Fisher considered that the communicators were in fact spirits motivated by a desire for the "psychic subversion" of the living, that they were earthbound entities that exerted their influence through the medium rather than by direct contact with the minds of the sitters. His term for them, "hungry ghosts," is the Tibetan Buddhist term for so-called earthbound spirits, spirits of the dead that remain fixated by the earth and obtain their gratification vicariously by dominating the living. Fisher sought to warn those interested in mediumship and communication of the dangers of spirit contact – dangers that have been emphasized many times by those who counsel against the use of ouija boards and of other homegrown attempts such as hypnosis to make spirit contact.

Was Fisher correct in his conclusions? His attempts to check up on the personal details were thorough and painstaking. And his attempts to confront the various "guides" who communicated through the medium with the discrepancies between their personal details and the true facts of the situation gave them every opportunity to explain themselves correctly. Yet he was met with nothing other than evasion – sanctimonious attempts to put the blame upon him for being too literal in his thinking, futile claims that the evidence would check out if he looked hard enough, and blatant denials of the facts used by him to expose the communicators' duplicity. If indeed the paranormal explanation for the details that did turn out to be correct is accepted – and at face value it seems difficult to quarrel with this explanation – the idea of mischievous earthbound spirits intent upon manipulating and if possible possessing the living would seem to fit the facts. More will be said about supposed earthbound spirits when we discuss the nature of an afterlife in Chapter 18, but the point to stress here is that if Fisher was correct in his diagnosis we need not take this to apply to other – perhaps most other – mediumistic communications. No question of attempts at gaining power over sitters emerges from the work of the other mediums we have discussed so far. Fisher's group was unusual in that the communicators all claimed to be the "guides" of members of the group, rather than simply friends and relatives. A "guide" was individually identified for each group member, who was then referred to as the "charge" of the guide concerned. Also unusual were the attempts by the "guides" to enter into close emotional relationships with their "charges" (Fisher's earthly relationship even broke up due to his emotional over-dependence on his "guide" Filipa).

The idea that spirits can willfully deceive mediums and sitters is supported by the Reverend Aelwyn Roberts, a Welsh Anglican priest whose diocesan duties included working with people who feared they were the victims of hauntings. Over 40 years Roberts built up a dossier of literally hundreds of cases working in harness with a successful medium, the similarly named Elwyn Roberts. Convinced by his experiences of the reality of the spirit communication, the Reverend Roberts notes in one of his books (Roberts 2002) that spirits can be jokers, out to trick gullible mortals, not necessarily maliciously but much in the way some humans enjoy taking a rise out of the serious-minded. He gives an example of a deceased communicator, contacted through the medium Elwyn Roberts during one of their joint investigations, who claimed to be a nurse who had committed suicide in 1934 on finding herself pregnant. She gave many apparently accurate details of herself, including the place of her suicide (now covered by a housing estate but found marked on an old ordnance survey map by the Rev. Roberts) and the non-conformist chapel (named 'Capel Coch' in Welsh, which means "Red Chapel" – very unusual as Welsh chapels are customarily given biblical names) where she was buried. Roberts excitedly followed each clue, and finally tracked down the chapel, which agreed with her description in every detail – except one. There was no burial ground there. The nearest was fully two miles away in another village. The whole episode seemed like an elaborate treasure hunt, with a metaphorical slap in the face and loud spirit laughter at the end of it.

If these are earthbound spirits who have once had a physical existence, what might their true identities have been? It is tempting to suppose, as demonstrated perhaps by "Earnest," that some of them were involved in the environments to which they referred but that there were things about themselves that they wished to hide, hence their reluctance to give their true identities. In the case of "Earnest" at least, there seem to have been attempts to glamorize their life histories. "Earnest" may indeed have been a member of 99 Squadron (whether as Sergeant Scott or not); the ex-members of the

Squadron interviewed by Fisher certainly thought so. By claiming to be a Flying Officer (equivalent to an army lieutenant) did he wish to hide the fact that, although a pilot, he had failed to obtain a commission? Habitual liars in this life often invent false life-histories for themselves, and not only do they have a total disregard for the truth, they actually appear sometimes to believe their own falsehoods. Those who work with communicators sometimes insist that people do not change their natures simply by dying. Dr. Carl Wickland, who we mention in the next paragraph, puts it that "Death does not make a saint of a sinner, nor a sage of a fool. The mentality is the same as before and individuals carry with them their old desires, habits, dogmas, faulty teachings, indifference, or disbelief in a future life." To this the Reverend Elwyn Edwards, whom I know personally and whose work I respect, might add that they also seem to retain their pleasure at making a fool out of an honest hard-working clergyman. If this is indeed the case, the dissembling of "Earnest" and of his fellow self-styled "guides" makes perfect, if discreditable, sense.

Some groups sitting regularly with mediums act as "rescue circles," intent upon encouraging earthbound spirits to contact them in order that they may be convinced of the fact of their deaths, and encouraged to move on to higher things. Many examples of such rescue work are given in Dr. Carl Wickland's *Thirty Years Among the Dead* (1978). Wickland, a medical doctor specializing in psychiatry, sitting with his wife Anna Wickland who was a medium, apparently contacted an impressive number of deeply disturbed spirits, many of them criminals in their earth lives and apparently now possessing some of his psychotic patients, and persuaded them to move on. The book makes interesting reading, but regrettably no real attempt was made by Wickland to check on the identities and personal details given by communicators. This is always a problem when sitters are so convinced of the reality of survival and of spirit communication that they take communicators at their face value. The argument put forward by sitters in defense of this practice is that their intention is to be helpful to communicators, not to ply them with questions about their earth lives that might discourage them from maintaining the contact.

Wickland puts forward two arguments against the possibility that the extensive number of communications received during his work among the "dead" can be explained by the medium's sub-personalities. The first is that "it is manifestly impossible that [Anna Wickland] should have a thousand personalities," and secondly that by allowing the spirits to speak through Anna Wickland he was able to communicate with them and persuade them to move on, with the result that his patients were healed. Such healing, he insisted, could not occur if the voices were simply Anna Wickland's sub-personalities. Similar successful results in healing psychotic patients by freeing them from possessing entities were reported by Dr. Morton Prince (1927), who even without the presence of a medium decided to take the possessive "voices" speaking through two of his patients at face value, and talk to them as if they were real people present in the room with the patient and himself. Morton Prince reasoned with these voices, pointing out that they were causing great suffering to the patients, and at the same time inhibiting their own spiritual development. The voices belonged to people known to the two patients when alive, and known to have some kind of grudge against them. Morton Prince assured the voices that they had a reason for the grudge they were carrying, and requested their forgiveness. He then asked them to see things from the viewpoint of the patient, and counseled them that "there is a power in the universe" which responds to spirits prepared to forgive in this way, and that "there are kindly intelligences about you who will gladly be of assistance to you." The patient was then instructed not to reply should they hear the possessing voice again. The treatment, it seems, was successful.

In the case of both Wickland and Morton Prince we could quite reasonably argue that the whole thing was psychological, i.e. that the patients concerned had in the past experienced overpowering guilt about certain tendencies in themselves, and could only deal with this guilt by massively repressing it into the unconscious. This repressed guilt then re-emerged into consciousness, personified as an accusing and invasive "voice" and producing classic symptoms of paranoid schizophrenia. The patient was then cured, according to this explanation, by the fact that in their different ways both Wickland and Prince, with the patient present, allowed themselves to respond to the "voice" as if it was a credible fact, thus satisfying the patient's need to be taken seriously, an important ingredient in any attempt to heal mental disorders. Against this explanation is the fact that if the "voices" were simply symptoms of deep-seated mental disorders in the patients rather than the cause, then we would expect their removal to be followed by symptom substitution. That is, other symptoms of paranoia would emerge. The alternative explanation, that the "voices" really were those of earthbound spirits, is supported by the apparent absence of symptom substitution. Further support, if of a limited kind, is provided by the fact that Prince's method failed to work with two of his other patients whose "voices" were said to come from a number of spirits whose identities were not known. This prevented Prince from addressing them with the same directness that he employed in the successful cases. Wickland, we can suppose, was more effective than Prince because he allowed the "voices" of unidentified spirits to possess his entranced wife so that he could hold long conversations with them, invite them to give their names and personal details, and then speak directly to them.

Not the least of the impressions left with the reader after studying *Thirty Years Among the Dead* is the dedication that Anna Wickland brought to the task of rescuing supposed earthbound spirits and freeing Dr. Wickland's patients from their apparent possessive power. For 30 years and more she sat entranced while unfamiliar voices spoke through her, and her husband patiently conversed with them. Was the whole thing a charade on her part undertaken simply to please her husband? Three things suggest otherwise. Firstly, as we have already said, Dr. Wickland's patients appeared to recover – no easy matter at the end of the nineteenth and the beginning of the twentieth century, before the development of modern psychotropic drugs. Secondly, Wickland, who had had plenty of professional experience at identifying and analyzing the vagaries of human behavior, clearly never suspected that Anna Wickland was play-acting. And thirdly, if play-acting she was, Anna Wickland must have had a very robust psychological constitution to take the role of supposedly severely disturbed earthbound spirits for 30 years, improvising all her lines as she went along in her pretended trance, without it taking a toll on her own mental stability.

The unfortunate fact is that more steps were not taken to apply the scientific method – inimical as it might have been for the primary purpose of providing treatment for deeply troubled patients – and thus demonstrate the extent of Anna Wickland's mediumistic gift. Opportunities were lost in other areas of her work as well. For example, she made an agreement with a close friend of hers, Mrs. Lackmund, that whichever of them died first would return to give the message "spirit return is true." In the event, Mrs. Lackmund was the first to go, and subsequently returned in a dream to give the agreed message. How much better it would have been if each lady had decided on her own message, told no one, and left it in a sealed envelope in the hands of an attorney. The protocol would still not have been perfect. We would have to rely on Anna Wickland's word that Mrs. Lackmund's message had been kept secret from her. But if Mrs. Lackmund had managed to communicate a message that, on opening the envelope turned out to be accurate, how much more convincing this would have been. Many attempts have been made by others to convey post-mortem messages, but no unequivocally successful case has as yet been reported.

A different kind of rescue work is reported by Air Chief Marshall Lord Dowding, Head of Fighter Command during the Battle of Britain in the Second World War (Dowding 1945). Dowding, a member of a regular home circle and a guest at many others, was particularly concerned to provide support for young servicemen who had died in the war and whom he feared were still in a state of confusion and despair. Dowding's interest in survival had led him to write an earlier book, *Many Mansions*, which looked at possible spirit communications from a purely theoretical point of view. The book resulted in his receiving invitations to attend sittings with various mediums, and on accepting one of these the medium's guide quoted to him the final line of another book he had just finished writing, namely "Now, therefore, as I lay down my sword, I take up my pen and testify." The book was still awaiting a publisher, and Dowding assures us that nobody present at the sitting knew of this sentence or even of the book's existence. Further communications, through independent voice and materializations, enabled him to make contact with his dead parents, his wife, and with other relations and friends. One deceased friend, a Colonel Gasgoine, communicated with him through four separate mediums, three of them unknown to each other. It was these experiences that convinced him of the reality of survival and the possibility of communications with those in the next world.

Dowding appeared to believe that his readers were already convinced of survival, thus he gives no evidence that those communicating with him were who they said they were. This is particularly unfortunate, as due to his role in the Battle of Britain Dowding was a national hero, a man of international standing well known at the time both in Britain and abroad. Had he produced firm evidence to support his conviction that survival is a fact, the impact upon public opinion would have been impressive. As it is, Dowding is virtually ignored, and those few who do know his writings mostly dismiss him as a harmless eccentric, a sensitive, humane man who, deeply disturbed by the loss of so much young life during the Second World War and the part he perforce had played in this loss as head of Fighter Command, had turned to a belief in survival in an attempt to reassure himself that those who had died had not simply been snuffed out for ever. It is true that people can turn to spiritual beliefs as a way of compensating for existential anxieties, but in my review elsewhere of the relevant research (Fontana 2003) I summarize extensive evidence that does not support the view that fear of death is a frequent factor in bringing people to spiritual beliefs and to the attendant belief in a life after death.

The Cross-Correspondences

Similar in some ways to drop-in communications in that the communicators were in some cases not well known to the mediums and did not make contact in order to communicate with sitters, the *Cross-Correspondences* are considered by many knowledgeable judges to be among the very best – if not *the* very best – evidence we have for survival of death, and moreover for survival of death with memory and intellectual vigor apparently undimmed. They appear to represent an ambitious experiment from beyond the grave, daring and imaginative in scope and designed not only to provide this evidence but to do so in a manner that defies explanation by the Super-ESP hypothesis.

This experiment took the form of elaborate puzzles¬, depending for the most part upon an erudite knowledge of Greek and Latin classic texts and English poetry, to which clues were given by the communicators through a number of different people with mediumistic abilities, all working in isolation from each other. By themselves, none of the clues made much sense. Only when put together did they make clear the solution to the puzzle. As a variant of this puzzle, the same piece of information, again typically based upon the classics, was communicated to each of the recipients, still working in isolation from each other, and attention then drawn to this fact by one of the communicators. The experiment was even more impressive in that it went on not for weeks or even months, but for some 30 years (1901–1930).

The experiment began at a time when many of the founders of the Society for Psychical Research had passed away. These included Frederick Myers, who died aged 58 in 1901 during his term as serving president, Professor Henry Sidgwick the founding president who died in 1900 aged 62, and Edmund Gurney the founding honorary secretary who died in 1888 aged only 38 (it seems ironic in some ways that three men, so interested in the question of survival, should all have died before their time). Later, in 1910, another leading figure in the SPR, Professor Henry Butcher, passed away, and he was followed in 1912 by Professor A. W. Verrall (not a member of the SPR but interested in its work). All five of these men were gifted classicists, a breed of scholars with a breadth and depth of scholarship rarely seen now in our more hurried, information-sodden, and inescapably superficial age. In addition to these five, two further individuals took part in the experiment, Professor Francis Maitland Balfour, brother of Arthur and Gerald Balfour (both eminent politicians who later became 1st and 2nd Earl Balfour respectively), one of the most brilliant men of his generation and by all accounts one of the most generous and courteous, who died in a climbing accident aged only 31, and Catherine Lyttelton, who died of typhus at 25, and who is the main figure in one of the cases I summarize below.

The principal mediums in receipt of communications from these seven gifted individuals, were Mrs. Margaret Verrall, lecturer in Classics at Newnham College, Cambridge and wife of Professor A. W. Verrall; her daughter Helen Verrall (later the wife of W. H. Salter, who served as Honorary Secretary and subsequently as President of the SPR); Mrs. Holland (a pseudonym for Alice Kipling, sister to Rudyard Kipling, whose married name was Alice Fleming), who lived in India; Mrs. Willett (a pseudonym for Mrs. Coombe-Tennant, a Justice of the Peace and a leading figure in Welsh cultural and political life – a closely guarded secret at the time); Mrs. King (a pseudonym for Dame Edith Lyttelton); and Mrs. Leonora Piper. Only the last-named was a professional medium, and it would be difficult to find a more illustrious group of Victorian ladies. Writing of them in his excellent, if brief, summary of some aspects of the cross correspondences, H. F. Saltmarsh (1938), a notable member of the SPR at the time, put it that:

> ... the question of fraud can hardly arise; no reasonable person could suggest that a group of ladies of the culture and intelligence of those here involved, would combine together to carry out a scheme of concerted cheating ... and persist in the practice for over 30 years. Moreover,

it is hard to assign any motive for such conduct ... had it been for the sake of "showing up"
the investigators, the scheme missed fire for the plot was never divulged.

All the ladies practiced automatism in addition to any other mediumistic gifts they may have had. Automatism, more popular among mediums then than it is now, involves holding a pen or pencil in contact with a sheet of paper, and allowing the hand to move of its own volition. Although initially the hand is likely to remain still, it is said that with patient daily practice many people eventually find their hand starts to move, producing intelligible sentences. Usually the writer is unaware of what is being written until the session is over. Gifted automatists, such as Mrs. Leonora Piper, are able to produce evidence in this way that appears to originate from discarnate minds.

In view of the importance of automatism to the cross-correspondences it is worth summarizing what three of the women said about their work. Mrs. Verrall reported that she did not look at the paper as she was writing, and although she was usually aware at the time what language her hand was using she consciously perceived only a word or two of it, and on completing the script had often even forgotten these words, so quickly did her recollection of the experience fade. Even when she made a conscious effort to remember what it was her hand had been writing, she was unable to do so. Mrs. Willett reported that she first discovered she could produce automatic writing in childhood, but abandoned the practice until personal circumstances prompted her to take it up again in adult life. Unlike Mrs. Verrall and Mrs. Holland, each individual word (though not the sense of what was being written) seemed to form in her brain a fraction of a second before being written by her hand. Later she began to receive mental communications, which she wrote down as she received them, and later still sometimes went into trance and spoke these communications. The third automatist, Mrs. Holland, revealed that her first experiences of automatic writing were through poetry, which her hand produced far more rapidly than her attempts at conscious composition (she was in fact a poet of some note). She noted that after reading Myers' *Human Personality and its Survival of Bodily Death* an immediate change took place in her scripts in that they now appeared to be communications from Myers himself and from Sidgwick and Gurney. Like Mrs. Verrall, Mrs. Holland was unaware of what was being written, and although fully conscious in the early years, later had to use auto-suggestion to prevent herself falling into trance while the writing was taking place.

Mrs. Holland's automatic poetry is a convenient place at which to start summarizing the cross-correspondence case. She herself considered that the verses she wrote automatically were "often childishly simple in wording and jingling in rhyme," but "rarely trivial in subject," and noted that sometimes they appeared to touch on survival and even on spirit communication. Reading them now the poems are certainly not without merit, as we can see if I quote two of the examples she sent to Alice Johnson, then Honorary Secretary of the SPR, who was one of the chief investigators of the cross correspondences. In her letter to Alice Johnson, Mrs. Holland wrote that her automatic verses rarely included facts but that on one notable occasion, while staying at a palazzo in Italy for the first time, she felt the impulse to write, and did so while keeping up a conversation with the two friends who were with her. The result, with its strangely haunting quality, was:

Under the orange tree
Who is it lies?
Baby hair that is flaxen fair,
Shines when the dew on the grass is wet,
Under the iris and violet,
'Neath the orange tree
Where the dead leaves be,
Look at the dead child's eyes!

"This is very curious" remarked one of her friends when the poem was completed and read to her, "there is a tradition that a child is buried in the garden here, but I know you have never heard of it." Not only had Mrs. Holland never heard of it, she had not at that point even been into the garden (Johnson 1908). Here is the second example of Mrs. Holland's automatic verses sent to Alice Johnson.

I whom he loved, am a ghost,
Wandering weary and lost.
I dare not dawn on his sight,
(windblown weary and white).
He would shudder in hopeless fright,
He who loved me the best.
I shun the paths he will go,
Because I should frighten him so,
(weary and lacking rest).

I whom he loved am a shade,
Making mortals afraid,
Yet all that was vile in me,
The garb of mortality,
The body that I used to be,
Is moldering out of sight.

I am but a waiting soul,
Pain-purified, seeking its goal,

Why should he dread the sight?
If I showed him my white bones
Under the churchyard stones,
Or the creatures that creep and rest
On what was once my breast,
He who loved me the best
Would have good cause for fright,
But my face is only pale,
My form like a windblown veil,
Why should he dread the sight?

Should I beat on the window pane,
He would think it the wind and rain,
If he saw my pale face gleam
He would deem it a stray moonbeam
Or the waft of a passing dream.
No thought for the lonely dead,
Buried away out of sight.
And I go from him veiling my head,
Windblown weary and white.

The poem was written down by Mrs. Holland exactly as it came to her, without polishing or altering it in any way, and with her hand moving so rapidly that she was rarely aware of any word that was being formed. Reading it through afterwards she was surprised to find it had a form of its own. Personally I would not class this form as childishly simple, but rather as resembling good verse written for children (after the manner, for example, of Frances Cornford), which requires no little poetic ability on the part of the writer. Produced as automatic writing it either demonstrates the remarkable creative powers of the unconscious, or provides evidence of genuine spirit contact. If the latter, then it reminds us we have no need of the superstitious dread with which much of the human race regards ghosts and apparitions. Perhaps more importantly, it seems to tell us that love survives death, and that there may be a yearning by the deceased to communicate this love to those on earth.

This yearning is particularly evident in one of the most evidential of the many cases that occurred during the years of the cross-correspondences and in which five of the automatists (but principally Mrs. Willett) featured, the so-called *Palm Sunday Case*. The case is long and complicated and was set out in full by Jean Balfour (The Countess of Balfour) in 1960, and an excellent summary appears in Roy (1996). Briefly, it concerns Mary Catherine Lyttleton (known as "May" to her family), who died in 1875, and Arthur Balfour (First Earl Balfour), Prime Minister of Britain 1902–1905 and Foreign

Secretary 1916-1919. Balfour fell in love with Mary Lyttleton and it seems that she returned his affections, but before he could propose she died tragically of typhus on Palm Sunday, which in 1875 fell on March 21st. Heartbroken, Arthur Balfour never married, but unless prevented by urgent political matters spent every Palm Sunday in contemplation and remembrance of Mary Lyttleton with Lavinia Talbot (Mary's elder sister) and her husband Edward Talbot, Warden of Keble College Oxford and afterwards Bishop of Winchester.

Throughout the 30 years of the cross-correspondences, communications were registered by the automatists that seemed to indicate Mary Lyttleton's love for Arthur Balfour was as steadfast after her death as was his love for her, and that she wished that he should be assured of this. However, it was not until Mrs. Willett produced an automatic script on March 31, 1912 (interestingly also a Palm Sunday) that Mrs. Sidgwick and Gerald Balfour, both of whom were closely following the cross-correspondences, finally recognized the communicator appeared to be Mary Lyttleton, and that it was her relationship with Arthur Balfour to which reference was being made. Mrs. Willett's script implied Palm Sunday (*"the day to which an allusion is wanted ... not the date but the day – It moves according to ... the Moon – but it is the day, that is full of meaning"*), and referred to memory casting *"down thy wreathed shell"* (the Lyttleton coat of arms contains shells), and to *"graves of long ago."* It also made an implied reference to *The Blessed Damozel,* a poem by Dante Gabriel Rossetti (*"what is the poem where Rossetti speaks of a dead sister?"*), mentioned *"an old story yet ever new,"* *"the love that waits beyond death,"* *"roses for a maiden dead,"* *"My love involves the love before – I shall not lose thee though I die,"* and *"the spirit broke the bonds – soared and yet hovers."*

Gerald Balfour was careful not to mention that the communicator might be Mary Lyttleton – or that a romance had existed between her and his brother Arthur – to Mrs. Willett or to the other automatists until July 1912, prior to which they had no knowledge of either piece of information. And from 1912 onwards, as a matter of policy, he and the other SPR members investigating the case (principally Alice Johnson and Mrs. Sidgwick) kept all the automatists in the dark about any of their interpretations of the scripts.

It was after Mrs. Willett received a script in July 1912 containing the words *"Look back, far back I come. Years ago have I been at the door. Shall I ever reach him?"* that the investigators looked back at the scripts received from 1901 to that date in the light of the knowledge that it appeared to be Mary Lyttleton and Arthur Balfour to whom reference was being made, and it was only at this point that it became clear that cross-correspondences received by the other automatists had also been referring to this very material. I have space for only small extracts from the many communications that finally convinced Arthur Balfour and others associated with the case that Mary Lyttleton had indeed survived death and wished the fact to be known. The extracts are necessarily much abbreviated, but they give something of the flavor of the case.

The first thing that the investigators noticed when they looked back at the early scripts written by the automatists between 1901 and 1912 was that those by Mrs. Holland and Mrs. Verrall and her daughter contained references to *"something laid aside with care that once was worn,"* to something treasured in a metal box or chest associated with a lock of hair – *"lying in a chest it gleams," "the lock of hair – that is the link," "ask about the chest," "love is the bond," "the hair of Berenice," "hair in the temple."* There were also references to a line from Rossetti's *The Blessed Damozel*, to *"her hair had grown just long enough,"* to "King Arthur," to periwinkles, to a *"small gold box highly ornamented and embossed,"* to *"royal purple,"* and to *"scallop shells"* (which feature in the arms of the Lyttleton family). In addition there were numerous classical references that related back to these various topics.

All these references were highly relevant to Mary Lyttleton, and those to the lock of hair and the casket particularly so because in 1888, three years after Mary Lyttleton's death and during Arthur Balfour's Palm Sunday visit to the Talbots, her sister Lavinia had shown him (in Lavinia's words) "a beautiful thick and long strand of May's hair, with the pretty wave and gold color in it." Mary Lyttleton had been particularly noted for her beautiful hair, and some of it had been cut off to ease her discomfort during her last illness. Arthur Balfour then had a lovely bronze and silver box made in which to keep the hair, lined with purple and decorated with periwinkles and other flowers and engraved with the quotation from Corinthians beginning with the words " ... this corruptible must put on incorruption and this mortal must put on immortality." In the context of this lock of hair and the silver box, the relevance of the reference in the scripts to Berenice, who in *De Como Berenices*, a poem by the first-century BCE Roman poet Catallus, cut off her hair and dedicated it in the temple for the safe return of her husband, became clear. Clearer still was the relevance in the 1912 script of the reference to Dante Gabriel Rossetti's poem to his dead sister, *The Blessed Damozel*, the most apposite lines of which tell that she:

.... *leaned out*
From the gold bar of Heaven

Surely she lean'd o'er me – her hair
Fell all about my face ...

'I wish that he were come to me:
'For he will come,' she said,
'Have I not pray'd in Heaven? – on earth,
'Lord, Lord, has he not pray'd?
'Are not two prayers a perfect strength?

'And shall I feel afraid?
'When round his head the aureole clings,
'And he is clothed in white,
'I'll take his hand and go with him
'To the deep wells of light;
'As unto a stream we will step down,
'And bathe there in God's sight'.

This strain of longing runs through all the remaining verses. I know of no poem in the English language that speaks more strongly or more beautifully of the wish of a spirit to be reunited with a loved one still on earth (and around whom she lets fall her hair). Note also what may be Mary Lyttleton's attempt to communicate her feelings for Arthur Balfour in the poem that had come through Mrs. Holland's automatic writing and which I quoted earlier. Alice Johnson had published the poem in 1908, but the investigators only recognized its significance when looking back through the scripts in 1912, and did not discover the existence of the lock of hair and the silver box until 1916 (Arthur Balfour was not himself one of the investigators of the case, and – an intensely private man – had kept the fact of the construction of the box to himself until that date. At no time during the remaining 20 years or so of the cross-correspondences were the automatists told of the lock of hair and the silver box.

All these various symbolic references to Mary Lyttleton appear highly significant, as are the references that continued to come in the following years. For example, in 1916 the following words appeared in a trance utterance from Mrs. Willett:

The May Flower ... but it is not of a ship but of a person I want it said ... A slender girl with quantities of hair worn in heavy plaits ... And add to that Silvery Sirmio ... The lock of hair - that is the link ... Berenice's vow. She cut the lock from her head. It had been there ... through the years of the past ... All these classical allusions are scattered about and disguise a reality which touches the Blessed Damozel ... The May blossom has never ceased to bloom unfading there ... And through another sonnet "And if God will, I shall but love thee better after Death" ... The Lock of hair Berenice. The symbol but oh! behind it lay the beating human heart with all its faithfulness and love, and its passionate belief in the faithful knight.

It will be remembered that Mary Lyttleton was known as "May" rather than "Mary" to her family, hence the appropriateness of "The May Flower," which the communicator insists through the entranced Mrs. Willet is "not a ship but a person." Note the appropriateness of many of the references in the communication, particularly those to the lock of hair, to the "Blessed Damozel," to the line of poetry (from one of Elizabeth Barratt Browning's *Sonnets from the Portuguese*, published incidentally the year Mary Lyttleton was born) that speaks of love continuing after death.

As already made clear, the above quotations are only samples of the many references that convinced Arthur Balfour, his brother Gerald, and the other distinguished investigators of the paranormality of the *Palm Sunday Case* and of much else of the cross-correspondences. The material contained in the cross-correspondences also provided further confirmation of survival for Sir Oliver Lodge, who took a close interest in the case. For those who may question why so much symbolism was used in the scripts when Mary Lyttleton and the other communicators might simply have given her name and spoken openly of her undying love for Arthur Balfour, the answer seems to be that their intention throughout the cross-correspondences was to bring through information in such a way that no paranormal explanation (such as the Super-ESP hypothesis) short of survival would suffice to account for it. The classical references and symbols relating to Mary Lyttleton in the *Palm Sunday Case* that had come through the automatists from 1901 to 1912 carried no meaning at the time either to them or to the SPR investigators to whom they sent each of their scripts as soon as it was received. This effectively rules out telepathy from the living. What living mind could have been responsible for successfully sending carefully designed snippets of information independently and selectively to each of the automatists for these 12 years and the years that followed?

Similarly it seems we can rule out the suggestion that the automatists received their material through clairvoyance. No source existed in the environment that contained all the relevant references, carefully put together and available to be picked up paranormally by automatists who had no link with it, no motivation to make contact with it, and no knowledge even of its existence. We can also rule out precognition. The notion that the automatists may have precognized the moment in the future when the meaning of the *Palm Sunday Case* became clear is patently absurd. The references relevant to the case in their scripts are quite unlike the actual future events surrounding the attempts by the SPR investigators to unravel the various clues given by the scripts. If the automatists could see the future, their scripts would have been about these attempts rather than containing only the obscure references themselves.

Thus it seems, as with many of the other elaborate puzzles that made up the cross-correspondences, that the *Palm Sunday Case* succeeds in fulfilling the apparent intention of the communicators to eliminate any paranormal explanation for the scripts other than that of survival. The only possible alternatives to survival would be that the apparent cross-correspondences between the snippets of information (and their relevance for example to Mary Lyttleton) noted by the investigators were due purely to chance, or that the automatists practiced fraud. The second of these possible explanations would, for the reasons quoted earlier, seem so unlikely as to be effectively beyond consideration, and no hint appears in the literature that fraud was thought by the investigators to be a possibility. Quite apart from the integrity of the ladies concerned and the lack of any motive for fraud, we cannot seriously believe that for 30 years, and at a time when communications between continents (Mrs. Holland was in India, Mrs. Piper in America, and the others in Britain) were very much more difficult than they are now, that the automatists would have managed to remain in constant touch with each other in order to carry out their deception.

In addition, only Mrs. Verrall (a classics lecturer at Newnham College, Cambridge) and Helen Verrall (a classical scholar from the same College) would have had the necessary knowledge to construct the elaborate classical allusions that appeared throughout the scripts. Can we suppose the two women masterminded the whole thing, sending regular quotations to the other automatists to be included in their scripts? Mrs. Verrall was a highly respected member of the SPR, serving on its Council and on its Committee of Reference for many years, and publishing a number of important papers in the *Proceedings*. In her obituary (*Proceedings* LXXII, Vol. XXIX, 1916) Mrs. Sidgwick said of her that it was "the combination in a high degree of two qualities – sympathy and the critical faculty" that made her "so valuable as an investigator." Helen Verrall, Mrs. Verrall's daughter, seems to have inherited her mother's ability both as a classical scholar and as an investigator. She held a number of important posts at the SPR, including in her younger days that of assistant research officer. She contributed many paper to the *Proceedings*, and later became the wife of W. H. Salter, who as mentioned earlier had periods of office both as Honorary Secretary and as President of the SPR, and who was a major investigator of the cross-correspondences and author of *Zoar* (1962), a classic text on survival (which he dedicated to Helen Verrall). Could the two Verralls have wished not only to mastermind the fraud, but to keep it from their highly qualified colleagues for so many years?

What of the other possible normal explanation, namely that the cross-correspondence scripts were so extensive that the same material was likely to appear in several of them by pure coincidence? One could test for this by looking for cross-correspondences between passages taken at random from works of fiction. As the cross-correspondence scripts were written by seven automatists working in isolation from each other we would have to take seven works of fiction by different authors for this exercise, and give different weightings to each of them to mimic the fact that some of the automatists produced far more scripts than others. We would then have to compare the number and nature of the cross-correspondences generated by these meaningful coincidences with those generated by the scripts. Alternatively, we could go through the cross-correspondence scripts and see if they supported a number of purely fictional scenarios. This number would have to be quite extensive, since the scripts are full of apparently meaningful references in addition to those associated with the *Palm Sunday Case*.

Moreman (2003 and 2004) has demonstrated that passages taken at random from a number of books do reveal some cross-correspondences by chance coincidences, and has suggested that together with telepathy and other PSI manifestations by and between the mediums concerned, such coincidences could account for at least some of data even in the best cross-correspondence scripts. This conclusion has been contested by Keen and Roy (2004) who point out not only the voluminous nature of the cross-correspondences but the fact that they are linked together by patterns and specific messages, and that there is nothing approaching a message in the chance coincidences between passages identified by Moreman and others in the random book-based material used by them.

Those who researched the cross-correspondences for the SPR over their many years of production were men and women of outstanding ability both as investigators and as classical scholars. We cannot fall back upon the argument sometimes advanced by critics that such people are just as prone to malobservation as anyone without their background knowledge and meticulous attention to detail. And if one wishes to propose alternative theories to those they advanced after many years spent studying the scripts, then one would at least have to devote to the task something of the care and attention they expended upon it. For the present, the last word seems to belong to Professor Roy, who puts it that "I find that after careful study of the case and the scripts I have to dismiss any question of coincidence or fraud as being wildly improbable" (Roy 1996).

The Cummins-Willett Scripts

Although not involved in the cross-correspondences, Geraldine Cummins (1890–1969) was another noted automatist who produced scripts particularly relevant to the case for survival (see Fryer 1990 for a good account of her life and work). It is convenient to deal with her here, as her most notable scripts consisted of apparent post-mortem communications from Mrs. Willett, who features so prominently in the cross-correspondences (see Cummins 1965 *Swan on a Black Sea*). The starting point for the scripts was a letter written to Cummins in August 1957 by W. H. Salter (mentioned earlier in connection with the cross-correspondences) of the SPR to the effect that a member of the Society who had lost his mother a few months previously would like to give her the opportunity to send him a message. Salter informed Cummins that the case was a particularly interesting one, and that "by the end of the year the evidential significance of the case will probably have declined through the publication of some facts at present known to very few persons" (these facts – still a closely guarded secret at that time and unknown to Cummins – were that "Mrs. Willett" was a pseudonym for Mrs. Coombe-Tennant). In a subsequent letter Salter indicated to Cummins that the SPR member concerned was Major A. H. Coombe-Tennant, but did not give his first names or any other details about him.

Geraldine Cummins agreed to co-operate in trying to contact the Major's mother. At the time Cummins was living in County Cork in Ireland. She had never heard of the Coombe-Tennants, and had no connections with Wales, where Mrs. Coombe-Tennant had lived, or with anyone who might have known her or her family. She did not know what the initials 'A. H' in Major Coombe-Tennant's name stood for. Nevertheless, in her very first script after accepting the assignment, Mrs. Coombe-Tennant (C-T) appears to have made contact. Astor, Geraldine Cummins' control, gave several relevant facts about her, and none that was incorrect (my comments appear in brackets after each of these facts). The most important were that *T-C was old when she died* (she was 81), that she had *lost a son in the First World War aged 19 or 20* (George Christopher Coombe-Tennant was a month short of his twentieth birthday when he was killed in action in 1917), the name of the communicator was *Wyn or Win – can't get more ... may be mistaken* (C-T's first name was Winifred, though this was never shortened to "Win" during her lifetime), and that *there is someone still in the physical body ... Henry or is it Harry?'* (Major A. H. Coombe-Tennant was always known by his second Christian name, Henry).

Geraldine Cummins produced 40 scripts in all (44 if one includes the fact that some scripts were completed in two sessions on the same day) during the assignment, from August 28, 1957 to March 6, 1960. In the second of them Astor reports that "W" was one of the of the communicator's initials, and after this he referred to her again as "Win." Other relevant facts given in the second script were that *Win did automatic writing* (correct; Cummins had not even been told by Salter that she was a medium), that *an old friend of hers named "Gerald" was present with her* (almost all C-T's sittings during the years of the cross-correspondences were carried out with Gerald Balfour, who was an intimate friend, as the sitter), that *Gerald appears as a very old man on the verge of 90* (he died in his ninetieth year), and that *he was a scholar* (correct). *A young man "Francis" was also present with her, a scholar like Gerald, who had died in a fall in a foreign country while engaged in sport* (Francis Balfour, mentioned briefly in the last section as one of the communicators in the cross-correspondences, was Gerald's younger brother and one of the most brilliant men of his generation who had died aged 31 in a climbing accident in the Alps), and that *he and C-T had met and talked on a number of occasions in some odd, unusual circumstances* (Francis Balfour was one of the communicators through C-T during the cross-correspondences – surely "odd unusual circumstances").

During the second script C-T also gave permission *for some papers to be published which when alive she had insisted be kept confidential* (this may refer to her desire to keep her mediumship secret, or to some papers dealing with highly personal matters that are currently being studied with a view to publication by Professor Roy). Many descriptive details of C-T's personality were also given in the script, all of which were recognized as correct when shown by Salter to Major Henry Coombe-Tennant.

In the third script, Astor correctly gave C-T's name as Winifred, and informed Cummins that she [Winifred] now wished to control the automatic writing herself, rather than working through him. From this point onwards C-T does so throughout the script. She communicated that *she was an automatist like Cummins, and that this was "an engrossing interest"* (correct, as we saw from her work with the cross-correspondences) *though she remained "a mere amateur"* (correct – she never took money for her work, and during her lifetime her gift at her own request was a closely-guarded secret known only to Gerald Balfour, Sir Oliver Lodge, Mrs. Sidgwick, and the other SPR investigators of the cross-correspondences), and that *she had been a magistrate* (correct).

In the fourth script "Gerald" (Gerald Balfour) himself communicated and gave some of the difficulties faced by C-T in communicating:

She is "extremely nervous" ... as in the case of old people in the physical body "those who have experienced the full span of life on earth when they come here recall most easily fragmentary memories of the distant past and fail to recollect near events ... we seem to swim in the sea of the automatist's subliminal mind, and any strong current may sweep us away from the memory objectives we have in view ... At any rate the automatist is more isolated in this country – quiet from other human beings than in a town, so [C-T] is less likely helplessly to drift in the strong pull of tide or current ..."

Later on the same day C-T communicated that she *spent many happy years in Morganwg in Wales* (correct; "Morganwg" is the Welsh name for Glamorgan, where C-T spent many years), that her *mother came from there* (correct), that *she met her husband and gave birth to her children in Morganwg* (correct), that *she lived the first seven years of her life "mostly elsewhere"* (probably correct; she was born in England in Gloucestershire), that she and her husband *lived at "Cadox Lodge"* (she had difficulty getting this name through – she and her husband lived at Cadoxton Lodge – though she incorrectly says this was her husband's family home), and that *there was Dorothy ... Eveline and ... Fred* (the names of her two sisters-in-law and her brother-in-law, who was in fact F. W. Myers).

In the fifth script Astor was initially in control again, and although referring to C-T as "Winifred" also wrote that *She tells me she is Mrs. Wills, and she smiles* (this seems like an attempt to get through the name "Mrs. Willett"). C-T herself then refers to *Cambridge ... Cherry, Cherries. Yes, Cherry* (C-T had a great love for Cambridge, where her father was born, and for the church at Cherry Hinton where her forebears were buried and towards whose upkeep she subscribed), that she is *directed by a group who once lived at Cambridge or were connected with it* (the founders of the SPR involved in the cross-correspondences were Cambridge men) and that she *stayed in Cambridge with "good friends"* (she stayed there with the Myers family). She reported that she *had experiences of "celestial places" as a child*, that she *received automatic "scribbles" at that time*, that *her first sitting as an adult was with "a scientist"* (correct; it was Sir Oliver Lodge), that she did her *best work for Gerald* (correct), that *Gerald's wife Betty was particularly kind and supportive* (correct, both as to the name and the behavior). She finished by reporting that *the Cambridge group who were her communicators during her mediumship were still together, and had been joined by Gerald and by "Portia"* (thought to refer to Mrs. Verrall) and *by "the scientist"* (presumably Lodge). She again insisted *I am Mrs. Wills. That is not quite right. Never mind, press on ...*

It was during the writing of this script that Geraldine Cummins realized that C-T was also Mrs. Willett, whose work as a medium Cummins knew from her studies of the SPR publications on the cross-correspondences. There were plenty of clues – her ability as an automatist, her involvement with "Gerald," her links with "Betty" his wife and with "Francis," her links with a "Cambridge group" who were her communicators, and with a "scientist" (Lodge), and her attempt at communicating the name she used as a medium, "Mrs. Wills." Cummins knowledge of Mrs. Willett did not, of course, tell her anything of the life of C-T, and she could not have known the details about C-T given in the scripts.

In the sixth script, "Gerald" is even more directly identified as Gerald Balfour by being referred to as "Gerald B." The bulk of the script consists of a personal letter by C-T to her son, Major Henry Coombe-Tennant, in which C-T speaks of her relationship with him and her other children and gives many details of her emotional life, all of which appear to Major Coombe-Tennant to be correct. She also mentions names and initials correctly, i.e. "your aunt Eveleen" (Myers' wife) and Aunt Eveleen's unhappy son "L" (Leopold Myers), who she correctly says took his own life. The sixth script, written on the September 26, 1957 was the last one before the publication of C-T's obituary in the *SPR Proceedings* in October of that year, in which her identity as Mrs. Willett is revealed. Too many facts about her dual role were now accessible to Cummins by normal means, and accordingly from the seventh script onwards (written in February of the following year) C-T switches her attention from demonstrating her survival to writing with painful honesty of her earthly behavior, her emotions, her perceived shortcomings, her relationships, and her experiences in the afterlife.

The remaining scripts represent an extraordinary document in themselves, and seem to indicate that earthly memories remain after physical death, that emotions are felt as keenly as ever, and that ruthless self-examination is a feature (perhaps an essential feature) of afterlife development. *Swan on a Black Sea* contains comments by Major Coombe-Tenant on the appropriateness or otherwise of this material, and there are also further comments from his elder brother, Alexander. These comments indicate that although not all the communications seem characteristic of their mother (and there are a few errors of fact), the great majority of them do. Taken together with the fact that C-T appears to have effectively demonstrated her identity as C-T and as Mrs. Willett to Cummins in the first six scripts, *Swan on a Black Sea* is a record of mediumship that nobody interested in the possibility of survival can ignore.

A close study of the book leads to the conclusion that the only reasonable alternative explanation to the survival of C-T, with her memories and emotions intact, is that Cummins gained her knowledge by normal means, and kept very quiet about it. Cummins herself gives reasons why this was not the case, and it is difficult to doubt her. For example, in the case of C-T's identity as Mrs. Willett, we would have to suppose that Cummins gained her knowledge from the SPR investigators of the cross-correspondences, even though there is no evidence as to how and when this might have happened, as she had no direct contacts with them. In the case of C-T's personal life and life history, we would have to suppose that Cummins was given these details by people who knew C-T well. Again there is no evidence as to how and when this might have happened. Those who are intent on closing every possible loophole for sensory leakage might argue that the opportunities for Cummins to obtain her information by normal means did exist, however wildly improbably they appear to be. One can only answer that this is so, but such an argument is difficult to sustain with any credibility after a careful reading of *Swan on a Black Sea*.

CHAPTER 9
PROXY CASES

The Edgar Vandy Case

Proxy sittings, in which the sitter deputizes for someone who hopes for information from a deceased, are of particular interest to investigators, as they are intended to avoid the possibility that the medium may get her information telepathically from the mind of the sitter, or simply from what is called "cold reading" (i.e. by picking up clues from the sitter's body language, facial expressions, nods or shakes of the head, age, sex, or even style of clothing and objects such as wedding rings). Many instances of evidence suggestive of survival have come from proxy sittings. One of the best examples – and in the view of some commentators one of the best pieces of evidence for survival available to us – is the Edgar Vandy case (Gay 1957, Broad 1962, McKenzie 1971, Keen 2002). Edgar Vandy, a 38-year-old engineer – and by all accounts a brilliant inventor – was taken on the morning of August 6, 1933 by a friend (NJ) for a day out at a country estate where NJ's sister worked as secretary. The owners of the estate were away at the time, and although Vandy was a poor swimmer he and NJ decided to bathe in the swimming pool in the grounds. Both men changed into swimsuits in some bushes approximately 200 yards from the pool. Vandy was ready first and went on his own to the water, unseen by NJ. When the latter followed him two or three minutes later, he found Vandy face down in the pool and in obvious difficulties. The pool was fed by an underground stream, and the cement bottom was slimy and the water cloudy, and in spite of NJ's attempts at rescue, Vandy slipped from his grasp and began to sink. NJ went to obtain help (the sister only came on the scene at a later stage), but this took time, and it was over an hour later before, in the presence of the police, the pool was half drained and dragged and poor Vandy's body recovered.

At the subsequent inquest it was reported that there were slight abrasions under Vandy's chin, on his right shoulder and on the left side of his body, and his tongue was bitten through. Medical evidence suggested he had entered the pool from the diving board, hit his chin on the bottom, stunned himself, and drowned as a result. The theory that he had been stunned was supported by the fact that less water was found in his lungs than would otherwise have been expected. Vandy's two brothers, George and Harold, were dissatisfied with this verdict. In particular they knew Edgar could not dive, and doubted if he would have used the diving board. A cousin who was an expert swimmer and life-saver visited the pool and suggested it was more likely he had entered at the shallow end and lost his footing on the slippery, steeply-sloping cement bottom. George thought he might have slipped while trying to climb out of the pool, and had hit his chin on the edge. As a member of the SPR, George considered that a medium might be able to obtain more information on the exact cause of death, and six sittings were held with four different mediums, one of whom was Gladys Leonard. False names and addresses were given to the mediums, and the sitting with Mrs. Leonard was a proxy one, with Drayton Thomas deputizing for the Vandy brothers. Thomas had never met the Vandys, and was simply told by letter that they were trying "to obtain more information about a brother who had died recently, and that there was some doubt in the minds of relatives as to the cause of the death." No names or other details were given. Thomas was also asked if he could recommend mediums, and it was he who suggested Mrs. Leonard and the other three mediums (Miss Campbell, Mrs. Mason, and Miss Bacon) used by the Vandys. Careful records were kept of the sittings, and these, with George Vandy's comments, are in the possession of the SPR.

No report of Edgar Vandy's death had appeared in London newspapers, though a brief account of it was given in local newspapers, including the *Sussex Gazette*. Drayton Thomas had a sitting with Gladys Leonard on the September 6, 1933, but as his intention on this occasion was to receive details relating to some of his own relatives, he did not intend to use this as a proxy sitting for the Vandy brothers. Consequently Edgar Vandy was not in his thoughts, and after the exchange of letters he had not been in contact with the Vandy brothers. However, during the sitting Feda, Gladys Leonard's control, suddenly mentioned two initials which fitted respectively the first name of one of the two Vandy brothers interested in the case, Harold Vandy, and that of their recently deceased sister, Minnie Vandy. Feda then added "This may be a proxy case about someone who went out through falling." Thomas replied that this could refer to a case about which he had been asked, but he knew nothing of a fall. Feda than gave the following details:

- *the person concerned was not a boy but not old, and had met with a tragic accident involving a fall* (Thomas replied this might relate to a person with two brothers still living, and asked Feda if light could be thrown on the mysterious circumstances surrounding his death.)

- *no one was at fault; he had had a funny feeling in his head, which he had had before ... he realized the importance of air ... at the dragging, something was ... wrong interpretations given to certain proceedings.*

Taken independently, these communications may not be very impressive. But in the context of the sittings the Vandy brothers subsequently had with the other mediums recommended by Drayton Thomas, they contribute importantly to the case. At the sittings held with the Vandy brothers, shorthand writers were present and a careful record was kept of all that was said. At George Vandy's sitting on September 24, 1933 with Miss Campbell (who was told nothing about Edgar or his death) the shorthand writer was NJ, who was the friend with Edgar Vandy on the fateful day, but who was not known to Miss Campbell. At the sitting Miss Campbell said to George "You have a brother in the spirit world who died as the result of an accident." She then gave the following statements about him, with George Vandy providing only confirmation or rejection to each of them.

- *he shows himself holding a tennis racquet, which is odd as he didn't play tennis* (GV could not confirm this, but subsequently discovered that Edgar had recently been persuaded by his sister to have his photograph taken while he was holding a tennis racquet)

- *there were five children in his family;* (this was then corrected to six – one child had died in infancy)
- *he had a watch* (not a particularly common possession in the 1930s, and a fact unknown to GV at the time but which was subsequently found to be true)
- *his death was quite sudden*
- *he disagrees with the verdict*
- *the shorthand writer (NJ) was with him on his last day*
- *he used to go into NJ's shop* (NJ had two bicycle shops, one of which was frequented by Edgar Vandy).
- *he was taller than GV and ten years younger* (Edgar was eight years younger than George)
- *he had a tooth missing* (Edgar had a broken tooth)
- *he was a wireless expert* (he was involved in inventing and manufacturing machines – see later)
- *he was a competent violinist and also played the banjo* (he played the violin)
- *GV now had two violins that belonged to him, a standard one and a sort of comic instrument* (one was a standard violin, the other a one-stringed fiddle)
- *it was a very sunny day*
- *no one saw him fall*
- *he shows me water. Was there water in connection with his death?*
- *he was dressed in a short swimming suit* (he had borrowed a swimsuit from NJ's sister that did not fit him well).
- *his clothes were at some distance from where he was*
- *he struggled to get his breath*
- *the body was in the water for some time before it was found*
- *he shows me a cigarette case and says it is in his room in a chest of drawers near the window under some carefully folded things* (Edgar Vandy was a non-smoker, but in the chest of drawers near the window and under

some carefully folded underwear GV subsequently found an aluminum soap dish resembling a cigarette case.

At Harold's sitting with Miss Campbell (George and Harold were said not to look alike, and as both gave false names and the shorthand writer was not NJ, there was no reason for Miss Campbell to suspect they were related) on September 30 the medium said:

- *there is a man who passed over very suddenly ... anxious to communicate with you ... as if he passed over feeling he would like to get back to clear matters up ... He is your brother. He says brother*
- *he shows me water. He dived naturally and was killed*

She also made a number of references which seemed to apply to a machine invented and constructed by Edgar, and on which he was working at the time of his death, for drawing accurately letters and decorative work from which copies could then be made by lithography.

- *there were red and green pilot lights on a machine he was making* (George: Vandy was working on such a machine; no details had been published; the machine was a secret and only one prototype had been built)
- *he had been helped in the construction by someone called Mac* (Mr. MacNamara, known familiarly as Mac, had worked with him on the machine)
- *would lithography or something of the sort come into it? lithograph or something to do with printing*

Details unknown to Harold but which turned out to be correct were also given of the method used by the machine to ensure the correct position of the lines of printing and of the pen carriage used for producing them.

On October 15 George Vandy had a sitting with Mrs. Mason the medium. As in all the sittings, no details of Edgar were given to the medium. In the course of the sitting Mrs. Mason gave the name of the deceased Vandy sister, "Millie." George then asked "Has she met anyone yet?" and obtained the reply " ... seen her brother ... passed out young ... she passed out before him ... young man ... I should think 34" (Vandy was 38). George handed her an envelope containing a drawing and two words made by Edgar's machine. Mrs. Mason commented that:

- *he was suffocated ... showing me a scene as if he could have been near water – not the sea, a little amount of water*
- *was he drowned?* (GV answered yes) *Of course he was ... I don't know how he*

came to get this blow, but he was found in the water ... semi-conscious when he was in the water

- *it is to do with machinery is it not? He says there is some drawings ... there is a tiny bit of writing ... but I think ...more drawings.*

At Harold's sitting with Miss Bacon on October 19 Miss Bacon said:

- *I feel as though I were going under somewhere*
- *the one you want has only just recently passed out ... you are not sure of the way he did so*
- *I am getting a sensation of floating out on water ... I am in water*
- *it was an accident*
- *I feel as if I had been drowned*

Harold then handed her, without explanation, a roll of paper from the machine on which Edgar was working and asked if the owner had passed out in a very tragic way. Miss Bacon agreed that he had, and then gave a detailed description of Edgar, which was taken as correct. She then returned to Vandy's death:

- *don't think it was a swimming bath ... a private kind of pool ... like a private swimming pool*
- *had a blow on the head before he passed over ... not diving*
- *catching his foot on the bottom ... drawn under ... there was a diving board and whether someone knocked him or not I don't know*
- *he remembers going under and feeling a distinct blow on the head*
- *the water should have been transparent ... bottom not bricked in ... grass at the bottom ... open air pool ... someone swimming there at the time* (NJ was only about to swim with him)
- *open air pool ... would this pool belong to a certain place?*

At George's sitting with Miss Bacon on November 11 he was told:

- *whether he had been swimming I can't say*
- *he went into the sea or near the sea ... got caught under or in the turn of the tide* (incorrect, but corrected later).
- *there were people beside the water* (this may have been a reference to NJ, who was of course in the water with him while trying to save him)

Drayton Thomas had another proxy sitting with Gladys Leonard on July 27, 1934. Again Mrs. Leonard was not told any details of the family for whom the proxy sitting was held. This time Drayton Thomas' father was the communicator, and commented that:

- *the young man had a lot of papers he kept in a flat book form ... one of them with writings and drawings ... some brown ... some ... almost like black covers* (12 notebooks belonging to Edgar Vandy were found among his possessions some years later at a Pickfords' store, all with black covers except one with brown. The books contained numerous sketches of mechanisms and electrical circuits)

The above summary does not cover all the correct details given in the case, particularly those relating to the machine invented by Edgar and on which he was working at the time of his death. Not all the statements made by the mediums were correct, though the errors seem to have been more to do with details than with major issues. However, the above details are sufficiently extensive to demonstrate that fishing, guessing, cold reading, or luck on the part of the mediums could not account for the production of so much material relevant to Edgar Vandy's tragic death. Prior knowledge or research into the case by the mediums or collusion between them can also be effectively ruled out. Drayton Thomas and the Vandy brothers took care to ensure no information about Edgar or about their own identities was leaked by them. Keen (2002), who has made a particular study of this case, stresses this point in reply to critics who have tried to dismiss the case on the above grounds. In particular, Keen points out that cold reading is precluded as an explanation a) where proxy sittings are involved, b) where correct information is given which is unknown to the sitters at the time, and c) where different mediums, without collusion, provide the same specific and correct information. Each of these conditions was satisfied at the Vandy sittings (Keen lists the correspondences between the statements made by each of the mediums, giving many extra details for which I have no space here). Particularly important are the frequent references to water and drowning, to a pool, to the condition of the pool and to the state of the water, to the fact that Vandy (although his name was not given) was in the water for some time before he was found, to the fact that it was no one's fault, and to the machine on which he was working when he died.

No serious attempt has been made by critics to suggest fraud or misrepresentation on the part of Drayton Thomas, of the mediums or of the Vandys, and indeed it would not be easy to see how such a suggestion could be made to appear credible. However, could the mediums have gained their information by telepathy and clairvoyance? Both these abilities would have had to come into play if the medium's own psychic powers, rather than any communication from the deceased Edgar Vandy, were responsible for the wealth of information given to the Vandy brothers and Drayton Thomas. However, the events surrounding Vandy's death were not recorded anywhere. Are we to suppose some psychic record of them existed somewhere or somehow into which the mediums were able to peer? In addition, it is notable that the mediums gave their information as if it came from Vandy himself – and clearly believed that it did – rather than from their own telepathic or clairvoyant abilities. If the mediums were using psychic rather than mediumistic abilities, it seems strange that they were not aware of the fact, and created instead the fictitious persona of Edgar Vandy.

Furthermore, if the mediums were using clairvoyance, it is surprising that they were unable to give objective accounts of the events surrounding Vandy's death. Instead, the details they gave seem more consistent with the confusion shown by the drowning man himself. There is also the suggestion that Vandy was anxious to avoid suspicion attaching to anyone else, and to exonerate others from any charge that they could have done more to save him. This again seems more in keeping with communications from Vandy himself than with clairvoyance from the living. Again, unless one rejects the possibility of survival on principal, survival is, as Broad (ibid. 1962) says of this case, much the simplest and most natural explanation.

There have only been two credible attempts to dismiss the importance of the Vandy case as evidence for survival. In the first of them philosophy professor Arthur Miller (1998), who accepts the reality of the paranormal but who baulks at the idea that consciousness could survive the death of the brain, suggests that the information given about Vandy's death could have come from Vandy himself during the diminished period of consciousness that may intervene between apparent and actual death. This is simply a variant of the Super-ESP hypothesis which has the added weakness that it overlooks the fact that the information given by the mediums extended over a period of 18 days to more than three months after Vandy's death, and that a final piece of important evidence was given by Gladys Leonard at the end of July of the following year. One cannot seriously suppose that Vandy's telepathic impressions – if such they were – given out in the few instants between apparent and actual death would have lingered on for this period of time, or even that in those few fatal moments he would have been thinking of the kind of information received by the mediums

The second attempt comes from William Oldfield, a professor of public administration (Oldfield 2001), and is based on the charge that all the relevant information could have been acquired by the mediums by "cold reading" (i.e. by picking up clues from the appearance and behavior of sitters), by lucky guessing, by previous research, or by common parlor tricks. This charge has been fully and persuasively dismissed by Keen (2002). Cold reading, much beloved by skeptics as an explanation for successful mediumship, can hardly apply to the two proxy sittings Drayton Thomas held with Gladys Leonard at which important evidence, unknown to Thomas, emerged. Nor can it apply to occasions when the Vandy brothers as sitters were given evidence that was also unknown to them (a sitter can hardly give clues to the correctness of material when he is unaware that it is correct), or to the numerous occasions (all fully cross-referenced by Gay) when different mediums gave the same or similar information as each other and to different sitters. Previous research by the mediums can also be ruled out as the mediums had no idea of the identity of the deceased individuals or of the brothers (who gave false names and addresses, different for each medium). Lucky guessing is such a palpably absurd explanation that it hardly needs serious attention. It would only be credible if the correct pieces of information given about Vandy were embedded in a mass of incorrect details, which they were not. Good luck only stretches so far. Parlor tricks such as mind-reading can be dismissed out of hand. Oldfield gives no examples of the tricks that might have been used, or of occasions when parlor tricks have been shown to yield evidence of the quality forthcoming in the Vandy case.

The Edgar Vandy case has been in the public domain for more than 60 years, and I can only say that if this is the best that the critics can do even given all this time it simply confirms the strength of the case. In his critique of Oldfield Keen asks why "a prominent academic ... should have suppressed or denied so much evidence inconsistent with his reasons for dismissing the Vandy case." This question could be asked of many other skeptics who choose to attack the evidence for survival and for the paranormal in general. It is a sad fact that all too often they do not seem fully familiar with the material to which they are taking exception.

The Bobbie Newlove Case

Another excellent proxy case is also connected with Gladys Leonard and Drayton Thomas (Thomas 1935). Like the Edgar Vandy case, this also centers on a tragedy, though of a rather different kind. In September 1932 Thomas received a letter from a stranger, Mr. Hatch, writing from Nelson in Lancashire, a town some 200 miles away from where Thomas lived, and which he had only once briefly visited ten years previously. Mr. Hatch wrote that his stepdaughter (Mrs. Newlove) and her son Bobbie had lived with him and his wife for ten years, and that Bobbie had recently died from diphtheria. Bobbie was described as a "particularly intelligent and extraordinarily loving and lovable" child and the "life and center" of the family. The loss of him, wrote Mr. Hatch, "is so dreadful that we feel we must ask if you can in any way obtain comfort similar to that recounted in your book, *Life Beyond Death*."

Despite his doubts as to whether a child of ten could communicate Drayton Thomas, acting as proxy sitter, mentioned the child during a sitting to the entranced Gladys Leonard, inadvertently getting his name wrong by saying "Truelove" for "Newlove" – an error that was not corrected until the third of the ten sittings he had with her on this occasion. The only other detail Thomas gave was that he had had an earnest request for news of the little boy, who had died a few weeks previously. He then gave the letter from

Mr. Hatch, folded so as not to reveal any information, into the hand of the still entranced Gladys Leonard. Many statements concerning Bobbie were subsequently communicated through Feda, Mrs. Leonard's control, at this first sitting and at the ten that followed, all of which were taken down for Thomas by an expert shorthand writer. Feda claimed that throughout these sittings Bobbie was being helped by Thomas' deceased father and by Etta, his deceased sister. These statements were so numerous that I can only give a few examples, together with the results of Thomas' subsequent enquiries when he visited the Newlove/Hatch family in Nelson. However, at the end of each sitting the number of statements out of the total rated by Drayton Thomas and by Mr. Hatch and the family as right or otherwise are given, together with a brief indication of the content of those that were rated poor or wrong.

First sitting, November 4, 1932

At the first sitting Feda, through the entranced Gladys Leonard, questioned the reference Drayton Thomas had made to "a few weeks" since Bobbie's death, and said *"Feda feels it would be several months now"* (it was in fact some three months). Although she had not been told where Bobbie lived, Feda then gave some accurate descriptions of Bobbie's home town, and then proceeded to more personal matters.

- *Will you find out whether this boy had a pain in his hand* (Bobbie sometimes lost the use of his right hand, and although he did not complain of pain he could not write while the condition lasted)
- *Did he have anything the matter with his glands?* (the glands are affected in diphtheria)
- *... a little while before he passed over I get such a feeling of a lot of cakes and cooking going on as if for some special occasion* (meaning unclear: the only possible connection was that Bobbie and a friend had been making toffee some six months before he died)
- *... the family [of the boy] have a comfortable home and nice surroundings* (*correct*)
- *Ask if the boy's neck or throat were affected* (diphtheria principally affects the neck and throat)

Thirteen statements were made during this first sitting, of which Mr. Hatch regarded eight as "right," one as "good" (the first three letters of the name of a friend), two as "fair" (the initial of a friend, and an apparent reference to the cross made for Bobbie's grave), one as "doubtful" (the pain in the hand), and one as "poor" (the cooking). He concluded that coincidence could not explain the results, but suggested that psychometry might be involved as Mrs. Leonard was holding his letter when the statements were made, and he did not feel that the statements were ones that Bobbie himself would have made.

Second sitting, November 18, 1932

- *He was very pleased at winning something not very long before he passed* (Not long before he died Bobbie had come top of the class in the half-yearly examinations, and also received top marks for the term; nine weeks before he died he had also won a competition with a salt-sifter shaped like a dog, of which he was very proud)
- *.... played with something with numbers on ... curved lines ... grooves ... and numbers ... evenings after tea* (Bobbie was particularly successful with a machine at a local fair which rewarded him with money for shooting into numbered circles; he played the game several times in the evenings after tea)
- *played indoors with marbles on a table* (correct)
- *was he interested in rabbits?* (correct; he often visited a neighbor who kept rabbits)

Of the 20 statements made as this sitting, eight were right, four good, three fair, one doubtful (a recent gift), two poor (money put aside for him and a person he was said to like), and two wrong (both of which concerned Feda's attempts at a physical description of Bobbie).

Third sitting, December 2, 1932

- *... a photograph of Bobbie ... full-faced ... with something in front of him ... a board in front of him ... like at the back of a board or a tray ...* (the last photograph of Bobbie ever taken was of him in fancy dress as the knave of hearts, with boards in front and behind him representing playing cards)
- *... something he has been given ... a joke ... wearing on his head ... something round ... new ... just like a ring ... no peak at all* (the knave of hearts costume had a round crown, which Bobbie was so fond of putting on that his mother stopped him for fear of wearing it out)
- *An event nine weeks before his death for which "the pipes" will give the clue* (correct in the light of later communications, returned to in due course)
- *went to a place where there was a broken stile ... footpath ... a church with trees ... something dangerous near the stile ... you would say to the children "Now don't go that way" ... something you could fall down ... wet ... can't see the water but I think they want me to say that ... sticky and wet there ... place he knew well ... has been thinking of it when he has been with his people on earth* (regarded as very good by Mr. Hatch; one of Bobbie's favorite walks was by a broken

stile, since removed, beyond which was a church with trees and a churchyard. Past the stile there was a quarry with water in it, where Bobbie wanted to go; this was forbidden because of the danger)

- *he would go near a collapsed building* (an old barn, partly ruined, was near the house)
- *his nose hurt* (Bobbie was learning to box and his instructor gave him a blow on his nose that hurt; he had written in his diary "The instructor ... burst my nose")
- *... some food he did not like ... given only a little while before he passed over ... a food that many boys would like* (Bobbie's pet aversion was the white of egg, and his mother was trying to insist he ate it)
- *... not a naughty boy ... very nice nature ... very affectionate ... very appreciative of his mother and of his relations and his home life* (all correct)

Of the 21 statements made 18 were considered right, one good, one fair, and one wrong (the first two letters of a place name that could not be recognized).

Fourth sitting, January 13, 1933

Mr. Hatch asked if three questions could be put to Bobbie, namely "what did he keep in the bathroom cupboard?", "where did he go with his mother last winter in the evenings?", and "what did he do in the attic besides boxing?." A number of other statements were made before these questions were addressed.

- *... interested in something to do with mice ... someone else mixed up in this ... another child* (Bobbie was interested in the mice kept by a friend, and brought some of them to show his family)
- *Bobbie did some funny things for a boy ... pulling something from the wall ... thick string or rope ... the pulling out seems important ... drawing it out as far as possible, and then letting it go back to the wall ... something he seemed to do rather regularly* (in the attic Bobbie had an arrangement for strengthening his muscles that consisted of a thin rope that ran through a pulley fixed to the wall and was attached to a heavy weight: pulling the rope from the wall raised the weight; Bobbie exercised with this rather regularly; this appears to be in anticipation of the question as to what Bobbie did in the attic)

Later, when Thomas put to Feda the question about the attic, she answered that he was:

- *lying on the floor ... flat on the floor or something ... sort of squirming about ... hands and feet going* (a correct reference to the exercises Bobbie's boxing instructor gave him, and which he did in the attic – raising legs while on his back etc.)

- *he remembers having his teeth looked at and that something was to be done* (he needed to visit the dentist and the family was rather worried about this)
- *his mother had a rather important engagement before he passed over ... he thinks it was a Saturday ... his being ill would have interfered with it* (Mrs. Newlove had an engagement with the Brownies, of which she was an officer, arranged for the Saturday before he died; she postponed it when he fell ill)
- *bad handwriting ... trying to improve it ... spoken of lately* (bad handwriting held Bobbie back at school; the family had even spoken of this after his passing when trying to read his diary)
- *ask his mother if she has been thinking of doing something about Rosemary* (not recognized at first, but Mrs. Newlove then recalled she was receiving letters from a Lady Rosemary Stopford connected with her work with the Brownies, in which Bobbie took an interest)
- *he keeps on saying he has met Arthur there* (Arthur, Bobbie's uncle by marriage, had died suddenly two years previously).
- *... another doctor to look at him ... I keep getting a mix-up between two doctors* (a throat specialist who lived next door to the Newlove/Hatch family had been called in to give a second opinion a few hours before Bobbie died).

In answer to the question what he did with his mother the previous winter Feda referred to *"carrying something ... holding his mother's arm ... thoughts of buying something new ... rather expensive ... enjoyed going to this place ... rather a bare place ... a place where they cleared the furniture ... lot of other people there ... hoped to go again after buying something special ... getting warm there ... did she ask him to buy new boots for it ... a discussion about boots or shoes."* In reply to the question as to what he kept in the bathroom, she spoke firstly of a balloon, then rejected this and said *"light and round ... like something that floats in the air."*

Neither of these answers was precise. The place Bobbie visited with his mother was a roller skating rink, and there was talk of her buying skates for herself, instead of borrowing them at the rink. The description of the rink as rather a bare place was correct, as was "getting warm there." The object kept in the bathroom cupboard was a boat, but although Feda got the idea of roundness and floating, she mentioned "air" rather than "water."

Consequently only one in three of the questions suggested by Mr. Hatch was answered fully, though this answer was particularly impressive. One would not readily guess the existence of the homemade muscle-strengthening apparatus, or the exercises carried out on the floor. In the light of this, the failure accurately to answer the other two questions is surprising.

But Feda, like many controls, often claimed to be shown pictures by communicators instead of being given words. It was rather as if, as suggested when discussing the images reported by mental mediums, her position between the spirit world and the material world only allowed her tenuous contact with the communicators, and images shown to her by the latter worked better with her than words. In addition, if she was who she said she was, she would have been unfamiliar with some of the modern or technical words that communicators may have wished to use. However, although inconclusive, the seeming references to the skating rink are suggestive of how Feda might have interpreted the images shown to her. For example, unfamiliar with roller skates, she may have interpreted them as boots. Something that floats might be an obvious guess for what is kept in a bathroom cupboard, but the fact that Feda mistakes the object concerned for something floating in the air suggests this may have been an effort to interpret the image that was being shown to her. The image may also not have been particularly clear in Bobbie's own mind. Some 10-year-old children are able to visualize things with great clarity, others are still rather vague, as one soon discovers if one asks a young child to draw an everyday object from memory.

Of the 25 statements given at the sitting, 16 were considered right, four good, three fair, one doubtful (the name of someone at the rink), and one poor (reference to a toy that was "something like a duck"). The descriptions of the skating rink were classified as right, but although correct as far as they went it is doubtful that somebody reading them would deduce that they referred to a skating rink. This highlights the difficulties sometimes met in classifying statements from communicators, but ambivalent statements of this kind were few in number over the course of the sittings.

Fifth sitting, January 27, 1933

- *did he use something made of celluloid ... they wanted to stop him using it ... might make a flame or explosion* (Bobbie had bought a second-hand cinematograph lantern, and the family was nervous about the fire risk from the celluloid films)
- *did [his mother] have the bathroom walls done after he passed? ... he remembers she wanted to have them done* (parts of the bathroom walls and ceiling needed attention, and this was done after Bobbie's death)
- *his mother had folded up ... tissue paper ... something he wore ... conical shape ... several of them ... pink, green, blue, white ... an occasion since he passed when they could have used them but did not* (the paper Christmas hats had been put away the previous year, and would have been used again for Christmas 1932 had Bobbie lived; the descriptions of the shape and colors of the hats were correct)

Of the 16 statements, nine were right, one was good, two were fair, two were doubtful (one relating to bowing movements Bobbie was said to make in the attic and which Feda could not understand, but which Mr. Hatch thought should have been rated as "good" because the bowing was "a good description of Bobbie's movements as he lifted weights"; the other related to the claim that improvements had been made to the pipes that are discussed in due course below), one was poor (a reference to water "swilling" from these pipes, although Thomas later accepted that this was a good description of what would happen in winter), and one was wrong (a reference to the doors having been changed at the place – i.e. the rink – Bobbie used to visit with his mother the previous winter).

Sixth sitting, February 16, 1933

The communications all related to events that supposedly weakened Bobbie's resistance to diphtheria, and these communications, more of which occur in later sittings, are in view of their importance best dealt with separately. Accordingly they are summarized later in the chapter, together with the necessary explanatory comments.

Seventh sitting, March 10, 1933

- *he had very good powers of observation and perception ... boys are usually very careless in many things, and Bobbie was not* (Bobbie's powers of observation were certainly above average)
- *he would have had a rather scientific mind* (correct; he pored over books on paleontology, mastered the names of extinct monsters, and loved chemical and electrical toys)
- *... strongly artistic side ... he is not telling you this, Etta* [Thomas' deceased sister who, with Thomas' father, was said to be helping Bobbie] *... someone connected with his mother became known for some special artistic work connected with drawing or designing* (Bobbie was not artistic, but an uncle of his mother was a well-known architect)
- *exceptionally good idea of form and perspective* (incorrect; Bobbie was not even up to the standard of boys of his age in these skills)
- *... he had a wooden box ... inside was a collection of metal things ... Etta can't remember what he said ... I think some kind of tools ... had to be exchanged* (Bobbie had no tools but had been given a Meccano set which was too difficult for him and which had to be taken back and exchanged)
- *... Are his people helping a very old person? ... forget what he told me ... special help for the time being* (at the time Bobbie's family were considering sending daily dinners to a widow who looked older than her 63 years – shortly afterwards they commenced to do so)

Of the six statements at the sitting four were right, one was poor (the box of tools), and one was wrong (the claim that Bobbie was good at artistry and perspective, though this should perhaps have counted as two errors; one can be good at art yet poor at perspective. Note however that the reference to art was said by Feda to come from Etta and not from Bobbie, as did the reference to tools. Note also that Bobbie himself does not appear to have been "present" at the sitting – Feda speaks of both Etta and herself "forgetting" what he had told them). Feda, and possibly Etta, would not have understood an image of a Meccano set, and might well have interpreted it as "tools."

Eighth sitting, March 24, 1933

Again the communications had to do with the events supposedly predisposing Bobbie to diphtheria, returned to later.

Ninth sitting, April 10, 1933

Only one statement was not to do with these predisposing events, namely:

- ... was Bobbie very interested in ... place where there are bottles? ... like a chemist's shop but not a chemist's shop ... bottles and weighing things ... instruments and things of that kind ... liked going there ... clean white place ... taps and bottles and measuring things (*Mr. Hatch had a great deal to do with a laboratory in the town, and Bobbie liked to go there with him; reference to taps, bottles, and weighing things all correct, though the reference to cleanliness a little over-done*)

Tenth sitting, May 19, 1933

- *a polite boy* (Bobbie was very polite)
- *His mother thinking something about a cap ... thinking something rather special of it lately ... a little thing but wants her to know it* (his mother had been thinking about the crown he wore with his costume as the knave of hearts)
- *She came across something with a special badge on it ... not a heart exactly, but the lower part is rather shaped like a heart ... straight line through the top ... a little upstanding piece comes out of the top* (a good description of the crown he had worn with his knave of hearts costume; the crown had a large heart on the front but it was upside down, hence perhaps the slight confusion over this; the base of the reversed heart protrudes above the top of the crown, as is apparent in the picture of Bobbie taken in his costume)
- *a church and a churchyard ... the right hand side of the church as you face it ... ground slopes down a bit just there ... somewhere his mother has been lately, and*

where she was thinking of him very much (Bobbie's grave is in the position indicated, and the ground slopes downwards at this point; his mother frequently went there thinking of him)

- ... *mother thinking very much of apples in connection with him* (correct; Bobbie was very fond of applies and his mother had often thought of this lately)
- ... *he thinks his mother wants a new dressing gown* (Bobbie's mother had recently purchased the material to make a dressing gown, though it was for her mother not for herself)
- ... *ask if cardboard boxes make her think of him* (correct in connection with her recent Spring cleaning)
- ... *close relationship with his mother ... like chums... she was like another boy as well as a mother ... he says "I could always talk to her like I could to another boy" ... "always talked to me as if I was a grown-up" ... etc. etc.* (a remarkably accurate description of Bobbie's relationship with his mother).

In the eighth, ninth, and tenth sitting 25 statements were made, many of them referring to circumstances concerning his contraction of a predisposing condition before he went down with diphtheria, which is returned to in the discussion of the "pipes" below. Of these 25 statements 18 were right, three fair (all related to the diphtheria and dealt with in due course), three doubtful (ditto), and one wrong (the dressing gown was not for his mother but for his grandmother).

Eleventh sitting, June 2, 1933

- ... *a special photograph of him down to the waist ... a sweater on that his mother likes ... "my hair coming down at the side" ... "not exactly frowning but drawing my eyebrows down over my eyes"* (among the many photographs of Bobbie there was one that answered the description, with the boy screwing up his eyes to face the sun; it was not a favorite of his mother as his hair needed cutting, but she did like the sweater)
- ... *something belonging to him ... can't show Feda the shape ... yellow varnished wood ... something he was very fond of* (possibly a stool that he considered belonged especially to himself and his mother)
- ... *connection between photographs and this wooden thing* (in one of his full-length photographs he is shown standing on it)
- *swings ... he used to go there and his mother did not like it much ... jolly at this time of year* (Bobbie loved the swings at the fair that came to the town at that time of year, but his mother did not much like him going on them)
- ... *does she remember the track where there was some racing? ... rather dangerous ... circular track ... don't think mother liked it* (there was a kind of motor cycle racing at the fair which he wanted to see; his mother did not like it)

- *... an accident there ... dangerous and unpleasant ... we saw it* (an accident did happen at the race track, though Bobbie never actually saw the racing)
- *a place called something like Catelnow, Castlenow* (Bobbie went to Catlow, with Mr. Hatch on the day he was taken ill – the last time in fact he left the house)
- *his mother's neck, throat has been worrying her lately* (correct)

Mr. Hatch had asked Drayton Thomas by letter to question Bobbie about the whereabouts of a garden in which he used to cycle. The reply at the sitting through Feda, was:

- *... Bicycle through a gate ... turn to the left down a side path ... Is there a clergyman, minister connected with this place? I don't think he lives there, and yet I get a feeling of clergy and ministers ... a tall lady and another boy* (the position of the garden is correct; also correct is the fact that it belonged to the family of a minister who no longer lived there as he had died three years previously; the reference to the tall lady is correct, Bobbie had brought another boy to the garden gate and tried unsuccessfully to obtain permission for him to cycle there too)

Fifteen statements were made at the sitting, nine were correct, five were fair, and one was wrong (an attempt to get the name of the minister's family). The reference to "Catelow" for "Catlow" was regarded as very good, particularly as Bobbie was there on the day he was taken ill with the sore throat at the start of his diphtheria. The answer to the question about the garden where he cycled was also excellent, and acknowledged as correct in every detail by a member of the minister's family. In the 11 sittings there are thus 141 statements (not counting those made at sittings six and eight, which are looked at in the next section). These break down as follows:

Right	Good	Fair	Doubtful	Poor	Wrong
90	10	21	8	5	7

Thus 121 were positive (right, good, fair) and 20 were negative (doubtful, poor, wrong). One way of seeing if the medium could produce results of this kind by chance or guessing would have been to present the statements to a sample of 10-year-old boys from the area where Bobbie lived, and see how many applied to them. Unfortunately the gap of time (boys in the 1930s lived very different lives in many ways from those in the twenty-first century) renders this inappropriate, but even without a test of this kind it would be hard to argue that results of this nature could have been produced by chance. Many of the statements are particularly striking – for example those referring to Bobbie's temperament and behavior, to the fact that his death concerned his throat and neck, to his abilities, interests, and relationship with his mother, to the knave of hearts costume, to the crown that went with the costume, to the apparatus and activities in the attic, to his favorite walk near the quarry, to the ruined building near his house, to the laboratory he liked to visit with Mr. Hatch, to the position of his grave, to the fact that he was taken ill on a Saturday and his mother postponed an important engagement that day, to the visit to "Catelow," to the garden where he cycled and to the connection between the garden and a clergyman who was no longer there (i.e. who had died). By contrast the poor, wrong, and doubtful statements are not only far fewer in number, but have to do with relatively minor matters.

Bobbie's correct responses to two of the questions Mr. Hatch suggested be put to him (his activities in the attic and the location of the garden in which he cycled) are also highly significant, and although the details about the roller-skating rink in response to another of the questions put to him were not specific enough, they were correct as far as they went. His answer to the fourth of the questions, the one concerned with the bathroom, is the only one that would seem a failure.

It is unlikely in the extreme that Gladys Leonard could have obtained results as detailed as this by carrying out her own research into Bobbie and his background. She was given Bobbie's name by Thomas, but no other details. Much of the information she provided was known only to the family, and the idea that she or an accomplice could have tracked down the family and then questioned them closely about Bobbie without arousing their suspicion is hardly credible. Bobbie's family lived in a respectable area of the town (a throat specialist lived next door), and Mr Hatch was clearly an educated man and, on his own admission in a letter to Drayton Thomas, not at all credulous. Such a family can hardly be regarded as easily duped. Drayton Thomas only visited them after the sittings were over, and prior to his visits was given no information about Bobbie apart from the written comments made by Mr. Hatch in response to the record sent to him of each sitting (a study of these comments reveals that they gave away nothing that Thomas could have fed back to Mrs. Leonard, consciously or unconsciously, as clues).

Mention has been made of the information provided by the communicators during the sittings of the circumstances that may have predisposed Bobbie to contract diphtheria, and this information, which relates primarily to a location frequented by Bobbie, is so significant that it will be now looked at in some detail.

Bobbie Newlove and the Pipes

At the second of Drayton Thomas' proxy sittings with Mrs. Piper on November 18, 1932, Thomas' father answered Feda's comment about Bobbie's throat trouble by implying that Bobbie had died of diphtheria. During the third sitting on December 2, his father communicated and expressed an opinion that there was a cause that happened nine weeks before Bobbie's death that contributed to his catching diphtheria. When asked by Thomas what this was, his father answered *"pipes – he just says this – pipes. That word should be sufficient."* At the same sitting Feda mentioned that *"There was something that weakened his system before,"* and suggested it might be to do with his heart. When commenting on the records of this sitting, Mr. Hatch confirmed that Bobbie's illness had started with tonsillitis, which turned to quinsy (an abscess around the tonsils), "and no doubt these weakened the heart."

At the third sitting Feda insisted that Thomas' father was telling her

There was something behind that condition; he would not have passed over with that condition alone, there was something before that ... Will you ask if there is anything they can trace to nine weeks before, something that at the time might not have seemed important ... it was not the thing that weakened him, but nine weeks before Bobbie passed ... something very significant that had a link with his passing.

In reply to a query from Thomas as to what this was she replied *"he says pipes, pipes ... "* She makes it clear that "he" in this instance refers not to Bobbie but to Drayton Thomas' father, who had *"asked Bobbie a few questions before the sitting that I thought might have a bearing on his earth life, and this was one of them."* Drayton Thomas queried this with Mr. Hatch, who answered that the family could not trace the reference. Nine weeks before Bobbie's death he had been taken to Morecombe for a very short holiday. The word "pipes" meant nothing, and they were very doubtful if Bobbie had ever heard of someone catching diphtheria from pipes. However, in subsequent sittings the issue was returned to repeatedly. At the fourth sitting on January 13, 1933 Feda says Bobbie has been told (it seems by Mr. Thomas Senior) *"that there was something in his case which was making it not only easy ... for him to get [diphtheria] but not to be able to throw it off."* She adds that he tells her he got it *"from the pipes."*

The family were still unable to trace this. At the fifth sitting on January 27, 1933 Feda again returned to the theme.

It was not his home ... not a place where he went regularly ... he went to it not from his home but while he was in a second place he went to a third one ... through these – what he calls pipes – he picked up the condition which was not the cause of the trouble in the first place, but it introduced a destructive element which resulted in diphtheria ... poisonous condition that infected his system.

In reply to a question from Drayton Thomas as to the location of this place Feda told him

... animals there you call cattle ... two or three friends of his who have passed over are also helping ... the matter will be brought to light in what will appear to be an accidental and yet natural manner ... after Bobbie caught it something was done to improve matters with regard to those pipes ... made safer ... animals will be the best clue ... his parents not familiar with this place ... another boy mixed up in this ... [he] seemed to be the reason for Bobbie going ... not quite a country place ... stables there ... like barns and stables ... straw in big bundles ... got to call it a barn, with one side nearly, or all, open — more like a shelter place ... water running ... kind of gutter or drain ... like a swilling.

At the sixth sitting on February 16, 1933 Bobbie was said to be pleased with the results of his messages, but could not understand why they could not fathom it out. Asked for a place name, Feda replied

... like Bentley and Stoo ... Stock, Stop, begins Stoo ... down hill ... shops and houses ... come to a cross road ... think there is a big station there; because there is a bridge just down that turning ... trains ... [go] straight up a hill opposite ... more towards houses and less shops ... cleaner ... name again that sounds like Ben or Bentley.

In response to the notes of this sitting sent to him by Thomas, Mr. Hatch enclosed a sketch map of the lower part of town and commented that "the description of the town is quite a good one. The name Bentley is particularly good ... as there is a Bentley Street near our house and adjoining Bobbie's school ... we can see no connection ... [with] ... 'pipes,' though it is cleaner and brighter as you go up the hill." Mr. Hatch added that it seemed from the description of the route given by Feda that Bobbie went from his school to the place where the pipes were, "But as far as our knowledge goes, the only place answering to this description is the Baths, and this does not fit in with the account [from the previous sitting] of a barn-like place with hay etc." Feda's attempt at a word – "Stoo, Stock, Stop, begins Stoo" appeared to refer to the fact that soon after Bentley Street the route passed the churchyard, where just inside the entrance some stocks are preserved.

During the sixth sitting Feda mentioned the names " ... *something like 'Phil' ... and a boy called Peter who knew this place too ... not sure whether his real name was Peter but they called him Peter ... and another boy whose name sounds like Eric or Alec.*" Mr. Hatch commented that these names were unknown to the family, but they did not know all of Bobbie's school companions. Mr. Hatch suggested that the location to which Bobbie was referring seemed to point to a place that Bobbie and a friend had visited, but to which the rest of the family had never been. He declined to say more in the hope that Bobbie might communicate more details. Similarly the family had decided not to question Bobbie's friend

Jack about the names mentioned, as Bobbie himself might say more about them himself.

Nothing of consequence in connection with this location came through at the seventh sitting, but at the eighth, on March 24, 1933, Feda commented that Etta, who appeared to be the link between her and Bobbie at that stage, was certain they would verify the evidence about them. She asked Thomas to instruct the family not to tell him anything they discovered until *"we have given you a little more about it."* Early in the ninth sitting, on April 10, 1933, Feda referred to *"a brook or inland water"* in some way connected with the pipes, and *"a swampy condition."* Mr. Hatch thought this might refer to a boating pool, which Bobbie liked to visit, but "swampy condition" was incorrect. The tenth sitting on May 19, 1933 brought further references to the locations during which Feda announced that " ... *Bobbie is not disappointed about* [the difficulties] *as he felt it was going to be difficult ... two different bodies of people to contend with ... neither of them would make it easy, but one might make it easier than the other"* (Mr. Hatch considered that the "two different bodies to contend with" might refer to the fact that the family were currently divided as to the places meant).

Feda also referred during the sitting to *underground*, but Thomas thought this vague. Thomas then addressed Bobbie directly, asking how he would find the place if he wished to start from the railway station. "I should walk past your house ... and a little uphill, what ought I to do then?" Feda replied

Yes and there is another way ... past the school ... I should think past the house and straight on [the significance of this will be made clear shortly] *it seems to be on the right ... [not] far from the main road. I think it is on it ... On the main road it goes uphill, all the way, not just a little bit of hill ... for a good distance it is more open on the left than the right? ... not all built up ... lots of spaces as well ... a mixture ... at one time not much built up, but built on lately ... an address on "B"? ... He went to this "B" place at certain times ...*

At this point Thomas considered that Feda became a little confused as a result of his incorrect assumption that "B" stood for "Baths" and his subsequent misleading question "Is it within the same walls, under the same roof?", because she then tended to use his word "baths" (possibly not knowing of the existence of public baths, and assuming people washed under "pipes"). Thomas considers that he then may have added to the confusion by asking if Bobbie drank the water at the "Baths". However, Feda continued to give some useful descriptions

... something that had to be added on afterwards ... when it was thought to be complete there was something added to it, quite a big portion ... Is there a district there that begins with the letter "H" ... a longish name ...He calls it the district ... he knew somebody living in the "H" part that used to go to the same place ... you have been going up hill ... go down to the right, like a side way ... you come to a place ... a kind of abrupt drop down ... still some evidence of it being there, but

not quite as it was ... you can get to that place by walking up the hill and turning to the right near the baths [i.e. pipes]; *not perhaps the best way, but you could get so.*

Thus ended the sittings and the references to the mystery of the pipes. Thomas paid two visits to the Hatch family in June and July 1933 and together they attempted to see if the mystery of the location could be solved. There was no doubt that the references to a "predisposing condition" to Bobbie's diphtheria could be correct. He had had tonsillitis, which led to quinsy, which was followed by the diphtheria. Whether these illnesses "weakened his heart" or not is unclear (although as already mentioned Mr. Hatch thought they did), but they certainly set up an infected throat condition that may have made it easier for the diphtheria to take hold. Diphtheria was prevalent in the 1930s, but in response to Thomas' inquiries the Medical Officer of Health for the Nelson district informed him there were only two other cases of the disease in Nelson at the time of Bobbie's death, and only three in the adjoining urban district of Brierfield. Thus there was no outbreak of the disease and, as already made clear, Bobbie's home was in a pleasant and, we are assured, healthy part of the town.

In the light of this, Thomas wondered if Feda's reference to Bobbie's having contracted his predisposing condition "nine weeks" before might provide some clue. He asked to see the diary that Bobbie used to keep, and turned to the entries nine weeks before Bobbie's death on August 12, 1932, which took him back to June 10. Five days after this, on June 15, he found something he thought could be relevant, namely an entry to the effect that on that day Bobbie had written *"joined gang."* The family informed him that the "gang" was a secret society formed by Bobbie and one or two of his close friends, which in the way of young boys' gangs used to play at having "adventures." The family had found out by chance in March 1933 that the gang's chosen place for these adventures was called "The Heights." Although the gang may have decided on some formal joining ceremony on June 15, again in the way of young boys, they had actually chosen The Heights in March 1932, and the family now knew that they had played there during the early summer, i.e. in the weeks leading up to June 15. Thus it seemed possible to Thomas and to the family that Bobbie's predisposing condition had something to do with The Heights.

Accordingly, when visiting the family for the first time in July 1932, Thomas accompanied them to The Heights (i.e. Marsden Heights), an open area above the part of Nelson in which the family lived. On their second visit they investigated a disused and overgrown quarry there known as "The Delf" (not the quarry mentioned in Sittings Three and Eleven in connection with one of Bobbie's favorite walks), where they noticed a shed higher up the hill and near the road. Approaching it they saw the marks of animals, and on entering the building found that part of it was used as a stable, while another part contained straw and hay for bedding. One end of the shed was open, which further aroused their interest, as one of the clues they had been given spoke of "an open end." By chance a woman then approached them, and after exchanging casual greetings Thomas asked her if children came to play in the quarry. She answered that they did, and that they got up to mischief and had "broken the pipe."

Further questions revealed that there was a spring part way down the hill, and that water from it previously issued through this pipe. Given directions, Thomas and the family found the pipe, made of iron and several feet in length. It had been displaced, presumably by the mischievous children, and the water from the spring now ran down the slope in a channel of its own making. This pipe may have been to what Bobbie was referring, but during the sittings the word "pipe" had consistently been given in the plural. Nothing to explain this discrepancy was found at the time, but Mr. Hatch subsequently paid a number of visits to the area, and in September of 1933 the reason for the use of the plural became apparent. Accompanied by Bobbie's boxing instructor he discovered a second pipe, undamaged this time and discharging its water into a "kind of trough." Neither of these pipes was shown on any map of Nelson and the surrounding district.

Drayton Thomas makes the point that these events bear out two of the pieces of information that had come from Bobbie, firstly that *"the matter will be brought to light in what will appear to be an accidental and yet natural manner,"* and secondly that *"animals you call cattle"* were involved. The meeting with the woman who informed them of the first pipe had indeed been accidental, and without it Thomas doubted if they would have found the pipe. And animal tracks were discovered outside the shed used as a stable/barn. A third piece of information from Bobbie, namely that his family were not familiar with The Heights during his lifetime, also proved correct. His grandparents had never visited them, and although Bobbie had once brought his mother to view them from a lower road, the weather had been bad at the time and they had returned home without visiting them. Another of Bobbie's statements that appeared correct was that he had not gone to The Heights from home but from "a second place," which was probably a reference to his school, as The Heights were only a short walk away.

In the sixth sitting on February 16 (*before* the family learnt in March that the gang frequented The Heights), Bobbie had given directions through Feda on how to get to the "pipes." On being informed of these directions by Drayton Thomas, Mr. Hatch had sent him a sketch map (reproduced in Thomas 1935), which showed they were quite a good description of the relevant part of the town. The crossroads, the railway station, the railway bridge, the uphill road beyond the station (which passed Bobbie's house), Bentley Street, the stocks just inside the churchyard, and the fact that the road becomes cleaner and brighter as one goes up the hill, were all correct.

Following the route given by Bobbie took one up the main road as far as the churchyard, just beyond which the road ran past The Heights. His mention of going past the railway station was strange, however, as this would have meant going down hill to the station, doing a short detour around it, then going back again past his house and up the hill. The boys mentioned, Phil, Peter, and Eric (or Alec) could not be placed.

At the ninth sitting there had been a mention of a "brook or inland waterway," which could not be placed at the time, but with the discovery of the second pipe Drayton Thomas tells us that it "perfectly applied to the place where we saw water issuing from the pipe. The water made a small pool and swampy area around the spot where it issued from the hill" (the term "inland waterway" may seem a little grand for this, but taken literally it clearly fits the area around the pipe). At this ninth sitting there was also a reference to "underground," which Thomas had found vague at the time, but once they visited the site the meaning became clear; as both pipes were positioned to take water from underground streams running down the hillside.

At the ninth sitting Bobbie gave a further set of directions on how to get to the pipes, explaining " ... *I should think past the school and keep straight on ... It seems to be on the right. I don't think it is very far from the main road. I think it is on it.*" This is correct. It is clear from Mr. Hatch's sketch map that the road veers round to the left, and on the right there is a blind alley leading into The Heights – which are indeed bounded by the main road as Bobbie implied. The rest of the description given in this sitting, though more general (*"goes uphill ... not all built up there ... more open on the left than the right ... lots of spaces"*), is also correct. Bobbie then tries to convey the idea of "an address on 'B'," which Thomas mistakes for the initial letter of "Baths." In fact The Heights are in the urban district (the administrative district) of Brierfield, which adjoins Nelson, and it was probably to this that Bobbie was referring. Bobbie's description then implies that the pipes themselves are near a building *"not all built at the same time, there was something added on afterwards,"* which is a correct description of the barn/stables near the pipes. The letter "H" is then given during the sitting, which seems to refer to The Heights, and a reference is made by Feda to the fact that Bobbie *"knew someone living in the 'H' part that used to go there too"* (presumably a member of the "gang").

In describing the walk up the hill to the Heights there is also a reference by Feda to " ... *a place that was – there are no cliffs there, are there? – ... a peculiar place ... almost like a drop ... a kind of abrupt drop down, not an ordinary hill ... some evidence of it being there, but not quite as it was.*" Drayton Thomas considers this applies to the disused and now overgrown quarry (*"not quite as it was"*) referred to in Sittings Three and Eleven, which one would pass just before reaching The Heights, and this is strengthened by the fact that Feda also says *"you have been going up hill ... suppose you were to go down to the right, like a side way ... you wouldn't go very far to the right before you come* [to the place]." Feda goes on to say that *"You can get to that place by walking up the hill and turning to your right near the baths* [pipes], *not perhaps the best way, but you could get so."* This seems accurate, as there is a turning to the right further up the hill that would also lead to the quarry, although it is *"not perhaps the best way,"* as by taking the earlier turning one would not need to walk so far uphill.

The mysterious pipes and their surroundings, together with the route to them, are therefore quite well described by Bobbie, though in the rather general way that we would expect from a 10-year-old boy trying to give directions. In all, 33 statements were made on the subject during the sittings, and Thomas scores them as:

Right	Good	Fair	Doubtful	Poor	Wrong
10	3	4	5	1	0

The only statement rated "poor" by Thomas was the use of the word "swilling" in connection with the water emerging from the pipes, but this is somewhat strange, as in the text he remarks that the water would indeed be "swilling" out in the winter. The five statements rated "doubtful" were: (i) an alteration had been made to render the pipes less dangerous, (ii) the name "Phil" is a clue, (iii) the names "Peter and Eric" for the other boys, (vi) the use of the term "underground", and (v) someone living in the "H" part used to go there too. Of these, the name Phil and the names of other boys could have applied to comrades (possibly from another school, as Bobbie is unsure of the names), and the same could be true of "someone living in the 'H' part who used to go there too." As I have already made clear the word "underground" is not doubtful at all. Thomas says elsewhere in the text that it applies accurately to the fact that the streams ran underground and emerged at the pipes. (In the summary of the statements given by Feda relevant to the possible connection between Bobbie's illness and the pipes there appears to be a discrepancy between the dates for the relevant sittings and those given for the same sittings earlier in the text. It is unclear why these errors were not corrected, and anyone reading Drayton Thomas' report of the case needs to check back to the dates originally given by him for each of the sittings.)

Concluding his report on the Bobbie Newlove case, Drayton Thomas goes through all the various explanations that might be advanced (including telepathy from the living and clairvoyance) and dismisses each of them in turn as without basis. His own conviction at the end of the case was that "Bobbie Newlove and his friends in the Beyond gave the messages." However, what of Bobbie's apparent belief that the pipes were responsible in some way for the predisposing condition that led to his diphtheria? Drayton Thomas contacted Dr. Wilson, the Medical Officer of Health for Brierfield, and inquired as to the purity of the water at the pipes. In response Dr. Wilson and his Sanitary Inspector visited the two springs at The Heights that issued through the pipes, and took away samples of the water for analysis. They found that although the springs themselves were suitable for drinking when they emerged from underground, the water in the pools that they formed on the ground was "obviously liable to contamination from surface water and [was] not fit for drinking purposes. Any person, child or adult, might develop a low or even an acute infection from the drinking of such water." Although Dr. Wilson does not elaborate on the nature of the contamination present in the surface water, part of it would seem to have come from the cattle who drank at the pools, part of it from bacteria naturally present in the soil, and part of it from the children and adults who used The Heights for recreation.

In addition to publishing the letter from Dr. Wilson containing this report, Thomas includes a photograph of the second of the two pipes – the one that was not displaced by childish mischief – that shows clearly it discharges only just above the ground (he also includes a photograph of the stable/barn which bears out the description given by Bobbie, and one of the quarry). One would not easily be able to drink from it without also taking in some of the surface water. In the case of the displaced pipe, drinking uncontaminated water would have been even more difficult, as the water was discharging directly onto the ground. We do not know for certain that Bobbie drank any of this contaminated water, but when asked by the family, his friend Jack confirmed that the two boys used to play at the pipes. In the course of their play, which probably involved a certain amount of splashing and certainly a wetting of hands, it is almost certain that some of the surface water would have found its way to Bobbie's mouth. Certainly in the communications through Gladys Leonard he seems clear that he was infected by the water.

Not surprisingly, there were those who disagreed with Drayton Thomas that the information given by Gladys Leonard came from the afterlife, and various letters to this effect were published in the *Journal of the Society for Psychical Research*. Eric Dingwall, at one time research officer of the SPR and a consistent critic of mental mediumship, considered that Thomas may have given sufficient information away during the sittings for Gladys Leonard to have guessed the rest. It is unclear what prompted Dingwall to arrive at this consideration, and the suspicion is that he did not read Thomas' report of the case with sufficient care. He claimed to have "made a very careful study" of the case, but doubt is thrown on this claim by his example of how Thomas may have leaked information to Mrs. Leonard. He writes that " ... the transformation of the drains to the pipes through the kind assistance of Mr. Thomas will, I think, remain a classic instance of a principle which, I suspect, runs all through the mental phenomena, namely that it is the sitter who produces the results, not the medium." This suggests that Mrs. Leonard first used the word "drains" and that Thomas somehow prompted her to substitute it with the word "pipes." This is untrue. The first mention of "pipes" comes from Mrs. Leonard (with Drayton Thomas' father the apparent communicator) at the third sitting (*"An event nine weeks before he died for which 'the pipes' will be the clue"*). I can find no mention in the transcripts of the word "drains" before this. The next mention, at the fourth sitting, again comes from Feda, apparently listening to Bobbie (*" ... Bobbie, you say you got yours from the pipes"*). There is again no mention of drains at the sitting. Thomas does remark that after Feda spoke of "pipes" in the third sitting it occurred to him that the word might refer to defective drainage, but when he put this possibility to the family "they refused to accept any suggestion of the kind ... the word 'pipes' meant nothing to them."

The only other criticism of note came from Dr. Soal, who referred to Drayton Thomas' report as "vague" (again it seems unclear that he had read it with any care), and wonders if, on a brief visit to Nelson some years before the Bobbie Newlove case, Thomas had heard the words "Bentley" and "Catelnow," and hearing vague approximations to them during the sittings had assumed that these were the names communicated by Bobbie. Thomas answered this by referring Soal to the shorthand records of the sittings which contained both of the place names and which had been written down at the time exactly as the stenographer heard them pronounced.

The 33 statements concerning the pipes remain impressive in their accuracy, particularly when taken with the rest of the material produced at the sittings. They cannot readily be attributed to lucky guessing by Gladys Leonard, or to research by her into the Newlove/Hatch family. We can dismiss any suggestion that Bobbie may have told one of his friends (certainly he did not tell his family) that he feared the water from the pipes had predisposed him to diphtheria. No child would have been near Bobbie once he went down with such an infectious and dangerous disease as diphtheria. The statements also pose great difficulties for the Super-ESP hypothesis. Could Gladys Leonard have got the idea telepathically that the pipes caused a condition predisposing Bobbie to diphtheria? If so, from where could she have got it? It was not in the minds of any of the family, or in that of Drayton Thomas. It was Bobbie himself who raised the matter during the sittings, and he appears to have been prompted in part at least by Mr. Thomas Senior. During the third sitting, Feda says that the word "pipes" comes from Mr. Thomas Senior who "asked Bobbie a few questions before the sitting that I thought might have a bearing on his earth life, and this was one of them." Can we suppose that he told one of his friends that the tonsillitis from which he was suffering prior to diphtheria might have been due to the water at the pipes, leaving the friend (or someone to whom the friend may have spoken) subsequently to deduce that the tonsillitis lowered his resistance to diphtheria, and leaving Gladys Leonard to pick up the deduction telepathically? Unlikely, and there is surely a point where speculation becomes so tortuous that it has no place in any serious discussion, and this seems a good example of such speculation.

If Gladys Leonard could not have got the idea of the pipes by telepathy, could she have done so by clairvoyance? Unlikely, as the information was not recorded anywhere, and one cannot reasonably suppose that she found her way (with no link) clairvoyantly to the pipes, then clairvoyantly assessed the quality of the water and recognized it as likely to predispose anyone who drank it to diphtheria. Precognition by her of the moment when Drayton Thomas learnt from the Medical Officer that the surface water was contaminated can also be effectively ruled out. Drayton Thomas only checked on the quality of the water with the Medical Officer of Health *as a direct result of what he had been told at the sitting*. Surely we cannot suppose that Gladys Leonard precognized an action of his – i.e. consulting the Medical Officer about the state of the water – which he only undertook as a direct result of what she had already told him about the pipes. Even if we were prepared to make this absurd supposition, we would then have to explain why, instead of speaking of the Medical Officer's report and the contaminated surface water, her supposed precognition was communicated to Thomas dressed up in several layers of fantasy purportedly to do with an attempt by Bobbie to convey the idea of "pipes," much to the puzzlement of both Thomas and of the Newlove/Hatch family.

Quite different issues are raised if we ask why Bobbie did not mention The Heights and Brierfield by name during the sittings, and only referred to them by initials. Mentioning them by name would have saved everyone a great deal of trouble. But as already pointed out, difficulty with names is a common feature of mediumship. Communicators frequently offer clues (initials, misspellings, parts of words, symbolic visual images) to the names concerned rather than give them in full. This suggests that the name is often known to the communicator, but that he or she cannot recall it fully or get it through to the control or the medium. Communicators have suggested that the difficulty partly arises because names, which are simply labels and often arbitrary ones at that, mean little to the deceased, who are much better able to remember deeper and more meaningful aspects of their earthly existence such as feelings and experiences, hopes and aspirations, relationships and interests, personal strengths and weaknesses. Be this as it may, what seems clear is that although Bobbie could only communicate the initial letters of "Heights" and "Brierfield," he otherwise comes across during the sittings very much as a 10-year-old boy recalling his earthly memories, interests, and favorite things, and giving descriptions and explanations very much as would a 10-year-old boy.

However, we may still be left wondering why Bobbie did not give clearer statements during the sittings, and why the puzzle of the pipes went on so long. There are two possible answers. One is the perhaps confused state of Bobbie himself. He was only ten years old when he died, and he began communicating only three months after his unexpected and painful death. Those who have worked with young children will know only too well the rather muddled way in which they give accounts of themselves and descriptions of their doings. In view of this, Bobbie might be said to have performed rather well. The second possible answer was given by Drayton Thomas' father (who it will be remembered was one of those helping Bobbie) when Thomas put this question to him through Mrs. Leonard's mediumship after the conclusion of the case. The Reverend Thomas Senior said in sum that each piece of information from the communicators could only be filtered through the mind of the control or of the medium at opportune moments. "I should wish," he is reported as saying, "to start with that piece which will enable me to proceed methodically, but I may find that I cannot convey it to Feda, or that she cannot convey it to the medium. So I have to give just whatever happens to fit at the moment." He likened the whole thing to a jigsaw puzzle, with the pieces presented in a rather jumbled fashion. Only at the end could the sitter put all the bits together and make proper sense of what is being conveyed.

Drayton Thomas and the Newlove/Hatch family were clearly in no doubt that all the pieces of the puzzle did finally fall into place.

CHAPTER 10.

ARE STATEMENTS BY MEDIUMS TOO GENERAL AND TOO TRIVIAL?

Could Statements by Mediums Apply to Everyone?

A frequent criticism of mediums is that the messages they give are so general that they could apply not just to the sitter but to almost everyone. Statements for example that "your grandfather is here" could safely be given to any elderly man or woman, and messages such as "he knows you have had some difficulties lately, but these will pass," or "he is telling me he had some chest trouble before he died," or "he wants you to know that he is helping you, and sends you his love" could fit almost any deceased grandfather. Similarly, critics claim that mediums often "fish" for information by asking questions like "Is your father in spirit?," or "Who are the two men in your family or who are connected to you in some way?," or "Were you close to your mother?," and then use the sitter's response as a clue on what to say next. For example, the medium may ask "Was your grandfather very particular about his dress?," and when told by the sitter that he was, will follow up with "Yes I thought so, because he's wearing a very smart suit." Or the medium may ask, "Is someone you know connected with the sea?," and if this is denied may then change tack and ask "Well does someone live near the sea?," to which the answer is almost bound to be "yes." Even if the statement by the medium is wrong, it is claimed by critics she will wriggle out of it. Thus if a statement such as "There is a date in April that was important to your mother" is met with blank looks, this may be supplemented with "Well remember I told you this, and ask someone in your family about it."

It would be easy to reply to this criticism by saying that only very poor mediums would resort to this kind of behavior, but the skeptic will answer that the difference between poor and good mediums is simply that the latter are less obvious in their generalizations, in their fishing, and in their ability to cover up their mistakes. The skeptic will add that the good medium is also adept at reading the sitter's body language, and that on the strength of this language can deduce a great deal about the sitter and use this as a clue to what "communications" to give. Thus the only suitable reply is to put these criticisms to the test. Suppose therefore that we ask a sitter to tell us how many of the statements made to him or her by a medium are accurate, and we then give the same list of statements to a number of other people who were not sitters, and ask them how many of these statements would apply to them. If significantly more statements are claimed as appropriate by the sitter than by the non-sitters, then it looks as if the charge that statements are so general they could apply to anyone is incorrect. However, if the sitter *knows* he is the sitter, he may be more inclined to rate statements as correct than if he were a non-sitter. Accordingly, we need to tighten up the experiment, so that no one knows whether he is the sitter or the non-sitter. At the same time, we can ensure the medium does not fish for clues, does not ask questions of the sitter, and does not observe body language, by placing the medium on one side of a screen and the group of individuals who will constitute the sitter and the non-sitters on the other side, out of the medium's sight. We can place the group in numbered chairs, then select a number at random and designate the individual in that chair as the sitter. This number can then be communicated to the medium but not to the members of the group, thus ensuring that no one knows whether he is the sitter or not. The medium now has the task of conveying messages to an unknown, invisible, and silent sitter known only to her by a number, while on the other side of the screen the whole group is in ignorance as to who amongst them is the sitter, and therefore in ignorance as to whom the messages are supposed to apply. We can even ensure that those conducting the research do not know who the sitter is by arranging matters so that they do not see the number when it is being given to the medium.

This experimental methodology effectively ensures that the medium cannot make use of fishing and questioning, and cannot obtain clues from the sitter's replies and body language. At the end of the session, and still in ignorance as to who was selected as sitter, all members of the group are given copies of the statements given by the medium and asked to rate them for applicability to themselves. If the person designated as sitter accepts significantly more of these statement than do the other members of the group, we can, provided all the controls have been strictly maintained throughout, suppose that the medium has gained her information paranormally. The experiment also poses difficulties for the Super-ESP theory because, if it were to operate, the medium, without any assistance from the group or the investigators, would have to obtain the identity of the sitter clairvoyantly and then switch to telepathy in order to read his or her thoughts before dramatizing them into a fictional communicator, or alternatively to obtain the identity of the sitter by clairvoyance and then precognize the moment when the sitter sees and accepts as correct the statements intended for him. Braude's so-called "magic wand" hypothesis, mentioned in Chapter 5, would explain how this could happen by arguing that paranormal abilities arise from a common source and therefore act in concert rather than separately. The reply to this, given earlier, is that if mediums do indeed possess this "magic wand," are we supposed to believe they cannot use it to determine from where their information actually comes? Until this question can be answered, and experiments set up that demonstrate that those insisting they use only psychic abilities (unfortunately for supporters of the "magic wand" theory their number is unlikely to be large) can produce similar results to those employing mediumship, it is difficult to place much credence in magic wands.

Experimental Evidence: The Work of Robertson and Roy in the UK and of Schwartz and Russek in the USA

The first recorded attempt to carry out the kind of experimental methodology I have detailed was published by H. F. Saltmarsh, a prominent member of the SPR, as long ago as 1930. Saltmarsh gave the statements communicated through medium Mrs. Warren Elliott by an airman killed in the First Word War to six individuals who had also lost a young relative in the same war, and invited them to score these statements for applicability to themselves had they been the sitter. Only 8 per cent of the statements turned out to be applicable to these individuals, as opposed to the 72.8 per cent rated as applicable by the sitter who had actually received them. However, the six non-sitters knew the statements were not intended for them, and this may have led them to respond more negatively to them. To avoid this danger, Dr. J. G. Pratt, a colleague of Rhine in the parapsychology laboratory at Duke University (and one of the few who took an active interest in survival research) arranged for medium Eileen Garrett to be located in a separate room while she gave 15 sittings to 15 different sitters. The transcripts of all 15 sittings were then passed to the 15 sitters, who remained in the dark as to which of them was intended for him or her. The sitters then rated the statements in each of the 15 transcripts for applicability to themselves. Results showed that the sitters scored the statements in the transcript intended for themselves significantly higher than the statements in the other transcripts (Pratt 1936). A follow-up study using a more sophisticated rating system produced similarly significant results (Pratt and Birge 1948). Another important study was carried out in 1958 by Professor Gertrude Schmeidler, working with medium Mrs. Caroline Chapman. The methodology involved Mrs. Chapman in giving sittings in which Professor Schmeidler acted as proxy sitter – i.e. acted in place of the recipients for whom the communications were really intended – thus avoiding the risk that the medium might fish or pick up clues from the sitter. Sixteen sittings were held, four for each of four recipients, and the recipients asked to rate all 16 transcripts without knowing which ones were intended for them. As in the previous studies, recipients rated significantly more statements in their own transcripts as correct.

The above studies suggest that the communications given by the mediums concerned could not be attributed to lucky guessing on their part, or to over-generalizations or clues obtained from sitters. However, this line of research was then neglected for a number of years, and it is only recently that similar studies have begun to appear using more extensive trials and more tightly controlled methods. These studies, by Professor Roy of the University of Glasgow and physicist Patricia Robertson, provide further support for the argument that mediums' statements are not so general that they could apply equally well to anyone. In their initial studies Roy and Robertson (Robertson and Roy 2001, Roy and Robertson 2001) used ten mediums, 44 people for whom the mediums' messages were intended (the "recipient group") and 407 people for whom the messages were not intended (the "non-recipient" group). Results showed that the recipient group accepted far more of the messages as appropriate to themselves than did the non-recipient group, with odds against the differences between the two groups being due to chance more than a million million to one against. Thus the messages did indeed seem specific to the recipient group, and not so general that they could also be accepted as relevant to themselves by the non-recipient group. However, the weakness of this protocol was that not only were the mediums allowed to see the recipients and may in consequence have gained clues from their body language, but people who know messages are intended for them may be more inclined to accept such messages as relevant than are people who know the messages are not intended for them. Accordingly, in further studies Roy and Robertson progressively tightened their protocols, and established that even when firstly the medium and the sitters are isolated from each other, secondly the medium does not know the identity of the person for whom the messages are intended (recipients are identified to the mediums only by a number), and thirdly recipients and non-recipients do not know whether they belong to the recipient or the non-recipient group (and thus no one in either group knows whether the messages are intended for them or not) individuals in the recipient group still accept significantly more of the messages intended for them than do individuals in the non-recipient group. The odds against the differences in acceptance and non-acceptance by the two groups being due to chance are smaller than in the earlier experiments but they are still huge, and of the order of a million to one against chance (Robertson and Roy 2004).

In a recent study, Professor Schwartz of the Human Energy Systems Laboratory at the University of Arizona and his colleagues (Schwartz *et al* 2001) used a different approach, involving only one sitter (known to have experienced six significant bereavements over the previous ten years) and five well-regarded mediums. The sitter, who was unknown to the mediums, had sittings with each of them, separated from visual contact by an opaque screen. She was allowed to say only "yes" or "no" by way of verbal response to any questions asked of her by the mediums. Analysis of the sittings revealed that on average 83 per cent of the mediums' statements were rated correct by the sitter. But could their success have been due simply to clever guessing? To test this possibility, the investigators prepared a questionnaire based on 70 of the correct statements made by the mediums, re-worded to act as questions (for example the statement by the medium that correctly gave the name of the sitter's child was re-worded as "What is the name of the sitter's child?," and the statement giving the cause of death of the sitter's mother became, "What was the cause of her mother's death?"), and the questionnaire was then given to 68 non-sitters acting as controls who were asked to *guess* the correct answers. Results showed that their average success rate at doing so was only 36 per cent. The difference between the 83 per cent success rate of the statements made by the mediums and the 36 per cent success rate of guesswork by the controls was significant at the ten million to one level against chance.

Comparisons between these success rates must be treated with some caution, as the controls did not have the benefit of hearing the sitter's "yes/no" answers to questions, which by tone of voice may have given the mediums some clue as to whether or not they were on the right track. The controls, who were undergraduate students, were also younger than the sitter and the mediums, which could mean that they had a different mind-set when it came to guessing such things as names. Nevertheless, it is difficult to explain away differences of this magnitude between the two success rates by normal means. Even the highest scorer among the controls did not approach the success rate of the least successful of the mediums (54 per cent for the guess-work of the control as opposed to 80 per cent for the medium), and in a partial replication of the experiment that did not allow 'yes/no' responses from the sitter (who had tragically lost her husband in a car accident in the period between the initial experiment and the partial replication), the mediums still obtained a success rate of 77 per cent.

In a further series of experiments by Schwartz, Russek and Barentsen (2002) three mediums each gave sittings to five female sitters unknown to them (15 sittings in total), with each sitting consisting of two ten-minute periods. In the first period the sitter, again hidden from the medium by a screen, remained silent and the medium was allowed to ask no questions, while in the second questions were allowed to which the sitter, still behind the screen, responded only with nods or shakes of the head which the experimenter sitting with her verbalized as "yes" or "no," thus ensuring the mediums did not hear the voice of the sitter. At the end of the experiment, each sitter was given her own transcript together with those of the other four sitters, without knowing which was which, and asked to rate the statements in all the transcripts on a scale (from "plus 3" – a definite hit, to "minus three" – a definite miss) as if they applied to herself. Results showed that on average the sitters rated 40 per cent of the statements in their own transcripts as plus 3, as compared to only 25 per cent of the statements rated as "plus 3" in the transcripts of the other sitters. They rated only 29 per cent of the statements in their own transcripts as "minus 3," as compared to rating 42 per cent of the statements "minus 3" in the transcripts of the other sitters.

The odds against these results being obtained by chance were three in a hundred. The fact that these results, although significant, are not so impressive as those from the other studies just mentioned may be explained by the small size of the sample (only 15 transcripts) and by variations in the success rate among the mediums, one of whom averaged 54 per cent accuracy in statements made, another of whom averaged 40 per cent, and the third of whom averaged only 28 per cent. This variation is of interest in itself, and suggests two conclusions. The first is that for any experiments into mediumship the quality of the individual mediums involved must be taken into account. The second is that the conditions under which mediums work may affect their performance. The medium obtaining only a 28 per cent success rate may have performed much better in different circumstances. In addition, some sitters appear to work better with some mediums than do others. In the present experiment, the mediums had no obvious links with the sitters, and were unable even to hear their voices. Many mediums would doubtless refuse to work under these conditions. We could argue that failure to see and hear the sitter removes the visual and verbal clues upon which the medium depends for "guessing" her information. But equally we could say that the medium requires some form of emotional rapport with the sitter, and that a particular frame of mind in the sitter (objective rather than gullible or hostile) may be essential if successful results are to be obtained.

There is an obvious necessity to have trial runs with mediums when developing experimental methodologies of the above kind, and then to work only with those mediums who appear to perform well under these methodologies. It is little use attempting experiments with unsuitable or untried mediums, and there is a danger that inexperienced investigators, anxious to replicate the work of Schwartz and his colleagues, may attempt to do just this, inevitably producing non-significant results that will call into question the successful findings already obtained. The investigators I have just referenced are fortunate in having the co-operation of apparently gifted mediums who are able to work under the very stringent conditions imposed, and if the results so far obtained with these mediums continue to be replicated, then they will present us with some of the most important evidence yet available in favor of the survival hypothesis.

In another experiment, using only one medium and one sitter, Schwartz and Russek (2001) made use of the telephone. Both medium and sitter, who had never met and who did not know each other's identities (though the sitter had been given the name of the medium as one of those who might be involved) were separated by hundreds of miles, and with only the telephone as a link between them. Before the telephone connection was made, the sitter was asked to "invite" the deceased people with whom he wished to make contact, while the medium attempted to link in to the sitter mentally, and to give the names of these people and of any other communicator who appeared to come through. The telephone connection was then established, but the mute button was depressed at the medium's end of the line by the investigator and kept depressed during this phase of the experiment. Although the telephone was live at the sitter's end, he was instructed to say nothing, and his compliance with this instruction was monitored by the investigator. At the end of the session the transcript of the statements made by the medium both before and after the establishment of the telephone link was checked with the sitter. The four people "invited" by the latter to communicate (two friends, Michael and Jerry, an aunt called Alice, and his father called Bob) were all correctly named by the medium, although the relationships were not specified. The medium also correctly gave the Christian name of the sitter, and referred to a dog whose name began with "S" (the sitter confirmed that a dog, Suzanne, of special significance to him, had indeed died). Critics may suggest that as the sitter was given instructions to "invite" communicators during the period prior to the opening of the telephone connection, the medium may have picked up their names telepathically. This is true, and the experiment could be repeated without these instructions being given.

The research reported by Roy and Robertson and by Schwartz and his colleagues in the above publications is too detailed to receive full justice in the space available here. But these various outlines suggest that research of the kind that they are pioneering may do much to substantiate further the reality of mediumship. As more becomes known, it may even help us to find answers to some of the questions that have puzzled investigators since the days of the Fox sisters in the mid-nineteenth century. For example, although the percentage of correct statements given by mediums is high, there is nevertheless a sizeable percentage that is wrong. In the Schwartz, Russek, and Barensen research, an average of 29 per cent of the statements were rated as definitely incorrect by the sitters for whom they were intended. Why should this be? As they were rated "definitely" wrong we must assume that the sitter realized that no amount of checking after the sitting could turn up evidence to vindicate them. Did the medium lose contact with the communicator when giving these statements, and unwittingly simply present personal thoughts? This is possible. I have had sittings with some mediums at which every statement given has been wrong (just as I have had sittings where most statements have been right), and the mediums concerned seemed incapable of recognizing their errors.

Another possibility is that the medium, when in the receptive state of mind seemingly necessary in order to receive communications, may also be particularly open to telepathic impressions, whether from the sitter or from people in general. Thus together with genuine contacts some apparent facts may be oddments culled unwittingly from living minds. Yet another possibility – at least in the instances when most of the other statements are correct – is that the communicator gets things wrong. There may be failures of memory on his or her part, or the communicator may be confusing the sitter with somebody else, or may even intentionally wish to mislead, like some of the supposed earthbound spirits discussed in some detail in Chapter 8. Yet another possibility is that the medium may from time to time pick up statements from another communicator who is trying to make contact (and who may even be confusing the sitter with somebody else).

If research of the kind undertaken by Roy and Robertson and by Schwartz and his colleagues builds up a sufficiently large data bank of statements known to be correct, we may find that it is of equal interest to study those rated incorrect in some detail. What relationship, if any, do they bear to correct statements? Do they show any particular patterns of their own? For example, do they mostly concern names or the sitter's earlier years or the sitter's relationships or current life events or the communicator's own life history? Could it be that some of them represent the communicator's fantasy life, things he or should would like to have done while on earth or qualities he or she would like to have possessed? If we could answer some of these questions, we would be a step closer to understanding what really goes on during mediumship. Research conducted by investigators such as Roy and the others mentioned who are known to be sympathetic to mediumship and not merely intent on exposing it as spurious, may also encourage more mediums to become involved in serious research. Most of the mediums to whom I have spoken are only too anxious to find our more about their gifts, but unfortunately have only a hazy idea of what is meant by "research." It should not be difficult to obtain their co-operation. I sometimes wonder how many mediums of the caliber of Leonora Piper, Gladys Leonard, and Eileen Garrett are living and working in obscurity. But for the discovery of Mrs. Piper and the many years of patient, time-consuming, and costly research carried out with her by leading members of the SPR such as Sir Oliver Lodge, Frederick Myers, and Richard Hodgson, we may have heard of her abilities only at the anecdotal level, and learnt little of her ability to produce successful results under tightly controlled conditions. The same can be said of some of the other mediums who will be described in the book. Since interest shifted towards psychic abilities such as telepathy, clairvoyance, and precognition in the 1930s, scientific research into mediumship has steadily declined. It looks now as if it is in the process of being restored.

Before accepting the evidence yielded by this research, the critic will quite rightly want to be assured that all possible precautions were taken to prevent the mediums obtaining their information by normal means. Is it certain the sitters were unknown to the mediums? What if anything did the investigators tell the mediums about the sitters? Were all opportunities for sensory leakage eliminated? For example, is it certain the screen between the medium and the sitters really was opaque? Is it certain the sitters did not whisper reactions to the investigator during the experiments, which the medium may have heard? Was there any chance the mediums might have caught sight of the sitters arriving for the experiment? The critic will also want to know whether or not the mediums knew anyone connected with the sitters who might have provided information about them. Some of these criticisms are difficult to meet. One can never be sure that a medium has not met a sitter at some point before the commencement of an experiment, even though the meeting may have been many years ago and consciously forgotten by both medium and sitter. The possibility that the medium has met someone connected with the sitter is equally impossible to eliminate. But steps can certainly be taken virtually to rule out sensory leakage (the risk that during the experiment the medium may receive clues from the sitters), and it looks as if investigators are now well on the way to doing so.

Are Communications Through Mediums Too Trivial?

In attempting to answer this question we must first ask another one: what is the purpose behind communications from the deceased? There can be only one answer. If we travel to a distant country in this life, our first thought on "phoning home" is to assure everyone that we have arrived safely. How much more would this be true if we find ourselves still existing after death. However trivial it might sound to others, the message that we are all right is also the message that those at home most want to hear. As part of this message, we would in addition want to assure those at home that it is really we who are talking. Normally we do this by giving our names. Sometimes simply the sound of our voice is enough. So to go back to our original question, the purpose behind communications from the deceased is to assure us of their safe arrival and of their identity. However, the deceased face a problem. They cannot simply pick up the telephone and talk to us (although there have been some reports of brief messages apparently from the deceased coming through by telephone – see e.g. Rogo and Bayless 1979). They have to try to impress their message upon the mind of the medium or, as recent experiments in ITC appear to show (Chapter 14) upon electronic media. A particular difficulty arises with proof of identity. Even if, after death, you are able to remember arbitrary labels such as names and succeed in getting them through to the medium, how are we to know that you are who you say you are?

Professor Oliver Lodge once sat his children down around the table and attempted, as a game, to convince them that he really was Oliver Lodge. It seems he was unsuccessful. In an even better test, Professor James Hyslop set up a telegraph link between two widely separated buildings on the campus of Columbia University, and manned one end of the link himself while some of his students manned the other. The purpose of the experiment was to determine whether or not the students could prove their individual identities to the professor, who did not know in what order they would contact him and who of course could not hear their voices across the telegraph link. When it was the turn of Louis Ansbacher, who tells of the experiment in his book *The Challenge of the Unknown*, he telegraphed a number of erudite statements about philosophers well known to Hyslop and himself, but to no avail. Hyslop had no idea who he was. Ansbacher then thought of telegraphing "Coming up in the Amsterdam Avenue car, you and I discussed Bergson's *Creative Evolution*. The conductor was amused at our barbarous French. We both tried to pay the fare. Your dime dropped into the mat." Hyslop immediately telegraphed back "Ansbacher."

Medium Arthur Ford (1969) tells how one of his sitters, Professor Jerome Ellison, received the name "Burch" from Ford's control Fletcher while Ford himself was in trance. Ellison remembered having a Sunday-school teacher of that name when he was a boy. Fletcher went on to say that "Burch" was also giving him something about a white rabbit. Ellison replied that he had a white rabbit when a boy, but that this was nothing to do with Mr. Burch. Fletcher persisted that the rabbit "was related somehow to you and to Mr. Burch," and asked if perhaps Mr. Burch was nicknamed Bunny. Professor Ellison rejected this, and was then told by a frustrated Fletcher to "check it out." A year later, on a visit to his mother, Ellison related the incident. "You mean you don't remember" his mother said in surprise, "The white rabbit was given to you as an Easter present by Mr. Burch." Professor Ellison comments that for small children the gift is usually much more readily remembered than the giver. To illustrate this he reminds us that when writing thank-you letters children frequently appeal to their parents to be told who gave them what. Thus although he remembered the white rabbit from childhood, he did not recall until his mother mentioned it that it was from Mr. Burch that he received it (notice out of interest how Fletcher, having given the correct information, then entered into a speculation of his own when introducing the incorrect word "Bunny" and suggesting erroneously that it might have been a nickname. Mediums can often confuse sitters in this way when they fail to restrict themselves simply to what is given to them by communicators).

The incident, trivial as it was, was sufficient to convince Ellison that Mr. Burch had been in contact. Checking up on trivial incidents in this way can be very important. Once, just after I had given a lecture I was told by medium Brian Gledhow, who had been listening to me, that he had seen the spirit of a clergyman standing beside me. People have told me in the past that they have seen exotic figures like Tibetan Llamas standing near me when I have been lecturing, and although I do not take these tales seriously, my immediate reaction was that a clergyman was rather less exciting. Brian then handed me a drawing he had made of the gentleman concerned, which I glanced at and put in my briefcase without another thought. However, a few days later I came across the drawing and looked at it closely for the first time. Immediately I recognized it resembled a deceased uncle of mine, Ben, who had been a clergyman. I took the drawing to my mother, and without mentioning how I came by it asked her who it looked like. As soon as she set eyes on it she said emphatically "Ben." Brian had never seen my Uncle Ben, who had lived many miles away while alive, and had no idea that I had a relative or friend who was a clergyman. The incident, trivial to an outsider, was nevertheless important evidence to me.

The great majority of communications between people while alive consists of small talk, the recall of little incidents, a shared joke or two, enquiries about mutual friends, anecdotes of daily happenings, references to mutual interests, etc. This also helps explain the apparent trivia of many mediumistic communications (though by no means all, as we shall see from those summarized in Chapter 18). Arthur Oram, a senior Council member and former Honorary Secretary of the SPR, who has for many years been sitting regularly with a number of well-regarded mediums, insists that it is often trivia such as a characteristic turn of phrase, a particular sense of humor, a trait of personality, a certain way of thinking that are most important in helping him recognize that communicators are indeed who they say they are. The consistency shown by the same communicator over a number of sittings also provides good evidence. Even as in life we recognize our friends for whom they are partly because they have enduring personal qualities, so do we recognize them, Arthur Oram insists, after death.

The point often stressed by mediums is that people are still people, whether on earth or in the afterlife. The afterlife does not suddenly make saints of sinners, or wise men and women out of the ignorant, or peaceful people out of violent people. As we shall see in Chapter 18, we are told that much learning awaits us after death. Our interests, our concerns, our way of thinking go with us to the afterlife, at least for a time, and it is these interests and concerns and ways of thinking that lie behind the great majority of communications of the deceased. And often in the very trivia of these communications resides the best proof of the reality of survival.

CHAPTER 11
PHYSICAL MEDIUMSHIP: INDEPENDENT VOICE PHENOMENA

Independent (Direct) Voice Mediumship

Among the many interesting features of Gladys Leonard's mediumship (Chapter 7) was her development of what is known as independent voice phenomena, that is phenomena in which supposed spirit voices are heard coming from thin air rather than from the medium's mouth. At one time commentators (e.g. Drayton Thomas) used the term "direct voice" for this, but currently there is a tendency to reserve "direct voice" for those occasions when communicators speak through the medium's voice box rather than simply conveying ideas to her which she then relays to sitters. On balance this distinction between independent and direct voices seems a useful one, and accordingly I shall use "independent voice" for those utterances that seem to have an objective existence distinct from the medium herself.

Drayton Thomas, who worked extensively with Gladys Leonard, gives many examples of the independent voices that sometimes occurred during her sittings, all of which took place in good light, and he is categorical that the voices concerned were not her own.

I hasten to assure [the critic] that there is no question possible in the mind of those who have heard it often. The direct [independent] voice does not proceed from [Mrs. Leonard's] lips, neither is it possible to confuse it with any whisper which Feda may make through those lips ... Feda's whisper proceeds from Mrs. Leonard's lips; the direct [independent] voice comes from a spot some two feet to three feet in front of the medium (SPR Proceedings Vol XLVIII, Part 173, 1947).

Others also reported hearing the independent voice during Mrs. Leonard's mediumship (e.g. Blatchford 1925). In 1933 two SPR members, using two pairs of microphones set up at different points in the room, found no evidence that the independent voice really was independent of Mrs. Leonard, but acknowledged that their method was "unsuitable for the observation of sounds ... produced from different and alternating sources." They also recognized that fatigue on the part of the investigators listening to the voices through headphones "supervened fairly rapidly and produced serious errors."

A notable feature of Mrs. Leonard's independent voice mediumship was that the voice, from its apparently separate location, was reported as heard variously to supply the correct word when Feda hesitated, to give the required word when Feda requested it, to supply the correct word without being asked, to address Feda directly, to correct her mistakes, to correct her pronunciation, to contradict her, and to remonstrate with her. The independent voice was also sometimes heard to start a new line of thought, which Feda then took up, and sometimes to say things unheard – or only partly heard – by Feda. To all intents and purposes therefore it was as if two quite separate people were operating during the sitting. The idea that Gladys Leonard was using ventriloquism to produce this effect seems to be absurd. As is well known, even when speaking for his dummy the ventriloquist's words issue from his own mouth. There is no such thing as literally "throwing the voice." The ventriloquist's trick is to keep his lips still while speaking and to distract attention from himself to his dummy, situated literally a few inches away from his mouth, by manipulating the lips and the face of the latter in all sorts of supposedly interesting and amusing ways. In the case of Mrs. Leonard, not only did the independent voice appear to come from some two to three feet away from her, but she was apparently in trance and there was no dummy to distract attention.

Genuine independent voice mediumship adds materially to the strength of the survival hypothesis in that there is no laboratory evidence to suggest that psychic abilities alone can produce independent paranormal voices. Independent voice mediumship is rare (though I have been fortunate enough to experience it myself, as I discuss later), but among the good, well-reported examples mention must be made of the American medium Etta Wriedt, and of two British mediums, Leslie Flint and John Sloan.

The Independent Voice Mediumship of Etta Wriedt

Etta Wriedt, from Detroit, Michigan, was investigated by, among many others, Professor Sir William Barrett, who together with Dawson Rogers provided the impetus behind the founding of the SPR. Initially skeptical – for scientists like Barrett Etta Wriedt must have sounded too good to be true – Barrett became convinced of her abilities, writing that "she is a genuine and remarkable medium, and has given abundant proof to others besides myself that the voices and the contents of the messages given are wholly beyond the range of trickery or collusion." But the most extensive investigation of Etta Wriedt's mediumship in Britain was by Vice-Admiral Usborne Moore (Moore 1913), who gives the above quotation from Barrett. Moore reports hearing three independent voices talking simultaneously to him during his sittings with her, one in each of his ears and one through a trumpet (the simple cone device sometimes used by independent voice mediums to amplify the voices, and that seemingly floats around the room of its own accord, halting in front of each sitter for whom there is a message).

At various times independent voices were reported to be heard speaking in Dutch, French, Spanish, Norwegian, Serbian, Croatian, and Arabic, although Mrs. Wriedt herself is said to have spoken only English. The deceased Professor Sidgwick communicated to Sir William Barrett at one of the sittings, and although Barrett doubted that Mrs. Wriedt knew that when alive, Sidgwick had a speech impediment, Sidgwick volunteered that he no longer stuttered. Frequently Mrs Wriedt, fully conscious or in trance, was heard speaking to sitters with her normal voice while simultaneously independent voices were audible. She is also reported as sometimes conversing with the independent voices herself, and materializations were said sometimes to be visible to the circle while she continued talking. For example, when, on one of Mrs. Wriedt's five visits to Britain, Admiral Moore took a friend of his, a man unknown to Mrs. Wriedt, to a séance he was immediately greeted with his name by one of Mrs Wriedt's controls, Dr. Sharp, through the independent voice. Mrs. Wriedt, perfectly conscious at the time, immediately demanded to know how Dr. Sharp knew this name, and was met with the reply "His dear wife and children told me he was here."

It is unfortunate that we have no recordings of Mrs. Wriedt's independent voices (her last visit to Britain was in 1919). Thus we cannot be certain of the accuracy of the various languages in which the voices were said to have spoken. However, Countess Nora Wydenbruck, an Austrian living in Britain, an experienced investigator and fluent in a number of European languages, reports hearing lengthy communications in good French, Italian, and German during one of Wriedt's séances (Wydenbruck 1938). Countess Wydenbruck writes that all the voices she heard "had distinct, different timbres, and the different languages and accents were most remarkable." She even heard the independent voice of a German soldier apparently killed in the First World War speaking in a "most peculiar [German] accent impossible to imitate" and characteristic of soldiers from German frontier regiments who were of Slav origin. Like Admiral Moore, Countess Wydenbruck reports hearing "two or three direct [independent] voices [speaking] simultaneously in the air, while the medium in trance was also speaking." Both she and her husband received lengthy independent voice communications (her husband in German, French, and Italian and in the Slav-accented German) containing information apparently known only to them. She examines the theory that the sitters subconsciously influenced the ectoplasm produced by Mrs. Wriedt, thus forming whatever mechanism was needed to produce the many and various voices in foreign languages, but concludes that "Somehow it seems simpler to accept the incredible."

If Countess Wydenbruck is right in her statement that the independent voices spoke correctly in foreign languages, and if Admiral Moore is right that many sitters vouched for this – then the evidence provided for survival is strengthened. We have Sir William Barrett's word for it that there was "no risk of trickery or collusion," at least in his experience of Mrs. Wriedt, and indeed it would be difficult to imagine how she, a visitor to Britain and

Northern Ireland, could have roped in (let alone paid – she charged only nominal fees for her sittings) accomplices with a good grasp not only of the sitters and their affairs but of the various languages spoken by them. We are also told by Admiral Moore that although the majority of the sittings took place in darkness, communicators who manifested physically were able to find sitters unerringly when they wished to touch them (and this in the days before infra-red viewers or image intensifiers). Admiral Moore gives written testimony after testimony from sitters – many of them people of status – to the effect that communicators proved their identity by talking of personal details unknown to Mrs. Wriedt, and that some of the voices resembled those of the communicators in life. It has already been pointed out that there is no evidence that the living can produce independent voices by psychic means, and after studying the accounts of Mrs. Wriedt's mediumship one is seemingly left with only two realistic explanations, firstly that in spite of the almost overwhelming difficulties involved, trickery of some kind was used, or secondly that the communicators were who they claimed to be.

The Independent Voice Mediumship of Leslie Flint

We can reach a similar conclusion with the second of our independent voice mediums, Leslie Flint. Living in a time when modern research methods were becoming available, Flint regarded himself as one of the most carefully tested of all British mediums, and we have a large number of audio tapes of the voices at his sittings. Although originally a trance medium voicing the words of the communicators, Flint went less often into trance once the independent voice phenomena began. Like Etta Wriedt, he sometimes remained conscious throughout, and he too was often able to engage in conversations with the spirit voices. In his autobiography (1917) Flint tells us that his first psychic experience occurred in 1918, when he was seven. An aunt of his, Aunt Nell, entered the kitchen in tears on having heard of the death of her husband, Flint's Uncle Alf, in France. Flint reports that she was followed into the kitchen by a soldier carrying Uncle Alf's personal effects in a kitbag, and a second soldier who stood in the kitchen looking sad and lost, and who tried to attract Aunt Nell's attention by pulling at her sleeve. Both soldiers were ignored, and when the young Flint later saw a photograph of the dead Uncle Alf – who he tells us elsewhere in the book he never saw in life – he recognized him as the second of the two soldiers. Needless to say he was soundly punished for lying when he tried to tell his family of his experience. (If the story is correctly told, the first soldier may have been one of the "helpers" said to be witnessed at deathbeds.)

Flint tells us that, following on from his trance mediumship, his independent voice mediumship commenced with persistent whispered paranormal voices around him when he was sitting in the darkness of a cinema (not surprisingly it seemed that such whispers caused great annoyance to fellow cinema-goers). Prompted by this experience to try for independent voices, he found that sitters assured him not only of the genuineness of the phenomena but that the voices concerned were recognized as those of deceased friends and relatives. So strong and consistent were the voices that Flint soon attracted the attention of researchers, and three of the experiments set up by them to test him deserve mention. In the first of these, organized by the Reverend Drayton Thomas in 1948, Thomas closed Flint's mouth with adhesive surgical tape over which he secured a scarf, then tied Flint's hands to the arms of his chair. Another cord was tied at his forehead so that he could not bend his head and attempt to remove scarf and tape by rubbing his mouth against his shoulders. The sitting proceeded as normal, and Drayton Thomas reported that independent voices were heard with all their usual clarity, sometimes even shouting loudly. At the close of the sitting, it was found that everything securing Ford was still firmly in place.

This appeared to dispose of the theory, held by some researchers, that although Flint might perhaps receive genuine spirit communications, the supposed independent voices were not independent at all but came from his own lips. A few weeks later Drayton Thomas arranged for the Research Officer of the SPR, Dr. Donald West (subsequently Professor of Psychiatry at the University of Cambridge and twice President of the SPR) and other SPR members to attend a sitting of Flint's circle. Donald West was invited to secure Flint's arms to his chair and to seal his mouth with both horizontal and vertical strips of adhesive tape, and to trace around each strip with indelible pencil to ensure that any movement of the tapes during the sitting would be readily apparent. Flint, entranced on this occasion, sat in the darkness of a cabinet as it was agreed that the lights would remain on in the room. Again voices were heard, and Dr. West was given permission by the communicators to raise the curtain of the cabinet briefly during the sitting, with the lights still on, to check that everything securing Flint was still intact. All seemed well, but on checking at the end of the sitting Donald West discovered that one of the pieces of tape was no longer in line with his pencil markings. Although no suggestion was made that this was Flint's doing (one of the tapes may have moved slightly with Flint's labored breathing) this invalidated the test.

The test took place long before my own involvement in psychical research, but I still hear criticisms of Donald West's actions. This criticism misunderstands the nature of the scientific method. Having decided on the protocol to be used in a test, the scientist is bound to measure success in terms of whether or not this protocol is satisfied. In the experiment with Flint, the protocol depended on there being no disturbance to the adhesive tape around Flint's mouth and to the cords securing him. In the event, there *was* some disturbance to the tape, although there was no claim that Flint himself was responsible, and no explanation as to how, bound as he was, he could have displaced the tape deliberately or of how, with only a small displacement, he would have been able to fake independent voices. Nevertheless, Donald West's concern was to close every loophole that might permit critics to argue a normal explanation for the voices, no matter how unlikely this normal explanation might be. He was also doubtful that the cords binding Flint were fully secure owing to the thick coat that Flint insisted on wearing even though the cabinet was hot and stuffy, and would have preferred that the medium's hands were held throughout the sitting by disinterested observers.

Donald West attended two other sittings of the Flint circle, both of which took place in darkness and both of which left him unable to reach conclusions as to the genuineness or otherwise of the phenomena; he then invited Flint to participate in a more thorough investigation at the SPR offices. The conditions he suggested for the test were that the sitters would include "a majority of sympathetic spiritualists," that the medium should have his lips sealed and his hands held by sitters on either side, and that he should wear a throat microphone. The sitting could take place in complete darkness if Flint preferred, but in this case he should be under observation through an infrared viewer. Disappointed that he had not already satisfied Dr. West that the voices were genuine, Flint tells us in his autobiography that he refused.

It is a pity that Flint did not agree to be tested under Dr. West's conditions, none of which was in any sense unreasonable (a decision that he tells us in his book that he subsequently regretted). If satisfactory results had been obtained under these conditions it would have amounted to one of the most important validations of independent voice mediumship yet available to us. It is understandable that mediums feel inhibited by the presence of skeptics, but scientists involved in psychical research are rarely drawn to the subject by reason of skepticism. Their concern is simply that, if we wish to convince the scientific community in general of the reality of paranormal phenomena, then this can only be done through use of the scientific method, which is designed to eliminate alternative explanations for observed phenomena.

However, two years later Leslie Flint again agreed to be put to the scientific test, this time under the supervision of Professor Bennett, an electrical engineer from Columbia University, and under the aegis of Drayton Thomas and Brigadier Firebrace, another prominent researcher. This time, in addition to the usual taping and trussing, Flint was fastened to a throat microphone wired to an amplifier that would detect even the slightest attempt to use his voice; his hands were held by investigators, and an infrared viewer that detects movement even in the dark was trained upon him throughout. Once again independent voices were heard, though more faintly than usual, and Professor Bennett was able to confirm that Flint's vocal chords were not involved in their production. Very near the end of the sitting the infrared viewer failed, and immediately the voice heard speaking at the time increased in volume. Flint tells us that Brigadier Firebrace confirmed these facts in writing to him, and testified that the medium could have had no knowledge that the viewer had failed, yet the independent voice "immediately doubled in volume." Firebrace concluded from this that infrared may weaken mediumship in some way.

This last conclusion, if correct, is of some interest. In the various sittings I have had with mediums producing physical phenomena – of which more later – infrared viewers have never been permitted, apparently on the instructions of the spirit communicators, even though such viewers do not serve as a source of light or indeed add to the electrical energy in the room in any way. In our sittings with the Scole Group, detailed in due course, both the Group and we as investigators were puzzled by the refusal to let us use infrared. Skeptics predictably claim that such refusals are designed to safeguard the mediums from detection during their (allegedly) clandestine acts of trickery, but the experience with infrared at the Flint test provides some suggestion to the contrary. It need hardly be said of course that if we were able to use infrared, and no movements by the mediums were observed, the same skeptics would brush this fact aside with the comment that good conjurors can fool people under their noses in broad daylight, and that therefore the vague images shown up by infrared, however seemingly above suspicion, mean nothing. However, if Brigadier Firebrace was correct in his suggestion that infrared may have inhibited the phenomena at the Flint sitting, it would seem as if the general embargo said to be placed by spirits on infrared may have some justification.

Unlike Etta Wriedt, Flint worked at a time when it was possible to tape record independent voice sittings, and two of Flint's regular sitters, George Woods and Betty Greene, were able to put on record over 500 of their conversations with communicators. These were later transcribed, and a selection published by Neville Randall (Randall 1975). George Woods and Betty Greene were concerned primarily to investigate the experience of dying and the nature of the afterlife (Betty Greene's opening question to communicators was "Can you describe your reactions when you found yourself alive?"), and although this material carries its own interest, it is regrettable that once again no consistent attempt was made by investigators to obtain the kind of personal details from communicators that could be verified later. It also seems odd that communicators did not themselves offer these details, and request that contact be made with their surviving relatives and friends. As many of the communicators were what is now generally called drop-ins (i.e. unknown to anyone present, and thus immune to the charge that their details came telepathically from the sitters), this failure to collect verifiable information is doubly disappointing.

The Independent Voice Mediumship of John Sloan

Flint was never identified in fraud, and his mediumship further supports the survivalist argument that communications through at least certain mediums do not appear to be due to any psychic abilities in the living so far identified in laboratory experiments. Similar support comes from the work of John Sloan. Sloan was extensively studied by Arthur Findlay, a highly successful stockbroker, a Justice of the Peace, holder of the M.B.E. for his services to society, and the founder of the Glasgow Society for Psychical Research (who bequeathed his stately home, Stansted Hall, to the Spiritualist National Union who now use it as the Arthur Findlay College). Sloan was not sufficiently investigated by the scientists of his day, which means that his mediumship is less well known than that of the others I have mentioned in this and previous chapters. Findlay attributed the scientific neglect of Sloan to the latter's persistent refusal to become a public medium, to take money for his work, or to give demonstrations. Despite this refusal, Sir William Barrett, Sir Arthur Conan Doyle, Dr. Abraham Wallace, together with Sir Oliver Lodge and The Honorable Everard Feilding, Hon. Secretary of the SPR and the leader of the SPR team sent to investigate Italian medium Eusapia Palladino (Chapter 12), all had sittings with him. Feilding was sufficiently impressed by Sloan to send the Controller of Queen Alexandra's household incognito to a sitting at which Queen Alexandra's late husband, King Edward VII, apparently communicated, impressing the Controller with his identity. Sir William Barrett was equally impressed by Sloan, and put to the SPR Council of the day Findlay's offer to pay all Sloan's expenses for a sojourn in London in order that the SPR could test him under strictly controlled conditions. To Sir William's anger the SPR Council refused the offer. Findlay reports that no reason was given to him by the Council for this refusal, and no formal word of thanks was offered. Bitterly disappointed, he resigned his membership of the Society, and an opportunity to test an apparently gifted medium under strict conditions was lost. (Findlay also deplores the fact that although most of Sloan's sittings took place in proximity to Glasgow University, not one member of the academic staff volunteered an interest in attending, or responded to an invitation to do so.)

We thus have to rely primarily upon Arthur Findlay's own investigations for our knowledge of Sloan. Yet anyone who has read the extensive material he published on these investigations (particularly 1931, 1951, 1955), much of it containing accounts by other seemingly reliable eye-witnesses, can hardly fail to find it of interest. Sloan, like Flint, began as a trance medium, but later was able to remain conscious during some sittings, often commenting wryly upon things said by the communicators. He himself had little interest in mediumship, and conducted sittings solely for the benefit of others. Findlay describes him as "an upright, good, honest man, with little learning, a poor memory, and ... average intelligence ... This was the opinion of the very many other people who knew him, and I never once heard a word of suspicion about the honest conduct of his séances." At Findlay's first sitting with Sloan (at which he kept his identity from all those present), his deceased father communicated, gave his full name – Robert Downie Findlay – and announced that he had with him his deceased business partner, whose name, David Kidston, he also gave. Kidston then spoke, and between them the two men apologized for the fact that 14 years previously they had, at Kidston's insistence, refused to take Findlay into the family stockbroking and accountancy business on the grounds that it was not generating enough income to justify appointing another partner. According to Findlay, only three people ever knew of this refusal, he himself and the two dead men.

Findlay had 39 sittings with Sloan, and gives many details in *On the Edge of the Etheric* (1931). Frequently he tested Sloan, while independent voices were communicating, by holding Sloan's hands and placing his ear against Sloan's mouth. No movement of Sloan's lips was detected during these tests, and no sound emerged. One of the best cases indicative of survival during his investigation of Sloan occurred in 1919 when he took his brother John Findlay, demobilized from the army a few weeks previously, to a Sloan sitting. Findlay did not introduce John, and no one present knew that he had been a soldier, or that he had spent part of his time training machine gunners at Lowestoft on the East Coast and at Kessingland, a small village near Lowestoft. During the sitting the trumpet tapped John Findlay on the knee and a voice announced itself as "Eric Saunders." The former confessed he knew nobody by that name and asked Saunders where they had met. The ensuing interaction, which for convenience I present as a continuous conversation, went as follows ("JF" denotes John Findlay, and "S" Saunders):

S: *In the army.*
JF: *Aldershot? Bisley? France? Palestine?*
S: *No, none of these places. I knew you when you were near Lowestoft.*
JF: *Near Lowestoft?*
S: *You were not in Lowestoft then, but at Kessingland.*
JF: *To which company were you attached?*
S: *B? C?* (answer not clear)
JF: *Can you remember the name of your Company Commander?*
S: *MacNamara* (correct for Company Commander of B Company).
JF: (testing Saunders by pretending to remember him) *Oh yes, you were one of my Lewis gunners were you not?*
S: *No, you had not the Lewis guns then, it was the Hotchkiss* (the Hotchkiss machine gun replaced the Lewis gun in 1917).

JF then asked Saunders two or three leading questions, such as the name of

JF's own billet, all of which Saunders answered correctly. Then Saunders went on to say:

S: *We had great times there, Sir; do you remember the General's inspection?*

JF: *To which inspection do you refer?*

S: *The day the General made us race about with the guns.* (JF remembered this incident well, and the fact that it had caused a good deal of amusement among the men at the time.) Saunders then said that he was killed in France.

JF: *When did you go out to France?*

S: *With the big draft in August 1917.*

JF: *Why do you call it the big draft?*

S: *Don't you remember the big draft, when the Colonel came on the parade ground and made a speech?* (JF remembered that a particularly large draft had indeed gone out to France in August 1917, and that this was the only occasion on which he recalled the Colonel ever personally saying good-bye to the men.)

Saunders then thanked JF for the gunnery training, and said it had been most useful to him when he was in France. JF asked him why he had come through to speak with him.

S: *Because I have never forgotten that you once did me a good turn.* (JF had a hazy recollection of obtaining leave for one of the gunners, owing to some special circumstance, but whether or not his name was Saunders he could not remember.)

Six months later, JF was able to arrange a meeting with the corporal who had been his assistant with the light guns at Kessingland. The corporal consulted a pocket diary in which he had kept a full list of the men under training with JF, and looked up the records for B Company in 1917. Sure enough "Eric Saunders, fully qualified August 1917" appeared, and the corporal's notes also told him that Saunders had gone out to France with the draft that same August. Enquiries by Findlay at the War Office revealed that some 4,000 men of the name of Saunders had fallen in the war, and that without the details of Eric Saunders' regiment it was impossible to check further. It was indeed unfortunate that Saunders was not asked for the name of his regiment, but in my view even more unfortunate was that he was not asked for his army number (or at least the last three digits of it), which no soldier is ever likely to forget, and the date of his death. Had Saunders given these, and had enquiries at the War Office shown them to be correct, this would constitute one of the very best cases supporting survival in the literature. Even without this additional proof, it stretches the bounds of credibility to assume that telepathy from the living could be responsible, with Sloan contacting obscure memories hidden so deeply in JF's unconscious that JF could not himself recall them even when provided with the relevant details at the sitting and the confirmation of these details by his corporal. Arthur Findlay tells us that hundreds of men completed the short gunnery courses under JF, and although all of them would have known JF well as the officer in charge, JF had had little opportunity to get to know them individually.

Further and more detailed accounts of Sloan's work with his circle appear in *Where Two Worlds Meet*, edited and with lengthy commentaries by Findlay (Findlay 1951). This is a remarkable document, containing as it does verbatim accounts, taken down in shorthand at the time by an expert stenographer Miss Jean Dearie, of 24 of Sloan's séances held between April 11, 1942 and July 10, 1945. There were between seven and eleven sitters at each séance, all held in Glasgow at the homes of various of the sitters and none of them in Sloan's own house. Arthur Findlay sent copies of Miss Dearie's shorthand accounts to seven of the regular sitters who testified to her competence and confirmed that the accounts agreed with their own notes taken at the time (Findlay publishes all seven of these testimonials).

Many of the communicators referred to in *Where Two Worlds Meet* were well known to the sitters, but others were drop-ins who were unconnected with anyone present and who claimed to be attracted to the sittings through their wish to make their survival known. The weakness of the sittings is that more attempt was not made to establish – and subsequently check on – the identity of these drop-ins. Even communicators well known to sitters were not usually pressed by the sitters for detailed accounts of their earth lives, an omission explained by Findlay in his Introduction to *Where Two Worlds Meet* as due to the fact that the sittings had been going on for many years before Miss Dearie began her records, by which time regular communicators had already amply established their identities. In addition, the sitters claimed that they could recognize the identity of regular communicators by the persistence of their earthly personalities and habits of speech, and by their references to shared memories. For the most part therefore, the communicators were allowed to talk about the kind of mundane things that occupy much of the usual conversation between those who know each other well, or about the conditions in the next world (to which we return in Chapter 18), interspersed with short sermons full of pious uplift. But there are a few exceptions to this general unconcern with identity. For example, at a sitting in April 1942 an unknown communicator, having confessed that he did not always "walk in the right path," was asked by a sitter if she might know who was speaking, to which he replied:

Mr. Moritz [one of the other sitters present] *should know. I will mention the Central Hotel and he can take Greenock along with that. You knew my wife and myself – Wink is the name.*

Mr. Moritz acknowledged these clues and the name Wink, and expressed his pleasure at the contact. Mr. Wink then mentioned the center of Glasgow and Vincent Street, and ended with the words *"J. D. Wink, Union Bank."*

Mr. Moritz informed the other sitters that John D. Wink was the man who had succeeded him as Head Office Manager of the Union Bank of Scotland at 110 Vincent Street, Glasgow, and that he had died in June 1936. As hard evidence for survival this is of limited value, as Mr. Moritz knew all these details beforehand and could perhaps have mentioned them to Sloan (although this is unlikely and not suggested as a possibility by Moritz or by Findlay), but it leaves us wishing that more details of this kind had been sought and had been given. As it is, the most interesting evidence provided by Sloan's work, as with the other independent voice mediums mentioned in this chapter, is that he was able to give séances for some 50 years, usually in other people's homes rather than his own, and in front of many seemingly reliable witnesses, without any charge of trickery ever being made against him. Indeed Findlay discusses what would have been necessary if trickery were to take place, and the points he raises can be summarized as follows:

1. Sloan would have had to engage a script writer to help him think up a new script for each sitting that reflected a knowledge of the lives of the many sitters who at different times regularly attended his séances over some 50 years, and a knowledge of the details of any dead friends and relatives who might communicate. Such knowledge would have had to include pet names used within families, together with other details of intricate family relationships.

2. The scripts would also have had to include appropriate material for many hundreds of other sitters who came as guests of the regular circle members, many of whom protected their anonymity before and during the sitting and yet still received satisfactory communications.

3. Accomplices would have been needed for each sitting in order to impersonate, from different positions in the room, the 40 or so characters who appeared in the script for each sitting and spoke through the independent voice method.

4. The accomplices would have had to be smuggled into the various private houses where the sittings were held, bringing with them any necessary props. In addition to using their voices, they would have had to keep two trumpets flying around the room, frequently at great speed, and even touching the ceiling and beating on it, ring bells, and make small lights dance so expertly here and there that they were never caught by the sitters.

5. The accomplices would have had to manage all this in the dark, and in small rooms where most of the space was taken up by sitters, and without bumping into the sitters or into each other.

6. In addition, the accomplices would have to find sitters unerringly in the dark in order to touch them – often on request – and to stroke and caress their faces.

7. Finally the accomplices would have had to escape undetected from the room before the electric lights were switched on at the end of the sitting.

Quite apart from all these obvious difficulties, Findlay points out the costs that would have been involved in all this. As already made clear, Sloan did not take money for the séances or seek publicity or status, and had no financial resources beyond the small wage he earned from unskilled work. In addition, none of the sitters capitalized on his mediumistic abilities or sought reflected glory of any kind. Even Findlay, who wrote extensively about Sloan, made no profit from his books, which on his instructions were sold only at cost price. Nevertheless, critics are still likely to insist that fraud was possible at Sloan's sittings as there was no team of investigators present to put in place strict controls. To this it might be replied that it is hardly conceivable that fraud could have gone undetected for some 50 years under the conditions operating at Sloan's séances. In reply, critics would insist that fraud is more conceivable than that something non-physical survives the death of the body and can return to earth and talk to sitters from thin air. Further, it would be pointed out that people are easily deceived, that many of those who sit with mediums have a strong wish to believe and are subject to wishful thinking, and that in any case science insists that extraordinary claims – such as the claim that survival is a fact – require extraordinarily strong proof if they are to be accepted.

These arguments deserve to be heard, and we shall have more to say about them in the context of the investigations into other forms of physical mediumship in the next chapter. But it is relevant to introduce at this point the concept of the balance of probabilities. This concept underlies not only the way in which we make judgments in daily life, it is the principle upon which judgments are made in courts of law (and, it has to be said, in some branches of science). All the possible explanations are weighed in the balance, and the scales allowed to tip in the direction of the one that seems most likely. Unless we decide in advance, on the basis of the materialist-reductionist philosophy adopted by much of modern science, that nothing can survive the death of the body and that no voices can talk from thin air, then the balance of probabilities would come down in Sloan's favor. That Sloan may have been able to deceive sitters on any one occasion is possible, but that he could do so over the course of hundreds of occasions in different venues with very many different sitters, decreases this possibility to the point where it become difficult to maintain.

This is of course the well-known, bundle of sticks argument. A single stick can be broken easily, but place a number of sticks in a large bundle and they can defy the most determined attempts to snap them in two. Let us take an example. Suppose I see a figure across the road one morning and wonder if it is that of a friend of mine. I cannot see the face clearly, but the figure is obviously male, as is my friend. He is wearing a distinctive blue coat identical to one favored by my friend, and carrying a striped golfing umbrella, just as my friend usually does. In the other hand he has a leather briefcase like the one owned by my friend, and is walking in my friend's characteristically urgent way. The time in the morning is exactly that at which my friend goes to catch the bus that takes him to his office, and I see him halt at his usual bus stop. As he does so he opens a copy of a pink newspaper resembling the financial broadsheet my friend is in the habit of reading, and I note he is wearing black shoes and a soft peaked cap in the style of my friend. By this time, even if I still cannot see the face, I would be justified in concluding that the figure is indeed who I think it is, and in calling out a greeting to him. If the figure had manifested only one of the characteristics of my friend (i.e. he had metaphorically provided me with only a single stick) I would certainly not have greeted him, recognizing that he might be a perfect stranger. But as he had many of these characteristics (i.e. had provided me with a substantial bundle of metaphorical sticks) the balance of probabilities was overwhelmingly in favor of his being my friend.

Similarly if we pile instance after instance after instance of Sloan (or any other medium) producing satisfactory phenomena under a range of conditions in each of which trickery would have presented major difficulties, we end up with such an impressive bundle of sticks that it cannot readily be rejected on the grounds of fragility.

244 | *Is There An Afterlife?*

CHAPTER 12.
PHYSICAL MEDIUMSHIP: MATERIALIZATIONS AND OTHER PHENOMENA

In the context of mediumship, the term "physical phenomena" refers not only to the independent voices covered in the last chapter, but to supposedly paranormal lights, movement of objects, raps on the walls and tables, levitations of objects, apports (inexplicable arrival of objects such as flowers and jewelry), ringing of bells, and materializations (sometimes visible, sometimes purely tactile) of what are said to be spirit forms. At one time, following on from the raps and other manifestations at the house of the Fox sisters (Chapter 5), physical phenomena of this kind comprised the stock in trade of many mediums. The medium, usually in a state of trance, was said to release a substance known as "ectoplasm," a semi-physical material that may derive from the vivifying energy body said to permeate the physical body and to leave it at death (see Chapter 18), and the claim was that this substance is then used by the spirits to build up their materialized forms and to allow them to interact with physical matter.

With the exception of a very few mediums such as Daniel Dunglas Home, who sometimes worked in the light, physical phenomena were and still are usually produced in complete darkness apart from the luminous bands around the trumpet that amplifies the independent spirit voices, and luminous plaques that spirits sometimes use to help illuminate their features. It is said that darkness is essential, and that if light is suddenly introduced into the room the ectoplasm will recoil violently into the body of the medium, causing serious physical injury. Sometimes a dim red light is permitted, but even this can only be turned on with the express permission of the spirit communicators.

The need for darkness is regarded as highly suspicious by critics. Under cover of darkness all kinds of fraud and subterfuge may be taking place and in the past many fraudulent mediums have in fact been detected by alert investigators (see e.g. Podmore 1902). Yards of cheesecloth have been used to mimic ectoplasm, crude dolls have substituted for spirits, finger and toe joints have been used to produce realistic-sounding raps, tables have been "levitated" by rods protruding from the medium's sleeves, and trumpets manipulated by the same means (such rods can even be used when the medium's hands are being held by sitters on either side). Attempts to guard against fraud by tying the medium to a chair have been shown in some cases to be ineffective, and even when the knots used are escape proof, charges have been made that shadowy accomplices lurking in the darkness have been responsible for the effects. The fact that many mediums also insist on sitting in cabinets curtained off from the room (allegedly because this helps the build-up of spirit energies) adds fuel to the suspicions of critics. Even when no actual evidence of fraud is forthcoming, skeptics have dismissed the whole thing as no more than clever conjuring on the grounds that fraud theoretically *could* have taken place. They have also frequently ridiculed the ability of scientific investigators to act as reliable observers, arguing that conjurors would do a much better job.

In view of the scope for fraud, the reader may wonder why it is worth investigators pursuing the search for mediums who claim to be able to produce physical phenomena. There are several reasons why it is worth it. Firstly, because, if genuine, it provides an additional and very powerful argument against the Super-ESP theory. Psychokinesis (PK), the paranormal interaction between the mind and physical objects, has been demonstrated in the laboratory (see e.g. Radin 1997 for an excellent summary of the evidence), but the effects are minute, and only show up as small significant variations from chance after large numbers of trials involving such things as dice-throwing and attempts to influence random number generators. Such results bear no comparison with the macro effects witnessed as part of physical phenomena. As in well-authenticated poltergeist cases (Chapter 4), even large and heavy objects are sometimes violently displaced during physical phenomena séances, and there is no evidence that PK effects from the living can produce anything remotely comparable. Thus if physical phenomena can be clearly established as paranormal, they support the argument that some unknown agency seems to be involved. It is true that this agency may not be that of departed men and women. If spirits are involved, they still need to prove that they are who they say they are, and this has not proved to be an easy task.

The second reason why physical mediumship remains important is that, unlike mental mediumship, the phenomena which they manifest are purely objective. All those present when these phenomena occur see the same thing (although inexperienced witnesses may differ wildly in their descriptions of it). Again unlike mental mediumship, the phenomena do not appear to be filtered through (and perhaps distorted by) the medium's own unconscious mind, though whether this applies to the independent voices heard at physical séances or not is unclear. Supporters of physical phenomena claim that, in the case of the independent voice, the spirits use ectoplasm to manufacture "voice boxes" through which they can speak, which means they do not have to use the medium's mind or vocal cords, which if correct would seem to indicate that apart from providing the ectoplasm the medium is not actively involved. A piece of evidence in favor of this is that in independent voice séances such as those held by Etta Wriedt, many languages were used

246 | Is There An Afterlife?

which were apparently unknown to her. By contrast, when speaking through mediums, spirits are said to be able to use only the languages and the vocabulary that mediums already have in their heads.

A third reason for the importance of physical phenomena is that during physical séances the investigators can *request* certain phenomena which, if produced, indicate that some responsive intelligence is at work. Such requests need not be verbalized. For example, I have held out my hand in the darkness of a séance and sent out a mental wish to be touched in the middle of the palm by the supposed materialized spirit present, and had the request instantly and unerringly granted (the critic may suggest this was coincidence, and ask me how many times at séances with the medium concerned I sent out mental requests that were not granted; the answer is that this was the only time I used such a request). If the sitter's requests are met, this also weakens the argument that clever conjuring can account for everything that takes place during a physical séance. Provided the medium has had no prior warning of the request, she can hardly have prepared the necessary trick to meet it.

The fourth reason is that, if genuine, physical phenomena have important implications for the relationship between discarnate minds and physical matter. How can a discarnate mind, which by definition is non-physical, influence objects in the material world? As already mentioned, we are told that this is done by making use of ectoplasm from the medium, but if ectoplasm is supposedly partly physical in composition, it is still true that a disembodied mind is interacting with the stuff of the physical world, i.e. that some form of non-physical energy is interacting with matter. Such interaction is not inconsistent with findings from quantum physics that suggest the distinction between energy and matter is at a fundamental level illusory. But if spiritual energy is capable of interacting with the material world, what kind of energy is it? Is it the energy of pure mind, whatever that might be? If it is, in what way if any does this energy differ from the mental energy of the human mind? And if thought is indeed possible without the activity of the human brain, what does this imply about the relationship between the mind and the brain, something to which we return at several points in the book?

A fifth reason for taking an interest in physical phenomena is that – again provided these phenomena are genuine – they offer the sitter what seems to be much closer contact with the deceased. Instead of listening to the medium relaying spirit messages, the sitter can actually be physically touched by what are claimed to be spirit hands, can actually see what are claimed to be visual materializations of the deceased, and can actually shake hands with and even embrace the deceased. For those with a particular emotional need to make contact with departed loved ones, this is likely to be a particularly moving and reassuring experience.

These five reasons are certainly sufficient to keep serious investigators interested in physical phenomena. But each of them carries the proviso *if physical phenomena are genuine.* What evidence is there that they are or might be genuine? Can we accept their reality, or are we driven to the conclusion that all is due to the dishonesty of the medium and the gullibility of the sitter? It is frequently said that the reason physical phenomena are very much rarer these days than they once were is that modern methods of detecting fraud are so much more effective than in the past. Few mediums dare risk the almost inevitable exposures that will now follow their efforts. How much easier it is, argue the critics, to keep to the vague generalizations of mental mediumship. Let us therefore look at the evidence for genuineness, and try to gauge what it is worth.

The Mediumship of Daniel Dunglas Home

If poltergeist phenomena are genuine – and in the face of the evidence from many cultures and down through the centuries it is difficult to argue that they are not – then we already have some grounds for supposing that physical phenomena in the séance room might be a realistic proposition. Mention has already been made of the Fox sisters, and the effects associated with them during their years as professional mediums, but the most celebrated of the physical mediums investigated by psychical researchers in the early years of investigations is surely the Scotsman Daniel Dunglas Home (1833–1886), pronounced in the Scottish way as "Hume." In fact, even at this distance Home remains arguably the most noted physical medium ever to be put extensively to the test. After a boyhood in Scotland, Home spent his teens in the USA, firstly in Connecticut and then in Troy, New York State, under the care of an aunt, Mrs. McNeil Cook. It was in Troy, at the age of 13, that he had his first vision, that of a deceased classmate with whom he had once made a pact that whoever died first would return to the other, and who appeared to him in a bright cloud. His second vision followed four years later, when his mother came to him to announce her death, apparently at the precise hour at which it took place. Paranormal rappings occurred subsequently in his vicinity, and alarmed by these happenings (it was only two years after the commencement of the rappings at the home of the Fox sisters) and afraid that he was possessed by the devil, his aunt turned him out of the house.

News seems to have spread of Home's experiences, and in the light of the publicity surrounding the Fox sisters he was investigated by Professor Wells of Harvard University and by Judge Edmonds of the USA Supreme Court, both of whom testified to the genuineness of the rappings (Judge Edmonds even subsequently became a spiritualist). In 1855 Home returned to Britain, but spent virtually the rest of his life traveling around Europe and America, holding séances not only with eminent scientists but with emperors and royalty, including Napoleon III of France, the King of Bavaria, the King of Naples (in the years before the unification of Italy), the Emperor of Germany, the Queen of Holland, and the Czar of Russia. Apparently so impressed with Home was the Czar and his court that he was permitted to marry into the nobility, in the person of Alexandrina de Kroll, sister of Count Koucheleff-Besborodka. The wedding was held in St. Petersburg, with Count Alexis Tolstoy, one of Russia's greatest writers, and Count Bobrinsky, Chamberlain to the Czar, as groomsmen. However, Home continued to practice mediumship, and he did not escape controversy. The poet Robert Browning, whose poet wife Elizabeth Barratt Browning was convinced that Home was genuine, wrote *Mr. Sludge the Medium*, which is an ill-disguised attempt to portray Home as fraudulent (although Browning never claimed he had caught Home in trickery). By contrast, the equally illustrious writer William Thackeray, who had many sittings with Home, was convinced of his genuineness, and said so in print.

Home seems to have been a victim of tuberculosis from an early age, and his powers apparently fluctuated, but he insisted on holding most of his séances in a good light, and was highly critical (particularly in *Lights and Shadows of Spiritualism*, which followed his earlier book *Incidents in My Life*) of those who relied upon darkness. Nevertheless, he continued to have detractors. The eminent scientist Michael Faraday, for example, who was invited to séances, apparently declined to attend unless Home acknowledged that the phenomena were "ridiculous and contemptible." Wild stories also circulated about his private life. An attempt was made to assassinate him, a successful law suit was brought against him by a Mrs. Lyon for the return of £60,000 that she had given him, and another law suit (which he won) was brought against him by his wife's family to prevent him from inheriting her fortune after her death in 1862. In 1864 he was even expelled from Rome for practicing sorcery, which I suppose at least means he received the stamp of authenticity from the Church.

Home's career took a significant turn, however, in 1869 when Lord Adare privately published a careful record (*Experiences with D. D. Home in Spiritualism*) of 80 séances that he had had with him, spread over two years. The original printing was intended only for a few of Adare's friends, but he agreed in 1924 that it be reprinted for public consumption both by Glasgow University Press and by the SPR, who brought it out as a copy of the *Proceedings* (Vol. XXXV, Part XCIII). This reprinting – a bold step for a respected peer of the realm (Adare had now succeeded his father as the Earl of Dunraven) – attests to the continuing confidence that Adare had in the genuineness of the phenomena. The fact that the prestigious Glasgow University Press and the Council of the SPR thought it worth publishing also says much for the regard that serious scientists still had for Home, 38 years after his death.

Experiences in Spiritualism with D. D. Home is a remarkable document by any standards, and essential reading for anyone with a serious interest in Home. Lord Adare catalogued an amazing range of phenomena over the sittings. In his preface to the SPR edition Adare says cautiously "I was very young at the time ... and was not trained in scientific observation. All that I desire to say is that, to the best of my ability, I scrupulously examined certain strange phenomena ... and faithfully recorded the facts." He also said of Home, who he reports took no money for séances during the two years in which he kept his records, that:

He was proud of his gift, but not happy in it. He could not control it and it placed him sometimes in very unpleasant positions. I think he would have been pleased to have been relieved of it, but I believe he was subject to these manifestations as long as he lived.

Adare was Home's close companion throughout these two years, and had as assistant investigators his cousin Captain Charles Wynne, and his friends the Master of Lindsay (later the Earl of Crawford and Balcarres), and Captain Gerard Smith of the Scots Guards. The phenomena recorded by Adare

... occurred at all times and seasons, under all sorts of conditions – in broad daylight, in artificial light, in semi-darkness, at regular séances, unpredictably without any séance at all, indoors, out of doors, in private houses, in hotels – at home and abroad.

They included among many other things full materializations. On one occasion, when sharing a room with Home at the home of a friend, Adare saw at the foot of his makeshift bed "a female figure standing in profile to me, and asked Home if he saw anything. He answered 'A woman looking at me ... It is my wife; she often comes to me.' And then she seemed to fade away." Adare saw the features perfectly, and the following day recognized the face in a photograph of Sacha, the deceased Mrs. Home. On another occasion, in Adare's rooms in London, he, Captain Smith, and another friend Dr. Gully were present when Sacha

... slowly, very slowly revealed herself beside Home, who was standing at the window. She moved close to Home and kissed him. She stood beside him against the window, intercepting the light as a solid body, and appeared fully as material as Home himself ... It was too dark, however, to distinguish features ... Her hair was parted in the middle and flowed down her shoulders, or ... she had on what appeared to be a veil.

There were levitations of Home in which the investigators saw him rise four to five feet from the floor. For example, Adare tells us that on one occasion, when the room was "nearly dark" Home while in trance

... was lifted up to the back of my chair. "Now" he said, "take hold of [my] feet." I took both his feet in my hands, and away he went up into the air so high that I was obliged to let go his feet; he was carried along the wall, brushing past the pictures, to the opposite side of the room; he then called me over to him. I took his hand, and felt him alight upon the floor.

On another occasion, while out of doors, Lord Adare and Captain Charles Wynne saw Home floating above the ground and being carried over a two-foot broken wall – in Adare's view "There could not be a better test of his being off the ground." But the most dramatic of his levitations was the reported occasion when, while in trance he was lifted up and taken through a third floor window at Ashley House in London, and re-entered through a window in the next room. It was night time, but we are told that some light was coming from outside. Adare tells us that there was a ledge outside each window 19 inches deep, bounded by two balustrades 18 inches high. The distance from the balustrade of one window to the nearest balustrade of the next was seven feet and four inches. Between the window at which Home went out and the one at which he came back in, the wall receded six inches. The only masonry connecting the windows was a stone string course four inches wide running from the bottom of one balustrade to the bottom of the other, and another string course three inches wide running between the windows at the top. The idea that anyone could have used these protrusions to pass from one window to the next seems highly unlikely, and Home – still entranced – demonstrated to Adare how he had been taken through the window. This sash window was open less than a foot, and Home was drawn rapidly through this aperture head first, his body rigid and horizontal, and brought back in feet first.

Various suggestions have been made over the years as to how Home might have managed this feat by normal means, but none of them is particularly convincing. They also ignore the fact that the Master of Lindsay, who it seems had some psychic abilities of his own, told Adare before Home went to the window in the next room what he was going to do, the information apparently being conveyed to him by Adah, Home's control, in "tones that were whispered or impressed inside his ear." Of course, if trick it was, Lindsay may have been Home's accomplice and therefore party to what was about to take place, but in the two years of Adare's investigation there was never any suggestion that Home engaged in trickery, and never any suggestion that the Master of Lindsay was anything other than an honest investigator. Furthermore, in writing his preface to the reissue of his report in 1924, over half a century after the events concerned, Adare clearly had no reason with hindsight to suspect Home or Lindsay of trickery.

Other phenomena witnessed by Adare and his companions, all of which Home claimed were accomplished by the spirits, included elongation, in which with his feet held firmly on the floor by two investigators while the other two measured the height of his head against the wall he was seen to be "stretched" by more than a foot. Another bizarre phenomenon was his apparent ability to withstand heat. In trance he buried his face in red-hot coals without injury, held burning coals in his hands, and even seemed able to communicate this immunity temporarily to the investigators. "Tongues of flame" were also reported proceeding from his head, gusts of wind were said to blow through the room, and on one occasion a bird was heard flying round the room, whistling and chirping, although only Lindsay, with his presumed psychic abilities, was able to see it. Home also caused apports of flowers to be brought to sitters, withdrew the scent from flowers at will, and caused his head or hands to become luminous. In his presence chairs and tables were moved by unseen hands or levitated (on one occasion a heavy table was raised three feet, with all its legs off the ground), and a harp in the gallery of the Dunraven home played, even though it was under its cover and some distance from him.

None of these phenomena took place in Home's own home. All happened in the properties of Adare or his friends, and none of the objects that moved or levitated belonged to Home. Thus he had little chance of bringing his own trick props or of secreting accomplices around the room. Often when entranced the spirits would speak through him and give notice of what was about to happen, thus giving the investigators every chance of observing closely. Adare and his colleagues could be accused of inexperience in their investigations, and of lacking any equipment for maintaining control over Home. As much of the phenomena happened to him personally, there were limited opportunities for securing him to a chair while paranormal events happened around him. Even so, the recorded phenomena were at such a dramatic, macro level that it seems unlikely that four intelligent and observant young men would not have spotted fraud at some point in the two years of their investigation had it existed, or that with hindsight they would not have realized that certain events looked suspicious.

The charge could be made that Adare and his colleagues were young men intent on being party to practical jokes in order to make fools of the gullible, but this seems unlikely. Adare's record of events – mostly in the form of letters originally intended to be read only by his serious-minded father – was only circulated to a small number of friends, and was never intended for publication. No money was involved. And at no time, either during the two years of the investigation or subsequently, did Adare or his colleagues admit to being involved in tomfoolery – hardly the behavior of high-spirited young men determined to play a series of pranks on the world.

In 1871 an even more important series of investigations commenced with Home, this time carried out by Sir William Crookes. Crookes at the time was already a Fellow of the Royal Society, a top honor for a British scientist, and although many of his other honors (including his knighthood, which came in 1897) lay in the future, he was already bidding fair to become one of the greatest physicists of the nineteenth century. His interest in psychical research, which seems to have begun with the death of a much-loved brother, was aroused by sittings with mediums Mrs. Marshall and J. J. Morse, and in 1870 he expressed his determination to bring mediumship under the scrutiny of science. As he put it in an article entitled *Spiritualism Viewed in the Light of Modern Science* in the *Quarterly Journal of Science*, "Views or opinions I cannot be said to possess on a subject I do not pretend to understand ... I prefer to enter upon the inquiry with no preconceived notions whatever ... The increased employment of scientific methods will produce a race of observers who will drive the worthless residuum of spiritualism hence into the unknown limbo of magic and necromancy."

Crookes' intentions were well received by both the press and fellow scientists. Here, it was thought, was the death blow to this nonsense of talking with spirits. In the event, the exact opposite turned out to be the case. Crookes was assisted in his investigations by his chemical assistant, Williams, by his brother Walter, by the eminent physicist and astronomer Sir William Huggins (former President of the Royal Society), and by the leading lawyer Serjeant Cox, and his report was presented to the Royal Society in 1871, which together with the British Association for the Advancement of Science had refused to send observers to the investigations. The report was refused by the Royal Society, and it was left to Crookes to publish it in the July 1, 1874 issue of the *Quarterly Journal of Science*, of which he was co-editor, under the title *Notes of an Inquiry into the Phenomena called Spiritual*.

One of the phenomena reported was the playing in a good light of "a sweet and plaintive melody" on an accordion supplied by Crookes and placed in a specially made wooden cage situated under the table while Home's hands were held by the investigators on the table top. The accordion was also seen to float about in the cage. The cage was wound round with insulated copper wire which was connected to two Grove cells to form an electric circuit, thus ensuring that any attempt to tamper with the cage would be immediately detected. Another was an alteration in the weight of bodies placed on specially designed and fraud-proof apparatus. Crookes was adamant that his experiences with Home enabled him "to confirm ... conclusively the existence of [a psychic force]." He also reported seeing "luminous points of light darting about and settling on the heads of different persons ... a luminous cloud hover over a heliotrope on a side table, break a sprig off, and carry [it] to a lady" and also condense "to the form of a hand and carry small objects about." He further described

A beautifully formed small hand [rise] up from an opening in a dining-table and [give] me a flower; it appeared and then disappeared three times at intervals, affording me ample opportunity of satisfying myself that it was as real appearance as my own. This occurred in

the light in my own room, whilst I was holding the medium's hands and feet.

Crookes' reference to holding the medium's hands and feet suggests that he had four hands and was capable of extraordinary contortions, but I take it he meant *controlling* rather than holding, and the usual way to do this was to grasp the medium's hands while placing both feet over his.

Crookes also held materialized spirit hands on occasions, and try as he might to keep them captive they resolved themselves "into vapor, and faded in that manner from my grasp." He witnessed repeated levitations of Home and was able to feel under his feet, over his head and all around him to ensure there was no mechanical means of support. Once his own wife was levitated while in her chair. In the "dusk of the evening" the form of a man materialized, "took an accordion in its hand, and then glided about the room playing the instrument. The form was visible to all present for many minutes, Mr. Home also being seen at the same time." The figure then vanished. The accordion also played while Crookes was holding it, with the keys downwards, some distance from Home, and on another occasion floated about the room with no visible means of support. Like Adare, Crookes witnessed Home's fire-handling. Home stirred the fire with his hand, "took out a red-hot piece nearly as big as an orange, and putting it on his right hand, covered it over with his left hand ... and then blew into the small furnace thus extemporized until the lump of charcoal was nearly white-hot ... [then] he took out another hot coal with his hand ... "

Crookes gave fuller accounts of his experiences with Home in *SPR Proceedings* Volume VI, Part XV, 1889 and in *Researches in the Phenomena of Spiritualism*, published in 1874 (reprinted 1953), but unfortunately, as Medhurst and Goldney (1964) point out, his family destroyed his voluminous collection of papers on psychical research after his death, and much detail of his work with Home has undoubtedly been lost (how many families have destroyed the papers of great men after their deaths in the mistaken belief that by doing so their reputations would be protected!). In answer to the ridicule that was heaped upon him by colleagues (none of whom had been present at the sittings) Crookes demanded "Will not my critics give me credit for the possession of *some* amount of common sense?" He also asked reasonably why they could not "imagine that obvious precautions, which occur to *them* as soon as they sit down to pick holes in my experiments, are not unlikely to have also occurred to me in the course of prolonged and patient investigations?"

Many of the phenomena reported by Crookes were similar to those described by Lord Adare. In addition, to reduce any risk of fraud he had a special room constructed for séances, with a concrete floor to guard against vibrations, and with iron shutters on the windows. A massive table, which could neither be moved nor made to produce creaking or cracking noises by any one person, was installed, and it was this that was levitated on several occasions by Home. The Reverend Stainton Moses, in one of his notebooks preserved at the College of Psychic Studies in London, records of this table that while attending a séance

The movement of the table was very remarkable. The very heavy mass moved with a sort of ponderous sliding motion, and once rose and vibrated heavily in the air. The whole room shook, in spite of its solid foundation and vibrated throughout, the pictures shook, and the chairs on which we sat oscillated strongly.

Another sitter at a Home séance was Sir Francis Galton, noted for his pioneering work on genius and for founding the science of eugenics (in the attempts by psychologists to assign IQ ratings to great men of the past based upon their work, Galton comes out on top, with a massive IQ of over 200 points). Writing to his friend Charles Darwin (see Medhurst and Goldney 1964) Galton reports that in full gas-light the accordion played without apparent human agency under the table, away from the table, behind the chairs and in the hands of Serjeant Cox, one of the investigators. "The playing was remarkably good and sweet ... [and] ... there were other things nearly as extraordinary." The accordion was even placed in Galton's hands by the spirits, though it did not play for him. Galton concluded that "I am convinced, the affair is no matter of vulgar legerdemain and believe it well worth going into on the understanding that a *first rate medium* (and I hear there are only three such) puts himself at your disposal." Galton says in the same letter to Darwin that "I really believe the truth of what they [the mediums] allege, that people who come as men of science are usually so disagreeable, opinionated and obstructive and have so little patience, that the séances rarely succeed with them" (words which might still apply today). In a further letter to Darwin, Galton expressed his regret that "I can't myself get to these séances as often as I like – indeed I have had no opportunity for a long time past." The correspondence was sparked off by Darwin's earlier letter to Galton in which he asked "Have you seen Mr. Crookes? I hope to Heaven you have, as I for one should feel entire confidence in your conclusions." We can assume from this that Darwin accepted Galton's conclusions that "no matter of vulgar legerdemain" could account for the phenomena he had witnessed with Home.

Home's marriage and withdrawal from public mediumship meant that Darwin himself never saw him in action, but together with Galton he had earlier attended a séance with the medium Charles Williams (whose honesty was vouched for at the time by Home, a discerning critic of other physical mediums), held at the house of his brother. In a letter to Thomas Huxley, Darwin wrote that "We had grand fun ... Charles Williams made the chairs, a flute, a bell and a candlestick jump about ... in a manner that astounded everyone, and took away their breath," while the medium's hands and feet were controlled by the philologist Hensleigh Wedgwood on one side and by George Huxley (brother of Thomas Huxley, Darwin's greatest champion) on the other. Darwin may also have been influenced by the fact that Alfred Russell Wallace, who developed the theory of evolution at the same time as himself and with whom he was on the best of terms, was converted from initial skepticism by his many experiences with mediums, as witnessed by his *On Miracles and Modern Spiritualism*, published in 1874. However, Thomas Huxley subsequently attended a further séance with Charles Williams, at which he concluded, although without positive evidence, that the medium was a cheat and an impostor. Darwin, it seems, was much relieved by this, and considered that it rid him of the necessity to believe that Williams was genuine. He preferred to ignore a séance that Crookes and Serjeant Cox had with Williams a few days later behind locked doors, at which heavy objects were brought and placed upon the table from a distance of seven feet away, a musical box was wound up and conveyed around the room playing all the time, and a hand bell was taken from the table and rung at each corner of the room near the ceiling (Inglis 1977).

Like Lord Adare, Crookes never wavered in his support of the genuineness of Home's phenomena (and, it seems, of that of Charles Williams). In his Presidential Address to the British Association years later in 1898 he affirmed that psychical research was not only "the weightiest and farthest reaching" of his interests, and that

Thirty years have passed since I published an account of experiments tending to show ... there exists a Force exercised by intelligence differing from the ordinary intelligence common to mortals. I have nothing to retract. I adhere to my ... published statements. Indeed I might add thereto.

In an interview published in *The Psychic Gazette* in 1917, two years before his death, he went further and affirmed his continuing belief in survival:

I have never had any occasion to change my mind on the subject. I am perfectly satisfied with what I have said in earlier days. It is quite true that a connection has been set up between this world and the next.

At the age of 38, after re-marrying (to another aristocratic lady, the daughter of a Councillor of State to the Czar of Russia – Home seems to have had a special affinity for Russia), Home retired from public life. His decision to do so was not just a consequence of married bliss, but from concerns for his health, which had never been strong. By all accounts his mediumship took a great deal out of him, and on one occasion the spirits had withdrawn his gift from him for a year in order to allow him to regain his strength. His retirement may have prolonged his life, but in 1886 his lungs were in such a bad condition that specialists in Paris held out little hope for him, and he died there in June of that year at the early age of 53, presumably confident in his reception by his spiritual friends. In 1888 Julie, his second wife, published her *D. D. Home: His Life and Mission*, a lengthy and somewhat rambling but totally supportive account of her husband's life and work, and of his conviction that he had been given a divine mission to convince the world of the truth of the spirit world.

In his 1889 article in the *SPR Proceedings* Sir William Crookes wrote of him:

During the whole of my knowledge of D. D. Home, extending over several years, I never once saw the slightest occurrence that would make me suspicious that he was attempting to play tricks. He was scrupulously sensitive on this point, and never felt hurt at anyone taking precautions against deception. To those who knew him, Home was one of the most lovable of men and his perfect genuineness and uprightness were beyond suspicion.

The only published attempt to discredit Home on the basis of direct observation in the séance room is a letter from a Mr. Merrifield published in the SPR *Journal* in 1903 but written in 1855, the year that Home arrived in London from America and in which several attempts were made, without supporting evidence, to dismiss the 19-year-old newcomer as a fraud. Merrifield claims to have seen a connection between Home's arm and a spirit hand during a séance, and to have seen his shoulders "rise and fall" in concordance with the movements of the hand. On the strength of this Frank Podmore, in his *The Newer Spiritualism* (1910), changed his earlier favorable opinion of Home and accused him of being a practiced conjuror, though even Podmore, who throughout his work with the SPR remained skeptical of survival, concluded by confessing that "We don't quite see how some of the things were done, and we leave the subject with an almost painful sense of bewilderment." This same bewilderment is also apparent in Jean Burton's account of Home and his work (*Heyday of a Wizard*) published in 1948. Burton gives no evidence to support charges of fraud against Home, yet adopts a somewhat frivolous attitude to the phenomena, as if to imply we all know it must have been fraud really, although we can't think how it was done. By contrast Harry Price in his long Foreword to Burton's book, states that "Home was a great medium [who] produced genuine phenomena at times." He speaks of him as one in ten thousand among physical mediums, and – although not noted for commending the work of investigators other than himself – he extols "the classic experiments" with Home of Lord Adare, Sir William Crookes, "and a host of other serious inquirers." Price ends his Foreword with the words of Home (which we have in his own handwriting) that his strange powers were a "gift from God."

Nevertheless, some critics have dismissed Crookes' work with Home by referring to what, without the benefit of being present, they regard as weaknesses in his experimental methods. For example in 1933 H. G. Wells (no friend of psychical research) wrote in his *The Science of Life*, published over half a century after these experiments were completed, that Crookes' "experiments have been submitted to searching criticism and it is now seen that they have no claim to be in any way scientific." Other critics have insisted that the methods of investigation available in Crookes' day were inadequate, and that had Home been working in later years his tricks would quickly have been found out. This kind of reasoning is little more than speculation, and I doubt very much if the critics concerned read the work of Adare or of Crookes on the subject in any detail or with any care. If they did so, they could hardly fail to be aware that Adare and Crookes had little need of modern infra-red cameras when many of the phenomena were produced in good light, had little cause to wire the medium up to modern electrical circuits and circuit breakers when the phenomena occurred on the opposite side of the room from him, and little reason to suspect the kind of elaborate modern stage props and hidden accomplices necessary for levitating the medium nearly to ceiling level when these levitations occurred on the home territory of Adare and Crookes respectively rather than in Home's lodgings.

If critics were to study the reports of Adare and of Crookes they would also be aware, from the descriptions given, of the apparent quality of the observations concerned. They would then be faced with explaining how even the most accomplished conjurors could duplicate Home's achievements under the conditions in which they occurred. If trickery there was, no one has so far provided convincing chapter and verse as to how it might have been done. The best way of demonstrating its existence would be for critics to duplicate the phenomena under the conditions described by Adare and by Crookes. To my knowledge no attempt has yet been made to do this. But we can still wait and see. For those wishing to duplicate Home's phenomena it is worth concluding this section by listing the 13 different kinds of physical phenomena that Crookes reports witnessing. The list is abbreviated from the summary given by Inglis (1977).

Home's Phenomena Witnessed by Crookes:

- *Movement of heavy bodies (e.g. the heavy table), with human contact but without human propulsion.*
- *Percussive and other sounds (e.g. raps).*
- *Alteration in the weight of bodies (e.g. the medium's own body weight).*
- *Movement of heavy bodies without human contact (e.g. chairs moving from the far side of the room).*
- *Raising of furniture off the ground without human contact (e.g. the heavy table rising one and a half feet off the floor under conditions that "rendered trickery impossible").*

- *Levitation of human beings (e.g. Home, another medium, and children).*
- *Movement of small objects without human contact (e.g. knots tied in handkerchiefs, a pendulum enclosed in a glass case, the keys of an accordion, a fan which fanned sitters).*
- *Luminous appearances (e.g. points of light and a cloud "that visibly condensed into the form of a hand").*
- *Materializations (e.g. a hand grasped and held firmly by Crookes that then faded like vapor from his grasp).*
- *Writing by materialized hands.*
- *Phantom forms.*
- *Demonstrations of intelligence not attributable to the medium (e.g. answers the medium could not have known given to questions put by investigators).*
- *Translocation (e.g. a bell in Crookes' library disappearing and reappearing in the séance room though the door was locked).*

The Mediumship of Eusapia Palladino

Eusapia Palladino (1854-1918) (the name is sometimes spelt "Paladino") was probably second only to Home in the thoroughness with which she was investigated by competent observers. Born near Bari in Italy, she was left an orphan at the age of 12, and taken as a nursemaid into a wealthy family. From an early age she experienced raps and other spirit manifestations, and the story goes that in 1872 Madame Damiani, the English wife of a noted Italian psychic investigator, was told by the control, a certain John King, at a sitting in London that a medium in Naples called Eusapia was his reincarnated daughter. John King gave Madame Damiani the Naples address of the medium, and she dutifully paid a visit there on her return to Italy, and met Eusapia Palladino, who was unknown to her at the time.

The London medium may have been Charles Williams, who was active in London at the time and who claimed John King as his control. In this Williams was not alone, for King was claimed by so many successful mediums that it would be interesting to know if he had time for much else in the spirit world, so busy was he as a control. In addition to Charles Williams, the mediums who claimed he worked with them included the Davenport brothers, Mary Marshall (the medium who introduced both Dr. Alfred Russell Wallace and Sir William Crookes to spirit phenomena), Agnes Guppy, Mrs. A. H. Firman (who was reported as having materialized four spirits while her entranced or sleeping form was visible), Georgina Houghton (who specialized in the automatic drawing of spirit faces), Frank Herne, William Eglinton (who was accused of fraud but was said to materialize spirits even in the open air), Mr. and Mrs. Nelson Holmes, W. T. Stead (the journalist and investigator mentioned in Chapter 11, who was not a professional medium), Cecil Husk (the materialization medium who produced supposed matter through matter phenomena while in trance), Etta Wriedt (during her visits to London – see Chapter 11), and even the enigmatic Madame Blavatsky. King claimed to have been Henry Owen Morgan, the buccaneer who had plundered Jamaica in the seventeenth century, was knighted by Charles II, and made governor of Jamaica for his pains (an odd person for a spirit control; but he claimed to be making up for misdeeds in his earthly life).

John King, who controlled the Davenport brothers from 1850 throughout their career and materialized at an Ira Davenport séance in the flash of a pistol shot (possibly thinking of old times), claimed descent from a race of men said to be called Adam, insisted he was head of a band of 160 spirits who had strayed from the path of virtue in their last incarnations, and was the first to use the trumpet for independent (direct) voice phenomena. He was also said to materialize fully at the séances of Agnes Guppy, and at those of Frank Herne and Charles Williams (who usually worked together). Katie King, the spirit whom we shall meet shortly in connection with the mediumship of Florence Cook, claimed to have been one of his daughters, Annie Owen Morgan, who was also making up for former misdeeds.

The common feature among the galaxy of mediums claiming to be controlled by John King – all of whom operated in the years from 1850 to 1920 – was the production of physical phenomena. So it is perhaps not surprising that the trail led from John King in London to Eusapia Palladino in Naples, since her ability to produce these phenomena had revealed itself from such an early age. If John King was her control, he hardly seems to have been a reformed character. Palladino was several times caught in crude attempts at faking on occasions when her own powers seemed inadequate, and made no attempt to disguise the fact, admonishing her investigators to "Watch me or I'll cheat." Her defense was that John King (who continued to claim her as his daughter) "makes me do it." Carrington had a different explanation (Carrington 1909):

She depends for successful results on a power over which she has little or no voluntary control ... When [it is forthcoming] the phenomena begin at once, and nothing can stop them ... practically all the phenomena seen are genuine. At other times ... the power ... is weak ... after waiting for an hour or more, with no result, Eusapia will insist upon less light, and will then resort to fraud ... Her vanity is the cause of all the trouble ... It is a great pity, but no amount of argument will influence her in the least or induce her to act otherwise.

Palladino was by all accounts uneducated and almost illiterate, kind-hearted but given to fits of rage, cunning but ingenuous, and described as "coarse featured" but with large compelling eyes. One of her first investigators was the noted Italian psychiatrist and criminal anthropologist Cesar Lombroso. Initially highly skeptical, Lombroso became convinced that Palladino was genuine, in spite of her attempts at times to cheat, all of which he carefully chronicled. Among her phenomena were levitations of her own body and of objects, elongations of her body by as much as four inches, the ability to attract articles to her from across the room even when securely held by investigators, raps on walls and ceilings, materializations of spirit hands, flashes of electricity from her body, and music from bells and tambourines at some distance from her. Eventually so impressed was Lombroso that he even became converted to the idea that spirit agency was responsible for the phenomena. This led him to embark upon an extensive study of mediumship, and to conclude by accepting the hypothesis of survival. In *After Death – What?* (1988), first published in 1909, he writes that "If ever there was an individual in the world opposed to spiritism by virtue of scientific education and I may say by instinct, I was that person." Yet he reaches the conclusion that

... the spiritistic hypothesis seems to me like a continent incompletely submerged by the ocean, in which are visible broad islands raised above the ground level, and which only in the vision of the scientist are seen to coalesce in one immense and compact body of land, while the shallow mob laughs at the seemingly audacious hypothesis of the geographer.

It would perhaps have been more accurate for Lombroso to speak not just of the scientist but of the scientist who has taken the trouble to make an extensive study of the evidence, preferably bolstered by direct personal experience and the courage to speak as he finds. Lombroso was warned by his friends that as a result of his decision to publish his findings in psychical research he would "ruin an honorable reputation – a career in which after so many contests you have finally reached the goal; and all for a theory which the whole world not only repudiates but, worse still, thinks to be ridiculous." Lombroso was undeterred, and history perhaps shows that although neither his theories of genetic factors in criminality nor his endeavors in psychical research have had the impact for which he hoped, his reputation as a pioneer in his chosen fields remains intact.

Palladino was thus from the first subjected to research by a range of scientists. In addition to Professor Lombroso, these included at various times Professor Camille Flammarion the leading astronomer, Professor Morselli professor of psychology at the University of Genoa, Professor Schiaparelli Director of the Milan Observatory, Professor Charles Richet the physiologist and well-known psychical researcher, Professor Brofferio and Henri Bergson the philosophers, and Professor Gerosa a physicist. The general conclusion of these luminaries seems to have been that phenomena witnessed in good light could not be explained by trickery, although in poor light the attempts to control Palladino's hands were less than satisfactory. Professor Richet's conclusions in the 1893 issue of the French publication *Annals des Sciences Psychiques* were that Palladino may have succeeded in getting one of her hands free (perhaps by the so-called substitution method in which the medium surreptitiously moves her hands closer and closer together until the two investigators holding them on either side of her end up unwittingly both holding the same hand while she frees the other and gets on with her deceptions). Nevertheless, "Absurd and unsatisfactory though [the conditions] were, it seems to me very difficult to attribute the phenomena produced to deception ... [although] ... conclusive and indisputable proof that there was no fraud on Eusapia's part ... is wanting."

A series of sittings organized by the eminent Polish psychical researcher Dr. Julien Ochorowitz in 1893 to 1894 with a jury of 22 fellow investigators and summarized by de Krauz in the July–December issue of the *Renue de l'Hypnotisme*, produced ten members (including Ochorowitz) convinced of the paranormality of Palladino's phenomena, seven who considered that at least some of them could not be explained by normal means, two who were inclined to a normal explanation, and three who considered the whole performance fraudulent. Things became even more interesting in 1894 when Professor Richet invited Sir Oliver Lodge and F. W. Myers to join him in four private sittings with Palladino on the Mediterranean island of Roubaud, where the fortunate man had his summer retreat (Richet 1923). Isolated from any possible props or accomplices, Palladino produced phenomena which convinced all three men that some at least of the phenomena were genuine. Lodge was again present for three quarters of the time when Professor and Mrs. Sidgwick enjoyed Richet's hospitality at eight sittings with Palladino. This time the phenomena were not so impressive, but the Sidgwicks nevertheless concluded that provided Palladino's hands were, as they appeared to be, adequately controlled, supernormal explanations were the only way of accounting for the phenomena.

Dr. Richard Hodgson, investigating Mrs. Piper for the American SPR at the time, was dissatisfied with Lodge's report of his sittings, and in 1895 a series of 21 further sittings were arranged with Palladino in Cambridge, UK, at which Hodgson, Myers, and Lodge (for two sittings only) were all present, together with the conjuror J. N. Maskelyne. The sittings were a disaster. The investigators claimed that most of the sittings were held in the dark, that the medium placed limitations on their attempts to control her hands and feet, and that she refused to allow them to grab at the supposed materialized hands. In the end, they were reduced simply to trying to ascertain how she carried out her tricks. However, investigators who had obtained positive results with Palladino tended to lay the blame on the conditions under which she had to operate. Dr. Ochorowitz pointed out that Palladino needed to release her hands from time to time to clutch her head, which was always in pain during materializations. Lodge protested he saw no similarities between the phenomena he witnessed at the two sittings he attended and those on the island of Roubaud. Dr. Joseph Maxwell, Attorney General at the Court of

Appeal in Bordeaux, who had obtained genuine phenomena with Palladino in good light, wrote in his *Metaphysical Phenomena* published in 1903, that "the Cambridge experimenters were either ill-guided or ill-favored ... " This may have been an implied criticism of Hodgson, who was deeply suspicious of physical phenomena, and who may have attempted to impose impossible conditions upon Palladino. Ida Goodrich Freer, a leading if controversial SPR member (Hall 1980), seems to have thought so. In her *Essays in Psychical Research* published in 1899 she wrote, without expressing an opinion on the genuineness or otherwise of Palladino's phenomena, that "she never had a fair chance in England. Even her cheating seems to have been badly done. The atmosphere was inimical; the poor thing was paralyzed."

The scene was set for a final resolution. In 1908 the SPR elected to send a team of investigators to conduct a number of sittings with Palladino in Naples. The team was well chosen. It was led by the Honorable Everard Feilding, then Hon. Secretary of the Society, about whom Dr. Eric Dingwall, one of the most demanding critics ever to serve in the SPR and a man never lavish in his praise, wrote "In over fifty years of psychical research I found Everard Feilding to be the most acute and well-balanced investigator I ever encountered, and, in addition, one of the noblest characters I ever met" (see his Introduction to Feilding's posthumously published papers, *Sittings with Eusapia Palladino and Other Studies* 1963). His two co-investigators were Hereward Carrington and W. W. Baggally. Carrington was already the author of *The Physical Phenomena of Spiritualism* (1908), and one of the prime advocates of a controlled, scientific approach to the investigation of mediumship. He also had an expert knowledge of conjuring tricks (though by all accounts his performance of them left something to be desired). Henry Gilroy, who worked for many years with Carrington after the latter moved to the USA, said of him "He was a great man. He knew his business far better than most people ever will – he went on to the end of his life as a true pioneer and an indefatigable searcher for truth ... " (in Tabori 1972). Baggally was regarded as an expert at both the theory and practice of conjuring. In his preface to Baggally's *Telepathy, Genuine and Fraudulent* (1917) Sir Oliver Lodge described him as "a careful, conscientious, and exceptionally skilled and critical investigator. It would be difficult to find anyone more competent by training and capacity to examine into the genuineness of these subtle and elusive phenomena ... " All three investigators had had numerous sittings with physical mediums (Baggally in particular had investigated virtually all the mediums active since the days of D. D. Home). Up to that point none of the three experts had seen anything he could not explain by trickery.

The three investigators thus traveled to Naples in what appears to have been a corporate skepticism. They were there because, as they stated in the Introduction to their Report (Feilding, Baggally, and Carrington 1909, Feilding 1963), "one of [the] objects [of the SPR] is to investigate physical phenomena." They were disposed to be fair, but not generous. Eleven sittings were held, and although Palladino was allowed to specify the conditions, when she was in a good mood the investigators were free to use their preferred methods of control. These included holding her hands and covering her feet with their own, or tying her hands to theirs and her feet to the chair. They state that *"We never found, however, that the adequacy of the control influenced unfavourably the production of the phenomena"* (original italics), and later that "the occurrence of the phenomena appeared to depend entirely upon her own condition, to the 'psychic trim' in which she happened to be, and not at all upon the severity or laxity of the control or the degree of light permitted at the time, or upon the closeness of our attention." The degree of light permitted varied from sitting to sitting, and from time to time within the sittings themselves. It ranged from good to very dim and on occasions to darkness. All the sittings were held in Feilding's room on the fifth floor of the Victoria Hotel in Naples (Carrington and Baggally had the two rooms on either side). The investigators sat with Palladino at a small table provided by Palladino, and which they satisfied themselves was simply of plain structure (she offered them the option of providing their own table, but they preferred to use hers as they wished to see if she tried to produce anything in the way of trick apparatus – the table was left in Feilding's room between séances, allowing ample time to examine it at will). Behind her was a small curtained cabinet, made by hanging thin black curtains on a wire stretched across a corner of the room. Palladino remained outside the cabinet throughout, with the curtains closed and with the back of her chair a foot or a foot and a half away from it. Inside the cabinet the investigators placed tambourines, a toy trumpet and piano, a guitar, a bell, a small table and a flageolet, all procured by themselves. Light was supplied by electric lights that could be dimmed as necessary. A shorthand writer was present to record all the descriptive and other remarks of the investigators, and at some séances a small number of other invited investigators was present.

Some highly skilful substitution of hands (the main charge against Palladino at the Cambridge sittings) was noted by the investigators at certain points in the séances, but their conclusions on the genuineness or otherwise of the phenomena were based on those séances "in which, on account of the degree of light and of the adequacy of control, substitution of hands was not possible and – unless our coincident sensations of both sight and touch were constantly hallucinatory – certainly did not take place, and of such séances the bulk of our series of experiments was composed."

Anyone interested in this series of sittings and in reaching their own conclusions as to the results, is urged to study the investigators' Report. In summary, however, the report catalogues the following phenomena apparent at various times during the 11 séances, many of them repeated on separate occasions.

- *Movement and levitation of the séance table without apparent contact.*
- *Raps on the table.*
- *Movement of the cabinet curtains.*
- *Touches by invisible or unseen fingertips.*
- *Movement of objects inside the cabinet.*
- *Loud noises and raps inside the cabinet.*
- *Pulling of sleeves as if by fingers.*
- *Movement of a small table situated in the room three feet from the medium.*
- *Movement of a tambourine in the room a similar distance away.*
- *Levitation of the small table from inside the cabinet, through the curtains and onto the séance table*
- *Appearance of hands, arm, and a head through the curtains of the cabinet.*
- *Cold breezes from the medium's brow.*
- *Bulging of the medium's dress.*
- *Grasps by a hand through the cabinet curtains.*
- *Guitar music from inside the cabinet.*
- *Continued movements of various objects outside the cabinet.*
- *Ringing of bell inside cabinet even before arrival of medium.*
- *Appearance of lights.*
- *Appearance of hand bringing bell from cabinet.*
- *Untying of knots (expertly tied before the séance by Carrington) securing the medium.*
- *Transportation of objects from inside the cabinet.*
- *Grasp by a visible hand outside cabinet.*
- *Slow climbing of a stool up the outside of the curtain.*

Not a particularly impressive array of phenomena when compared with Home or the reported doings of other physical mediums active at the time, or of Palladino herself under different circumstances. But as the investigators say in their Report, their function was not to examine the nature (or I presume the extent) of the possibly supernormal manifestations, but to use their technical expertise, including "the experience in 'spiritualistic' conjuring possessed by two of our number to attempt to determine the preliminary question of whether the manifestations themselves were or were not merely attributable to *legerdemain.*" Thus they were less interested in the variety of genuine phenomena that could be obtained in the séances than in whether or not genuine phenomena could be produced at all.

Their conclusions were that "a large proportion of the manifestations of which we were the witnesses in Naples were clearly beyond the possibilities of any conceivable form of conjuring [we] entertain no difficulty in saying so in precise terms ... " These conclusions are among the most important to have emerged from investigations into physical phenomena. They do not say that all of Palladino's phenomena produced elsewhere were genuine " indeed they knew perfectly well that they were not – or that the phenomena produced by other physical mediums could be taken at face value – they knew perfectly well from extensive experience that they could not. What they were saying is that phenomena do occur in physical mediumship that cannot be dismissed as clever conjuring and therefore as fraud. By extension, we could suggest that as mediums such as Palladino and Home who produced physical phenomena under carefully controlled conditions were adamant that these phenomena were due not to their own abilities but to those of spirits, this might just be the case.

The only serious attempt to discredit the Feilding Report is by Wiseman (1992), who suggested that an accomplice could have gained access to Carrington's room, sawn through a panel in the locked door that connected it with Feilding's room and which was partly obscured by the curtains of the cabinet, crawled into the cabinet (or fished into it with a stick from Carrington's room) and produced the phenomena by normal means. I have set out several reasons why this argument is unconvincing (Fontana 1992 and 1993), as has Barrington (1992). There was never any evidence of this vandalism to a door at the prestigious Victoria Hotel, or any evidence that Feilding and Carrington, who were the people who used the door, would have been so obtuse as not to notice it if it had been tampered with. Similarly there is no evidence that the intruder could have gained access through such a panel, shown by photographs taken at the time to be only half-covered by the curtain, without being seen by the investigators, or that poking a stick through the aperture could have produced the hands, arm, and head seen to appear through the curtain. And no evidence that the intruder could have caused the movement of objects seen in the séance room, the levitations of the table, the lights, the touches by unseen fingers, or the untying of Carrington's knots in the cord securing Palladino (a cord incidentally brought by Carrington for the purpose and that made knots particularly difficult to untie). An attempt by Polidoro and Rinaldi (1998) to argue that the phenomena may have been due to Palladino's hypothetical ability to free one of her feet, and to do everything with its help (including poking false heads and hands at head height out of the cabinet situated over 12 inches behind her, and moving objects in the room more than three feet away) is even less credible, as I have made clear elsewhere (Fontana 1998).

After the séances in Naples Palladino went to the USA, where the first 26 séances she held were, with one exception, relatively satisfactory, some of them markedly so. Carrington (1918) gives a full account of these séances, some of them held in full light, which convinced Howard Thurston, one of the leading conjurors in America at that time, that "the phenomena [he saw] were not due to fraud and were not performed by the aid of her feet, knees, or hands" (Fodor 1933). Thurson even offered to donate $1,000 (an immense sum at that time) to charity if it could be proved that Palladino could not levitate a table without trickery. It seems there were no takers. Fraud was, however, detected in séance 14 and at a later sitting at Columbia University, where observers hidden under the table or under the chairs apparently saw her using her foot to manipulate objects. A great fuss was made of these discoveries in America, but European investigators were not impressed. As Carrington (1918) put it,

Fraud was discovered it is true, but it was also found by practically everyone who has ever investigated Eusapia's powers seriously ... trickery of a type well known to exist and described by Richet, Morselli, and others, years before ... Yet in spite of these facts when trickery was discovered [in America] it was heralded forth as a great discovery. Had the investigators in America studied the case more carefully ... they would have ascertained – as did their European confreres – that genuine phenomena were also produced, and that their task was to sift and separate the two classes of phenomena.

Carrington had in fact even described Palladino's fraudulent methods in a circular letter sent to potential sitters before she even landed in America. So much for what has since been regarded by Hansel (1989) and by Polidoro and Rinaldi (ibid. 1998) and others as the breathtaking discovery that Palladino did at times resort to cheating. Is it too much to ask that people who wish to speak of cheating, in this and in other cases of physical mediumship, at least read all the available literature before assessing the seriousness of these charges?

Relevance of Home and Palladino

What can be learnt from these studies of two of the most important mediums to flourish in the heyday of physical phenomena? Firstly, has enough been said to suggest we should take the various investigators seriously? It is all too easy, from the standpoint of the present, to allege there were faults with the methods used by investigators in the past, all of whom conveniently are in no position to answer their critics. It is all too easy, from our armchairs and in many cases with little knowledge of the literature and even less personal experience of investigating physical phenomena, to think we know their business better than they did. It is all too easy to fasten upon one apparent weakness in the methods of investigation and use it to discredit the whole endeavor, conveniently ignoring a range of reported happenings to which it could not possibly apply. It is all too easy to insist we have discovered procedural errors that were not apparent to those directly involved, and all too easy to give the impression we are cleverer than they were. It is all too easy to accuse others of gullibility, and to argue that scientists of the caliber of those mentioned in this chapter are unable to spot tricks that the conjuror would identify from a mile away. It is all too simple to ignore the fact that in the Feilding investigation Carrington and Baggally were in the team precisely because of their expertise in conjuring, and their long experience in using this expertise to spot the tricks of fraudulent mediums.

In short it is all too easy to suggest that the investigators involved with Home and Palladino were gullible – even to imply that the very wish to investigate physical phenomena is sufficient evidence of this gullibility. It is all too simple to suggest methods by which fraud could have taken place, without recognizing that under the conditions obtaining at the time such methods were impossible or so unlikely as to be barely credible. And it is all too easy to accept that once a charge of fraud has been made, no matter how unsubstantiated, that is the end of the matter, and the whole case can be safely dismissed.

In the case of Palladino a legitimate criticism is that she frequently dictated the conditions under which séances should take place (though as Feilding and his colleagues point out, the severity or laxity of the control or the degree of light permitted at the time or the closeness of the investigators had no influence upon the quality of phenomena. Nevertheless, the question of whether or not physical mediums should be able to determine the conditions under which they can produce phenomena is an important one, and one which I and my colleagues have met in our own work. Typically mediums claim that it is not they who determine the conditions, but their spirit controls. To the skeptic this looks highly suspicious, but two points should be made. Firstly there are many circumstances in which it is accepted that individuals have a right to say under what conditions they can and cannot work (though these conditions may of course influence the investigator's attitude to results obtained). Writers, poets, musicians, painters, sculptors, and most creative artists are a good example. There is a level of eminence at which many scientists also become autonomous enough to dictate their working schedules and conditions and sometimes even their methods. Athletes know what training schedules work for them and what do not. Therefore we should not be too surprised that mediums (or their controls) claim to know what is possible for them and what is not. Secondly, in working with mediums (and I would say in many situations involving scientific work with people) it is important to regard investigator and medium as co-researchers. The idea of the researcher as a remote Olympian figure and the medium as a humble servant to be trussed and bound or linked up to electrical circuitry at the whim of the former is unacceptable. We are not doing the medium a favor by working with him or her – rather it is the other way around. Many mediums, whether physical or mental, have spent many years and made many sacrifices in order to develop their gifts. To their own satisfaction at least they know that their gifts are real. They are not particularly beholden to the scientist to come and prove it to them. Mediums also have a natural dislike of scientists who seem to be intent only on catching them out in fraud, and who are not interested in them as people or in what they consider to be their genuine gifts.

The important thing therefore is not whether or not one can dictate all the conditions for experimental work with mediums, but that one is alert *under the conditions that obtain* to recognize whether any possibilities for trickery exist. If there are such possibilities, the next questions becomes does the medium take advantage of them? If the investigator is unsure, this must be made clear in his or her report. And the report must also outline fully and accurately all the conditions under which the experimental séance took place. Readers of the report can then make up their own minds as to how much credence to place in any phenomena that are described.

The only adequate conclusions that we can draw from the reports of work with Home and with Palladino are firstly that the investigators appear to have been suited to their task, secondly that no one has yet duplicated the phenomena they witnessed under the conditions that they describe, thirdly that although weak psychokinetic effects have been observed under controlled conditions in the laboratory nothing comparable to those produced by Home and Palladino has been witnessed, and fourthly that Home and Palladino were both convinced, as were other physical mediums, that the effects seen during their mediumship were produced by spiritual agencies.

Other Physical Mediums

Whole books could be and have been devoted to physical mediums, but space does not allow me to make more than brief mention of the other men and women whose phenomena attracted so much attention and controversy in the latter part of the nineteenth and the early twentieth century.

We can start with Florence Cook. William Crookes was one of those fortunate individuals who seemed to find no shortage of apparently successful mediums, and after reporting positive results with Kate Fox (one of the Fox sisters) and Mrs. Annie Fay, he was introduced to another seeming superstar, a young woman called Florence Cook (1856–1904), who eventually featured even more prominently in his experimental life (and arguably did more to threaten his scientific reputation) than Daniel Home. W. H. Salter, a former President of the SPR and one of its most respected commentators, wrote when reviewing in the *Journal of the Society for Psychical Research* Trevor Hall's book on Crookes' experiments with Cook (Hall 1962) that "In the long history and pre-history of psychical research there is no single episode of more crucial importance than the series of sittings held by Crookes with Florence Cook as medium ... " Many authorities would agree with this, though with certain reservations that will I hope become clear in due course.

One of the best accounts of Cook's mediumship and her work with Sir William Crookes is given by Medhurst and Goldney, in their *SPR Proceedings* paper (1964). It seems that spontaneous physical phenomena had happened in the proximity of Florence Cook since childhood, and at the age of 15 she was dismissed from her teaching post at a school in Hackney, London, because, as the headmistress explains in her letter to Florence's mother, books and pencils flew around in her presence, chairs followed her about, and tables moved without contact. The headmistress was particularly concerned because all this was said to happen during school hours, but she laments having to let Florence go because "I am so fond of Florrie and I have such a high opinion of her ... She has always been so willing to do anything and everything for me ... ," but "a report is spread in Hackney that I am a spiritualist because Florrie comes to my school, and my friends have told me that my school may be injured as a consequence." She also writes of her "deep sorrow that Florence is engaged so much ... [in mediumship] ... for she is fitted for something far higher and nobler."

Florence Cook then seems to have spent some time on the Isle of Wight, where she was investigated by a Dr. Purdon and apparently produced elongations and, while bound hand and foot in the cabinet, a full materialization of a woman clad in white and with the hands and arms bare who identified herself as "Katie King." A reporter from the *Daily Telegraph* actually photographed this figure, and the resultant publicity brought Florence to the public eye. Among those who thought her genuine was Alexander Aksakov, Councillor to the Czar of Russia and a relative of Home's by marriage, who reported asking the materialized Katie King, standing outside the cabinet, if he could see the medium. After one unsuccessful attempt in the darkness she told him to bring the phosphorescent lamp that sometimes dimly illuminated the séance room. In his own words he was inside the cabinet "within a second" (swift going if he was carrying the lamp), to find that although Katie had disappeared Florence was slumped in her chair in deep trance, dressed in black and tied hand and foot. At the end of the sitting he found that the knots in the cords, marked with a seal, were undisturbed.

For a short time Florence also held joint séances with medium Frank Herne at which both Katie King and her father John King were said to appear, though the controls seemß to have been few and far between and not everyone was convinced. One of the doubters was Mrs. Agnes Guppy, who at the time was the most celebrated medium in London (it was she, as Miss Nichols, who had convinced Alfred Russell Wallace of the reality of spiritualism). Reported among her phenomena were levitations and spirit music, but her best-known phenomena were apports. It is said that fruit and flowers, sometimes in great quantities, fell onto the séance table. A mass of snow and hothouse flowers appeared at a sitting in Serjeant Cox's home. Often the apports came in response to requests by sitters. Married to a wealthy husband she lived for a time on the Continent, and when in Naples

Princess Marguerite asked for prickly cactus (presumably to test whether or not Mrs. Guppy secreted the apports about her person). Twenty plants descended on the table and had to be removed with tongs. The Duchess d'Arpino asked for sea sand, which duly appeared together with seawater and live starfish. It is also said that eels and lobsters were sometimes brought, and that back in her own house in London three ducks appeared, while in the house of Catherine Berry (who chronicles many of these experiences in her *Experiences in Spiritualism*) a cat, a dog, and butterflies appeared (Catherine Berry suffered for her friendship with Mrs. Guppy, who at one point asked for tar, which was duly deposited over the unfortunate Mrs. Berry, much to her discomfort).

To cap all these supposed marvels, it is reported that when Frank Herne and Charles Williams, well-regarded physical mediums at the time (though Herne was later caught out in fraud), who along with Mrs. Guppy claimed John King as controls, were holding a joint séance with eight sitters three miles away from Mrs. Guppy's house in Highbury, someone jokingly asked for Mrs. Guppy, whereupon it is said that three minutes later the astonished lady was deposited on the table clad in her dressing gown and slippers, and still clutching her account book and her pen. The incident was vouched for by those present and by Mrs. Guppy herself, who it seems was not at all amused by it. If so, she was one of the few people in London who did not explode with laughter at the thought of Mrs. Guppy, one of the largest women around, being teleported over the rooftops. Not surprisingly, this bizarre story did much to discredit both physical mediumship and Mrs. Guppy personally. Presumably the story was regarded as an ill-judged publicity stunt.

The alleged incident took place in 1872, the year after Florence Cook's mediumship became publicly known, and Mrs. Guppy, perhaps badly damaged by the teleportation story, may have become jealous of this young upstart. By all accounts Florence was an attractive young lady, and stories of her being stripped of her clothes by spirit hands during sittings with the Dalston Association probably helped her growing fame (and presumably assured her of a ready audience of sitters if need be). Be this as it may, Mrs. Guppy is said by Mr. and Mrs. Nelson Holmes, American mediums who also claimed John King as their controls and who were visiting London in 1873, to have informed them she was trying to persuade confederates to throw acid in Katie King's face when she materialized, presumably in the suspicion that Katie was Florence in disguise. The Holmes were outraged, and the scheme came to nothing. But Mrs. Guppy wasn't done yet. William Volkman (who turned out to be a close friend of hers and who subsequently married her after the death of her first husband) actually caught hold of the materialized Katie King at a séance in the same year, again on the suspicion that the materialization was Florence Cook herself. In the scuffle that followed, Katie

King seems to have eluded his grasp and disappeared, and on opening the cabinet Florence Cook was found to be in deep trance, with all her cords, knots, and seals intact. A search revealed no trace of the white material worn by Katie King.

In spite of the lack of hard evidence, the incident was published by Volkman and widely held to be proof that Florence was fraudulent. This is where Crookes enters the picture. He had attended her séances in 1872 and the medium, made ill by the Volkman incident, approached him and asked him to investigate her claims. Crookes agreed, and for good measure wrote to the spiritualist press championing her cause. Thus began Crookes' series of investigations with Florence Cook. At one of the first he searched the séance room as usual and fastened the doors and windows, while Florence was searched by Mrs. Crookes and other ladies. She was then tied in her chair, and the knots sealed with wax impressed by Crookes with his own signet ring. Katie King duly appeared in her flowing white robes while Crookes could still hear Florence moaning in trance behind the curtains of the cabinet.

In subsequent sittings in Crookes' house he was invited into the cabinet by Katie King, who promptly vanished. Entering immediately he found Florence Cook in her black dress, a shawl over her face to shield her from the lamp, and still moaning in trance. On other occasions, still in his own house, some sitters claimed to have seen both figures simultaneously and photographs were taken, although none of those obtained in Crookes' house showed the faces of the two girls together. There then followed two séances in the medium's own house in which she used her bedroom (hardly the most secure of locations) as her cabinet. At the one held on March 29, 1874 Katie is reported to have walked about the room for nearly two hours, talking to those present and several times taking Crookes' arm – we are left wondering what was said during this lengthy perambulation. She then told Crookes he could enter the cabinet with his lamp, and this time he saw the medium crouching on the floor in her black dress, with Katie standing close beside her. There is a photograph of this event, though the spirit's face is hidden. Three separate times he examined Florence by the light of the lamp and took her hand to make sure she was real, "and three times did I turn the lamp to Katie and examine her with steadfast scrutiny until I had no doubt whatever of her objective reality." The novelist Florence Marryat also claimed she saw Florence and Katie together. Called into the bedroom which Katie was using as a cabinet, she writes in *There is No Death* that Katie then dropped "her white garments and stood perfectly naked before me. 'Now' she said, 'you can see that I am a woman.' Which indeed she was, and a most beautifully made woman too."

On May 21, 1874 Crookes was present, again in the bedroom/cabinet at Florence's house when Katie roused Florence in order to bid her an affectionate farewell. The latter shed many tears, Crookes found the scene moving, and Katie dematerialized for good. Another control, calling herself Leila, subsequently made her appearance, only to be replaced by Marie, who apparently danced and sang for the sitters (possibly as a reflection of Florence's happiness, for in 1874 she became the wife of Captain Corner). This phase of her mediumship lasted until 1881, when Florence began to withdraw temporarily from public mediumship. A possible reason for this withdrawal was an incident that happened at a séance organized by the British Association of Spiritualists in 1880 (another possible reason was that, as we know from her letters, her husband was against her giving more public séances). In the course of this séance Sir George Sitwell (father of the literary trio of Osbert, Sacheverell, and Edith Sitwell, and a noted Victorian eccentric) grabbed hold of Maria, and discovered her to be no other than Florence, dressed only in her corsets and a white petticoat (though some sitters claimed she was also enveloped in white drapery that vanished when Sir George made contact).

Florence did hold a few more séances after this demonstration of fraud, insisting on at least one occasion that someone must sit with her in the cabinet presumably to guard against further charges of trickery. Florence Marryat was chosen for the purpose, and she and Florence Cook were tied together throughout the time, while Marie is said to have materialized outside the cabinet. Florence Marryat, at least, was fully convinced the phenomena were genuine. Florence then disappeared from the public scene for some eleven years, only to reappear during the 1890s and to continue to give séances until a few months before her death in 1903. By all accounts some remarkable phenomena took place in the course of them, but there are so few details of controls that with one exception we have no idea how much attention to pay to them. This exception was a series of séances arranged over three months by the Battersea Spiritualist Society. These are reported by Harry Boddington (1938), a Vice President for many years of the Spiritualists National Union, and a respected commentator. Unfortunately his book was published 40 years after the events, and although he may well have been relying upon records made at the time, he gives no details of these and his report is more in the nature of a brief summary than a scientific account. The sittings were held in his own kitchen, and the cabinet formed by a curtain stretched across one corner of the room. The walls of the kitchen were solid, and for many of the séances the medium's chair was placed inside a large purpose-made muslin bag, which, after she had taken her seat and been tied to her chair, was drawn up around her and secured with a drawstring over her head. The drawstring was knotted and the knots marked with seals, and the end loop of the cord was hung on a hook in the ceiling visible to all the sitters.

Boddington tells us that on occasions the bag, with all the knots and seals intact, was thrown out of the cabinet as soon as those who had secured it around the medium had withdrawn, although the medium could still be seen tied to her chair. But usually the bag remained in place until the end of the séance, with all the knots and seals undisturbed. The main phenomenon was the apparent materialization of Marie, who in "face, form and height [was] in every way different from the medium." At one séance Boddington measured her height against the wall, and it was found that she was several inches taller than Florence. Some of the sitters were allowed to touch Marie, and reported that she felt like real flesh and blood. She appeared to breathe naturally, and her eyes were clear and bright. Towards the close of the series of séances the bag and the tapes securing the medium to her chair were dispensed with, but the phenomena did not improve "and steadily decreased in intensity as the weather got warmer." During the series a total of 80 members of the Battersea Spiritualist Association attended the séances, all of which were held in "good photographic red light." Unfortunately Boddington gives none of the names of the sitters or any of the dates of the sittings, and one can only regret that what may have been such an extraordinary and well-controlled series of séances was not properly documented.

Was Florence Cook a fraud? Or was she, like Palladino, an example of a mixed mediumship, with fraud and genuine phenomena mixed up together? If John King was involved – remember that Palladino insisted it was he who made her cheat – then perhaps he is the one to blame. But the fact remains that Florence was only once caught out in fraud (if we dismiss the Volckman incident as inconclusive), at the hands – literally – of the eccentric Sir George Sitwell. The incident is described by his son Osbert Sitwell in the first volume of his autobiography *Left Hand Right Hand*, and it is not in dispute as the exposure was witnessed by members of the British National Association of Spiritualists, and the Council of the Association discussed it fully at their subsequent meeting. However, in a statement to the Association, Carl von Buch, who had accompanied his friend Sir George Sitwell to the séance and who had been responsible for tying the knots securing Florence to her chair, made clear that he had deliberately left them loose enough to be slipped. This raises the possibility that Florence left the cabinet unwittingly in trance, though why she should have removed most of her clothes before doing so (unless we are to believe the spirits were up to their tricks again, as reportedly happened when they stripped her in the early years of her mediumship) remains unclear.

The pity is that we do not have more details of the séances with Florence held by Crookes. Crookes wrote them up in three articles in *The Spiritualist* magazine of 1874 (February 6, April 3, and June 5), and referred to them again in a letter to the magazine (June 19, 1874) and in his *Researches in the Phenomena of Spiritualism*, also published in 1874, but we are given summaries rather than careful records. In his letter to *The Spiritualist* he mentions having had "between thirty and forty séances with Miss Cook," and we would like appropriate details of each of these, particularly as he goes on to say that this was the number of séances he attended *before* he felt "justified in coming to a positive opinion" about Florence. He explains that "with every new medium only one or two séances leave suspicion in the mind," and that this was the case with Home and with a number of other mediums, but that "In all instances where a great number of séances have been available, this suspicion has been replaced by belief." He also confesses that he had been "misled" in Florence Cook's case into holding strong grounds for suspicion at first, but that subsequently "I am satisfied that Miss Cook is true and honest. I have had too many séances with her, and have tried too many tests ... to leave any doubt on my mind." This is an important statement, but his experiments with Florence Cook are nowhere near as well documented in the published literature as are those he had with Home. Quite possibly the full details were destroyed by his family along with his other manuscript material on psychical research after his death. We shall probably never know.

It may be that, satisfied of the genuineness of physical phenomena by his work with Home, Crookes was over-disposed to accept Florence Cook. The séances held in her own house, where Crookes saw her together with Katie King in her bedroom/cabinet, contain too many possibilities for fraud to be taken as conclusive. Florence's family were among the sitters, and although we cannot suppose that Crookes did not search the bedroom thoroughly before the sitting began, there are too many hypothetical possibilities that a member of her family impersonated Katie. Yet we cannot dismiss so readily the very many séances held with Florence in Crookes' own house. In his own house Crookes had undisputed control of the séance conditions (as he did with Home, Kate Fox, Charles Williams, and Mrs. Annie Fay, all of whom he investigated and considered genuine), and it is unlikely that he would have put his scientific reputation at such grave risk over Florence if he was not satisfied he could reply to all charges of operating insufficient controls.

Unless, that is, we agree with Trevor Hall, who in his extensive study of the Cook-Crookes case (Hall 1962), advances the view that Crookes was infatuated with the 18-year-old Florence, and that she became his mistress and he collaborated with her in fraud in order to cover their relationship and protect her reputation. Hall's book is carefully researched, but in places it is difficult to separate fact from personal opinion. Medhurst and Goldney (1964) consider that it reflects the prevailing tendency to take any or all published accounts of exposures of mediums at their face value and as damning to the medium, instead of subjecting them to proper scrutiny. It seems also that Hall was incorrect in the suggestion made in his book that a letter that had surfaced from an unnamed medium confessing fraud came from Florence Cook. Medhurst and Goldney (ibid. 1964) put forward a more convincing case that it originated with Rosina Showers (sometimes referred to as Mary Showers), a medium with whom Crookes had sittings but of whose genuineness he retained doubts. It is also worth remarking that Hall, in his various books on psychical research, takes a particularly critical view of the investigators about whom he writes. It was his books that did much to discredit – possibly harshly – both Harry Price (Hall 1978) and Ada Freer (Hall 1980). It is also revealing that the blurb inside the dust cover of the latter book contains a quotation that not only suggests Ada Freer had a love affair with Frederick Myers, but accuses the latter of being "a psychopath a good deal more deadly than she was." The words are not Hall's own but from a certain Dr. Eliot Slater, but presumably Hall regarded them as accurate enough to sanction their use in connection with his book. Many would regard them as more of an indictment of their writer than of Myers or of Freer.

As Medhurst and Goldney make clear, Hall seems to have taken for granted that fraud occurred in Florence's séances with Crookes, and that as Crookes was too experienced to have been deceived he must consequently have been an accomplice, perhaps as a consequence of a hypothetical sexual relationship between Florence and himself. He bases his suggestion of this illicit affair upon such things as the trip Crookes and Florence made together to the Continent after Florence's marriage, but this seems flimsy evidence given that Florence was accompanied by her sister-in-law, and that as Crookes was bound for Brussels and the two women were going to Weisbaden, he accompanied them for only part of the way. The charge that Crookes engaged in this affair also has its origin in a statement made in 1943 to Eileen Garrett by Jules Bois, who in his *Miracles Modern* published in 1907 claimed he had detected Florence in fraud, ostensibly impersonating the materialized Katie King herself or using one of her sisters in the role. Bois informed Eileen Garrett that Florence had confessed to him that the Crookes séances had been fraudulent, and that she and Crookes had used them as a cover for their sexual liaisons (Zorab 1972).

Crookes knew of these charges against him and Florence. In a letter to Sir Oliver Lodge, dated July 5, 1909 and in the possession of the Lodge family, he explains that it was in fact the innuendos about his relationship with Florence that deterred him from giving the fuller details of his séances with her. In his letter he also deplores the implication in an article in the *Annals of Psychic Science* that Palladino ensnared Feilding, Carrington, and Baggally (and Lodge himself) with her sexuality, and then goes on to say "This is the tax one has to pay for investigating phenomena with female mediums. Hints and innuendoes have been freely circulated about all previous investigators … For myself I have been so troubled by hints and rumors in connection with Miss Cook, that I shrink from laying stress on what I tried with her mediumship and rely on phenomena connected with Dan. Home's mediumship when saying anything in public." If these hints and rumors, taken up years later by Hall, were to blame for Crookes' failure to give us the details we would like of his experiments with Florence Cook, then one can not only deplore the damage done to Crookes by what may have been nothing more than unsubstantiated gossip, but the fact that they have deprived us of a full account of what is potentially one of the most interesting cases of spirit materializations.

So we come back again to the question, was Florence Cook a fraud? In addition to the charges against her arising from Sitwell's exposure of her impersonation of Katie King, it is often said that there is a highly suspicious resemblance between her face and that of Katie King in the photographs of materializations taken by Crookes and others. Nothing conclusive can be said about this resemblance (which seems to be rather less obvious in the photographs of Marie, who succeeded Katie as the control). Critics suggest it shows Cook impersonated King, supporters of Cook suggest that as King was using ectoplasm taken from Cook, some resemblance was inevitable. But another point against Cook is that none of the photographs taken of Katie and herself together show the faces of both women clearly. The face of one or the other is always obscured. Critics suggest this looks suspicious. Supporters say that it is remarkable that photographs were obtained at all, since the light could have injured the medium, and that Florence had to draw her shawl over her face to protect herself. It is also argued that the photographer of materialized spirits can hardly pose his subjects as can the professional in the studio.

The verdict on the photographic evidence must remain an open one. Some commentators have suggested that ectoplasm exteriorized by the medium should really be called ideoplasm, to indicate that in their view it can be molded by the thoughts of the medium and the sitters. The ideoplasmic theory, if true, would weaken the case for survival, but would explain the resemblance between Katie and Florence, and the rather bizarre and artificial looking quality of many materializations that nevertheless were said to have been produced in conditions that made fraud unlikely. However, the ideoplasm hypothesis seems to have little to commend it. Ideoplasmic images have never been demonstrated under laboratory conditions, so we have no direct evidence to suggest the mind can produce thought forms (I am not here considering the Tibetan *tulku*, which is said to be a materialized thought form created by the advanced practitioner after long periods of intensive meditation specially designed for the purpose).

Among the points in Florence Cook's favor is that at two of the séances Crookes was able to use electrical equipment specially designed by Cromwell Varley and described by him in *The Spiritualist* of March 20, 1874 (see also Broad 1964). In sum, the equipment wired the medium into an electrical circuit. Any attempt by her to leave the cabinet would break the circuit, and the fact would be registered on a galvanometer situated outside the curtains, the needle of which would fall to zero. Trevor Hall points out that if the medium was equipped with a resistance coil that provided the same resistance to the current as did her body she could substitute this for herself, and thus leave the cabinet without affecting the circuit and the needle of the galvanometer. However, even if Hall is correct, there would be some deflections in the needle of the galvanometer as the medium extricated herself from the circuit wires and replaced herself with the resistance coil. It is hard to believe that Varley, a Fellow of the Royal Society, did not know his job well enough to be alert to such a possibility.

At the first séance in which the equipment was used there were in fact some deflections, and Kate only showed her face and her arms and hands at the curtains and did not advance into the room. However, Varley was able to feel her hand, and then enter the cabinet (Kate having disappeared) and feel the hand of the medium. He reported that while the first hand was long, cold, and clammy, the second was small and dry. Varley also writes that when Florence moved her arms around before the séance began this caused deflections in the needle, but when Katie moved her arms around outside the cabinet there was no such deflection, which seemed to indicate that Florence had not somehow managed to leave her seat in the cabinet while still remaining wired into the circuit. He therefore concluded that the medium and the materializations could not be one and the same (presumably he also noticed that there were no wires attached to Katie's wrists).

In addition, Crookes seems to have considered that the substitution of a resistance coil for the body of the medium was never a feasible proposition. Resistance coils were hard to come by at the end of the nineteenth century, when work with electricity was in its infancy. It was also unlikely that Florence would have had the necessary knowledge to obtain such equipment, or to be able to substitute it for her own wrists without the needle of the galvanometer dropping to zero, at least briefly, as the contacts with her wrists were broken and those to the resistance coil made. Hall recognizes this, but seems to imply that Crookes must therefore have been Florence's accomplice, and to have provided both the resistance coil and the expertise in how to use it. There seems to be no evidence for this supposition, and I do not see how it can be taken seriously. However, as always in psychical research, it is assumed by critics that explaining how fraud *could* have been carried out is, no matter how unlikely the explanation, the same as proving it *was* carried out.

At the second séance at which the equipment was used Varley was absent (apparently he had found the first séance exhausting for some reason), and Crookes was in sole charge. Crookes took the added precaution of making sure the wires attached to Florence's wrists were so short that she could not leave the cabinet without their becoming detached, and this time is seems that Katie did come fully into the room. Unfortunately, as with so much of Crookes' work with Florence, we only have a short popular report (the article in *The Spiritualist*) to go on. Thus we cannot attach the importance to this séance that we would like, particularly in view of Hall's accusations that Crookes was a party to fraud. Nevertheless, unless we take the charges of complicity against Crookes seriously, Katie's emergence from the cabinet while Florence was still behind the curtains wired up to the Varley apparatus would, on the face of it, appear to demonstrate that the two women were not in fact one and the same. It could still be argued that Florence may have had an accomplice who took the part of Katie, but the séance was held in Crookes' own séance room, and one would assume he had taken sufficient precautions for this argument to be discounted.

In sum, although the genuine nature of the phenomena associated with Home and with many of those associated with Palladino cannot be in reasonable doubt, question marks must remain in connection with Florence Cook, primarily because of the lack of full details of the procedures and controls operated by Crookes in the séances he attended with her. On the basis of the details that we do have, it seems unlikely that she could have been consistently fraudulent. The dual accusation against Crookes of fraudulence and of a sexual affair with the teenage Florence could only be seriously entertained if we were given more evidence. We should also remind ourselves that Mrs. Crookes was closely involved in her husband's psychic investigations, was present during some of the séances with Florence, and appears to have regarded her as genuine and as no threat to her marriage. Charges of fraud and adultery would not be made against any other eminent scientist on the basis of what little we know of the relationship between Crookes and Florence, and it is hard to escape the conclusion that such charges are leveled at him because they appear to represent the only way of denying the paranormality of the phenomena he witnessed with Florence, and the support such phenomena seems to give to survival of death.

The Mediumship of Stella Cranshaw

It is difficult to regard the mediumship of Stella Cranshaw (Stella C) as anything other than providing some of the best evidence for physical phenomena available to us. This is not because the phenomena associated with her were very spectacular – they were not. Or because she had a lengthy career as a medium – she did not. Or even because she provided valuable insights into how the phenomena were produced – she did not. But because she was tested under conditions that – assuming they were properly reported – rendered fraud out of the question. The only reason why her mediumship is not better known is that the principal investigator was Harry Price, founder of the now defunct National Laboratory of Psychical Research and of the Harry Price Library at London University, to which he bequeathed his personal collection of over 7,000 volumes on psychical research.

Harry Price was a controversial figure, partly because of his apparent love of publicity which led to such forays as the Brocken Experiment, a tongue-in-cheek attempt on the Brocken Mountain in Germany in 1932 to enact an ancient magical ritual (*The Blocksberg Tryst*) designed to turn a goat into a handsome prince (not surprisingly, the attempt failed). Price seems to have undertaken the experiment partly to put a stop to such occult nonsense and partly through his love of self-publicity but the press, never reluctant to make fools out of anyone involved in psychical research, preferred to regard Price as serious in his intentions and he was much lampooned as a result – to such an extent in fact that in the Harry Price Library at London University there are over 1,000 newspaper cuttings relating to the incident. Another reason for the controversy surrounding him is that he concentrated almost exclusively on investigating physical phenomena, in the belief that, if genuine, physical phenomena provided objective proof of the reality of the paranormal. Price brought a number of new scientific methods into the investigation of these phenomena, and used some of these methods to cast doubt on the work of many highly regarded mediums such as William Hope, leader of the famous Crewe Circle at which so-called "spirit extras" were claimed to occur on photographs taken of sitters (during investigations it is claimed that Hope switched Price's secretly marked photographic plates for fraudulently produced ones of his own).

Price was also involved in controversy over his long investigation of the reported hauntings at Borley Rectory, about which he wrote two books (Price 1940 and 1946). An investigation by Dingwall, Goldney, and Hall (1956), threw doubt on much of the evidence produced by Price at Borley, virtually accusing him of concocting it in the interests of publicity, though a later report by Hastings (1969) makes the case that the charge of fraud against Price cannot be sustained, and that the allegations against him by Dingwall, Goldney, and Hall stand discredited. Many of these allegations appear to have originated with the third of these joint authors, Trevor Hall, to whose various attacks against Crookes, Myers, and Ida Freer I drew attention earlier in the chapter. But further controversy surrounded Price's work with the Austrian physical medium Rudi Schneider, younger brother of Willi who was also a successful medium. Price was in no doubt that Rudi produced genuine phenomena during the two series of sittings he held with him in 1929 and in 1930 at which the strict test conditions included wiring the medium and all the sitters (via metallic gloves and slippers) into an electrical circuit that registered immediately if anyone left their place. Writing of these sittings, Price (1930) put it that

Not only was it physically impossible for the boy to have produced one single phenomenon fraudulently under our severe conditions, but it would have been difficult for him to have simulated some of the phenomena if all his limbs were free and if he was totally uncontrolled.

As a lifelong student of methods of deception, I know the apparatus that would be required ... I am speaking as one with complete knowledge of what can and can not be done by means of legerdemain. If we had detected Rudi in any fraudulent action we would have exposed him.

However, Price backed up the above claim that he would have exposed Rudi if fraud had taken place when, in a later series of sittings in 1932, one of the three cameras designed to fire by flashlight if infrared detectors registered movement – and which at one point obtained remarkable photographs showing a test handkerchief levitated by no visible means from a table behind Schneider – took a photograph at the twenty-fifth séance that appeared to show Rudi freeing one of his hands from Price and reaching out to move the test handkerchief fraudulently (the photograph is reproduced in Gregory 1985). Controversy still surrounds this photograph. From the position of his arm it would seem impossible for Rudi to have reached the handkerchief, and suggestions have been made that Price may even have faked it in order to discredit Rudi at a time when the latter had angered him by agreeing to hold sittings with Lord Hope, between whom and Price there was some animosity at the time. Certainly Price was capable of very angry behavior when crossed, and seemed to regard Schneider as his own property. For example, on an earlier occasion when Schneider had sought to impose financial "conditions" for agreeing to continue with experiments Price had written to a colleague that "We have been put to endless trouble and expense and then Rudi plays a filthy trick like that. If a son of mine did such a thing I would thrash him within an inch of his life" (see Tabori 1972). But Price was a humane man, and if he had had a son I doubt if the unfortunate youth would have been subjected to quite such barbaric treatment. In addition, his suspicion that Rudi had freed a hand during the twenty-fifth séance did not cause him to change his view that all the previous phenomena produced by Rudi had been genuine. Indeed, if anything, the incident only went to show the effectiveness of his controls against fraud.

The whole Schneider incident and much else is summarized and discussed by Gregory (ibid. 1985), and is only mentioned here as another of the possible reasons why Price's work is not taken as seriously by many psychical researchers as it might be. His taste for self-publicity and his readiness to take offence have even led some to doubt if he can be regarded as a "serious" investigator. This is unfair. Price was an expert electrical engineer, if largely self-taught (as were many men of his day fortunate enough to enjoy a private income). Furthermore he was an expert conjuror, whose skills were recognized by the Magic Circle and the Magicians Club (of which he was a Vice President), and an adept at identifying how fraudulent mediums, many of whom he claimed to have exposed, produced their tricks. On balance, there is no valid excuse for the way in which his investigations with Stella C, which are among the best conducted into physical phenomena, have been largely neglected in the years following his death.

Price met Stella, a hospital nurse and dispenser, by chance on one of his journeys from his National Laboratory in London to his home in Pulborough. She asked if she could look at a copy of *Light*, the journal of the College of Psychic Studies (then known as the London Spiritualist Alliance), which she saw that Price had with him, and in the ensuing conversation she told him that although not interested in psychic matters, strange events happened near her from time to time. Strong breezes blew through her room, especially when she was in the proximity of flowers; a matchbox would move independently away from her when she stretched out her hand towards it; raps and occasional flashes of light would also occur. Price was intrigued, and invited her to co-operate with him in investigating the phenomena. She agreed, and throughout the three series of sittings that were held (40 sittings in total, although the third series was arranged by Lord Hope, with Price present only once, perhaps due to his strained relationship with Hope) he found her to be the most co-operative medium with whom he had worked, despite the fact that she had no enthusiasm and little interest in the proceedings (see Price 1924 or Turner 1973 – who reprints and edits all Price's material on Stella – for an account of these sittings with Stella C).

The séances began on March 22, 1923, and Price assembled a group of serious-minded sitters that included the medium Eileen Garrett, who attended all but two of the 13 sittings in the first series, and experienced investigators such as Eric Dingwall, Research Officer of the SPR, who attended three, and two authors of the *Feilding Report* on the mediumship of Eusapia Palladino, the Honorable Everard Feilding and W. W. Baggally who each attended one. The most impressive phenomena were observed during the first series, occurring both in red light and in darkness (when the effects were more marked). During this series, the medium, who was frequently in trance, was controlled hands and feet by Price on one side and usually by Mrs. L. E. Pratt, experienced in nursing, on the other. The séances took place in a locked room loaned for the purpose by *Light* magazine, with the sitters grouped around a table with hands linked and resting on the tabletop. Communications from the medium's control, who gave the name of "Palma" and claimed to be a child, were by raps and by movements of the table (the so-called "Sloan" table, weighing 43.5 pounds, was used at first), which in good red light was seen during the second séance, with six sitters present, to levitate completely on six occasions and to move three feet laterally while levitated. A thermometer registering room temperature dropped by 11.5 degrees during the séance (at one point in the series it was found to drop by as much as 20.5 degrees). The table also produced what is described by Price as "a curious pulsating effect ... as if charged with running water, the rhythmical effect of the 'waves' being particularly noticeable."

At the third séance a lighter, three-legged "strongly constructed" deal table (known as the "Crawford" table), used in place of the "Sloan" table, was levitated in the full red light used throughout the sitting "several times, remaining in the air for several seconds on each occasion," and once rising "completely above the heads of the sitters." Levitations were observed when only the medium's fingertips were touching the table, and some way into the séance two of the table legs broke away "with a percussion-like noise," and this was followed shortly afterwards by the tabletop breaking into two pieces "with a violent snap," while the remaining support crumpled up so that *the whole* [thing was] *reduced to what is little more than matchwood*" (Price's italics – his accompanying photograph confirms the "matchwood" description). Colonel Hardwick, one of the sitters, confirmed that splitting the tabletop, which was nearly half an inch thick, would have required considerable pressure and the "use of two hands with a wrenching action." Even this seems to be something of an understatement.

At the fourth séance, held on April 12, 1923, the medium, in a semi-trance, reported that she could "see" a copy of the *Daily Mail* newspaper dated May 19, 1923 which bore in large letters the name "Andrew Salt," and that she had the "sensation" of seeing a boy falling, and a man bending over him and "pouring a white powder out of a bottle or tin which he was giving the boy." None of the sitters recognized the name, and little importance was attached to the event. However, on May 19, 1923 the whole of the front page of the *Daily Mail* was found to be taken up by an advertisement for ANDREWS LIVER SALT. The picture shows a boy in tears who has spilled a tin of the salt, which is scattered on the ground. The advertisement explains that the picture is intended to form an advertising poster, and offers a prize of £100 (a fair sum in 1923) for a title.

Enquiries made by Price from the manufacturers of Andrews Liver Salt, based in Newcastle-upon-Tyne, ascertained that until the month of May no exhibition of the advertisement had taken place. The *Daily Mail* affirmed that until about three weeks before the advertisement appeared in the paper (i.e. two weeks *after* the séance of April 12 at which the medium reported seeing it) the manufacturers of the Liver Salt had intended to use an advertisement featuring a picture of Abraham Lincoln, and had not communicated any intention to the paper of using the one that actually appeared. Thus unless we suppose that Stella C, based in London, had somehow obtained, by normal means, information about an advertisement being prepared many miles away for publication, and moreover had discovered that the manufacturers intended to substitute it for one already scheduled to appear on the date concerned (and seemingly before they themselves had decided on the substitution), the incident bears all the marks of paranormality. In a letter to Price dated 7, June 1923 and preserved in the Harry Price Collection at London University, the News Editor of the *Daily Mail* expresses himself "quite convinced by the evidence [Price had} submitted."

At the fifth séance, in good red light, the Sloan table, pressed back into service, not only levitated with only the fingertips of the sitters in contact with it, but turned completely over, before righting itself upon request. When Palma was asked to manifest by raps, "she" (her sex was later said by another control, "Hendras," to be female) obliged with simultaneous raps on various parts of the table, and with raps on the chairs and walls as well. The sitters and medium then moved well away from the table, linked hands, and held them high in the air. The table, in response to a request to the control for levitation, was then seen to move without contact for 10 minutes, apparently making decided attempts to levitate. Once the sitters' hands were replaced on the table it "charged" Colonel Hardwick, pinning him against the wall and hammering with the edge of the tabletop at his knees, which in his report he described as still red and painful from the blows when he arrived home two hours later. It then reared up on two legs, and the combined strength of the sitters proved unable to force it down again. Its movements then became so destructively violent, striking Eileen Garrett on the head and nearly felling another sitter, that it was decided to end the séance (would that the sitters had been more courageous). In his report, Colonel Hardwick confirmed that "Considering the weight and awkwardness of the table ... it would have required a very strong and tall man to produce the violent movement experienced; in addition to which he would have required full freedom of movement – an obvious impossibility under the circumstances."

For the sixth séance Colonel Hardwick, perhaps to get his own back on the aggressive Sloan table, designed his own wooden version (the "Hardwick" table), weighing 18 pounds and with three-inch sides to the tabletop that prevented the sitters from placing their hands under the top and exerting upwards pressure. Nevertheless, in a good red light, the table manifested behavior as previously, moving around the room, levitating completely, and even turning upside down. While in this position, the medium was asked to place her hands upon the base of two of the upturned legs, while two of the sitters lightly placed their hands over hers, with the other sitters standing clear. Again the table levitated, although this seemingly could not have been due to any physical action on the part of the medium. When the circle was re-formed, Everard Feilding asked the control to imitate various complicated sequences of raps which he tapped out, and this the control accurately did, thus demonstrating to the satisfaction of the sitters the operation of intelligence.

At the seventh séance in the series, again with the red light full on at 60 watts, a toy trumpet, a bell, a mouth organ, a set of Pan Pipes, a blank writing pad, and two pencils were placed under the table. With the hands of all the sitters visible on the table and linked together, and with each sitter's feet touching those of neighbors on either side, sounds from the bell, the Pan pipes, and the mouth organ were nevertheless all heard, and when the light was turned off a number of brilliant flashes of light were seen by all those present. Eileen Garrett, whose own mediumship was discussed in Chapter 7, reported seeing an ectoplasmic cloud hanging over the medium, and a tall girl of Italian aspect wearing a bright robe standing behind her. It was assumed this was Palma. At the end of the sitting all the objects under the table were found to have moved, and pencil marks were apparent on the writing pad.

At the eighth séance a new purpose-built table (the Pugh table) was used which had trellis down to the ground on all four sides, thus forming a cage. Enclosed inside the cage and thus inaccessible to the sitters was an inner table that could only be levitated by upward pressure from some unknown force within the cage. The inner table was the same height as the outer table, which had a square opening cut in the center into which the top of the inner table fitted exactly, thus making it possible for the sitters to see by any upward movement of this top if levitations of the inner table took place. In addition, the inner table had a trapdoor cut in the top, which could only be opened upwards (i.e. from within the cage). Various musical instruments, toys and a writing pad were placed within the cage, some on a shelf that formed part of the inner table, and some on the floor. During the sitting the red light was turned out as the controls imposed by the Pugh table were considered adequate. The mouth organ, an autoharp, and the trumpet placed inside the cage were all heard to play, and the hinged trapdoor in the center of the inner table was heard to open several times. Finger-like forms were felt reaching upwards through the open trap, a rattle that had been placed in the cage was thrown out, and a rubber dog that was also in the cage was "handed" out to a sitter. The inner table was heard to move and creak violently, as if with efforts at levitation, and flashes of bright light were seen both within and outside the cage.

At the ninth séance the usual objects were placed in the cage, together with what Price called a "telekinetoscope," an instrument designed to demonstrate psychokinetic phenomena (paranormal movement of objects) without risk of fraud. The instrument (Price gives full details) consisted of a contact breaker inside a cup-shaped holder. Across the top of the cup was drawn a thin liquid "bubble" made from glycerine, distilled water, and soap, and the instrument was then topped off by a glass shade. If the contact breaker was depressed it completed a battery-driven circuit, which then illuminated a small red bulb situated on the outer table. It was impossible to depress the contact breaker (which required two ounces of pressure) without penetrating the cage, removing the glass shade, and breaking the soap bubble (which normally remained intact for some hours). Similar phenomena to that recorded in the previous séance were noticed, and for approximately one second the red light connected to the telekinetoscope was illuminated, although the glass shade and the soap bubble were found to be in place at the end of the séance.

In the next séance the telekinetoscope produced no results, but a bell in a sealed box prepared by Colonel Hardwick and placed on the table was heard briefly. Phenomena with the musical instruments in the cage were as before, and the rubber dog was squeaked. This time a shadow apparatus, consisting of a pencil of light that passed through the cage and threw a disc of light onto a screen on the far side, thus projecting the silhouettes of all the objects in the cage, was used. Crouching on the floor in order to see under the table and towards the screen, Eric Dingwall saw when the red light was switched on "an egg-shaped body beginning to crawl towards the center [of the cage] under the table ... To the end nearest the medium was attached a thin white neck like a piece of macaroni. It advanced towards the centre and then rapidly withdrew to the shadow."

In the eleventh and twelfth séances the usual phenomena were again witnessed, but the power appeared weaker, and no results were obtained with the telekinetoscope. However, at the thirteenth séance the shelf of the inner table gave way with a rending sound. Musical instruments in the cage under the table were played, and the rubber dog was flung out violently, striking two of the sitters (it seemed the sitters still went in some danger to life and limb). All seemed to be going well, but the thirteenth séance was to be the last of the series. Shortly after the twelfth séance Stella had dropped a bombshell, informing Price by letter that in view of the demands made upon her by her employment, she would have to discontinue the sittings. Price must have been devastated by the news, and it is clear from the subsequent correspondence between the medium and himself that they were never again to be on the close friendly terms that they at first enjoyed. However, Stella was eventually prepared to resume working with Price, and the second series of séances, 18 in all, commenced in 1926. The difference this time was that the setting was a room in Price's own National Laboratory for Psychical Research, but the Pugh table was again used, and the phenomena found to be much the same as during the first series. One new precaution was to place the musical instruments and toys in a sealed chamber rather than in the cage under the table, but again they were heard to play at various times during many of the sessions. Flashes of light were again seen, the trapdoor on the inner table was opened, and vigorous raps were given in response to questions.

The third series took place in 1928, but as already mentioned Price was present on only one occasion, and Lord Hope was this time in charge. There were nine séances, and the phenomena were generally weaker, although there were the customary raps and movements of the table. Palma appeared, as usual, to be the medium's main control.

These descriptions of the séances held with Stella can become tedious to read and to write, but they are of great importance to our subject. The precautions put in place by Price appear to have been very thorough. Price himself was meticulous about such matters, and investigators of the caliber of Feilding, Dingwall, Baggally, and Hardwick would have been quick to identify flaws in them. At no time has there been any suggestion that the phenomena were not genuine, that Price practiced deception during them, or that Stella herself was in any position to perpetrate fraud. Thus the séances serve as important evidence for the reality of physical mediumship. But what of their relevance for survival? No details relating to earthly lives were given from the deceased (and none as far as I know were requested), and consequently there was no opportunity to check on whether or not such details were correct. The communications from Palma were in the form of raps rather than vocalizations through the medium or through independent voice, and apart from the shapes reported by Dingwall from under the Pugh table and the fingers and hands felt obtruding through the trap door of the same table there were no materializations. Thus the direct evidence for survival would appear to be slim.

However, there was no evidence that Stella could produce phenomena of the kind witnessed at the séances by her own psychokinetic abilities. Her experiences before the commencement of the séances, at least at related to Price, had not been particularly extensive, and the only psychokinetic effects were those involving the slight movements of the matchboxes. In addition, she had little interest in mediumship and in the paranormal, which further points to the limited nature of her personal paranormal powers. Thus there must be some suggestion that the phenomena were produced by energies other than her own. These could have come from the sitters, yet the composition of the sitters varied from séance to séance. Only Price, Hardwick, and two other sitters were present for the whole of the first series, and none of these four was present throughout all sittings in the second and third series. Thus unless we are to suppose that fortuitously there were various individuals present at every séance with powerful psychokinetic abilities, the suggestion that the energies concerned may not have come from the living is not an unreasonable one. In further support of this is the fact that many of the phenomena took the sitters by surprise on first appearance. The violent behavior of the tables (and the destruction of the Crawford table and of the shelf of the inner Pugh table), were as far as we know completely unexpected. And if there are individuals around who, by psychokinetic abilities, are able to affect the electrical contacts under the soap bubble in Price's telekinetoscope, then it is not unreasonable to suppose their powers would have been identified on other occasions.

There is a further important point. Stella had not been a medium before the sittings began, and there had been no talk of her "controls" (indeed she may not even have been familiar with the concept). Yet "Palma" announced her presence early on, and was later joined by a second control, "Hendras." By copying complicated series of raps, and by responding to other requests, the controls evidenced intelligence. Eileen Garrett reported seeing a figure thought to be Palma standing behind the medium. A thought-form projected by one of the sitters? Perhaps, but it is difficult to see why this possibility should be preferred to the conclusion reached by the sitters, namely that it was probably one of Stella's controls.

As for the two controls whose names were given, can we suppose they were simply Stella's sub-personalities? Sub-personalities have already been discussed in Chapter 7, but it is worth repeating that in the absence of any identified psychiatric problems it is rare for sub-personalities with apparent independent existence suddenly to manifest themselves. Stella had no previous history of such things, in spite of her psychic experiences, and in every respect she appears to have been a normal young woman. Her experience in nursing would, it seems fair to suppose, have given her at least some knowledge of how to identify psychotic states, whether in others or in herself. And if sub-personalities they were, it seems strange that they confined themselves to paranormal raps in answer to questions put to them by the sitter. Crabtree (1985), to whose standard work on sub or multiple personalities I have already referred, defines them as "the splitting off of a group of ideas and emotions which then proceed to carry on a life of their own in the subject's subconscious, sometimes to re-emerge in his consciousness in automatic actions of some sort." It would take a considerable leap of the imagination to suppose that this definition fitted the responsive behavior of Stella's controls.

Nothing that happened during the three series of séances with Stella is proof of survival, but the apparent weakness of alternative explanations means that these séances add materially to the evidence arising from the other examples of physical mediumship detailed in this book. There for the moment we must let the matter rest, and turn to another question that arises from Stella's mediumship.

Violent Events at Séances – the Mediumship of Indrid Indridason

The question is, why should a number of such violent incidents have taken place during the first series of her séances? It will be remembered that at the third séance of this series two of the legs of the Crawford table broke away with what is described as "a percussion-like noise," the tabletop nearly half an inch thick broke into two pieces "with a violent snap," and the rest of the table was reduced to "little more than matchwood." At the fifth séance in the series the Sloan table charged the luckless Colonel Hardwick, pinning him against the wall and hammering with the edge of the tabletop at his knees, which were still red and painful two hours later. It then became even more violent, rearing up on two legs with such force that the combined strength of the sitters could not bring it back down again, and striking Eileen Garrett on the head and nearly knocking another sitter to the ground. So dangerous did matters become that the sitters hurriedly ended the séance (one wishes their courage had matched their interest in psychical research).

This is reminiscent of what has been reported in some poltergeist cases. If spirits were involved, what was happening? Did they take a dislike to the sitters, particularly the unfortunate Colonel Hardwick? We can only speculate, but one possible answer is that the spirit energies, if such they were, proved unable to control their actions. Interacting with the physical world perhaps for the first time, they had little or no idea of the effects they could produce. Another possibility is that the séances were taken over by hostile drop-in communicators. Something of this kind seems to have happened during the phenomena witnessed at séances held with the extraordinary Icelandic medium Indrid Indridason (1883–1912), who was exhaustively investigated by Professor Gudmunder Hennesson, shortly afterwards to become professor of medicine at the University of Iceland and Iceland's most prominent scientist, Professor Haraldur Nielsson, professor of theology at the same university and one of the greatest theologians and preachers in Icelandic history, and members of the Experimental Society in Reykjavik, the first society for psychical research founded in Iceland (Nielsson 1924, Gissurason and Haraldsson 1989). Initially a trance medium and automatist, Indridason soon began to produce levitations, materializations, apports, luminous phenomena, and independent voices. Most of his séances were held in darkness, although he did produce reduced phenomena in red light, and sometimes spontaneously in daylight. Indridason was non-professional, and only discontinued his five-year mediumship in 1910 because of ill health, dying two years later (like Home, of tuberculosis) at the early age of 29. Initially Indridason's séances were held in the home of members of the Experimental Society, and here he was reported as levitating, sometimes to the ceiling and sometimes together with the sofa on which he was lying, remaining airborne long enough for the sitters to feel under and all around the sofa to check for possible fraud. The sitters were also able to inspect the genuineness of his levitations by the illumination of match light. Indridason's primary spirit control was said to be his deceased great uncle, who had been a professor at the University of Copenhagen, and 26 spirits were said to speak through him.

No violence was involved in any of this, but in 1907 Indridason is reported as seeing clairvoyantly the figure of a man who, unknown to him, had recently committed suicide, and about whom he made some mocking remarks. The man appears to have been Jon Einarsson, and Indridason's spirit controls said during a séance shortly afterwards that "Jon" was now present and in control of the "power," and that they did not know how the séance would end. The sitters' chairs were then thrown around the room, Indridson was tipped out of his own chair and onto the floor, a coal scuttle full of coal was hurled at the spot where a moment previously one of the sitters had been standing, and the clothes of sitters were clutched by unseen hands. In view of the disturbances it was agreed to discontinue the séances (discretion once again sadly getting the better of the true spirit of the researcher), but disturbances continued in Indridason's living quarters. So alarmed was Indridason by these that members of the Experimental Society stayed with him overnight and compiled written reports of the happenings, which Indridason's spirit controls, speaking through him in trance, once more attributed to "Jon," insisting that he now had more power than they. Professor Neilsson (1924) tells us that on one occasion:

[Indridason] *shouted that he was being dragged out of bed ... He implored Mr. Oddgeirsson* [the member of the Society with him at the time] *to hold onto his hand. Mr Oddgeirsson took his hand, pulling with all his might, but could not hold him. The medium was lifted above the end of the bed ... and was pulled down onto the floor ... At the same moment a pair of boots, which had been under Mr. Oddgeirsson's bed, were thrown at the lamp, breaking both the glass and the shade.*

Indridason was then dragged head first through the door and along the floor into the front room, in spite of his attempts to hold onto things, and the efforts of Oddgeirsson and Kvaran (another member of the Society also present) to hang onto his legs. The three men then fled to Kvaran's house, but violent disturbances, all of which were carefully documented at the time in the Society's Minute Books, continued there for much of that and subsequent nights. For example, Indridason was levitated and the unseen power appeared to be attempting to throw him out of the window until he was pulled down by his companions, on this occasion Mr. Oddgeirsson and Mr. Thorlaksson. Heavy objects were violently thrown about, sometimes aimed at the men, and things were smashed. "Jon" then appeared to gain control of Indridason's body, claiming he wanted to use him "as a trained instrument," and that he "wished to kill him and to do all possible harm to those in the so-called upper world."

Eventually Indridason's spirit controls appeared able to drive "Jon" out, and normal séances were resumed. However, "Jon" now spoke through the independent voice, and more violent disturbances took place. Heavy objects were thrown about and smashed, the cabinet in which Indridason sat was destroyed, a musical box was wound up and levitated around the room, a hand bell was rung violently in the face of sitters, and "Jon" shouted and abused people through a trumpet that flew around the room. At this point, Professor Hannesson (skeptical up to this point) enters the picture, and is permitted by the Society to use proper controls during the séances, which by now are held in the hall of the Society's own purpose built Experimental

House. Hannesson, together with his chosen assistant Bjorn Olafsson, an ophthalmic surgeon, satisfied himself that there was no cellar under the floor, which was made of wood and covered with linoleum, and no space above the ceiling (the roof was flat) that could have been used by accomplices. He divided the hall into two parts by firmly nailing a strong, close-meshed net from ceiling to floor and from wall to wall. The sitters were placed on one side of the net, and the medium and the human control on the other. The hall was searched minutely by Professor Hannesson and Dr. Olafsson, and the space behind the net emptied except for a lectern, a musical box, a cupboard that was locked and sealed, chairs, and a table. All the objects, with the exception of Indridason's chair and that of Professor Neilsson, who was acting as the experimental control, were placed eight to ten feet away from the medium, and the slit in the net through which Indridason and Neilsson entered was closed and sealed by Hannesson.

The séance was held in darkness, but throughout it Professor Neilsson called out exactly what was happening behind the net. Professor Hannesson reports that:

Suddenly we are startled by hearing the music-box ... play a tune and circle around ... at great speed. [Professor Neilsson] says the medium is sitting motionless in the chair and ... he is holding both his hands. If [Professor Neilsson] were not a man of unquestionable integrity we should have no hesitation in calling him a liar... then ... every movable thing goes mad and tumbles about.

At the end of the séance the seals on the net were found to be intact, and the possibility of an accomplice was ruled out. However, at the second of the experimental séances under Professor Hannesson's control even stricter precautions were taken. Only five sitters were allowed on this occasion, and there was to be no music or singing which could cloak suspicious sounds. The medium was undressed and searched, Professor Neilsson was also examined, and the doors to the hall were locked and sealed. Professor Hannesson, still skeptical, explained in his report that "It is a life-and-death struggle for sound reason and one's own conviction against the most execrable form of superstition and idiocy." Through the entranced medium the spirit control then warned those present that it might be a noisy séance as some uninvited spirit visitors were present. Independent voices were then heard swearing, and objects were thrown about behind the curtain with great force. Hannesson and Olafsson checked by match light and ascertained that Indridason was still in his chair, with his hands held by Professor Nielsson. The chair was then roughly snatched from under Indridason and thrown into a corner with great force. Nielsson, still holding onto Indridason who seemed very weak, stood up to support him and immediately his own chair was thrown away. In order not to leave hold of Indridason Nielsson called out for help in retrieving the chairs, and Hannesson entered the net through the slit, his match light allowing him see "the two men standing in the centre, and every article inside the net." He could make out Indridason's chair in the corner, and went to pick it up. It became dark again, but as he turned away from the corner with the chair he was struck "a heavy blow in the back … Yet a few seconds previously there was nothing to be seen in that corner."

Hannesson then left the net via the slit, and a moment later Professor Nielsson called out that

The medium is now drawn up into the air with his feet turned towards the ceiling and his head downwards … We hear a great deal of struggling going on … [Professor Neilsson] says that the medium is pulled with such force that he is put to the limit of his strength to keep hold of him.

Things then briefly quietened down, and Indridason's spirit control observed that the unwelcome visitors had gone away temporarily to "get more power."

Suddenly the commotion starts afresh and the [independent] voices speak again. The chairs under the medium and [Professor Neilsson] are … snatched away and finally broken to pieces. The medium is pulled up into the air with such force that [Neilsson] is repeatedly almost lifted off the ground … the medium's legs were then pulled down into the lectern while the small of his back is resting on the edge … [Neilsson] fears … that it will end in disaster, for while he is pulling at [the medium's] shoulders "the others" are pulling at his legs.

Independent voices are then heard speaking rudely and threatening the medium. Things once more quieten briefly and Indridason's control informs the investigators that "the others" have again gone for more power. They return and even louder crashes are heard. Both Indridason and Neilsson are thrown into the air. The lectern is torn loose, although it had been firmly nailed to the wall and to the floor when the hall was built, and while the indefatigable Neilsson is still holding on to Indridason it is thrown at the net. Professor Hannesson feels it hit the net, takes hold of it, and challenges the entities to pull it away. He is told to "eat hell" (a somewhat impractical invitation) and the lectern is dragged with considerable force a little way across the floor away from him, and some of the broken rubbish now behind the net is thrown into his face. The table, which Neilsson was holding onto with one hand while hanging onto Indridason with the other, was then wrenched from his grasp and hurled noisily to the floor.

Things then grew quieter, and when the lights were turned on the floor was seen littered with the broken lectern and the wreckage of the other items that had been behind the net. The place on the wall where the lectern had been securely nailed and the place where it had been nailed to the floor were clearly visible, and it was found that the lectern was so heavy that even three strong men could not shake it.

Further sittings were held under Hannesson's control, some in the hall of the Experimental Society, some in other houses including Hannesson's own house and the home of the Bishop of Iceland, and a range of phenomena were witnessed including levitation of the medium, levitation of a zither marked with phosphorescent tape while its strings were plucked paranormally, trumpet levitation accompanied by independent voices both male and female, movement of objects, and partial materializations and touches by spirit hands. Sometimes two investigators sat on either side of Indridason rather than one. On occasion the investigators turned on lights (with and without permission – the latter surely a dangerous practice) to ascertain that Indridason was in his place. Phosphorescent tape, which at that time could only be bought in Europe, was attached by Hannesson to objects behind the net, to Indridason, and to the investigators acting as controls. A string, so short that movement to reach the objects behind the net would be instantly detected, was attached to Indridason and held by the control, and frequently he was body searched by Hannesson and asked to change his clothes before the séances commenced. Among the many tests used by investigators was to request that raps take place at certain places in the room, requests that were immediately satisfied. It was also noted that two or more of the phenomena sometimes occurred simultaneously, and two independent voices were also heard singing together. Hannesson also attempted to replicate by normal means the spirit lights seen during the séances, and reports that he was unable to do so successfully. None of the objects moved during the séances were owned or provided by Indridason, and many were not even the property of the Experimental Society, and all of them were carefully inspected by Hannesson to ensure they had not been tampered with in any way.

However, there was little further violence at the séances, although the language used by some of the spirits could hardly be called celestial in content. At the end of his investigation, Hannesson, whom we are told was well aware of the tricks used by conjurors, concluded that:

At almost every séance I noticed something which I considered suspicious, sometimes very suspicious, and at the next one I would be specially vigilant on that particular point. But in spite of all, I was never able to ascertain any fraud. On the contrary, the bulk of the phenomena were, as far as I could judge, quite genuine, whatever their cause may have been.

Of Professor Neilsson, who usually served as the human control behind the net (although Hannesson himself also took his turn), Hannesson said

... as far as I was able to judge, his observations were very keen and accurate ... This man

has had better opportunities than any other to observe the phenomena. To be constantly deceived he would therefore have had to be more than blind. His verdict of the phenomena is that there can be no doubt whatever of their actuality, and he is a trustworthy man, highly respected by everybody.

For himself, Professor Hannesson assured Neilsson, nearly ten years after Indridason's death and when he had had ample time to reflect, that "You may state as my firm conviction, that the phenomena are unquestionable realities" (Neilsson 1922). The reason why Indridason's remarkable mediumship is not better known outside Iceland is probably because it took place too far away for European investigators such as Sir Oliver Lodge and Sir Arthur Conan Doyle to become directly involved. But there seems no doubt that the investigations of Hannesson, Neilsson, and others were as well conducted as any at the time, and the case has been thoroughly reviewed by Professor Haraldsson of the University of Iceland, himself once of the most highly respected figures in modern psychical research (Gissurarson and Haraldsson 1989). Gissurarson and Haraldsson give a range of reasons why the phenomena are likely to have been genuine, including the fact that Hannesson found no evidence of fraud, that the investigators and the members of the Experimental Society were men of integrity and among the most educated citizens in Iceland (most of them academics and some holding the highest offices in the country), that the reports of witnesses agreed as to what was observed, that the precautions taken by Haraldsson were thorough, that many skeptics such as the Bishop of Iceland, the British Consul, and a Magistrate who later became a Supreme Court Judge who attended the séances apparently became convinced there was no fraud, that some of the phenomena took place in full light, and that many of the physical phenomena were unwelcome and seem genuinely to have frightened Indridason.

To this we can add that although many of the phenomena did in fact take place in darkness, darkness is less of an obstacle for skilled investigators than might at first sight be thought (more will be said on this point in the next chapter). On the question of possible fraud it is also worth adding that Indridason, the uneducated son of a farmer, reportedly had never seen a conjuror at work and knew nothing about trickery. His gifts were discovered by accident at the age of 22 when he innocently attended a newly formed circle that was trying for table-tilting. Furthermore, any suggestion (never made to my knowledge) that he had sub-personalities that chose to impersonate spirits, and that he had psychokinetic abilities that could produce such violent and extraordinary phenomena, would seem implausible.

Let me conclude by returning to the issue with which I commenced the discussion of Indridason's mediumship: who or what is responsible for the violence experienced at some physical séances? If we can believe what we are told by Indridason's spirit controls, uninvited spirits may find a way of taking over the séances concerned. It is a pity that we have no details that those investigating the Indridason mediumship pursued the matter of the identities of these uninvited spirits and of the other communicators who spoke through Indridason more closely (unfortunately the detailed records kept by the Experimental Society, which may have contained these very details, were lost in 1942). We would very much like to know why and how these uninvited spirits, if such indeed they were, were able to gain access to the séances, and what is meant by the statement from Indridason's own spirit control that they went away temporarily to "obtain more power." Where did they go and of what did this power consist? And if they were earthbound spirits (such spirits are discussed more fully in Chapter 18), why were they earth bound and could nothing be done to help them? The case leaves many unanswered questions, though that of genuineness does not appear to be one of them.

CHAPTER 13

PHYSICAL MEDIUMSHIP: MORE RECENT EXAMPLES AND THE QUESTION OF FRAUD

The Harrison Home Circle

I have already spoken of the reasons why many scientists find it difficult to accept the possible reality of physical phenomena, and why even parapsychologists would prefer the subject not to feature within the parameters of respectable psychical research. Little needs to be added on this point, except to emphasize that the attitude of scientists and parapsychologists has tended to impede research into the phenomena concerned. One wonders how many private circles at which physical phenomena are witnessed are never made public due to the reluctance of those concerned to lay themselves open to suspicion and possible charges of fraud. A good example of the work of one of these circles, which took place over a ten-year period from 1946, has been published in a slim monograph by Tom Harrison (Harrison 1989). It details the mediumship of his mother, Minnie Harrison, sitting once a week with a small home circle of eight regular sitters – the medium herself, Tom's father, and Tom's late first wife Doris (a State Registered Nurse and Midwife), Sydney and Gladys Shipman close family friends of the Harrisons, Gladys Shipman's mother Mrs. Florence Hildred, and Dr. William Brittain Jones, FRCS, who was for many years Medical Superintendent of Middlesborough General Hospital. All of them, including Dr. Brittain Jones, were fully convinced by their experiences of the genuineness of the phenomena.

Recently demobilized as a young army officer, Tom Harrison kept careful records in his army field service notebooks of the phenomena witnessed at each sitting. As detailed by him, these phenomena included spirit voices of known deceased individuals – both male and female – speaking through a trumpet paranormally suspended five feet from the floor; materializations of hands and of whole bodies, initially in a subdued red light but later in what Tom Harrison describes as a bright red light. Some of the materializations were photographed. Written spirit signatures and messages were also received, as were spirit lights, and a range of apports including coins, flowers, sweets, lapel and shoulder badges, an Indian bell, and a host of personal items. The materializations, which included Dr. Brittain Jones' mother, were of both male and female individuals, all of them known to and recognized by the sitters. Some of the materializations were frequent visitors, in particular

Tom Harrison's aunt, Agnes Abbott, who had been a noted trance medium herself while alive. Arthur Findlay described his sitting with her in 1936 during her lifetime as 'amongst the most evidential ever recorded.' In the course of it his deceased mother communicated through the entranced Agnes Abbott, and no fewer than 92 facts were given, including names and intimate family details, all of which were correct and none of which in his estimation could have been known by Agnes (Findlay 1955).

One of the many impressive features of the Harrison home circle was a young drop-in communicator who spoke to the sitters through the trumpet. He gave his full name, James Andrew Fletcher (a pseudonym used by Tom Harrison to protect the family concerned), his age at death (12 years), the fact that he was an only child but had had a pet dog, the date of his death (June 6, 1941), the name of his village (Haverton Hill), and a street name (Coniston Avenue) about which he was rather unsure. He spoke of unsuccessful attempts to contact his parents, and asked the sitters to help him reach them. None of the sitters had heard of the boy or of his family. With some trepidation Tom Harrison visited Haverton Hill, and ascertained from a local shopkeeper that there was no Coniston Avenue in the village, although there was a Collinson Road. Full of misgivings Tom found the road, and asked a resident where the Fletchers lived. To his surprise she directed him to a nearby house, number 20. There was no reply to his ring on the doorbell, but he returned later that evening, and after a suspicious reception the name 'James Andrew' was accepted and he was invited in. During the course of an initially apprehensive conversation, it transpired that not only was the name given by the drop-in communicator correct, so was the date of his death, his age at death, the fact he was an only child, and the fact that the pet dog had belonged to him.

The conditions obtaining at the weekly Harrison séances, discontinued only when ill-health forced Minnie Harrison to give up active mediumship, were not controlled in the manner of scientific investigations, but they nevertheless appear to have been such as to render fraud unlikely. Minnie Harrison had been operated on for breast cancer in 1942, before the séances began, and her left arm was so impaired by the operation that she could not raise it above waist height. During the years of the sittings she had numerous follow-up operations (she died in 1958), and was clearly in no state of health to produce the wide range of physical phenomena witnessed at the séances. In addition, she sometimes sat in the circle instead of in the improvised cabinet formed by a curtain placed across the corner of the room, and was in full view of the sitters while materializations were taking place. If fraud there was, the only possibility is that it was perpetrated by accomplices, but this seems difficult to accept. For some years the sittings took place in the Shipmans' small living room behind their baker's shop. With eight people present, the possibility of accomplices entering and remaining undetected over many séances over many years, most of them in a good red light, stretches credulity.

Could one of the sitters have been responsible? Again unlikely. The circle consisted of a close-knit group of family and friends, well known to, and well trusted by, each other. In the good red light that attended many of the materializations it again stretches credulity to suppose one or more of them could have left the circle undetected, retreated behind the curtain of the improvised cabinet in which Minnie Harrison usually sat, pulled on sheets or robes of some kind, and re-emerged sufficiently disguised to be taken for the spirits they were impersonating, then withdrawn behind the curtain, divested themselves of their robes, and returned unseen to their place. To make things more difficult, some of the materializations appeared in Tom Harrison's words to 'gradually sink towards the floor and appear to be going through a trap door' [which did not exist] in ... the carpeted living room.' It has been demonstrated that this disappearing feat can be done fraudulently in darkness, when the 'spirit's' face is seen only in the reflected light of a luminous plaque, but the disappearances in the Harrison circle took place in good red light, inches away from the sitters, one of whom, Dr. Brittain Jones, was a respected surgeon and retired Medical Superintendent of a major hospital. Aged only 68 at the start of the sittings it cannot easily be supposed he was likely either to be easily deceived or to risk his reputation by becoming involved in fraudulent mediumship. He is described by Tom Harrison as 'an enthusiastic and lively man' and as having 'a wealth of investigative experience.' Sydney Shipman was equally experienced. The monograph tells us he was 'very mediumistic,' 'certainly not given to self-deception or naivety,' and as having been brought up in a Spiritualistic environment. His wife Gladys was also a 'keen worker for the Spiritualistic movement.' Of the other four regular sitters, Tom, his father, and his wife Doris all had years of experience of mediumship, as will be made clear shortly. Thus the sitters were hardly the people to be readily taken in by deception carried out by any of their number. It might of course be argued that people with this background were predisposed to believe in the phenomena, and therefore more easily deceived. I would question this. My many years spent investigating mediumship has taught me that experienced individuals identified with the subject are by no means easily duped. Quite the contrary. This was one of the things that most surprised me when I began my investigations. I had expected to find a gullible, naive group of people, all too ready to believe anything that fitted in with their wishes and expectations. Instead I found those involved to be well-informed, hard-headed, honest, and sensibly guarded, very ready to be perceptively critical both of themselves and their colleagues, to entertain alternative explanations for the mediumistic phenomena, and to recognize the first signs of anything suspicious. My impression is that the sitters in the Harrison circle came into this category. It is true that there are many highly impressionable and easily deceived people interested in the various movements associated with mediumship and with psychic abilities, real or imagined. But these are not the real practitioners, the men and women with years of experience at practicing and/or observing mediumship at close quarters, and in the great majority of cases dedicated, patient, and pains-taking in their approach to the subject.

If the sitters in the Harrison circle were not involved in deception, the only remaining possibility is that Tom Harrison has exaggerated the phenomena he witnessed, or worse still fabricated the whole thing. Again this seems unlikely. In addition to Tom, Sydney and Gladys Shipman are surviving members of the circle. Interviewed in recent years by Mary Rose Barrington, a lawyer and one of the most experienced and respected members of the SPR Council, they turned out to be adamant as to the truth of the facts recorded in Tom's monograph, and transparently clear in their recollection of them. Subsequently BBC Radio producer Chris Eldon Lee, in the course of his research for a program on Minnie Harrison's mediumship in which I took part, also interviewed the Shipmans, and confirmed to me that he too found them adamant and unshakeable about what they had experienced. In addition, during the course of the Harrison séances guests were sometimes present, and one of these, Colonel Roy Dixon Smith, has left a record of happenings in his *New Light on Survival* (Dixon-Smith 1952). Dixon-Smith saw six materializations, including that of his deceased wife, Betty, whose 'hand was just like Betty's and quite unlike the medium's.' He reports that he 'stared into the face and recognised my wife.' They spoke a few words together, he was invited to kiss her, and 'she then sank. I watched her form right down to the level of the floor at my feet where it dissolved ... ' The other materializations seen by Colonel Dixon-Smith (all deceased friends or relatives of the sitters) ' ... were solid, natural, and ... exactly like ordinary living people; [had they been dressed like the sitters] it would have been quite impossible to distinguish [them] from the rest of the company.' He was encouraged by Dr. Brittain Jones to touch the materializations and found that 'Their hands felt perfectly natural and life-like in every respect ... They smiled, laughed, and chatted to me and the others, all their features, complexions, and expressions being perfectly clear in that ample [red] light.' He also found that they 'all differed drastically in face, figure, voice, and mannerism [from each other], and in every case their eyes were open ... the movements of their features ...by itself disposes of the suggestion of a set of masks.' On another occasion the guests were the Matron of Middlesborough General Hospital, who had worked with Dr. Brittain Jones for many years, and a Chartered Accountant. It is reported that the former recognized the materialized form of a deceased nursing colleague, and the latter recognized a materialization of his mother.

I was fortunate enough to meet Tom Harrison some years ago – quite by chance – after reading his monograph, and we have remained firm friends ever since, so that I have had many opportunities to talk to him about the Harrison circle. I do not believe I have met a man of greater integrity and gentle compassion in the course of my research into any area either of psychical research or of my own subject, psychology. Years after the events detailed in his monograph, he is as clear as ever on all the details. He knows what he experienced, and has never sought to gain prestige or make money from these experiences (all proceeds from his monograph go in fact to a charity he founded some years ago for the care and support of those with cancer). I have inspected Tom's army field service notebooks in which he kept his records, and can vouch firstly that his monograph is a faithful reflection of these handwritten records, and secondly that the yellowing pages of the notebooks and the faded writing provide good evidence that these records were all made during the period concerned. I have also listened to the audio tapes, made on an old reel-to-reel recorder, of some of the events during the séances. The quality of the tapes is commensurate with their age, but they stand as further evidence of the authenticity of Tom's records. Recently, I have read relevant sections of a more lengthy account of the Harrison Circle that he is preparing for publication, and the details here amply, without any attempt at exaggeration or over-statement, reflect those given in his monograph.

It is of course unfortunate that Tom Harrison did not obtain signed statements from all the sitters after each séance, but it must be realized that during the years concerned he had no idea that his records might one day be published, and be the subject of scrutiny by investigators. For him mediumship was a simple fact of life. He grew up in a family where its reality was taken for granted. Both his mother and his aunt, Agnes Abbott, were mediums (the reactions of Arthur Findlay to his sitting with Agnes Abbott, one of the best-known mediums of her day, have already been described). Tom's father accepted the reality of mediumship, took a keen interest in the subject, and was said to provide strong psychic energy during the séances. Tom's wife Doris was mediumistic and came from a well-known local Spiritualist family, and Tom himself confesses to 'some mediumistic awareness.' The family never set out with the intention of convincing others. For them, the Saturday séances were regarded simply as an opportunity for a weekly meeting with departed relatives and friends.

The Question of Fraud in Physical Mediumship: Mina Crandon and Helen Duncan

I have devoted some space to the mediumship of Minnie Harrison, as it is one of the best examples of a successful private home circle for physical phenomena in the literature. Some critics may dismiss it on the grounds of insufficient controls against fraud. This is their right. Others will prefer to take the evidence seriously. This also is their right. As I have tried to show, fraud seems a highly unlikely explanation for the Harrison case. And while on the subject of fraud – a charge that is brought so frequently against physical phenomena – it is fair to say that in most cases it is impossible to guard against every possibility – however implausible – that fraud may take place in the séance room. However, the bundle of sticks principle, mentioned earlier (Chapter 11), and certainly applicable to the phenomena witnessed in the Harrison circle, is one of the best safeguards we have that physical phenomena are genuine. In addition, unless one accuses Tom Harrison of suppressing unwelcome facts, there is no evidence that Minnie Harrison's mediumship was of the mixed variety, with genuine phenomena alternating with fraud, as in the case of Eusapia Palladino and some other physical mediums. No suspicion ever surrounded her work, and it must be remembered that she never took money for it or sought publicity. Could she simply have been out to impress her family and friends? If so, one would still have to explain how she managed to produce the phenomena under the conditions operating at the home circle, and under the restrictions imposed by her own physical disability.

The same cannot unfortunately be said of two other physical mediums regarded by some as among the finest in the history of the subject and by others as not worthy of serious consideration. I refer to the mediumship respectively of Mina Crandon (known at the time under the pseudonym of 'Margery') and of Helen Duncan. But for the controversy surrounding both of them, which sadly is too extensive to be dealt with fully here, they would merit fuller coverage in the present chapter. On the other hand their prominence in the history of psychical research is such that they cannot be passed over without comment.

Mina Crandon (1884-1941), the Canadian wife of Boston physician Dr. Leroy Crandon, came to the attention of American psychical researchers in 1923 as a consequence of her apparent ability to produce a range of séance room phenomena with the co-operation of her deceased brother, Walter Stinson, who acted as her control and who was said to have had psychic abilities himself during his lifetime. These phenomena involved levitations of the table and of objects, raps, spirit music, psychic breezes, including the trumpet which touched sitters and through which Walter spoke, raps, touches by unseen spirit hands, spasmodic control of the Victrola (the gramophone) used at the sittings, spirit lights, music, psychic breezes, measurable pressure by Walter upon the pan of a set of scales, sounds from a bell placed in a specially made bell box, materializations in the form of so-called 'teleplasm,' a flesh-like substance that molded itself into crude representations of a hand and apparently emerged from her vagina, and much more besides (see Bird 1925 for a full account). Such was the immediacy of her impact upon the world of psychical research that she visited Europe in the same year and was tested by both Geley and Richet under strict conditions in Paris, and seems to have largely satisfied them that she was genuine.

In the USA an investigation into the mediumship was carried out by three Harvard scientists, Professor MacDougal (who also features in the *Scientific American* investigation of her mediumship, dealt with below), Dr. Gardner Murphy who worked with MacDougal and like him was favorably disposed towards the paranormal, and a doctoral student, Harry Helson. The Harvard scientists witnessed a range of phenomena, including the dismantling of the cabinet in which Mina and MacDougal were sitting at the time, the movement of a table, and the jigging of a piano stool in time to the music from the Victrola phonograph and the subsequent movement of the stool by some eight feet. Nevertheless the scientists remained unconvinced as they considered that the phenomena could have been faked by an accomplice. The only evidence for this was the discovery by Helson of an eight-inch piece of string at the end of the sitting, which convinced MacDougal that one end had been attached to the piano stool and the other threaded down a hot air conduit to the supposed accomplice on a lower floor. When Mina pointed out that an eight-inch piece of string, which she described as an unraveling from the carpet, would not have reached down to a lower floor or proved able to move the piano stool by eight feet the absurdity of the charge against her became apparent, and MacDougal, ever the gentleman and one of the finest scientists ever to be attracted to psychical research, subsequently apologized for it.

In 1924 she took up the challenge thrown out by the *Scientific American* in 1922, which offered a prize of $2,500 to the first person who could produce 'a visible psychic manifestation – to the full satisfaction' of 'the eminent men who will act as judges.' Hereward Carrington, a member of this committee of judges and one of the team that had investigated Eusapia Palladino in Naples (Chapter 12), became convinced she was genuine on the strength of 40 plus sittings with her (Carrington 1930), as did Malcolm Bird (Bird 1925), assistant editor of the *Scientific American* and secretary to the committee (to whose deliberations we will return shortly). Hamlin Garland, chairman of the research committee of the American SPR and a vastly experienced investigator, who had sittings with her under his own test conditions in 1927, was also satisfied there was no fraud (Garland 1936). The American SPR as a body were in fact very interested in her mediumship, did much to bring it to the attention of researchers, and published three lengthy copies of *Proceedings* detailing their exhaustive experiments with her (1928, 1933a, and 1933b) and their conclusion that she was genuine.

Mina Crandon's early sittings with her home circle all took place in a good red light, but on Walter's instructions the later ones were mostly in the dark except when he asked for the red light. Usually Mina, often in deep trance, was controlled by her husband Dr. Crandon on one side and by one of the other sitters, often another medical doctor Dr. Mark Richardson, on the other. Richardson also devised various pieces of equipment as additional controls, including an elaborate device that involved Mina blowing continuously into a tube in order to keep a small ball in the air while Walter was talking through the trumpet in order to demonstrate that she was not responsible for his voice. However, not everyone was satisfied she was genuine. Although during her European visit in 1923 she had held a sitting for Eric Dingwall, research officer of the SPR, in his room at the SPR at which a six-inch levitation of a supposedly fraud-proof table took place in full light – a result that he found 'very striking and, if fraudulent, involved some skill in performance' (Dingwall 1926) – his subsequent sittings with her in Boston led him to produce a guarded report (ibid. 1926) which only succeeded, in the Hon. Everard Feilding's wry words, 'to box the compass of most opinions and to end with none' (Feilding 1926). Professor William MacDougal, who was a strong supporter of psychical research (and later responsible for setting up the parapsychology laboratory at Duke University where J. B. Rhine did most of his work) and who was a member along with Hereward Carrington and James Malcolm Bird of the Scientific American committee investigating her attempt at securing the $2,500 prize, fluctuated from indecision to deep suspicion throughout, although never finally committing himself one way or the other. Two other members of the *Scientific American* committee, Dr. Daniel Comstock a retired physicist from the Massachusetts Institute of Technology and Dr. Walter Franklin Prince, a minister of religion and research officer of the American SPR and considered to be America's foremost psychical researcher at the time (and President of the British SPR in 1930-31), were also suspicious of her and wanted more evidence before reaching decisions. Another member of the committee, Harry Houdini the well-known magician who attended only a few of the sittings, was hostile and dismissive (of which more shortly). The upshot was that the committee concluded that she had not succeeded in demonstrating genuine phenomena to their satisfaction, and she was refused the $2,500 prize.

Later, a group of enthusiastic but inexperienced researchers from Harvard University led by Hudson Hoagland carried out a second series of investigations under allegedly carefully controlled conditions and came down against Mina, though their report and their conclusions (Hoagland 1925) were described by Everard Feilding (ibid. 1926) as:

almost preposterous ... (and leading) ... one to doubt (the investigators') competency, and ... so surprising as to leave one with a conviction that in order to make the whole story at all vraisemblable, we must supply some fact or motive hitherto undisclosed and one which, if known, may go to the root of the whole matter.

I am bound to agree with Feilding, and it is difficult to accept that anyone could take their contributions as a serious contribution to the case. Nevertheless, by this time the Margery mediumship, as it came to be called, had divided the American SPR into two camps, one in favor of the genuineness of the phenomena and one against, and his membership of the second group prompted Dr. Walter Franklin Prince to resign and to form an alternative organization, the Boston Society for Psychic Research, in 1925. In 1931, a telling finding against Mina was that thumb prints in dental wax allegedly made by Walter's materialized hands during séances turned out in fact to be those of her dentist, Dr. Frederick Caldwell, who was one of the sitters and who had initially supplied the wax. Nevertheless, the séance conditions under which the prints were obtained appeared to be fraud-proof. In addition, the prints of Walter's other fingers failed to match those of Caldwell (although it could not be proved these prints were those of Walter, as only a single thumb print, found on his razor, survived from his lifetime), and there were also some grounds, hinted at by the American Society for Psychical Research (1933b) to suspect that the apparently incriminating evidence had been tampered with by someone bent on discrediting Mina. However, thumb prints obtained during another visit to the SPR in 1929 were also apparently found to be those of Dr. Caldwell (Cummins 1935), though again the conditions under which they were obtained appeared to exclude fraud. So the mystery remained. Over 50 years afterwards Marian Nester, then director of education at the ASPR and daughter of the Crandons' close associate Dr. Mark Richardson, who herself had many sittings with Mina as a teenager, rejected the idea that her trances were not genuine – 'That's hard to believe when you were there ... I feel the things Walter did were not explained away by fraud' (Brian 1982). Other quotations from Marian Nester in support of Mina are given in Beloff (1993). Dr. John Crandon, Margery's son by her first marriage, was another who still took the view half a century after the events that 'some of the stuff was genuine, particularly in the early years' (Brian 1982).

The enigma of the Margery mediumship is still unsolved to the satisfaction of researchers. There are several accounts of her mediumship, some of them favorable to her (Bird 1925, Brandon 1982, Inglis 1984) and others more ambivalent (Tietze 1973). The former are more extensive and more detailed than the latter, and make it well nigh impossible to dismiss all of Mina's mediumship as fraudulent. It was Houdini's accusations against her that did most to ruin her reputation, in spite of the fact that these accusations were supported by no real evidence. Houdini was a major public figure in the USA at the time, and had a renowned reputation for unmasking fraudulent mediums, and his word thus carried even more weight than the evidence of the dubious thumbprint.

Despite the scandals surrounding her, Mina Crandon continued with her mediumistic work, producing by all accounts some remarkable phenomena (see e.g. Beloff ibid. 1993 for some details) until her premature death in 1941 – the year incidentally when J. B. Rhine, having left the ASPR over the Margery affair, considered it had purged itself sufficiently of any connection with 'spiritualism' for him to rejoin. Together with his wife Louisa, Rhine had had a single sitting with Mina Crandon on July 1, 1926, and although apparently predisposed in her favor, concluded to his disappointment that the séance was fraudulent from start to finish. His only concrete charge of fraud was a glimpse of what appeared to be Margery's freed foot silhouetted against a luminous plaque 'kicking the megaphone within her reach' (Rhine and Rhine 1927), but he listed a range of what he took to be other suspicious circumstances, and proposed a normal explanation for all the phenomena he had witnessed. Although Louisa Rhine, who had been sitting further from Mina throughout the séance, had seen nothing to arouse her own misgivings, she subsequently became convinced by the strength of her husband's doubts. It was this experience with Mina that helped persuade the Rhines that physical phenomena were too susceptible to fraud, and that the new science of parapsychology should steer well clear of them if it wished to be taken seriously by the rest of the scientific community. One may wonder a little that Rhine, who was only 30 years old at the time and had no track record as an investigator of physical mediumship, should draw his conclusions after only a single sitting, while cautious and highly experienced investigators like MacDougal and Carrington felt the need to attend scores of Mina's séances before coming to any conclusion. However, his friendship with Dr. Walter Franklin Prince and with Houdini (to whom Prince introduced him, and who showed him many of the alleged tricks used by mediums), both of whom regarded Mina Crandon with deep suspicion, further strengthened this resolve to ignore physical phenomena.

Which brings me back to Houdini. Houdini's only hard evidence to support his charge of fraud against Mina during the *Scientific American* sittings was that she had moved her leg, which he was controlling by pressure from his own leg with the trouser bottom rolled up to improve sensitivity. Once Mina had freed her leg, Houdini considered that she could have used it to effect the movement of physical objects and to operate the bell box, which was placed on the floor nearby. However, he had no evidence that she in fact did so, and a photograph published by Bird (1925) of the respective positions of Houdini's leg and that of Mina during the sitting concerned suggests that unless he first moved his leg from his position Mina's foot could not have reached the bell box without the whole maneuver being detected. Furthermore, Mina apparently produced phenomena while enclosed in the special fraud-proof box designed by Houdini in which she sat for three other sittings and which only left her head and hands free. Houdini remained silent about this, perhaps because a charge was made against him that he deliberately attempted to incriminate Mina by planting a ruler in the box (a charge ostensibly supported by his assistant, who later 'confessed' to doing the actual planting on Houdini's instructions). He also remained silent about those séances with Mina when impressive phenomena had been produced and when, along with the other members of the *Scientific American* committee, he had signed a statement affirming that the controls were perfect. However, whatever the rights and wrongs of all this, Houdini published a pamphlet entitled *Houdini Exposes the Tricks Used by the Boston Medium 'Margery'*, which seems more concerned with self-publicity than with making a serious appraisal of the case.

If the Margery mediumship was genuine – even Bird, one of its strongest supporters, accepted that it may have been 'mixed' at times, with both genuine phenomena and trickery – then who was Walter, Mina's control? Was he her older brother (by five years) as claimed, who had been killed at the young age of 29 in a tragic accident on the railroad? Certainly he gave every impression of being an intelligent and witty young man, outspoken and often short on patience, practical and resourceful and always ready to try something new, protective and concerned toward Mina, and immensely likeable. In fact he emerges from the transcripts of the séances as surely one of the most humorous, inventive, and iconoclastic of all controls. He swears at the apparatus in the séance room when it does not behave according to plan, makes unprintable remarks about Mina's critics, invents execrable verses as comments on proceedings, frequently refers to the sitters as 'damn fools' for some trivial failure on their part, taps them rather too hard over the head with the trumpet, and awards them with nicknames (for example Dr. Mark Richardson, known for his research into infectious diseases, becomes the 'Bugmaster') Walter talked almost continuously during some of the séances, often while Mina could be heard snoring away in her trance, and took a particular pleasure in whistling, which he seemed to do well. The voluminous transcripts of the sittings are almost worth reading just for the amusement provided by Walter. In the early sittings some 30 controls communicated, but once Walter took over, the strength of his personality was such that they all fell silent with the exception of John and Mark, Dr. Richardson's two young sons who had sadly died from infantile paralysis (poliomyelitis) some time before, and who seemingly served as his assistants in the production of some of the phenomena.

Mina herself was an intelligent and outspoken young woman, somewhat flirtatious and given to teasing, and brother and sister (who had been very close to each other in life) were similar in many ways, yet it seems unlikely that Mina could have gone on successfully impersonating a young man throughout the many years of her mediumship and doing so in such a way as to convince the regular sitters. As befitted the Crandons' social and professional status these sitters were all intelligent and presumably perceptive individuals. Dr. Le Roi Crandon, Mina's husband, was a well-respected Boston surgeon from an affluent family, a demonstrator of surgery at Harvard Medical School and author of a textbook for medical students, *Surgical After-Treatment*. Dr. Mark Richardson was a Boston physician who had done important research into typhoid and who after the death of two of his sons was devoting his professional life to research into the organism responsible for infantile paralysis. His wife and their son and daughter were also sitters. Other sitters included Mrs. Mark Richardson's two sisters, Dr. Edison Brown another Boston medical man and his wife, Dr. Frederick Caldwell a Boston dentist and Mrs. Brown's brother, and Frederick Adler a businessman and agent-superintendent of the building in which Dr. Crandon had his consulting room. It was Dr. Le Roi Crandon who, after reading Crawford's research with the physical phenomena reported at the Goligher Circle (Crawford 1916 and 1921), had the idea of bringing this group together and starting the home circle at which Mina Crandon's gifts were developed. It seems unlikely that over a number of years a circle such as this would have consistently been deceived by Mina Crandon not only into believing faked physical phenomena were genuine but into believing Walter was not the result of clever impersonation.

Could Walter have been Mina's secondary personality? We have no evidence that a secondary personality can carry out all the paranormal phenomena witnessed at the séances, some of which were at times violent and destructive (though never harmful to sitters), and impersonate in trance, consistently and successfully, the personality of a deceased brother. It must also be remembered that highly experienced investigators such as Hereward Carrington and Hamlin Garland were convinced they witnessed genuine phenomena and never suggested that a secondary personality was responsible. In addition, it should be borne in mind that Mina Crandon suffered from accusations of fraud rather than from solid evidence of fraud. Even the thumb print which turned out not to be that of Walter but of the dentist Dr. Comstock could possibly have been accidental rather than fraudulent. It was Dr. Comstock who supplied the dental wax and his thumb print could have been there before it was given to Mina. Subsequently he insisted that he had not touched the wax after handing it to Mina, and his word as far as I can ascertain was never doubted.

Subsequently, Walter has announced himself at the séances of Stewart Alexander (Chapter 13), a leading physical medium currently active in the UK, and I can vouch from personal experience of these séances that he appears to have lost none of his ingenuity and acerbic wit. But the Margery mediumship was in its way something of a double tragedy. Firstly it was a tragedy for Mina Crandon, a non-professional medium who never received payment, who cheerfully co-operated with every attempt to put her to the test, who suffered unsubstantiated attacks on her reputation (e.g. she has been accused variously of being 'flirtatious,' of having illicit relationships with named sitters, of taking up mediumship only in order to keep her husband's affections), and who for her pains was charged on rather dubious grounds of being a consistent cheat and a liar. Secondly because the controversy surrounding her mediumship gave parapsychologists an excuse for dismissing physical phenomena for the following half century, much to the detriment of further advances in our understanding of this controversial area of research.

Helen Duncan (1897?-1956), a Scottish woman based in Dublin, was another physical medium whose career was the subject of major disagreements. However, one thing about her is beyond much dispute, namely that if genuine she was one of the greatest materializing mediums of all time. She came to wide public attention as a result of a series of séances she held for the London Psychic Laboratory, the research department of the London Spiritual Alliance (now the College of Psychic Studies) in 1930 and reported in their journal *Light* for May 16 the following year. In some of these séances she was sown into a sack with sleeves ending in stiff buckram fingerless gauntlets, and the sack was fastened with tapes and cords to her chair, yet despite these controls, ectoplasm was seen in quantities, materializations of robed adults and children were obtained, movements of objects well beyond the medium's reach took place, and on occasions she appeared outside the sack although the ties and cords remained intact. The investigators were favorably impressed although they reached no final conclusions and did note some possibly suspicious circumstances, one of which was an analysis by the Charing Cross Hospital of a sample of ectoplasm obtained at one of the séances that proved to be paper and cloth pulp bound together with albumen (probably egg white).

However, when Harry Price (whom we met in Chapter 12 in connection with his work with Stella Cranshaw) tested her at his National Laboratory of Psychical Research his claim, printed in *The Morning Post* of July 14, 1931 and later in one of his books (Price 1931) was that she was 'one of the cleverest frauds in the history of spiritualism.' One of the photographs he published in support of his claim appeared to show that her 'ectoplasm' was simply cheesecloth swallowed by her prior to the séance and regurgitated at the appropriate moment (although the photograph appears to show the cheesecloth coming from her nose rather than her mouth). An X-Ray was also said to show that she possessed a remarkable faculty of regurgitation, although in fact an X-ray taken at the Dundee Royal Infirmary showed her stomach and esophagus to be normal.

Price appears to have based his charge largely upon the suspect ectoplasm, as he seems to have seen little of the materialization phenomena witnessed on other occasions. In fact the five séances he held with Helen seem to have been an unmitigated disaster for her. A safety pin was found attached to the cabinet curtains, another pin showed up on one of Price's photographs as did a face that looked to have been cut from a magazine. A dangling spirit hand had all the appearance of being a glove tied to a piece of muslin. At the conclusion of the fourth séance Helen refused to be X-rayed, and ran screaming into the street where she apparently had a fit of hysterics. On returning she then insisted on being X-rayed, having in Price's opinion had the opportunity to regurgitate during her hysterics and hand the incriminating evidence to her husband Henry, who then refused Price's request that he be searched. At the following séance a piece of ectoplasm cut by one of the doctors in attendance turned out to be folded paper. However, worse was to come. The London Psychic Laboratory had arranged a second series of séances with Helen in 1931, at one of which it was reported that her clothes were apparently thrown into the room, leaving her naked at the end of the sitting although the ties on the sack in which she had been sitting remained intact. However, in their subsequent report on her mediumship, published in the July 1931 issue of *Light* just two days after Price's newspaper article, they now changed their tune and accused her of clear-cut fraud, quoting in support a confession by her husband in which although he claimed that her phenomena were genuine he admitted she did sometimes conceal things, albeit 'unconsciously.' On the occasion when she had been asked to swallow a staining tablet of methylene blue before one of the London Psychic Laboratory séances to guard against regurgitation no ectoplasm was produced. The Laboratory then cancelled the remainder of Helen's contract to hold more sittings, allegedly because she had been holding unauthorized sittings with Price, and Helen and her family returned abruptly to Dundee, although £500 (a considerable sum in those days) the richer from their stay in London.

Many of those who had attended Helen's séances before the London fiasco were outraged by these charges of fraud made against her. Helen's gifts – of seeing deceased people, of clairvoyance and precognition (the Scottish 'second sight') – had in fact been evident since childhood. In the early 1920s, struggling against poverty and with a growing family (she had eight children of whom six survived) and with her husband stricken with ill-health from his time in the First World War trenches, she began to give private clairvoyant and psychometric (the paranormal acquisition of information by holding objects owned by the deceased) sittings. Encouraged by her husband Henry, who also had psychic gifts, she then began to sit with a home circle, and soon developed trance mediumship and acquired a spirit control, Dr. Williams. Around the year 1925 physical phenomena began to manifest, initially of a poltergeist form with violent disturbances and the presence of seemingly malevolent entities. At this point Dr. Williams gave Helen a new control, Albert Stewart, who remained with her for the next 30 years and proved successful in keeping undesirable elements away. Soon afterwards ectoplasm began to make its appearance in red light, flowing out from the cabinet within which Helen now sat until there seemed to be at least ten yards of it in a soft pile (Brealey 1985). As the mediumship developed, the ectoplasm was seen to take the form of materialized spirits, sometimes as many as 14 in a sitting. Particularly noticeable was Albert himself, described as bearded and over six feet tall. The materializations were said to give their names and to answer questions, but sadly most of the copious notes that Henry kept throughout Helen's mediumship were lost in a house fire after passing to his son on his death, though a few of the photographs of materializations taken respectively by Harvey Metcalfe an amateur photographer and by Harry Price (some of the latter photographs looking like crude puppets, still survive and are reproduced by Cassirer 1996, Gaskill 2001 and others).

Helen's children were allowed to attend the séances, and her daughter Gena Brealey (Brealey 1985) gives many accounts of their experiences. Harry, one of Helen's sons, recalls seeing at his first séance, in the light of a lamp, 'people dressed in white shimmering nightgowns' coming out of the curtains that were stretched across a bed recess and disappearing into the floor.' Ectoplasm, which he saw in profusion in the very many séances he attended over the following years, seemed to him like 'driven snow with bright sunshine shining on it. It appeared to sparkle with a million sequins' (an odd description if we are to believe that it was nothing but regurgitated cheesecloth). The first full materialization was said to be that of the deceased son of one of the sitters who sang a hymn and threw his arms around his mother, fully convincing her that it was indeed he. Numerous other materializations followed over the subsequent séances, and Brealey reports that once the materialized Albert held a chair above his head to amuse the children. There were also trumpet phenomena, and unable to control his curiosity one of the Duncan boys once took hold of it as it flew around the room. Immediately his entranced mother let out a fearful groan, and at the end of the séance there was a burn mark on her left cheek. Dr. Montague Rust, a physician from Fife, Scotland, was so impressed by Helen that he became a staunch supporter, and it was he indeed who introduced her to London and the sittings with the London Psychic Laboratory and with Harry Price. Dr. Rust angrily rejected the charge of fraud leveled against her by both the Laboratory and Harry Price, and continued to give her his full support, acting as a witness when she was eventually tried under the Witchcraft Act, an event to which I return in due course.

By 1930 Helen had gained an enviable reputation among those interested in establishing the survival of deceased friends and relatives. Unlike many mediums, she proved able to produce phenomena wherever she happened to be, and tirelessly traveled the country, usually accompanied by her husband but carrying with her to séances only a small attaché case containing her séance clothes, black dress, knickers, and court shoes. Her energy in view of her bulk and her increasing ill health was remarkable. By this time, although only five feet six inches in height she weighed 17 stone four ounces (later in life she was said to have increased to 22 stone but to be only 12 stone at her death), and already showed signs of the heart trouble and the diabetes that were to make her life increasingly difficult. Some of her weight gain was said to be due to edema (fluid retention), and she was also reported as having lung, bladder, intestinal, glandular, gynecological, and kidney problems. A sterilization operation after her eight pregnancies also left her gravely ill. Physically she was described as coarse and gross, and by no means a magnetic personality. In spite of her bulk, she was nevertheless seen to levitate in her chair to one foot in height, and it is claimed that the bulk made it increasingly unlikely that she could have impersonated the various spirits said to materialize during her séances.

However, although short neither of work nor of public esteem, Helen was anxious to gain recognition by the Spiritualist National Union (SNU), the main body for Spiritualists in Britain, and it was for this reason (together perhaps with financial inducements) that she agreed to Dr. Rust's suggestion that she make the journey to London in 1930 in order to be tested by research bodies such as the London Psychic Laboratory. Can we reconcile what happened there with the reports of successful séances both before and after this unfortunate adventure? One possibility is that she had genuine gifts, but resorted to cheating when these gifts deserted her in the harsh glare of publicity at the Laboratory and under the critical scrutiny of Price. Price in particular seems to have terrified her. The room in which she sat for him was decorated with photographs of supposedly fraudulent mediums and even with one of Houdini. The sitters seem to have been critically inclined. Price hired two doctors from St. Thomas Hospital to carry out an intimate and intrusive clinical examination of her before one of the séances (the examination turned out to be negative, as did the séance). Flashlight photographs were taken of her while she was in trance, attempts were made from the start to capture samples of ectoplasm, and X-rays of her digestive system were demanded. For someone from a humble background new to all such pressures it was hardly surprising that any gifts she might have had would have deserted her. Her early successes at the London Psychic Laboratory did not continue, and the pity was that she may have resorted to cheating in a forlorn attempt both to protect her reputation and to continue to earn the large sums of money on offer to her in London. Price's claim in his newspaper article that Helen was 'one of the cleverest frauds in the whole history of Spiritualism' seems to have been an attempt to demonstrate how clever he was in catching her out. In fact, if his account of the séances is accurate, the fraud was clumsy and readily detected – hardly that of someone with several years practice in deluding people.

On her return to Scotland there was no shortage of people prepared to champion her cause. Arthur Findlay (Chapter 11), Vice President of the Scottish SPR, sent Price a collection of testimonies to her genuineness, which he dismissed curtly. Dr. Rust pointed out that it was known all along that the London visit would be a fiasco for such 'a very sensitive creature' (a strange comment in view of his earlier support for the visit). Writing to Mollie Goldney, a leading member of the SPR, he referred sarcastically to the fact that if regurgitation was the explanation for her phenomena

... she regurgitated my brother-in-law, Charles Ross, and my driver, Andrew Barclay, and my dog Hector. We had long conversations with them in their own characteristic voice and varying memories, Hector being lifelike in all his actions and ran about the floor as he did in life. Forms came out [of the cabinet] and sat on some of the sitters' knees and spoke and ate apples and drank water, and ... removed my boots forcibly and put them on and walked about with them.

It is unclear what to make of the apples and water, though presumably if the deceased could materialize and clump about in Rust's boots they could at least simulate a bite or two of an apple (Rust does not tell us if the resultant pieces were found on the floor at the end of the evening). The SNU also appeared to consider Helen genuine, awarding her the diploma she so much coveted. An expert also testified that Price's photo of Helen with her cheesecloth ectoplasm was a fake, and solicitors wrote to Price that Helen affirmed she had never been photographed in the position shown, and that the photograph was posed by Ethel, Price's secretary. She also thanked the London Psychical Laboratory for putting her on the map as a medium, and work continued to flood in. Will Goldston (Chapter 13), one of the leading magicians in Europe, stated in *Psychic News* – after attending séances where he had been responsible for securing her with cord and handcuffs – that he could not duplicate her phenomena. Spiritualist churches in various parts of the country pronounced themselves convinced by her. Even disinterested bodies were cautious about siding with Price. Reviewing Price's book for the London SPR, Count Berovsky-Petrovo-Slovovo (a serious and highly respected commentator in spite of his somewhat over-theatrical title) considered it lacked research content and failed to prove regurgitation. The American SPR refused to publish Price's findings in their journal on the grounds that the major facts were a subject of controversy. The editor of *Luce e Ombra*, the well-respected journal of the leading Italian society for psychical research, also found the research unimpressive.

Price, however, was not finished with Helen, and invited her maid, Mary McGinlay, to London, where the girl confessed she had seen rubber gloves, a doll, and masks in the bathroom, and that Helen gave her cheesecloth to wash after her séances. It seems then that Price refused McGinlay money to get married, and she subsequently confessed to J. D. McIndoe, President of the SNU, that she had no reason to think Helen fraudulent. Nevertheless, disaster for Helen was to follow. At a séance held in the home of Esson Maule, who had her own séance room, Helen was thought to be impersonating the materializations, and when Miss Maule grabbed at the materialization of a young girl called Peggy it turned out to be an undervest apparently manipulated by the medium. A struggle ensued, Helen tried unsuccessfully to hide the vest, was accused by Miss Maule of producing fraudulent materializations, became violent and abusive, and the police were called. Eventually Helen left in her taxi, but not before picking up her £4 fee and signing a receipt. Eleven days later Miss Maule and five of the other sitters appeared before a magistrate to testify that Helen had been caught perpetrating a criminal fraud. The undervest was produced as evidence, and on May 3, 1933 Helen appeared before the Sheriff Summary Court to answer the charge that she had pretended to be 'a medium through whom the spirits of deceased persons were – materialised – [and] did pretend to hold a séance – and to materialise the spirits of certain deceased persons including that of a deceased child named Peggy.' Helen pleaded not guilty, and a number of witnesses spoke up in her favor. However, her counsel gave the defense that this was the first time she had 'stooped to manipulation' (a statement which Helen vehemently and immediately denied), and the Sheriff concluded that 'Whatever psychic powers the accused may possess, I find that this charge against her has been proved.' Helen was fined £10 or one month's imprisonment. She paid the fine.

Suspicions were immediately voiced however that the séance organized by Miss Maule was a trap specially set to catch Helen, and evidence emerged that suggested Harry Price, who had been in contact with Miss Maule, may have been behind the whole thing. Helen continued to protest her innocence, and continued her work. Some of her supporters even considered the court case, in view of the statements by witnesses for the defense, had been good publicity for the Spiritualist cause. A vote of confidence in her mediumship was carried by 57 votes to two at the Annual General Meeting of the SNU, and her SNU diploma was renewed. Fresh reports of the wonders of her séances continued to appear. Sitters testified that they were reunited with and embraced deceased loved ones, dead pet animals were said to appear, and Albert continued to hold court, predicting the inevitability of the Second World War when the general feeling was that it would be averted. Helen even began to fill large theatres with her demonstrations, and the audiences she attracted greatly outnumbered those who turned up for Harry Price's lectures (which must have mortified him). The beginning of the Second World War, with its growing list of casualties, added further to the demand for Helen's mediumship, and she became able to command a fee of £8 for each séance, four times the weekly state retirement pension at the time.

It was not to last. For a year or more Helen had been in the habit of visiting Portsmouth, one of Britain's premier naval ports, where she gave séances at the Master Temple. At one of these in late 1941 a dead sailor with the name HMS Barham on his cap-band apparently materialized for his mother, one of the sitters. Not knowing that anything had happened to the Barham, a British battleship whose home port was Portsmouth and which was currently serving in the eastern Mediterranean, the woman telephoned the Admiralty in London the following day and asked for details. The result of her call was a visit from two naval officers demanding to know the source of her news. The problem was that although the Barham had indeed been sunk (on 25 November with the loss of 868 of her crew) the news was top secret. The German submarine, U-331, that had done the damage had dived immediately in order to avoid retaliation by the rest of the British battle fleet, and her crew were unaware of the name or nature of their victim. The loss of the Barham necessitated a reorganization of the seriously weakened Mediterranean battle fleet, and the Admiralty considered it crucial that this should be completed before the Germans came to know the importance of the sinking. Thus the news of the Barham's fate was kept secret until late January 1942. Military Intelligence already had Helen's name on their files after the revelation by her control Albert in May 1941 that a great British battleship has just been sunk, information that proved correct as HMS Hood, the pride of the British navy, was sunk on May 25. News of the sinking was not however made public by the authorities until after Helen's séance. Military Intelligence were not unnaturally alarmed, and with the Barham case were confronted by an even more important reason to be deeply suspicious of Helen.

There is a belief therefore that after her revelation of the sinking of the Barham Helen was seen as a security risk – either through her mediumship or because she had clandestine access to secret information. Be this as it may, a number of mediums were in fact being brought before the courts at the time to be charged under the 1842 Vagrancy Act, convicted, and fined £10. It certainly seemed as if those responsible for intelligence were, for whatever reason, becoming increasingly nervous of mediums. On January 14, 1944 a naval officer, Lieutenant Worth, who had already attended several séances given by other mediums at the Master Temple, turned up to Helen's séance with his friend Surgeon Lieutenant Elijah Fowler. Both men were given seats on the front row, and Worth apparently saw a materialized figure who claimed to be his deceased aunt, although in fact he knew all his aunts were still alive (it is said he deliberately set a trap by asking the figure if she was his aunt and took her muffled answer for assent). Next day he went to the police where he consulted Detective Inspector Ford, and by agreement with Ford attended another of Helen's séances on the 19th of the month armed with a torch and a whistle and accompanied by War Reserve Constable

Rupert Cross. At an agreed moment and after watching materializations, Cross got to his feet and pushed his way into the cabinet followed by Worth, whose torch revealed Helen allegedly trying to hide several yards of cloth. Cross grabbed for the cloth but lost his grip on it. Worth blew his whistle, and as agreed Inspector Ford entered with three other detectives, switched on the light, and arrested Helen on suspicion of contravening the Vagrancy Act by 'pretending to communicate with the spirits of deceased persons.' There was no sign of the supposed yards of cloth on Helen's person, but Ford refused offers by the sitters to be searched to prove she had not passed it to them in the confusion. Helen was taken to the police station, and formally charged. She spent the night in the cells, and the following day the magistrate remanded her in custody until January 25, transferring her from Portsmouth to Holloway Prison in London, from where after five days she was released on bail.

Deeply concerned by this turn of events, the SNU immediately came to Helen's support and appointed Charles Loseby, a barrister who had already acted for a number of mediums, to defend her against the charge. Charles Loseby, a 62-year-old distinguished First World War hero who had served as a Member of Parliament for both the Tory and the Liberal Parties, was a natural choice in this role. A Spiritualist himself, he had for some years fought a passionate campaign against what he saw as official discrimination against mediums. Meanwhile, in preparing the case against Helen, the Assistant Director of Public Prosecutions decided that in view of her previous conviction for fraud she should be charged under the more serious count of Conspiracy to Defraud rather than under the Vagrancy Act, thus ensuring a trial by jury instead of a hearing before a magistrate, and a mandatory prison sentence rather than the option of a fine if found guilty. The ensuing publicity, the involvement of the Director of Public Prosecutions (the DPP), the strength of the protests in Helen's favor, and the petitions lodged in her defense escalated matters to the point where it became inevitable that Helen's trial would be held in the Central Criminal Court in London (the Old Bailey, the top court in the land). It then became clear to the DPP that it might be difficult to obtain a conviction for conspiracy to defraud, as to do so it would be necessary to prove that Helen had taken money from those at the séance on the promise of producing materialized spirits, whereas the séance organizers, Mr. and Mrs. Homer who were also to be tried with Helen along with Mrs. Brown, Helen's traveling companion, had been scrupulous in never promising anything of the sort. Therefore an even more serious charge was needed, and this was identified in Section IV of the obsolete 1735 Witchcraft Act, which in summary was designed to prevent and punish anyone pretending to the 'arts or powers' of witchcraft in order to delude and defraud ignorant persons. The use of this ancient Act, the re-location of the trial to the Old Bailey, the furor in defense of Helen, and the heavy involvement of the press all ensured that the trial would attract maximum attention.

The trial, which opened on March 23, 1944, was far too convoluted and confused to be dealt with fully here. Excellent accounts are given in Gaskill 2001 and Cassirer 1996 (both books are in fact essential reading for anyone wishing to take further their studies of Helen Duncan; Brealey 1985, Helen's daughter, also gives an illuminating account). Suffice it to say that although there is no doubt of Charles Loseby's total commitment to Helen's cause and his great skills in court, he has been criticized on four major counts for his handling of the defense during the trial. Firstly, as noted by the Recorder (i.e. the Presiding Judge) he called too many witnesses for the defense – 19 primary and some 22 secondary. All testified to having seen genuine phenomena at Helen's séances, but it is thought that the large number confused the jury, and with hindsight Loseby might have been better advised not to call as witnesses people who had only attended previous séances and not been present on the fateful day in Portsmouth. The second criticism was that he failed to anticipate that a reference by one of his witnesses, Alfred Dodds, to séances attended in the early 1930s, would allow the prosecution to refer to Helen's 1933 court conviction as evidence that she was not a genuine medium at the time. But for the references back to these early séances the prosecution would not have been allowed to raise this previous conviction in court. The third criticism was that Loseby did not make sufficient use of the alleged inaccuracies and possible falsehoods of some prosecution witnesses such as Lieutenant Worth, who proved an articulate and otherwise convincing witness, and the police. And the fourth one was that he did not call Helen or her three co-defendants to the witness box to testify.

In reality, Loseby seems simply to have been out-gunned by John Maude, who led the case for the prosecution. Maude was a King's Counsel and top barrister who had already acted as counsel for the Treasury and who seems to have been cherry-picked by the prosecution – and who commanded fees far beyond the resources of the SNU, who were paying for the defense. Loseby confessed afterwards that Maude spoke with 'such adroitness, skill, and economy of words that any ill-informed person might well imagine that there could be no effective answer to the case as he set it out.' It might also have been better had Helen's co-defendants been represented separately. Loseby had the job of defending all four, which inevitably put extra pressures upon him. In addition the presiding judge, Sir Gerald Dodson, although even-handed and fair throughout, seems to have become bored by the large number of witnesses for the defense, and this boredom probably communicated itself to the jury. However, Loseby did his best, and moreover produced a masterstroke – the offer by Helen to demonstrate materializations to judge and jury. The offer caused a sensation. Initially the judge rejected it, then agreed to allow the jury to decide. They also rejected it. But the significance of this offer remains to this day, and more will be said about it shortly.

At the end of the trial the judge, in his summing up, commented that Loseby may well have defeated his own case by 'being too prolix and multiplied.' The jury made up for this by taking only 24 minutes to reach their verdict, finding all four defendants guilty. Inspector West, called upon to comment on the records of the defendants before sentences were passed, not only spoke of Helen as having deluded confirmed Spiritualists but as having 'tricked, defrauded, and preyed upon the minds of a certain credulous section of the public – many of whom left [her séances] with the firm conviction that the memory of the dead had been besmirched.' Finally and amazingly he added that Helen had 'transgressed the security laws – in a naval connection, when she foretold the loss of one of His Majesty's ships long before the fact was made public.' Mr. and Mrs. Homer were simply bound over, Mrs. Brown was sentenced to four months in prison for aiding Helen's offence, while Helen herself was given nine months. Loseby's plea that in view of her health problems she be given a non-custodial sentence was rejected.

I have dealt with Helen Duncan's case at some length not only because many of her materializations were vouched for by so many witnesses of good standing that it is difficult to dismiss all her work as fraudulent, in spite of the fact that she appears to have resorted to crude trickery at times, but because of the significance of some of the events at the trial. These are firstly that the Council of the SNU were sufficiently convinced by her to fund her defense. The SNU was not then and never has been run by people readily taken in by fraudulent mediumship, whatever may be true of some of its members. In fact those responsible for the organization – which is a recognized religion in the UK – have more knowledge of mediumship, good and bad, than the scientists and conjurors who have over the years carried out research into it. The SNU, which is still campaigning for a pardon for Helen Duncan, would not have gone to the expense of defending her – and courting possible bad publicity – had they not been satisfied that the charges against her were false. The second significant feature of the trial is that 41 witnesses went into the witness box in a court of law prepared to swear on oath that they had witnessed genuine phenomena. The number may have been too large for the patience of the presiding judge, but the fact that 41 witnesses were prepared to risk charges of perjury by speaking up for Helen in court speaks volumes for their confidence in her. The third was that a serious offer was made in the twentieth century on behalf of a medium in a court of law to produce materializations. Unless both Helen and Loseby knew that the offer would be turned down (by no means certain; there was nothing in law to prevent such an offer being accepted) this speaks volumes for Helen's conviction of her own abilities. Even the most vehement of her critics would hardly suppose that she would have attempted – or been able to accomplish – trickery in such an arena. The fourth significant feature was that a police officer not only spoke of Helen's 'foretelling' the loss of the Barham but did so in the context of her alleged 'transgression of the security laws,' thus adding strongly to the suspicion that it was the threat posed by Helen's mediumship to national security that was the real reason for the charges against her. On the one hand it seems therefore that Helen was brought to court because the reality of her mediumship was officially recognized (and feared), and on the other that she was sent to prison because her mediumship was officially regarded as fraudulent. Military Intelligence, the DPP, the courts of justice, and the police therefore seemed to succeed in both having their cake and eating it.

To these four significant features we can add a fifth, namely the repeal of the Witchcraft Act. Prime Minister Winston Churchill, who it seems was open-minded in his attitude to the paranormal, was said to have been outraged by the trial, and the process that led in 1951 to the repeal of the iniquitous Act may have been put in train at this point. However, most credit for repeal goes to the SNU who campaigned tirelessly against the Act, Chuter Ede the reforming Home Secretary of the Labour Government that came to power after the end of the Second World War and who piloted the Bill repealing the Act through the Commons, and Air Chief Marshall Lord Dowding who gave the Bill its reading in the House of Lords. The Act was replaced by the Fraudulent Mediums Act that stipulated 'intent to deceive or defraud' on the part of mediums would now have to be proved in court before a conviction could be obtained, that all prosecutions would need the consent of the DPP before they could proceed, and that 'anything done solely for the purposes of entertainment' could be used as a defense. With the exception of this last proviso, which may have been included more to protect magicians than mediums (no serious medium would claim he or she was simply 'entertaining' the public), mediumship was therefore, for the purposes of fraud and deception, put on very much the same footing as any other profession.

The matter was not quite done with, however. For some unknown reason police raided a séance Helen was holding in a private house in Nottingham on Sunday October 28, 1956 just at the point when materializations were taking place. Amid the shouting and police flashlights Helen fell to the floor, where she was pinned by police officers anxious to confiscate any incriminating evidence. None was found. A doctor, called to attend to the sick and deeply distressed woman, refused a request by the police to carry out an intimate physical examination in order to find this incriminating material. Helen was not arrested but allowed to return home, which she did with great difficulty on October 30. Gena, her daughter, a trained nurse, was appalled to find an angry burn the size of a tea plate on Helen's right breast and a smaller one on her stomach, both apparently caused by the recoil of ectoplasm consequent upon the abrupt intrusion of the police. A doctor who examined her described the burns as electrical, and doubted that they could have been self-inflicted. In view of Helen's diabetes, her heart trouble, her injuries, and her desperate physical condition he had her admitted immediately to hospital. The SNU and other supporters promptly took up her case once again, but shortly after her return from hospital at the end of November a letter was received informing her that her case had been passed to the DPP. By this time Helen, now in great pain, was being given morphine by her doctor, and in the early hours of December 6 she quietly slipped into the spirit world that she had sought all her life to serve. Her husband Henry, devastated at her death, began to prepare a case against the police, but was advised that there was insufficient medical evidence to prove they had actually caused Helen's death.

The reason for the police raid remains a mystery. There is some suggestion that a complaint had been made to the Nottinghamshire police by person or persons unknown (Harry Price was certainly not involved; he had died in 1948 from the heart trouble that had prevented his giving evidence against her at her trial). Gaskill (2001) draws attention to what he calls the coincidence that the surprise Anglo-French invasion of Egypt in an abortive and wholly misguided attempt to reclaim the Suez Canal took place less than 36 hours after the police raid. Was it considered that Helen might once again pose a security risk? Who can say? One thing is clear. The DPP was very unlikely to have sanctioned another trial on the strength of the evidence (or rather lack of it) gathered by the Nottinghamshire police during their raid. However, it may have been considered that the raid itself, plus the warning that the case had been sent to the DPP, would be sufficient to prevent Helen from continuing with her work.

One thing is clear. The treatment received by Helen was a disgrace by any standards, and coming on top of the prosecutions of other mediums under the Vagrancy Act, seems to indicate that there was indeed a recognition by some of those in authority that mediumship was genuine and could pose a very real threat to national security in times of war. Spiritualists regard Helen Duncan as a martyr to their cause, and rightly credit her death as leading to the repeal of the Witchcraft Act. It would, of course, have been far better for the government to remove this infamous Act from the statute book without waiting for the impetus given by the unnecessary death of an unfortunate woman.

Mediums and Magicians

It is often argued that credibility cannot be attached to accounts of physical phenomena unless magicians are included in the circle of sitters and are satisfied that no sleight of hand was being used. This argument can be disputed. The role of magicians in detecting fraud at physical séances has been somewhat exaggerated. In many cases magicians have merely pointed out how they think fraud could have taken place, rather than directly identified it. It is natural that magicians, well-versed as they are in conjuring, are likely to suppose that trickery of some kind is taking place, but it is notable that few of them, when challenged, have been prepared to stage fake séances under the conditions operating at the original sittings, and in the presence of the investigators who have pronounced these sittings as genuine. The great escapologist Harry Houdini is said to have exposed any number of frauds, and his book *A Magician Among the Spirits* (1924) is often referenced in this context. The book is in fact little more than a weak attempt to discredit individuals – who are given no chance to defend themselves – on the basis mostly of speculation. As already mentioned it was Houdini who, on very dubious grounds, did much to discredit Mina Crandon and to scotch her attempt to win the $2,500 prize for a successful demonstration of physical mediumship offered by the *Scientific American*. A charge often made is that scientists are not qualified to act as investigators and that magicians should be invited to do the job instead. This is usually followed up by a second charge to the effect that no leading magician has ever been convinced of the truth of physical phenomena. Let us take these two charges in turn. In reply to the first it should be said that what is needed is a knowledge firstly of the kind of tricks that could be used in the séance room, secondly of how to spot if they are being used, and thirdly of how to guard against them. The inability of some investigators to perform these tricks convincingly themselves is less important. Knowing about tricks and performing them successfully are two different things. For example, Carrington, who with Baggally (another expert on magic tricks) and Feilding made up the SPR team sent to investigate Palladino (Chapter 12), was a recognized expert on magic tricks and on the ways in which they could be used in the séance room, but by all accounts he was indifferent when it came to demonstrating them. In addition, it is important to remember that much of a magician's time is spent practicing tricks suitable for his or her own act, and not in studying others that are irrelevant to it. Thus a magician who has not taken a detailed interest in physical phenomena may have far less knowledge of possible tricks associated with it than the scientist who has. There is no need for the scientist to be good at actually demonstrating a trick for him or her to know how it is done.

It is true that some magicians have unmasked fraudulent mediums, but so have some scientists. And it is worth remembering that not only are many of the magicians who dismiss all physical mediumship as trickery unread in the subject and inexperienced in its observation, some of them also have a professional interest in branding it as fraud and in claiming that they could easily perform the same tricks. Possibly they could, but it would be interesting to see them doing so, under the conditions that were observed by the investigators during the production of the original phenomena. I would even like to see them reproduce, by normal means, one of Uri Geller's effects that I witnessed at close quarters. This is not the place to make any pronouncements on Uri Geller, who does not claim to be a physical medium and who does not try to produce séance room phenomena, but who has been roundly criticized by certain fellow magicians and scientists alike. When Uri Geller was a guest in the offices of the SPR in London I took one of our teaspoons and he and I each held an end, lightly balanced only between the fingertips of our index fingers. Any significant downward pressure on a spoon held lightly in this position would cause it immediately to fall to the floor. Uri did no more than very gently stroke the shaft with the tip of the index finger of his other hand, and while I watched closely the shaft bent through a near 45-degree angle. I kept the same light pressure upon the spoon throughout and at no point was it pressed hard against my finger by Uri (thus causing us to produce the curvature ourselves). The spoon was isolated from any object that Uri could have used to provide the purchase necessary to bend it by sleight of hand, and in addition Uri had no opportunity to weaken the spoon beforehand (chemically or otherwise), and he did not ask to retain it afterwards. I still have the spoon, and was free to apply any subsequent test that I liked to the metal. The whole thing took place in broad daylight, without props or subterfuge of any kind, and Uri made no attempt to divert my attention or disarm my critical faculties by calling out excitedly that it was bending, as is sometimes claimed when he produces similar effects elsewhere. Two of my colleagues, both of them highly experienced investigators, watched the whole process closely from only inches away. One of them, Guy Lyon Playfair, has a particular knowledge of tricks done by sleight of hand, and has made a special study of Geller and has co-authored an important book about him (Geller and Playfair 1986). Both of them were convinced that nothing suspicious took place. No magician has as yet attempted to produce the same effect for me under these conditions by normal means, or tried to explain how the effect could be produced.

The second charge, that no magician has ever been convinced by physical phenomena, is equally misleading. Over the last half century and more a number of the magicians who have looked closely at physical phenomena have concluded that they appear genuine. Fodor (1933), that extraordinary encyclopedist of psychic phenomena, collected and published a range of examples. For example, Robert Houdin, the leading magician of his time (and the man from whom Houdini, out of admiration, borrowed his own stage name) gave Dr. Edwin Lee a signed statement after witnessing the work of clairvoyant Alexis Didier (who was not a physical medium but who, among other effects, carried out a successful book test with Houdin) that the more he reflected upon the things he had witnessed 'the more impossible do I find it to class them among the tricks which are the objects of my art.' He added in a letter to de Mirville that the more he reflected upon what he had experienced with Didier, the more 'fully convinced [he became] that it would be impossible for anyone to produce such surprising effects by mere skill.' Of a séance with Home, Houdin wrote that he was 'as astounded as I could be, and persuaded that it is perfectly impossible by chance or adroitness to produce such marvellous effects.' Bosco, who himself performed before royalty, was convinced that D. D. Home was genuine. Canti, another magician who was intimate with the great (and sometimes good) informed Prince Napoleon that 'he could in no way account for the phenomena ... on the principles of his profession.' Houdin's stage successor, Hamilton, wrote to the Davenport Brothers after attending one of their séances that the 'phenomena are inexplicable, and the more so by such persons as have thought themselves able to guess your supposed secret.' Harry Kellar, one of the best-known conjurors of his day, testified that the medium Eglinton (another individual who appears to have used a mixed mediumship, with both genuine phenomena and fraud) was levitated while he held his hand, and that he was pulled to his feet 'and subsequently compelled to jump on a chair and then on the table in order to retain my hold of him. That his body did ascend into the air. with an apparently utter disregard to the law of gravity, there can be no doubt.' Even J. N. Maskelyne, the founder of the famous Maskelyne dynasty of expert stage magicians, confessed firstly that he believed in table-turning (the paranormal partial levitation of a table to tap out spirit messages with its legs while the medium and the sitters have their hands on its surface), and that although he could imitate any example of séance room phenomena he would need the help of his own apparatus which in many cases weighed more than a ton. 'Professor' Jacobs testified that the phenomena of the Davenport brothers was genuine, and that attempts to imitate it by Robert Houdin were 'an infantile and grotesque parody' of their phenomena. Will Goldston, one of Europe's leading professional magicians, author of 40 works on sleight of hand, and founder of the Magicians' Club of London, testified in a national newspaper (the *Daily Sketch*) that 'I am convinced that what I saw [at a Rudi Schneider séance organized by Harry Price] was not trickery. No group of my fellow-magicians could have produced those effects under such conditions.' Goldston also spoke up for independent voice medium Hazel Ridley and for Helen Duncan (who may have been another who used mixed mediumship) and was sufficiently impressed by physical phenomena actually to become a spiritualist. Both David Abbott and Howard Thurston, contemporaries of Houdini and two of America's best-known magicians, confessed their conviction in the genuineness of physical phenomena (like Goldston, Thurston also became a spiritualist).

Harry Price, an expert amateur magician himself and Vice President of The Magicians Club, reports that Will Goldston, a personal friend, assured him that both J. N. Maskelyne and his son Nevil Maskelyne were secret believers in spiritualism, and that Houdini's claimed exposures of mediums were simply part of a great publicity stunt. Goldston further assured Price that Houdini, like the Maskelynes, was a clandestine believer in spiritualism, and Price himself possessed a letter from Houdini in which the great man stated that a 'spirit extra' (i.e. a materialization) he had witnessed of Professor James Hyslop was genuine.

As Fodor points out, the difference between magicians and mediums is that the former are always masters of ceremonies at their own performances, whereas during investigations mediums are expected to submit themselves to the conditions imposed upon them. To this we can add that although a magician never repeats his tricks over and over again, simply on demand, mediums are required by investigators to replicate their phenomena at sitting after sitting. The attempt by magicians to respond to the challenge to reproduce physical phenomena under the same conditions as mediums has not been particularly successful. Archdeacon Colley offered J. N. Maskelyne a thousand pounds (a princely sum in the late nineteenth century) if he could duplicate the materialization phenomena of the Rev. Francis Monck (who at one point was found guilty of alleged fraud and sentenced to three months in prison). Maskelyne accepted the challenge but his performance was considered unsatisfactory and the money was refused. Maskelyne took Colley to court but lost the case, and Colley was awarded £75 (still a considerable sum at the time) plus costs against Maskelyne. Interestingly, another member of the Maskelyne 'family,' Captain' Clive Maskelyne was offered, in a national newspaper, a hundred guineas by Dennis Bradley if he could reproduce the phenomena of George Valiantine under the same conditions. Maskelyne agreed at first, then withdrew when he learnt the nature of these conditions. Yet another member of the Maskelyne family, J. N. Maskelyne's grandson Noel Maskelyne, who produced a supposed reproduction of Rudi Schneider's phenomena for public entertainment at the London Coliseum theatre, was challenged on stage by Harry Price, with a wager of £250, to do so under the conditions imposed by Price on Schneider during their work together. Noel Maskelyne publicly and humiliatingly refused, and also did not take up Price's public offer of £1,000 for any magician who could reproduce Schneider's phenomena under the conditions that Price imposed upon him during the séances held at Price's laboratory in London (Price 1930). Revealingly Maskelyne was not alone. No other magician was prepared to take up up Price's offer. Finally, although the result of attempts by the conjuror Selbit to reproduce on stage the effects of the Bangs sisters (whose mediumship involved producing portraits of the deceased by apparent spirit agency) impressed Carrington, Admiral Usborne

Moore, who made a particular study of this aspect of the Bangs' mediumship, reported that the conditions under which Selbit did so 'were as different to the conditions of the Bangs sisters as a locomotive boiler is different from a teapot.'

The charge that all magicians dismiss physical phenomena as fraudulent and can reproduce any of the effects concerned under the same conditions is thus clearly unfounded. It is perfectly possible for competent magicians to reproduce many of these effects if they are allowed to install their equipment in the séance room beforehand and clear it away afterwards, but these are not the conditions enjoyed by the mediums pronounced genuine by serious investigators after months and years of careful research. It is also worth repeating that, as with Palladino and some of the other mediums mentioned in this book, evidence of fraud under lax conditions does not automatically invalidate evidence of genuineness under strict conditions. The SPR had for many years a policy of never investigating a medium who had been detected in fraud. The file was automatically closed on him or her. This policy was understandable but in the light of the findings of Feilding and his colleagues with Palladino, misguided. It is not unlike arguing that a footballer sent off the field for foul play can never subsequently be believed to play fairly. Certainly, if fraud is detected at any point, suspicion attaches to the medium concerned until he or she has been found to produce phenomena under conditions that preclude its repetition. But it would be unscientific to discontinue work with a medium on the strength of a single instance of fraud, particularly if the medium is in trance at the time and therefore may not necessarily be fully responsible for his or her movements.

Many of those who raise the cry of fraud against physical phenomena appear to have only a very limited idea of what goes on in a séance. Two colleagues of mine – one particularly well known for his public skepticism – conducted an experiment a few years ago in which an actor, posing as a medium, faked a physical séance in darkness but under the gaze of a hidden infrared video camera which made a tape of the proceedings. I watched the tape after the experiment was over. The sitters all sat around a table on which were objects of various kinds such as children's toys, and from his seat the actor pushed some of these objects onto the floor with a long rod, to the accompaniment of shrieks and cries from the sitters who were in total darkness and who had apparently been deceived into supposing that they might be present while something genuine was taking place. The whole purpose of the exercise was to show how easily people are fooled, and in this it clearly succeeded. However, the sitters were young students who knew little or nothing of physical phenomena, and apart from the darkness the whole thing was as unlike any séance I have attended or read about as it could possibly be. No serious séance to my knowledge consists primarily of things falling off a table, and no serious séance to my knowledge consists only of naive sitters. The whole thing, as an attempt to throw doubt on physical mediumship, was meaningless.

I pointed out to my colleagues that their mock séance told us nothing about the real thing. I was listened to with great courtesy, and nothing further was said. However, to my surprise I saw the very same video tape shown some time afterwards as part of a supposedly serious scientific program on mediumship broadcast by one of the UK's most respected television channels. Viewers were led to believe that the tape was serious evidence demonstrating how readily sitters can be fooled at séances. My colleagues were not involved in the making of the program and were blameless in the way their tape was presented, yet this stands as good evidence of how misleading information about physical phenomena can become public and be believed by millions. On the same program, one of the many supposed 'experts' interviewed made the ludicrous – and patently actionable – statement that 'all mediums except one have been caught out in fraud,' which provides equally good evidence of how mediumship itself is given a bad name. Needless to say my letters of protest to the program's producers and to the television watchdog yielded evasive replies as ill informed as the program and its contributors, and no apology was ever broadcast. In no other field of serious research would viewers of a respected television program, screened at a peak time, be given the erroneous impression that science has 'shown' that the evidence upon which much of it depends can all be dismissed as due to a combination of fraud and human gullibility.

Physical Phenomena at Scole

It is now nearly eight years since I was invited by the late Montague Keen, Secretary of the Survival Research Committee of the SPR, to join him and the late Professor Arthur Ellison in an investigation into a group of four people, led by Robin Foy, who had been sitting regularly over many months with a view to producing physical phenomena. Robin Foy (Foy 1996) is a man who has dedicated some 30 years of his adult life to investigations into physical phenomena, and together with his wife Sandra and a husband-and-wife team of mediums, Diana and Alan Bylett, he now reported obtaining significant results with the help, we were told, of a spirit team on the other side. Members of the team were said to communicate through both of the entranced mediums, but also to produce independent voice phenomena, spirit lights, and much else besides. Of particular interest to us were photographs obtained by the group on unexposed film left on the table around which they sat during the séances. The group had no intention of making money from their work or of obtaining prestige for themselves in the field of psychical research. Their objective was to obtain physical phenomena with a view to supporting the concept of survival.

Reports by Monty Keen and Arthur Ellison after their early visits to the group (known to us as the Scole Group, from Scole the small town in Norfolk where the Foys lived and where the group met), together with those by the late Ralph Noyes, at that time Hon. Secretary of the SPR, made it clear that they were impressed by their experiences with the Group, and when Ralph Noyes resigned as an investigator for health reasons I was pleased to accept the invitation to take his place. For two years Monty Keen, Arthur Ellison, and I sat with the Group at least once a month, 31 séances in all, though only Montague Keen, who had a number of additional sittings both in Britain and abroad, was present at all of them. Two fellow-investigators, Dr. Hans Schaer a lawyer from Switzerland and Walter Schnittger an engineer from Germany, with whom we worked closely, also attended séances at which we were not present, gathering highly important data, one example of which I give later.

My difficult in writing about Scole is not because the experiences we had with the Group have faded. They are as clear as if they happened only weeks ago. The difficulty is to make them sound believable. It is a strange fact of life that whereas most psychical researchers interested in fieldwork are able to accept – or at least greet with open minds – the events of many years ago connected with the mediumship of physical mediums such as Home, Palladino, and Florence Cook, a strain of skepticism bred by scientific training makes it much harder for them to accept that similar events may happen today, and may even be witnessed by those of us fortunate enough to be there when they occur. I mentioned in my discussion of the Cardiff poltergeist case (Chapter 4) the struggle I had with my own belief system after seeing the phenomena concerned. When in the room while they were taking place I had no doubt they were genuine, but as soon as I began the drive home I started to doubt. Surely stones and other objects could not be thrown without human agency, things could not fall from the ceiling apparently materializing on the way down, unseen intelligences could not unerringly hit a target nominated by me with their stones. In spite of the absence of any evidence of trickery – or any motive for it – on the part of the owners of the premises, the whole thing seemed simply unbelievable.

It took a lengthy investigation, including an occasion when I witnessed phenomena while I was on my own in one of the rooms where the disturbances took place and the owners were two hundred miles away on holiday, before I could full accept that poltergeist phenomena can indeed be genuine, and provide evidence not only of paranormality but, at least in some cases, of survival. However, at Scole things were rather different, not only because I knew by this time that physical phenomena are possible, but because I was fortunate enough to work with two other highly skilled investigators, now sadly both no longer with us. Professor Arthur Ellison, twice President of the SPR and Emeritus Professor of Electrical and Electronic Engineering at the City University, London, was widely experienced in the investigation of physical phenomena, having found his first case some 50 years previously. Montague Keen, an agrarian scientist, Secretary of the SPR Survival Research Committee and the Society's Honorary Media Relations Officer, was one of the most knowledgeable authorities on psychical research in the UK, and someone with a longstanding interest in physical phenomena. Both were men of unimpeachable integrity, positive towards the existence of physical phenomena, yet careful and cautious as researchers, well aware of the possibilities of fraud, and alert to any possibility that it might be taking place. I could not have wished for wiser companions or truer friends.

Thus the three of us were able exhaustively to compare notes after each séance, to agree on what we had seen, to discuss possibilities for deception, and to decide upon further controls that we hoped might be acceptable to the Scole Group. And here it is appropriate to say that we were unable to introduce all the controls that we deemed necessary if critics of the investigation were to be satisfied when we published our report. We knew that critics would fasten upon the smallest loophole in our report, and claim that in spite of all the many precautions we were able to put in place, fraud could still just have happened. And for critics the fact that fraud could just have happened provides more than enough grounds for assuming that it did. We have often been asked why it was that the Scole Group could not agree to all our suggested controls (details of which I will outline in due course), and the answer is that their primary purpose was not to satisfy us. Their primary purpose was to pursue their own work with those they claimed to be their spirit group, and to refer all our suggestions and requests to this group before agreeing to them. It is a necessary lesson for scientists to learn that when they are invited to join a group sitting for physical phenomena, things do not automatically revolve around them. The group has its own agenda, and its members may, after years of dedication to physical phenomena, regard themselves not only as having done more hard work (for example sitting regularly in the dark for months or even years before phenomena begin to occur) but as being more knowledgeable than the scientists invited in as investigators.

It has been said to me that if investigators are not allowed to control all the conditions at a séance, then they should not take part in it. This view is deeply mistaken. We have no real idea of the difficulties and constraints faced by communicators if they are indeed speaking from the next world, and no idea of the difficulties and constraints they may have when producing physical phenomena in a material dimension. The laws of material science, as we understand them, clearly do not operate in these cases, and it is arrogant to suppose that we as scientists are in a position to dictate our own terms during investigations. Perhaps in any case we are destined never to achieve absolutely watertight conditions when investigating survival. Professor

William James may have been right when he lamented that it rather looks as if the Almighty has decreed that this area should forever retain its mystery. If this is indeed the case, then I assume it is because the Almighty has decreed that the personal search for meaning and purpose in life and in death are of more value than having meaning and purpose handed down as certainties from others. If the certainties of life and death were so well known that they appeared in every school textbooks, there would no longer be scope for the personal search, and for the inner development that may be possible only as a product of such a search.

Be this as it may, the realistic aim of investigators into physical phenomena is not to insist upon imposing all their own conditions and stipulations upon the conduct of the séance room, but to introduce as many of these conditions and stipulations as are acceptable to the group concerned. If these conditions and stipulations are so lax as to leave ample opportunity for fraud or for other normal explanations, then little credence can be put upon reports of the phenomena that occur. If they leave few opportunities, then the credence placed upon these reports increases accordingly. But it is a different matter if they leave room for rejecting paranormal explanations only by stretching the bounds of credibility beyond what is reasonable. In the case of physical phenomena, these conditions should involve numerous sittings by experienced investigators without any detection of fraud, the presence of a very wide range of phenomena all of which would need different tricks if performed fraudulently, a range of safeguards to render the performance of each of these tricks difficult if not impossible, a consensus of positive conclusions among the investigators themselves, and the known integrity of the medium or mediums. .

However, even with these conditions in place, accounts of physical phenomena arouse intense suspicion among critics – for the most part, it has to be said, among critics who have never experienced these phenomena for themselves. They who have seen nothing claim to know everything, or at least to know much more than those who have seen a very great deal. This is to some extent understandable, for in the area of physical phenomena there is absolutely no substitute for practical experience. Nevertheless, some critics seem more interested in rejecting the accounts of physical phenomena than in keeping an open mind about them. On occasions the impression is given that they do not want such things to be true, as this would suggest that our known laws of science are not yet fully comprehensive (as surely they are not). The result of this is that to speak or write of experiencing physical phenomena is to risk being met with disbelief and even downright hostility. It is to suggest one is naive and given to extremes of wishful thinking. It is to experience something of the ridicule experienced by great men of the past such as Sir William Crookes when he published his findings with Home and with Florence Cook. Inevitably one becomes tempted to remain silent, and to pursue opportunities for witnessing physical phenomena for purely personal reasons (I wonder indeed how many investigators have taken this line in the past, and how much valuable material has been lost as a consequence). My fellow investigators and I at Scole took a different view, hence the publication of our extensive findings under the title of *The Scole Report* (Keen, Ellison, and Fontana 1999). A popular book on the Scole phenomena, which gives an accurate account of some of the events and which contains contributions from my fellow investigators and myself, is also on the market (Solomon and Solomon 1999).

The Scole investigation constitutes the most extensive and carefully investigated example of research into physical phenomena undertaken in recent years. Thus it adds substantially to what we know of physical phenomena and, like all the cases of such phenomena reported in this book, provides us with a range of phenomena far outside any known psychokinetic abilities in human beings. If Scole was genuine – and no one has demonstrated anything to the contrary – it thus provides us with further evidence that some intelligent source of unknown energy is occasionally at work within our material world.

BACKGROUND TO THE SCOLE INVESTIGATION

The four members of the Scole Group had been sitting together two or three times a week, for some two hours each time, over a period of many months before we began our investigations. Robin Foy in particular was highly experienced in the investigation of physical phenomena (Foy 1996), and all four members of the Group had a long interest in psychical research and in mediumship and the possibilities of survival. After very many hours of this patient work they had begun to experience physical phenomena, and as these phenomena developed two of the Group, Diana and Alan Bylett, began to manifest deep trance mediumship. Through their mediumship, communicators explained that they were members of a spirit team, and it was implied that certain deceased members of the SPR were working with this team from the afterlife. These phenomena then rapidly increased – so much so in fact that the Group were prompted to found the Spiritual Science Foundation to share with others the methods used in their work, some of which represented new developments in physical mediumship. One of the most important of these was that although both mediums were in deep trance during the séances, and knew nothing of what took place, no ectoplasm was used. Ectoplasm (Chapter 12) is said to be a quasi-physical substance exuded by the medium while in trance and connected with the so-called energy body that serves as an intermediary between the physical and the spiritual bodies. It is this substance that is then said to be used by the spirits to allow them to produce materializations and to interact with the physical environment in the course of the séance. In the case of the

Scole Group it was said that ectoplasm was no longer necessary as a new form of energy was being used, contributed principally by the spirits themselves but also taken from the sitters and from the energy of the earth itself (the village of Scole was claimed to be situated on a geophysical energy point).

Our experiences with the Group during the two years of our investigation gave us no reason at any time to entertain the smallest doubt as to their total sincerity and honesty. Monty Keen in particular spent a great deal of time with them even outside the séance room, traveling with them to the USA (a trip he organized in order to give American researchers an opportunity to observe the phenomena) and to Ibiza, where the sittings were arranged on his own premises by our colleague, Dr. Hans Schaer. Furthermore, it was clear to us that the Scole Group had no discernible financial motive for practicing deception. In fact they were considerably out-of-pocket as a result of the work of their Spiritual Science Foundation, and steadfastly refused financial assistance from the SPR even to cover their expenses. Publicity could also be ruled out as a motive for deception, particularly in the case of the two mediums, who remained anonymous at their own request throughout the investigation, and would have continued to do so but for a report in the national press which betrayed their confidence.

All the sittings we attended with the Scole Group in the UK took place in the windowless cellar in the Foys' house, converted by the Group into a specialist séance room. The walls, floor, and domed roof of the cellar were constructed of solid brick, and the only access to it was by means of a staircase with a lockable door at the top. A door at the bottom of the stairs led into the cellar, and although this was not lockable it creaked so loudly on opening that it could not be used without detection. The brickwork of the walls and roof of the cellar was in excellent condition, and the whole was painted a deep blue, thus allowing any attempt to loosen bricks in order to create hiding places readily apparent. The cellar had a small opening in one wall that had once served as a coal shoot, but this was securely blocked up, allowing no possibility of access. The cellar was freely available to us for a thorough search at all times, including before and after each of the séances. It contained only a round wooden table (approx. 1.2m in diameter) fully obstructed underneath by legs in the form of screens that prevented clandestine movement; upright plastic stacking chairs; and a trolley holding two audio tape recorders, one to play music during the séances, and the other to record the communications through the mediums, the independent voices, and the verbal descriptions we three investigators and Robin and Sandra Foy gave of the phenomena as they occurred. Both machines were operated by Robin Foy. The four members of the Scole Group, together with Monty Keen, Professor Ellison, and myself, sat on the plastic chairs around the table. The members of the Group all wore luminous armbands that identified their positions throughout the sitting. Fastened with powerful and extensive Velcro strips, the armbands could not be removed inaudibly.

EXPERIENCES AT SCOLE

The Scole Group, reportedly on the instructions of their spirit team, were able to agree to most of the controls we requested, but not to all of them. And here was our first problem, for as in most physical séances (those held by Home and Palladino were two exceptions) proceedings are held in darkness. More than any other single factor, this arouses the suspicions of critics. Darkness is seen as highly convenient for covering up fraudulent behavior, and one can appreciate the point. All the physical phenomena I have seen, at Scole and elsewhere, have been in darkness (except on one occasion for a dim red light, switched on for a short period). The explanation given by communicators through mediums is that spiritual energy, coming as it does from another dimension, cannot function in our world in the presence of the energy we call light (where ectoplasm is involved it is also said that this will immediately recoil into the medium if light is introduced, causing physical damage). On the face of it this seems not unreasonable. I have already said that, assuming physical phenomena are indeed due to spirit energies, we are in no position to know the conditions under which it can operate. However, there is no denying that darkness is very convenient if fraud is to be attempted, and certainly makes things much more difficult for investigators.

One solution is to use infrared viewers. We repeatedly requested to be allowed to use these at Scole, but our request was politely refused by the spirit team. Professor Ellison pointed out that infrared viewers do not introduce any additional energy into the room; they simply respond to energies that are already present. Thus it is difficult to see how they could interfere with spirit energies, or pose any kind of threat to the mediums. The response we were given by the spirit team is that nevertheless it would have an inhibiting effect. Furthermore, they assured us that they intended to bring their own light and eventually to produce phenomena in daylight, and that in addition peering through infrared viewers would distract us from the business of the séance and disrupt the harmony and the focused, communal energy so necessary among the sitters if results were to be obtained.

The first of these two intentions was fulfilled in that many of the 'spirit lights' referred to in due course were sufficiently bright and sufficiently sustained to allow us restricted viewing of the séance room, and so was the second in that a final sitting, attended only by Dr. Hans Shaer, one of our two fellow-investigators, was held in good electric light. In any case, the use of infrared viewers would not have convinced critics that no fraud was taking place, as they would have insisted that clever conjurors can deceive the unwary even in daylight, and that the fuzzy images seen by means of infrared provided little by way of safeguard. However, the refusal to allow us to use infrared certainly provided critics with ammunition with which to attack the investigation.

Every séance was preceded by our thorough search of the room in full electric light. This involved moving and looking under the table and under each chair to check that they had not been tampered with, checking the trolley on which the two tape recorders were placed and making sure nothing was hidden there, and checking the brickwork of the walls to ensure no tampering had taken place. If there were objects on the table such as the glass dome that the Group used in the earlier sittings (in order, it was said, to help concentrate paranormal energies), quartz crystals which were frequently present, and a Pyrex bowl (the purpose of which is explained later), these were also carefully checked. If experiments with unexposed film cassettes were to be used, these were also checked by us and the tubs in which they were contained sealed and marked (later we were able to bring our own films, which we sealed into our own tubs, using marked sticky paper, before we took them into the séance room).

When everything was checked to our satisfaction and the door at the top of the stairs leading down to the cellar had been locked, seats were taken around the table. The two mediums sat next to each other facing the three investigators, while Robin Foy sat on our right and Sandra Foy on our left. The mediums and the Foys wore their luminous armbands on each arm in order to enable us to keep a check on their position. Doubts have been raised as to the adequacy of these armbands as a means of controlling the position of the members of the Group, but they were more effective than might at first sight be realized. Attempts to remove them would have been readily detectable due to the noise made by the Velcro, and the only way in which fraudulent movement could have taken place undetected would have been surreptitiously to cover them up and place substitute armbands on the table. However, this would have been a risky maneuver. The armbands would have had to be covered up before the substitutes were placed on the table, and their momentary disappearance from view on the countless occasions when the members of the Group would have needed to leave their seats in order to produce fraudulent phenomena would not have gone unnoticed by the investigators. Phenomenon followed phenomenon in quick succession and we engaged the communicators (speaking through the mediums) in almost constant conversation, in which the Foys joined throughout. If any one of the Group was not in his or her place when they spoke to us we would have quickly detected this (experience of sitting in the dark sharpens the ears' ability to ascertain direction). Thus constant comings and goings by the Group members, with constant obscuring of armbands and constant revealing and hiding of substitute armbands throughout the two to three hours of each séance, would have been required, and the likelihood of Group members being able to accomplish this without being detected was remote.

After taking our places the lights would be extinguished, and Robin Foy would begin proceedings with the customary simple prayer for protection before switching on a tape of soft music on one of his tape recorders and starting a blank tape to record proceedings in the other. We were always encouraged by Foy to hum along with the music (which I rather enjoyed, though the faltering sounds from my two fellow investigators suggested a measure of genteel embarrassment), and to converse together in normal tones. The human voice is said to help concentrate the 'energies' upon which the spirits are said to rely. After a relatively short period, the sound of deep breathing from both mediums would indicate that they were in trance. A masculine voice, said to be that of a spirit known as Manu, would then come through Diana, welcoming us and asking us to visualize 'energy' (as white light) running around the circle. He or she was then usually followed by the cultured tones, again through Diana, of a communicator known as Mrs. Emily Bradshaw, who acted as Mistress of Ceremonies throughout, and by one or other of the three male communicators, Patrick, Raji, and Edward, who spoke through Alan (all three, plus some 'spiritual scientists' who also spoke through Alan, were said to relay communications from early members of the SPR who were supposedly at a more advanced level and consequently unable to speak to us directly).

The phenomena usually began with lights. So-called spirit lights have been reported at séances for many years. Some of the best examples were those reported by Crookes during his investigations of Home, described on occasions as 'luminous points of light darting about and settling on the heads of different persons.' This description exactly fits what we saw at Scole. The points of light were usually the size of a pea, though we sometimes saw them the size of a large grape. Although points of light, they seemed to have a substantial form. They would land on the table in front of us and appear to roll forward towards us before moving swiftly back into the air. Sometimes – this could happen in response to requests – they would land upon the palms of our hands, exerting a gentle pressure, as if they carried weight, and allowing us to examine them from close quarters. On occasions one of them would move at great speed, forming an unbroken circle of light, symmetrical and perfect in every respect and with a diameter of a foot or more. As we watched, one of the segments of the circle would then disappear, as if the light extinguished itself for a fraction of a second at precisely the same spot during each revolution. This segment would then become light again, only for another segment to become darkened. On many occasions the lights would also hit the surface of the solid wooden table with an audible sound only to appear almost instantaneously underneath the table, as if they had passed through solid matter. Once under the table they illuminated our feet, in positions inaccessible to the members of the Scole Group due to the position of our feet under the tabletop and the solid, screen-like legs of the table. An experienced colleague of ours, Professor Ivor Gratton Guiness, who was invited to attend one séance, even closed his hand over one of the lights when it landed on his palm to satisfy himself that it was not connected in any way to rods or wires, although as the lights were seen at times traveling rapidly in far corners of the room the notion of rods or wires was in any case untenable.

Once, troubled by a dry cough, I was sipping from a glass of water taken into the cellar when one of the lights entered the water at some speed. I watched it, as did my colleagues, submerged in and illuminating the water and moving around vigorously. I brought the glass close to my mouth to ensure It was not connected to the rigid structure that would have been required to produce this movement by normal means. The light then left the glass and I drank the water (which for one reason or other put paid to my coughing). On another occasion Robin Foy mentioned that the lights, which appeared able to pass through matter, had actually entered the bodies of sitters at one of their other séances. I at once invited it to enter mine, and a light struck me in the center of my chest and disappeared. A moment later, totally unexpectedly, I felt the pressure in the middle of my palm characteristic of times when the lights landed on our hands, but this time the sensation was pushing outwards from within my palm rather than inwards. A moment or so later the light reappeared, as if from my chest.

There is a great temptation not to report incidents like this for fear of ridicule, but this is nothing less than a form of dishonesty. I know what I experienced, and my account of it is accurate in each detail, and my description of the incident, made at the time, is captured on tape. It seems absurd to suppose that the light actually entered my body, but if the light was able to go through the table, as it appeared to do, then there would seem no reason why it should not enter the body. In addition, we also saw it enter the crystals on the table, and not only brightly illuminate them but apparently move freely around inside, even levitating the crystals some inches above the table on occasion. Critics will say that the light was merely drawn across the face of the crystals by whatever device the Group was using to fake the phenomena, but my reply is that this happened under the noses of the three investigators, and all three of us were in no doubt that we saw it within the depth of the crystal. The crystals were all carefully examined by us before and after the séances and found to be normal. Even if a member of the Group had been able, undetected, to substitute a trick crystal for a genuine one only inches away from the three of us, and then switch them back again before the lights were put on, this does not explain how the trick was performed. On occasions the light appeared to enter a table tennis ball, placed on the table on the instructions of the spirit team, which then levitated and moved around the room.

Even more difficult to explain was an instance when the crystal itself seemed to dematerialize. There was on the table a Pyrex bowl, mentioned earlier, placed there on instructions from the spirit team. Normally this was upside down, and one of the lights would apparently enter the bowl and illuminate it from within, producing an effect like a low-powered light bulb. On this occasion the bowl was illuminated in this fashion when, in the light thus provided, a dark hand, visible only as far as the wrist, appeared to materialize just above the bowl, turn it the right way up, and then place one of the crystals, also apparently illuminated from within, inside it. The hand was then withdrawn, and the whole outline of the brightly illuminated crystal was visible in the bowl. The light was in fact sufficiently bright for me to see the faces of my fellow investigators as they lent forward, inches above the bowl. We were then told by Emily Bradshaw, speaking through Diana, to feel the crystal, which we all three did, noting its solidity. The next instruction was to remove our hands and we did so, leaving the crystal shining brightly as before. There then followed an immediate instruction to feel the crystal again, but this time when we did so, although it still appeared solid as ever, our fingers passed through it as if there was no substance there. Once again we were instructed to remove our hands and then immediately to replace them, and this time, although there was no observable change in the illuminated crystal, it felt once more solid as normal.

We found no normal explanation for this. There is a trick apparatus on the market that produces the illusion that an object, placed within a bowl, is floating solidly just above it, but this bears no comparison with our experience. Even with his 50 years of experience of electrical devices and with his international reputation in his subject, Professor Ellison could advance no explanation, either then or subsequently, for how such a phenomenon could be produced by normal means. The explanation we were offered by the communicators was that they had indeed dematerialized the crystal, leaving only its 'essence' in the bowl (a kind of ghostly crystal if you like). To this day no one has advanced ideas on how this effect might be produced normally – or better still demonstrated how it could be done – and the experience remains one of the most baffling of those we encountered at Scole.

Throughout the investigation, we questioned the communicators on all aspects of the phenomena. On one occasion we asked how the small points of light were produced. The answer, given through the mediums, surprised us. We were told they had not been brought by the spirit team, but that they were attracted to the séances and that the team had found they could make use of them as aspects of the physical phenomena. Although it was not made clear to us, it was implied that they in some way represented, or were manifested by, the spirits of departed individuals. Less spectacular but equally difficult to explain were the diffused lights. These would gradually build up in mid air, often at some distance from the table, and then move slowly around the room. It is easy enough to project a diffused light onto a surface, but not so easy to produce a patch of this light in mid air. This diffused light was also associated with materializations. Sometimes it would slowly form into what appeared to be small robed figures, with oval patches of brighter light where the face would be. Once I asked one of these figures to touch me, and it moved towards me before brushing my hands with part of the 'robe,' which felt like gossamer drapery. On other occasions the lights appeared to take the shape of faces, not fully formed but unmistakable, with mouths that seemed to move in attempts at speech. At one séance the light, more blue than white this time, gradually built up on the table into a rock-like or flower-like shape, which then levitated and passed just in front of me before coming to rest in front of a colleague invited by us to be present on that occasion.

Hands frequently materialized, sometimes visible as dark silhouettes in the illumination from the spirit lights (as in the case of the phantom crystal mentioned earlier), at others invisible but touching us on the arms or hands or legs (which were under the table and inaccessible to members of the Group. Hands caught hold of both of mine and lifted them high into the air, and pulled hard at the sweater I sometimes wore. On one memorable occasion I was addressed by what seemed to be an independent voice, speaking firmly and clearly from just in front and above me (trumpets were not used at Scole). In reply to my question the voice told me it was a scientist involved in helping produce the phenomena. I asked if I could shake the owner's hand and held out mine in the darkness. Immediately and unerringly my hand was firmly clasped and shaken, then the spirit hand was withdrawn effortlessly from mine (I have had my hand shaken on request in a similar fashion during a sitting with another physical medium). Sometimes we asked the hands to place certain objects taken from the table (crystals, tubs of film) onto our palms, and this also was unerringly done in the darkness. There was never any fumbling or groping for us. The hands that touched us were invariably gentle, and we all three remarked on the unexpected but seemingly objective feeling of tenderness that they conveyed (a phenomenon described by Robin Foy as an expression of spiritual love).

Other materializations took the form of apports, though I was only present on one occasion when an apport arrived. Emily Bradshaw had jokingly bet Montague Keen half a crown (an old coin no longer used) over some factual matter on which they had disagreed, and when she was proved wrong (much to Montague's triumphant amusement) we heard something clatter onto the floor. After the séance was over Montague found it was the promised half a crown. The Scole Group had a wide range of even more impressive objects that had apparently arrived during their own private séances (which they continued to hold throughout the two years of our investigation). One of the most notable of these was a copy of the Daily Mail newspaper of April 1, 1944 containing an account of the celebrated trial of medium Helen Duncan. The newspaper was in pristine condition, the paper on which it was printed was as white as if it had been printed only that day. Our supposition was that it might be a modern facsimile edition of the kind that can be bought from some newspaper publishers. However, analysis of the paper and of the newsprint by the prestigious Print Industry Research Association (PRIA), carried out at the request of Montague Keen and handled by him throughout, revealed that this supposition was incorrect. The PRIA confirmed that far from being modern, the newspaper was in fact printed by the old-fashioned letterpress method in use in 1944, and that the paper on which it was printed dated from the same era. The PRIA expressed themselves baffled by the newspaper's perfect condition. Dating from 1944, it should have shown the ageing and yellowing inevitable in a newspaper of that age. Unless an explanation can be found, the newspaper may therefore be what is known by psychical researchers as a PPO (a Permanent Paranormal Object – an object apparently produced or modified paranormally that remains with us as a subject for study), and thus represent one of the Holy Grails of psychical research.

Examples of other phenomena witnessed at Scole included the fact that at relatively frequent intervals the table commenced a very rapid vibration, which could both be heard and felt by each of us. When this happened the whole structure of the table was affected. Four luminous tabs were secured to it at the cardinal points of the compass, and on occasions, in spite of its solid base, movement of the tabs showed that it was not only vibrating but swiveling round, passing through some 20 degrees each time before returning to its original position. Another example involved music that emanated from an audio tape recorder from which the microphone had been removed by the Scole Group. The tape recorder was a relatively cheap instrument but Arthur Ellison and I dismantled it and ascertained that the microphone had indeed been removed and that there was nothing in the machine that could reproduce or receive sound. In our experiments with the recorder we then used one of our own audio tapes, secretly marked by myself. In the séance room the recorder was connected to a primitive germanium semi-conductor device that Professor Ellison had designed in an attempt to improve the quality of communications following earlier instructions from the spirit team (full details of this and all the other occurrences during our investigations at Scole are given in *The Scole Report*). Throughout the séance the tape recorder was under my immediate control on the table in front of me, and I was able to ensure that it was not touched by anyone except myself throughout (a bright red LED light on the front provided illumination that assisted me in this). We were told through one of the entranced mediums that music would come from the recorder as a special treat for Montague Keen, and we then heard from the recorder

Rachmaninoff's Second Piano Concerto, which has deep and meaningful boyhood associations for him (a fact that he had divulged to no one present).

After the conclusion of the séance we found that the marked tape I had put into the recorder had recorded the Rachmaninoff music but none of the comments that we or members of the Group were making while the music was playing. By contrast, the tape recorder used by Robin Foy to record all that happened during the séance had recorded both the music and our voices. This provided further confirmation that the depleted tape recorder under my control, even though connected to the germanium device (which we had already established was not capable of acting as a rectifier) could not record sound by normal means. Another important example was the apparently paranormal production of images on cassettes of films placed by us on the table, either still in their own tubs or in a locked wooden box, at the start of the séances. The Scole Group had themselves obtained a number of such images before our investigation commenced. These took many forms, including photographs of unknown groups of people such as First World War soldiers or airmen, a view of St. Paul's Cathedral in London with subtly incorrect dimensions, and unknown faces surrounded by cloud-like structures. Initially the films used by the Group were Polaroid, developed by them on the premises at the end of each séance, but subsequently Polychrome, Polapan, and Kodachrome were used.

It was clear to us that the possibility of obtaining paranormal images on films in fraud-proof conditions would provide a major breakthrough in psychical research. And if the phenomena could be repeated to order – e.g. at séances to which a range of skeptical scientists could be invited – this might lead at long last to the unequivocal acceptance of paranormal phenomena by the scientific community, and allow important scope for further investigation. Our proposal was for a four-step protocol that would consist of (i) a film provided by ourselves as investigators, (ii) a secure container provided by us in which to place the film, (iii) our control of this container throughout the séance, and (iv) our control of the subsequent development of the film. If convincing images were obtained on film using this four-step protocol little scope would be left for argument. Three secure containers were used. The first was a special security bag provided for us by Professor Richard Wiseman from the University of Hertfordshire that could not be opened without detection, the second was a wooden padlocked box made by the Group (referred to here as the 'Scole' box, but as the 'Alan box' in *The Scole Report*), and the third was a similar box prepared by Montague Keen (the Keen box). But in the event, although we got tantalizingly close to obtaining successful results with all four steps of this protocol in place, we never quite achieved it, which was a major disappointment to ourselves and to the Scole Group.

Let me give two instances. In the first of them we used our own film and the security bag provided by the University of Hertfordshire and steps three and four of our protocol, and obtained (or the spirit team succeeded in giving us) three or four very small star-shaped symbols on the film. Since the film had been put in the bag unexposed, on development it should have been totally blank. Thus these stars seemed indicative of paranormality, but we considered their quality as images was not sufficient to convince critics. In the second instance, conducted by our co-investigator Walter Schnittger, the only deviation from the protocol was that the Scole box (padlocked with his own padlock, the key of which was locked in his car and firmly held by him throughout) was used as the secure container instead of one provided by ourselves. On development, the film – provided by himself, secretly marked, and under his control throughout – was found to contain a poem of considerable merit in German, whose author we still have not been able to identify. This second example was therefore again strongly indicative of paranormality, as there seems no possibility that the film could have been tampered with, but the weakness was the use of the Scole box rather than the Keen box, although as it was held firmly by Walter throughout no one other than himself had access to it. The problem with the Scole box, admittedly no more than a theoretical one, was that it was vulnerable in that the two arms of the hasp that held it closed could be forced out of the brackets securing it to the lid, thus allowing the box to be opened without disturbing the padlock. This could only be done by forcing the brackets to swivel forward, then squeezing the hasp so that the arms could be maneuvered free from them, and we had ensured that paint seals were placed on the heads of the nails holding the brackets in place so that we could detect if any attempt was made to tamper with them in this way. Nevertheless the box did have this weakness, hence Montague Keen's decision to have an alternative box constructed to his own fraud-proof specifications (the Keen box).

On other occasions we got results with films secured in the Scole box when it was placed on a sheet of paper on the table and its outline clearly marked in pencil to reveal if any attempt was made to move it during the séance under cover of darkness. This precaution meant that even had the Scole Group had access to infrared or image intensifiers (and there was no evidence that they did) it would have been well-nigh impossible for them to ensure the box was replaced exactly in its correct position after their having tampered with it). However, we were unable to obtain results when films were placed in the Keen box, which was unfortunate particularly as Dr. Alan Gauld, a past President of the SPR and one of the most experienced and careful of investigators, took the view that the Scole box could be opened without breaking the paint seals and demonstrated this to his satisfaction, in the presence of Howard Wilkinson, an audio-visual aid technician and also a highly experienced investigator, when the box was loaned to him after the termination of the investigation. However, when the box was returned to us by Dr. Gauld we found that the paint seals were in fact broken, which suggested to us that even if it could be opened once without them breaking, they would not survive subsequent efforts (attempts to repair the paint seals had they been broken would have been immediately obvious to us). Our own experiments also revealed that even had the Scole Group been able to abstract the box from our control in the darkness of the séance room, to open it by removing the hasp from the brackets without breaking the seals, to remove our film, and to substitute it with one of their own prepared beforehand (a difficult substitution to accomplish as our films were sealed in their tubs and marked) without our detection, it would have been virtually impossible in the darkness to thread the arms of the hasp back into the brackets before surreptitiously returning the box to our control.

Nevertheless, the fact that the Scole box was theoretically vulnerable and that we did not fully achieve our four-step protocol was a drawback (the premature ending of the investigation prevented us from returning to this protocol). Nevertheless, with the safeguards that were in place, the results with the films qualify as among the best evidence obtained for the reality of physical phenomena. Many of these results were also of considerable interest in themselves, and these will be discussed in due course.

EVIDENCE FOR SURVIVAL FROM THE SCOLE INVESTIGATION

I have already stressed that part of the evidence for survival provided by physical phenomena is the very fact that it occurs. We have no indication from laboratory experiments that human psychokinetic abilities can produce anything approaching the effects produced during physical séances. Thus at the very least there appears to be some unknown energy at work in the séances that does not come exclusively from the medium or sitters. The argument for survival provided by physical phenomena is further supported by the fact that those most directly involved, namely physical mediums (including those of the caliber of Home and Palladino), are adamant that the energy comes from spirits and spirit controls rather than from themselves.

In the case of Scole, the highly dramatic physical effects witnessed by us had further relevance for survival in that they appeared to be fully under the control of the communicators. Usually the communicators made clear in advance what phenomena they intended to produce, and frequently they responded to our requests for specific effects. Only on one occasion in my experience did we have an almost blank sitting. On all other occasions the phenomena continued intermittently for the full three hours or so of the sitting. In addition, the communicators often referred to events and facts unknown to us, which suggests that we were not the telepathic source of their information. The level of mature intelligence displayed by them throughout was also impressive, as was their apparent knowledge of the history of the SPR. Everything said by them and by us was tape-recorded and subsequently transcribed and studied by us, and we considered that the possibility that they were secondary personalities of the mediums could be safely dismissed. Emily Bradshaw, who spoke through Diana, was invariably cultured, highly knowledgeable, and with an attractive, dry wit. Her accent was quite different from Diana's own, and never varied throughout our investigation. Similarly, her personality remained consistent, as did her ability to remember what had taken place during previous séances. She was to all intents and purposes who she claimed to be (although she made clear that Emily Bradshaw was a pseudonym used to protect members of her family still alive). The same was true of the controls who spoke through Alan. Each had his own distinct personality, and this never varied. There was no confusion between the personalities, and none of them made mistakes when recalling things he had said on previous occasions. Again the impression was of highly intelligent entities, consistently friendly, courteous, and patient towards us, and strongly motivated by their desire to prove survival. In technical discussions they (or the more advanced beings whose thoughts and ideas they claimed to be relaying to us) proved invariably accurate, and Professor Roy, a leading astronomer and former President of the SPR who attended one séance, was highly impressed by the conversation on relatively obscure matters in his own subject that he was able to hold with one of them.

At no time, therefore, did we detect any sign in the communicators that suggested they might be secondary personalities. Furthermore, they did not simply deliver set pieces through the mediums, they engaged with us in lengthy and spontaneous conversations, often of our own choosing, that ranged over a number of erudite subjects. Diana and Alan Bylett, the mediums, were intelligent and deeply thoughtful people with great natural charm and compassion (both worked as healers, and neither was a professional medium), but their backgrounds were not academic. Thus had the communicators been mere pretence on their part, it is inevitable that their lack of knowledge would have revealed the fact to us during the conversations we held at each séance over the two years of our investigation.

The communicators also gave us messages from time to time purportedly designed to strengthen the evidence for survival, and consisting for the most part of enigmatic snippets of information relating to the writings and doings of the deceased SPR members who it was claimed were primarily responsible for the work at Scole. These pieces of information were effectively in the form of puzzles, which we then attempted to solve by studying early copies of the SPR *Proceedings* or books written by the founders of the SPR. Opinions differ as to the value of these messages as evidence for survival. Puzzles which prove difficult to solve may not be difficult to set, and although considerable research by us was required in order to find the answers to some of them, the availability of the necessary information in publications held by the SPR (albeit in publications nearly a century old and relatively difficult to find outside the SPR library) lessens the impact of this evidence. Critics claim that since the Scole Group could have had access to SPR literature in their own possession, they could have made up the puzzles themselves. However, although it would have been more impressive had the messages related to unpublished rather than published SPR records, these messages nevertheless add a further dimension to the evidence provided at Scole.

Space allows only one example. At our 14th séance with the group, on August 10, 1996, Manu, who was always the first to speak through Diana, said 'Somebody is nudging at my side, and says "Tell them to remember the Albemarle Club. Your colleagues used to meet there." Nothing was known by us of any connection between the Albemarle Club (not to be confused with the hotel of the same name) and SPR members, but subsequent research by Montague Keen revealed that the Albemarle was in fact an obscure gentlemen's club no longer in existence that receives no mention in many reference books on London clubs past and present, its only claim to fame being that it was while on the premises that Oscar Wilde received the letter from the Marques of Queensberry that led to his subsequent trial. However, in Lodge's *The Survival of Man*, published in 1909, I came across the fact that during a sitting with medium Mrs. Thompson, Lodge received a message purportedly from the deceased F. W. Myers:

Lodge, it is not as easy as I thought in my impatience. Gurney says I am getting on first rate. But I am short of breath. Oh Lodge, what is it when I see you! Was it the Albemarle Club we went to when I talked about ... oh it leaves off. Sidgwick knows. I am with him. He said that he saw me in the morning of ... Oh dear, it always leaves off in the interesting places.

The other names mentioned in this communication, Gurney and Sidgwick, were also among the founders of the SPR, and together with Myers they had been prominent in the group of deceased SPR members apparently responsible for the cross-correspondences (Chapter 8). A reference to the communication was also made by Lodge in a paper in the SPR *Proceedings* shortly afterwards. Following up the clue further, Dr. Alan Gauld found an entry in Myers' diary for 1880, held in the library at Trinity College, Cambridge, that records 'Lunch Albemarle,' though whether this refers to the Club or to the Hotel is not stated. No other references to the Club appear in any of Myers' diaries, but it seems clear that the meeting with Lodge did indeed take place there, otherwise Lodge would have commented on the fact when quoting Myers' communication. Full details of this and the many other puzzle messages received through the mediums are given in *The Scole Report*, and a close study of these details is necessary before conclusions can be drawn on the degree of importance that should be attached to them.

The messages, referred to earlier, that appeared on the unexposed films taken by us into the séance room and either left in their sealed tubs on the table or locked in the Scole box, also provide some further evidence that the communicators really were intelligent surviving personalities. Some of these messages were in the form of words, while others consisted of drawings and vague hermetic symbols (we received no photographs of the kind obtained by the Scole Group when they were working on their own). We were told through the mediums that much of the material contained in these messages was taken from existing sources, and my impression was that the content was therefore considered by them to be less important than the fact that the messages were received at all under the conditions obtaining during the séances. In many cases it was not difficult to find the origin of the material. For example it was discovered that some of the drawings and symbols appeared to have been copied from *A Pictorial History of Magic and the Supernatural* by Maurice Bessy, published in 1963; a fragment of writing was found to come from Myers' classic *Human Personality and its Survival of Bodily Death* (first published after his own death in 1903); and another fragment came from an early draft of Wordsworth's poem *Ruth* which had been published in a Christies catalogue in 1983 when some of Wordsworth's manuscript material was sold to the USA

What evidence is there that the messages imprinted on the films were in fact paranormal? It is not difficult to imprint images on unexposed film by normal means. The late Ralph Noyes, who was one of the investigators at Scole in the early days, established after experiments carried out for him by a commercial photographer that one of the ways in which this can be done is to cut a strip of acetate to fit the emulsified area of the film, and write images on it with a felt-tip pen. Working in the dark, the film is then pulled out of its cassette and the acetate placed over the emulsified area. Finally a flashgun is fired which imprints the images onto the film, and the film is wound back into the cassette and developed in the normal way. Could the Scole Group have used this method to fake the films? Not easily. It will be remembered that even when using their own film they obtained images showing old photographs rather than drawings or handwriting, and that in at least one case the image (of St. Paul's Cathedral) showed subtle differences from a photograph taken of the real thing. It is not impossible to transfer images from photographs to unexposed film if one first makes a negative of them and uses this instead of acetate but difficult when the images were made to distort them as with that of St. Pauls. And it would be very much more difficult to impress images on film provided by us rather than by the Group, and placed in sealed tubs or in a locked box that in the instance already described was held firmly in the hand of our fellow investigator Walter Schnittger throughout the séance, and on other occasions in a locked box placed by us on a sheet of paper on which its outline had been carefully delineated. And even if the film could have been abstracted in some way under these conditions, an accomplice would have been needed to take it elsewhere in the house in order to tamper with it, and for reasons already explained no accomplice could have entered the séance room without detection.

Could the Scole Group have abstracted our films, and replaced them with exposed films of their own? Unlikely. To do so they would have had to conceal their armbands and leave substitutes on the table, silently leave their places, and come round to our position at the table, remove a film secured in a box or placed on the table only inches away from us, open the box if it was being used, take out the sealed tub, remove the film from the tub, and replace it with their own, study our film to detect if we had placed secret markings on it, reproduce these markings as necessary, replace the film in the tub, seal the tub in such a way that there was no sign of disturbance, and replace the film in the box (carrying out the delicate task of replacing the hasp) or in its correct position on the table as necessary, all the while joining in the conversation that was almost continuous between us and the Foys and the mediums. This tricky maneuver would have had to be accomplished not once but on each of the seven occasions that images were produced on our films. Furthermore, as the Group never stipulated what kind of film we should use at each séance, and never inspected our films before we sealed them and placed them in the Scole box or on the table, they could not be certain what film we were using or what markings we might or might not have put on it. Thus it is hardly credible that even if they had been able to switch the films without detection under the conditions obtaining in the séances they would always have provided a fraudulent film of the same type and the same manufacture as our own, and with the same markings.

If this is barely conceivable, it is even less so on the occasion already quoted when our co-investigator Walter Schnittger supplied his own secretly marked film, locked it in the Scole box with his own padlock (the key of which he locked in his car), and held the box firmly in his hand throughout the séance. If a conjuror could demonstrate how the films could be switched under these conditions without detection, or if a psychic could demonstrate how the same results can be produced using nothing more than his or her psychokinetic ability, then the possibility of fraud or of human paranormal abilities would be established. To date no such demonstrations have taken place.

FINAL THOUGHTS ON SCOLE

A brief summary such as this does inadequate justice to our long and detailed investigation of the phenomena produced at Scole. A careful reading of *The Scole Report* is necessary for all those wishing to know the whole picture, including the views of critics and our attempts, as investigators and authors of the *Report*, to answer these criticisms. All such criticisms have centered upon the way in which fraud might have been able to take place. No direct evidence for fraud was ever discovered at Scole, either by ourselves and our co-investigators, or by the very many other people (some highly experienced) who are mentioned in *The Scole Report* as having attended other séances held by the Group. Thus any criticisms can only focus on how fraud could have taken place, rather than upon revelations that it did take place. Identifying how fraud could have taken place is not the same as proving that it did, although many critics fall into the trap of confusing the two. They also confuse the fact that suggesting how fraud could have taken place is not even the same as demonstrating that fraud was feasible. I have already given arguments to support the view that at Scole it was not feasible, but let me conclude by re-emphasizing these arguments.

For fraud to have taken place, two things remained essential throughout the séances, namely the presence of the necessary equipment, the scope for undetected movement in order to operate this equipment, and of course strategies to circumvent the controls put in place. The infrared or image intensifying equipment needed to see and move in the dark, and the equipment required to produce the phenomena of the lights and the materializations, the sustained high-frequency vibrations of the table and its swiveling movements on solid legs, the levitation of objects, the apparent de-materialization of the crystal, and the beaming of radio signals to a tape recorder from which the microphone had been removed would, assuming it all existed, have been elaborate, ingenious, expensive, and probably highly conspicuous. To smuggle it in without our seeing it (it could not have been previously hidden in the séance room, as this was searched by us before each sitting) on every occasion during our investigation, including the occasions when séances were held abroad, would seem to have been out of the question.

The movement needed in order to operate this equipment and to touch us frequently on various parts of our bodies, including our legs under the table, would also have presented major difficulties. Robin Foy is not built for agile and stealthy movement around a dark room. In addition, his seat at each séance was only inches away from Professor Arthur Ellison, who was free to reach out and touch him unexpectedly at any time. Hemmed in as Robin Foy was on the other side by the unit bearing his tape recorders, silent movement of any kind would have presented him with many challenges. Sandra Foy, the other non-medium member of the Group, was invariably on my left, again only inches away and vulnerable to touch by me at any moment. To remove or cover her armbands and frequently absent herself undetected by me would have presented her with challenges only marginally less than those facing her husband. In addition Robin and Sandra were constantly engaged in conversation by us without warning throughout the séances, and replied unfailingly and promptly from their correct positions.

What of the mediums? If they were responsible for the necessary movements they would, without detection, not only have had constantly to be removing and replacing armbands without detection, they would have had to manipulate lights at ceiling level one moment then at table level the next, and make them hit the table and reappear instantaneously underneath, near our legs and in positions inaccessible without detection. They would have had frequently to move around the table (the supports prevented access from underneath) in order to touch our legs in similarly inaccessible positions, again without detection. They would have had to levitate crystals under our noses, apparently dematerialize and re-materialize a crystal literally under our noses, fabricate illuminated materializations on the opposite side of the table from themselves and move these materializations up to the ceiling or across our hands, stand soundlessly on the middle of the table in order to fake direct voices from above our heads, masquerade as spirits by shaking or touching – promptly and on request – our hands, and put objects from the table in these same hands (again on request and without fumbling). They would also have had to lean across the table to do nefarious things with films variously secured in a locked box (even when held firmly by Walter Schnittger) or placed on the table directly in front of us.

They would have had variously to bombard us with lights which rested on our hands and appeared to enter our bodies and simulate internal movement, manipulate the diffused patches of light that traveled the length of the room in mid air, materialize – only inches in front of us – simulated human hands which appeared to end at the wrists and which picked up crystals and were clearly visible in accompanying 'spirit' lights, and lift up, simultaneously and to full stretch, my two arms and those of another investigator. They would have had to perform perfect and sustained circles in the air with pinpoints of light above the table so fast that the circles appeared unbroken, illuminate large crystals from within, and put in place and operate the machinery for vibrating and swiveling the table, and much more besides. Before the end of the séance, they would have had to secrete all the equipment about their own persons and the persons of the Foys, and they would have had to do this while impersonating communicators from their usual positions across the tables from us, frequently doing so promptly and calmly in response to our questions and comments.

These arguments against fraud are further strengthened by the fact that a very experienced and well-qualified professional stage magician (James Webster, an Associate and Silver Medal Holder of the British Inner Magic Circle) who has been studying mediumship for more than 40 years, attended three of the séances organized by the Group for other guests. James Webster testified to us that, in his professional opinion, even leading magicians could not duplicate the phenomena he witnessed at Scole even after lengthy and expensive preparations. He further testified that any magician who could produce the Scole effects would rapidly make a fortune on the professional stage. James Webster's presence at séances defeats the frequent criticism that investigators never seek the expertise of conjurors. It is true that even highly experienced conjurors cannot always spot the tricks of their colleagues, but James Webster's particular interest in psychical research meant that he was well aware of supposed séance room trickery. Thus his views carry particular weight. Professor Arthur Hastings, of the Institute of Transpersonal Psychology in the USA and another expert conjuror with a longstanding interest in psychical research, also testified to us that even a careful study of *The Scole Report* is sufficient to reveal that the Scole phenomena, under the conditions obtaining at Scole, could not be duplicated by conjuring skills.

As authors of the *Report* we invited any conjuror to attempt such duplication and have offered to assist them in every way we can. At the time of writing, we have had no takers. In fact, beyond the claim that the Scole box was vulnerable to fraud (though no explanation has been given as to how it could have been manipulated by fraud under the conditions obtaining at the séances) and an attempt to explain away the lights as faked by an LED on the end of a wire (a device that can be bought in any magic shop, and that can achieve nothing like the effects at Scole), and endeavors to show how some of the abstract images obtained on films could be faked by tampering with the films (though no explanation as to how this could be done when the films were our own and under our control), we have received so far no suggestions as to how any of the phenomena could have been produced by normal means.

The Scole investigation ended prematurely. The Scole Group informed us that their communicators wished to bring moving images from the spirit world which could be captured on video tape (a practice similar to some of the ITC experiments surveyed in the next chapter). We were not involved in this new development, as we were told that it required the full attention of the Group. Once the work was well under way, we would once more be invited to sittings. Reports from the Group, who kept us fully informed, indicated that progress was good, with the receipt of abstract colored images and strange mask-like images. Our co-investigator Dr. Hans Schaer, who provided one of the video cameras required for the new work, was able to attend one sitting at this point, and this turned out to be one of the first at which recognizable human faces were captured on tape. Dr. Shaer reported that these faces were the profile of a man aged between 50 and 60 with dark black hair and metal-rimmed spectacles, and of a man wearing what appeared to be a Russian fur hat. We were subsequently shown these pictures, which agreed with his description, and Dr. Schaer was of the opinion that as he had unwrapped the new video tape from its sealed shrink-wrapped plastic wrapper prior to the experiment, marked it secretly and kept it under his control throughout the proceedings, there was no possibility for trickery.

Disappointingly, we were then told by the Scole Group that some form of 'interference', which disrupted the experiments, was being experienced, and that after some time the communicators had finally confessed they were unable to put a stop to this, and that in view of the spiritual dangers posed by this interference all sittings must cease. As we were not involved at this point I cannot comment on the nature of this interference, but as investigators we were certainly aware of the devastating effect that the termination of the work had upon the Scole Group. So ended one of the most remarkable investigations into physical phenomena undertaken in recent years. The Scole Group experienced none of the violence possibly caused by mischievous, poltergeist-type entities reported in some investigations. Yet their work came to a premature end through reported interference of some kind. Does this mean that all physical mediumship runs the risk of attracting undesirable influences? Possibly. No mediumship, including mental mediumship, is said to be free from risks of this kind. If this is indeed the case, the warnings sometimes given against treating this area too lightly may be well founded.

Phenomena Not Present at Scole

Scole was untypical of physical phenomena in many ways. For example it was reported to us by the communicators that no ectoplasm was involved (certainly neither of the mediums showed any signs of the exhaustion usually present in mediums after they are said to have produced ectoplasm), and that instead of ectoplasm new forms of more subtle energy were used. In addition, the mediums did not sit in cabinets, and the materializations built up at some distance from them (usually on our side of the table) and did not return to them as they dissolved. There was none of the violence reported at the séances of Stella C or of Indrid Indridason, and a feature of the spirit voices was their consistently high intellectual level of communication, which contained none of the banal and trivial messages that characterized many séances in the past. And what were described as independent or direct voices came from in front and slightly above us, rather than through trumpets.

Trumpet phenomena are, however, of interest in themselves, not only because they have been so consistently reported in the past, but because they raise a number of issues to do with fraud. We are told that the trumpet is used because it amplifies the often faint independent voices of communicators, and that it is carried around the room on extending ectoplasmic 'rods' extruded from the medium's body. Be this as it may, the trumpet phenomena that I have witnessed at a number of séances other than those at Scole have been spectacular to say the least. Although the séances concerned took place in the dark, the trumpets were identified by luminous bands, making it easy to track them during their movements and levitations. At each of the séances the trumpet sailed high over the heads of sitters while the medium was secured in his chair. The normal explanation for this is that the medium – or an accomplice – uses extendable rods to hold the trumpet and send it into the air. Although I have carried out searches of mediums before the commencement of physical séances thorough enough to ensure that at least there were no rods hidden on their persons, an accomplice could easily secret one without much risk of detection. However, there are certain difficulties in the accomplice theory. For example, séances held by Stewart Alexander, a highly respected medium from the north of England, take place with his home circle in a small upstairs room in the house of one of the circle members. The room can hold no more than ten people, and it is difficult to conceive of an accomplice moving freely and silently about such a small room, waving a trumpet above the heads of sitters on an extending rod, and then bringing it rapidly down and close to their ears in order to whisper words through it, and remaining undetected while doing so throughout the many years in which the circle has been meeting. Stewart, at his own wish, is strapped into his armchair with plastic straps that, when secured, cannot be undone and have to be cut through and discarded. I have been present when his long-sleeved sweater has been removed from him while he is strapped down in this way, an apparent demonstration of matter through matter. While with Stewart's home circle the trumpet has circled above my head while my chair has been backed against the wall making it impossible for an accomplice to move behind me. I have had somewhat similar experiences at the séances of Colin Fry, and also at those organized by Margaret Wehling, with Dinesh as medium (see below).

Claims for the existence of ectoplasm are also of interest. Sitting with Stewart Alexander I have seen, in a dim red light, a cloud of what is apparent ectoplasm form itself into the shape of a hand whose fingers I have touched. At a Colin Fry séance I have also, at my request, shaken the hand of a materialization (said by his supposed independent voice speaking in front of me to be that of the deceased Harry Boddington, well-known researcher and author of yesterday) supposedly formed by ectoplasm. Although some distance from Colin Fry and invisible to myself and other sitters, the materialization at my request found my hand unerringly in the dark. Without the presence of adequate controls, it is easy to dismiss experiences of this kind as purely anecdotal. Yet they defy ready explanation, particularly when, as in the case of Stewart Alexander, the medium is well known to me and I have never heard his integrity questioned or any accusation of fraud made against him, and as in the case of Colin Fry the medium has gone on to make a name for himself as a mental medium and been given his own television series.

One of the most interesting experiences of this kind I have had was at the home circle arranged by Margaret Wehling with Dinesh, a non-professional medium whose abilities had only been discovered as a member of Margaret Wehling's home circle. During the course of the séance a materialization unexpectedly touched my neighbor Veronica, the wife of Montague Keen with whom I worked extensively at Scole and elsewhere. Veronica gave a shriek of surprise, whereupon I opened my right hand and held it below my knee, palm uppermost, and sent out a mental request to be touched in the center of my palm. Almost immediately I felt a firm pressure precisely in the designated spot. Critics might argue I imagined the whole thing. My reply would be that as a psychologist with over 30 years' experience of the foibles and oddities of the human mind I am well aware of the powers of imagination, and well able to guard against the most obvious of them. There is no doubt that the touch on my palm was objective, and no doubt that in the concealed position in which I held my hand an accomplice, even with night vision equipment, would not have been able to see it. There was a chair directly in front of me and almost up against my knees, for reasons which will become apparent in a moment, and if there was an accomplice, he or she would only have had room to stand in front of this chair, from where my hand would not have been visible. (Critics might ask how many times I sent out a similar request at the sitting but without response; the answer is that this was the one and only time.)

There were eight people present at the séance in question: the four members of the home circle including the medium, and three experienced colleagues (Montague and Veronica Keen and Maurice Grosse) and myself from the SPR. Our main aim was to investigate the production of allegedly paranormal images on unexposed Polaroid films, and for this reason my colleagues and I, on the initiative of Montague Keen who led the Scole investigation and who was the principal investigator on this occasion too, secured a net across the width of the room as in the investigations with Indrid Indridason. Behind the net we placed the camera, which was our own and loaded with our own film – together with the bells, the tape recorder, and all the other paraphernalia that the spirits were said to use during the séance, and all eight sitters, including the medium, sat on the other side of the net in two rows closely together. During the séance all the various objects on the far side of the net were heard being brought into use. The tape recorder was turned on and off at request, and we heard the films being ejected one by one from the Polaroid camera.

At the end of the séance we found that apart from a small burned area some four inches in diameter the net was intact. However, the Polaroid films audibly ejected from the camera were found to have abstract images covering in each case the whole of the emulsified area. The camera had not left our possession until it was placed behind the net and the net secured in place. The film had been identified by us with secret markings. We had taped over the lens of the camera before we arrived at the séance, and the tape and adjoining area of the camera had been marked indelibly by us in a way that would reveal any attempt at tampering. It is possible to fake the photographic effects obtained at the séance fairly easily, but not under the conditions we put in place (details of which had not been previously disclosed to the home circle). Thus even if an accomplice had been able to enter the room through one of the windows behind the net (soundlessly and without admitting light, and in spite of the tapes we placed to guard every point of access and which showed no sign of disturbance at the end of the séance) he or she could only have achieved these effects by taking the camera out of the room, removing the film, placing it in another camera, exposing the film, replacing it in our camera, returning it to the table where we had placed it, and ejecting films from another camera in order to fake the sounds heard by us. As this would have taken some time, a second and possibly a third accomplice would have been required to manipulate the objects behind the net during the absence of the first one.

It is always interesting to know who these alleged accomplices might be, and why they carry out their shadowy unsung work in the background, particularly in the service of mediums who either refuse to take money for their services or take so little that they could hardly distribute much in the way of largesse. I have been present at Colin Fry séances where at the conclusion, with a loud crash, the medium still entranced and strapped to his heavy wooden armchair with similar straps to those used at Stewart Alexander's séances, has been thrown out of his cabinet and into the center of the room. At least two accomplices would have been needed to carry medium and chair out of the cabinet and drop it from a sufficient height to cause the crash. By no means impossible, but difficult to stage manage without detection.

If accomplices were not involved, how could supposed spirit energies have lifted a weighty chair along with the medium and hurled it into the room (by the same token, how could they have carried out the mayhem reported at the séances of Stella C and Indrid Indridason?). It has been suggested that, assuming the paranormality of these phenomena, the physical objects were rendered momentarily weightless, but an alternative suggestion is that it may be the medium who briefly loses weight, thus providing the energy necessary to levitate them. The latter suggestion is supported by findings published by Dr. W. J. Crawford, whose work with the Goligher home circle was mentioned earlier as inspiring the Crandons to start their sittings. Crawford found that when the medium, Kathleen Goligher, was placed on a highly accurate weighing machine tested and loaned to him by the leading firm of W & T Avery, she briefly lost up to 20 pounds (9.07 kilograms) in weight when the raps in the room that were a feature of her mediumship 'reached sledgehammer' intensity. When the raps ceased, her weight returned to normal. Crawford, who held posts in mechanical engineering at both the Municipal Technical Institute in Belfast and at Queens University, Belfast, concluded from this that ectoplasm was drawn from the medium in order to make each of the raps (Crawford 1921).

In sum, the cases summarized in this chapter make it difficult to argue firstly that the physical phenomena observed on at least some occasions can be explained by normal means, and secondly that they can be accounted for solely by the action of living agents. These phenomena do not conclusively demonstrate the reality of survival, but it would be hard to argue that they do not add materially to the case in its favor.

CHAPTER 14
INSTRUMENTAL TRANSCOMMUNICATION

Electronic Voice Phenomena

I first became interested in what is known as electronic voice phenomena (EVP) in 1971, with the publication of the English translation of *Breakthrough* (the German edition had appeared in 1968) by a Latvian philosopher with a keen interest in psychology and parapsychology, Dr. Konstantin Raudive. Dr. Raudive, who had lived in Sweden and Germany since the end of the Second World War, was the author of four previous books in which the fundamental problems of the relationship between death and life was one of the themes, and he seemed to be generally well regarded by his fellow philosophers. I learnt from *Breakthrough* that what subsequently became generally known as EVP are the faint inexplicable voices that some researchers appear to capture on tape recorders and which they claim are communications from the deceased.

To clarify what is meant by EVP I can jump ahead of myself for a moment and explain that one of the methods for trying to obtain these voices is to tape record the hiss of static heard when a radio is tuned to a frequency carrying no transmissions. When the tape is played back, the hope is that the inexplicable voices will be heard against the background of static. Referred to sometimes as "white noise," radio static is in fact a random mixture of sounds of many different wavelengths. The sounds made by a waterfall are a purer example of this kind of randomness since they are uncontaminated by the non-random sounds of voices or music that, although inaudible to the human ear, may be present in radio static. But radio static, provided the radio is tuned far enough away from wavebands used by transmitting stations, is an acceptable example of white noise. The claim is made by EVP researchers that the communicators appear able by some unknown means to abstract sounds from this white noise in order to fashion the sounds of their voices.

The Work of Raudive and Jürgenson

Using this method among others, Raudive found he did in fact receive such voices, which in his view could not be accounted for as snatches of normal radio transmissions misinterpreted by the human ear as they used words – such as personal and place names – and left messages that were directly applicable to Raudive himself. They also appeared to use his own native language, Latvian, even though there were no radio transmissions in Latvian anywhere near the waveband to which his radio was tuned. Another anomaly suggestive to him of paranormality was that the voices spoke at a speed at least twice that of the normal human voice. In an attempt to confirm that he was not mistaken in all this, Raudive invited panels of listeners to hear his tapes of the voices and then inform him what words they thought they had heard. The level of agreement between panel members was sufficient to satisfy him that the voices were not readily explicable by normal means. By the time *Breakthrough* was published Raudive had recorded some 72,000 of the brief messages given by the voices, of which 25,000 were said to contain identifiable words. His panels included highly respected scientists and parapsychologists such as Professor Hans Bender, Dr. Jule Eisenbud, Dr Karlis Osis, Molly Goldney, and Professor Walter Uphoff, together with a wide range of other professional people. In all cases a high percentage of the voices were said to be heard clearly.

Raudive gave examples in *Breakthrough* of transcripts of a number of his recorded voices, and also included in the book a phonograph record of some of them (though this was of limited value to those unfamiliar with the languages concerned). In translation some of the messages given by the voices seem to make little apparent sense, while others are more coherent. The effect sometimes is like reading snatches of conversation half-heard between people who do not know they have an audience. But at other times the communications do indeed appear to have been intended for Raudive himself. In addition to Latvian, many of the voices spoke in German, Raudive's second language, while a communicator whose voice he recognized as belonging to his mother often used Latgalian, the dialect of Latgalia, a province in Latvia, and also spoke in Spanish and in Swedish, languages with which she was unfamiliar in life. In translation, some examples of her messages taken from several different recording sessions were:

Your mother ... Mother is here. Tekla ... Kostulit, (a term of endearment) this is your mother ... Here is mother, Kostja (a diminutive of Konstantin) ... Mother is with you ... Let mother through – Kosta! ... Koste, your mother speaks ... Speak, Kosti, Mummy ... Kostja, mother is in the room.

In some of the examples his mother expresses very human feelings, speaking of having a "headache," and of being "sick." She also says that she "cries," and that she "cried over her lost son." Speaking of Raudive's collaborators she protests that she likes "none of them," and even speaks variously of being "lonely" and of being "strong."

Raudive first became interested in EVP research after hearing of the results obtained by the Swedish singer, artist, and documentary film-maker Friedrich Jürgenson. Two books by Jürgenson, written in 1964 and 1967 respectively and subsequently privately translated into English as *Voices from the Universe* and

Radio Communications with the Dead, detail how while recording the songs of night birds for the sound track of one of his documentaries he was irritated to find the results spoilt by intrusive human voices. Supposing these voices were of normal origin he made further recordings, only to obtain similar results. At this point he recognized, to his apparent surprise, that far from being stray conversations picked up by his tape recorder, the voices seemed to be addressing him directly, calling him by his pet name and using the names of deceased members of his own family. Fluent in eight languages, Jürgenson identified words in German, Italian, Hungarian, and Swedish, and concluded that the voices were indeed addressing him from beyond the grave.

Jürgenson's findings apparently aroused little interest when he presented them to the Swedish Parapsychological Society, but he determined to devote much of his time to studying the voices, spending for the purpose long solitary periods at his country retreat, largely neglecting his family and his professional life in the process. This dedication appears to have paid off, because consequent upon the publication of Jürgenson's two books Professor Hans Bender, Director of the Institute of Parapsychology (at that time part of the University of Freiberg) and one of Europe's most respected parapsychologists, began to pay serious attention to his work. With a team of technicians and fellow scientists from the University of Freiburg, Bender carried out a number of experiments with Jürgenson at various locations, using many different tape recorders, the shortest possible connecting cables between items of equipment, and precise unidirectional microphones in order to minimize the possibility of picking up stray sounds from any normal source. Oscilloscopes and electromagnetic wave detectors were even used to ensure that the equipment was set up in areas least likely to suffer from interference (Bender 1985).

Anomalous voices continued to be recorded even under these strict control conditions. However, in Bender's view, although the voices appeared to be paranormal, they were not communications from the deceased, but sounds impressed upon the tapes in some way by Jürgenson's own unconscious psychokinetic (PK) abilities. Bender was in fact noted for his skeptical views about the possibilities of proving survival, and preferred the Super-ESP hypothesis as an explanation for all apparent communications from the deceased, whether through mediums or through Jürgenson's tape recorder. In his view, all supposed contact from spirits was probably due to what he called "psycho-mechanic automatism," which he described as a pathological condition in which psychic material leaks from the medium's unconscious mind and is then unwittingly personified into "spirit" communications. He argued that such leakage can express itself in any of the phenomena associated with mediumship, whether trance voices, automatic writing, direct voice, psychokinesis, or whatever. For Bender, "the superstitious attitudes built on misunderstood communication with 'spirit-beings' ... carry, as case-histories show, the seeds of mental illness" (Bender 1966).

Bender was deservedly a highly influential figure among psychical researchers, but his theory of "psycho-mechanic automatism" has not attracted much serious support, and the "case histories" that he claimed show that superstitious attitudes towards supposed communications with the deceased carry the "seeds of mental illness" remain hard to find. Reasons for dismissing the Super-ESP hypothesis have already been given (Chapter 5 and elsewhere), and the notion that Jürgenson had psychokinetic abilities powerful enough to produce sustained, repeated, and often coherent voices on audio tapes, although these abilities had hitherto failed to reveal themselves during his many years work with audio tapes as a documentary film maker, may seem to many people harder to swallow than the spirit communication hypothesis. In addition, neither Jürgenson, Raudive, nor anyone to my knowledge involved in EVP research has developed the "seeds of mental illness" as a result of their activities. It is also odd that, as far as I know, Bender never attempted to put the supposed psychokinetic abilities of either Jürgenson or Raudive to the test at a time when the work of Rhine and his colleagues at the Parapsychology Unit at Duke University had demonstrated the possibility of researching psychokinesis under laboratory conditions.

Jürgenson and Raudive carried out a number of experiments together, both in Sweden and in Germany, and confirmed each other's results. For example, after repeated visits to Germany, Jürgenson wrote in 1967 that he could understand clearly the 300 or so voices recorded by Raudive to which he had listened, and that he was "able to verify and confirm them without assistance." He added that "The fact that Dr. Raudive's questions receive clear and unequivocal answers from the voice-entities – as if a telephone link had been established – is enough in itself to indicate that a direct contact exists. I found that some of the male and female voices which appear frequently in my own recordings manifested also in Dr. Raudive's experiments" (see Raudive 1971). In Jürgenson's view "There can be no doubt whatsoever that the phenomenon manifesting in Dr. Raudive's experiments is the same that manifests in my own ... The voices describe themselves as 'the dead,' but always stress most emphatically that they are very much alive; 'the dead live,' they say ... I can state with the utmost conviction and certainty: these messages stem without doubt from our so-called dead."

In 1970 David Ellis, now Production Editor of the *Journal of the SPR*, embarked on an intensive three-year investigation of EVP, funded full-time by his tenure of the prestigious Perrot-Warrick Studentship, a trust set up by two SPR members interested particularly in survival research and administered by Trinity College, Cambridge. David Ellis published his results in 1978, and although privately printed they proved influential among SPR members. The Perrot-Warrick Studentship is an award much sought after by young psychical researchers, and David Ellis spent some time in Germany interviewing and attending recording sessions with Raudive and Professor Bender. While there he heard samples of Raudive's recordings that included what he considered to be "very clear [ones] ... These voices are interesting in that their interpretation is almost unambiguous ... they appear to be in German [and] contain neologisms and corrupted German words." Ellis reports that Bender informed him that the counter-hypotheses of subjective misinterpretation of the recorded sounds, uncontrolled utterances by the researchers themselves, and stray fragments of radio broadcasts could not explain some of the results obtained, which were almost certainly paranormal, but that Bender still held to the view that Jürgenson and Raudive "functioned as mediums, and produced the effects by psychokinesis" (strangely Bender made no reference to the fact that frequently visitors to Raudive's studio had apparently obtained voices in Raudive's absence). While with Bender and Raudive, Ellis and his German-speaking colleague were present when a quite clear voice, giving a single name, was recorded.

However, over the course of his research, Ellis gradually became doubtful of the paranormality of the voices, particularly perhaps because his own listening tests, using individuals who independently heard samples of Raudive's clearest voices, revealed an absence of significant levels of agreement as to what was actually being said. His conclusion was that "in most cases there does not seem to be anything paranormal about the sounds" on the tapes that he studied. Most if not all of these could be explained away as stray radio transmissions and misinterpretations on the part of the listeners. This conclusion served to convince many British psychical researchers who had not themselves had experience of the EVP phenomena that there was little point in pursuing the matter further, and in Britain the subject was largely allowed to fade into the background.

However, although David Ellis was accompanied during his research in Germany by a German-speaking colleague (the late Manfred Cassirer, a highly respected member of the SPR Council), his own lack of facility in the languages used by the voices received by Jürgenson and Raudive seems to me to have been an unavoidable handicap – a handicap apparently shared by the individuals who took part in his listening tests. Studying Ellis' book soon after it was written, it also seemed clear to me that the controls imposed by Professor Bender in his work with both Jürgenson and Raudive should have been effective in screening out the stray radio transmissions to which David Ellis refers. In spite of his conclusions, I therefore kept an open mind on the possibility that EVP voices might be paranormal.

Three British Researchers

In 1989 my attention was drawn once more to the subject of EVP by a small book I came across by chance entitled *Whispers of Immortality* by Samuel Alsop, published by Regency Press, a so-called vanity publisher that produces books only at the author's own expense. Seeing that it was about EVP I bought it, and read it with interest. There is a tendency among some scientists interested in psychical research to dismiss any book written by someone who does not possess recognized academic qualifications. This is misguided and can be a hindrance to further advances in the subject. Psychical research is one of the few areas of science where those without what are regarded as relevant scientific qualifications can still engage in potentially valuable investigations. Much of the work in EVP carried out since the days of Jürgenson and Raudive (again I am jumping ahead of myself) has been carried out by technicians, electrical engineers, and men and women who do not profess to be scientists. It is arguable that some of these people are in fact better qualified to attempt EVP research than are professional psychical researchers. Alsop himself had an engineering background, and although not highly qualified his book gives evidence that he was a painstaking and committed researcher, well aware of the possible dangers of picking up stray radio transmissions and misinterpreting the sounds concerned.

One of Alsop's communicators appeared to be an old friend of his whose name, Lucy Price, was apparently given. Alsop decided to test her identity by asking her for her burial place, which was unknown to him. After posing the question on several occasions without results, the word "Ashcroft" was heard on playback of the tape. The word meant nothing to Alsop, who had never heard of a cemetery by that name. At subsequent EVP sessions he heard on tape the words "In Bush" and "I'm on Bush." This still meant nothing, but enquiries with living people who had known Lucy Price revealed that her remains were at a cemetery called Bushbury Hill. Visiting the cemetery, Alsop discovered that Lucy had been cremated not buried, and that her ashes were scattered in what was indeed a croft, a small open space in the cemetery surrounded by hedgerows and reserved exclusively for ashes. In his view, this explained the earlier reference to 'Ashcroft'.

After reading Alsop's book I wrote to him, care of his publisher, and enquired if I could have copies of his tapes, for which of course I would pay. In due course I received a letter from his daughter Gillian, giving me the sad news that her father had died at the time his book was published. Gillian Alsop is mentioned in *Whispers of Immortality* as having helped Sam Alsop in his work, and she proved most co-operative, informing me that she was carrying on with the research, and sending me copies both of voices received by her father and those received by herself. Most of these voices were faint, and the words delivered at speed and with a rather unusual rhythm, but some were clearly audible and quite impressive. The language was English, and the voices appeared to respond to questions put to them by the Alsops, and on occasion to address them by name. It seemed apparent that results of this nature could not easily be dismissed as stray radio transmissions misinterpreted by listeners. Either they were as claimed, or they were fraudulent.

In psychical research as elsewhere in life, it is inappropriate to assume dishonesty simply on the basis that what is reported appears not to accord with existing information. No paranormal phenomenon accords with existing information, if by existing information we mean in this case the accepted laws of science. The assumption of dishonesty in the absence of supporting evidence can lead us to reject evidence that may prove worthy of serious study, and can deter some independent investigators from informing us of their results. Much scientific progress in the past has come from those prepared to entertain anomalous views, and to go by the evidence in front of them rather than by conventional wisdom. There was no evidence that either of the Alsops were dishonest, or had any motive for being engaged in fraud. Certainly money was not involved. I wrote a review of Sam Alsop's book for *Light*, the journal of the College of Psychic Studies, who were sufficiently interested in the work concerned to offer Gillian Alsop financial assistance to purchase new audio-visual equipment in order further to develop her work. This she refused, on the grounds that if her communicators wanted her to have the new equipment for which they had apparently been asking, they would find a way to provide it for her themselves.

The interest aroused by the Alsop tapes prompted me to identify other researchers who were apparently producing similar results in Britain, and I then wrote to two of them, Gilbert Bonner and Raymond Cass (an audiophonics expert) to enquire if they might be agreeable to sending me samples of their respective results. Both men responded immediately and generously, providing me with the requested samples, which I found contained recorded communications that could not be dismissed as due to stray radio transmissions. In addition, Gilbert Bonner provided me with details of his working methods and of the advances he felt he had made over many years of research in improving the quality of the voices received. Raymond Cass's voices were particularly clear, so much so that few people with average hearing could mistake any part of the communications. As with the Alsop tapes, the voices were heard to respond to questions and comments from the researcher.

It is true that in each of the three cases just mentioned, the researchers sent me some of their best examples of voices. Not all of their results were up to the same high standard. It is also true that from other researchers I have heard recorded voices that I find so faint or so indistinct that they command little or no credibility. Nevertheless, on the strength of the examples received from Sam Alsop, Gillian Alsop, Gilbert Bonner, and Raymond Cass it seemed clear to me that it was worth continuing to take an interest in EVP.

The Work of George Meek

In 1985 Roy Fuller, a well-known American investigative writer, published *The Ghost of 29 Megacycles* in which he detailed results arising from a very different approach to EVP. The approach was that of an American engineer, inventor, and highly successful businessman, George Meek. Meek, whose interest in the possibilities of survival of death led him to retire from business in 1970 at the age of 60 and to devote the rest of his life to a study of the subject, conceived the idea of using mediums in the hope of contacting scientists in the next world in order to request instructions on how to build a machine to facilitate the reception of EVP-type communications. Thomas Edison is said to have tried to construct just such a machine for contacting the spirit world, but without success. To this end Meek embarked on an ambitious program of investigation, setting up a network of international contacts with like-minded medical doctors, psychologists, psychiatrists, and scientists. He organized and led research teams to interview mediums and healers, and co-authored with 14 members of this network a book on healing (*Healers and the Healing Process*) which was recommended by the World Health Organisation for health professionals in developing countries. Concurrently with this endeavor, he founded a laboratory (later called the Metascience Laboratory) staffed by a team of technicians who began experimenting on building machines to improve the reception of EVP. Early results held out some promise (see Fuller 1985 and Meek 1987) but real progress only started when, in 1973, Meek began working with healer and medium William O'Neil who apparently was then contacted by a deceased scientist, Dr. George Mueller. Mueller gave O'Neil a number of personal and seemingly obscure details about his life on earth, many of which were found on subsequent investigation by Meek and his colleagues to be correct. Meek claims none of these details was known by himself, by O'Neil, or by their colleagues, and he concludes that the Mueller case provided "one of the best documented cases of survival for more than 100 years." A summary of some of these details is given below, together with their verification.

Details Given by Mueller	Verification
Social security number	*Confirmed as correct by Meek from Enquiries at the Social Security Department*
B.Sc. in Electrical Engineering, University of Wisconsin at Madison 1928 (graduating in the top 20 per cent of his class)	*Confirmed as correct by Professor Walter Uphoff from records at the University Registry*
M.Sc., Cornell University 1930	*Confirmed as correct by Professor*

	Uphoff's son, Professor Norman Uphoff, a Faculty Member at Cornell
Ph.D. in Experimental Physics, Cornell University	*Confirmed as correct by Professor Norman Uphoff*
Member of the Haresfoot Club while at Wisconsin	*Confirmed as correct by Professor Walter Uphoff from an old photograph which the University archivist discovered*
Address of Daughter	*Incorrect (or no longer correct)*
Meritorious Civilian Award,	*Confirmed as correct by Tom Beardon, by Secretary for the US Air Force intelligence service Army and US Army (retired)*
Top Secret Clearance from US Army	*Confirmed as correct by Tom Beardon US Army*

Other details given subsequently by Mueller of his career were also found to be correct, including a Research Fellowship he had held while at Cornell University, and his design and development work for the United States Signal Corps and for the NASA Space Program at Cape Canaveral. Also verified and found to be correct were the details he gave of the unlisted telephone numbers of two of his old colleagues, of his place and cause of death (confirmed from his death certificate), of the names of four family members (confirmed by his wife, who was traced through the Social Security Office), and of his physical appearance and his personality (confirmed by his wife and others who knew him). Some of these details came through O'Neil's mediumship, others through the "Spiricom" machine that Mueller subsequently instructed O'Neil and Meek to build, and which is referred to in more detail below.

There is no doubting the strength of all this evidence, but is the case for Mueller's survival as strong as Meek claimed? All the details given by him were already in the public domain, and could have been discovered by O'Neil by normal means. However, many of them were apparently obscure and only obtained after extensive investigation. For example, Mueller's membership of the Haresfoot Club and of the Triangle Fraternity were only confirmed by Professor Uphoff with the discovery of old photographs (more than 30 years had passed since Mueller's membership of these undergraduate societies). It took a retired nuclear scientist who had worked with the service to confirm the details of his work with US military intelligence. The personal and family details were only obtained after Meek traced the Mueller family.

Subsequently Mueller also gave details of a booklet he had written in 1947 for the US Army, *Introduction to Electronics*, of which the Library of Congress had no record and whose existence was only confirmed after a two-year search by Meek from the Wisconsin State Historical Society archives (the material on the two pages of the book to which Mueller drew particular attention was found to be significant for the construction of Spiricom). Mueller also gave details – details that this time did not appear to be in the public domain – of a machine he had invented for the treatment of arthritis and which had never been published and which were apparently known only to himself. Meek's team constructed the device, and reported they found it to be effective.

It seems unlikely that O'Neil, who was a High School dropout and who eked out a somewhat impecunious existence in an isolated farmhouse, would have had the knowledge and the money to undertake the many investigations needed in order to come by all this material. Could Meek himself have obtained it by normal means? Possibly. But no grounds for being suspicious of Meek have ever been advanced. It could be argued that he knew someone who had been well acquainted with Mueller and obtained details of him that way, or that he chanced upon the draft of an autobiography that Mueller may have been writing, but suggestions of this kind could be made in connection with a large number of the investigators whose word has not been doubted. In the absence of evidence – for example even when Meek's work became well known nobody came forward to claim they had provided him with details of Mueller, or that Mueller was known to have been writing an autobiography – we have no grounds for impugning Meek's veracity. However, if he did not obtain details of Mueller by normal means, what of the ubiquitous Super-ESP explanation? Could O'Neil perhaps have obtained some of the information clairvoyantly from the environment and some of it telepathically from Mueller's surviving family? Apart from the various weaknesses of the Super-ESP hypothesis already discussed in earlier chapters to the point of tedium, a particular problem for the hypothesis in the present instance is that O'Neil had no apparent link with Mueller. What therefore would have set him off on his clairvoyant and telepathic quest? And if for some reason he had decided to embark on such a quest he would have had conscious knowledge of the fact, and would have known that any information obtained as a result of it was a consequence of his own abilities rather than those of a deceased Dr. Mueller

The critic might suggest that O'Neil did nevertheless obtain the information by Super-ESP, and for some unknown reason decided to keep quiet about it, but if so, how are we to explain the fact that Mueller subsequently gave O'Neil the very instructions on how to build the EVP-type machine (christened "Spiricom" by Meek) for which he had been seeking? The instructions on how to build and progressively improve the machine came over a period of time, firstly through the mediumship of O'Neil and subsequently apparently through Spiricom itself (at which point all communications were audio taped by Meek). From where did these instructions for Spiricom originate if not from Mueller? And if O'Neil obtained them clairvoyantly or telepathically from physical sources why not say so and gain the resulting prestige, if any? Meek was only too ready to experiment with machines that might prove capable of receiving spirit voices, so why would O'Neil attribute Spiricom to fictitious communications from Mueller, communications which he would in fact have had to fake once they began to come through Spiricom itself, rather than to his own psychic abilities? O'Neil was already financially supported by Meek to carry out technical work before Spiricom came on the scene, so O'Neil had no need to pretend to receive instructions from spirits in order to capture Meek's patronage. We can never be categorical about what leads people to behave as they do. Men and women are capable of very strange actions. But in the absence of supporting evidence it is always premature to assume strangeness rather than normality when seeking for people's motives.

If fraud by O'Neil – or by O'Neil and Meek in conjunction – is regarded as unlikely it seems that survival serves as a strong possible explanation for the contacts from Mueller. But what of Spiricom itself? It is claimed that not only was it successful in receiving communications, but that it allowed much longer and more coherent messages to come through than had proved possible by existing EVP methods. The audio tapes I have heard of these communications confirm their length and coherence, although the voice of the communicator sounds robotic and artificial. Spiricom also appears to have allowed direct two-way conversations between the communicator and the researcher, an impossibility with the normal EVP method, which required the investigator to wait until the tape was rewound and played back before discovering whether or not there were replies to his questions and comments.

In the course of the initial instructions for the construction and operation of Spiricom given mediumistically through O'Neil, Mueller stipulated that an audio tape containing 13 of the tones between 121 and 701 cycles per second that make up the adult male voice be used as an acoustic background for the machine instead of white noise (Meek 1982). Using this tape, Mueller apparently spoke loudly and clearly through Spiricom on September 23, 1980, and a lengthy conversation was recorded between him and O'Neil. In the course of it Mueller can be heard reciting the nursery rhyme "Mary had a Little Lamb," then asking O'Neil to play the tape back for him and giving instructions on improving the sound. In later communications, Mueller can also be heard giving detailed guidance on the construction of a videocom that O'Neil was building in the hope of receiving video images from the spirit world.

Meek (1987) gives many lengthy transcripts of the conversations between Mueller and O'Neil through Spiricom. In these samples Mueller comments on his liking for various foods, remarks on his lack of any awareness of time, assures O'Neil that he should not worry about a pending surgical operation, stresses the importance of knowing about survival so that one is not confused on entering the next world, and gives evidence of his ability to "see" everything taking place in O'Neil's workshop. Meek reports that O'Neil would sometimes place letters or magazine articles in his workshop which Mueller would apparently "read" and comment on through Spiricom, and at other times Mueller would refer to items of electronic equipment also present. His interest in removing what he called the "zombie-like" quality of the voices received through Spiricom was also evident. For example he commented that " ... we are going to have to have a more stable frequency. By more stable, I mean we have to do away with the AC frequencies in the background ... to eliminate the fractional frequencies." In this context he made his first reference to his book *Introduction to Electronics* and to pages 66 and 67, which he considered relevant to the matter of frequencies (as mentioned earlier it took Meek two years to trace a copy of the book).

Meek presented details of Spiricom in April 1982 at the National Press Club in Washington, and played extracts from the tapes. More importantly, he had the tapes analyzed at the University of Tokyo, where it was confirmed that Mueller's recorded voice was not that of either O'Neil or Meek. The report on Mueller's voice prints suggested that the voice might possibly have been computer-generated, but pointed out that computer-generation of this kind would require a million dollar computer set-up (remember we are talking about the equipment costs obtaining in 1982) and many hours of complex rehearsal and adjustments far beyond Meek's financial resources and O'Neil's competence. Alexander MacRae, a leading voice expert and a consultant to NASA who has worked on the problem of unscrambling the distorted speech of astronauts and of divers when working in a helium–oxygen environment, also concluded in favor of the paranormality of the voices, writing to Meek that "EVP is unquestionably paraphysical ... there is something there not recognized by science ... communication rules exist that, when known, may alter appreciably our world view" (Meek 1987). I know from recent communications with Alexander MacRae that after extensive research of his own into voices received through electronic media he is still fully convinced of their paranormality. Recently MacRae has published detailed findings of a series of experiments he has conducted that capture anomalous, EVP-type voices when background sound is provided by a device of his invention originally designed to use electro-dermal skin activity (EDA) to simulate vowel sounds (this is possible because the voltages produced by EDA cause oscillators to vibrate in the same frequencies as the basic voice pitch). MacRae discovered that the higher harmonics thus produced by his device are prominent enough to be picked up by a radio receiver, and it is these harmonics that appear well suited to function successfully as background noise for EVP voice reception (MacRae 2004).

Spiricom thus appeared to be the major breakthrough in communications with the next world for which Meek and many others had been waiting. Unfortunately, things did not continue in this way. Meek was aware throughout that the work with Spiricom "depended considerably on O'Neil acting as a psychic channel as well as building the equipment. Meek had still not been able to separate the two" (Fuller ibid. 1987). He also had intimations from Mueller that Mueller himself "would not be here forever." Sure enough, as 1981 wore on, it became clear from Mueller's communications that "he was beginning to shed his dense earthly vibrations and was starting his progression upwards" through the various levels of consciousness said to exist in the next world. It became increasingly difficult for him to communicate through Spiricom, and he began to give instructions on how to build a more advanced model that would enable him to remain in contact. However, before these instructions were complete, Spiricom fell silent.

Meek's hope throughout had been to dispense altogether with mediums as the channels between this world and the next, and to bring communications through by electronic means alone. This would in theory allow anyone, whether he or she had mediumistic abilities or not, to receive voices from the next world. The loss of contact with Dr. Mueller was therefore a major disappointment to him, particularly as no other communicators seemed able to speak through Spiricom. The project thus reached a dead end. True, a wealth of taped material from Dr. Mueller exists, and as we have seen voice print analysis suggests that Mueller's voice is not readily explicable by normal means. However, science demands that results be capable of replication by other researchers if they are to be accepted as valid, and the hard fact is that the Spiricom results have not been replicated. But if Mueller could no longer communicate through Spiricom, why could no other spirits take his place? One of them, who claimed the name of Fred Ingstrom and reported that he had died 151 years previously in Virginia (the scanty birth records of that period have not confirmed his existence), did in fact supposedly communicate in the days when Mueller was in charge. Why could he not have continued to make contact?

There is no easy answer. Possibly the design of Spiricom suited the "frequencies" used by Mueller, but were unsuitable for anyone else unless Mueller was present to facilitate them in some way. Perhaps some special relationship existed between Mueller and O'Neil's mediumistic abilities, and it was this that allowed them to work together with Spiricom. Perhaps, as William James suggested, the Almighty may have decreed that we are never going to receive the final element of proof for which survival researchers have been looking, and that Spiricom was in danger of giving this proof.

New Developments – Instrumental Transcommunication

Fortunately for supporters of EVP research, evidence has continued to come not only through the traditional EVP method of white noise and tape recorder, but through a range of other electronic devices including radios, computers, video tape, fax machines, and telephones (see e.g. Butler and Butler 2003 for a survey of much of this evidence). A broader term, translated into English as *Instrumental Transcommunication* (ITC), proposed by German physicist Professor Ernst Senkowski (Senkowski 1989) of the Mayence Higher Technical Institute, is now used to cover this whole range of communications. In order to survey some of the evidence yielded as a consequence we have in fact to go back even beyond Jürgenson and Raudive, in fact to September 17, 1952, when Italian Roman Catholic priests Father Ernetti of the Abbey of San Giorgio Maggiore in Venice and Father Gemelli, a medical doctor at the Catholic University of Milan, were investigating in the University's Experimental Physics Laboratory ways of filtering the taped sound of Gregorian chants in order to enhance their acoustical purity. The efforts of the two priests were hampered by the fact that the wire used by tape recorders before the invention of magnetic tape broke frequently, and required constant and delicate repair work. Finally Father Gemelli, as was his habit when exasperated, called on his deceased father for help. On starting the machine again, the Fathers heard, not the Gregorian chant upon which they were working, but the voice of Gemelli Senior, "Of course I'll help you! I am always with you."

The astonished priests obtained an audience with Pope Pious XII to acquaint him of the incident, and were reassured by his strongly positive response. He considered that the reception of the voice through an electronic machine might initiate "a new scientific study for confirming faith in the afterlife." Professor Francois Brune, a leading theologian and himself a Roman Catholic priest and expert on ITC who details these facts (Brune 2002), reports that although the Church still remains neutral on whether or not ITC really represents contact with the dead, seeing this as a matter for scientists and technicians, he himself is convinced of the strong support that it provides for survival (e.g. Brune 1993, Brune and Chauvin 1996).

If Brune is correct in his conviction, we are bound to ask why nobody had received apparent ITC communications before Fathers Ernetti and Gemelli, since electronic media had been around for many years before their experience. The answer is that there is some evidence that they may have done so. Guglielmo Marconi, the inventor of wireless, is reported as receiving Morse code signals of unexplained origin during his experimental transmission and reception of radio signals in the first years of the twentieth century. As Marconi at the time was the only person with the experimental radio equipment through which such signals could be sent, there was speculation that these may have come from "spirits." Nikola Tesla, another leading inventor and a pioneer in the field of Direct Current and high voltage oscillations, also apparently received signals of unknown origin while attempting to transmit electrical energy without cables (see e.g. Cardoso 2003). The American ethnologist Waldemar Borogas, using one of the first rudimentary phonographs in 1901 to record the ritual chants of shamans of the Tchouktchis tribe, apparently found voices inexplicable by normal means on the recorded material (Grandsire 1993). Ferdinando Cazzamatti, an Italian doctor, reported receiving strange paranormal voices on a radio receiver placed in a Faraday Cage while researching telepathy in psychotics (Fernández 2002). There is no guarantee that any of these unexpected results provide early examples of ITC, but since the circumstances in which they were obtained seem to have precluded normal explanations, it is suggested by Cardoso and others that they may indeed do so.

Be this as it may, ITC research certainly grew rapidly in the latter part of the twentieth century, inspired particularly by the work of Jürgenson and of Raudive. Many of the researchers involved have been – and still are – electronic engineers and technicians rather than parapsychologists. The late Professor Arthur Ellison, who we met in Chapter 13 as one of the investigators at Scole, always insisted that engineers are in many ways more open to phenomena of this kind than are researchers from other disciplines (see e.g. Ellison 2002), and receive less opposition from colleagues than do scientists in other fields. In his view this is because engineers, by the very nature of their profession, are interested in what works, whether or not there happen to be existing theories to explain why it does.

A good example of the eclectic approach adopted by many ITC researchers is provided by United States researcher Raymond Bayless. Bayless first became interested in the possibilities of capturing paranormal voices on tape in 1956, when he met and began work with Attila Von Szalay, a commercial photographer and psychic. In 1938 Von Szalay had heard a disembodied voice, which he considered was that of his deceased son, calling out his name loudly and distinctly. Other voices followed, and he noticed the effect was particularly pronounced after his periods of meditation and yogic practice. Bayless was interested to establish firstly if the paranormal voices were genuine, and secondly if they were independent of Von Szalay himself. The results of their first experiments together were published by Bayless in 1959 in the *Journal of the American Society for Psychical Research*, but aroused no apparent interest in the parapsychological community. However, the two men persevered, working together for over a decade, basing some of their research in a Hollywood studio rented by Bayless for the purpose. At first Von Szalay was placed in a wooden cabinet equipped with a microphone (sometimes situated in the mouthpiece of a trumpet, such as that used in séances for physical phenomena), while a loudspeaker and a tape recorder outside the cabinet allowed Bayless to hear any sounds from within.

Whispered voices, apparently both male and female, were heard and recorded by Bayless, and these were still heard when, later in the experiments, Von Szalay sat several feet outside the cabinet. Even on the occasions when no sounds were heard, the tape was found to carry voices when played back after the session. Low whistles produced by Von Szalay from outside the cabinet also produced answering whistles from inside. The room was normally illuminated during the experiments, von Szalay was kept under close observation by Bayless, and the controls were such that, in Bayless' words, " ... fraud, under such conditions, is completely eliminated."

In subsequent experiments Bayless placed the microphone and trumpet in an inner box, which was then enclosed in an outer box covered with sound-deadening material and the whole arrangement suspended then from the ceiling above the cabinet. Bayless and Von Szalay sat three feet away from the cabinet, with the recording equipment some further foot or two away (Rogo and Bayless 1979). Even under these conditions a clear human whisper was nevertheless recorded. Later, Bayless even established that the voices appeared able to answer specific questions. For example, when he asked where his medical doctor brother who had moved away from the area was now located, the answer "Bridgeport" was received. Several days later Bayless was able to confirm the truth of this. Bayless also asked for the name of his grandmother, which although known to him was unknown to Von Szalay. The correct answer, "Emma," was given. The voices even seemed aware of distant events. On September 30, 1971 Bayless, during a private conversation with his wife, spoke despondently of withdrawing from the craziness of the human race and becoming a recluse. Von Szalay, 15 miles away, was experimenting with a tape machine and recorded a male voice saying "Bayless is virtually become a recluse." Von Szalay reported this to Bayless before hearing of the latter's conversation with his wife.

In 1968 Scott Rogo, well known for his published work on psychical research, began experiments with Von Szalay, achieving similar results to those of Bayless. Over a period of three years (and sporadically thereafter) Rogo and Von Szalay recorded many voices, and noted that the length of the utterances increased as the work progressed. Reporting these results (Rogo and Bayless 1979) Rogo dismisses as "frankly ridiculous" the criticism that the tapes were only picking up "random radio broadcast fragments or calls from overhead aircraft." He points out that Von Szalay's voices answered questions and used the names of the researchers, and that results were only obtained in Von Szalay's presence. He also dismissed the suggestion that the voices were too faint to be properly interpreted. Some of them were as loud and clear as normal human speech, and although others were not it was claimed that they were nevertheless recorded under conditions that ruled out normal interpretation (see also Smith 1977). Discussing whether the voices came from the deceased or from the living by psychokinesis, Rogo inclined towards the former explanation, pointing out that the voices invariably gave the names of those who were known to have died, and that when Von Szalay's father (one of the frequent communicators) spoke, the timbre of the voice was recognized as exactly that of the dead man. Regrettably, although the voices were said to answer questions, no attempt seems to have been made by the investigators to invite them to prove their identities.

More will be said about these results shortly, but for the moment it is relevant to point out that, assuming their paranormality, they appear to show a clear link between ITC and physical phenomena. Von Szalay appears, initially at least, to have had some of the attributes of a physical medium, hearing apparent independent voices and making use of a trumpet. It is also worth noting that on the strength of his work with Von Szalay, Rogo reached the conclusion that physical mediumship was of value in facilitating the reception of the paranormal voices. Unlike Jürgenson, Raudive, and many later researchers, neither Bayless nor Rogo used white noise as background when working with Von Szalay. Their method, referred to as the "open microphone" method, simply relied upon picking up air-born sounds.

Hans Otto König

Another good example of this eclectic approach to ITC research is provided by Hans Otto König, a consultant electrical-acoustic engineer, who experimented with a number of different sources of background noise such as running water, in addition to radio static. In the course of his work König noted that his equipment showed that these various sources of noise all carried sounds that stretched into the ultrasonic range. Since most magnetic tape recorders cannot register sounds above the 15,000 to 20,000 Hertz range, this prompted him to design a source of noise that used four sound generators producing a complex mixture of frequencies and harmonics reaching beyond the audible range of human hearing. Like Meek's Spiricom, this equipment was intended to allow direct two-way contact between the experimenter and the supposed communicators. Results, it seemed, were so promising that König was invited to give a demonstration live on Radio Luxembourg, at that time one of the most popular radio stations in Europe and normally transmitting in English. The equipment was set up under the scrutiny of the Radio Luxembourg technicians and of the program's presenter, Rainer Holbe. As a further safeguard, the equipment was operated only by the technicians, not by König himself.

One of the technicians then asked if a communicator could make himself heard, and a clear voice was received saying "Otto König makes wireless with the dead." The technician asked a further question, to which the reply came "We hear your voice." The two replies were as clear as the voice of the technician asking the questions. It is reported (Fuller 1985) that Rainer

Holbe's voice was shaking when he assured listeners "I swear by the life of my children nothing has been manipulated. There are no tricks. It is a voice and we do not know from where it comes" (see also Holbe 1987). Subsequently Radio Luxembourg put out an official statement emphasizing that the program was carefully supervised, and that the staff and the engineers were convinced that the voices heard during the program were paranormal. Subsequently König demonstrated his equipment before the German EVP Association, and it is claimed that the deceased Raudive communicated, and that when analyzed his voice print was found to tally with that recorded during his lifetime. The equipment was also successfully demonstrated in the presence of Professor Senkowski and George Meek. On this occasion Senkowski asked the unknown communicator to give the code word that he used in his own ITC experiments ("Aurora"), and this was correctly given. Professor Senkowski attested that "König recorded voices at many different locations ... some ... under controlled conditions. The content of the messages and the process of communication leave no doubt about the paranormality of the voices ... we must conclude that the origin of the voices is in the spirit area in which our departed now reside" (Senkowski 1989; see also Locher and Harsch-Fischbach 1997). When König was challenged over the possibility of fraud, his equipment was exhaustively tested by Professor Senkowski, by physicist Dr. Ralph Determeyer, and by communications expert and electrical engineer R. M. Schaeffer. Their report confirmed the absence in the equipment of any mechanical or electro-magnetic manipulative elements.

How much credibility can we attach to these various results and the supporting statements? The temptation is to dismiss all those involved as too prone to be deceived by stray radio signals captured by poorly constructed amateur equipment all too likely to pick up even local police radios. Or we might prefer the alternative explanation that the researchers concerned were fraudulent, intent on deceiving the public for reasons best known to themselves. There is no denying that it is tempting to write off the above ITC research in either of these ways. Yet the facts suggest otherwise. Firstly, we are not dealing with well-meaning dabblers. Hans Otto König is an engineer working in the field of electro-acoustics who serves as a consultant on acoustics to many leading German business organizations. Scott Rogo was well versed in the controls necessary in good psychical research. Professor Senkowski and Dr. Ralph Determeyer are physicists, and R. M. Schaeffer was a communications expert. Such men would seem unlikely to be too easily fooled. Secondly, there is no evidence that they themselves have ever been involved in fraud of any kind, and no evidence that they had any motive for fraud.

Similarly, the technicians at Radio Luxembourg who supervised König's experiments live on air were hardly likely to be easily deceived, or to hazard their position with their employers or their status with their listeners by conniving in fraud. Furthermore Rainer Holbe, the presenter of the Radio Luxembourg program, was a well-known broadcaster with a reputation to lose. So convinced was he in fact by König's results that he subsequently hosted other Radio Luxembourg programs dealing with ITC, and wrote a book describing his experiences with König and with another leading ITC researcher, Klaus Schreiber (Holbe 1987). While on the subject of the involvement of independent technicians we can also hark back to the demonstration of EVP organized by Raudive and supervised by technicians from Pye Records that convinced the well-known publisher Colin Smythe to bring out the English translation of Raudive's book *Breakthrough* (see Raudive 1971, Bander 1972). In this demonstration, attended by Smythe and other independent observers, four tape recorders, all suitably shielded from radio interference and supervised by the technicians, recorded between them over 200 paranormal communications of which 27 were accepted by those present as clearly understandable.

In addition to supervised experiments of this kind, over the last 30 years there has been a wide range of carefully controlled and conducted investigations that have further supported the paranormality of ITC communications. One of the most interesting was that by Dr. Sinesio Darnell. Darnell's procedure (Darnell 1979) was to invite a colleague to collect, from 30 individuals in Spain and elsewhere in Europe – and to whose identity he remained blind – separate unlabelled audio tapes on which they had each recorded questions of their own choice that could be put to supposed spirit communicators by means of ITC. The individuals were instructed to allow two minutes of silence on their tapes after each of their questions in order to permit ITC answers, if any, to be recorded. The tapes were then randomized. On receipt of the tapes, to whose content he remained blind, Darnell set up two audio tape recorders in his studio, one to play the questions on each of the tapes in turn, and the other to record the questions and the responses, if any, given to them by communicators. No white noise was used. A timer was programmed to switch on both tape recorders simultaneously at random intervals during periods when no one was present in Darnell's studio. Experiments with each of the tapes were allowed to run for several weeks, with each tape played through several times to allow extended opportunity for communicators to respond to the questions concerned. The whole series of experiments took two years to complete.

Results revealed that a number of the questions received audible tape-recorded replies, usually in Spanish although the questions were in a number of European languages. The experiment thus seemed not only to demonstrate paranormality, but to challenge any suggestion that the replies were impressed upon the tapes by psychokinesis from the living. For psychokinesis to have been responsible, one would have to assume that Darnell first used clairvoyance to identify the random moments when the tape recorders were being switched on in his empty studio, and then to identify what questions were being asked (despite the fact that the questions were in a number of different European languages). Following this, he would have had to decide on appropriate answers, and then to impress these answers psychokinetically on the recording tape. Those who prefer this explanation are free to adopt it, but the onus of proof then rests upon them to demonstrate its credibility. Commenting on Darnell's results, Dr. Anabela Cardoso (2003) reports that she has also received ITC communications while leaving tapes running during her absence from her studio (Dr. Cardoso's work will be returned to in due course).

Much of the most challenging research into ITC has been carried out in non-English speaking countries such as Germany, Italy, France, Portugal, and Spain, and it is unfortunate that psychical researchers in other European countries and in the USA who have no familiarity with the languages concerned have been unable to keep abreast of published results. These results are too extensive for me to do more than draw attention to some of the most important of them, such as the work of Franz Seidl, an Austrian electronic engineer at the Vienna College of Science and Technology best known for his pioneering work on the use of tone-modulating high-frequency electrodes in the treatment of deafness (for which he was nominated for the Getty Prize, the engineering equivalent of the Nobel Prize), and who sought like Meek to develop a machine that would facilitate the reception of paranormal voices. The result was the *Psychophone*, a broadband radio receiver designed to receive simultaneously a mixture of different languages that together might provide communicators with a better opportunity to construct their voice sounds than the melange of frequencies present in white noise (Schaeffer 1989, Senkowski 1989, Locher and Harsch-Fischbach 1997). Seidl was convinced that the voices received through the psychophone came from dimensions beyond our space-time continuum and could not therefore be explained in terms of classical physics. Several other experimenters, including Raudive, also claimed to obtain good results with the psychophone, which unlike Meek's Spiricom seemed able to prove helpful to more than one operator.

Anabela Cardoso and Direct Radio Voices (DRV)

Among current researchers, the work of Dr. Anabela Cardoso merits particular mention, not only for the quality of the results obtained but because it provides a valuable insight into the way in which the researcher can progressively develop his or her experience and expertise (Cardoso e.g. 2000a, 2000b, 2003a, 2003b). Dr. Anabela Cardoso, a linguist fluent in six languages and Portugal's senior woman diplomat who has served as Portuguese Chargé d'Affaires in Japan and India and as Consul General in a number of countries including the USA, first became interested in ITC in an attempt to help friends who had recently lost their son in a sailing accident. After familiarizing herself with the work of previous researchers, she began weekly experiments in EVP in 1997 with her two bereaved friends and with electronics expert Carlos Fernandez. Instead of using white noise as background, Dr. Cardoso chose to follow a method pioneered by Friedrich Jürgenson and tune her radio to a short wave foreign language station. After ten weeks without results, the group heard on playing back their tape – recorded against the background noise of a German radio program – the single Spanish word "Si" ("yes") in reply to Dr. Cardoso's recorded question asking if the group was being protected from negative influences.

Her interest aroused, Dr. Cardoso began an intensive experimental program, holding regular EVP sessions on her own three times a week. Switching to white noise as background rather than foreign language broadcasts, she began to use old valve radios as her source, as these were reported as producing better results than solid state receivers. In the course of the experimental program she received a number of EVP voices, but on March 11, 1998, there came a new and totally unexpected development. Recording a question as usual on blank tape she heard an immediate answer given through one of the valve radios. The voice spoke in Portuguese interspersed with Spanish, in both of which languages she is fluent. The experience, startling as it was, led to her switching from EVP to what is known as the Direct Radio Voice (DRV) method. This method, similar to one of those also used by Friedrich Jürgenson, involves asking questions not into a tape recorder as in EVP but directly to a radio tuned to white noise. A tape recorder with an open microphone is kept running in order to capture both the question and any replies that come from the radio. It is claimed by researchers that this is a more advanced method than EVP since it opens up the possibility of direct dialogue with the communicators, but it is said that it is only likely to be successful for those who have already been receiving regular EVP responses.

Successful results with the DRV method prompted Dr. Cardoso to establish, at her own expense, an international journal published in Portuguese, Spanish, and English (*The ITC Journal*), and this now provides a regular forum for the publication and discussion of serious research findings. Her own results included repeated communications from a number of named individuals unknown to her, and also short messages that announced themselves as coming respectively from her deceased grandmother, father (who used the pet name he called her in her childhood), and brother.

After hearing some of Dr. Cardoso's tapes I visited her both in Lyon, where she was Consul General at the time, and in Vigo, Spain, where she has her private residence. In order to study her results more closely and in the hope of being present when further results were obtained. I listened to many of the EVP and DRV tapes in Dr. Cardoso's collection, some in the form in which they were received, and some after software reduction of the background white noise. Many of the voices were indeed loud and relatively clear just as claimed, and some were heard not only to give their names but to respond to questions and even to comment upon events and equipment in Cardoso's studio, just as Dr. Mueller had apparently commented on the events and equipment in O'Neil's workshop. For example, a voice on one of Dr. Cardoso's DRV tapes was heard giving the full name of a maid she had just appointed at the time of the recording, even before she knew the full name herself. Later, on another tape, a voice was heard commenting on the maid's first arrival in the house. DRV voices were also heard commenting on Dr. Cardoso's dogs, and on the presents she had bought for friends. Unlike the EVP voices, which apparently can sometimes be recognized as resembling those of the deceased communicators when alive, these DRV voices, although recognizably male or female, tend to be more uniform, with a characteristic speech distortion. Most of the voices are in Portuguese, a language of which I have sufficient command to identify what is being said, but there are also words in German, Spanish, and English, all languages spoken by Dr. Cardoso.

For Dr. Cardoso, the fact that DRV communications take place at all provides sufficient proof of survival, and the purpose of her research is less to ask communicators personal questions about their past earth lives than to request details on the nature of the next world. The recorded replies to this request insist that survival is a natural law for all beings, including plants; that fundamentally all beings are equal; that this world and the next are very similar; that beings in the next world still have "bodies"; that suffering in this world is very important for spiritual development; that people in this world should always think of the next world because "Whoever thinks of [the next] world reduces the distances"; that reincarnation is a sporadic event and happens "only when there is no other way"; that Group Souls (groups to which like-minded souls belong) are a reality; that mediumship in the investigator is not necessary in order to receive EVP or DRV communications; and that entities in the next world are "outside time" and live "on an edge of space" (whatever that means).

Some of the recorded DRV replies taped by Dr. Cardoso take the form of single words of assent or disagreement in response to her questions, others introduce concepts of their own. In many cases the clarity, though not perfect, is good. In general, the connection between question and answer, and the relevance of the statements relating to Cardoso's personal life, make it clear that the recordings cannot be dismissed as stray radio broadcasts misinterpreted by listeners. Further confirmation of this comes from the fact that the communicators claim to belong to a group in the next world intent upon demonstrating survival that calls itself *Rio de Tempo* ("River of Time" or "Timestream"). This name is in fact used as the group's call sign, and I have heard it repeated very many times not only on the recordings but when I have been in Dr. Cardoso's studio (sometimes alone) when the radios have been left switched on. The words are unmistakable.

One of the most consistent of Dr. Cardoso's communicators – and certainly the clearest and most articulate – named himself as Carlos de Almeida, and reported that he had died as a political prisoner in a Portuguese prison at an unspecified date in the past. Sometimes, to judge by the DRV recordings, the background white noise fell almost completely silent while he was speaking. At other times his voice was so loud that a member of Cardoso's domestic staff heard it clearly while some distance away in the garden. Unfortunately, as so often happens in psychical research, this promising period during the investigation came to an end when Almeida ceased to communicate, and Dr. Cardoso was told by other voices that he had moved on to a higher plane of the afterlife from where communication by ITC is not possible. ("Almeida" is a relatively common Portuguese surname, and records held of political prisoners who died in captivity are few and far between, but attempts are still being made to check the details given of his life.)

The great majority of Cardoso's DRV recordings have been made while she is working on her own, and the possibility of fraud or interference by other people can be effectively ruled out. Dr. Cardoso herself is regarded by all who know her as a person of unimpeachable integrity, and the notion that a high-ranking diplomat in her position would compromise herself by faking supposed spirit communications is out of the question. There can be no doubt that the recordings made by her and to which I have listened are genuine. Nevertheless, I was naturally anxious to be present when further results were obtained, and I have subsequently had many opportunities to observe Dr. Cardoso at work. Her studio (at one time she had studios both in France and in Spain, but is now based in Spain) is equipped with two ICF SW77 state of the art Sony short wave radios, one Sony ICF SW7600GR short wave radio, and two elderly valve radios. Sometimes the radios, each of which is tuned to a different short wave band, are left on day and night, as apparently this facilitates the work of the communicators. While staying in the house I have frequently heard voices from the radios at unexpected times of the day or night that are so loud and seemingly insistent that I have entered the empty studio in the hope of hearing communications. Typically the speech has proved too distorted for me to make out individual words apart from "Rio de Tempo," and the impression given is more like someone testing the line than someone attempting to communicate.

More importantly, I have also been present on several occasions in Dr.

Cardoso's studios both in France and in Spain when she has carried out conversations in Portuguese with communicators, many of which I was able to follow. As with the recordings to which I have listened, there seems no doubt that the communicators are responding directly to comments and questions from Dr. Cardoso, although sometimes she has to repeat the same question several times over before a reply is heard. The distortion characteristic of many of the communications presents a problem for the listener, but the volume is that of a normal human voice. It is impossible to convey in print the exact nature of this distortion, but it is unlike that heard from badly tuned short wave stations. It is perhaps best described as nasal, with heavily slurred enunciation. During all the sessions at which I have been present the communications have come through only one or other of the array of radios (though Dr. Cardoso reports that on occasions a reply has started to come through one radio and then been completed through one of the others, even though they are both tuned to quite different frequencies on the short wave band).

A thorough examination of all the equipment in both the studios, which on every visit I have been free to make at my leisure and in my own way at any time of the day or night, has revealed no cause for suspicion. The radios are all mains operated, and each of the Sonys had its own external aerial. Two air microphones are used, one placed near the investigator and the other near the radios. The sound picked up by the microphones is then conveyed via a mixing table to a high quality Panasonic tape recorder. Apart from the radios and these other items of equipment, the studio are kept intentionally bare. There are no other tape recorders or other items of audio equipment present. I have also been free to examine the grounds outside the studios (both in France and in Spain the studios are in detached houses set in their own gardens well back from the road) and found nothing to arouse any suspicion. In any case, it would be unrealistic to suppose that, even were it feasible for a hidden accomplice to transmit spurious material for reception by the radios during my presence, he or she could have been nearby, undetected, during each of the lengthy experimental sessions in which I have taken part.

Nevertheless, it was clearly important to ascertain whether or not I was able to obtain results for myself, and under my own conditions. The protocol I used was very simple. During one of the sessions in the studio in Lyon, when several communications in Portuguese had been obtained, I broke in to ask if the communicators could speak to me in English (using English myself). The reply, although distorted, both Dr. Cardoso and I agreed seemed to be "Help me prove I'm alive." I then asked the communicators if they could repeat two phrases that I offered to them, namely "Hello David" and "How are you?" In reply there came a sentence in English, the only words of which I could understand were " ... there will be no time until tomorrow ... ", and this was followed, much more clearly, by "Hello David," and by "How are you?" There is no question other than that these replies came through the radio that was receiving all the communications at the time. The radios are placed separately in the studio, and it is possible to identify which of them is receiving the voices at any one time.

An important feature of this test was that I had said nothing about it beforehand to Dr. Cardoso or indeed to anyone else, and had never suggested that it would be useful to see if the communicators could repeat words offered by me. Thus it would have been impossible for Dr. Cardoso to have made provision in advance to fake these results by pre-recording the replies and, for reasons already outlined, the suggestion that an accomplice might have been involved in any of the work carried out in the studio is untenable.

I tried the same test on a separate occasion, in Dr. Cardoso's Spanish studio. She was of course aware that this was the test I had tried in the past, but not that I intended to repeat it. I used the same words as before in order to ensure that, if they were repeated, there would be no question of mistaken interpretation of what was heard. Once again "Hello David" and "How are you?" were repeated at my request. The tape of this test has been played to the five members of the Survival Research Committee of the SPR, which I currently chair, and all have confirmed they hear the relevant words. I am continuing to work with Dr. Cardoso and the hope is that the communicators, who report they are experimenting with ways to improve the sound quality of their messages, will succeed in their endeavors. However, psychical research is a particularly uncertain field, and there are periods of time when no communications of any kind are received. It is Dr. Cardoso's hope that at some point the communicators will make clear what environmental conditions facilitate or impede their efforts. There is some suggestion that atmospheric conditions may play some part, but the reasons for this are unclear.

Another experimenter reported to have obtained successful results with DRV is Italian researcher Marcello Bacci. For over 35 years Bacci and a small group of colleagues at the Psychophonic Center in Grosseto, Italy, have been receiving communications by this method, using an old valve radio tuned to the short wave band. Bacci's particular concern is to obtain communications from children for their bereaved parents, and in this he has apparently met with considerable success. His method is reported as turning the dial of his radio slowly through the wave band until he finds a point at which the white noise changes to a noise resembling the sound of the wind. Communications then become possible. Professor Mario Festa, professor of nuclear physics at the University of Naples, began researching the Bacci voices in 1996, and is in no doubt of their authenticity (Festa 2002). In the presence of colleagues from Il Laboratorio, an Italian research center founded specifically to test the authenticity of paranormal acoustic phenomena, Professor Festa has carried out tests on the electric and magnetic high frequency fields registered by Bacci's radio while the paranormal communications are being received, and has ascertained that there is no significant variation in either of them. In his view this validates the authenticity of the voice phenomenon, because if the voices were transmitted fraudulently from a terrestrial source both these fields would show a measurable increase.

Festa also details an experiment in which, in his presence and on his initiative, both the frequency modulation valve and the local medium frequency oscillation valve were removed from Bacci's radio by electronic engineer Franco Santi while the communications were being received. Removal of these two valves would silence reception of radio transmission across all wave bands, yet even in their absence the communications continued without any loss of signal and continued to do so when, as a further test and with the valves still absent, Festa moved the tuning up and down the frequencies. His conclusion was that these results turn upside down the standard laws of physics (Festa ibid 2002).

Visual ITC Images

ITC therefore appears to have come some way from the early experiments of Jürgenson and of Raudive, when critics suggested that the voices could be stray radio transmissions. Further progress is claimed to include the reception of paranormal images through the television. The name particularly associated with such images is that of Klaus Schreiber, a German saddlesmith whose life was visited by almost unbearable tragedy. His first wife, Gertrude, died young, and he lost his son Robert at age 22 and his daughter Karin at age 18. Shortly after Karin's death his nephew and his sister (the boy's mother) died, and his brother-in-law committed suicide. Some ten years later he lost his second wife, and suffered from a great deal of ill health himself. It might be supposed that faced with these sad events Schreiber was exactly the kind of man who would visit mediums and become too readily persuaded of survival. In fact his interest in survival research was aroused not through these events or through research into mediumship but through one of the Radio Luxembourg programs presented by Rainer Holbe, mentioned above in connection with the work of Hans Otto König. Inspired by this to try his own experiments, Schreiber succeeded in recording voices using Seidl's psychophone instead of white noise as background. Some of the voices were recognizable as those of deceased individuals known to Schreiber, and his results were subsequently confirmed as genuine by Professor Senkowski (Senkowski 1989).

In 1985, allegedly at the suggestion of his communicators, Schreiber then attempted to obtain their images through his television set or through video tape. His first two methods involved respectively simply gazing at empty TV channels and leaving his video camera hooked up to the TV and trained upon an empty chair. When these two methods proved unsuccessful he developed more sophisticated techniques, eventually using a combination of equipment consisting of a television set, a black and white video monitor, a number of video recorders, two separate video amplifiers, and a video camera aimed at an angle and slightly off center at the television screen. The output from the video camera was then fed back into the monitor, forming an electro optical feedback loop. The first successful result was of a hazy image repeated many times, as when one stands between two mirrors. Adjustments to the distance between the camera and the screen and to the camera angle and the video output led to the recording of light patterns which he then played back at very slow speed, often frame by frame. This produced some washed out images that looked promising, and these were then videoed from the screen, often several times, using the same procedure. This time-consuming process produced recognizable human faces from the washed-out images. Some of these were of Schreiber's deceased relatives, others of deceased public figures such as film stars Romy Schneider and Kurt Juergens.

Studying these photographs, Professor Senkowski considered their resemblance to photographs of the same individuals taken during their lifetimes was sufficiently close to allow them to be dismissed as images picked up from stray television transmissions. Apparently as a result of information from the communicators that he was still receiving through ITC audio recordings, he then tried video-taping a normal TV channel, and playing back the tape until he noticed what appeared to be a small, brief change in the picture. During very slow playback of the five or six frames concerned, the paranormal face of his deceased daughter appeared. Continuing to use this method he subsequently received images of his first wife, of his father, and of his deceased sister and brother-in-law. A month after her death an image of his second wife also appeared. After his own death in 1988, Schreiber's friend and collaborator, Martin Wenzel, continued his work, apparently with successful results.

Rainer Holbe, the Radio Luxembourg presenter who had been so impressed by the on-air demonstration of ITC by Hans Otto König, also took an interest in Schreiber's work, and his book (Holbe 1987) contains many of Schreiber's video images. A number of them also appear in Locher and Harsch-Fischbach (ibid. 1997). There is no doubt of the quality of these images, or of their close resemblance to the photographs of the same people taken in life. If, as Senkowski suggests, this resemblance does indeed rule out the accidental capture of stray television transmissions we are left once more with only two plausible explanations, either the images are genuinely paranormal or they are faked. If the former, are they best explained as psychokinesis from Schreiber or as evidence for survival? Schreiber did appear to have some psychic abilities, and we know from Eisenbud's work with Ted Serios (Eisenbud 1989) that some individuals appear able to impress images on film by thought alone. But there is a difference between capturing images on video tape that only become visible when subsequently put through the processes used by Schreiber, and the still images captured directly on film by Ted Serios. Another difference is that not only did Schreiber receive his video images, he also reported receiving messages on audio tape that referred to the images and gave guidance as to how they could best be obtained.

In addition, could Schreiber have obtained his complex and detailed results yet at the same time remained unaware that he was the agent? Ted Serios produced his "thoughtography" images by gazing with intense and sustained concentration into the camera lens. Schreiber by contrast made no attempt to influence the images he received, and far from looking into his video camera it was turned away from him and towards the television screen. On balance it would seem difficult to sustain psychokinesis from the living as the preferred explanation to that of survival for Schreiber's images. What of the possibility of fraud? Video tapes can be readily faked, and unlike audio tapes which can be subjected to acoustic analysis they are not easy to subject to scientific test. However, experienced investigators such as Professor Senkowski and Rainer Holbe who knew Schreiber personally and made a close study of his work were satisfied that his results were genuine. And Schreiber is not the only one to have received apparently paranormal images in the course of ITC research. In Luxembourg Maggy and Jules Harsch-Fischbach, teacher and civil servant respectively, who have spent many years experimenting with ITC and who are regarded by those working in the area as two of the leading pioneers, received images on a television screen in 1987 – having previously been alerted by ITC audio communications of the hour at which these would appear – in the presence of Professor and Mrs. Senkowski., Professor Resch, professor of clinical psychology at the Lateran University in Rome, and George Meek. These images were of the same quality as those recorded by Schreiber. One of them was that of an unknown man, and a little later his name and date of death were given during an audio recording (Henri Sainte-Claire de Ville, died 1881). It is reported that none of those present had heard of the name, and that subsequent research confirmed a French chemist of that name had indeed died in the year given.

At various times the images of both Jürgenson and Raudive have appeared during the experiments by the Harsch-Fischbachs (reproduced in Locher and Harsch-Fischbach, 1997, together with other examples), and although the likeness in each case with photographs taken of the two men during their lifetime is readily apparent, it is claimed that no photographs identical to those received are in existence. In 1988 the Harsch-Fischbachs received both sound and paranormal image simultaneously during their TV experiments, and also received at least one image of a person in movement, said to be recognizable as Maria Jakubowski, the deceased relative of friends of the experimenters. Images of pastoral scenes, claimed to be of the next world, were also received, as were a number of computer images of comparable clarity, including one of Schreiber himself after his death. Professor Francois Brune, who reports these events and who was present when some of the images were received, is in no doubt that normal explanations can be ruled out (Brune 1993).

Criticisms of ITC Research

A major problem for those hearing about these various results is that they sound quite simply too good to be true. And there are two obvious problems with many of them, namely that they were not produced under conditions controlled by independent observers, and that some of the researchers are unfamiliar with the need to give full details of all their experimental procedures and protocols. This means that in many cases it is all too easy to suggest there were inadequacies in these procedures and protocols that could have allowed error to intrude. In addition, there is often little attempt by ITC researchers to persuade communicators to give the kind of personal details that would enable their claimed identities to be verified. These details would strengthen the evidence for survival, and also counter the charge that although the communications may be paranormal, those from whom they come may be impostors of the kind that have sometimes intruded into physical séances. Locher and Harsch-Fischbach (1997) give a warning in fact of the "dangers that are threatening us from deceased low-level earthbound beings ... [who] ... continue indulging in their desires; inclinations or passions by influencing sensitive people on Earth," and to the fact that some ITC researchers have come "under the control of low-level beings who are able to imitate the voices of higher beings."

A further problem is that disagreements among some of the leading ITC researchers have disturbed the co-operative spirit in which much of the early work was carried out (see Macy 2001 for a discussion), leading to a breakdown in consensus on methodology and protocol. The enthusiasm of many researchers has also led them to neglect the cautious, objective approach that is so much a part of scientific methodology, and/or to overlook the fact that many apparent communications from the deceased, even if paranormal, cannot be taken at face value. Nevertheless, in spite of these reservations, there is enough data to show the potential importance of ITC for survival research and for parapsychology in general. As always in psychical research there is no substitute for personal experience, and I have been fortunate in gaining this experience while observing and participating in the work of Dr. Anabela Cardoso. Along with other researchers she takes the view that ITC offers an ideal opportunity for individuals, provided they take the necessary safeguards against self-deception and possibly intrusions from unwanted communicators, to engage in their own research. Mediumship is seems is not essential in order to obtain results, and if George Meek is to be believed ITC has an advantage over mediumship in that communications are not channeled through the human mind, with all the possibilities for error that this channeling may involve.

In conclusion, it seems appropriate to say that, assuming results continue to be obtained through ITC (all too often in the past we have seemed on the verge of a major breakthrough in psychical research only to be frustrated by a weakening of the phenomena), there seems every possibility that an important new chapter in survival research is in the process of being written. Acoustic analysis of some of the voices received by Dr Cardoso and by the other researchers reveal that they contain acoustic anomalies incomparible with the human voice. Further analysis of this kind is clearly a priority, and if earlier results are confirmed, such anomalies will help to put the paranormality of ITC communications further beyond question.

CHAPTER 15

NEAR-DEATH EXPERIENCES

The Process of Dying as Communicated Through Mediums

An interest in survival usually involves not only the question whether or not we survive, but what is the nature of this survival and what form does the transition between life and death take. The nature of a possible afterlife is returned to in detail in Chapter 18, but what can we say about the transition and the extent to which our knowledge of it adds to the evidence that life goes on after death?

The literature on mediumship contains many accounts of this transition supposedly given by communicators. One of the most comprehensive collections of these accounts is by Dr. Robert Crookall. A distinguished botanist, geologist, and Doctor of Science who also had a degree in psychology, Crookall was Principal Geologist in the Department of Scientific and Industrial Research at Her Majesty's Geological Survey, UK. His longstanding interest in the question of survival led him, after retirement, to collect first-hand accounts of communications by the deceased through mediums in which they described the process of dying. Together with these accounts, he also collected first-hand descriptions of what have come to be called Out of the Body Experiences (OBEs) and Near-Death Experiences (NDEs), some from the literature (stretching back to the early twentieth century) and some from reports collected in the course of his personal research. Crookall published these accounts in a number of books (e.g. Crookall 1961, 1965, 1978) which have never achieved the attention they deserved, perhaps because on the one hand his rather dry and over-academic style does not appeal to popular readers, while on the other his populist titles are too sensationalist to capture the attention of scientists.

Crookall analyzed the accounts of the dying process in order to identify the various common features arising from them, and these features are worth looking at. Firstly, Crookall found that communicators frequently mentioned being aware of leaving their physical bodies at the moment of death, and seeing around them relatives and friends known to have died, much as are reported in deathbed visions. Here are three examples.

1. *I saw about me those that had been dead for a long time ... Then I seemed to rise up and out of my body and come down quietly on the floor ... There seemed to be two of me, one on the bed and one beside the bed ... I was gently told [by those who had died] what had happened.*
2. *... I saw that I was not lying in the bed, but floating in the air, a little above it. I*

saw the body stretched out ... My first idea was that I might re-enter it, but all desire to do this soon left me ... I saw my [deceased grandfather], he had been with me all through.

3. I seemed to be lifted above the usual surroundings. I was ... with those who had passed over recently ... I was not conscious of any change or of anything abrupt ... I knew I was not on earth because of the long-lost people around me.

A second common feature identified by Crookall from the accounts given by the deceased was the frequent mention of doors and tunnels.

1. When I was dying there was a door I could see in the corner of the room. I knew that when it was open wide, I would go through.
2. ... I felt as though I had gone through a door ...
3. I remember a curious opening, as if one had passed through subterranean passages and found oneself near the mouth of a cave ... the light was much stronger outside.

Thirdly, there were many references to an expansion of consciousness.

1. Then there was relief, expansion, a sense of being freed from an intolerable weight. I came out into a strange clearness and could not believe that I had died.
2. The transition was interesting and delightful. I expanded in every direction. I was boundless, was infinite ...
3. After you die the soul suddenly seems to expand.

In the great majority of accounts collected by Crookall there is no mention of any pain or alarm during the dying process, while any physical pain that was being experienced before death disappears. The physical body, which is still visible to the deceased until they leave the sick room or are transported away from it, appears to them like a discarded garment in which they have no interest and for which they have no further use. The process of dying seems so easy and so natural that in some cases the fact that death has taken place is not at first realized. Often there are references to attempts to talk to living relatives and friends grieving at the bedside, but without result. It is said not surprisingly that if the grief observed by the deceased appears unduly strong this can be distressing for the deceased, as can their inability to attract the attention of those concerned and assure them that all is well.

The majority of accounts speak of the deceased possessing a body analogous to the physical body, and although initially this may be naked, it is reported that should this cause any embarrassment in the owner it immediately becomes clothed, usually in normal everyday dress. Sometimes the deceased are said to have been held near the physical body by a connecting cord or thread of some kind (said to be the "silken cord" referred to in Ecclesiastes 12:6), and that when this connection between the two bodies is finally loosened they are free to go, usually to be conducted by spirit "helpers" away from the sick room and towards the next world. Accounts of what is said to transpire from this point onwards will be looked at in Chapter 18.

It could be argued by critics that although all this sounds interesting, it may provide less evidence for survival than it does for the medium's over-active imagination, and that in any case there is no way in which we can check on their reality. However, although the above accounts were collected before the current publicity given to so-called near-death experiences (i.e. experiences reported by some individuals who have been briefly at or near clinical death and then revived), they show in some cases marked similarities with them. These similarities will become more apparent when we look at near-death experiences in a moment, but they include the sense of consciousness being located outside the physical body, the ability to see one's own body from this externalized position and to see bystanders but not to make contact with them, the awareness of spirits known to the deceased in life and of a tunnel or door, and the sense of peace and tranquility and of a disinclination to return to the physical body.

Near-Death Experiences (NDEs)

The dividing line between life and death has never been clear-cut, and with modern resuscitation methods it is now less so than ever. People are regularly revived after their breathing and their hearts have stopped, and even the absence of brain activity (known as "brain death") may not be an infallible indication that death has taken place. What happens to the mind of the individual at the shadowy borderline between life and death, when to all intents and purposes the person has breathed or is about to breath his or her last? What happens during the interval when the heart has stopped beating and but for speedy medical intervention would never start again?

If there is only a period of oblivion, this does nothing to support the idea that anything is likely to survive death. On the other hand, if there is a continuation of consciousness, then this looks promising for those who consider survival is a possibility – even more so if this continuation of consciousness is lucid and coherent, and consists not just of earth-memories but of the apparently objective experience of leaving the body. In addition, if consciousness persists at this time it deepens the mystery as to what consciousness is and where it is located. If the body appears not to be essential for the continuation of consciousness during apparent physical death, this strengthens the possibility that it is not essential for the continuation of consciousness when actual death occurs, and the possibility that consciousness – mind, soul, call it what we will – can then continue into whatever new form of existence awaits it.

The evidence that consciousness does indeed appear to persist during the moments either when the body is clinically dead or near death has been mounting steadily in recent years. A new set of research studies has in fact grown up around these so-called near-death experiences (NDEs), although the first extensive account of a return from apparent death in fact occurs in Plato's *Republic*, dating from the fourth century BCE. Plato tells us that a Greek soldier, Er, was apparently killed in battle, and his body taken home 12 days later for burial. On the funeral pyre (in the nick of time one might say) he suddenly revived and told a strange story. After his apparent death his soul had left his body, and together with the soldiers killed around him he found himself traveling to a strange country where he witnessed his companions choosing their next lives (whether in this world or in the next world is unclear). This may have been a form of the "life review" or "self-judgment," to which we return in Chapter 18. Subsequently they drank from the river of forgetfulness in order to discard memories of their past lives (if such a river, symbolic or otherwise, exists this may explain the strange memory lapses reported all too often in those who communicate through mediums!). However, Er was not allowed to drink from the river, and hence on his return was able to recall what had happened to him during his apparent clinical death. The implication is that he was deliberately sent back to share his experience of survival with others.

We can come forward some two thousand years to our next example of an NDE, that of the American doctor, Dr. A. S. Wiltse, who was in a near-death coma from typhoid fever, without perceptible pulse for four hours and without detectable breathing for 30 minutes. His doctor, named as Dr. S. H. Raynes, pronounced him dead, and the village church bell began to toll for him. An account of Dr. Wiltse's experiences during this time appeared in the *St. Louis Medical and Surgical Journal* for November 1899, and is quoted by F. W. H. Myers, one of the founders of the SPR (Myers 1903) and many years later by Rawlings (1978), a doctor of medicine who made a special study of NDEs. In this account, Wiltse relates that he felt himself separating from his body "like a soap bubble," and floating up and down laterally until the separation was complete. He then fell lightly to the floor, and seemed now to have resumed the shape of a man.

I seemed to be translucent, of a bluish cast, and perfectly naked. As I turned, my elbow came into contact with the arm of one of two gentlemen standing near the door ... his arm passed through mine without resistance ... I looked quickly up at his face ... but he gave no sign ... [I] saw my own dead body ... lying just as I had ... [composed] it, partially on the right side, the feet close together and the hands clasped across the breast ... I was surprised at the paleness of the face ... [I] attempted to gain the attention of the people [at the bedside] with the object of ... reassuring them of my own immortality ... but found they gave me no heed ... the situation struck me as humorous and I laughed outright ... I concluded that they "are watching what they think is I, but they are mistaken." That is not I ... I am as much alive as ever. How well I feel ... Only a few minutes ago I was horribly sick and distressed. Then came the change called death which I have so much dreaded. This has passed now, and here I am still a man ... thinking as clearly as ever ... how well I feel ... I shall never be sick again, I have no more to die.

Dr. Wiltse then describes being lifted up by unseen hands and transported along a beautiful road until he finds his way barred by rocks and is told that if he crosses this barrier he will not be able to return to his body. However, he is also told that if he feels his work is not yet complete on earth he can return. He attempts to cross but at that point the decision is made for him, and he is stopped by a "small black cloud." The moment it touches his face he finds himself back in his body.

... in astonishment and disappointment I exclaimed "What in the world has happened to me? Must I die again?"

He relates his experiences to those around him, who testify both to his physical condition during the interlude and to the account he gives of his experiences.

This experience provides us with a number of the features reported in the modern NDE cases that we shall be looking at shortly, and has several things in common with the accounts of transitions given through mediums. For example, Wiltse experienced no pain on separation from his physical body; once the separation was complete he found he possessed a body analogous in shape to his physical body; he was able to see his physical body on the bed; he was able to see the people in the sick room but unable to attract their attention; he felt no fear or alarm; all his feelings of sickness left him; he was taken away by helpers (represented by unseen hands rather than by deceased relatives and friends); he was sent back to his body by some force that appeared to recognize he still had work to do on earth; he was reluctant to return; and on regaining consciousness he was convinced that he had indeed been dead during the NDE experience.

Now for a more modern case. Like Wiltse and many others, Damian Brinkley was also convinced of the reality of his NDE. Struck by lightning and in terrible pain (even the nails of his shoes were welded to the floor by the heat), Brinkley suddenly found himself "engulfed by peace and tranquility. It was a feeling I had never known before and have not had since. It was like bathing in a glorious calmness." Below him he saw his own body, with his shoes smoking and the telephone he had been holding melted in his hand. He saw his wife run into the room and try to revive him by pumping his chest, but his own feelings were "as dispassionate about watching my own death as I might be if I were watching actors re-enact it on television." He revives briefly under treatment from paramedics, but then leaves his body again, and hears himself pronounced dead. He then goes through a tunnel, meets a being of light, and eventually agrees reluctantly to come back to undertake a mission he feels has been given to him. Some time later he has another near-death experience as a consequence of coronary arrest, and again returns reluctantly to his body in order to fulfill his mission, which he is convinced is to work with the dying (Brinkley and Perry 1994).

The experience of being sent back to their bodies in order to complete a mission of some kind (usually involving service to others) is a particularly common feature in reported NDE cases. Sometimes the force that sends the person back – or gives them the choice whether or not to return – is unseen, sometimes it is described as a "being of light," sometimes as deceased relatives or friends. The individual is often given a choice, as initially was Wiltse, and elects to return because of family or professional commitments (presumably this choice is only given where the physical body remains viable). At other times they are simply told, gently but firmly, that it is not yet time for them to make the transition, and that they must go back. In the great majority of cases, subjects report returning with great reluctance. Eadie (1995) writes that her mission on earth was explained to her, and she was told she must decide whether to return in order to carry it out, or remain in the next world.

Afterwards, I knew that I had to come back. Although I would hate to leave that glorious world of light and love for one of hardship and uncertainty, the necessity of my mission compelled me to return.

Joe McMoneagle, one of the most successful participants in the Stargate remote viewing program funded by the US Military, the FBI, and the CIA, also had the experience of being sent back during an NDE. After a heart attack McMoneagle watched from outside his body while paramedics took him to hospital. Once there he saw the doctors attempting to restart his heart by shocking it, and then felt himself leave the hospital and pass through a tunnel before finding himself in the presence of a being of light. At this point he recognized that "There is no comparable place in physical reality to experience such total awareness. The love, protection, joy, giving, sharing, and being that I experienced in the Light at that moment was absolutely overwhelming and pure in its essence." But McMoneagle is told by the being of light that he must go back, and in spite of his attempts to argue against the decision he finds himself once more in his body (McMoneagle 1997). McMoneagle now devotes his life to teaching remote viewing skills as a way of expanding human awareness of other levels of reality.

In spite of earlier accounts of NDEs such as that by Wiltse and those published in Crookall's various books, the experience did not attract much general interest until 1975 when Raymond Moody, another medical doctor, wrote *Life After Life* in which he presented a range of case studies. Moody's book performed a valuable service in bringing such case histories to general attention. Of particular importance was the fact that many of the individuals presented in his case studies also reported observing, from a position outside their bodies, verifiable visual details of some of the events apparently taking place around their beds while they were unconscious. This is in fact a common feature of NDEs, and provides us with evidence that the people concerned may actually have been outside their bodies. A good example of one such case is given by Clark (1984). It concerned a woman, Maria, who suffered a cardiac arrest while being operated on in a Seattle hospital. During the arrest, she felt herself leave her body, and found herself outside the building where she was able to see in great detail a tennis shoe on the window ledge outside a third floor window. On regaining consciousness she related the incident to Kimberly Clark, a social worker at the hospital, who went up to the third floor and was able to verify the existence of the shoe and retrieve it for closer inspection. The details given by Maria of the position and the appearance of the shoe were correct. Maria had been admitted to hospital during the night and had been on her back in bed or in the operating theatre ever since, and Clark verified that even if she had been outside the hospital in daylight the shoe was not visible from ground level. In addition, some wear on the toe of the shoe which featured in Maria's description could have been seen only from a position outside the window and not from inside the hospital. For these various reasons Clark was satisfied that Maria could have had no opportunity to see the shoe by normal means (Clark 1984). Thus it appeared as if Maria had indeed been out of her body during the NDE as claimed. The only other paranormal explanation would be that she saw the shoe clairvoyantly without leaving the operating theatre, but this is not how the patient herself reported and interpreted the experience, and clairvoyance does not normally involve feelings of leaving one's body or the lengthy and coherent sequence of events that Maria described while she was out. In addition, unlike clairvoyance, she had no particular target in mind. She decided to leave the hospital and travel outside, but she had no particular aim in mind, and certainly no intention of searching for a tennis shoe of whose existence she was in ignorance.

The Research of Martin Sabom

One of the most thorough early investigations into NDEs was by Dr. Martin Sabom, a cardiologist who specialized in resuscitations. Sabom, whose interest in the subject was aroused by Moody's book, embarked on a five-year study of NDEs that involved interviewing resuscitated patients in order to establish whether or not they reported similar experiences to those collected by Moody (Sabom 1982). Sabom recognized the difficulty, still not resolved by the medical profession, of determining whether or not resuscitated patients had been clinically dead or near death, and decided to use as a criterion "any bodily state resulting from an extreme physiological catastrophe ... that would reasonably be expected to result in irreversible biological death in the majority of instances and would demand urgent medical attention." Such conditions would include cardiac arrest, severe traumatic injury, and deep comatose conditions resulting from metabolic derangement or systematic illness. With the exception of individuals with known psychiatric illness, Sabom contacted all intensive care patients in the two Florida hospitals who had survived the near-death condition and requested interviews. Patients were not told the purpose of the interview and there was no prompting from Sabom during it. They were simply asked whether or not they had had any experiences while unconscious. If they had and were prepared to talk about them, these were tape recorded.

Of the 78 patients interviewed by Sabom, 34 (43 per cent) reported an NDE. There was no overall difference in religious belief or observance between the group that reported NDEs and the group that did not. In addition, more of those without NDEs had prior knowledge of such experiences than did those with NDEs, which suggests that the expectation that one might have an NDE played no part in whether the experience occurred or not. Initially, Sabom assumed that the accounts given would contain "obvious inconsistencies ... which would reduce these purported [bedside] visions to no more than an educated guess on the part of the patient," but contrary to his expectations he found a high degree of agreement among the accounts given by the 34 patients. All of them reported that they were conscious of apparent separation from their physical bodies, and that the predominant emotions experienced during the NDE were calmness and peace. Ninety-two per cent (29) of them reported a subjective sense of being dead, 53 per cent of them reported an awareness of their physical bodies while separated from them, and 54 per cent reported traveling to transcendent realms ("paradise conditions"). Fifty-three per cent experienced both physical and transcendental conditions, while 33 per cent experienced only physical conditions, and 48 per cent only transcendental. Twenty-eight per cent saw a bright light, and 48 per cent were aware of meeting other beings or deceased people. Twenty-three per cent reported encountering a dark region or void at some point at the start of their transcendental experiences that seemed analogous to the "tunnel" experience.

All those reporting NDEs were aware of a return to their bodies. Sometimes this return was instantaneous, but in most cases there was a sense of being sent back, often against their will, by deceased relatives or other beings, usually because it was "not yet their time" or because they had "unfinished business" to attend to. Those reporting an awareness of their physical surroundings sometimes gave clear details of the resuscitation equipment and methods used, although they claimed to have no prior knowledge of any of these. Not surprisingly, Dr. Sabom was also interested in the after-effects of the NDE upon those who had had the experience. After all, how would you feel if you were convinced that you had died, that you had remained conscious and felt calm and peaceful, that you had left your body and seen the room in which you died from a vantage point outside your body, that you had traveled to what seemed like paradise conditions and met there people you knew to have died before being sent reluctantly back to your body? Would life ever seem the same again? Would death carry the same meaning as before? Results from Sabom's sample showed that 82 per cent of those in his sample who had had NDE experiences now had less fear of death, and 77 per cent had an increased belief in an afterlife. By comparison, figures for a reduced fear of death and for an increased belief in an afterlife for those in the sample who had not had an NDE were just over two per cent and zero per cent respectively. Conviction that one had died therefore was indeed life changing.

Psychologists are naturally interested in any event that produces such a marked and abrupt change in core human beliefs such as the meaning of life and death. Fear of Death (or FOD as we psychologists like to call it – and we have tests designed to measure the level of this fear) is known to be generally lower in those with religious beliefs than in those without (Koenig, McCullough, and Larson 2001), but in the case of Sabom's sample, there was no difference in prior religious belief between those who had experienced an NDE during their medical emergency and those who had not. Therefore Sabom attributed the decrease in this fear and the increase in belief in an afterlife among the NDE group to the NDE itself (we are not told whether or not those in the NDE group who did not register an increased belief in an afterlife already had a strong prior conviction of its reality, so that the NDE simply corresponded to what they already knew).

The Work of Kenneth Ring

This radical change in the belief systems of those who have experienced NDEs was subsequently explored in even more detail by Professor Ken Ring. Ring, who had written an earlier book on the subject of NDEs that helped establish the consistent nature of the experience and confirm the work of earlier researchers (Ring 1980), now carried out extensive interviews with 111 people who reported having had NDEs. Full details of his research methods are given in Ring (1984), but the responses of his sample revealed a consistent range of important after-effects. Characteristically all fear of death had been removed; life goals and values had changed in more spiritually attuned directions; greater emphasis was now placed upon love and compassion; and belief in spiritual realities had increased, a belief that tended to be broadly based rather than narrowly religious. Some of the sample even reported they were now aware of possessing significant psychic abilities. Those who had experienced their NDEs many years previously insisted that the experience remained fresh in their minds, as did the conviction that they really had died and now knew the reality of survival. (Further examples of the transforming power of near-death experiences are given in Moody and Perry 1989.)

Ring subsequently set out to try to answer another intriguing question, do those who are born blind and who have NDEs experience vision during them? If they do – having never known what sight is like – the case for the reality of the NDE is greatly strengthened. With the help of eleven American Associations for the Blind and a newspaper advertisement followed by screening interviews, Ken Ring and his co-researcher Sharon Cooper identified 21 blind individuals who satisfied Ring's criteria for having had NDEs, namely conscious experiences associated with unquestionably life-threatening conditions (Ring and Cooper 1999). Not all the 21 were born blind. Nine had lost their sight after age five (and were classified by the researchers as "adventitiously blind"), and two were severely visually impaired. The remaining ten had never experienced sight, however limited.

In-depth interviews with those reporting NDEs established that of the ten individuals blind from birth, five reported they were sighted during the experience. The other five either had no sight or were unsure whether they had sight or not. Of the 11 adventitiously blind or severely visually impaired, all except one reported having what seemed to be normal vision during the NDE. In addition, of the total sample of 21, ten claimed to have seen their bodies after leaving them during their NDEs. The interviews also established that the experiences of those who claimed to have sight during the NDE – feelings of separation from the physical body, journeys through a tunnel or dark space, feelings of peace and well-being, encounters with a bright light, and a life review – were virtually indistinguishable from the experiences reported by sighted people.

Two of the case studies of those born blind, those of Vicki Umipeg and Brad Barrows respectively, contain accounts of particularly clear vision of both earthly and "paradise" conditions during the NDE. The details given of the earth conditions are seemingly accurate, but due to the time elapsing since the experiences the researchers could not confirm this. Both Vicki Umipeg and Brad Barrows reported that their experience of sight was initially confusing, but while Vicki found this disorientating Brad was less worried by it, and his descriptions of his visual perceptions during the NDE are striking and precise. He comments for example on the "brilliance" of the colors he experienced, more "brilliant" than any of the descriptions of color given to him by sighted people. He describes the snow he "saw" when his consciousness was apparently out of his body and above the street during the

NDE as "very soft," and goes on to say that:

It had not been covered with sleet or freezing rain. It was the type of snow that could blow around anywhere. The streets had been ploughed and you could see the banks [of snow] on both sides of the streets. I knew they were there. I could see them.

Several other subjects also give clear descriptions, sometimes involving seeing apparently correct details of other people's behavior or of their surroundings. One of the most closely corroborated cases among the adventitiously blind was that of Nancy (second name not given), tragically and permanently blinded by a mistake during a surgical operation. While Nancy was in the recovery ward after the operation that cost her sight, the medical staff recognized there were complications and she was wheeled out of recovery and taken to have an angiogram. At this point she regained consciousness, realized she had lost her sight, and immediately found herself out of her body, from which position she was able to "see" again much that happened to her on her way to have the angiogram, including "seeing" her then lover Leon, and Dick the father of her child, standing further away down the corridor. She then went into what she describes as "the light," where she was persuaded to return to her body. Medical records essentially confirm the external aspects of these experiences, but the best confirmation comes from Leon, whose account of his actions when Nancy "saw" him as she was taken for the angiogram square with hers in virtually every important detail. Though more hazy over details, Dick also substantially corroborates her account.

However, did those born blind really "see" during their NDEs? Professor Ring considers that the argument that they dreamt their visual experiences can be effectively ruled out. Not only did the individuals concerned confirm that their NDEs were quite unlike their dreams, research studies with the congenitally blind assure us that they have no vision while dreaming, and indeed that there is very little vision in the dreams of those who lose their sight before the age of five. Ring argues that the possibility that the blind constructed an imaginary visual experience from auditory information heard by them during or after the NDE seems equally unlikely. Only one of the individuals in the NDE group mentioned that the experience might have been imaginary, and imagination fails to explain those accounts in which members of the group reported "seeing" during their NDE unusual objects or events that were some distance away from them and that would not, for this reason, have featured in auditory information. In addition, although the blind subjects may on other quite different occasions have sometimes constructed imaginary experiences from information given to them, they confirmed that the NDE experience was unlike any of their imaginings.

A remaining possibility is that the subjects were experiencing so-called "blindsight," the baffling but well-researched condition that sometimes enables blind people to reach correctly towards objects whose exact location is unknown to them, and to assume the appropriate shape with their hands to pick them up even though they are ignorant of their size and shape. However, Ring and Cooper feel this can be ruled out as individuals with blindsight do not claim to see – and cannot visually describe – the objects to which they are relating. For similar reasons the authors consider that the suggestion their subjects were using some form of skin-based vision (the ability shown by some blind people to identify colors by touch) can also be effectively ruled out.

Having eliminated alternative explanations for the reported experiences, Ring and Cooper then address the central issue of whether or not the experiences reported by their blind NDE group can really be classed as "seeing." In some cases members of the group, when pressed on this point, said their "seeing" was more a form of awareness than of visual perception. They "knew" what was there, but the sensation was more a tactile one, though no touching was actually involved. They used the word "see" because this is the linguistic convention. This indecision over what is meant by sight is not surprising (and in any case does not discount the paranormality of their experience), as those born blind cannot be sure what sighted people "mean" by the word sight. But Ring and Cooper point out that their use of words like "brightness," and their references to colors, seem much more related to vision than to touch. Interestingly, the authors also give examples from Ring's previous research of people with poor eyesight who yet in NDEs found they could see perfectly, and could obtain veridical details that would normally have been outside their restricted powers of sight. This accords with the findings reported by one of the first systematic investigators of experiences in which the consciousness appears to be outside the body, Celia Green. In her large group of subjects, Green (1977) found that not only sight but all deficient senses appeared to be fully restored while out of the body, though on return these senses were again lost.

The kind of "vision" experienced by the blind when out of their bodies may, however, be at times different from that of normal sight in one important respect. Some subjects studied by Ring and Cooper gave accounts of omni directional vision – the ability to see through 180 degrees at one and the same time. After reviewing these experiences the authors conclude that their blind subjects had a kind of transcendental vision, which they term "mindsight," during the NDE. This is in fact a highly evidential point, as this kind of all-round vision is also reported by some normally sighted people during NDEs, as is the ability to see through walls and doors and other apparently solid objects. Mindsight would thus seem not to be specific to blind people, but to represent the enhanced potential for vision experienced when out of the body, and thus outside the constraints experienced by the physical senses. Such vision seems to be synesthetic in that it appears to combine the abilities of sight, hearing, and touch into one comprehensive modality that is greater even than the sum of these sensory parts.

Abilities Experienced During the NDE

It is interesting to note that in many of the accounts of NDEs assembled by Green (1968), Crookall (1964 and 1978), Black (1975), Greyson and Flynn (1984), Zaleski (1987), Lorimer (1990), Morse and Perry (1990), Fenwick and Fenwick (1995), Bailey and Yates (1996), Peterson (1997), Fox (2003), and many others, sighted individuals, like those born blind, also report the ability to behave in ways impossible while in the physical body, even seeing through solid objects. A good example is quoted by Tyrell (1943) and by Findlay (1961) and concerns Sir Alexander Ogston who, during the South African War, was admitted to Blomfontein Hospital at death's door, like Dr. Wiltse, from typhoid fever. In sum, Sir Alexander reported that:

I lay, as it seemed, in a constant stupor ... Mind and body seemed to be dual and to some extent separate. I was conscious of the body as an inert, tumbled mass near a door; it belonged to me but was not I. I was conscious that my mental self used regularly to leave the body ... and wander away from it under grey, sunless, moonless, starless skies, ever onwards to a distant gleam on the horizon, solitary but not unhappy ... In my wanderings there was a strange consciousness that I could see through the walls of the building ... and that everything was transparent to my senses. I saw plainly, for instance, a poor Royal Army Medical Corps surgeon, of whose existence I had not known, and who was in quite another part of the hospital, grow very ill and scream and die; I saw them cover his corpse and carry him softly out on shoeless feet, quietly and surreptitiously, lest we should know that he had died, and the next night I saw him taken away to the cemetery. Afterwards when I told these happenings to the sisters, they informed me that all this had happened just as I had fancied ...

Further examples of the ability of those experiencing NDEs to behave in ways impossible while in the physical body are given in the books just referenced above. Individuals speak variously of moving rapidly through space, of traveling to distant locations, of experiencing colors and scenery of enchanting beauty, of hearing the thoughts of others, and of encountering a light of unearthly brilliance that yet does not hurt the eyes. In view of these extended abilities, it may not be surprising that sensory experience can become synesthetic as Ring suggests. Thus in a sense it is as unrealistic to ask if the blind during NDEs and OBEs "see" in the way that sighted people see in normal life as it would be to ask whether or not sighted people in NDEs "see" as they do when in the body.

NDEs in Young Children and Visions of the Deceased

In addition to the question whether or not those born blind experience NDEs, we can also ask what of young children? Too young in most cases to be familiar with the literature on NDEs or to be over-influenced by adult conditioning on the meaning of life and death, the experiences of young children who have come close to death are of particular interest. Research in this area is not easy, as there are relatively few young children who have gone through the process of cardiac arrest followed by resuscitation. However, after combing ten years of medical records Dr. Melvin Morse (Morse and Perry 1990) was able to identify and interview 12 children who fitted the criteria. He made no mention to them of NDEs, but simply asked them a list of simple questions designed to find out what it was like to be very ill. Only two of the questions, "do your remember being unconscious?" and "what do you think happens when we die?" were directly relevant to possible NDEs.

The results of these interviews were astonishing. Eight of the 12 reported the experience of leaving their bodies and traveling to other realms that are a feature of adult NDEs. By contrast, none of a control group of 121 children who had been very sick but not near death reported NDE experiences when interviewed by Dr. Morse. In addition, a further 37 children treated during their illnesses with "almost every kind of mind-altering medication known to pharmacology" and who were also interviewed, reported no incidence of NDEs, which indicated that medically administered drugs do not in themselves give rise to the experience. Ten years later, Morse conducted a follow-up study with the children who had experienced NDEs in order to assess the effect that their experiences appeared to have had upon them. Results showed that they had all "become special teenagers who have excellent relationships with their families. They share a maturity and wisdom that is humbling." There was a conspicuous absence of drug use or even drug experimentation in the group, of excessive risk-taking, or of rebellion against authority, and at school they had "good grades and fine behavior." We would need further studies with larger samples before we are in a position to draw firm conclusions on NDEs in children, but Morse's results add further to the evidence that whatever else they may be, NDEs are not imaginary experience prompted by expectation based upon previous knowledge.

A feature of NDE reports already mentioned is that people who are known to have died are sometimes seen by the individual while out of the body. An example of this in my files was reported to me by Hilda, an excellent witness who has had a number of psychic experiences during her life. Traveling by car with her family in South Africa at the time of the incident she was involved in a serious car accident in which both she and her husband, who was driving, were thrown from the car. She relates that:

I found myself out of my body and saw both my children [who were in the back of the car and unhurt] *get out of the wrecked vehicle and run to where I was lying. I watched them trying to help me, and whilst still out of my body I saw my husband, who was also lying in the road, leave his body and travel towards a bright light in the distance. I knew that he had died.*

Sadly, her vision of her husband's death proved correct, although she recovered in due course from her injuries.

The Work of Peter Fenwick

A number of large-scale studies into the NDE phenomena are currently underway. Notable among them is that being undertaken in some 20 hospitals in the UK for the Horizon Research Foundation by Dr. Sam Parnia of Southampton General Hospital and neuropsychiatrist Dr. Peter Fenwick of London University's Institute of Psychiatry. A recent survey commissioned by the Foundation and involving a random sample of 1,000 UK residents also reveals that no fewer than ten per cent claim to have had an experience in which, although not necessarily involving clinical death, the individual experienced consciousness as located outside the physical body (Parnia 2001). Another example of a current large-scale study is that of Van Lommel and colleagues at Rijnstate Hospital in the Netherlands, involving 344 cardiac arrest patients all resuscitated after clinical death. Results reveal that 18 per cent report NDEs, and the authors conclude that medical explanations such as the chaotic activity of the dying brain or hallucinations consequent upon medical drugs, or upon anoxia (lack of oxygen) or vagaries of bodily chemistry cannot account for these experiences.

Fenwick and Fenwick (1995), from a study of 300 NDE cases, arrive at the same conclusion. Only 14 per cent of their sample was receiving drugs at the time of their NDEs, and in any case the hallucinations experienced by patients losing consciousness due to drugs are reported as chaotic and disorganized, whereas NDEs are vivid and coherent. In dismissing anoxia, Fenwick and Fenwick point out that the condition is regularly induced in airline pilots as part of their training and at one time was also a feature of the training of medical students, yet none of those concerned appears to have reported an NDE. In addition anoxia, like drugs, leads to brain disorientation and confusion. Fenwick and Fenwick accept that a build-up of carbon dioxide in the blood (hypercarbia) of patients can lead to dream-like experiences that sound similar to NDEs, but point out that no Hospital Intensive Care Unit would allow hypercarbia to occur in the blood of those for whose lives they are responsible. In addition, hypercarbia produces convulsive muscle movements, in some cases so violent that the patient seems to be acting out their dream-like experiences. However, no such convulsions have ever been reported in the case of patients claiming to have undergone NDEs.

Fenwick and Fenwick also dismiss the theory that NDEs are simply hallucinations brought on by the patients' medical condition. They point out that NDE subjects all have very similar experiences whatever their medical condition, whereas the hallucinations that occur during physical illness are typically highly personal. Fenwick and Fenwick regard as inadequate another explanation sometimes advanced in an attempt to explain away NDEs, namely that they are caused by the release of endorphins, the brain's own pain-killing drugs. Endorphins are similar to opiates in that they can lead to feelings of bliss and calm, but many groups of people experience high levels of endorphins without having NDEs. Athletes release endorphins during sustained physical activity and this lessens their sensitivity to the pain of exertion, but although these can lead to euphoric feelings – the so-called runners' high (Murphy and White 1995) – they do not appear to prompt NDE-type experiences. Patients with grand mal seizures also have a high release of endorphins, which can persist in the brain for several hours, but again these do not lead to experiences similar to NDEs. In fact, patients typically report feeling tired and exhausted after the seizure rather than ecstatic. In addition, endorphins do not appear to be potent hallucinogens (Oyama et al. 1980). Thus even if they play some part in the blissful feelings reported by some NDE subjects, they seem unable to account for the experience itself.

Skeptics point out that stimulating certain parts of the brain with weak electrical currents can also produce some mystical-type experiences, but Fenwick and Fenwick point out that these experiences tend to be disorganized and fragmentary. By contrast, the NDE is a whole and integrated experience that typically makes good sense to the patient both while it is happening and for years afterwards. Furthermore, those reporting NDEs have not been subjected to brain stimulation in this way. What of the possible relationship between self-administered drugs and NDEs? Psychedelic drugs such as LSD and mescaline can certainly produce vivid hallucinations, but again these hallucinations have an intensely personal quality (see e.g. Groff 1975). Such hallucinations may have a spiritual content and can be life changing, but they do not show the clear stages often reported in the NDE. And although people sometimes report negative and frightening experiences after ingesting psychedelics, negative experiences (discussed in more detail shortly) are relatively infrequent in NDEs, and generally take a rather different form from the bad LSD trip. To this we can add that people who experience NDEs are not under the influence of psychedelics, and that there is no evidence that the natural substances that mimic the chemical composition of psychedelics are released into the bloodstream during the NDE.

The Ketamine Explanation of the NDE

Recently some authorities have claimed that ketamine – a short-acting, hallucinogenic, dissociative anesthetic used principally in veterinary medicine – is capable of "reproducing all the features of the NDE" (Jansen 1996). They also point out that although those reporting NDEs were not receiving ketamine at the time, their brains may have been in a similar state to that associated with ketamine ingestion. Ketamine appears to act by inhibiting the action of the amino acid glutamate, which is the key neurotransmitter in the temporal and frontal lobes of the brain and that plays a vital role in all cognitive processes involving the cerebral cortex such as thinking, memory creation and recall, and perception. If glutamate is present in excess it can damage brain cells, and in defense the brain produces a substance that protects the receptors in these cells from binding with it. The result may be that data from the outside world, which is usually registered upon the brain by the action of glutamate, is blocked, and the brain becomes flooded instead with stored memories and perceptions, which it then organizes into experiences resembling NDEs. In the actual near-death situation, the argument goes, there may be the same excessive release of glutamate, which prompts the same defensive blocking mechanism to come into operation, prompting the NDE.

The first objection to this is that drugs do not "reproduce" NDEs or any other mental states. They may facilitate the conditions under which these states can occur, but this is not the same thing as "reproducing" them. Thus whether or not glutamate inhibition (or any other abnormal chemically induced brain process) is present during the NDE, it cannot be said to have caused it. We are thus no closer to knowing whether the mind that experiences the NDE is caused by abnormal brain activity or is simply facilitated by it. If the latter, it is possible that the way in which drugs facilitate the operation of the mind during the NDE is by inhibiting those brain processes that would otherwise prevent NDEs from emerging into – or perhaps remaining in – consciousness. This is a point to which we will return in the next section that deals with out-of-the-body experiences (OBEs) in which, as with NDEs, the consciousness is seemingly located outside the physical body.

Secondly, we do not as yet know if the experiences reported by those who have taken ketamine are real or imagined. That is, do they, as in NDEs, sometimes produce information about the environment that could not have been obtained if the consciousness had remained within the body? If they do not, then they would appear to be due only to imagination, and thus have no relevance to NDEs. If they do, then the analogy with the NDE would become a real one, as would the possibility that ketamine inhibits those brain processes that normally prevent the mind from leaving the body. It is said that ketamine may allow sufficient sensory input for those under its influence to allow them to obtain normal knowledge of what is going on around them even when they are seemingly unconscious, but there is evidence that both in the NDE and the OBE (out-of-the-body experiences unconnected with imminent risk of death) accurate information is sometimes acquired of physical realities that are too remote from the individual to be reached by his or her normal sensory awareness – the case of Maria to which reference was made earlier is one example. Thirdly, looking ahead again to the OBE, there is no evidence to suppose that during these experiences the individuals concerned are suffering from the physical conditions that lead to an excessive release of glutamate. OBEs can occur when the individual is perfectly well both physically and mentally, and is not threatened with death or danger in any form

The Dying Brain and Other Normal Explanations for the NDE

Critics of the idea that consciousness may indeed leave the body during an NDE propose yet another possible normal explanation, namely that the NDE is simply the illusory processes that take place when the brain is dying. In support of this they suggest that the tunnel effect reported as occurring in some NDEs is caused by the progressive shutting down of parts of the brain responsible for peripheral imagery. As peripheral imagery disappears, the dying brain is able only to experience what seems to be a bright light surrounded by darkness, which generates the impression that one is traveling through a tunnel. The dying brain theory can however be faulted for several reasons. Firstly, if the brain is dying, one would expect the experiences generated by it to become increasingly chaotic. However, this is not the case. In fact in many cases the individual emerges from the tunnel, recovers full imagery, and enjoys visions of paradise conditions and of deceased relatives and friends, and the experiences become increasingly coherent. Secondly, if the brain is dying, one would expect each person to have highly personal chaotic experiences. But as we have seen, this is not the case in the NDE. Thirdly, many people do not report the tunnel effect during the NDE, but have full imagery immediately after apparently leaving their bodies. Fourthly, some report experiencing the tunnel effect on return to their bodies and not only on exit from them. We cannot suppose that the dying brain, having lost the ability to create peripheral imagery then for inexplicable reasons regains it as the dying process continues and the tunnel is left behind, then once more loses it again as it returns to the body. Fifthly, if the NDE is produced by the dying brain, it is strange that this dying brain then miraculously recovers once the NDE is terminated. This supposes that brain cells, once dead, are able to regenerate.

Another argument against NDEs as evidence of survival is that as those experiencing NDEs are successfully resuscitated they cannot really be said to have died, and therefore cannot tell us anything about life after death. The reply to this is that in many cases the patient undergoing the NDE did so when pronounced clinically dead on the strength of an absence of all the vital signs equated by the medical profession with life (as indeed was the case with all 344 patients in the Netherlands study). In one recent case (the Pam Reynolds case), the vital signs were even deliberately switched off by the medical team. This was done in order to carry out a very demanding brain operation to deal with a giant basilar artery aneurism (a ballooning out of the wall of the large artery at the base of the brain), which if it had ruptured would have proved immediately fatal. Before the operation could take place, it was necessary to drain Pam's brain of blood so that the aneurism could be collapsed and dealt with, but because starving the brain of blood in this way would have quickly led to irreversible brain damage, the body temperature had at the same time to be reduced so low (60F degrees) that the patient was literally placed in a state of suspended animation, and the heart stopped.

As a result of these procedures, all measurable brain activity was brought to a standstill. Yet after the completion of the successful operation and the restoration of body and brain activity, the patient reported she had experienced a coherent NDE in which she stood outside her body and had seen enough of the operation to be able to give details of the surgical instrument (the Midas Rex bone saw) used to cut into her skull, an instrument of which she apparently had no previous knowledge. She also reported some details of the conversations that had taken place between members of the medical team, even though throughout the operation molded ear speakers that effectively shut out airborne sounds were placed in each of her ears to monitor auditory and brain stem reflexes (Sabom 1998). It is impossible to say at what point during this lengthy clinical process the NDE actually took place, but since the Midas Rex bone saw described by the patient was used when no measurable brain activity was taking place, it seems that part of it at least encompassed this period of non-activity. In fact Pam Reynolds described the NDE as commencing only when she heard the sound of the bone saw, at which point she had been under anesthesia for about 90 minutes. Prior to that moment she states that she heard and saw nothing.

The significance of this case is that even if some brain activity had continued to take place at the cellular level of Pam's brain during the operation, this would not have been sufficient to generate consciousness. Yet the patient reported that consciousness took place, and that this consciousness was located outside the physical body. During the NDE she not only saw her body from the outside but was taken along a tunnel to where, coming out into the light, she saw her deceased grandmother, who was calling to her, and other deceased relatives. They prevented her from coming fully into the light, conveying to her that if she did so she would be unable to return. Then she had the feeling of being "nurtured" by them and made strong, before her deceased uncle took her back down the tunnel. Catching sight of her body again it now looked "terrible" to her "like a train wreck." In spite of her reluctance to return she feels her uncle pushing her – "I felt a definite repelling and at the same time a pulling from the body ... It was like diving into a pool of icy water ... It hurt."

Unless it is supposed that she fabricated the whole account, which seems unlikely in view of her ability to give some details of what she observed in the operating theatre while out of her body, it is difficult to explain away her experience by normal means. One of the many cases reported by Fenwick and Fenwick (1995) is equally difficult to explain away. The patient concerned, David Verdegaal, suffered a heart attack in which his heart stopped for a reported 30 minutes, and this was followed two days later by a stroke. He was left in a coma for two weeks from which he emerged blind and paralyzed, and with such widespread brain damage that he was left in a so-called vegetative state. Someone as severely brain damaged as this will almost certainly suffer from memory-impairment as well as loss of sight and movement. As Fenwick and Fenwick stress, even had a patient with this degree of mental impairment been able to form NDE memories during the heart attack and before the brain damage took place, this subsequent damage would mean that the memories would not have been retained. And the experience could hardly have taken place as he came out of his coma, as by this time not only memory function but the part of the brain responsible for creating visual imagery would have been damaged.

After a long period of gradual recuperation (said to be mostly due to his own extraordinary determination and perseverance), Verdegaal once more became an articulate, functioning human being and able to recount his remarkable NDE which included nearly all the typical incidents – realization that he was dead, a bright light, meeting a spiritual being, the realization of universal love, paradise conditions, the recognition that he would be given the strength to continue whether he lived or died, the instruction to convey his experience to others (in the form of a book), and the awareness of being gently guided back to this life. In the light of our knowledge of brain function and brain damage, neither the experience itself, so full of visual imagery, nor the memory of it should have been possible.

It is possible that convincing normal explanations for NDEs will one day be advanced, but even if this proves to be the case, it is likely that to accommodate them we will have radically to revise what we know of brain functions and of the relationship between the brain and the mind. Scientists are always wary of being too categorical in their statements in the fear that they will be proved wrong in the light of future discoveries. However, once again, as so often in this book, I think it appropriate to pay attention to what people tell us about their own experience. Those who have had NDEs are reported in all published research as insisting that they know they died, and that in consequence all fear of death has been removed. It is true that people diagnosed as suffering from schizophrenia recount illusory experiences that they subsequently maintain were real, but the subjects reporting NDEs are not schizophrenics, and it is misleading in this case to try to extrapolate from the mentally ill lessons for people suffering from no such affliction. In addition, although the hallucinations of schizophrenics are typically bizarre and personal, the accounts given by those who have NDEs show agreement on a wide range of details. Furthermore, in the great majority of cases, not only are the belief systems about death and the afterlife of those concerned radically changed, so also are their attitudes to life and to its goals and values and to the existence of a spiritual dimension to being. Years after their NDEs the memories seem undimmed, and their convictions as to what they experienced remain unshaken.

Commenting upon the argument that death has not taken place during the NDE, Moody (1999) likens this to "a stipulation that the goal post would be moved back if the athlete were to reach it." He further points out that " ... millions of people now alive have returned from a situation that a century ago was simply designated 'death,' and they have informed us that even after that point, they were very much alive, very acutely conscious ... comforted and welcomed and reunited with loved ones lost. So, by the criteria of 1890, even those of 1930, life after death has indeed been proven." Moody's argument is highly pertinent. He is saying that by the rules both of language and of medicine it is "impossible" to return from death, thus if anyone who has clinically died reports an NDE, we automatically say they have not died, even if this means redefining what we mean by death. I agree with him. Redefining it in what way? We have lost our yardstick of clinical death, i.e. the absence of any of the vital physical signs normally associated with life, and have put nothing in its place. It is little use saying that if a person is revived after clinical death this means they were not dead. It may indeed be that the boundary between life and death can be crossed, albeit briefly, in both directions. Why not? What is to stop us at least accepting this as a working hypothesis, and then studying what people have to tell us about their NDEs in order to learn what they have to tell us about this shadowy boundary between the two states?

A final criticism of NDEs, advanced particularly by Zaleski, is that there are significant differences between the accounts given by individuals from different cultures. This suggests to her that the NDE may in part be largely an imaginary experience. However, Osis and Haraldsson (1995), in a four-year study in the USA and India involving 877 detailed interviews with terminally ill patients, 120 of whom reported NDEs, found that there was a common core experience to the NDE in both these cultures. Their hypothesis was that if differences in the cultural content of the reported experiences were very marked between individuals in the USA and India, this would support the destruction explanation, while if these differences were only moderate, support would be provided for the survival explanation. Their conclusion after analyzing their data was that:

In our judgment the similarities between the core phenomena found in the deathbed visions of both countries are clear enough to be considered supportive of the post-mortem survival hypothesis.

Furthermore, although religious belief is very much a feature of both US and Indian cultures, Osis and Haraldsson found that "the phenomena within each culture often did not conform to religious afterlife beliefs." Several basic beliefs, such as judgment, salvation, and redemption in the case of Christians, and reincarnation and dissolution into Brahman in the case of Hindus, were notably absent. "We reached the impression," say the authors, "that cultural conditioning by Christian and Hindu teaching is, in part, contradicted in the visionary experiences of the dying."

Nevertheless, complementary to these findings by Osis and Haraldsson, we would expect that creative imagination, based upon preconceptions of how visual reality should appear, is likely to play some part in the NDE. Even our experiences in daily life are colored by preconceptions, and it seems unrealistic to suppose that we will abruptly be rid of these preconceptions at the moment of clinical death, and thus experience all things in their culturally neutral essence. This is an issue that has so many implications for survival that it will be returned to in more detail in Chapter 18.

Negative Near Death Experiences

Up to now, we have focused upon positive experiences during NDEs, but Rawlings (1978), Greyson and Bush (1992), Atwater (1995), and Storm (2000) all report cases where the experience has been frightening, even terrifying. Greyson and Bush point out that such cases are rare, but they nevertheless have some 50 of them in their files, and are able to divide them into three distinct types. The first is very similar to the positive NDE, the only difference being that the individual finds the prospect of death unwelcome, and returns eagerly to the body, sometimes helped by a spirit presence of some kind. In the second category are individuals who experience what appears to be a featureless void, and are told by mocking voices that this is all there is for the whole of eternity, and that everything they have previously learnt about life after death is a cruel joke. In the third category are individuals who hear moans and cries and who are appalled to see the apparent suffering of others, even though they themselves are not personally undergoing these sufferings and may be in the safe company of higher beings.

The reactions of individuals in the first of these three categories – who for some reason do not experience the more usual sense of tranquility once outside their bodies – can perhaps be best explained as a consequence of panic at the thought of death. The negative experiences of those in the second category sound very like the experiences reported in a small number of the communications through mediums from supposedly earthbound spirits (see Chapter 18). The remedy for these experiences is said to be to call for help from a spiritually exalted being, or even from deceased friends or relatives. Storm (2000), who initially went through apparently hellish conditions in his NDE, called for help in this way and was rescued from the beings intent on terrifying him (so convinced was Storm by his experiences that he subsequently left his university post and became a minister of religion). More will be said about these negative experiences in Chapter 18. In themselves they do nothing to weaken the evidence that NDEs may provide insight into the act of dying, and as identified by Greyson and Bush these experiences show a consistency which parallels that reported in positive cases, and which is at odds with the "striking differences in the reactions" shown by individuals who for example have so-called bad trips while under the influence of LSD (Groff 1979).

The experiences of those in the third category are more difficult to explain. If genuine and if accurately reported, they may represent a glimpse into the so-called lower astral regions, which earthbound spirits are said to inhabit until they fully recognize their predicament and call for help, or in the case of wrongdoers recognize and repent for the harm they caused to others during their earthly lives. Dante describes these realms in *Il Purgatorio*. If they exist they hardly sound inviting, and it is possible that some individuals are shown them during their NDEs in order to bring painful warnings back to those still on earth. Whatever the explanation, the subject will be returned to in Chapter 18.

Why Aren't NDEs Universal Among the Dying?

If NDEs are really experiences of crossing the boundary, albeit briefly, between life and death, why don't all those resuscitated from clinical death report them? Studies by Sabom (1982 and 1998), Ring (1984), Grey (1985), and Fenwick and Fenwick (ibid. 1995) report variously that between 12 and 40 per cent of those at or near clinical death go through NDE experiences prior to resuscitation. What of the percentage that do not? Do these findings suggest not everyone survives? One possible answer is that all who return from clinical death may have had the experience, but only a percentage remember it. NDEs do not appear dreamlike to those who have them, and there is no evidence that such people manifest the brain states or the Rapid Eye Movements (REMs) that characterize dreaming, but it is possible that the ability to recall NDEs has some similarities with the ability to recall dreams. Research suggests that we all dream every night, yet many people rarely if ever remember dreams. They can of course be helped through training to remember them (Tibetan Buddhists place great emphasis upon the importance of recalling dreams, which together with sleep they see as a dress rehearsal for death) and it is possible that people who recall their dreams also remember their NDEs (the field seems ripe for research). Thus memories of the NDE may for some people be lost at the point of re-entry into the physical body. Another possibility is that some individuals may not have left their bodies by the time they are resuscitated.

CHAPTER 16

OUT-OF-THE-BODY EXPERIENCES

Similarities Between NDEs and OBEs

There are many revealing similarities between NDEs and out-of-the-body experiences (OBEs). The term OBE represents those occurrences in which individuals feel they have temporarily left their physical bodies while in normal health and not threatened by death. OBEs happen spontaneously to some individuals but not to others. A number of people report having OBEs from childhood, but most people go through life with never a hint of such an experience (although some occult traditions claim we all leave our bodies during sleep, but fail to recall the fact). It is said (e.g. by Crookall 1961) that the reason for these differences is that some people have a "looser" connection between their vital and spiritual bodies (both of which are said to leave the body at death) and their physical bodies than others, and it is thus easier for them to experience OBEs. If this is the case, we would suppose that people who have NDEs are more likely to have experienced OBEs at some point in their lives than those who do not. More research is needed to clarify this supposition, and it would also be helpful, in view of the possible similarity between NDE recall and dream recall, to establish whether or not those who have OBEs are successful at remembering their dreams. Above all, more research needs to be done on the OBE itself. Current evidence suggests it cannot readily be explained by normal means, which leaves us with the suggestion that, like the NDE, it may give us an insight, however brief and confused, into what it is like to cross the boundary between this world and the next.

OBEs are also relevant to the discussion as to whether the mind is generated by the brain and entirely dependent upon it, or whether it exists independently of the brain and works through it. They have further importance in that, if they really happen, they indicate that it is not only the proximity of death that prompts consciousness temporarily to vacate the body. It may even do so when the individual is in good physical and mental health, and unthreatened by any external danger. This suggests, at the very least, that we must rethink our whole model of what it means to be human, and that if OBEs can be induced, as is claimed, through certain practices then potentially we each have a way of testing for ourselves whether or not consciousness is anything more than a part of material reality. Professor Charles Tart, who has made experimental studies of the OBE as we shall see in due course, puts it that if we are successful in experiencing OBEs ourselves, "Then 'soul' will not be just an opinion or speculation for us. Its reality and its implications for living will be experiential *data"* (Tart 1997).

Professor Ken Ring, mentioned earlier for his work on NDEs with those who are born blind, also investigated OBEs in the blind. Using the same methods that allowed him to identify a group of those born blind who had experienced NDEs, he found a sample of ten people (four blind from birth, two adventitiously blind, and four seriously visually impaired) who reported OBEs. Nine out of ten of this group claimed to possess what seemed to be normal sight during the experience, and the reports of their sighted experiences were similar in important respects to those of the NDE group (Ring and Valerino 1998). If the reports of Ring's two samples are accurate, then we can assume that, at least in terms of sensory awareness, those aspects of consciousness that leave the body during NDEs and OBEs are essentially the same.

Where is Consciousness?

Taken together, both NDEs and OBEs raise the question of where exactly is consciousness. Normally we seem to experience the outer world from inside our bodies, to such an extent in fact that we identify the one with the other. But if it is in the body, where exactly is it? Most people would say it is in their heads, yet as psychologists who have made a special study of consciousness remind us, we can be conscious anywhere in our bodies (e.g. Velmans 2000). If you have a pain in your foot you are conscious of the pain as being in your foot, not as being in your head. Why is it then that we assume consciousness is in our head? For most people, this is primarily because of the power of vision. We seem to look out at the world from behind our eyes. You may argue that even when you close your eyes your awareness is still in your head, but this is largely due to habit. Even when you close your eyes your attention remains with the sensations in your closed eyelids, in the sounds you hear, in the feeling of your tongue against your teeth, in the sensations around your mouth, in your nose as you breathe in and out and so on. Lots of sensations are felt in your head. But none of these sensations is consciousness itself. Consciousness is simply our awareness of these sensations, and this awareness can be anywhere in the body. There are certain meditation techniques in fact that encourage you to move the consciousness around the body. To feel it first in your toes as you move them gently, then in your feet resting on the floor, then in the sensations of your body seated on the chair or the floor, then in your solar plexus as you breathe deep down, then in the beating of your heart, and finally in the crown of your head.

Experience with these meditation techniques soon helps rid you of the idea that consciousness has a location in space, whether in the belly, the heart, or the brain. It can move around the body at will. But can it exist outside the body as appears to happen in the NDE and the OBE? Can consciousness even view the body from a position outside it in space? If so, then our whole concept of reality, of the relationship between mind and body, and ultimately of who we are, has to change. There is even a suggestion that not only may we be incorrect in assuming that consciousness is dependent upon the body and in particular the brain, but we may be wrong in supposing that consciousness is secondary to matter – i.e. that the material world and material life-forms were created first, and consciousness only arose much later as matter evolved. This suggestion, known as panpsychism, has it that consciousness pre-dates matter and was responsible for its creation. This has always been the teaching of the theistic spiritual traditions – i.e. that God, the divine consciousness, brought the material world into existence – but in the twentieth century the idea was also advanced seriously by some leading scientists, the best-known of whom was mathematician and astrophysicist Sir James Jeans, Gold Medallist of the Royal Astronomical Society, Royal Medallist, President of the British Association, Fellow of the Royal Society of which he also served for ten years as Secretary, and pioneer theorist on stellar structure and the origin of the solar system. Jeans, who became the UK's most popular scientist in the years leading up to the Second World War, put it that:

Thirty years ago, we thought, or we assumed, that we were heading towards an ultimate reality of a mechanical kind ... a fortuitous jumble of atoms ... destined to perform meaningless dances ... under the action of blind purposeless force ... One tiny corner ... had chanced to become conscious for a time, but was destined in the end ... under the action of blind mechanical forces ... to be frozen out and again leave a lifeless world.

Today there is a wide measure of agreement ... that the stream of knowledge is heading towards a non-mechanical reality; the universe begins to look more like a great thought than a great machine. Mind no longer appears as an accidental intruder into the realm of matter; we are beginning to suspect that we ought rather to hail it as the creator and governor of the realm of matter ... (Jeans 1932).

Sir James Jeans also made contributions to the development of quantum theory, and although to the pessimist the stream of knowledge of which he spoke looks at times more like a trickle, modern quantum theory – by recognizing that consciousness may be able directly to influence the behavior of sub-atomic particles – provides further support for his views (e.g. Goswami 1993). One thing at least is clear. We are a very long way from establishing the nature of the relationship between consciousness and matter, either at the macro level of the universe or the micro level of the individual, and the hypothesis that matter is primary to consciousness is subject to increasing assault even from within science itself. The implications of this for the survival of consciousness after the death of the physical body are not hard to seek.

Examples of OBEs

I first heard mention of the OBE when I was in my late teens, long before the wealth of books on the subject now in the bookshops became available. The brother of a friend of mine, while stationed with his army unit in Egypt, woke one night from sleep and found himself suspended in the air above his body. Panicking, he had the impression that unless he could get back into his body he would die. Abruptly, and with an impact, he was back once more, trembling and sweating with fear. I was intrigued by this account. Did it mean consciousness really could leave the body and return to tell the tale? This set me off on a search for anything written on the subject, and some while later I came across a book by Crookall, whose work in connection with NDEs has already been mentioned, with the rather fanciful title *More Astral Projections* (Crookall 1964). Crookall not only appeared to take out-of-the-body experiences (which he called by the earlier, occult name of "astral projections") seriously, he reproduced many accounts from people who claimed to have had these experiences. In a fairly typical example collected by Dr. Crookall, the subject, a Mr. Ernest Murray, reported that, after saying goodnight to his mother who was in bed with an attack of migraine, he went to his own room and fell asleep. After some hours he "got out of bed":

I walked through my bedroom door and through my mother's door. She was sitting up in bed ... with her head in her hands. I placed my hand on her head and said "Lie down - it's 2 a.m. and time you were asleep! She said "Thank you son!" I returned to my bedroom, walking through the two doors. I saw my body in bed, and climbed back into my body. The next thing I knew I was sitting up in bed.

Taking his mother her tea the following morning at 6.30 he asked her how she felt. She replied "It was nice of you to come to me. But what was I doing awake at two in the morning?" Mr. Murray considered this proved to him that he had not been dreaming.

As so often happens in these cases, the subject concerned did not obtain a signed statement from his mother confirming her side of the story, and again as in so many of these cases, it took place some years before it was reported to Crookall (people often express reluctance at telling others of these experiences for fear of ridicule, but as with NDEs, the memory is said not to fade with the years). But if the account is accurate, Mr. Murray's mother actually saw him while he was out of his body. Was he perhaps mistaken, and physically got out of bed and went to his mother? Some features of the experience argue against this. He was aware of passing through two solid doors on his way to his mother, passing through the same doors on his return, and of seeing his body in the bed before he was reunited with it. Is it possible that he was half-asleep and half-awake, and dreamt of passing through the doors while actually he opened them? Possibly. The case would have been stronger if, for example, his mother had been living some miles away from him at the time, and at a distance he could not possibly have covered while half-asleep.

The Experiences of Oliver Fox

There are in fact cases just of this kind. An interesting one, which has become something of a classic in the field, was published by Oliver Fox some years before Crookall's first book. Entitled *Astral Projection: A Record of Out-of-the-Body Experiences*, Fox's beautifully written little book has no date, but probably first appeared around 1940 (the most recent reprint known to me at the time of writing is dated 1993). Fox, who had enjoyed a vivid dream life as a child, discovered the ability to lucid dream – that is, to know while in a dream that he was dreaming, and to realize that he could take control of the dream and sometimes travel at will to wherever he wished to be (see Le Berge 1985 and 1990 for modern research into the lucid dreaming phenomenon). Later, while an engineering student at what is now Southampton University, Fox discussed these lucid dreams with two of his friends, Elkington and Slade, and the three young men agreed if possible to meet that night in their dreams on Southampton Common. Fox duly dreamt of being on the common and meeting Elkington, though Slade did not appear. The next morning, without first recounting his own experience, he asked Elkington if he had had any dreams the previous night. Elkington replied "Yes, I met you on the Common last night and knew I was dreaming, but old Slade didn't turn up." Enquiries of Slade revealed that he had no recollection of any dreams that night. (The boundary between lucid dreams and OBEs is unclear; it is uncertain whether Fox and Elkington were dreaming or were actually out of their bodies.)

Subsequently, another friend, Barrow, who was a Theosophist, undertook to appear to Fox while out of the body if possible. That night, while Fox knew himself to be awake, his friend appeared instantaneously by his bedside "in an intense cloud of bluish-white light" surrounded by bands of color. Mentally, Fox was aware of Barrow telling him not to be afraid, but before he could reply, his friend disappeared as abruptly as he had come. The following day however, Barrow had no recollection of having made the visit – a fact that has obvious bearing upon my earlier point that those resuscitated from clinical death who do not report NDEs may simply have forgotten them at the point of re-entry into the body.

It is easy to reject accounts such as this on the grounds that Fox, although insisting he was awake, was in fact dreaming. The same argument can reasonably be made against the earlier experiences of Fox and Elkington. Both men may have been dreaming. Alternatively, one or both of them may have made up the story of their meeting on the Common. What is really required is some hard evidence that the consciousness really does appear to have been outside the body. Evidence of this kind arises from a later experience detailed by Fox that took place in 1905. It concerns Elsie, a girlfriend with whom he was in love at the time. As a devout Christian, Elsie was firmly against Fox's experiments with his dream life (or with OBEs, whichever was the case). In her view they were "wicked" and "God would be seriously angry ... if [Fox] persisted." Fox's reply was that Elsie was ignorant and knew nothing of the matter, to which Elsie answered that indeed she did know about it, and "could go to you tonight if I wanted to." The argument went on along these lines until Elsie finally lost her temper and exclaimed "I'll *prove* it! It's wicked, but I don't care. I'll come to your room tonight and you shall see me there."

The boast seemed so childish to Fox that he forgot about it, and spent the evening studying for a forthcoming university exam. However, that night he awoke when it was already becoming light and he could dimly see the objects in the room. He lay there with the feeling that something was about to happen, although he did not associate this feeling with Elsie.

Suddenly there appeared a large egg-shaped cloud of intensely bluish-white light. In the middle was Elsie, hair loose, and in her nightdress. She seemed perfectly solid as she stood by a chest of drawers near the right side of my bed. Thus she remained, regarding me with calm but sorrowful eyes, and running her fingers along the top and front side of a desk which stood on the drawers. She did not speak.

At first, although full of wonder and admiration, he also was unable to speak. Finally he called her name, and she "vanished as suddenly as she had come." He attempted to note the time, but overcome by an irresistible drowsiness he fell back to sleep. The following day Else greeted him triumphantly with the words "I did come to you ... I went to sleep willing that I would, and all at once I was *there*." She went on to say that when she awoke she could remember all the details in his room, though some were now "slipping away." Nevertheless she was able to describe the relative positions of door, bed, window, fireplace, washstand, chest of drawers, and dressing table. She knew that the window was composed of small panes of glass, that Fox was on his side in a double bed with his eyes open and seemed dazed, that there was an old-fashioned pin-cushion in his room (unusual in a man's bedroom), that there was a black Japanese box covered with red raised figures, and that on the chest of drawers there was a leather-covered portable desk (we would call it a writing box) lined with gilt and with a sunken plate on the lid into which the handle was recessed. She also reported that while in the room she had run her fingers along a projecting ridge on the front of the portable desk.

Elsie had never visited Fox's room while in the body, and Fox insists there was no common friend who could have given her a description of it. Fox had not told her anything about his room (or even that he slept in a double bed), yet all the details given by Elsie were correct, with just one exception. There was no projecting ridge on the front of the portable desk. "What you took for a ridge is a gilt line on the leather" Fox assured her, but Elsie stuck to her story, claiming she felt the ridge, and challenging him to go home and look at the desk. Confident that he knew all the details of his own desk, Fox duly went to check up, and found that the hinges on the lid "made a continuous projecting gilt ridge just as she had described." Owing to the position of the desk, which Fox had placed with its front against the wall, "she had naturally mistaken the back of the lid for the front," and the continuous line of the hinges for a projecting ridge.

Fox concludes that:

I knew – and indeed I still know – that Elsie was in my room that night in her spirit, though her body was in bed a mile away ... And if the soul could leave the body while the latter still lived, was there not every reason to suppose man had an immortal spirit? ... it made the whole thing ... so much more probable.

The boot was on the other foot shortly afterwards. Elsie reported that she awoke one morning to see Fox standing by her bed, fully dressed and looking as solid as he did in life – so much so in fact that she assumed he had climbed in through the open window. Momentarily paralyzed and terrified of discovery, she heard her mother climbing the stairs to awaken her, but as the doorknob turned, Fox disappeared. Fox was able to verify that he was asleep at the time this happened, but he had no recollection of the experience (compare this once more with resuscitated patients who have no recollection of NDEs).

Scientific Research into the Reality of the OBE

We can still question whether or not these accounts are accurate. Are Oliver Fox and Elsie to be believed? Elsie certainly correctly reported the details of Fox's bedroom, including the raised ridge made by the hinges on his small portable desk. But there is no objective proof of this, beyond the word of the two young people. Have we any better evidence from elsewhere? Fortunately we have, even though it rather lacks the mystical touch of Fox's account. This evidence arises from an experiment conducted by Professor Charles Tart, formerly of the University of California at Davis and one of the most important modern pioneers in the experimental study of parapsychology and altered states of consciousness (Tart 1968 and 1989). Charles Tart was fortunate in obtaining a subject, referred to as Miss Z, who claimed like Elsie that she was able to leave her body at will. Unlike Elsie, Miss Z saw nothing wicked about this, and agreed to spend four nights in Tart's sleep laboratory at Davis, wired up to an electroencephalograph to monitor her brain waves and establish whether or not they showed any abnormal rhythms during her reported OBEs. In addition, Tart placed a different 5-figure random number every night high up on a laboratory shelf and invisible to anyone on the bed. His instructions to Miss Z were that if she could leave her body during the night she was to locate and read the number, note the time on the wall clock, and wake up to tell him about the experience.

On the first three nights Miss Z reported having a number of OBEs, but found herself unable to coordinate her movements sufficiently while out of the body to find her way to the number. On the fourth night, however, she was able to do so, saw the number, and was able to recall it for Professor Tart. The number she gave - 25132 – was indeed the number written down by Tart and placed on the laboratory shelf. The odds against getting a 5-figure random number correct by a single guess are 100,000 to one against. Such long odds suggest very strongly that the number was not guessed, but read paranormally. In addition, the electroencephalograph to which Miss Z was attached had recorded that at the time of the OBE her alpha brain waves slowed by one and a half cycles from normal. This was a highly unusual brain phenomenon. Tart had never seen it before, and its unusual nature was confirmed by a colleague at Davis who was the world's leading expert on EEG rhythms during sleep.

The number could only have been read by normal means by someone whose eye level was six and a half feet from the floor. Thus short of leaving her bed and finding something on which to stand, there was no way in which she could have read the number by normal means (the suggestion that it might have been reflected in the adjacent clock face was dismissed by Professor Tart as untenable). And far from leaving the bed, had she even raised her shoulders by two feet from where she was lying she would have dislodged the electrodes of the encephalograph, which would have interrupted the readings and immediately allowed the machine to register her absence. No disturbance of the electrodes had occurred.

Another interesting series of experiments into the objective reality of the OBE was carried out by Dr. William Roll, then Head of the Psychical Research Foundation associated with Duke University, assisted by Robert Morris, subsequently Koestler Professor of Parapsychology at the University of Edinburgh. William Roll had had a number of OBEs himself during which he affirms that "I had no doubt ... that my self had really left my body" (Duncan and Roll 1995). Anxious to research OBEs more objectively Roll, like Charles Tart, was fortunate in finding a subject, psychology graduate Keith Harary, who claimed the ability to leave his body at will. The ingenious experiments devised by Roll sought to establish whether or not Harary was able, when out of his body, to leave the laboratory, travel to his own home a quarter of a mile away, and make his presence felt to two pet kittens given to him for the purpose. One of the kittens was placed in a large box, the floor of which was divided into a grid of 24 numbered squares, and Bob Morris was given the task of recording how much time it spent in each of the squares, and the number of times it meowed during periods of 100 seconds each. The theory was that animals may be particularly sensitive to psychic impressions, and that if Harary was able to visit the box while out of his body the kitten's position on the grid might be influenced by his presence (see also Black, 1975, for a summary of this research).

Results showed that during the time when Harary was projected out of his body the kitten appeared to respond consistently to his presence. Instead of its usual behavior of wandering randomly around the grid and meowing on average 37 times during each 100-second period, it became much calmer, crossed few or none of the squares, and did not meow at all. The odds against this change in behavior being due to chance were calculated by the researchers as 200 to one, not as high as the 100,000 to one odds obtained by Professor Tart in the number-reading experiment, but highly significant nevertheless. There thus seemed little doubt that Harary really was out of his body, and that the kitten could sense his presence. On the strength of these various experiments, Harary then became a psychical researcher himself, and has since been involved in programs designed to help others develop OBE abilities (e.g. Harary and Weintraub 1991).

Another subject who was able to have OBEs at will, Ingo Swann, was extensively tested at both the American Society for Psychical Research and at SRI International, one of the leading research institutes in the USA. In the course of one of these experiments Swann was able successfully to identify objects placed on a platform so high from the ground that they could only be seen from the ceiling. The odds against these results being due to chance were calculated as 40,000 to one. Swann was also able to project to distant locations, given only the map reference, and produce accurate information of what he had seen (Targ and Puthoff 1975, Targ and Harary 1985).

OBEs in Different Circumstances

OBEs are reported as occurring under many different circumstances, including when one is sitting in meditation. One of my postgraduate students who had practiced yoga for many years, reported to me an occasion during meditation when he suddenly found himself sitting behind his physical body. The experience was entirely spontaneous and took him completely by surprise. He had no interest in OBEs and had never attempted any of the practices associated with them; in consequence he was alarmed to find himself staring at the back of his own body, so much so in fact that after he merged again with his body he abandoned yoga and the practice of meditation. In another of the cases in my files the subject told me that she was standing in front of her video recorder in the act of feeding a video tape into the machine when she abruptly found herself out of her body, standing to the right of herself, watching what she was doing. After a few moments she was once more back in her body. It was the only experience of the kind that had occurred in her life, and until she discussed it with me she knew nothing of such things and was completely puzzled by the experience. Another of my students, a mature psychology major and a qualified and experienced nurse, collapsed in her home and was in due course carried out by stretcher to the ambulance which took her to hospital. As the stretcher left her house she found herself out of her body and following along behind with the thought "Oh so that is what my head looks like from above."

On other occasions an OBE can occur during times of physical hardship. One of the most moving accounts concerns a French infantry soldier in the First World War (Muldoon and Carrington 1969). The infantryman reports that after

a dreadful march along a muddy road, mixed with melting snow ... we started for the firing line ... We entered a trench about a mile long ... The liquid mud was up to our knees [and] the frozen rain made it impossible to see. We were in one of the worst trenches ... H. and I were chosen for guard duty ... We were so fatigued that we had not the strength to curse our bad luck. We were prostrated and frozen to the bones, starving with hunger and with nothing to eat. There was no possibility of lighting a fire, and not an inch of dry ground on which to sit. Neither H. nor I would have thought before this time that human beings could suffer so much.

Several hours passed for the two men in these appalling conditions, when suddenly for the infantryman everything changed in what he describes as an "unforeseen manner":

I was conscious, absolutely conscious, of finding myself outside my body. I know that this was I – a real and conscious spirit – literally freed from the corporeal organism ... From without I examined my wretched body attired in green-gray ... But I looked at it with indifference ... I knew that my body had to suffer in an atrocious manner, but I ... my spirit, felt nothing. As long as I remained in this state ... it seemed to me that it was a perfectly natural happening ... It was only when I re-entered my body that I was convinced of having gone through the strange experience. Nothing could destroy the absolute, certain, and intimate conviction that on this night my spirit was temporarily separated from my body.

An interesting feature of all four of the above experiences is that they were totally unexpected. No drugs were involved, no special techniques for encouraging out-of-the-body experiences, and all four individuals were in apparently normal mental health. It could be argued that the infantryman was in such a desperate situation that he hallucinated, but this is simply to try to attach a label to his experience in order to argue that it was not what he thought it was. Labels, except when supported by hard evidence, are not explanations, and it is misleading to offer them as if they were. The infantryman knew what he experienced. He was awake (no guard in a front line trench would dare to allow himself even to doze – sleeping while on guard in the First World War was punishable by death – and as an extra safeguard against the risk of sleep sentries were always posted in twos), he was sober, and he was aware of what occurred. In the other three examples I have just quoted, it is even less appropriate to suggest hallucinations or dreaming. In the first of them the experience was so realistic and had such an effect upon the subject that he abandoned his yogic studies and his meditation. In the second, the subject was so anxious to find the cause of her experience that she embarked upon an extensive search for the answer, which led her in due course to consult me. In the third the subject was fully conscious when the ambulance arrived, and as an experienced nurse had some knowledge of her own condition.

Muldoon's Experiences

All four of these examples involve single experiences of OBEs. But there are in the literature many interesting first-hand accounts published by individuals who have had frequent OBEs. Oliver Fox is one such individuals but even better known is Sylvan Muldoon. In 1927 Muldoon, who had his first OBE at the age of 12, contacted Hereward Carrington, a leading psychical researcher and one of the authors of the Feilding Report into the mediumship of Eusapia Paladino (Chapter 12) to acquaint him with his numerous experiences out of the body. Carrington was impressed, and promised to co-operate with Muldoon in a book dealing with OBEs, a subject neglected up to that point by researchers. The book, which first appeared in 1929 and which has remained periodically in print ever since, was something of a revelation in that not only did it demonstrate that a highly-respected psychical researcher like Carrington was convinced that Muldoon's experiences were genuine, it approached the whole subject in a serious, analytical way, outlining in detail the nature of OBEs, their possible cause, their implications for an understanding of consciousness, their relationship with dreams and sleeping, and the techniques that could facilitate the experience.

After Muldoon's first spontaneous OBE at age 12, others followed so frequently that he "became so accustomed to them that ... [he] soon regarded them as nothing extraordinary and seldom mentioned them even to members of [his] own family." Subsequently, he learnt that what he called "the conscious projection of the astral body" was relatively common, and that many psychics could produce such experiences virtually at will. This started him experimenting – eventually successfully – with ways of producing intentional OBEs himself. However, with commendable prescience, he commented that "Although we are living in the twentieth century we still have with us the intolerance of the Middle Ages, and I am not optimistic enough to believe that a great many will read without prejudice what I have to say ... I am well aware ... that one must first experience conscious astral projection before he can believe it." Having had the experience himself, Muldoon was in no doubt of its reality, and his answer to the skeptic who demanded objective proof was "You cannot have objective proof. You must experience it, then you will have proof."

In a further book (Muldoon and Carrington 1987), the authors give numerous examples of OBEs reported to them by others. One of the techniques for inducing OBEs frequently reported to them is to start by imagining that one is looking at one's own body from a position outside it, as if viewing it objectively. Then at some point the consciousness is transferred to this image, from where one can now look back at the real physical body. In an old occult tradition, this is done, after intensive training in meditation, by imagining that a mirror image of oneself is sitting opposite during the meditation session, at which point the transfer of consciousness between the physical self and the imaginary self is attempted. Another of the techniques to which Muldoon and Carrington make reference is to imagine oneself ascending in a lift, upwards through several floors, and that on reaching the roof to imagine stepping out of the lift and in doing so out of the body.

Techniques for Inducing OBEs

Extensive guidance on other techniques is given by Harary and Weintraub (1991), Buhlman (1996), Slasher (1997), Peterson (1997), and Dack (1999). Like Muldoon and Carrington, all these authors stress the importance of visualization, in particular visualizing oneself from a point outside the body. Peterson also suggests that several times a day one visualizes oneself flying over valleys and seas. Frequent instructions to the unconscious are also stressed, so that the unconscious gets the idea variously that one wishes to remember dreams, to know during dreams that one is dreaming (i.e. to experience so-called lucid drams), and to leave one's body and return safely. Emphasis is also placed upon positive thinking (the unconditional belief that one *can* have OBEs), upon the ability to relax mind and body, and upon remaining conscious for as long as possible during the hypnagogic state (the state just between waking and sleeping), and upon meditation.

I can certainly vouch for the fact that practice in meditation appears to facilitate the OBE. There are two reasons why it does. Firstly, progress in meditation helps to still the distracting internal chatter of the conscious mind, thus allowing awareness of more subtle mental states, usually drowned out by this chatter, to emerge into consciousness. Secondly, progress in meditation helps one to become much more observant of both the inner and outer worlds. This awareness then persists even during dreaming sleep, so that one is better able to recognize the fact that one is dreaming and to experience the so-called lucid dreams that can act as triggers for OBEs (Fontana 1998, 1999). My own experiences of OBEs, limited as they are, have come during periods of my life when I have been devoting an hour a day to sitting in meditation. The first of these experiences developed out of a lucid dream. In the dream I was passing a small church on my right-hand side when I saw approaching me down the pathway from the church door a shadowy figure in a blue robe and a white headdress, who for some reason I associated with the Virgin Mary. Before she reached the gate of the churchyard I had passed on, crossing a road and looking up at another old stone building. In the tower of the building there was a clock, and around the clock was some writing which I was able to read. Before taking in the words the thought struck me "you can't usually read in dreams – oh, so I'm dreaming!" As typically happens in lucid dreams there came a great sense of excitement, and the colors around me became vivid and vibrant. My next thought was "so if I'm dreaming, what shall I do with the dream?" I decided I would like to fly, and immediately I was swept up from the ground, turned on my back, and drawn at great speed through a kind of velvet darkness. At the same moment I was aware of a roaring, rushing, vibrating sound that filled my whole body. The realization came to me that I was leaving my body. Nothing about the experience was in the least frightening, but the thought came that I ought to say a prayer for my safe return. By this I meant my safe return once the experience had run its course, but to my great disappointment it came to an abrupt end at the moment of saying the prayer, and I found myself awake and in my body.

I had read very little about OBEs at that time, but the following day I had a vague recollection that some time ago I had come across a reference to the fact that the feeling of vibration that I had experienced often accompanies an OBE. I turned up all the literature I could on the subject, and found this was indeed said to be the case. To my surprise I also read, for the first time, that any sign of fear leads to an abrupt return to the body. It thus seemed to me that my prayer for a safe return had been interpreted as fear by whatever mechanism was responsible for the experience, and that this was the reason for my abrupt return to the body. I make no particular claim for this experience or for any of my other brief personal encounters with OBEs. These encounters have been sufficient to demonstrate to me the reality of the experience, but they contain none of the veridical elements likely to convince others. One point to emerge from them, however, is that there does indeed appear to be a connection between the OBE and lucid dreaming. And from my own experience one of the triggers that converts a normal dream, in which one is not aware one is dreaming, into a lucid dream is the recognition of an anomaly of some kind in the dream that could not occur in waking life. For example, in one of my experiences, this trigger was the fact that I noticed, while my dreaming self was walking down a road that was strange to me but which I somehow knew was in Britain, that the signs above all the shops were in French. Immediately I realized that this could only happen in dreams, and with the usual flash of excitement the dream became lucid.

On this occasion I allowed the dream to take its course. There was no occurrence of the rushing, vibrating experience, but I nevertheless felt myself lifted up and floating gently and vertically just above the pavement. Passers-by seemed unaware of my presence, but I was conscious of trailing something behind me, which seemed like a fine white silken scarf, and when I passed two young girls the scarf gently touched the face of one of them and she looked up puzzled, as though she had felt the touch but could not see the cause. I mention this experience because on waking it occurred to me that the scarf was analogous to the silken cord that is said in some accounts of both OBEs and NDEs to connect the exteriorized body to the physical body while the consciousness is exteriorized. All I can say is that I was particularly skeptical about the existence of this silken cord, so my own expectations did not appear to play any part in the experience.

The Experiences of Robert Monroe

One of the most extensive and interesting published reports of personal OBE experiences is that of the late Robert Monroe, an American electrical engineer and President of two radio corporations. Monroe's first strange experience occurred in 1958 while he was resting on a couch in his living room. Without warning a beam of warm light like sunlight struck his entire body, causing it to vibrate violently. Initially unable to move, he forced himself to sit up and then get to his feet. The clock showed him that only a few seconds had passed since he went to lie on the couch, and he was sure he had not closed his eyes before the arrival of the beam of light. The experience was repeated nine times over the following six weeks when he lay down to sleep, and was only terminated each time when he sat up. Medical examination revealed no physical problem, so Monroe determined that if the experience happened again, he would simply observe it as objectively as possible (Monroe 1972).

It did indeed happen again, on numerous occasions, but each time the vibration died down of its own accord and nothing further occurred. However, some months later Monroe became aware during the vibration that he could move his right hand which was draped over the side of the bed and touching the floor. Tentatively he pushed with his fingers and felt them go through the floor and touch the top of the ceiling below. Then the experience ended and everything was back to normal. But four weeks later, when the vibration experience happened again, he idly started to anticipate a gliding trip he was to take the following afternoon. He then felt himself lying against a wall, and thinking he had fallen out of bed he looked in the dim light for the bedroom wall, but found it had no windows in it, no furniture against it, and no door. The realization then dawned that it was not the wall at all. He was up against the ceiling. There below him was the bed, and in it the recumbent figures of his wife and himself. The fear that this caused brought him immediately back into his physical body.

Thus began Monroe's series of extraordinarily vivid OBEs. He soon found that whenever the vibrations started all he had to do was to think of floating up, and the next moment he was in mid air. When he wished to return, he had only to think of himself back in bed, and next moment he was there. His first evidential experience came one afternoon when, out of his body, he thought of visiting his doctor, a Dr. Bradshaw, whom he knew to be ill in bed at the time and whose bedroom he had never previously seen. The sensation of going uphill then followed, and of being helped by some unseen lifting power, and this was followed by the sight of Dr. Bradshaw, dressed in hat and light overcoat, accompanied by his wife dressed in black. He watched them walk towards their garage before he returned to his office, where the experience had started, and felt himself back in his physical body. The time was four twenty-seven. He informed his wife of the details, and then telephoned the Bradshaws to ask, without mentioning his OBE, where they had been that afternoon. Mrs. Bradshaw replied that at four twenty-five she had left the house to drive to the post office, and that as her husband was feeling better he accompanied her. They had walked to the garage together. In reply to Monroe's query as to what they were wearing, Mrs. Bradshaw answered that she was in black trousers with a black coat over a red sweater, and that her husband was in a light-colored coat and hat.

Monroe gives a number of other examples of events witnessed during his OBEs, all of which were confirmed as correct by the people he recognized as involved in them. In some cases these events were unusual and very unlikely to have been the subject of good guesses. For example, he saw a friend, Agnew Bahnson, loading with some difficulty an awkward-looking device with wheels and an electric motor into the back seat of his car. Subsequently he saw Mrs. Bahnson dealing what looked like large white playing cards to members of the family seated around a table. Later, on asking the family what they were doing at the times concerned, Agnew Bahnson reported he was loading a Van DeGraff generator into the back seat of his car (Monroe was shown the device, which was unknown to him and which he recognized as the object he had seen). Mrs. Bahnson confirmed that, for the first time in two years, she had brought the morning mail to the breakfast table and was passing out the white envelopes to the family.

On occasions, Monroe was also able to make his presence felt to others while out of the body. On one of these occasions he decided to visit a woman friend, RW, who was away on holiday at the time, but in a location unknown to him. In response to the decision he found himself in a kitchen where RW and two teenage girls, one blonde and one brunette, were sitting together with drinking glasses in their hands. He sensed that RW was aware of his presence (although he had not told her of his intended visit), but to ensure she remembered the occasion he pinched her on her side, just above the waist and below the rib cage. When RW returned home after her holiday, Monroe asked her what she had been doing at the time concerned. It transpired she had indeed been sitting, for the very first time, with her niece, a brunette, and a friend of the niece, a blonde. Both girls were in their teens, and all three women had drinks in their hands. RW had no recollection of Monroe's visit, but when he asked her about the pinch she showed him the bruise on her side exactly where it had occurred, and reported that when she was sitting with the girls she "felt this terrible pinch," which she thought must have been inflicted by her brother-in-law who had crept up behind her, "I turned around, but there was no one there. I never had any idea it was you! It hurt!"

In two subsequent books (1985, 1994) Monroe recounts OBE experiences that apparently took him to other dimensions, and which he claimed are part of the route we all must take after death. But it is his first book that provides us with some of the most objective evidence that OBEs are real experiences, and that consciousness may indeed be able to leave the physical body while one is alive. It is unfortunate that he did not publish signed accounts from the various individuals he claimed to see while out of the body, and who confirmed as correct the reports he gave of their actions. But Monroe was well known to leading psychical researchers such as Professor Charles Tart and Professor Arthur Ellison, both of whom have featured in this book and both of whom had such respect for him and for his experiences that they served as advisors to the Monroe Institute, founded by Monroe to develop and teach practical methods not only for inducing OBEs but also for accelerated learning through techniques such as so-called hemi-sync which is designed to synchronize the activities of the two hemispheres of the brain. The Institute continues to thrive, and there are various interesting published accounts by those who have attended and benefited from its courses (e.g. Moen 1999).

Questions About the Nature of OBEs

The fact that many of the authors quoted in this chapter knew that they were out of the body during their OBEs argues against Louisa Rhine's suggestion (Louisa Rhine 1967) that OBEs (and for that matter apparitions) are all to do with the percipient not the agent. The number of occasions when individuals report experiencing OBEs far outweigh those occasions where – as in the case of three of the examples quoted in this chapter – the percipient saw the agent but the agent had no subsequent recollection of being out of the body. Even in the three examples quoted it is notable that the agents were asleep at the time. It is possible that had they been roused from sleep while the experience was taking place, they would have remembered it.

Monroe's references to OBEs that involve traveling to other dimensions rather than remaining within the physical world raise a different kind of issue, and one that puzzles some of those who have spoken to me about their OBEs or have read the relevant literature, namely that although on occasions the OBE appears to take place in this world, at other times it appears to take place in a world that seems to be at best only an inexact copy of this one (e.g. even if familiar sights are seen the details are not quite right) and even to extend to Monroe's other dimensions. Do the differences between these two types of OBE cast doubt on the reality of the whole experience? In fact explanations for these differences have been with us for many years. Muldoon and Carrington refer to them, as does Walker (1974) and many others. A common theme of these explanations is that humans have three bodies (in fact more than three, but for present purposes we can focus upon three), a physical body, a non-physical energy body, and an astral body. The physical body we know about. The energy body is said to permeate the physical body, and to be responsible for the subtle energies that animate that body (it is these energies that are said to form the chakras spoken of in the Eastern psycho-spiritual traditions, and the meridians that are needled in acupuncture). The astral body is said to be the seat of consciousness and of the soul and the spirit. At death the energy body and the astral body separate from the physical; three days later the energy body is said to disintegrate, leaving the astral body to continue a non-physical existence in other realms.

It is claimed that the astral body always leaves the physical during the OBE, sometimes alone but sometimes accompanied by all or part of the energy body. When it leaves on its own it finds itself in the astral world, which in places resembles the physical world (and which seems at times to create a copy of it, although with some of the details incorrect, as in dreams). When it leaves accompanied by the energy body, it remains in the material world and can view events in this world. If these explanations are correct, in his early OBEs Monroe's astral body left together with his energy body, enabling him to obtain apparently veridical details of what was taking place on earth, while as his abilities at leaving his physical body developed he left only in his astral body.

A further question sometimes asked is why, if the individual is in both the astral and the energy bodies and remains in the physical world, some people seem able to see him or her, while others are unable to do so. Possibly some psychic ability is needed in the observer, or possibly something depends upon how much of the energy body accompanies the astral body. The more of the energy body that is present, the more likely it is that the astral body becomes visible. Another question, namely why, if as it is sometimes claimed, we all experience OBEs while asleep we do not all remember them, has already been addressed. The possible answer is that, as in the case of failures to recall NDEs, the mechanism that prevents us from remembering many of our dreams comes into play. It does seem, however, that even if the person experiencing the OBE has no recollection of having done so, his or her astral body (let us use this term for want of a better one) may still be seen by others. One example, that of Fox seen clearly by his girlfriend Elsie even though he had no memory of the event, has already been given. I can add to this a very clear personal example of my own, which took place early one morning.

For some unknown reason I had woken early. I am unsure of the time but the room was becoming light. As I opened my eyes I saw a very dear friend of mine sitting on the left side of my bed, between me and the main bedroom window. She was in her nightclothes and was sitting with her back against the bed-head a foot or so away from me, and with her legs stretched out in front of her. In amazement, and sure she was present in the flesh, I turned fully towards her, raised myself on my left elbow, and resting my head on my hand said "What on *earth* are you doing here?" She seemed not to hear, and I looked steadily at her. She was as solid as if in the body, and was looking with a thoughtful, serious, rather preoccupied expression towards the foot of the bed. As I gazed at her, waiting for an answer, I saw that she was gradually becoming transparent, so that I began to see the outline of the window through her, then suddenly, like a light being switched off, she was gone.

One of my first acts upon rising was to phone her and recount the experience. She had no recollection of being out of her body or of visiting me. However, she had a clear memory of having had what she remembered as a "psychic dream," although the details now escaped her, and of waking from it as it was getting light with the idea "I must tell David about this." She thought, though was not certain, that she sat up in bed at that point. There is a possibility that her desire to tell me of the dream led to her appearance, out of the body, in my bedroom, but in my view a more likely explanations is that what she described as a "psychic dream" was in fact her OBE, and that it was this experience that on waking she identified with a dream that she could not quite remember. Either way, I know that the account of my own experience is correct. I know that I was awake, I know that I saw my friend sitting on my bed, I know that I raised myself on my elbow and looked at her closely, I know I saw her become transparent and disappear. The only thought in my mind until she began to disappear was that she was there in person. She has never been in my bedroom or even in my house, and I was naturally surprised to see her there early in the morning. She is a person with natural – if reluctant – psychic abilities and I have no difficulty in accepting that she might be able to leave her body, though she has never had any recollection of having done so, and has never made any conscious attempt to do so.

Experiences of this kind argue against the theory that nothing leaves the body during OBEs, and that the information gained in the course of them is due to clairvoyance. One could hardly suppose that my friend was being clairvoyant when she appeared to me. It is equally unlikely that I was clairvoyant, and actually saw her in her own bedroom and not in mine. She was sitting on my bed and not on hers, and as she became transparent it was my bedroom window that I saw through her and not her own. The other evidence so far quoted in this chapter also argues against clairvoyance. Keith Harary could hardly have influenced the behavior of his cats in Bill Roll's experiment by clairvoyance (though it is conceivable that he might have been in telepathic contact with them). If Elsie saw Oliver Fox's bedroom by clairvoyance, why was it that Fox saw her standing in the room? Can one clairvoyantly see one's own body from a position outside it? Could Monroe have been deceived, over a number of years and with hundreds of OBEs, into imagining he was leaving his body when all he was doing was practicing clairvoyance? Could Miss Z (who like Monroe had had many experiences of OBEs) have deceived herself into thinking she was leaving her body while asleep in Charles Tart's laboratory when all that happened was that she saw his random number by clairvoyance?

The distinction between OBEs and clairvoyance may sometimes be a confused one, but those who have regular OBEs are in no doubt that they are indeed out of their bodies. And clairvoyant experiences have no obvious reason to present themselves in the guise of out-of-the-body experiences. In two of the most veridical cases of clairvoyance in my own records, the subject concerned, one of my doctoral students, firstly saw a winning lottery number flashed up in front of her as on a screen (she was playing the Cyprus lottery at the time, and has had no such experiences, correct or incorrect, before or since), and subsequently in much the same way saw a telephone number of which she had no knowledge but which was of very great relevance to her (again a unique experience). On neither of these occasions was there any sensation of being anywhere other than in her physical body.

In recent years a range of books have appeared detailing personal experiences with OBEs. Slasher (1996) gives particularly extensive details of the various techniques that he has found effective in helping him leave the body. He also repeats the claim, referred to a little earlier in this chapter, that everyone leaves the body each night, sometimes in dreams and sometimes in dreamless sleep, even if no memory of the experience is retained. The esoteric and psycho-spiritual traditions have also long taught that the astral and energy bodies hover just above the sleeping physical body each night, and that clairvoyants can sometimes see this sleeping body, just as they are sometimes able to see the astral and energy body leaving at death. I once had an interesting experience that could be connected with this belief in some way. For many nights I had been waking briefly in the middle of the night with a clear awareness of a presence standing on the left side of my bed. I had no idea of the identity of this presence, and it seemed to vanish each time just as I became fully conscious. Every time this happened, I fell asleep again almost at once. There was nothing frightening about this seeming presence, but I was interested to find an explanation for it. One night when I awoke with a strong sense of it, I received simultaneously the clear impression that to find the answer I must think back to what had been happening just before I awoke, rather as one rewinds a film. I did so – many things seem possible in the moment of waking from sleep – and immediately became aware, to my utter astonishment, that the "presence" was in fact myself, in the moment of reuniting with the physical body.

I have no explanation for this curious experience. At the time I had not been giving any thought to out-of-the-body experiences, and certainly it had never occurred to me that the "presence" might have anything to do with them. The awareness that it was in fact myself came instantaneously, rather in the way that creative insights sometimes come to both artists and scientists in dreams or in the moment of waking (Fontana 1995). I don't make any claims for the experience, and simply record it as a matter of fact. Whether or not it supports the notion that consciousness leaves the body each night during sleep I cannot say. But I know that the experience happened, I know it was not a dream, and I know that, having had the curious insight into what might have caused the presence, the experience has never happened again – rather as if my unconscious mind, having succeeded in drawing the matter to my conscious attention in the hope I might learn something from it, no longer needs to disturb my sleep each time it occurs.

CHAPTER 17
REINCARNATION

The Concept of Reincarnation

Followers of Buddhism, of many schools of Hinduism and Taoism, of Jainism, of Sikhism, and of other Eastern traditions, regard reincarnation – or rebirth as the Buddhists prefer to call it, as they argue that the process is like a flame being passed from candle to candle rather than the reincarnation of an enduring self – as a simple fact of existence. The individual is born, dies, and is born again, and the cycle is repeated until he or she becomes free from the three hindrances of attachment, aversion, and ignorance. Attachment represents greed and the desire to cling to material things as if they are eternal, aversion is the drive to avoid or destroy those things that interfere with one's happiness, and ignorance is the mistaken view that the material world represents ultimate reality. Not only do these three hindrances lead to suffering, they prevent the individual from gaining so-called enlightenment or liberation.

Throughout each lifetime, the thread of personal karma is said to run. This means that good karma – good deeds – in one lifetime leads to a favorable rebirth, while bad karma leads to an unfavorable one. Advanced levels of good karma can even earn rebirth in the heavenly realms rather than back here on earth, but this is not necessarily a good thing, as it is said that since everything in the heavenly realms is perfect they provide no opportunity for facing challenges or for making choices between right and wrong, and consequently are devoid of opportunities for further progress and for obtaining enlightenment and leaving altogether the realms of form and passing into the formless Nirvanic realms (the realms of pure consciousness) where one ultimately becomes united with what Hindus refer to as *Brahman*, the absolute reality from which all things originally arise. Accordingly, when the length of time in heaven earned through good karma has been used up, one must again be reborn on this earth and must start afresh the process of seeking liberation (*moksha* in Hinduism). Similarly, it is said that an excess of bad karma can lead to rebirth in the hell realms or as an animal, but once one has expiated, through unimaginable sufferings, all the effects of bad karma, one will again be reborn on earth and have another chance to make the right kind of progress (see e.g. Fisher, 1993, for a summary).

A belief in reincarnation has also featured in many of the Western and Middle Eastern traditions. It was present in Egyptian beliefs, in the Orphic, Dyonisian, and Elusinian mystery schools of ancient Greece, in the teachings of Pythagoras (best known as one of the founders of geometry), in the writings of Plato and of Plotinus and of the Neo-Platonists. Head and Cranston (1968 and 1977) provide extensive surveys of the relevant Western and Eastern literature, and Christie-Murray (1988) examines some of the detailed differences between the various traditions. Until the Council of Constantinople in 553, when it was voted out by the unrepresentative delegates invited by the Emperor Constantine, reincarnation in one form or another was an acceptable part of Christian teaching, in particular of the Gnostic teachings associated with Origen, and there are hints of it in Augustine and Eckhart. It has also resurfaced from time to time in various Gnostic Christian heresies, such as that of the Cathars in thirteenth-century Europe (Guirdham 1977). But what exactly is the doctrine of reincarnation, and what if anything does it tell us about the possibilities of survival?

In most, though not all, traditions associated with a belief in reincarnation, it is taught that there is an interval spent in the spiritual realms between one incarnation and the next. In the Western traditions this interval is typically seen as an opportunity to learn the lessons of the previous life on earth before embarking on the next one (e.g. Whitton and Fisher 1986). In the Tibetan Buddhist teachings that have received much attention in recent years in the West it is seen as a chance to recognize and merge with the Clear Light of Bliss that represents ultimate reality, instead of being deceived into believing that the gods and demons witnessed while in the immediate afterlife are "real" instead of the creation of one's own mind, a deception that keeps one attached to the illusory world of form, and that leads inexorably to another lifetime here on earth (Evans-Wentz 1960).

The Evidence for Reincarnation

The immediate question is how can we attempt to ascertain whether the belief in reincarnation is supported by evidence? If there is such evidence, then although it would not demonstrate that everyone reincarnates, it would provide further support for some form of survival. Any answer to this question must rely to some extent upon the ability to remember past lives. If we have no memory of them can they be said to represent "our" lives? Even though our memories of the present life are fragmentary, we nevertheless rely upon them to give us a sense of continuity, a sense of persisting identity, a sense that we are the same people who lived through early childhood, went to school, made friends, fell in and out of love, obtained qualifications, built careers, had families, and so on. Without memories, we would be strangers to ourselves. Thus if we have no memories of past lives, we might just as well forget about the possibility that they ever existed. And since in our next lives we would not remember the present one, surely that would be tantamount to oblivion? It could be argued that past lives have made us what we are today, but what use is that knowledge, beyond perhaps giving us an excuse for blaming our present mistakes upon things that happened many lifetimes ago, and for assuming that people subject to extremes of suffering in this life must be working off the "bad karma" that they have earned for themselves? Even Buddhism, which rejects the idea that an enduring "self" goes from life to life, seems to recognize this, and to take the view that past lives can in fact be accessed (the Buddha is said after his enlightenment to have remembered 900 of his past incarnations).

One technique said to assist this recall is hypnosis. If someone is a good subject for hypnosis (as are some ten per cent of the population) they can be "regressed" back into childhood, recalling in the process memories that have lain buried in the unconscious for decades. The phenomenon is a curious one. They may begin to talk in childish tones, may apparently remember nothing of what happened in adult life, be unable to do simple arithmetic, and may draw like a child rather than an adult. Regression is sometimes used in psychotherapy in an attempt to uncover childhood memories that may be a cause of psychological problems in adult life, and there is some evidence that these childhood memories are accurate. One test of whether they are or not has been to establish if under hypnosis the individual is able to remember the day of the week upon which certain of their early birthdays fell. Few adults would remember details of this kind but they are important to young children, and some studies have shown that they can indeed be correctly recalled in response to questions by the hypnotist (Marcuse 1959).

What happens if we regress people to childhood, and then go on with the regression back down the years to their birth and then try to go back even before birth? Arnold Bloxham is a good example of a hypnotist who attempted past-life regressions of this kind (Iverson 1976). Once he had taken them through the pre-birth barrier, Bloxham's subjects went back, without further suggestion, to what appeared to be memories of lives often lived in distant centuries. What is more they reported events in these past lives that in some cases turned out to contain historically accurate – and sometimes obscure – details. Another hypnotist, Malcolm Price, from whom I learnt some of the skills of hypnosis, achieved a similar effect with his subjects. And not only were the historical details reported by individuals regressed by Bloxham and by Price correct, sometimes these memories were accompanied by powerful emotions that appeared to be connected with them in some way (see also Ebon 1969, Williston and Johnson 1988, Carpenter 1995, Stemman 1997).

One of the first hypnotists to attempt to obtain past-life regressions was Morey Bernstein who regressed a young woman, Virginia Tighe, to a past life in which she claimed to be a young Irish woman, Bridey Murphy, born in County Cork in 1798 to Duncan Murphy, a barrister (Bernstein 1956). She gave the name of her house, of her brother, of the teacher at her day school, of her brother's wife, of her husband, of the Catholic priest who married them (although she herself had been raised a Protestant), and of the church in which the wedding took place, together with many other obscure details. Many of the facts were found to be correct when checked by an Irish legal team appointed by Bernstein's publishers, but details of births, marriages, and deaths were not kept in Ireland until 1864, the year after Bridey supposedly died, so some of the most relevant details remained unconfirmed.

Many attempts were made when the case was first published to discredit the story, including charges that Virginia may have learnt details of Irish life from an Irish aunt who lived opposite her home, and that these may have unconsciously formed the basis for her story. However, it transpired that the aunt in question, Marie Burns, had been born in New York, had lived most of her life in Chicago, and had not met Virginia until the latter was 18. The paperback edition of Bernstein's book contains two additional chapters by journalist William Barker pointing out the many other errors made by critics in their attacks on the case, and these attacks were also refuted in a review of the whole case by Professor Ducasse, professor of philosophy at Brown University (reprinted in Ebon 1969 from the *Journal of the American Society for Psychical Research*). Ducasse's conclusion was that the case constitutes fairly strong evidence for paranormal knowledge of recondite facts, although since this knowledge could have been obtained by paranormal abilities other than those associated with a past life, it does not provide strong evidence for reincarnation.

An interesting feature of past-life regressions is that they may prove valuable in healing psychological problems experienced in the present incarnation. One of the first examples of this approach is that of psychiatrist Denys Kelsey, who was married to Joan Grant, an author whose widely acclaimed historical novels were said by her to be the result of her capacity, experienced from childhood, for what she called "far-memory," the apparent spontaneous recall of past lives. (Joan Grant's autobiography, published in 1975, is certainly one of the most engaging accounts available to us of the life of a gifted psychic.) Kelsey frequently regressed patients suffering from psychological problems to childhood, and as a consequence of becoming acquainted with Joan Grant developed an interest in possible past-life regressions. Using such regression with patients whose problems had hitherto proved resistant to normal regression and other psychotherapies, Kelsey discovered that these problems appeared to be associated with identifiable events in previous lives. On the basis of his own findings, Kelsey considered that "the recall of an event which occurred centuries ago can be as vivid as the memory of an automobile accident which occurred last week. In fact more vivid ... a regression can have a sense of immediacy which is enveloping and absolute" (Grant and Kelsey 1969).

Hurst (1982), another hypnotist and psychotherapist who has worked extensively with past-life regressions with a view to helping people handle their psychological problems, rejects the idea that the events recalled in the course of these regressions could be pure fiction on the grounds that when in deep hypnotic trance the mind is too relaxed to form the coherent thoughts needed for deliberate deception. However, if conscious deception is not involved, could unconscious fantasies be at work, much as they are in dreams? This is possible, but it would not explain the accurate historical details sometimes given by the subject while in trance. Subjects when they emerge from trance typically deny ever having encountered these details in waking life, and claim to have no conscious recollection of them. The normal psychological explanation for this is that a condition known as cryptomnesia may be at work, i.e. a condition in which, particularly under hypnosis, there emerge into consciousness memories for facts that have been buried so deeply and for so long in the unconscious that the owner does not recognize them as his own memories. There is little doubt that cryptomnesia may play a part in some supposed past-life memories, but the difficulty with it as a complete explanation is that sometimes the details given during the regression are so extensive and obscure that it is hard to accept that the subject would not remember at least having studied the area at some time in life, even if the exact details concerned have been forgotten. If the individual, for example, gives nautical terms associated with the eighteenth-century battleship on which he claims to have met his death in a previous life, it is difficult to accept that he would not recall having at some point studied details of eighteenth-century warships in some depth had he in fact done so. Perhaps people reporting past-life memories are being dishonest when they claim never to have encountered the subject of their memories in this life, but to dismiss all their accounts on the unproven explanation of dishonesty hardly counts as good science. Professor Ducasse makes a similar point when he insists that the attempt to dismiss all past-life memories containing accurate historical details on the grounds that the people reporting these details must have learnt them during their present lives is not "scientific ... but is just piously conservative wishful thinking" (Ducasse 1970).

A number of psychiatrists and counseling psychologists continue to use past-life regression in their work. Weiss (1988) devotes a large part of his book to a detailed report of his work with one patient, Catherine, who after 18 months of conventional psychotherapy under his care for her incapacitating panic and anxiety attacks was making no discernible progress until he attempted to regress her to childhood under hypnosis. After taking Catherine back to age three Weiss was astonished to hear her suddenly starting to speak of herself as a 25-year-old woman, and thus began a series of sessions in which Catherine recalled a number of past lives, many of them marred by frightening and tragic events. In the course of these regressions her panic and anxiety attacks progressively lessened, and finally ceased. Using regression techniques, Weiss then worked with a number of his other patients, and again uncovered events from previous lives that appeared to be the root causes of psychological difficulties in the present. Of particular interest to the question of survival he found he could take his patients back not only to previous lives but to the moment immediately after their deaths in these lives. Much as in NDEs, all apparently reported leaving their bodies with feelings of peace, and traveling towards a bright light. Catherine in particular was also able to remember details of the interval between death in one lifetime and rebirth in another. These included learning lessons from the life that had just ended, and receiving teachings from higher beings and apparently developing some psychic abilities in the process.

Clinical psychologist Dr. Edith Fiore (1978), on the basis of her own clinical experience, considers that there is no psychological problem that cannot be helped by good past-life therapy, and results certainly suggest that although "helped" may not mean cured in a physical sense, it does appear that the patient may feel he or she has a better understanding of the condition concerned, and can more readily muster the attitude of mind that assists positive progress. On the strength of thousands of hours watching and conducting past-life regressions, Fiore is in no doubt that "there is no deliberate nor conscious attempt to deceive." Many other therapists involved in past-life regressions appear to agree (Fisher 1993 gives examples), and even among some of those therapists who dismiss the idea that past-life regression has anything to do with real past lives there is a recognition that the therapy can prove helpful, perhaps because it provides subjects with an "excuse" for their present problems that render them more acceptable.

However, important evidence that memories of a supposed past life can emerge into consciousness outside the context of therapeutic work in the care of a psychiatrist or psychologist is provided by Professor Ian Stevenson, former Professor of Psychiatry at the University of Virginia, whose work will be described in more detail in due course. Stevenson reports that in his sample of children who recall past lives, those who have phobias arising from violent deaths in previous existences do not appear to be freed from these phobias despite now knowing and facing their apparent cause.

Personal Experiences with Regressions

I believe it is important for all psychologists working in clinical, psychotherapeutic, and educational areas to study hypnosis in order to establish whether or not it has any value as an experimental and therapeutic tool, and whether or not it can give us useful insights into the working of the mind. True to this belief, I myself trained in the theory and practice of hypnosis early in my career, and was a founder member of the British Society of Experimental and Clinical Hypnotists (a body open only to qualified psychologists and medical doctors), subsequently serving for some years as

Chairman of the Welsh Branch. As a consequence of my training I have induced hypnotic states in many subjects for experimental and therapeutic purposes, and experienced the hypnotic state myself. And let me digress for a moment and say that although some psychologists working in the area express doubts as to the reality of the hypnotic state, I can confirm from personal experience that there is no doubt that it is both real and remarkable. I can only assume that colleagues who doubt its reality have not experienced it for themselves, possibly because they have never attempted to do so, or because they are poor hypnotic subjects. Nobody can be hypnotized against their will, and some 50 per cent of the population find it hard even to achieve a light hypnotic trance. As a good hypnotic subject myself, the secret is to focus exclusively upon the suggestions given by the hypnotist, and ignore attempts by the mind to become distracted or over-analytical or fearful. End of digression.

I have never used past-life hypnotic regression as part of counseling or psychotherapeutic work, but I have used it (always with the consent of the subject) for experimental purposes. The results have been striking. When regressed, the subject's voice and manner of speech change. They speak haltingly (as always in deep hypnosis) but with apparent certainty of past events and places, of past emotions, difficulties, joys, and tragedies. After the regression is over, they may remark that the experience was one of the most extraordinary of their lives. As part of my own experimental work I have also been regressed, and I can testify that the experience is entirely realistic, lifelike and, perhaps most surprisingly of all, full of unexpected events that lessen the possibility that expectation could explain all that occurred. I can also report experiencing the feeling, mentioned by Dr. Weiss' subjects (though I was not familiar with Weiss' work at the time), of being out of the body at the moment of death during a past-life regression, of being taken upwards and away from the scene towards a light, and the presence of a wise and compassionate being.

Nevertheless, in spite of the vividness and seeming reality of this experience, I am not fully convinced that I was tapping into a past-life experience of my own, for reasons to which I will return in my conclusions later in the chapter. However, further light is thrown upon past-life regression by a lengthy series of experiments conducted by psychologist Dr. Helen Wambach, late of the Monmouth Medical Center in New Jersey (Wambach 1979a and 1979b). Helen Wambach developed what appeared to be a successful method of group hypnosis (though I think it doubtful that all the subjects in her groups would have achieved deep hypnotic states), and then attempted past-life regressions with whole groups of volunteers at a time. Her intention was less to build up a data bank of interesting cases than to look for similarities, differences, and trends between the reported experiences of large numbers of people. To this end, all group members were invited to fill in questionnaires at the end of each session of hypnosis, and the 1,088 responses obtained by this method were then analyzed. The results were striking.

One of the items in the questionnaire was designed to establish to which historical period and which location each subject had regressed. Firstly the results were analyzed to see if there were discrepancies between what is known of the architecture, climate, landscape, clothing, etc associated with the historical periods and the locations concerned and what was reported by subjects. Of the 1,088 responses, only 11 were found to show serious discrepancies, although the extent to which checks could be made on such things in the light of our historical knowledge and the details given by subjects was obviously limited. Next, the nature of the reported past lives was analyzed. In spite of the criticism made by skeptics that most people reporting past lives claim to be have been figures of importance, it was found that the majority of Wambach's subjects reported humble lives. Classifications were carried out on the basis of the reported occupations, clothes worn, dwelling places, food eaten, plates and utensils used, etc. and results showed only seven per cent belonged to the upper class, while some 23 per cent belonged to middle classes and 70 per cent to the lower class. Irrespective of class, most lives reported were bleak and barren and often unhappy. Nobody reported being a famous historical personage. There was no evidence of grand fantasies, and details of clothing and shoes worn and other domestic details were surprisingly accurate.

Another piece of evidence against the charge that her subjects were merely fantasizing their past lives was that, although more people in the general population are reported as preferring to be male than female given the choice, in all the periods of time to which Helen Wambach's subjects regressed – and despite the fact that many females reported lives as males and many males reported lives as females – the ratio of male to females remained consistent at 50.3 per cent males and 49.7 per cent females. This is close to the actual birth ratio between the sexes. Also significant was the finding that. although subjects were given the choice of regressing to one of ten time periods over the last four thousand years, the periods chosen replicated the graph of the world's known population during these times – i.e. more people regressed to periods when the population is known to have been high than to periods when it is known to have been low.

There are possible normal explanations for these various findings. Subjects may have had more prior access to historical data than Wambach supposed. Her methods of analysis may have been faulty. Her records may have been inadequate, both of past historical periods and of questionnaire data. Nevertheless, Dr. Wambach was a careful researcher, and none of those who have criticized her have bothered to go to the time and trouble of repeating her experiments in order to show the supposed flaws in them. And even if she did underestimate her subjects' historical knowledge, there is no doubting its extent and accuracy, even down to detailed items such as clothing and footwear. Her findings on the male-female ratio in past lives, and the close fit between the world population graph over the centuries and the number of reported past lives in each century cannot easily be explained away on the basis of historical knowledge. The absence of important or happy lives is also striking, and argues against the operation simply of pure fantasy. On balance, Helen Wambach's results do seem to add importantly to our knowledge of whether or not past lives are a fact.

There is another aspect of Wambach's research that deserves a mention, namely her attempt to gather accounts from her subjects of the moment of death and of experiences between lives. As with the accounts reported by Dr. Weiss, Wambach's subjects spoke of being taken to tranquil and peaceful surroundings, of learning while there the lessons of their past life, and of agreeing to return to earth when it was made clear to them that further lessons remained to be learnt. These accounts of death, although more general than those given by individuals reporting NDEs or those communicating through mediums, had similar elements to them – the release from the body, the feelings of peace and freedom, the absence of regret, the sense of traveling upwards. In fact 90 per cent of Dr. Wambach's subjects experienced death as pleasant. However, when she brought her subjects "forward" under hypnosis to their rebirth, most reported that the choice to return was made reluctantly. Only 26 per cent looked forward to rebirth; for the rest it was seen as an unhappy and frightening prospect – exactly the reverse of what Wambach had expected.

We can easily dismiss these findings as due to various psychological conflicts and problems faced by subjects within their present lives rather than to anything connected with possible survival and reincarnation. However, we cannot forget that the findings were gathered during the same sessions that yielded the significant historical, sex ratio, and other data. Wambach's subjects were self-selected in the sense that they were attending her workshops as volunteers for past-life regressions, but they represented a fair mixture of age and social class. If fantasy was all that was involved it seems a little strange that 90 per cent of them should conceive of death as pleasant, and only 26 per cent of them should view coming into the world in the same light. Science demands that experimental findings should be replicated by other researchers before they can be regarded as definitive in any way, and it is unfortunate that no large-scale attempt has been made to repeat Dr. Wambach's work. The investment of time, energy, and commitment needed to do so – with nothing to be gained in the way of financial support or of academic advancement – probably explains this.

However, other psychiatrists and psychologists using past-life regression as a form of therapy also report obtaining details from their subjects of the moment of death and the interval of time before the next rebirth. Williston and Johnstone (1988) present a number of such details, as do Whitton and Fisher (1986). Nearly all Williston and Johnstone's subjects speak without prompting of seeing their bodies after death and of moving away to other dimensions, sometimes in the company of deceased relatives and friends. There are no apparent differences between the accounts given by subjects who were agnostics and those who professed religious beliefs, and the similarity of these accounts to those given by individuals reporting NDEs and to those communicated through mediums is again clear, although there is no suggestion that the subjects giving them were familiar with these latter accounts.

Dr Guirdham and Jenny Cockell

Evidence for reincarnation does not come only from work with hypnosis. Some years ago Dr. Arthur Guirdham, a Senior Consultant Psychiatrist in Bath, wrote a series of books detailing a previous incarnation of his among the Cathars, a Gnostic Christian sect that believed one could have direct knowledge of God without going through the priesthood as intermediaries. The sect flourished in the twelfth and thirteenth Centuries in the Languedoc area of France until ruthlessly exterminated by the Albigensian Crusades instigated by Pope Innocent III (who obligingly forgave in advance any sins the Crusaders might commit in the course of their work) and supported by King Philip Augustus and his successor King Louis VIII of France (Guirdham 1970, 1973, 1974, O'Shea 2000). Guirdham's knowledge of this incarnation came initially through a patient of his, Claire Mills, who recalled her own apparent past-life in thirteenth-century France, and later through psychic experiences of his own – which included out-of-the-body experiences. What is unusual about this case is that it is reported to have involved eight people who had lived together as Cathars, and who had chosen to reincarnate in the present day. This group would appear to represent the so-called "group soul" to which we will return in Chapter 18, and Dr. Guirdham came to know each group member through a series of unusual coincidences. His books are far too extensive to summarize here, but in seven of the eight cases Guirdham was able to trace the identities of group members back to thirteenth-century France through obscure sources in the voluminous records of the thirteenth-century French Inquisition, instrumental in the trial and execution of many of the Cathars. He was also given details by Claire Mills and by other group members of historical details of the Cathars that appeared incorrect at the time but which, again from highly obscure sources that for various reasons group members were unlikely to have encountered and which Guirdham himself only discovered after considerable research, were eventually confirmed. (In a later book, Guirdham 1976, writes of other incarnations shared by this group plus some additional members.)

I must confess to being very puzzled by these books. When I first read them I wrote to the late Dr. Arthur Guirdham personally and was able to meet and interview him. He impressed me as a man of penetrating intellect and of complete integrity. I discussed his books with him, his past-life experiences, the group of people who he claimed had reincarnated with him, and his own psychic abilities, and he was consistent and unshakeable, both in the details which he had given in the books and in any others which he shared with me. For many years I have had an interest in the Cathars, and over a number of summers visited all the historical sites associated with them in the Languedoc area of France. Thus I can vouch for Arthur Guirdham's extensive and scholarly knowledge of all things associated with them. One thing was clear. He was not given to fantasy or deception. And he was not likely to be deceived by others. Another eminent psychiatrist, Dr. Ken Smith, one of the founders of the highly regarded psychological theory known as reversal theory (e.g. Apter 1989), who knew Guirdham for many years both professionally and personally, also vouched for his excellent good sense and undoubted integrity. Ken Smith, who I knew well, was a fine judge of his fellow men, and taken together with the evidence in Guirdham's books his good account of him supports the idea that at the very least Guirdham was involved in a series of events inexplicable by normal means.

Yet another kind of evidence for reincarnation comes from individuals who have intimations of their own past lives from dreams and from vivid spontaneous flashes of recall. Sometimes such cases yield details unknown at the time but which are confirmed by subsequent investigation. An example of such evidence is provided by Cockell (1993 and 1996). Jenny Cockell reports that throughout her childhood her dreams were "swamped by memories" of being another woman, Mary, and of dying of fever, terrified of what would become of the children she was leaving behind. During the day, strong memories would emerge of seven or eight children, the eldest a boy of 13, of a cottage standing sideways to a quiet lane and separated from it by a stone wall, of a gate and a farm track, and of details of the interior of the cottage. Clear images of neighboring houses, of a church, of a nearby village, and of surrounding countryside would also emerge. In addition she sometimes found herself doing the things that Mary would have done, such as sweeping and cleaning without the use of modern appliances, and remembering Mary's cooking and shopping chores. Repeatedly she found herself drawing maps of Mary's village, and there was a remarkable consistency to these maps and to the other memories over the years of her childhood and early adult life. When looking at a map of Ireland she would feel herself drawn intuitively to a village called Malahide, and experience the conviction that this was where she had lived as Mary.

Eventually she decided to submit to past-life regression under hypnosis in order further to explore these experiences. Once regressed she found herself as Mary, living through many other details of her past life. The family name O'Neil also came up during regression. There is no space to give details of all of Jenny Cockell's other attempts to check her past-life memories, but these included writing to all the people with the name of O'Neil living in the Malahide area, obtaining a street map of Malahide, visiting the village for herself, and securing a copy of Mary O'Neil's death certificate and the names of her children. Later, through the nationwide television network interested in covering the story, she met the eldest of Mary's four sons, Sonny (now aged 71), and the two of them were able to compare the descriptions they had each independently made for the televisions network of events and circumstances surrounding the family.

Cockell's extensive research and her meeting with Sonny confirmed that the great majority of the facts corresponded to those that had emerged in her dreams and during the past-life regressions. Her map of the village, the position and the internal layout of the cottage (which had been demolished in 1959), the cottage's immediate surroundings, the drunken violent behavior of Mary's husband, names and dates, and family events and experiences all proved correct. Many of these events and experiences were so personal that it seemed they could not have been accurately guessed or known by people outside the family. Sonny himself accepted that, incredible as it seemed, the facts pointed towards Jenny Cockell being the reincarnation of Mary O'Neil. When Mary had died, at the early age of 35, her children had been split up and sent to different orphanages, losing touch with each other. As a result of the publication of Jenny's book and the publicity given to her story on the television and in the national press, the surviving children once more came into contact with each other, and Jenny was instrumental in arranging a family reunion (Semman 1997).

What can we deduce from this story? Jenny Cockell was not and is not a gullible person. Her membership of Mensa (an organization that admits only those with high IQs) indicates that she is highly intelligent, and her book details not only a long and arduous search for what she considered were her lost children, but the painful emotions in which the search involved her. She is married in this life with children of her own, so there is no question of her unconsciously inventing the whole story as a compensation for a family that she does not have. Mary Rose Barrington, a lawyer, highly experienced researcher, and senior member of the SPR Council investigated the case, interviewed Jenny Cockell, and was impressed by her integrity. Stemman (1997) also interviewed Sonny and confirmed that he accepted Cockell's story. Gitti Coates, the researcher for the television network who became intimately connected with the case and investigated important details for herself, is known to colleagues and myself, and there is no doubt of the lengths to which she went to ensure the veracity of the story.

It would be professionally impertinent of me to try to insist that Jenny

Cockell is wrong to regard herself as the reincarnation of Mary O'Neil. Science knows so little about these experiences that we must take due note of what those who have them tell us, particularly when the person concerned is as credible as Cockell and the facts of the case are so clearly stated, and I will defer my comments until the end of the chapter. However, it would clearly be far-fetched to suppose that Cockell made clandestine trips to Ireland to learn details, which she then wove into a fictitious story. Not only is there no evidence that such trips took place (though there is evidence that her involvement in the case not surprisingly placed an emotional strain upon her present family), but many of the details of the O'Neil family which she relates were not public knowledge, and were only confirmed by Sonny O'Neil. The suggestion that Sonny agreed with Jenny's account out of sympathy for her or eagerness to be involved in the case is discounted by the fact that he and Jenny, at the instigation of the television network, wrote down all the details they could remember before they met each other. For these various reasons, the paranormality of the case therefore seems evident.

The Work of Ian Stevenson

Another class of evidence suggestive of reincarnation comes from the meticulous, painstaking work of Professor Ian Stevenson. With colleague Professor Bruce Greyson, whose work on near-death experiences was referred to in the last chapter, Professor Erlendur Haraldsson of the University of Iceland mentioned in connection with the Icelandic medium Indrid Indridason in Chapter 12, and Professor Satwant Pastricha of India, Ian Stevenson has identified many cases, particularly in India, Sri Lanka, Brazil, Alaska, and Lebanon, of children who have spontaneously referred to past lives in their early years, often long before they could either have visited the places and people to whom they refer, or learnt anything about them. Professor Stevenson is surely one of the finest and most gifted researchers ever to have devoted time to psychical research, and the results of his work with the young children in question is of such high quality that it cannot reasonably be questioned on methodological or other grounds. In a number of publications (e.g. 1974, 1975, 1977, 1980, 1983, 1987) Professor Stevenson presents case after case involving such children (together with some data from adults who spontaneously claim past lives). He never claims that any of the well over a thousand cases he has investigated "proves" reincarnation, as he identifies flaws in them (e.g. discrepancies sometimes between the accounts given by the children of their past lives and the facts as established by the researchers), but he is clear that they provide a body of evidence that taken together strongly suggest reincarnation as a likely explanation. In fact it would be correct to say that it is due to Stevenson more than to any other investigator that reincarnation research has come to be taken so seriously by scientists interested in survival.

There is only space for just one example from Ian Stevenson's work, though no single example can do justice to the quality and interest of his findings. However this one, taken from his first book on the subject (Stevenson 1974), is typical, and helped set the standard for his later work. The case concerns Parmod Sharme, a professor's son born in 1944 in Uttar Pradesh, India. When the boy was about two and a half years old he began to tell his mother not to cook because he had a wife in Moradabad who could cook. Between the ages of three and four he started referring to a large soda and biscuit shop that he said he owned in Moradabad, a large city over 60 miles away, and which he asked to go and see, claiming to be one of the "Mohan Brothers." Furthermore he claimed the Brothers to be well to do and to have had another shop in Saharanpur, over 160 miles away. He also claimed to have had four sons and a daughter in his previous life, and to own a hotel and a cinema in Saharanpur where his mother still lived. He also showed unusual interest in biscuits and shops, and related how in his previous life he had become ill after eating too much curd, and had died in a bathtub. There appeared to be no normal means by which he had acquired this knowledge and the related details which he spontaneously and insistently brought up in conversation. His parents were unfamiliar with any of these details, and had never heard of the "Mohan Brothers." Eventually his father and a maternal cousin took Pramod, by now aged just under five, to Moradabad, which he had never previously visited, in an attempt to check the truth of the things he had been saying.

In the event, as Stevenson discovered when he interviewed the father, the maternal cousin, and ten other people from Parmod's family and from his claimed family in Moradabad, many of these things were indeed verified. Stevenson established that Parmod had:

on arrival in Moradabad unerringly directed his father and his cousin the mile and a half from the railway station to the biscuit and soda shop, recognized several members of the Mehra family, known as the "Mohan Brothers" after the oldest brother, who owned the shop, together with various places in the town (e.g. he identified the Town Hall as they passed it, which is unsigned and resembles a mosque rather than a civic building, and claimed correctly that it was near the shop), recognized people when taken to Saharanpur, including Parmanand's mother.

It transpired that Parmod was also correct in his claims that the Mohans had indeed had a brother Parmanand who had developed a chronic gastrointestinal problem after gorging on curd. Parmanand had not actually died in a bathtub, but he had used naturopathic bath treatments for the appendicitis and peritonitis that had followed his gastrointestinal infection and from which he had died. He had been using these bath treatments during the days just before his end. Parmod's claim that the Mohan Brothers owned another shop, a hotel, and a cinema in Saharanpur was another detail that proved correct. Also notable was his ability to work the quite complicated soda water machine in the shop on his very first visit, although it had been disconnected from the water supply in an experimental attempt to mislead him.

Professor Stevenson also established that Parmod had correctly recognized:

- *Parmanand's bedroom and the fact that after his death a screen had been placed there to divide it.*
- *Parmanand's cupboard and his low eating table.*
- *Parmanand's wife, daughter, two sons, brother, and nephew.*
- *that some sheds had been added since his death to the Victory Hotel, owned by the brothers, and that some cupboards had been taken there from a previous hotel owned by the brother (which Parmod named correctly).*
- *a man called Yasmin, who owed money to Parmanand, and to whom Parmod said "I have to get some money back from you" (the debt was apparently unknown to the family, but Yasmin reluctantly admitted to it).*
- *two doctors and a lorry driver known to Parmanand.*
- *the rest house in which Parmanand used to stay, and the room there in which he used to sleep.*
- *the seat Parmanand had occupied in the shop, and the fact that its position, together with the layout around it, had been changed since his death.*

Professor Stevenson provides precise details of the circumstances in which each of these acts of recognition by Parmod had taken place. Even though it may be possible that some of the witnesses interviewed by him got certain of their details wrong, the case is therefore a remarkable one, and a tribute to Stevenson's research work and the apparent co-operation of the witnesses. As already mentioned, other cases chronicled by Professor Stevenson and exhaustively researched by him through interviews of the children's present and claimed past-life families show similar remarkable details. In some instances children claiming to have met accidental deaths in their previous lives even have birthmarks that correspond in position to the site of the fatal injuries concerned.

Does the Evidence Demonstrate the Reality of Reincarnation?

The various pieces of evidence summarized in this chapter, if correct, appear at first sight explicable only in terms of reincarnation. Nevertheless I am not necessarily convinced that these past-life memories are what they seem. Their paranormality would seem self-evident, but an alternative possibility to reincarnation is that the details of past lives relate not to the individuals reporting them but to the lives of other men and women now deceased. If this is the case, these details could perhaps be somehow stored in the environment and in the possessions of the deceased, or in the minds of the deceased themselves if they have survived death. The idea that they could be stored in the environment or in possessions seems unlikely, given that in many cases the person reporting these details lives far from the scenes of his or her supposed past life and has never come into contact with the possessions of the person they claim to have been. This leaves the possibility that the details come from the minds of the deceased. This explanation was first suggested to me by some of the mediums with whom I have worked, and who are in no doubt that were they not trained to avoid doing so they too could frequently mistake the data communicated by deceased individuals for details of their own past lives. In their view inexperienced men and women, encountering similar data in dreams, in spontaneous occurrences, and in hypnotic trance, may not be able to make the same distinction. Even Joan Grant (1975), who as we have seen used past-life memories as the subject for her novels, made it clear that the past lives concerned were not her own past lives. Each "has a soul [of their own], a personality if you prefer the word. The sum total of all these souls is the spirit they share between them." They are like "beads on the same necklace and the memory they share is contained in the string."

The explanation given to me by mediums does seem to account for at least some supposed past-life memories. It could even explain the birthmarks found by Professor Stevenson on some of his children if we accept the possibility that the deceased person, anxious to retain contact with earth, even impressed their memories upon the unborn child. Such a possibility is not entirely out of the question. If DMILS studies (Chapter 2) are correct in suggesting that the mind of one person can paranormally influence the physiological reactions of another, we clearly have a great deal to learn about the nature of this influence. In some very rare cases it could possibly result in the deceased, albeit perhaps unintentionally (just as the violent interaction between the deceased and sitters at some physical séances may be unintentional), impressing marks upon the skin of the unborn in the very place where they themselves received (and are still perhaps traumatized by) a fatal injury in their earthly life. Support for this possibility is also provided by the reports that hypnotists are sometimes able to raise temporary wheals on the skin of entranced subjects by suggestion alone.

This is not to dismiss the possibility of reincarnation. Indeed, it would be unwise to do so in the light of the strength of the evidence provided by Professor Stevenson, and the fact that over half the population of the world, including Hindu and Buddhist teachers who know far more about the matter than we Westerners, accept reincarnation almost as a demonstrable fact.

Reincarnation may indeed be a fact – although this does not mean that everyone is required by some natural law to reincarnate – or alternatively past-life memories may come from somewhere other than the minds of the living. What does seem clear is that the evidence produced by the studies summarized in this chapter and from many others is that supposed past-life memories, in one way or another, provide further potential support for survival. We clearly need a large-scale investigation into the subject by a research team involving psychiatrists and psychologists with experience of using past-life regression therapy, mental and trance mediums, and subjects who have undergone regression. Only in this way may we be able to find answers to the many questions raised by this fascinating area of enquiry.

CHAPTER 18
THE NATURE OF AN AFTERLIFE

Similarities and Differences

Without exception, all the great religions of the world (and many of their offshoots) teach survival of death, although not all of their adherents may necessarily believe it to be a fact. The purpose of this final chapter is to look at the nature of a possible afterlife as described by communications through mediums and by the teachings of the various spiritual traditions. However, in looking at communications that purport to tell us about the nature of an afterlife we must remember that many of the published collections of these communications are uneven in the sense that we are expected to take too much on trust – i.e. without evidence that the communicators are who they say they are (and not, for example, simply creations of the medium's unconscious). This is particularly true of some of the communications that purport to come from supposed wise higher beings but that contain no evidence for survival and consist of little more than pious uplift. "Channeling" is often now used as an alternative term to "mediumship," particularly in the USA, in relation to such communications but this grander label is no guarantee of better quality communications. If the higher beings concerned are really so wise, then they should have no difficulty in demonstrating the reality of survival before they go on to preach their message of supposed peace and light. If they do demonstrate it, then they deserve our respect and attention. If they do not, then suspicion remains that they may be no more than well-intentioned creations of the medium's unconscious mind.

Throughout the chapter I shall for the most part, to save tedious repetition of qualifications such as "if there is an afterlife," or "if there is a next world," simply use the terms "afterlife" and "the next world." This does not necessarily imply acceptance of their existence. We can now start looking at the nature of an afterlife by listing some of the features common both to communications linked to survival evidence and to most of the major spiritual traditions, namely that:

- *there is more than one level to the afterlife.*
- *a judgment of some kind determines the level to which one goes.*
- *belief in spiritual realities while on earth and the attempt to live by spiritual teachings favorably influence this judgment.*
- *as a result of this judgment the soul experiences either happy or unhappy consequences.*

We can also look at a number of the points of difference:

In the great majority of the communications and in some of the spiritual traditions (particularly those of the Eastern religions) the unhappy consequences (usually described as hell) are not permanent; repentance and atonement for one's misdeeds lead eventually to absolution. Some religions also speak of an intermediate realm between heaven and hell (purgatory) where this repentance and atonement can take place.

Some traditions (although a minority of communications) teach that after a period in the afterlife the individual returns to earth in order to learn further lessons and eventually to be freed completely from the shackles of earthly existence. Some traditions, most notably Buddhism, teach that even the sojourn in the happy upper levels of the afterlife (heaven) is not permanent; once all the merit gained from a good life on earth has been exhausted, rebirth takes place.

Other variations that exist between some traditions (e.g. some Hindu sects) are that reincarnation is instantaneous after death (one's behavior in this life determines whether one has a favorable or unfavorable rebirth), or that there is a long period of unconsciousness after death until all rise from the grave on the day of judgment (e.g. some Christian sects). These various differences may be partly explained by the possibility, as will be discussed in due course, that the expectations one holds at the moment of death help determine the precise details of what happens next.

Sources of Information on the Afterlife

There is an almost bewildering array of texts detailing communications from and about the afterlife. I have drawn on what I consider to be many of the most reliable of these. How do we know if they are reliable, since we cannot check them against the actual facts? The only criteria we can adopt is that they manifest a good measure of agreement in the descriptions and explanations provided, and present a picture that makes some sense if we assume that even in this life mind is non-physical and distinct in some understandable way from the material world (although we may accept that ultimately mind and matter arise from the same source). The standing of the mediums through whom the communications are given and of the various authors who bring these communications together and comment and enlarge on them also helps determine the amount of credence we are prepared to place in them.

Rather than pepper the chapter with references and cross-references, it seems more appropriate to give a selection in a separate section following the references at the end of the book of some of the most important of the texts upon which I have drawn. Some of these texts focus on communications from the deceased while others appraise the evidence and discuss the various issues that are associated with a possible afterlife.

Survival of a Body?

If we survive the death of our physical bodies, what might that survival be like? Many of those who hope for survival nevertheless find the concept of an afterlife extremely difficult. They confess themselves unable to imagine what it would be like to exist without a material body. A great deal of our experience in the present world is mediated through the body and its senses, and for some people the absence of such a body would seem to render any post-mortem existence so fragmented and ill-defined that it would hardly count as survival. How would we see, hear, feel, experience emotions, enjoy creature comforts and the pleasures of touch, of scent and of movement without a body? These questions are reasonable enough, and philosophers such as Professor H. H. Price (1995) have been quick to draw them to our attention. However, Sir Oliver Lodge, one of the most important scientists to turn his attention to psychical research, found them unconvincing. Lodge accepted that we need a "bodily vehicle of some kind for the practical functioning of intelligence," but insisted that such a body need not "be composed of [the] opposite electrical charges that we call matter." On the contrary, he regarded it perfectly possible to "imagine another structure just as solid and substantial as matter is, but making no appeal to our present sense organs" (Lodge 1928).

In other words, in his view we could exist after death in a body formed of something other than matter. This body, to which we made reference in Chapter 16 in the context of out-of-the-body experiences, is sometimes described as the *astral* or the *subtle* body (e.g. MacGregor 1992). The Western mystery traditions and Eastern psycho-spiritual traditions have long taught that on earth we possess not one body but at least three, a physical body, an energy body, and an "astral" or spiritual body. While on earth, each of these bodies is co-determinate with the other two. According to these traditions the physical body allows us to function in the material world, the energy body sustains our physical metabolism, and the astral body is the vehicle for mind, soul, and spirit. At death the physical body is discarded, and the energy body follows suit some three days later (one reason why in Tibetan Buddhism the body is not to be disturbed for three days after death). The astral body then proceeds to the next world, and remains the vehicle for mind/soul and spirit until we reach a stage in our development when it too can be discarded, and the spirit is free to move on to realms of pure consciousness.

If these ideas are correct, the body seen in apparitions and materializations is the astral body, a self-existent reality analogous in its own way to the physical body on earth. The astral body is said to resemble the physical body in appearance but to be free from its imperfections, and to be even more susceptible to our thought processes than is the physical body when we are on earth – thus it may in due course come increasingly to resemble the individual's ideal image of him or herself. It is said to contain the mental and emotional essence of the individual concerned (religious people might call it the soul), including memories, and to be capable of functioning in the afterlife very much as it did while in the physical body. Communicators go to tell us that it is made of a form of energy (just as is the physical body), but energy of a much more subtle kind, which renders it invisible to anyone without clairvoyant abilities.

The body we possess every night in our dreams may give us some idea of what the astral body, as described in these communications, may be like. During our dreams the dream body is typically as real to us as are our physical bodies in waking life. Thus, whatever the philosophical objections to talking about an existence distinct from the physical, it is in reality difficult to see why anyone – except perhaps those who cannot recall their dreams – has any great problem in at least conceptualizing a non-physical body. There are further possible examples of this astral or subtle body in the reports given to us by people who have experienced NDEs and OBEs (Chapters 15 and 16). In some cases they refer to being just "pure consciousness," but for the most part they report a clear awareness of being in a body of some kind, usually resembling the physical body. However, these reports raise an issue which for many people renders the reality of OBEs and NDEs – and indeed even more so the reality of apparitions – highly suspect, namely that usually the figures concerned are said to be clothed. Even those who might accept in theory that OBEs, NDEs, and apparitions could conceivably be real reject the idea in practice because they cannot conceive of the reality of ghostly garments.

Clare's Experience and the Question of Clothes

Interesting light is thrown on this issue from a case in my files that concerns Clare, a university psychology lecturer, who experienced an OBE as a result of a conscious experiment to verify at first hand whether or not it is possible for the consciousness to leave the body. The method Clare used was to lie comfortably on her bed in the afternoon, with the elbow of her right arm resting on the bed and her forearm raised in the air so that if she dozed it would fall and awaken her. The method also involved becoming particularly aware of the sensation of the body against the bedclothes, and then imagining that the body was sinking down through the bed. After persisting with this method for some time, Clare abruptly found herself out of her body, standing beside the bed and aware of the objects around her in her bedroom. Although she had taken off her clothes in order to be particularly sensitive to the sensation of the bed under her body, she now realized that although her legs and feet were still bare she was wearing a dress of which she had once been very fond, but which she had not worn for some eight years. She had not been thinking of this dress at the time, so why was she wearing it?

In his NDE Dr. Wiltse (Chapter 15) tells us that he found himself immediately clothed when he registered embarrassment at being naked – albeit in the spirit – in front of a room full of people. However, Clare is not a person who feels any embarrassment at nakedness in herself or in others (and I have in my files at least one example of a woman who usually sleeps naked and who finds herself naked during her experiences out of the body), so embarrassment does not appear to be the explanation. Clare herself considers that the reason may be that she regards herself as having been at her most physically attractive eight years ago, and as the dress in which she found herself when out of the body was one she had enjoyed wearing at the time it could therefore have symbolized this fact. Support for this possibility comes from communications through mediums which suggest, as mentioned earlier that in appearance people in the next world, whether they die young or old, either go forward to a time or revert to a time – usually in the early twenties – when they look their best (although when appearing as apparitions or materializations they may do so in the form in which they are best remembered by those still on earth). If Clare's dress was a symbol of herself at her physical best it appears to have been a thought-form, a facsimile, created for her for this reason by her unconscious. The alternative to this explanation would be that clothes, like bodies, have an astral self and that it was this astral dress that Clare was wearing, but this seems nonsensical.

Clare's experience, and much else that has been reported about OBEs and NDEs, thus suggests that the astral body (let me continue to use this term for want of something better) contains the unconscious as well as the conscious mind, and that the former, as for example in dreams and creative experiences, remains responsible for creating some conscious experiences. If the unconscious was indeed responsible for Clare's dress and for Dr. Wiltse's clothes, this extends the notion of what it is that survives physical death. Not only may the conscious mind and its memories survive, but so may the unconscious and some at least of the unconscious processes that help to make us who and what we are in our present lives.

Furthermore, if the unconscious was responsible for Clare's dress and for Dr. Wiltse's clothes we can argue, in response to critics who dismiss apparitions as hallucinations because they wear clothes, that these garments are in fact no more than stage props. Many apparitions, for symbolic reasons or because they have carried prudish attitudes with them into the next world (or because they wish to spare the blushes of those who see them) may consciously or unconsciously create images of suits of clothes for themselves. If you are able to make your body appear to those on earth, then it may be a simple matter to ensure that it comes complete with phantom clothes. In fact it might even be easier to materialize the clothes than the body. Tom Harrison (Chapter 13) reports that the materializations that appeared in good red light at his home circle wore "robes" (Harrison 1989), and that when asked the reason for this one of them replied that it was indeed easier to materialize robes than the whole body, and drew back the hem of her robe to show that she had no feet.

If it is possible for the unconscious or the conscious mind to decide to materialize spirit clothes, there may be no reason why it should not be able to materialize other props. Braude (2003) questions the fact that in one of the cases he quotes the spirit concerned appeared to be accompanied by a car of some kind. One can only ask why robes or a favorite dress or a tweed jacket should be easier for a spirit to create as a thought form, consciously or unconsciously, than a car or anything else associated with him or her in life. A more important question than a phantom car is what of the material objects *not* associated with individuals in life that yet accompany their apparitions? There are many cases of apparitions wearing garments they are very unlikely to have worn in life (Evans 2002), and of mediums who claim clairvoyantly to see spirits in adult clothes who are said to have died in infancy and grown to maturity in the next world (such cases are of interest if the sitter later discovers for example that a hitherto unknown sibling did die soon after birth). Why should such spirits be seen wearing clothes that had no associations to them when they were on earth? From where did they get the idea of these clothes? From other spirits? Or from observing people on earth? I know of no recorded attempt to put these questions to communicators, and it would be interesting to learn the answer to them.

The Nature of the Body After Death

In addition to the problem of clothes, a question that is often asked about the astral body is whether it has internal organs, or is it simply an outer shell? There are certainly accounts of spirits who materialize during physical séances and who feel warm to the touch and have a pulse that can be felt (e.g. Chapter 13). I have myself shaken hands (on cue and at my request) with supposedly materialized spirits during séances under conditions in which fraud would have been extremely difficult, and the hands concerned have felt warm and strong. I have also been touched many times by much smaller, more feminine hands, which I have also seen clearly silhouetted against bright spirit lights (Chapter 13). However, Sir Oliver Lodge's son Raymond, killed in the First World War, went much further when communicating through Gladys Leonard and spoke of soldiers in the next world who requested and were given cigars and alcohol (Chapter 7). Does this imply that they had, or at least thought they had, phantom lungs and stomachs? Other communicators have agreed with Raymond that although food and drink are not necessary in the next world, those who want them can have them. Islam also teaches that the blessed can enjoy food in paradise if they wish, and in Norse legends dead heroes are said to feast in Valhalla, while in Greek mythology the gods were described as eating ambrosia. Does all this imply internal spiritual organs? Hardly; the obvious answer is that if the food is non-physical it can hardly demand physical organs of digestion, although perhaps if one is under the illusion that it does, then the unconscious may obligingly provide facsimiles.

Alternative Explanations to the Reality of the Astral Body

Could it be, however, that, even though survival may be a fact, it does not involve a "body" of any kind, even in the initial stages of the afterlife? If so, the reported apparitions of bodies may simply be hallucinations projected from the mind of observers in response to telepathic impressions from the deceased. The idea that this might be the case took root at the end of the nineteenth century, when the Society for Psychical Research carried out and published two extensive surveys of hallucinations that made it difficult to explain them simply as mental aberrations by the living (Gurney, Podmore, and Myers 1886, Sidgwick et al. 1894). All the cases presented in these two mammoth publications (1,215 in total) were checked and double-checked for authenticity by the authors (very many more were rejected as unreliable), a colossal task by any standards and particularly so in the days before records could be computerized. This checking and double-checking ensured that the published cases were more than mere anecdotes. Nothing even approaching this effort has been carried out since, and the cases in these two publications remain the most extensive evidence we have for apparitions in all their diversity. The SPR, from its foundation, was interested in attempting to bring psychical research into the burgeoning scientific age, and in studying these cases some of its members considered that they could be effectively explained as telepathy plus hallucinations, a seemingly more scientific explanation than that the body could actually appear to those on earth after death. In the words of Sidgwick, the SPR's foundation President, all that telepathy had to do "is to introduce the idea," and the hallucination will be produced by the conscious or unconscious mind of the observer (Sidgwick et al. 1894). As Lang, an active member of the SPR put it at the time:

The modern doctrine is that every ghost is a hallucination; it gives the impression of the presence of a real person, in flesh, blood and usually clothes, though no such person in flesh, blood and clothes is actually there ...

For Lang, although he accepted that it might be "correct or erroneous," the idea that the hallucination actually was the spirit of the living or of the dead "represents the simple philosophy of the savage."

This attempt by the highly influential scholars responsible for the two SPR publications on hallucinations to equate everything with telepathy plus hallucinations was laudable enough, in that it contributed to the debate on the nature of survival, and probably helped some critics to accept that survival might be a possibility after all. But it had little to favor it over the idea that apparitions really are objectively present beyond the fact that it appeared to do away with the philosophical problem of how those who had left their physical bodies could appear as if still physical. In fact it seems to have been based more upon a desire to have done with this problem (Sidgwick himself was a leading and highly respected philosopher) than upon specific supporting evidence. No real attempt was made to discuss how telepathy, whether from the living or the dead, could prompt percipients who had never previously shown any ability at receiving telepathic impressions not only to do so but to then project a fully-formed, three dimensional, life-like figure into the space in front of them – in some cases a figure of someone who was not even known to them at the time, and with whom they had no close emotional link.

The explanation is particularly difficult to sustain in cases where apparitions are unexpectedly seen to be much younger than observers remembered them to be in life, or when apparitions convey the veridical fact of their unexpected deaths (why should this be done through inducing hallucinations by telepathy when telepathy alone would suffice?), or when they are seen by more than one observer either at the same time or on different occasions, or when they are seen in séances sometimes by many people over a number of years. Much as with the Super-ESP explanation, the assumption seems to have been that as we have evidence that telepathy exists and do not know its extent, we can propose it as an answer for everything to do with the paranormal, including the apparently solid appearance of the deceased.

What Might a Next World Be Like?

What of the environment of a possible next world? In attempting to answer this question I am summarizing what we have been told by communications through mediums, by mystics, by those who report near-death experiences, and by messages received more latterly through ITC. I am not presenting this summary as fact. I give it for what it is, although it is noteworthy that there is a marked degree of consensus between many of these accounts. However, before starting on the summary, it is worthwhile saying something about our present world. We tend to think of this world as a solid, objective reality "out there." What we see appears to be real, solid, and stable in itself, and not influenced in any way by us as observers. However, the atomic physicist tells us that this is not the case at all. The world "out there" (and in fact the world even of our own bodies) is in fact composed of atoms, all of which are in violent motion. The vast majority of it is made up by the empty space between the atoms, and its apparent solidity is the result of the fact that the atoms are in constant and violent motion. Thus the apparently solid desk in front of me as I write is almost entirely empty space, and not solid, or static at all. The quantum physicist, who studies the micro world within the atom, will go further still, and tell us that even the atoms aren't solid, but made up of bundles of energy, themselves in constant motion. Thus the world "out there" is not really as we see it at all.

So why do we see it as we do? The theory is that our act of observing it is in part responsible for what we see. We are, in a very real sense, co-creators of the "reality" that we experience as the physical world. What the physical world would really look like if we were not programmed to co-create it in the way we do, nobody can say for sure. All we know is that it would be a mass of whirling energies of some sort. Certainly there must be a "blue-print" of some kind, since we all tend to experience it in similar ways to each other. We don't each co-create it in our own way. Possibly, as Bohm (1980) argued, this "blue-print" arises from a much deeper underlying reality. But the important point is that if we are co-creators of the way in which this world is experienced, then it is less difficult to conceive that if there is a next world, we may be co-creators of the way in which we experience that as well. This seems to accord with what communicators tell us. They insist not only that we are co-creators of that experience, but that the next world is much more malleable by our act of observation and by the thoughts in our minds than is this world. Thus if we think, conditioned by our experiences in this world, that we see a world of houses, trees, and flowers that is what we will see, rather than the formless levels of pure consciousness which approximate closer to ultimate reality. Cultural factors also enter into what we see. One must not suppose that someone from the Far East would experience the next world in the same way as a Westerner. The *Bardo Thodol* (the Tibetan Book of the Dead) is a good example of how the Tibetan experience of the next world differs from our own. The *Bardo Thodol* insists that all experiences of at least the initial level of this next world, even visions of the Buddha, are creations of our own mind and must not be taken as ultimate reality. Such experiences are the observer's "personalization" of the transcendent spiritual energy that lies behind the illusory worlds of form represented by the earth and the lower levels of the afterlife (see Miller, 1997, for a survey of many other cultural differences).

The fact that the next world appears malleable by thought does not mean that each person creates their own environment. We are told by communicators that the way in which the next world – at least at the lower levels – is experienced by each individual is shaped not just by his or her own thoughts but by the thoughts of others who think in similar ways. Thus it is said we gravitate to that part of the next world where there are people of like mind to ourselves. Those who love trees and flowers, peace and harmony, go to a domain where the thoughts of others who love these things will have helped to create just such an environment. By contrast, if we prefer the city, we go to a city-like environment, and if we are identified with violence and strife we go to a place of violence and strife. There is a "blue-print" in the environment of the next world just as there is in this world. As in this world, the mind of the observer is only the co-creator, not the sole creator of what is experienced in the afterlife. But communicators assure us that thought plays a greater part in this formation of the afterlife than it does here on earth.

All this is difficult to accept. Even those of us who consider there may be a next world are likely to conceive of it as some spiritual dimension quite unlike the hard physicality of this world. The idea that there may not only be landscapes similar to our own but even houses and cities takes us way past the threshold of disbelief. Quite apart from anything else, who builds these houses? Of what are they constructed? Are there factories turning out bricks and mortar? Are these run by businessmen and operated by laborers? Is there competition and rivalry? Are the houses furnished? If so, who makes the furniture? Are there shops? Is there money? If so, do people have to work in order to get paid? The questions come thick and fast. Are we to leave one material world only to find ourselves in another one, with many of the same problems that confront us here?

All this seems so unlikely that we are prone to dismiss what communicators tell us about the next world altogether, even if the next world is indeed largely a world of thought. But before we do, it is worth remembering that our environment in this world is also largely created – if indirectly – by thought. If we wish to build a house we go to an architect with some ideas generated by our own creative thinking, and he or she, again through the power of thought, designs it for us. Materials are then purchased for its construction from brickworks and factories that have also been initially designed by thought. Builders then build the house, once again using thought in order to understand the architect's plans and to decide how to put them into practical reality. Communicators tell us that something rather similar happens in the next world. Prompted by the concepts and habits we carry over from this world, we once more – unconsciously or consciously – provide the ideas for a house which an "architect," who supposedly has more of the necessary powers of thought needed to bring it into being than we have ourselves, finishes the job for us. And just as houses are built in this way, so is the furniture.

Why should people operate as "architects" and "furniture makers" in the next world? Simply because they wish to do so, just as musicians and artists in the next world continue to create music and paint pictures if they wish to do so, and medical doctors (we are told) go on healing by working through mediums and spiritual healers on this earth. Not surprisingly, we are told that none of this is really necessary. We do not need houses or furniture in the next world, just as we do not need food or drink, but if we think we do, or if we get pleasure from these things, then we will continue to want them and use them until we decide to leave them behind and progress to higher levels of the afterlife where all such things are recognized as unnecessary.

Let me stress again (particularly in order to forestall criticism) that I am not saying any of this is fact. I am simply saying that communicators tell us it is fact. And if we like simply to play with ideas for the moment, it is worth remarking that if everyone when entering the next world had immediately to shed all his or her lifelong interests – whether these are to do with creating music or paintings or poetry or houses or gardens or any other seemingly life-enhancing undertaking – it would render these interests meaningless. If creative activity, and the work generated by creative activity, is of value for personal growth in this world, then it would be a little illogical to assume it ceases abruptly in the afterlife. However, what of the mysterious "material" used in this activity? Of what would a next world that enables creative activity to continue be composed? This question has already been partly answered in our reference to the material of which this world is composed. Thanks to the advances of modern science we know that this material is also mysterious, and more in the nature of energy than of solid substance. We do not know what it really is and we do not know from where it really comes. If the findings of modern quantum physics are to be believed and if it can indeed be directly influenced at some level by the consciousness of the observer, it may be rather nearer to a form of "mind stuff" than a form of inert matter. The more we ponder such possibilities, the more descriptions of the next world come to seem, if not credible, at least a little less incredible.

The Work of Rupert Sheldrake

Another insight into the power that thought may have upon our present world comes from Dr. Rupert Sheldrake's theory of *morphic fields* and *formative causation* (e.g. Sheldrake 1983, 1988, and most recently 2003). The theory is too rich and extended to be discussed at any length here, but as Dr. Sheldrake explains in his various publications, many experiments designed to put it to the test have yielded successful results. Put at their simplest, Sheldrake's ideas propose that everything is evolutionary in nature, constantly changing and developing from one state to another, and that intention, memory, and aspiration in all living systems, including humans, influence this evolution through a form of extended mind or collective consciousness (a kind of telepathic pooling of the mental life of a species). Thus each species is partly responsible for the evolution of its own behavior and possibly even its physical characteristics. Instances of this are apparent from the way in which new items of complex behavior learnt by some members of a species are suddenly duplicated by other members, even though there has been no physical contact between the two groups. Sheldrake supports this idea by presenting evidence to show that once new learning has taken place among a species it becomes easier for subsequent generations to acquire the same learning. A good example is the behavior of laboratory rats that learn to negotiate a maze in order to reach food. Careful records of the time taken to learn the maze have been kept since psychologists first attempted such learning experiments with rats in the 1930s, and these records show that the time has become progressively shorter, even though no selective breeding of the rats concerned has taken place. Even scientific laws, at one time thought to be immutable and unchangeable, may to some extent be subject to influence over the centuries by the concepts humans form of these laws. Sheldrake's theory remains controversial, but the supporting evidence continues to accumulate, and suggests that a radical rethink about our own nature and our relationship to each other and to the natural world is required.

If Sheldrake is correct, and each species influences the morphic field within which it evolves, it is not unreasonable to suggest that in the afterlife, where thought is said to have much more effect upon environmental change than it does here, the deceased do create some part of the world in which they find themselves. This makes better sense of the descriptions given by communicators of a world that resembles our own in so many respects.

Judgment

The belief held by the major spiritual traditions that there is a form of judgment after death, is supported by the communications received through mediums. Generally, however, these communications speak of this judgment as a form of self-judgment rather than as something handed down from on high. We are told that, sooner or later after death, the spirit must undertake the so-called life review in the course of which all the lessons to be learnt from the recent earth life must be confronted, which involves directly experiencing within oneself the emotional happiness and suffering caused in others – including non-human forms of life – by one's actions. No divine being hands out rewards and punishments. The rewards and punishments are implicit in the judgment process itself, and in the pleasure on the one hand and the remorse on the other that it brings. This judgment must sooner or later be faced if spiritual progress is to be made, and one is to be purified of the harm one has caused in the earth life. This purification process seems in fact akin to the "purgatory" of which some religions speak.

If this judgment sounds forbidding (and remember I am still summarizing what communicators have said through mediums, and not attempting to offer it as hard fact or as a preferred alternative to the teachings of the reader's own religious tradition), it is important to add that there is an almost universal emphasis, from mystics and communicators alike, upon the fact that ultimate reality is "love," and that the purpose of our life on earth is to learn how to love, how to behave selflessly and compassionately, and to overcome the ignorance, greed, and hatred to which material existence lays us open. The judgment is thus said to be to our own benefit, as it allows us to recognize our mistakes and our successes, and to become wiser in consequence. If this raises a theological question, namely why should we have to go through the learning experience offered by this world when presumably only the next world need have been created, all that can be said is that this is how things seem to be. The Hindus teach that we are all part of the infinite consciousness of the Divine, and that if we can liberate ourselves from the self-imposed limitations within which we live we can realize our own true nature. If we do so all things will become clear. Such liberation is known in Sanskrit as *moksha*, and we are told rather depressingly that few there be who find it, at least in this world.

However, there is a more practical question associated with judgment. If in the course of it we have to experience the emotional pain we have caused to others during our earth life, does this include the pain felt by people who took unnecessary offence, or who are so over-sensitive that even the mildest criticism leads to suffering? In the course of socializing our children and teaching them reasonable rules of safety, all parents will at some point have upset their children. Must we experience this upset? Throughout life others may make us suffer for our own good. During a meditation retreat a stern but necessary word from the meditation teacher, who sees us slipping into indolence, may cause us needless pain. Does he or she have to experience this pain during the judgment? One possible answer is that we may be able to recognize when the suffering of others was due to their own vulnerability rather than to error on our part. Another possibility is that the motivation behind our actions is what matters. If we did not intend to hurt others, then we will not have to experience their suffering (yet what of the occasions when we meant no harm but were too ignorant or insensitive to recognize the damage we were doing – surely this leaves us culpable?). A third possibility is that we are helped at each point to place our earthly actions in their true context, which might mean recognizing we were not to blame in circumstances when we seem to have been at fault – and perhaps at the same time recognizing when our "good" actions were motivated not by a real concern for others but by a desire for their gratitude.

Each of these answers is a possibility if we assume that there is some higher authority in the afterlife that organizes and arranges things for us. If there is, this supports the idea that pattern and purpose run through all existence, and that this pattern and purpose, as the mystics tell us, has to do with love. Each stage of our journey through the present world and the afterlife is a stage in learning how to love. Questions as to why this should be – if we come from an abiding source of love why should we have to relearn love? – must be left to theologians and philosophers. My own tentative contribution would be that if ultimate reality is infinite, all things are possible. Perhaps our task is to express the practical aspects of love. But as with so many ultimate questions, attempting to second-guess the purposes behind a reality that is so much vaster and more mysterious than we are serves little real purpose. As Candide said in Votaire's novel of the same name when treated to yet another theoretical diatribe by his philosophy tutor, "all that is very true, but we must cultivate our garden." Zen Buddhism places the same emphasis upon hewing wood and drawing water. Liberation and self-realization are far more likely to arise from interacting with the natural world and coming close to the creative force all around us, than from endless speculation, however much fun that may be.

After the judgment, some accounts suggest that if lessons still remain that can only be learnt amid the cut and thrust and challenges of this world, then one may decide – or be instructed by higher beings – to return to this earth and try again. Some communicators claim that this happens frequently, some rarely, and some virtually as a matter of course. Reincarnation is in fact one of the few areas where a significant measure of disagreement seems to exist among communicators. It is said that this disagreement is explained in part by the level of the afterlife that the communicating spirit currently occupies. Some spirits are indeed wiser and more knowledgeable about such matters than are others.

What Survives?

Is survival exclusive to humans? The answer from communicators seems to be no. Mediums sometimes claim to see or hear dogs, cats, and horses in the afterlife, and the descriptions given of these animals fit the deceased pets of sitters. Correct names of pets are also sometimes given. Communications reported as received by Cardoso (Chapter 14) tell us that all life goes after death to the next world. If we take "all life" literally, this means not only animals but plants and even microbes. This may sound fine in theory, but what does it mean in practice? Do humans eat the animals and do animals eat each other? Are plants grown just in order to be eaten? Do microbes create disease? These questions seem crucial, but in fact they only arise if we try to impose earthly conditions upon the next world. Firstly, "bodies" in the next world are not material and do not provide "food" for others, as they do on the earth. Secondly, as already mentioned, there is no need for food. Thirdly, if the next world is indeed much more a world of thought than is the present one, then the "food" and "drink" that some individuals are said to still crave in the lower levels of the afterlife are imaginary, that is images created by the power of thought. If this is indeed the case, there is no call and no opportunity for any creatures to live off each other – and that includes life forms such as bacteria which on earth act as parasites and cause disease (some members of the animal and plant kingdoms if they could use our language might describe the term parasite as most applicable to we humans).

It is sometimes suggested that if animals survive, they only retain their individuality in the afterlife if they have lived close to humans, and been "given" individuality through human love. Otherwise, they return to the collective consciousness of their species. This claim typifies our rather self centered way of thinking. As humans, we regard ourselves as lords of creation, with every other life form subservient to us, and open to our exploitation. But there is no special warrant for this view, and it would be arrogant to suppose that our assumed superiority will persist into the next world. It may be that one of the lessons we would have to learn in an afterlife is the unity of all existence, with all of creation arising from the same source. If we wish in this world to recognize the inherent sacredness of all things, we must not assume that there are any special privileges reserved for our species in the next.

Individuality in the Afterlife

However, this reference to individuality does raise the question whether or not we ourselves persist as individuals in the afterlife. Buddhist teachings in particular tell us that the individual self is a delusion, and that spiritual progress depends upon the recognition of this fact. Other Eastern religions such as the Advaita school of Hinduism and Jainism take a rather similar view. Yet in the West, individuality is prized as being of value in and of itself. Which of these views is correct, and what does this tell us about individuality in the afterlife? Any answer to this can only be tentative. Nevertheless, it is obviously true that as physical beings we are not separate from the rest of existence. The minerals that go to make up our bodies are taken from the environment, and after death they go back to the environment. We depend upon the environment for food, water, and air. And at a psychological level, much of our behavior and of our thinking is learnt from other people. Yet at the same time we do have a distinct self-awareness, and we do recognize individual differences between ourselves and others. I find it hard to believe that if there is a purpose to existence, then the struggle to learn that we have this degree of individuality is meaningless and an obstacle to spiritual progress, and that we after death we simply go back to the unity from which we arose. It seems to me more realistic to suppose that the infinite reality of which we are a part consists of both individuality and unity, the former existing within the latter. Possibly even the distinction between individuality and unity disappears when and if we progress beyond a certain point in the afterlife, but initially at least, it would seem that individuality still has a useful part to play.

If this is so, then the lesson is how to manage our individuality without harming others, how to use it to enhance rather than destroy life, how to learn to discard self-serving greed, in short how to make the world in our small way a better place. This does not mean that we are imprisoned within our own current very limited identity, that we have to spend eternity as ourselves. If everything is indeed evolving, then our selfhood is also evolving (which as I understand it is the real heart of Eastern teachings on the self), and at some immeasurable time in the future will recognize that human concepts such as self and other are limited and limiting, that our lives have been the expression of a universal life force, and that ultimate reality, in so far as our limited minds can at present conceive it, embraces all things.

Sex and Sleep in the Afterlife

This is surely something of a taboo subject. If the physical desire for food and drink, although illusory, persists for some time in the afterlife, what about sex, another of the driving forces behind human behavior? And what about the wider question of loving relationships formed in this world? Do they continue in the next? The question concerning loving relationships is easier to answer than that concerning sex. We are told that these relationships can continue if both parties wish it. Presumably, if we are to progress beyond our self-centered humanity, they do so without the petty jealousies that spoil so many relationships on earth. Spirits, we are told, do not "own" each other. Thus it seems as if people who have had more than one loving relationship on earth which transcends death can love and be loved equally in both relationships in the afterlife, experiencing a love that is genuinely non-possessive and that enhances the being of all those involved. Presumably new relationships can also be created, as one moves closer to the so-called group soul, of which more later.

We are told much less about physical sexuality, but what we are told suggests that the creative energy that is expressed through sexual union remains and is enhanced, and that this is experienced by proximity rather than by actual physical coupling. It seems that the latter, like food and drink, becomes unnecessary. It is not that the sensations associated with sex, food, and drink are lost or repressed, simply that they exist in and of themselves and are expressed through spiritual rather than just physical proximity to those we love. No communicators to my knowledge speak of procreation in the next world. Anabela Cardoso's communicators (Chapter 14) insist in answer to her question that all life comes to them from our world. This suggests that one of the functions of this world is to bring into being the world of form. Form has its origin in this world, and then becomes increasingly refined as it progresses through the various levels of the afterlife. This certainly seems to make sense. As in the teachings of the Kabbala, the mystical form of Judaism, this world is *Malkut*, the Foundation, the lowest level of being yet at the same time the base from which the ascent back upwards towards *Kether*, the Crown, has its start.

What of other physical pleasures such as sleep? We are told that, especially for those who die in advanced old age or after physical suffering, there is a period analogous to a long sleep on earth, during which the concept of oneself as old or as suffering or as tired can gradually fade, so that one can "awaken" refreshed and eager to start the new life. Subsequently, as with food and drink, one can sleep if one assumes the need for it. But we should remind ourselves that even in the present life the consciousness of the spiritually advanced person is said, both by the Eastern psycho-spiritual traditions and by the Western mystery traditions (e.g. Regardie 1972), to run continuously through dreaming and through dreamless sleep. The latter is akin to deep blissful meditation, in which the mind is clear and alert, but free from distracting thoughts or the other superficialities of waking life.

Occupations in the Afterlife

We have already touched on this in our discussion of the "houses" that are said to exist in the afterlife. Communicators generally tell us that spirits can pursue the interests they have developed on earth, though at a higher level. The arts and the sciences are therefore possible, and particular emphasis is placed upon music and upon the use of color. The gardener can garden, though presumably by doing many things by means of thought rather than through physical toil (unless such toil is still regarded as necessary). Gradually, many occupations particularly associated with the physical world are seen to be unnecessary and unfulfilling, and can be transcended. However, it may be at this point that reincarnation again becomes an issue. Those who for various reasons (to do not only with occupation but with other physical longings) cannot move beyond their preoccupations with the material world may choose, or be drawn inexorably, to further lifetimes on earth.

Reincarnation is also said to be entered into voluntarily by those who wish to help those still on earth. This is exemplified by the Buddhist teaching on beings known as bodhisattvas. The bodhisattva is one who has attained enlightenment and has nothing further to learn from life on earth, but who returns lifetime after lifetime to teach others until one day all beings achieve liberation. Whether one takes this teaching literally or not, it is surely one of the highest ideals of selflessness in any psycho-spiritual tradition. Having achieved entry into the ineffable bliss of Nirvana, the bodhisattva is said to turn aside and return instead to the challenges, difficulties, and sufferings of this world out of pure altruism. The fact that the human mind can even conceive of the possibility of such altruism presents something of a puzzle to those who believe humanity is driven only by a selfish gene.

No communication known to me has it that we suddenly become wiser, better, or enlightened beings immediately after death. We are told that we remain very much the people we were before dying, which explains why some earthbound spirits are said to be bent upon making difficulties for those still on earth. However, with the exception of traditions such as Buddhism that insist this world is the only level where progress can be made, most sources speak of the possibility of spiritual progress in the afterlife. Higher levels of learning are said to be available in the arts and the sciences for those who wish to follow the path of wisdom, while others can choose to devote themselves to helping the dying make their transition to the afterlife, or to influencing those on earth with new creative insights, or to working through mediums to spread the message of survival, or to countless other ways said to be of value to creation that is forever changing and evolving. Whether one accepts any of this as literal or not, it seems clear that communicators wish to rid us of the idea that the afterlife is either boring on the one hand, or full of celestial choirs devoting themselves to praising the Almighty on the other.

Memories of Earthlife

For some people, memories of their lives on earth may remain stronger than for others, for whom the earthlife is said quickly to resemble a dream. But we are told that for everyone it becomes increasingly difficult to remember details associated with this life, although emotional memories can remain strong. This may explain why, although communicators remember their loved ones still on earth and are anxious to make contact with them, they have difficulty in recalling mundane things like their date of birth, their house numbers, and their own and street names. Such things for them seemingly become unimportant. This is not too difficult to accept. It is worth reminding ourselves that our memories while on earth are much more fragmentary than we like to suppose. If we ask ourselves to remember exactly what we did from waking to sleeping on a certain day last month (or last week) we would be hard put to fill in many of the precise details. Even a review of the day each evening before we go to sleep sometimes proves difficult. Thus we can hardly be surprised that those in the next world do not recall some of the unimportant details we demand from them in order to establish their identity, particularly as they have to give these details through the mind of the medium or impress them on the energy fields of electronic media as in ITC.

Nevertheless, memory is an essential part of our identity. Thus we must assume that if survival is a reality the deceased must retain some core of facts that enables them to know themselves, even if other facts begin to slip away. Once having gone through the judgment process and learnt the lessons that the past life has to teach, it is in any case doubtful if many earth memories have any further part to play in the spirit's conscious progress. Whether or not these memories are retained at some unconscious level, as happens with so many of our memories during this lifetime, is another matter. If they are retained, this suggests they still have a role of some kind in sustaining individual identity.

However, what of those people who have lost their memories while on earth, either as a result of accident or a condition such as Alzheimer's? If they have no effective powers of memory before death, how can they be said to carry memories into the next world? To answer this question, we would have to know more about the nature of memory itself. In spite of our many advances in brain research, memory remains something of a mystery. We know that certain parts of the brain are more involved in the storage of memory than others, yet we also know that even if these parts are damaged, memory may slowly return after a period of amnesia. Does this mean that memory is also stored elsewhere in the brain, even perhaps throughout the brain? Or does it suggest that, if mind works through brain rather than being generated by it, memory may be stored not only in the brain? Pam Reynolds (Chapter 15) reported on returning to consciousness after her NDE that she could recall some of what had been happening during her brain operation even though there had been no measurable brain activity during this time. Where and how had the memories concerned been stored? Hardly in a brain that had been medically de-activated. The fact that nevertheless they apparently *were* stored somewhere suggests the possibility that while out of her body she not only possessed consciousness but the ability to retain memories of what was happening to her. If this us the case, it may also be that a person rendered unconscious by brain damage or handicapped by Alzheimer's disease is conscious at a level outside the brain, although unable to communicate this consciousness to us (rather as the television signal cannot communicate through a set that has broken down). In an attempt to research this possibility I have interviewed nurses who work with unconscious patients and have been assured by them that on recovery such patients have sometimes related details of incidents that took place around the bed while they were profoundly unresponsive to any of the medical procedures designed to establish if consciousness was present. Where was the consciousness that enabled them to register and remember these details even though they were deaf and blind to the outside world? Was it outside the brain?

We have of course no way of knowing how memories could possibly be stored outside the brain, but then we have no final explanation for how they can be stored within the brain. How can the biological material of which the brain is composed encode and retain abstract thoughts and impressions? How does this material remember emotions and feelings, sometimes experienced decades ago, and relive them with something of the same intensity of the original experience? Computers store memories by registering whether electrical switches are on or off, but the electrical activity within the brain is vastly more complex than the simple binary ("on" or "off") system of switching employed by a computer, and it consists of biological cells that are constantly dying off and being replaced rather than inert hardware like the computer. Thus the analogy between a computer and a brain breaks down at a number of points. They may, however, be alike in that external agents are needed to activate and operate both of them.

Communicators tell us that during episodes of unconsciousness the mind, though still linked to the body, is located outside it, as during NDEs and OBEs. They also tell us that in the days just before natural death the consciousness becomes increasingly disassociated from the body and, as we saw in Chapter 15, may be aware of unseen helpers and even of beautiful distant landscapes. In the case of those with conditions such as Alzheimer's or experiencing long periods of coma before death, the consciousness is said to have already virtually left the body, and to remain linked to it only by the flimsiest of connections, unable in any meaningful way to operate its various biological mechanisms. Before dismissing this kind of information as impossibly unscientific, it is right to remember that materialist explanations, which equate unconsciousness and death with oblivion, are not themselves based upon scientific evidence. Materialist explanations are in no sense "proved" by modern advances in brain research, and if we are mistaken into supposing that they are we may become further from, rather than nearer to, an understanding of what it means to be ourselves.

Other World Geography

Eastern psycho-spiritual traditions, Western mystery traditions, and communications through mediums all agree that there are many levels to existence, and the number seven is frequently mentioned (together sometimes with sub-divisions within these levels). Some of the names given to these levels and some of the other details associated with them differ, but the basic pattern remains reasonably consistent. This world is usually taken to be the lowest of the seven levels, and together with the next three to make up what are called the levels of form, above which are the three increasingly formless realms of pure consciousness. The next lowest level to earth – in fact usually spoken of as a part in fact of the earth plane – is usually said to be the domain of so-called "earthbound" spirits, those who either do not realize they have died and are unable to move on, or who are so intensely preoccupied with earthly affairs or material pleasures that they cannot let go of their earth lives or their appetite for physical gratification. In addition, it is said that spirits can sometimes remain earthbound if they are held there by the inordinate grief of their loved ones. Grief is an understandable and necessary emotion, and something to be lived through until one starts to adapt to the realities of the situation. But uncontrollable grief is said to hold the loved one close to the earth out of sympathy and a shared sadness with those who grieve. The advice given by communicators is that deceased loved ones should be gently allowed to move on to the next stage of their journey, and that this does not mean losing them as it may be easier for them to communicate with those left behind if they can free themselves from the deadening spiritual atmosphere close to the earth.

It is said that spirits held earthbound by their own inability to realize they have died exist in a foggy environment, solitary and confused, aware sometimes of their old earthly surroundings but confused and unhappy until they recognize their mortality and are ready to seek help in order to move on. The inability to realize one has died may be due to a refusal to accept the reality of an afterlife while on earth, or from a sudden, violent death, as in battle or in an accident. (Air Chief Marshall Lord Dowding, responsible for Fighter Command during the Battle of Britain in 1940, devoted much of his life after retirement to contacting through mediums young servicemen who had died in the war, and helping them to realize what had happened to them). Spirits held earthbound by their hunger for material existence (known as "hungry ghosts" in the Tibetan Buddhist tradition – "hungry" for the pleasures of the physical world yet unable, in the absence of a physical body, to partake of them) may still attempt to live in their old homes and follow their old interests, sometimes proving resentful of the new occupants who have moved in and who they see as invading their property. The result can be troublesome hauntings, sometimes of the poltergeist variety, and there are accounts of people actually driven from their homes by such spirits.

People who leave this world in a highly emotional state, or with feelings of anger towards others, may also remain earthbound (Tibetan Buddhism in particular stresses the importance of dying with a tranquil, composed mind, untroubled by earthly affairs or negative emotions). A psychiatrist friend of mine considers that such spirits can even be responsible for cases of possession wrongly diagnosed as mental illness, and in partnership with a medium she reports achieving cures in these cases by releasing the possessing spirit and directing it to ask for help and to move on. She agrees with those ancient traditions that claim possession is an attempt by an earthbound spirit, lacking a physical body of his or her own, to take over and control the body and mind of a susceptible person still on earth (see e.g. Smith 2002).

The next level above that of earth and the earthbound is usually referred to as the Lower Astral (this is sometimes said to be also the home of earthbound spirits), and it is here that individuals who have lived violent or otherwise negative lives create for themselves the "hell realms" spoken of in all the traditions. The Lower Astral is said also to be a place for those who manifested few redeeming attributes while on earth and pursued only greed and self-interest, and those who chose to live shallow lives with no interest in questions of meaning and value. If one shows no concern for the non-material dimensions of life while on earth, one will have little preparation for a non-material existence after death. Descriptions by communicators of the Lower Astral sound similar to what the Greeks called Hades and the Hebrews Sheol, a gray featureless realm peopled by pale shades wandering listless and lost, which is probably also akin to the Christian concept of Purgatory, a place of regret and repentance, where wrong-doers pass their days until purged and purified of their earthly wrongdoing. The very lowest level of the Lower Astral is said to be the abode of people responsible for great violence and harm while on earth, who together have created for themselves hellish conditions of mutual hatred and suffering.

I can find no mention by communicators of eternal damnation. They speak instead of redemption when the soul has suffered in the Lower Astral – and repented by living through it oneself – the pain it has visited upon others. There is no sense in which this is intended as punishment or revenge, simply a necessary part of spiritual growth.

Above the Lower Astral is said to be the Upper Astral. This is the Summerland of which Myers spoke when communicating through medium Geraldine Cummins (Cummins 1955). By all accounts the Upper Astral is an idealized version of how this world might be if we treated it and each other with appropriate love and respect. Communicators speak of landscapes of enchanting beauty, of mountains and rivers, of beautiful towns and cities, of wide horizons under a blue sky illuminated by a sun that warms but does not burn. It all sounds very much too good to be true, but if we are able to imagine the existence of such a beautiful and peaceful world, and if the next world is indeed more susceptible to direct influence by our thoughts than is this world, then the concept of the Summerland becomes a little more feasible. However, if it exists, it is presumably still very much culture bound, which suggests that each culture may have its own version. Communicators tell us that in the Upper Astral they can move from place to place by the power of thought (whereas in the Lower Astral some still prefer to imagine themselves using cars or other forms of transport known on earth). Increasingly those in the Upper Astral find themselves losing touch with the time/space continuum that defines earthly existence, which makes our concept of time irrelevant to them, hence their difficulty in speaking about time if they communicate. The Upper Astral is said to be the last level at which communication with those on earth is possible. Above the Upper Astral, beings have to "lower their vibrations" too much in order to harmonize with vibrations on the earth level. For beings beyond the Upper

Astral the world is said to appear as a gray, foggy, featureless place (it appears like this to some of us at times). Controlling the brain of the medium thus becomes particularly difficult for them, and they communicate instead with souls at lower levels of the afterlife, who can then relay their messages to those on earth. During our investigations at Scole (Chapter 13) we were told that this was what was happening. It seems that the same thing happens with ITC communicators (Chapter 14). When one of Anabela Cardoso's most regular communicators, Carlos de Almeida, whose recorded voice is the clearest example of any ITC I have heard, ceased communicating she was told by another communicator that he had moved to a higher level of the afterlife from where it was no longer possible to influence the physical energy systems involved in electronic media.

The Upper Astral appears to be the level at which new learning takes place. The past-life review has taken place in the Lower Astral, and it is there that the lessons contained in this review have to be learnt (and from where it is said some souls may have to reincarnate on earth if they are unable or unwilling to learn them). For those who reach the Upper Astral, opportunities to broaden and deepen understanding of spirituality, relationships, service to other life forms, and unimaginable areas of the arts and sciences open up, and it seems that the acquisition of wisdom is in fact one of the prime purposes of life at this level. We could question why, if this is indeed the case, there should be this need for further learning. Surely we already carry more than enough in our heads. One possible answer is that, in much the way that it does on earth, the quest for knowledge enriches the life of the individual and prompts greater levels of understanding in the Upper Astral. Knowledge in the Upper Astral may have nothing to do with the accumulation of more facts – it could indeed have more to do with the discovery of the ever-changing, ever-evolving nature of facts, and with the search for something unchanging behind the world of appearances. But whatever form it takes, the purpose of learning in the Upper Astral would seem to be to take further the wisdom acquired on earth.

Another of the prime purposes of the Upper Astral is said to have to do with enhancing the growth of harmony, beauty, and love. Frequent references are made by communicators to the fact that nothing is static and final in the Astral World. Everything there is developing, and just as the function of human life on this earth is to make choices that assist this development in positive rather than in negative ways, so in the Upper Astral it is to further the harmony between all living systems so that the fundamental unity that underlies all things can be better expressed. All existence plays its part in the development of this harmony (expressed in the biblical quotation much loved by Carl Jung as "the lion laying down with the lamb"), each in its own way, with no form of life dominating or abusing any other.

The three lower levels of existence, the earth plane and the Lower and Upper Astral Levels (together with their various sub-divisions) are said to be the realms of form or the planes of illusion. By "illusion" is meant the fact that they do not represent reality, but only our illusory way of experiencing reality. Reality itself does not consist of worlds constructed of separate distinct "forms," but rather of an ocean of pure, unitary consciousness of which each individual consciousness is an expression. It is we who, rather like magicians, create the illusion of a world of disparate forms by the way in which we use this consciousness. The earth is said to be the level of maximum illusion, but the Lower and Upper Astral are still illusory, albeit of an increasingly subtle form. Above the Upper Astral, one enters the last of the realms of form, albeit form of an increasingly rarefied and subtle nature, usually termed the First Heaven, above which are the three formless realms (though whether numbers have much meaning at these levels seems open to doubt).

Learning continues in the First Heaven, and the illusion that individuality implies separation and isolation from other beings fades. It is said that here the bonds between the so-called "group soul," which first become apparent in the Upper Astral, draw much closer. The group soul is said to be formed of beings who have a special affinity with each other. Members of the group soul, who may also have known each other while on earth, now become aware that they all, at a deep and subtle level, arise from the same stream of consciousness. The group soul is thus a taste of the fundamental unity that unites all beings, a unity in which individuality is not so much lost as extended, so that the boundaries between souls become fluid. At Scole we were told by the communicators that they "lived in each other's consciousness," which is perhaps a way of saying the same thing.

Those communicators who report that while at the Astral Levels they have glimpsed the First Heaven speak of seeing there beings composed of light and of shimmering fluid colors. Music, which exists at all levels, is said to be of such exquisite beauty there that those still in the lower levels find it impossible to experience it for any length of time. The same is said of the quality of light in the First Heaven. The whole level is described as of such perfection that those still carrying their earthly frailties are unable to bear it.

It seems that the length of time one spends in the Upper Astral and in the First Heaven depends to a great extent upon oneself and one's development. One does not move on before the time is right. But eventually a form of "death" is said to take place in the First Heaven as one finally leaves the realms of form and moves into the formless levels of the Second Heaven and beyond. Communication from these realms with those on earth is said to be increasingly difficult, though some highly advanced beings are described as able to lower their "vibrations" and once more take on form in order to transmit higher teachings to earth. There is little point in discussing the First

Heaven and the two that are said to lie beyond, since it is doubtful if we have the concepts to make much sense of them. Buddhism tells us that form is not entirely left behind until one enters Nirvana, and we can perhaps take this to mean that even at the exalted levels of the Second and Third Heavens some vestige of form may still remain. But at these exalted levels it seems that even concepts like individuality and unity cease to have any meaning, because all such concepts that imply the existence of opposites also imply the existence of a state of tension. The Second and Third Heavens seem to be a state beyond opposites, beyond tensions, beyond life and death, beyond unity and diversity, beyond the one and the many.

And with that we have to leave it. In what we are told by communicators and by the spiritual traditions, the afterlife appears to be a journey that takes the soul progressively beyond the domain of human understanding until it reaches a destination that is perhaps neither an end nor a new beginning, but beyond all ends and all beginnings.

CHAPTER 18
CONCLUSION

I always find it difficult to finish a book I am writing because inevitably there remains much more to be said, more to explain, more to clarify. The omissions often loom as large in my mind as the inclusions. Never has this been more apparent to me than in the present book. My mind is full of the many excellent cases that space has not allowed me to include, and of the many people whose work deserves to be described but who find no place in the text. Above all, I am left with an acute awareness of the vastness of the task that I or anyone else undertakes when they try to give a comprehensive but at the same time objective picture of the evidence for survival of death. There is no doubt in my mind that the question of whether or not we live after death is by far the most important that faces us, and that has always faced us. It is the most important not only because it has to do with our destiny and with the meaning and purpose of existence, but because it has implications for the way in which we live our present lives. Are we no more than biological accidents with nothing to motivate us beyond the struggle to stay alive, or is there more to it than this? Is there no purpose to our lives beyond self-interest, or are selfless ideals such as love and compassion, empathy and altruism, peace and harmony, the very stuff from which existence arises? Are our thoughts, our creative endeavors, our art, our poetry, our philosophy, our music no more than the byproducts of electro-chemical energy in a brain that would live out its earthly life just as well without them? Or are these creative masterpieces hints and whispers of a grander and finer reality of which we are all a part?

It would be too easy to let these questions remain unanswered, and after spilling so much metaphorical ink end the book by saying that no conclusions can be reached. This would be unfair, just as it would be unfair to attempt to make up readers' minds for them instead of allowing them to arrive at their own verdict on the basis of the evidence presented. But it is important to emphasize that all the evidence summarized in the book, from apparitions to NDEs and OBEs, from mental mediumship to physical mediumship, from past-life experiences to ITC, is either evidence for human deception backed up by human gullibility or is evidence in part or whole for the existence of psychic abilities. Having studied the evidence for these abilities for over 30 years and seen a significant amount of this evidence at first hand, I am in no doubt that the existence of psychic abilities can only be rejected on doctrinaire grounds and not on those of objective judgment. Psychic abilities are a matter of fact not of belief. What they are and what they mean for our view of reality is another matter, but one cannot dismiss them as fiction and yet retain credibility as an unbiased observer.

This brings us to a second set of alternatives. Given that the evidence supports the existence of psychic abilities, these abilities are either explicable as telepathy, clairvoyance, precognition and psychokinesis from the living (i.e. as Super-ESP), or as communications in one form or another from those who have survived death and live on in another dimension. There is no way around these two possibilities. The evidence either supports Super-ESP or supports survival. I have referred to the Super-ESP explanation at all relevant points in the book, and discussed its credibility or otherwise. In the course of these discussions it will have become clear that I do not think it is adequate to explain the evidence. Certainly some of this evidence could be due to the psychic abilities of living minds – albeit operating unconsciously – but to argue that such abilities explain all or even most of it stretches the hypothesis way beyond breaking point.

If this leaves me accepting survival, it does not resolve all the questions as to what form this survival may take. In Chapter 18 I have tried to summarize the information we have on the nature of the afterlife both from the major spiritual traditions and from communications through mediums and more recently from ITC. The degree of agreement between these various pieces of information does allow us to present a coherent picture, but a great deal still remains unclear. Doubtless we do not possess the concepts to understand or even discuss it. Perhaps we shall learn more from communicators in the future, particularly if ITC fulfils the promise that many researchers consider it holds out.

Ultimately our acceptance of the reality of survival may not come solely from the evidence but from personal experience and from some inner, intuitive certainty about our real nature. We are who we are, and at some deep level within ourselves we may be the answer to our own questions. If your answer is that you are more than a biological accident whose ultimately meaningless life is bounded by the cradle and the grave, then I have to say I agree with you.

REFERENCES

Alsop, S. C. R. (1989). *Whispers of Immortality: Electronic Voices and Images from the Dead*. London: Regency Press.

Alvarado, C. S. (2003). The concept of survival of bodily death and the development of parapsychology. *Journal of the Society for Psychical Research*, 67.2, 871, 65-95.

American Society for Psychical Research (1928). The Margery Mediumship, a complete record from January 1st 1925, Vol. 1. *Proceedings of the American Society for Psychical Research* 20 (whole issue; edited by M. J. Bird).

American Society for Psychical Research (1933a). The Margery Mediumship Vol. 2. *Proceedings of the American Society for Psychical Research* 21 (whole issue; no editor given but probably E. E. Dunlop).

American Society for Psychical Research (1933b). The Margery Mediumship: the Walter hands. *Proceedings of the American Society for Psychical Research* 22 (whole issue; edited by B. K. Thoroughgood).

Apter, M. J. (1989). *Reversal Theory*. New York and London: Routledge.

Baggally, W. W. (1917). *Telepathy, Genuine and Fraudulent*. London: Methuen.

Balfour, J. (1960). The 'Palm Sunday Case': New Light on an Old Love Story. *Proceedings of the Society for Psychical Research*, 52, 79-267.

Bander, P. (1972). *Carry on Talking*. Gerrards Cross: Colin Smythe.

Barrett, Sir. W. (1988). *Death-Bed Visions*. London: Aquarian Press (first published 1926).

Barrington, M. R. (1992). Palladino and the invisible man who never was. *Journal of the Society for Psychical Research*, 58, 324-340.

Beloff, J. (1993). *Parapsychology: A Concise History*. London: Athlone Press.

Bender, H. (1966). Mediumistic psychoses. *Parapsychology*, pp 574-604.

Bender, H. (1985). *Verbogene Wirchlichkeit*. Frankfort: Piper.

Bennett, Sir E. (1939). *Apparitions and Haunted Houses*. London: Faber & Faber.

Berger, A. S. (1988). *Evidence of Life After Death: A Casebook for the Tough-Minded*. Springfield Ill.: Charles Thomas.

Bernstein, M. (1956). *The Search for Bridey Murphy*. New York: Pocket Books (paperback edition).

Bird, J. M. (1924). *Margery the Medium*. London: Hamilton.

Blatchford, R. (1925). *More Things in Heaven and Earth*. London: Methuen.

Boddington, H. (1938). *Materialisations*. London: Psychic Press.

Bohm, D. (1980). *Wholeness and the Implicate Order*. London and New York: Routledge.

Bozzano, E. (1998). *Phénomenes Psychique au Moment de la Mort*. Paris: JMG (first published 1923).

Brandon, R. (1982). *The Spiritualists*. London: Weidenfeld & Nicolson; New York: Alfred Knopf.

Braude, S. E. (2003). *Immortal Remains*. New York and Oxford: Rowman & Littlefield.

Brealey, G. (1985). *The Two Worlds of Helen Duncan*. London: Regency Press

Brian, D. (1982). *The Enchanted Voyager: The Life of J. B. Rhine*. Englewood Cliffs NJ.: Prentice-Hall.

Britten, E. Hardinge (1996). *Autobiography of Emma Hardinge Britten*. Stansted Mount Fitchett: SNU Publications (first published in 1900).

Broad, C. D. (1962). *Lectures on Psychical Research*. London: Routledge & Kegan Paul.

Broad, C. D. (1964). Cromwell Varley's electrical tests with Florence Cook. *Proceedings of the Society for Psychical Research*, 54, 195, 158-172.

Broughton, R. (1992). *Parapsychology: The Controversial Science*. London: Rider.

Brown, R. (1984). *Unfinished Symphonies*. London: Corgi Books.

Brown, S. (1970). *The Heyday of Spiritualism*. New York: Hawthorn Books.

Brune, Father Francoise (1993). *Les Morts Nous Parle*. Paris: Philippe LeBaud.

Brune, Father Francoise (2002). Quelle est la position de l'Eglise sur ces communications avec les morts? *Cuadernos de TCI* (ITC Journal), 10, 22-26.

Brune, Father Francoise and Chauvin, R. (1996). *A L'Ecoute de l' Au-dela*. Paris: Philippe Lebaud.

Burton, J. (1948). *Heyday of a Wizard*. London and Toronto: Harrap.

Burtt, Sir Cyril (1967). Psychology and parapsychology. In J. R. Smythies (ed.) *Science and ESP*. London: Routledge & Kegan Paul.

Butler, T. and Butler, L. (2003). *There is no Death*. Reno, Nevada: AA-EVP Publishing.

Cardoso, A. (2000a). Preconceptions. *Cuadernos de TCI* (ITC Journal), 2, 14-18.

Cardoso, A. (2000b). Reflections. *Cuadernos de TCI* (ITC Journal), 3, 11-15.

Cardoso, A. (2002). Brief remarks on the concept of resonance or harmony in ITC. *Cuadernos de TCI* (ITC Journal), 10, 3-12.

Cardoso, A. (2003a). ITC voices: contact with another reality? *Proceedings of the Paradigma 2003 Conference, Finland*.

Cardoso, A. (2003b). Survival research. *Journal of Conscientiology* 6, 21, 33-36.

Carington, W. (1945). *Telepathy: An Outline of its Facts, Theory, and Implications*. London: Methuen (2nd edn.).

Carpenter, S. (1995). *Past Lives*. London: Virgin Books.

Carrington, H. (1908). *The Physical Phenomena of Spiritualism*. Boston: Small, Maynard & Co.

Carrington, H. (1909). *Eusapia Palladino and Her Phenomenon*. London: Werner Laurie.

Carrington, H. (1918). *Personal Experiences in Spiritualism*. London: Werner Laurie.

Cassirer, M. (1996). *Medium on Trial*. Stansted Mount Fitchett: PN Publications.

Christie-Murray, D. (1988). *Reincarnation: Ancient Beliefs and Modern Evidence*. Bridport, Dorset: Prism Press.

Cockell, J. (1993). *Yesterday's Children*. London: Piatkus.

Cockell, J. (1996). *Past Lives, Future Lives*. London: Piatkus.

Cornillier, P-E. (1921). *The Survival of the Soul*. London: Kegan Paul, Trench, and Trubner.

Crabtree, Adam (1985). *Multiple Man*. London: Holt, Rinehart & Winston.

Crawford, W. J. (1916). *The Reality of Psychic Phenomena*. London: J. M. Watkins.

Crawford, W. J. (1921). *The Psychic Structures at the Goligher Circle*. London: J. M. Watkins.

Crookes, W. (1874). *The Phenomena of Spiritualism*. London: James Burns (re-printed in 1926 by Two Worlds Publishing and in 1953 by the Psychic Book Club).

Crookes, W. (1953). *Researches in Modern Spiritualism*. London: Psychic Book Club (original edition published 1874).

Crossley, A. E. (1975). *The Story of Helen Duncan*. Ilfracombe: Arthur Stockwell.

Cummins G. (1933). *The Road to Immortality*. London: Nicholson & Watson (reprinted 1955 London: Aquarian Press).

Cummins, G. (1965). *Swan on a Black Sea: The Cummins-Willett Scripts*. London: Routledge & Kegan Paul (Book Club Associates Edition edited by Signe Toksvig, 1971, Pelegrin/Pilgrim Edn 1986).

Cummins, H. (1935). Notes on Walter thumbprints of the "Margery" Mediumship. *Proceedings of the Society for Psychical Research*, 39, 15-23.

d'Albe, F. (1923). *The Life of Sir William Crookes*. London: Unwin.

d'Esperance, E. (1898). *Shadow Land*. London: Redway.

Dallas, H. (192?). *Comrades on the Homeward Way*. London: Collins.

Darnell, S. (1979). *Voces sin Rostro*. Barcelona: Fausi (2nd edn.).

David-Neel, A. (1965). *Magic and Mystery in Tibet*. New York: University Books

Delanoy, D. (2001). Anomalous psychophysiological responses to remote cognition: the DMILS studies. *European Journal of Parapsychology*, 16, 30-41.

Dingwall, E. (1926). A report of a series of sittings with the medium Margery. *Proceedings of the Society for Psychical Research*, 98, 78-155.

Dingwall, E. (1927). *How to Go to a Medium: A Manual of Instruction*. London: Kegan Paul, Trench, and Trubner.

Dingwall, E. J. and Hall, T. H. (1958). *Four Modern Ghosts*. London: Duckworth.

Dingwall, E. J., Goldney, K. M., and Hall, T. H. (1956). *Haunting of Borley Rectory*. London: Duckworth.

Dixon-Smith, R. (1952). *New Light on Survival*. London: Dutton.

Dodds, E. R. (1934). Why I do not believe in survival. *Proceedings of the Society for Psychical Research*, 42, 147-152.

Dossey, L. (2002). *Healing Beyond the Body*. London and New York: TimeWarner.

Douglas, A. (1976). *Extrasensory Powers: A Century of Psychical Research*. London: Victor Gollancz.

Dowding, Air Chief Marshall Lord (1945). *Lychgate*. London: Rider.

Doyle, Sir A. Conan. (1989). *History of Spiritualism* (2 Vols.). London: Psychic Press (first published 1926).

Drayton Thomas, C. (1922). *Some New Evidence for Human Survival*. New York: Dutton.

Drayton Thomas, C. (1947). A new hypothesis concerning trance-communications. *Proceedings of the Society for Psychical Research*, XLVIII, 173, 121-163.

Ducasse, C. J. (1970). Bridey Murphy revisited. In M. Ebon (ed.) *Reincarnation in the 20th Century*. New York: World Publishing (revised edn.).

Duncan, L. and Roll, W. (1995). *Psychic Connections*. New York: Bantam Doubleday.

Dunraven, the Earl of (1924). *Experiences in Spiritualism with D. D. Home*. Glasgow: Glasgow University Press.

Ebon, M. (1969) (ed.). *Reincarnation in the Twentieth Century*. New York: New American Library (revised edn).

Eisenbud, J. (1989). *The World of Ted Serios*. Jefferson N.C: Mc Farland (2nd edn).

Ellis, D. J. (1978). *The Mediumship of the Tape Recorder: A Detailed Examination of the (Jürgenson, Raudive) Phenomena of Voice Extras on Tape Recordings*. Pulborough, West Sussex: D. J. Ellis.

Ellison, E. (2002). *Science and the Paranormal*. Edinburgh: Floris Books.

Evans, H. (2002). *Seeing Ghosts: Experiences of the Paranormal*. London: John Murray.

Evans-Wentz (1960). *The Tibetan Book of the Dead.* Oxford: Oxford University Press.

Feilding, Hon. E. (1926). Review of Mr. Hudson's Hoagland's "Report on Sittings with Margery". *Proceedings of the Society for Psychical Research,* 98, 156-170.

Feilding, Hon. E. (1963). *Sittings with Eusapia Palladino and Other Studies.* New York: University Books.

Feilding, Hon. E., Baggally W. W., and Carrington, H. (1909). Report on a series of sittings with Eusapia Palladino (the Feilding Report) *Proceedings of the Society for Psychical Research.*

Fernández C. (2002). *Apsicofonias y Psicoimágenes.* Madrid: Fausi.

Festa, M. S. (2002). A particular experiment at the Psychophonic Centre in Crosseto directed by Marcello Bacci. *ITC Journal,* 10, 27-31.

Findlay, A. (1931). *On the Edge of the Etheric.* London: Psychic Press/Headquarters Publishing Co.

Findlay, A. (1951). *Where Two Worlds Meet.* London: Psychic Press/Headquarters Publishing Co.

Findlay, A. (1955). *Looking Back.* London: Psychic Press/Headquarters Publishing Co.

Fiore, E. (1978). *You Have Been Here Before?* New York: Coward, McCann & Geoghega.

Fisher, J. (1990). *Hungry Ghosts.* London: Grafton Books.

Fisher, J. (1993). *The Case for Reincarnation.* London: Diamond Books.

Flint, L. (1971). *Voices in the Dark.* London: MacMillan (Psychic Press edition 1988).

Fodor, N. (1933). *Encyclopaedia of Psychic Science.* London: Arthurs Press.

Fontana, D. (1991). A responsive poltergeist: a case from South Wales. *Journal of the Society for Psychical Research,* 57, 823, 385-403.

Fontana, D. (1992). The Feilding Report and the determined critic. *Journal of the Society for Psychical Research,* 58, 341-350.

Fontana, D. (1992). The responsive South Wales poltergeist: a follow-up report. *Journal of the Society for Psychical Research,* 58, 827, 225-231.

Fontana, D. (1993). Palladino (?) and Fontana: the errors are Wiseman's own. *Journal of the Society for Psychical Research,* 59, 198-203.

Fontana, D. (1998). Polidoro and Rinaldi: no match for Palladino and the Feilding Report. *Journal of the Society for Psychical Research,* 63, 853, 12-25.

Fontana, D. (1998). Psychical research and the millennium: new light on the survival of man. *Proceedings of the Society for Psychical Research,* 58, 219, 125-147 (Presidential Address to the Society).

Fontana, D. (1999). Evidence inconsistent with the Super-ESP theory. *Journal of the Society for Psychical Research,* 63, 855, 175-178.

Fontana, D. (2000). Three experiences possibly suggestive of survival. *Journal of the Society for Psychical Research,* 64.1, 858, 39-45.

Fontana, D. (2001). The haunting of Maurice Grosse. *Paranormal Review,* 17, 10-12.

Fontana, D. (2003). *Psychology, Religion and Spirituality.* Malden MA. and Oxford: BPS/Blackwell.

Fontana, D. (2003). Apparent post-mortem communications from Professor Arthur Ellison. *Journal of the Society for Psychical Research,* 67.2, 871, 131-142.

Ford, A. (1969). *Unknown but Known.* London: Psychic Press.

Foy, R. (1996). *In Pursuit of Physical Mediumship.* London: Janus.

Fryer, C. (1990). *Geraldine Cummins: An Appreciation.* Norwich: Peregrin/Pilgrim Books.

Fuller, J. G. (1985). *The Ghost of 29 Megacycles*. London: Souvenir Press.

Fuller, J. G. 1979). *The Airmen Who Would Not Die*. London: Souvenir Press.

Gallup, G. and Proctor, W. (1983). *Adventures in Immortality*. London: Souvenir Press.

Garland, H. (1936). *Forty Years of Psychic Research: a plain narrative of facts*. New York: MacMillan.

Garrett, E. J. (1939). *My Life As a Search for the Meaning of Mediumship*. New York: Oquaga Press.

Garrett, E. J. (1949). *Adventures in the Supernormal*. New York: Garrett Publications (Paperback Library Edn 1968, Helix Press Edn, with additional material, 2002).

Garrett, E. J. (1968). *Many Voices: The Autobiography of a Medium*. New York: Putnam.

Gaskill, M. (2001). *Hellish Nell*. London: Fourth Estate.

Gauld, A. (1971). A series of 'drop in' communicators. *Proceedings of the Society for Psychical Research*, 55, Part 204 (whole issue).

Gauld, A. (1982). *Mediumship and Survival: A Century of Investigations*. London: Heinemann.

Gauld, A. and Cornell, A. D. (1979). *Poltergeists*. London: Routledge & Kegan Paul.

Gay, K. (1957). The case of Edgar Vandy. *Journal of the Society for Psychical Research*, 39, 1-64.

Geller, U. and Playfair, G. L. (1986). *The Geller Effect*. London: Jonathan Cape.

Gissurarson, L. R. and Haraldsson, E. (1989). The Icelandic physical medium Indrid Indridason, *Proceedings of the Society for Psychical Research*, 57, 214 (whole issue).

Goss, M. (1979). *Poltergeists: An Annotated Bibliography*. New York: Scarecrow Press.

Graff, A. (1998). *Tracks in the Psychic Wilderness*. Boston Mass.: Element Books.

Grandsire, J. M. (1993). *Le Transcommunication*. Agnieres: JMG Editions.

Grant, J. (1975). *Far Memory*. London: Corgi Books (first published in 1956 by Arthur Barker under the title *Time Out of Mind*).

Grant, J. and Kelsey, D. (1969). *Many Lifetimes*. London: Victor Gollancz.

Gregory, A. (1985). *The Strange Case of Rudi Schneider*. Metuchen N.J. and London: Scarecrow Press.

Grof, S. and Grof C. (1980). *Beyond Death: The Gates of Consciousness*. London: Thames & Hudson.

Guirdham, A. (1970). *The Cathars and Reincarnation*. Sudbury, Suffolk: Neville Spearman.

Guirdham, A. (1973). *A Foot in Both Worlds*. Jersey: Neville Spearman.

Guirdham, A. (1974). *We Are One Another*. Jersey: Neville Spearman

Guirdham, A. (1976). *The Lake and the Castle*. Jersey: Neville Spearman

Guirdham, A. (1977). *The Great Heresy*. Jersey: Neville Spearman.

Gurney, E., Myers, F. W. H., and Podmore, F. (1886). *Phantasms of the Living*. London: Trubner (2 Vols.).

Gurney, E. and Myers F. W. H. (1889). On apparitions occurring soon after death. *Proceedings of the Society for Psychical Research*, Volume V Part XIV.

Halifax, J. (1979). *Shamanic Voices: The Shaman as Seer, Poet and Healer*. Harmondsworth: Penguin.

Hall, T. H. (1962). *The Spiritualists: The Story of Florence Cook and William Crookes*. London: Duckworth.

Hall, T. H. (1978). *Search for Harry Price*. London: Duckworth.

Hall, T. H. (1980). *The Strange Case of Ada Goodrich Freer*. London: Duckworth.

Hansel, C. E. M. (1989). *The Search for Psychic Powers*. Buffalo: Prometheus Books.

Haraldsson, E. and Stevenson, I. (1975). A communicator of the 'drop-in' type in Iceland: the case of Runolfur Runolfsson. *Journal of the American Society for Psychical Research*, 69, 33-59.

Hardy, Sir A. (1979). *The Spiritual Nature of Man*. Oxford: Oxford University Press.

Harrison, T. (1989). *Visits By Our Friends from the Other Side: The Remarkable Mediumship of Minnie Harrison*. High Wycombe: Saturday Night Press.

Hart, H. (1959). *The Enigma of Survival*. London: Rider.

Hart, H. and Hart, E, B. (1933). Visions and apparitions collectively and reciprocally perceived. *Proceedings of the Society for Psychical Research*, 130, 41, 205-249.

Hastings, R. J. (1969). Reply to the Borley Report. *Proceedings of the Society for Psychical Research*, 51, 1-180.

Head, J. and Cranston, S. L. (1968). *Reincarnation, An East-West Anthology*. Wheaton Ill. and London: Quest Books.

Head, J. and Cranston, S. L. (1977). *Reincarnation: The Phoenix Fire Mystery*. New York: Julian Press/Crown Publishers.

Hoagland, H. (1925). Science and the medium: the climax of a famous investigation. *Atlantic Monthly*, 136, 666-681.

Hodgson, R. (1898). A further record of observations of certain phenomena of trance (Mrs. Piper). *Proceedings of the Society for Psychical Research*, XIII, XXXIII.

Holbe, R. (1987). *Bilder aus dem Reich der Toten*. Munich: Knaur.

Houdini, H. (1924). *A Magician Among the Spirits*. New York and London: Harper & Row.

Hurst, H. W. (1982). *The Thousand Year Memory*. London: Sphere Books.

Hyslop, J. H. (1905). *Science and a Future Life*. London: Putnam.

Hyslop, J. H. 1909). A case of veridical hallucinations. *Proceedings of the American Society for Psychical Research*, 3, 1-469.

Hyslop, J. H. (1918). *Life After Death*. New York: Dutton.

Inglis, B. (1977). *Natural and Supernatural*. London and Toronto: Hodder & Stoughton.

Iverson, J. (1976). *More Lives Than One*. London: Souvenir Press.

Jackson, H. G. (1972). *The Spirit Rappers*. New York: Doubleday.

Jacobson, N. O. (1973). *Life Without Death?* New York: Delacorte/Seymour Lawrence.

James, W. (1907). A case of clairvoyance. *Proceedings of the American Society for Psychical Research*, Vol. I, Part II.

James, W. (1909). Report on Mrs. Piper's Hodgson-Control. *Proceedings of the Society for Psychical Research*, XXIII, LVIII.

Johnson, A. (1908). On the automatic writing of Mrs. Holland. *Proceedings of the Society for Psychical Research*, LV, XXI, 165-369.

Keen, M. (2002). The case of Edgar Vandy: defending the evidence. *Journal of the Society for Psychical Research*, 66.4, 869, 247-259.

Keen, M. and Roy, A. (2004). Chance coincidence in the cross-correspondences. *Journal of the Society for Psychical Research*, 68.1. 874, 57-59.

Keen, M., Ellison, A. and Fontana, D. (1999). An account of an investigation into the genuineness of a range of physical phenomena associated with a mediumistic group, in Norfolk, England (The Scole Report). *Proceedings of the Society for Psychical Research*, 58, 220, 150-452 (whole issue).

Lang, A. (1899). *The Book of Dreams and Ghosts*. London: Longmans Green (2nd edn).

Larusdottir, E. (1946). Midillinn Hafsteinn Bjornsson. Iceland: Nordri.

Leonard. G. (1931). *My Life in Two Worlds*. London: Cassell.

Litvag, I. (1972). *Singer in the Shadows: The Strange Story of Patience Worth*. New York: Macmillan.

Locher, T. and Harsch-Fischbach, M. (1997). *Breakthroughs in Technical Spirit Communication*. Boulder, Colorado: Continuing Life Research.

Lodge, Sir Oliver (1909). *The Survival of Man*. London: Methuen.

Lodge, Sir Oliver (1916). *Raymond or Life and Death*. London: Methuen.

Lodge, Sir Oliver (1922). *Raymond Revisited*. London: Methuen.

Lodge, Sir Oliver (1928). *Why I Believe in Personal Immortality*. London: Cassell.

Lombroso, C. (1988). *After Death What?* Wellingborough: Aquarian Press (original edition 1909).

Lorimer, D. (1984). *Survival? Body, Mind and Death in the Light of Psychic Experience*. London and Boston: Routledge & Kegan Paul.

MacGregor, G. (1992). *Images of Afterlife*. New York: Paragon House.

MacKenzie, A. (1971). An 'Edgar Vandy' proxy sitting. *Journal of the Society for Psychical Research*, 46, 166-173.

MacRae, A. (2004). A means of producing the EVP based on electro-dermal activity. *Journal of the Society for Psychical Research*, 68.1, 874, 35-50.

Macy, M. (2001). *Miracles in the Storm*. New York: Penguin Putnam (New American Library).

Marcuse, F. L. (1959). *Hypnosis: Fact and Fiction*. Harmondsworth: Penguin.

McMoneagle, J. (1993). *Mind Trek*. Charlottesville VA.: Hampton Roads.

McMoneagle, J. (2002). *The Stargate Chronicles*. Charlottesville VA.: Hampton Roads.

Medhurst, R. G. and Goldney, K. M. (1964). William Crookes and the physical phenomena of spiritualism. *Proceedings of the Society for Psychical Research*, 54, 195, 25-156.

Meek, G. W. (1982). *The Spiricom Technical Manual*. Atlanta, Georgia: Ariel Press.

Meek, G. W. (1987). *After We Die, What Then?* Atlanta, Georgia: Ariel Press.

Miller, K. (1998). Survival and diminished consciousness. *Journal of Philosophical Research*, 23, 479-496.

Miller, S. (1997). *After Death: How People Around the World Map the Journey After Life*. New York: Touchstone.

Mishlove, J. (1975). *The Roots of Consciousness*. New York: Random House.

Moore, Admiral Usborne (1913). *The Voices*. London: Watts.

Moore, R. (1977). *In Search of White Crows*. New York: Oxford University Press.

Moreman, C. M. (2003). A re-examination of the possibility of chance coincidence as an alternative explanation for mediumistic communications in the cross-correspondences. *Journal of the Society for Psychical Research*, 67.4, 873, 225-242.

Moreman, C. M. (2004). Reply to Keen and Roy. *Journal of the Society for Psychical Research*, 68.1, 874, 60-61.

Morse, M. and Perry, P. (1994). *Parting Visions*. London: Piatkus Books.

Munves, J. (1997). Richard Hodgson, Mrs. Piper and 'George Pelham': a centennial reassessment. *Journal of the Society for Psychical Research*, 62, 849.

Murphy, G. (1945). An outline of survival evidence. *Journal of the American Society for Psychical Research*, 39, 2-34.

Murphy, G. (1945). Difficulties confronting the survival hypothesis. *Journal of the American Society for Psychical Research,* 39, 67-94.

Murphy, G. and Ballou, R. O. (1960). *William James on Psychical Research.* New York: The Viking Press.

Myers, F. W. H. (1903). *Human Personality and its Survival of Bodily Death.* London: Longmans Green.

Myers, F. W., Lodge, Sir Oliver, Leaf, W., and James, W. (1890). A record of observations of certain phenomena of trance (Mrs. Piper). *Proceeding of the Society for Psychical Research,* VI, XVII.

Nielsson, H. (1922). Some of my experiences with a physical medium Reykjavik. In C. Vett (ed.). *Le Compte Rendu Officiel du Premier Congres International des Recherches Psychiques a Copenhague,* 450-465. Conference Proceedings, Copenhagen.

Nielsson, H. (1924). Remarkable phenomena in Iceland. *Journal of the American Society for Psychical Research,* 18, 233-238.

O'Shea, S. (2000). *The Perfect Heresy: The Life and Death of the Cathars.* London: Profile Books, New York: Walker Publishing.

Oldfield, K. (2001). Philosophers and psychics: the Vandy episode. *Sceptical Enquirer.* 25, 6.

Owen, A. (1989). *The Darkened Room.* London: Virago.

Owen, I. M. and Sparrow, M (1976). *Conjuring Up Philip: An Adventure in Psychokinesis.* New York: Harper & Row.

Owen, R. D. (1860). *Footfalls on the Boundary of Another World.* London: Trubner.

Piper, A. L. (1929). *The Life and Work of Mrs. Piper.* London: Kegan Paul.

Playfair, G. L. (1980). *This House is Haunted: An Investigation of the Enfield Poltergeist.* London: Souvenir Press.

Podmore, F. (1902). *Modern Spiritualism.* London: Methuen (2 vols.).

Podmore, F. (1910). *The Newer Spiritualism.* London: Fisher Unwin.

Polidoro, M. and Rinaldi, G. M. (1998). Eusapia's sapient foot: a new consideration of the Feilding Report. *Journal of the Society for Psychical Research,* 62, 850, 242-256.

Pratt, J. G. (1936). Towards a method of evaluating mediumistic material. *Bulletin of the Boston Society for Psychical Research,* 23.

Pratt, J. G. and Birge, W. R. (1948). Appraising verbal test material in parapsychology. *Journal of Parapsychology,* 12, 236-256.

Price, H. (1924). *Stella C. A Page of Psychic History Compiled from the Records of Thirteen Sittings.* London: John M. Watkins.

Price, H. (1930). *Rudi Schneider.* London: Methuen.

Price, H. (1931). *Regurgitation and the Duncan Mediumship.* London: National Laboratory for Psychical Research.

Price, H. (1940). *The Most Haunted House in England: Ten Years Investigation of Borley Rectory.* London: Longmans.

Price, H. (1946). *The End of Borley Rectory.* London: Harrap.

Price, H. (1994). *Poltergeist.* London: Studio Editions (first published in 1945 under the title *Poltergeist Over England*).

Price, H. H. (1995). *Philosophical Interactions with Parapsychology: The Major Writings of H. H. Price on Parapsychology and Survival.* London: MacMillan (edited by F. B. Dilley).

Prince, M. (1927). The cure of two cases of paranoia. *Bulletin of the Boston Society for Psychical Research,* 6.

Prince, W. F. (1927). *The Case of Patience Worth*. Boston: Boston Society for Psychical Research.

Psychic Magazine. (1973). *Psychics*. In Depth Interviews from Psychic Magazine. London: Turnstone.

Radin, D. (1997). *The Conscious Universe*. San Francisco: HarperEdge.

Randall, N. (1975). *Life After Death*. London: Robert Hale (re-issued by Corgi Books 1980).

Raudive, K. (1971). *Breakthrough*. Gerrards Cross: Colin Smythe.

Regardie, I. (1972). *The Tree of Life*. New York: Samuel Weiser.

Rhine, J, B. (1937) *New Frontiers of the Mind*. New York: Farrar & Rinehart.

Rhine, J. B. (1948). *The Reach of the Mind*. London: Faber & Faber.

Rhine, J. B. (1949). Precognition reconsidered. *Journal of Parapsychology*, 9, 246-277.

Rhine, J. B. (1954). *New World of the Mind*. London: Faber & Faber.

Rhine, J. B. and Rhine, L. E. (1927). One evening's observation on the Margery Mediumship. *Journal of Abnormal and Social Psychology*, 21, 401-421.

Rhine, L. E. (1956 and 1957). Hallucinatory psi experiences: I. An introductory survey; II. The initiative of the percipient in hallucinations of the living, the dying, and the dead; III. The intention of the agent and the dramatizing tendency of the percipient. *Journal of Parapsychology*, 20, 233-256, and *Journal of Parapsychology*, 21, 13-46 and 186-226.

Rhine, L. E. (1961). *Hidden Channels of the Mind*. New York: William Morrow.

Rhine, L. E. (1967). *ESP in Life and Lab*. New York: Macmillan,

Rhine, L. E. (1977). *Mind Over Matter*. New York: Macmillan.

Richet, C. (1923). *Thirty Years of Psychical Research*. London: Collins (trans. by S. de Bratt).

Roberts, J. A. (2002). *Quiver of Guides and Poltergeists*. Bangor: Tegai Publishing.

Robertson, T. J. and Roy, A. (2004). Results of the application of the Robertson-Roy protocol to a series of experiments with mediums and participants. *Journal of the Society for Psychical Research*, 68.1, 874, 18-34.

Robertson, T. J. and Roy, T. J. (2001). A preliminary study of the acceptance by non-recipients of medium's statement to recipients. *Journal of the Society for Psychical Research*, 65.2, 863, 91-106.

Rogo, S. and Bayless, R. (1979). *Phone Calls from the Dead*. New York: Prentice Hall.

Roll, W. (1974). *The Poltergeist*. New York: Signet.

Roy, A. (1996). *Archives of the Mind*. Stansted Mount Fitchet: SNU Publications.

Roy, A. and Robertson, T. (2001). A double-blind procedure for assessing the relevance of a medium's statements to a recipient. *Journal of the Society for Psychical Research*, 65.3, 864, 161-174.

Saltmarsh, H. F. (1930). A method of estimating the supernormal content of mediumistic communications. *Proceedings of the Society for Psychical Research*, 105-122 and 126-128.

Saltmarsh, H. F. (1932). Is proof of survival possible? *Proceedings of the Society for Psychical Research*, 122, 40, 105-122.

Saltmarsh, H. F. (1938). Evidence of Personal Survival from Cross Correspondences. London: G. Bell & Sons.

Schaeffer, H. (1989). *Brücke Swischen Dicsseits und Jenseits*. Freiburg: Vorlag.

Schlitz, M. and Braud, W. (1997). Distant intentionality and healing: assessing the evidence. *Alternative Therapies*, 3, 62-73.

Schmeidler, G. R. (1958). Analysis and evaluation of proxy sessions with Mrs. Caroline Chapman. *Journal of Parapsychology*, 22, 137-155.

Schmidt, S., Schneider, R., Utts, J., and Walach, H. (2002). Remote intention on electrodermal activity: two meta-analyses. *The Journal of Parapsychology*, 66, 3, 233-234.

Schwartz, G. E. R. and Russek, G. S. (2001). Evidence of anomalous information retrieval between two mediums: telepathy, network memory resonance, and continuance of consciousness. *Journal of the Society for Psychical Research*, 65.4, 865, 257-275.

Schwartz, G. E. R., Russek, G. S., and Barentsen, C. (2002). Accuracy and replicability of anomalous information retrieval: replication and extension. *Journal of the Society for Psychical Research*, 66.3, 808, 144-156.

Schwartz, G. E. R., Russek, G. S., Nelson L. A., and Barentsen, C. (2001). Accuracy and replicability of anomalous after-death communication across highly skilled mediums. *Journal of the Society for Psychical Research*, 65.1, 862, 1-25.

Senkowski, E. (1989). *Instrumentelle Transkommunikation*. Frankfurt: F. G. Fischer

Sheldrake, R. (1983). *A New Science of Life*. London and New York: Granada.

Sheldrake, R. (1988). *The Presence of the Past*. London and New York: Collins.

Sheldrake, R. (2003). *The Sense of Being Stared At and Other Aspects of the Extended Mind*. London: Hutchinson.

Sidgwick, H. (1889). Addresses by the President, Professor Sidgwick, on The Canons of Evidence in Psychical Research and the Census of Hallucinations. *Proceedings of the Society for Psychical Research*, VI, XV.

Sidgwick, H. (1890). A second address by the President , Professor Sidgwick, on the Census of Hallucinations. *Proceedings of the Society for Psychical Research* VI, XVII.

Sidgwick, H. et al. (1894). Census of Hallucinations. *Proceeding of the Society for Psychical Research*, 10, 26, 25ff.

Sitwell, S. (1988). *Poltergeists. Fact or Fancy?* New York: Dorset Press (first published 1959).

Smith, S. (1964). *The Mediumship of Mrs. Leonard*. New York: University Books.

Smith, S. (1977). *Voices of the Dead?* New York: New American Library.

Smith, S. (2002). *The Afterlife Codes*. Charlottesville VA.: Hampton Roads.

Solomon, G. (1997). *Stephen Turoff Psychic Surgeon*. London: Thorsons.

Solomon, G. and Solomon, J. (1999). *The Scole Experiment*. London: Piatkus.

Spottiswoode, J. (1997). Association between effect size in free response anomalous cognition and local sidereal time. *Journal of Scientific Exploration*, 11, 2, 109-122.

Spottiswoode, S. J. and May, E. (1997). Anomalous cognition effect size: dependence on Sidereal Time and Solar Wind parameters. Brighton UK: *Proceedings of the 40th Annual Convention*, 399-409. New York: Parapsychology Association.

St. Theresa of Avila (1974). *Interior Castle*. London: Sheed & Ward (originally published in 1577).

Stead, W. (1891). Real ghost stories. *Review of Reviews*, December (whole issue).

Stemman, R. (1997). *Reincarnation: True Stories of Past Lives*. London: Piatkus.

Stevenson, I. (1974). *Twenty Cases of the Reincarnation Type*. Charlottesville VA.: University of Virginia Press.

Stevenson, I. (1975). *Cases of the Reincarnation Type: Vol. I: Ten Cases in India*. Charlottesville VA.: University of Virginia Press.

Stevenson, I. (1977). *Cases of the Reincarnation Type: Vol 2: Ten Cases in Sri Lanka.* Charlottesville VA.: University of Virginia Press.

Stevenson, I. (1980). *Cases of the Reincarnation Type: Vol 3: Twelve Cases in Lebanon and Turkey.* Charlottesville VA.: University of Virginia Press.

Stevenson, I. (1983). *Cases of the Reincarnation Type: Vol 4: Twelve Cases in Thailand and Burma.* Charlottesville VA.: University of Virginia Press.

Stevenson, I. (1987). *Children Who Remember Previous Lives.* Charlottesville VA.: University of Virginia Press.

Tabori, P (1974). *Harry Price, the Biography of a Ghost Hunter.* London: Sphere Books.

Tabori, P. (1972). *Pioneers of the Unseen,* London: Souvenir Press.

Tandy, V. (2000). Something in the cellar. *Journal of the Society for Psychical Research,* 64.3, 860, 129-140.

Thomas, Rev. D. (1935). A proxy case extending over eleven sittings with Mrs. Osborne Leonard. *Proceedings of the Society for Psychical Research,* XLIII, 439-509.

Thouless, R. H. (1963). *Experimental Psychical Research.* Harmondsworth: Penguin.

Tietze, T. R. (1973). *Margery.* New York and London: Harper & Row.

Turner, J. (1973) (ed.). *Stella C. An Account of Some Original Experiments in Psychical Research by Harry Price.* London: Souvenir Press.

Tyrell, G. N. M. (1953). *Apparitions.* London: Gerald Duckworth (rev. edn).

Wambach, H. (1979a). *Reliving Past Lives.* London: Hutchinson.

Wambach, H. (1979b). *Life Before Life.* New York: Bantam Books.

Weiss, B. (1988). *Many Lives, Many Masters.* New York: Warner.

West, D. J. (1954). *Psychical Research Today.* London: Duckworth.

Whitton, J. L. and Fisher, J. (1986). *Life Between Life.* London: Grafton.

Wickland, C. (1978). *Thirty Years Among the Dead.* London: Spiritualist Press (first published 1924).

Williston, G. and Johnstone, J. (1988). *Discovering Your Past Lives.* Wellingborough: Aquarian Press.

Wilson, C. (1981). *Poltergeist!* London: New English Library.

Wiseman, R. (1992). The Feilding Report: a reconsideration. *Journal of the Society for Psychical Research,* 58, 129-152.

Wydenbruck, Countess N. (1938). *The Paranormal.* London: Rider.

Yeats, W. B. (1961). *Essays and Introductions.* London: Macmillan.

Zorab, G. (1964). Foreign comments on Florence Cook's mediumship. *Proceedings of the Society for Psychical Research,* 54, 173-193.

REFERENCES FOR CHAPTER 18

The list shows the major references drawn upon for the descriptions of the afterlife given in Chapter 18

Borgia, A. (1970). *Life in the World Unseen.* London and New York: Transworld.

Cherie, M. (1987). *The Barbanell Report.* Norwich: Pilgrim Books (edited by Paul Beard).

Collyer, M. H. and Dampier, E. P. (1942). *When We Wake.* London and New York: Rider.

Cummins, G. (1955). *The Road to Immortality.* London: Aquarian Press.

Curtiss, H. A., and Curtiss, F. H. (1919). *Realms of the Living Dead*. Philadelphia: Curtiss Philosophic Book Co. Inc.

Delacour, J-B. (1974). *Glimpses of the Beyond*. New York: Dell.

Doore, G. (1990) (Ed.). *What Survives?* Los Angeles: Tarcher.

Ford, A. (1972). *The Life Beyond Death*. London: W. H. Allen.

Foreman, J. (1988). *The Golden Shore*. London and Sydney: Futura.

Grof, S. and Grof, C. (1980). *Beyond Death*. London and New York: Thames & Hudson.

Harlow, S. R. (1968). *A Life After Death*. New York: Doubleday.

Hart, H. (1959). *The Enigma of Survival*. London and New York: Rider.

Hyslop, J. H. (1919). *Contact with the Other World*. New York: Century.

Kardec, A. (1989). *The Spirits' Book*. Albuquerque: Brotherhood of Life (originally published 1857).

Liverziani, F. (1991). *Life, Death and Human Consciousness*. Bridport, Dorset: Prism, New York: Avery.

Matson, A. (1975). *The Waiting World*. London and New York: Touchstone.

Miller, S. (1998). *After Death*. New York: Touchstone.

Montgomery, R. (1973). *A World Beyond*. London: Souvenir Press.

Morse, D. (2000). *Searching for Eternity*. Memphis: Eagle Wing.

Murphet, H. (1984). *The Undiscovered Country*. London: Sawbridge.

Neiman, C. and Goldman, E. (1994) *Afterlife*. USA: Penguin.

Oram, A. (1998). *The System in Which We Live*. Purley, Surrey: Talbot Books.

Pauchard, A. (1987). *The Other World*. Norwich: Pelegrin/Pilgrim

Price, H. H. (1995). *Philosophical Interactions with Parapsychology*. London: MacMillan, New York: St. Martins.

Sherman, H. (1972). *You Live After Death*. New York: Ballantine.

Sherman, H. (1981). *The Dead are Alive*. New York: Ballantine

Sherwood, J, (1969). *The Country Beyond*. London: Neville Spearman.

Sherwood, J. (1973). *Peter's Gate*. London: CFPSS.

Stainton Moses, Rev. W. (1949). *Spirit Teachings*. London: Spiritualist Press

Thomas, C. Drayton (1955). *In the Dawn Beyond Death*. London: Psychic Press (new edn).

Toynbee, A. and Koestler (1976): *Life After Death*. London: Weidenfeld & Nicolson.

White, S. E. (1969). *The Betty Book*. London: Dutton.

INDEX